The International Tax Handbook

6th Edition

The International Tax Handbook

6th Edition

Bloomsbury
Professional

Bloomsbury Professional Ltd, Maxwelton House, 41–43 Boltro Road, Haywards Heath, West Sussex, RH16 1BJ

Nexia International is a leading worldwide network of independent accounting and consulting firms, providing a comprehensive portfolio of audit, accountancy, tax and advisory services.

Nexia International does not deliver services in its own name or otherwise. Nexia International and its member firms are not part of a worldwide partnership. Member firms of Nexia International are independently owned and operated. Nexia International does not accept any responsibility for the commission of any act, or omission to act by, or the liabilities of, any of its members. Each member firm within Nexia International is a separate legal entity.

Nexia International does not accept liability for any loss arising from any action taken, or omission, on the basis of the content in this publication. Professional advice should be obtained before acting or refraining from acting on the contents of this publication.

Any and all intellectual property rights subsisting in this document are, and shall continue to be, owned by (or licensed to) Nexia International Limited.

References to Nexia or Nexia International are to Nexia International Limited.

Nexia International also refers to the trading name of Nexia International Limited, a company registered in the Isle of Man. Company registration number: 53513C. Registered office: 1st floor, Sixty Circular Road, Douglas, Isle of Man, IM1 1SA.

ISBN: 978 1 78451 396 2

Printed and bound by CPI Group (UK) Ltd, Croydon, CR0 4YY

Contents

Introduction

This is the sixth edition of the International Tax Handbook that has been produced by Nexia International, Nexia International is a leading worldwide network of independent accounting and consulting firms, providing a comprehensive portfolio of audit, accountancy, tax and advisory services. I would like to thank all the contributors for their invaluable assistance.

This edition contains more chapters than previous editions of this book and each chapter provides an overview of the tax system in the relevant country and deals with information generally sought by businesses to understand the fiscal regime. This edition continues to include details of the withholding taxes applied to the major cross border transactions based on the double taxation conventions.

This book has been prepared in a tabular format to unify the content of each chapter and highlight the core tax aspects for each country. Each section is split into corporate, personal and indirect taxes which should provide the reader with an overview of the tax system in place in a specific country.

Every effort has been taken to ensure that the information provided in this book is accurate and up to date. However, it is only meant to provide a general overview of the prevailing tax systems and should not be used as a substitute for professional tax advice.

Neither the author nor the publishers can accept any responsibility for any loss sustained by any person relying on the information provided in this book and failing to seek appropriate professional advice.

Therefore, I would like to stress the importance of obtaining local advice before any action is taken or decision is made. Any queries can be addressed to the local Nexia offices directly, using the contact information provided in the Handbook. For a comprehensive list of Nexia International members worldwide, visit the Nexia International "Locations" section at www.nexia.com

James Wall
James.Wall@CohnReznick.com

Editor
January 2017

Nexia International
Tel: +44 (0) 20 7436 1114
Fax: +44 (0) 20 7436 1536
E-mail: info@nexia.com
Web: www.nexia.com

Glossary

CGT	Capital Gains Tax
CT	Corporate Tax (tax on income of corporation)
IHT	Inheritance Tax
PE	Permanent establishment (PE) is a fixed place of business, such as a place of management, a branch, an office, a factory, a workshop, an installation or structure for the exploration of natural resources, any place of extraction of natural resources, a building site or construction or installation project, through which the business is carried on. An agent acting on behalf of the company may also constitute a PE if he has and habitually exercises the authority to do business on behalf of the company.
SME	Small and medium-sized enterprise
VAT	Value Added Tax

Angola

*(Prepared by the Angolan desk of NG Auditoria e Consultoria Lda,
NG Auditoria e Consultoria Lda, Aviegas@ng-angola.com)*

I MAIN LEGAL FORMS

Legal form / Characteristics	General partnership (SENC) and Limited partnership (SEC)	Private corporation (SQ) and Public corporation (SA)
Partners/shareholders • Number • Restrictions	General partnership (*Sociedade em Nome Colectivo*): Minimum number of partners: two Limited partnership (*Sociedade em Comandita*): Minimum number of partners: two, or five if the capital is represented by shares	Private corporation (*Sociedade por Quotas*) (SQ): Minimum number of quotaholders: two Public corporation (*Sociedade Anónima*) (SA): Minimum number of shareholders: five
Directors	Management is attributed to the directors, independent of being partners	• One or more directors (independent of being quotaholders) • General meeting (for relevant decisions) • Board of Directors or a single director in the cases allowed by law, all controlled by an Audit Committee or an Individual Qualified Auditor (*Conselho Fiscal* or *Fiscal Único*)

Legal form Characteristics	General partnership (SENC) and Limited partnership (SEC)	Private corporation (SQ) and Public corporation (SA)
Registration	Companies have to register at: • National Private Investment Agency (Agência Nacional para o Investimento Privado - *ANIP*) in order to obtain the Private Investment Registry Certificate (Certificado de Registo do Investimento Privado - *CRIP*), licence for import of capital. The minimum value for the investment by the ANIP is US\$1,000,000 (only for foreign investment) • Registry of Company Names (*Ficheiro Central de Denominações Sociais or Guiché Único da Empresa*) • Commercial Company Register (*Registo Comercial*) • Tax authorities declaring the start of activity • Statistical Record (Instituto Nacional de Estatística) • Registration as importer/exporter (Direcção Nacional do Comércio) • Social security Registration (Instituto Nacional de Segurança Nacional) • Bank account opening in a company name; • Deposit of funds for capitalisation of the project where it is a private investment project	
Minimum capital	None	SQ: the amount in Kwanzas equivalent to US\$1,000 SA: the amount in Kwanzas equivalent to US\$20,000
Liability	General partnership: unlimited, subsidiary and joint liability Limited partnership: limited liability or unlimited, subsidiary and joint liability, depending on the type of partner	Limited
Governance	Partners	Board of Directors
Audit requirements	Not mandatory	Mandatory
Taxation	Corporation tax (*Imposto Industrial*)	Corporation tax (*Imposto Industrial*)
Usage	Minimal	SQ: mainly small and medium-sized companies SA: larger/listed companies

II CORPORATION TAX

Description \ Legal form	Resident corporation	Permanent establishment (PE)
General description	Corporation tax (*Imposto Industrial*): annual tax due for the income obtained by residents or non-residents as a result of any commercial or industrial activity. The income is classified into two groups (A and B), depending on the dimension of the activity and of the annual income	
Taxable entities	Corporations with headquarters, domicile or effective management in Angola	PE located in Angolan territory
Taxable income	Worldwide income	Income attributable to the Angolan territory
Calculation of taxable profits	Taxable profits are based on results arising from accounting records, adjusted for tax purposes due to different criteria	
Interest payments	Interest payments are deductible	
	Interest receivable on Government bonds which are part of technical reserves set up by insurance companies or by companies managing securities is deductible from income (tax exempt) in the cases stated by law [art 45°, 1, b) CII]	
Related party transactions	There are provisions in place allowing the tax authorities to adjust: • the taxable income because of related party transactions • the taxable income of foreign activities if not corresponding to income determined according to domestic rules	
Tax year, return and payment	The tax year corresponds to the calendar year Tax returns shall be filed: • Group A: in May following the tax year (or June where the taxpayer has premises or a permanent representation outside the province in which it has its head office) • Group B: in April following the tax year The payment shall be carried out as follows: • Group A: three payments during the year • Group B: only one payment[1]	
Capital gains	Included in the computation of the taxable income and taxable at the normal tax rate	
Losses	Tax losses may be carried forward for a period of three years	
Tax group	N/A	
Tax rate	30%, or 15% for agricultural, forestry and livestock activities	

---

1 Corporate tax has to be withheld on payments to companies and individuals including those which have headquarters, effective management or a PE in Angola, at a flat rate of 35% applicable to a taxable amount equal to 10% of the net value of any contract related to construction, benefitting or maintaining immovable assets, or 15% in all other cases.

III   TAXES FOR INDIVIDUALS

		Residents	Non-residents
Income Tax	General description	Tax on income received by individuals	
	Taxable entities and taxable income	Residents are taxed on their worldwide income	Non-residents are taxable on all income obtained in Angola
	Types of taxable income	Mainly income deriving from employment and independent workers, such as wages, salaries, fees, bonus and premiums Certain financial income and capital gains[2]	
	Calculation of income	The tax is applicable over the total monthly income and is calculated according to a progressive tax rate	
	Tax year, tax assessment and tax payment	Tax year – calendar year Income obtained by employees: employers are required to withhold tax over payments to employees and deliver the amounts withheld by the end of the following month Income obtained by independent workers: they must file their tax return during January of the following year	
	Losses	Losses may not be carried forward	
	Tax rates	Employees: the progressive tax rate is 0% to 17% Independent professionals: the progressive tax rate is 15% to 70%	

		Residents	Non-residents
Capital Gains Tax (CGT)	General description	There is no specific tax on capital gains. Capital gains / financial income may be subject to withholding tax[3]	
	Taxable entities and chargeable assets		
	Calculation of gain		
	Tax year, tax assessment and tax payment		
	Tax rates		

		Domiciled	Non-domiciled
Inheritance Tax (IHT)	General description	This tax is levied on the value of gratuitous transfers at progressive rates (from 10% to 15% in case of transfers in favour of spouses, ascendants or descendants, and from 20% to 30% in all other cases). Transfers in favour of descendants, ascendants and spouses with a value less than 500,000 Kwanzas are exempt from the payment of this tax	

---

2   Individuals are autonomously taxed on certain financial income/capital gains (see note 1 above).

3   See note 1 above.

IV WITHHOLDING TAXES

Under domestic law	Payments to residents	Payments to non-residents
Dividends	10%	10%
Interest	10% or 15%	10% or 15%
Royalties	15%	15%
On payments to artists and sportsmen	15%	15%

Note: Angola has not concluded any tax treaties with other countries.

V   INDIRECT TAXES

		Residents	Non-residents
Value Added Tax (VAT) / Consumption Tax	General description	There is no VAT in Angola, only consumption tax	
	Entities obliged to levy consumption tax	Individuals or companies	
	Taxable activities	• Production and import of certain products (such as automobiles, electronics and machinery) • sale or auction held by customs or other public services • water, energy and telecommunications consumption • hotel services and similar	
	Exemptions (examples)	• Goods imported by the producer or any other entity duly recognised • goods imported by diplomatic and consular representations as long as they have reciprocal treatment • animals used for reproduction • goods for domestic industry as long as they are duly certified by the competent Minister	
	Tax liability	Tax is paid on a monthly basis by those selling to the final consumers	
	Tax rates	Tax rates depend on the price of the goods, on the value of acquisition or on the customs value. In general, said values will be taxed at a rate of 10%, however this is variable (eg vehicles will be taxed at a rate of 20% or 30%, depending on their derived capacity)	
Real Property Taxes		Stamp tax is due on the acquisition of ownership or other rights on real estate – 1% Property transfer tax (*sisa*) is levied on the transfer of real estate at a flat rate of 10% over the value declared before tax authorities Municipal property tax (*Imposto predial urbano*) is levied on an annual basis at a flat rate of 30% over the effective or the potential rental value	
Stamp Duty		Levied on deeds, documents, books, papers, acts and other situations specified in the Code. Specific tax rates depend on the taxable event	

Argentina

(Graciela Valles, Bavastro, Delavault & Asociados, gvalles@bda-nexia.com)

I MAIN LEGAL FORMS

Legal form / Characteristics	Partnership and Limited Liability Partnership (LLP)	Ltd (private corporation) and Plc (public corporation)
Partners/shareholders • Number • Restrictions	• Minimum partners: two • LLP: maximum 50 • General partnership: no regulation applying maximum limit	• Minimum shareholders: two • No maximum limit
Directors	Partnerships are not treated as separate legal persons LLP: at least one manager must be appointed	Ltd minimum: single director with an alternate should be appointed. The majority of directors must be resident in Argentina Plc: directors, Statutory Auditors' Committee (SAC) and Shareholders' Surveillance Committee (SSC) are mandatory
Establishment	Partnership deed	Statutes approved by shareholders
Registration	Partnership, LLP and Ltd: with the Public Registry of Corporations Plc: with the Public Registry of Corporations and the National Securities Commission	
Minimum capital	Partnership: none LLP: ARS 100,000	Ltd: ARS 100,000 Plc: ARS 10,000,000
Liability	Partnerships: unlimited liability Limited to subscribed capital for LLP	Limited to subscribed shares
Governance	Partnership deed for Surveillance Committee	
Audit requirements	Annual audit report of financial statements is required	
Taxation	Companies are subject to corporation tax. LLPs are transparent for tax purposes	
Usage	Small businesses (defined by government regulations and for developing politics as those whose annual sales do not exceed ARS 10m, 14m or 4m for manufacturing, wholesale and service industries respectively)	Large capital businesses (defined by government regulations and for developing politics as those whose annual sales exceed the limits defining 'medium capital businesses' (ARS 82m, 112m and 28m for manufacturing, wholesale and service industries, respectively))

II   CORPORATION TAX

Legal Form / Description	Resident corporation	Foreign Corporation with Permanent establishment (PE)
General description	Corporation tax	
Taxable entities	Resident companies are liable to corporation tax on their worldwide profits	Non-resident companies are liable to corporation tax only on the profits derived in Argentina
Taxable income	Worldwide profits	Profits derived by PE in Argentina
Calculation of taxable profits	Accounting profit is adjusted for various tax add-backs and allowances to arrive at profits chargeable to corporation tax	
Interest payments	Interest paid or accrued is deductible Thin capitalisation rules apply to related party loans	
Related party transactions	All related party transactions must take place on arm's length basis	
Tax year, return and payment	Tax year is normally the financial year of the company Taxpayer must prepare a return determining taxable income and assessing the tax One part of the return provides figures from the taxpayer's financial statements and must be signed by an independent accountant 10-monthly advance tax payments, based on the previous year's tax liability are due commencing on the sixth month of the financial year	
Capital gains	Capital gains and losses are assessed to corporation tax Losses arising on the sale of shares may only be offset against similar profits	
Losses	The losses can be carried forward for 5 years	
Tax group	None	
Tax rate	35%	

III   TAXES FOR INDIVIDUALS

		Residents	Non-residents
Income Tax	General description	Tax levied on the chargeable income of a chargeable person for a year of assessment	
	Taxable entities and taxable income	Residents are taxed on their worldwide income	Non-residents are taxed on income arising in Argentina, through withholding
	Types of taxable income	• Property income (usually rent) • Income from capital investment (interest, sale of goodwill, dividends, royalties, annuities) • Income from business activities • Employment from personal services or pensions	
	Calculation of income	Tax is calculated on earned taxable income after deduction of necessary expenses to obtain and preserve the income Personal allowances (basic, family, etc) are available	
	Tax year, tax assessment and tax payment	• Tax year – calendar year • Tax assessment – returns must be filed in April of the following year	
	Losses	Tax losses can be carried forward for 5 years	
	Tax rates	(see table below)	

Taxable income		Basic tax	Plus	On the excess
From ARP	To ARP	ARP	%	ARP
0	10,000	0	9	0
10,001	20,000	900	14	10,000
20,001	30,000	2,300	19	20,000
30,001	60,000	4,200	23	30,000
60,001	90,000	11,100	27	60,000
90,001	120,000	19,200	31	90,000
120,001+	No limit	28,500	35	120,000

		Residents	Non-residents
Capital Gains Tax (CGT)	General description	Tax on increase in the value of assets between acquisition and disposal, not chargeable to income or corporate tax	
	Taxable entities and chargeable assets	As a general rule, capital gains are not taxable for individuals, although capital gains made in the course of business are assessed to income tax	

		Domiciled	Non-domiciled
Inheritance Tax (IHT)	General description	As of January 2010, inheritance tax has been re-established within the Province of Buenos Aires, exclusively	
	Taxable entities and chargeable assets	On most increases in value of any assets located in the Province of Buenos Aires and/or in the benefit of individuals or legal entities domiciled in that Province, including inheritance, inter vivos gifts and any other non-onerous wealth increase (eg forgiveness of debt)	
	Allowances	When the amount of the non-onerous wealth increase does not exceed the amount of ARS 50,000, then the beneficiary is tax exempt. The exempt amount increases to ARS 200,000 if beneficiaries are parents, children and spouse	
	Tax rates	The rate of tax is variable depending on the direct or indirect relation between the descendant and the heirs, as for example:	

Taxable amount		Parents, children and spouse		Other ascendant or descendant		Collateral of 2ª degree		Collateral of 3ª and 4ª degree and third parties (including legal entities)	
Higher than ARS	Lesser than or Equal to ARS	Fixed amount ARS	% on excess over	Fixed amount ARS	% on excess over	Fixed amount ARS	% on excess over	Fixed amount ARS	% on excess over
0	125,000	–	4%	–	6%		8%	–	10%
125,000	250,000	5,000	4.075%	7,500	6.075%	10,000	8.075%	12,500	10.075%
250,000	500,000	10,094	4.225%	15,094	6.225%	20,094	8.225%	25,094	10.225%
500,000	1,000,000	20,656	4.525%	30,656	6.525%	40,656	8.525%	50,656	10.525%
1,000,000	2,000,000	43,281	5.125%	63,281	7.125%	83,281	9.125%	103,281	11.125%
2,000,000	4,000,000	94,531	6.325%	134,531	8.325%	174,531	10.325%	214,531	12.325%
4,000,000	8,000,000	221,031	8.725%	301,031	10.725%	381,031	12.725%	461,031	14.725%
8,000,000	16,000,000	570,031	13.525%	730,031	15.525%	890,031	17.525%	1,050,031	19.525%
16,000,000	and over	1,652,031	15.925%	1,972,031	17.925%	2,292,031	19.925%	2,612,031	21.925%

IV WITHHOLDING TAXES

Under domestic law	Payments to residents	Payments to non-residents[1]
Dividends	10% payable by local beneficiary in annual income tax assessment[2,3]	10% income tax withholding[2,3]
Gain on sale of unquoted shares	15% payable by local beneficiary in annual income tax assessment	15% income tax withholding on assumed taxable income of 90%
Interest	6% income tax withholding	Tax rate 35% on assumed taxable income of 43%
Royalties	6% income tax withholding	Tax rate 35% on assumed taxable income of 60% (technical assistance) or 80% (licences)
On payments to artists and sportsmen	2% income tax withholding	35% on assumed taxable income of 70%

1 Reduced rates of withholding tax may apply where there is an appropriate double tax treaty.
2 Individuals only.
3 Excess of book profit dividends over tax profit are subject to full and final payment of 35% on such excess.

Reduced rate available under the relevant Double Taxation Treaty			
Country	Dividends	Interest	Royalties
Austria	(5)	(5)	(5)
Australia	10%/15%[3]	12%	3%/10%/15%[2]
Belgium	10%/15%[3]	12%	3%/5%/10%/15%[2]
Bolivia	(1)	(1)	(1)
Brazil	(1)	(1)	(1)
Canada	10%/15%[3]	12.50%	3%/5%/10%/15%[2]
Chile	(5)	(5)	(5)
Denmark	10%/15%[3]	12%	3%/5%/10%/15%[2]
Finland	10%/15%[3]	15%	3%/5%/10%/15%[2]
France	15%	20%	18%
Germany	15%	10%/15%	15%
Italy	15%	20%	18%
Netherlands	10%/15%[3]	12%	3%/5%/10%/15%[2]
Norway	10%/15%[3]	12.5%	3%/5%/10%/15%[2]
Russia	10%/15%[3]	15%	15%
Spain	10%/15%[3]	12%	3%/5%/10%/15%[2]
Sweden	10%/15%[3]	12.5%	3%/5%/10%/15%[2]
Switzerland	(4)	(4)	(4)
United Kingdom	10%/15%[3]	12%	3%/5%/10%/15%[2]
United States	(4)	(4)	(4)
Uruguay	(1)	(1)	(1)

Note: the above rates are only available provided the specific Treaty criteria are satisfied. As treaties will not be identical, guidance should be sought in all cases.

1 General rates of the country are applicable. Different tax credit schemes are applicable.
2 Rate varies if related to the use of, or the right to use of:
   • news;
   • copyright of literary, dramatic, musical or other artistic work;
   • any patent, trademark, design or model, plan, secret formula or process, or for the use of, or the right to use, industrial or scientific equipment, or for information concerning industrial or scientific experience, or the rendering of technical assistance; or
   • all other cases.
3 Rate varies if the beneficial owner is a company which controls, directly or indirectly, at least 25% of the voting power in the company paying the dividends or more.
4 Not ratified by law.
5 Double Taxation Treaties not currently effective as they have been terminated by Argentine Government decision during 2012 or prior year, willing to enter into new convention terms.

V   INDIRECT TAXES

		Residents	Non-residents
Value Added Tax (VAT)	General description	Tax on the supply of goods and services	
	Entities obliged to levy VAT	Individuals, partnerships and corporations supplying goods and services in Argentina	
	Taxable activities	Supply and import of goods and services	
	Taxable activities – zero-rated (examples)	N/A	
	Exemptions (examples)	• Exports of goods and services are tax exempt • Books, publishing, newspapers are exempt • Life insurance and annuities are exempt • Educational services provided by authorised institutions are exempt	
	Refund of VAT	Exporters' VAT on purchases is reimbursable	
	Tax liability	• VAT on supplies must be paid in the following month. VAT incurred by businesses can be offset against VAT invoiced to clients • Withholding schemes on VAT invoiced are applicable	
	Tax rates	• General tax rate: 21% • Gas, electricity and telecommunication are taxed at 27% • Certain farming products: 10.5% • Machinery and spare parts specifically designated: 10.5%	
	Administrative obligations	Recording of sales and purchases on special forms	
Real Property Taxes		Covered by Stamp Duty below	
Stamp Duty		The City of Buenos Aires and the Provinces apply a stamp tax on contracts, transfer or lease of real estate, promissory notes, banker's drafts, and certain other documents. The most common rates range from 1%/1.2% to 3.6%	

Australia

(Stephen Rogers, Nexia Sydney, srogers@nexiasydney.com.au)

I MAIN LEGAL FORMS

Legal form / Characteristics	Partnership	Limited partnership	Private and public companies
Partners/Shareholders	Two or more	At least one general partner, at least one limited partner	One or more
Maximum Number	20 (other than certain professional partnerships)	20 general partners (no restriction on limited partners)	None
Restrictions	None	None	None
Directors	Management by partners		Private: one or more / Public: three or more
Foundation	Partnership deed		Constitution
Registration	None	Registration required with Fair Trading	Registration required with ASIC
Minimum capital	None	None	None
Liability	Unlimited to all partners	Unlimited for general partner, limited to capital for limited partner	Private: Limited to capital for all shareholders / Public: Generally limited to capital for all shareholders / Companies limited by guarantee limited to members' respective contributions
Governance	Partners' meetings	Partners' meetings	Directors' meetings / Shareholders' meetings

Legal form Characteristics	Partnership	Limited partnership	Private and public companies
Audit requirements	None	None	Private: None – but if over any two of following must audit: • consolidated revenue $25m • consolidated gross assets $12.5m • the company and any controlled companies have 50 employees or more
Taxation	Pass-through entity	Corporate limited partnerships effectively treated as companies for tax purposes. Partners' drawings deemed to be dividends Foreign limited partnerships – such as a US LLC or UK LLP, can be treated as 'flow-throughs' in Australia in certain circumstances Venture capital limited partnerships treated as ordinary partnerships	Subject to company tax, but can pay franked dividends to shareholders

II CORPORATION TAX

	Resident corporations	Non-resident corporations
General	30% federal tax 27.5% federal tax for companies classified as small business entities (aggregated turnover of less than $10m) for 2016–17. (Aggregated turnover threshold will increase to $25m for 2017–18)	Australian permanent establishment (PE) and sale of taxable Australian property
Other	No state income taxes or trade taxes	
Taxation in Australia	Incorporated in Australia, or management and control in Australia – worldwide income	Australian PE or management and control in Australia
Calculation of taxation income	Accounting profit X Plus/Minus Tax timing differences Y Plus/Minus Tax permanent differences $\underline{Z}$ Australian taxation income $\underline{I}$	
Interest payments	Thin capitalisation rules: De minimis exemption: rules do not apply where debt deductions are less than $2m Debt deductions are disallowed where the adjusted average debt is greater than maximum allowable debt determined under either a *safe harbour test* or an *arm's length debt test*	
Related party transactions	Strict adherence to the arm's length principle Very detailed transfer pricing methodologies, procedures and requirements	
Tax year and tax payments	• Tax year = 1 July to 30 June • Annual federal tax return • Quarterly prepayments, final payment or refund after tax assessment	
Capital gains	Taxable at regular company tax rate (30% or 28.5%) (no concessions as for individuals and trusts)	Since December 2006 capital gains are now limited to Australian land, shares in land-rich companies, sale of Australian branch assets and Australian mining/ prospecting rights and information
Losses	• No carry back allowed; • Must satisfy Continuity of Ownership (COT) (generally greater than 50% underlying individual ownership) Concessions on COT test for public companies; or • Same Business Test (SBT)	
Tax group – prerequisites	Tax consolidation rules for 100% wholly owned Australian entities – Head entity must be a company	Special rules for PEs and foreign-owned multiple entry groups
Company tax rate	30% (28.5% for small business entities)	
Wealth tax	No wealth tax in Australia	

	Resident corporations	**Non-resident corporations**
Real Estate Taxes		
1. Stamp duty on transfer of real property	Yes – levied by the Australian state where the relevant land is situated – range of 1.25–7% of value of real property	
2. Annual land tax levied by states on commercial and investment properties	Land tax levied by the Australian state where the relevant land is situated, with tax-free thresholds ranging from $25,000–$599,999 and tax rates ranging from 0.02–2.67% per annum	

III TAXES FOR INDIVIDUALS

	Residents	Non-residents
General	Australian resident – worldwide income	Australian source income
Calculation of income	Generally cash for salaried employees – accruals if running a business	
Tax year	• Tax year = 1 July to 30 June • Sole individual annual return • Quarterly prepayments (unless salary and wage income which is subject to withholding when paid)	
Capital gains	• Starting point – same as other income • 50% reduction in gain if asset held for more than 12 months	Since December 2006 capital gains are now limited to Australian land, shares in land-rich companies, sale of Australian branch assets and Australian mining/prospecting rights and information Non residents can no longer access the 50% CGT discount
Losses	• No carry back • Unlimited time in which to utilise	
Tax rates as at 1 July 2015	*Income ($)* *Tax (%)* 0–18,200 Nil 18,201–37,000 19 37,001–80,000 32.5 80,001–180,000 37 180,001+ 45 The above rates do not include the: • Medicare levy of 2% • Temporary Budget Repair Levy; this levy is payable at a rate of 2% for taxable incomes over $180,000	*Income ($)* *Tax (%)* 0–80,000 32.5 80,001–180,000 37 180,001+ 45 Foreign residents are not required to pay the Medicare levy The above rates do not include the Temporary Budget Repair Levy; this levy is payable at a rate of 2% for taxable incomes over $180,000
Tax rates as at 1 July 2016	*Income ($)* *Tax (%)* 0–18,200 Nil 18,201–37,000 19 37,001–80,000 32.5 80,001–180,000 37 180,001+ 45 The above rates do not include the: • Medicare levy of 2% • Temporary Budget Repair Levy; this levy is payable at a rate of 2% for taxable incomes over $180,000	*Income ($)* *Tax (%)* 0–80,000 32.5 80,001–180,000 37 180,001+ 45 Foreign residents are not required to pay the Medicare levy The above rates do not include the Temporary Budget Repair Levy; this levy is payable at a rate of 2% for taxable incomes over $180,000
Other	No wealth tax and no inheritance tax in Australia (but there are CGT issues on the death of an individual). Note also there are minimum superannuation employer contribution requirements for Australian employees	

IV   WITHHOLDING TAXES

Under domestic law	Payments to residents	Payments to non-residents
Employment income	Yes at source	Same for employment in Australia
Dividends	None at source	• Nil if fully franked • 30% to non-treaty country • 0%–15% for treaty country (depending on treaty terms) and depending on percentage of ownership
Interest	None at source	Generally 10% for treaty and non-treaty
Royalties	None at source	• Between 5% and 15% for treaty countries • 30% for non-treaty countries
Payments to artists and sportsmen	None at source	• Company tax rate for payments to companies • Foreign resident marginal rates if paid to individuals • Need to also consider relevant Double Taxation Agreement (DTA) article (where appropriate)

Australia has entered into a number of comprehensive Double Taxation Treaties and the following table lists the rates applicable			
Country	Unfranked dividends	Interest	Royalties
Argentina	15%	12%	15%
Austria	15%	10%	10%
Belgium	15%	10%	10%
Canada	15%	10%	10%
Chile	15%	10%	10%
China	15%	10%	10%
Czech Republic	15%	10%	10%
Denmark	15%	10%	10%
Fiji	20%	10%	15%
Finland	15%	10%	10%
France	15%	10%	10%
Germany	15%	10%	10%
Greece[1]	–	–	–
Hungary	15%	10%	10%
India	15%	15%	15%
Indonesia	15%	10%	15%
Ireland	15%	10%	10%
Italy	15%	10%	10%
Japan	15%	10%	10%
Kiribati	20%	10%	15%
Korea	15%	15%	15%

1   The Agreement with Greece deals with airline profits only.
2   Australia has signed limited Agreements with Aruba, British Virgin Islands, Cook Islands, Guernsey, Isle of Man, Jersey, Kiribati, Marshall Islands, Mauritius and Samoa.
3   Australia also has Tax Information Exchange Agreements in force with a number of countries.

Australia has entered into a number of comprehensive Double Taxation Treaties and the following table lists the rates applicable			
Country	Unfranked dividends	Interest	Royalties
Malaysia	15%	15%	15%
Malta	15%	15%	10%
Mexico	15%	10%	10%
Netherlands	15%	10%	10%
New Zealand	15%	10%	10%
Norway	15%	10%	5%
Papua New Guinea	20%	10%	10%
Philippines	25%	15%	25%
Poland	15%	10%	10%
Romania	15%	10%	10%
Russia	15%	10%	10%
Singapore	15%	10%	10%
Slovakia	15%	10%	10%
South Africa	15%	10%	10%
Spain	15%	10%	10%
Sri Lanka	15%	10%	10%
Sweden	15%	10%	10%
Switzerland	15%	10%	10%
Taipei	15%	10%	12.5%
Thailand	20%	25%	15%
Turkey	15%	10%	10%
United Kingdom	15%	10%	5%
United States	15%	10%	5%
Vietnam	15%	10%	10%

Note: the above rates are only available provided the specific Treaty criteria are satisfied. As treaties will not be identical, guidance should be sought in all cases. It is possible that lower rates than those shown above may be available provided certain criteria are satisfied.

V INDIRECT TAXES

		Residents	Non-residents
Value Added Tax (VAT)	General description	Goods and services tax (GST) on the supply of goods and services	
	Entities obliged to levy GST	Federal tax levied by way of GST at all levels of the production/service chain with right to tax credit	
	Taxable activities	All types of services and goods	
	Taxable activities – zero-rated (examples)	A zero rate (known as GST-free) applies to the export of goods and services	
	GST free supplies (examples)	Food, health, education, exports, charitable activities, going concerns, farmland, precious metals	
	Refund of GST	By way of tax credit in the chain of entrepreneurial activity	
	Tax liability	Strict liability with entity rendering service or effecting sale	
	Tax rate	10%	
	Administrative obligations	Precise accounting and documentation required	
Real Property Taxes		Levied at State level on land used in business – subject to minimum threshold values	
Stamp Duty		Imposed at State level on various transactions and conveyances at either a fixed rate or at ad valorem rates	

Austria

(Hannes Greimer, K&E Wirtschaftstreuhand GmbH, hannes.greimer@ ketreuhand.at)

I MAIN LEGAL FORMS

Legal form Characteristics	Partnership (OG) and Limited Partnership (KG)	Private Corporation (GmbH) and Public Corporation (AG)
Partners/ shareholders • Number • Restrictions	• Two or more • No restrictions	• One or more • No restrictions
Directors	Management by partners One or more	Management by directors, no restrictions in number of managers
Establishment	No formal requirements	Notarial deed
Registration	Commercial Register at law court – exceptions due to size	Commercial Register at law court Annual accounts to be published 9 months after end of commercial year
Minimum capital	None	GmbH: €35,000 (€10,000 between 1 July 2013 and 28 February 2014 – has to be made up to €35,000 by 1 March 2024); from 1 March 2014 onwards, there is a possibility to reduce the paid minimum capital for 10 years AG: €70,000
Liability	OG: Unlimited for all partners KG: Limited to capital, at least one partner has unlimited liability	Limited for all shareholders/ stockholders
Governance	OG: Partner/s KG: General partner/s	• Managing director • Supervisory board (AG, GmbH in some cases) • Shareholder/Stockholder meeting
Audit requirements	Normally, no audit requirements, but required for companies with corporation as general partner	Yes, exemptions for small GmbH[1]

---

1 Small companies are companies which do not exceed two of the following criteria: turnover of €10m; total assets of €5m; and 50 employees on average per year.

Legal form / Characteristics	Partnership (OG) and Limited Partnership (KG)	Private Corporation (GmbH) and Public Corporation (AG)
Taxation	• Partnership considered transparent/no taxation • Partners subject to income tax on their profit share	• Companies are subject to corporate tax
Usage	Professional services	• Small and medium-sized enterprises • Plcs (AG) used for larger companies seeking to be listed on stock market

II CORPORATION TAX

Legal form / Description	Austrian resident corporation	Permanent establishment (PE)
General description	Tax on income of corporations	
Taxable entities	• Companies incorporated in Austria • Foreign companies with central management and control located in Austria	• PE located in Austria
Taxable income	Worldwide income	Income derived by PE in Austria
Calculation of taxable profits	Income for corporation tax = Accounting profit +/- tax adjustments	
Interest payments	Deductible, no capitalization rules	
Related party transactions	All related party transactions must take place on arm's length basis, special documentation required in some cases	
Tax year, return and payment	Calendar year, but the financial year of a company may be any fixed 12-month period Tax is payable in advance in quarterly instalments on the estimated profit. Final payment or refund after tax assessment for the tax year. Interest after September of the following year on the final payment	
Capital gains	Included in normal income. Profits or losses on the sale of investment shares of more than 10% in foreign companies are tax-free (it has to be hold more than one year)	
Losses	Carried forward unlimited, annual maximum offset is normally 75% of the year's profits. No carry back	
Tax group	A group comprises an Austrian parent company and its controlled subsidiaries or PEs, which can be foreign (only EU countries) or domestic, the share-ownership ratio has to be more than 50%	
Tax rate	25%	

III TAXES FOR INDIVIDUALS

		Residents	Non-residents
Income Tax	General description	Tax on the chargeable income of a person	
	Taxable entities and taxable income	Residents and individuals with habitual abode in Austria are taxed on their worldwide income	Non-residents are taxed on income arising in Austria
	Types of taxable income	• Property income (rent and transfer) • Income from capital investment (interest, sale of goodwill, dividends, royalties, annuities) • Income from business activities • Income from previous or current employment	
	Calculation of income	Profit in seven so-called schedules (agriculture, professional service, business, employment, rental, capital and 'other') Non-residents have to add €9,000 to their taxable income	
	Tax year, tax assessment and tax payment	• Tax year = calendar year. Tax return due 30 April of the following year or, if electronically filed, 30 June • Quarterly prepayments, final payment or refund at the end of the year • Employment income – tax payment usually from employer • Interest Tax – tax deduction from bank or to be declared individually • Special tax for selling real estate since 2012	
	Losses	Deductible against income from the same category. Generally compensable but many specific rules Carry forward unlimited for Austrian trade losses. No carry back of losses	
	Tax rates	*Band of taxable income (€)* *Rate of tax applicable to band (%)* *0–11,000* *0* *11,001–18,000* *25* *18,001–31,000* *35* *31,001–60,000* *42* *60,001–90,000* *48* *90,001–1,000,000* *50* *Over 1,000,000* *55 (for the years 2016 till 2020)*	
Capital Gains Tax (CGT)	General description	Under the new taxation regime, from 2011 onwards capital gains are taxable independent of the holding period	
	Taxable entities and chargeable assets	All capital gains are taxable at a tax rate of 25%/27.5%. No more speculative period in use	
	Calculation of gain	Sales minus acquisition costs	
	Tax year, tax assessment and tax payment	• Taxable chargeable gains are part of year's income • Tax to be deducted from the capital gains when capitals gains are paid from bank institutes or part of the tax assessment	
	Losses	• Deductible from taxable chargeable gains of the same quality • No carry forward	
	Tax rates	• 25% for bank accounts and saving books, all other 27.5%; or • part of total income	

		Domiciled	Non-domiciled
Inheritance Tax (IHT)	General description	There has been no IHT since 1 August 2008	
	Taxable entities and chargeable assets		
	Calculation of charge		
	Taxable events		
	Allowances		
	Tax rates		

IV   WITHHOLDING TAXES

Under domestic law	Payments to residents	Payments to non-residents[2]	
		Natural persons	Legal entities
Employment income (wage tax)	Same tax rates as tax rates for individuals	Same tax rates as tax rates for individuals – only for income in Austria	No wage tax for legal entities
Some specific incomes	No withholding tax for residents and individuals with habitual abode in Austria	20% – 25%	25%
Dividends	27.5%	27.5%	27.5%
Interest from banks	25%	Since 30 June 2011: 35%	Nil
Royalties	subject to income tax	20%	20%

Reduced rate available under the relevant Double Taxation Treaty (Examples)			
Country	Dividends[3]	Interest[4]	Royalties[5]
Albania	15%	5%	5%
Algeria	15%	10%	10%
Armenia	15%	10%	5%
Australia	15%	10%	10%
Azerbaijan	15%	10%	10%
Bahrain	Nil	Nil	Nil
Barbados	15%	Nil	Nil
Belarus	15%	5%	5%
Belgium	15%	15%	Nil
Belize	15%	Nil	Nil
Bosnia and Herzegovina	10%	5%	5%
Brazil	15%	15%	15%
Bulgaria	5%	5%	5%
Canada	15%	10%	15%
China	10%	10%	10%
Croatia	15%	5%	Nil
Cuba	15%	10%	5%
Cyprus	10%	Nil	Nil
Czech Republic	10%	Nil	5%
Denmark	15%	Nil	Nil
Estonia	15%	10%	10%

2   Reduced rates of withholding tax may apply where there is an appropriate double tax treaty or according to Directive.
3   General reduced rate. Reduced rates (for example, intercompany dividends) may apply. This has to been checked for individual cases.
4   General reduced rate, with many exceptions.
5   General reduced rate. In some cases, there are exceptions.

Reduced rate available under the relevant Double Taxation Treaty (Examples)			
Country	Dividends[3]	Interest[4]	Royalties[5]
Finland	10%	Nil	5%
France	15%	Nil	Nil
Georgia	10%	Nil	Nil
Germany	15%	Nil	Nil
Greece	15%	8%	7%
Hong Kong	10%	Nil	3%
Hungary	10%	Nil	Nil
India	10%	10%	10%
Indonesia	15%	10%	10%
Iran	10%	5%	5%
Ireland	Nil	Nil	Nil
Israel	25%	15%	10%
Italy	15%	10%	Nil
Japan	20%	10%	10%
Kazakhstan	15%	10%	10%
Korea	15%	10%	10%
Kuwait	Nil	Nil	10%
Kyrgyzstan	15%	10%	10%
Latvia	10%	10%	10%
Liechtenstein	15%	10%	10%
Lithuania	15%	10%	10%
Luxembourg	15%	Nil	Nil
Macedonia	15%	Nil	Nil
Malaysia	10%	15%	10%
Malta	15%	5%	10%
Mexico	10%	10%	10%
Moldova	15%	5%	5%
Mongolia	10%	10%	5%
Morocco	10%	10%	10%
Nepal	15%	15%	15%
Netherlands	15%	Nil	Nil
New Zealand	15%	10%	10%
Norway	15%	Nil	Nil
Pakistan	15%	15%	10%
Philippines	25%	15%	15%
Poland	15%	5%	5%
Portugal	15%	10%	5%
Qatar	Nil	Nil	5%
Romania	5%	3%	3%
Russia	15%	Nil	Nil
San Marino	15%	Nil	Nil
Saudi Arabia	5%	5%	10%
Serbia	10%	10%	10%
Singapore	10%	5%	5%
Slovenia	15%	5%	5%
South Africa	15%	Nil	Nil

Reduced rate available under the relevant Double Taxation Treaty (Examples)			
Country	Dividends[3]	Interest[4]	Royalties[5]
Spain	15%	5%	5%
Sweden	10%	Nil	Nil
Switzerland	5%	5%	5%
Tajikistan	10%	8%	8%
Thailand	20%	25%	15%
Tunisia	20%	10%	15%
Taiwan	10%	10%	10%
Turkey	15%	15%	10%
Ukraine	10%	5%	5%
United Arab Emirates	20%	Nil	Nil
United Kingdom	15%	Nil	Nil
United States	15%	Nil	Nil
Uzbekistan	15%	10%	5%
Venezuela	15%	10%	5%
Vietnam	15%	10%	10%

Note: the above rates are only available provided the specific treaty criteria are satisfied. It is possible that lower rates than those shown above may be available provided certain criteria are satisfied. As treaties will not be identical, guidance should be sought in all cases.

V INDIRECT TAXES

		Residents	Non-residents
Value Added Tax (VAT)	General description	Tax on the supply of goods and services (VAT)	
	Entities obliged to levy VAT	Sales tax at all levels of the production/service chain with right to tax credit	
	Taxable activities	Delivery of goods and services in Austria	
	Taxable activities – zero-rated (examples)	A zero rate applies to the export of goods and services, including transport	
	Exemptions (examples)	• Transactions related to the sale or lease of any property located in Austria (option to VAT possible) • Banking and insurance services • Educational supplies • Certain welfare services, including hospital and medical care services • Small business entrepreneurs (limit up to €30,000)	
	Refund of VAT	By way of tax credit in the chain of business activity – no credit for tax paid on tax- exempts	For foreigners, electronic VAT refund procedure • EU: Tax refund in the home country • Non-EU: Tax refund to be claimed in Austria (Graz)
	Tax liability	• Normally the supplier of goods and services is responsible for charging VAT • Reverse charge for certain supplies of goods and services (eg consultancy services received from businesses established outside Austria)	
	Tax rates	There are 3 tax rates at present: 10%, 13% and 20%. Most goods and services in Austria are taxed at 20%, but certain essential goods and services are taxed at 10%. From 2016 onwards, there is a tax rate of 13% for some agricultural products, works of art and sporting events; and, from 1 May 2016, also for lodging, theatre and musical performances and entrance fee in museums	
	Administrative obligations	• Formal requirements concerning invoices • VAT identification number must be shown on all invoices • Monthly self- assessment VAT return plus VAT payment (smaller businesses quarterly) • Recapitulative statement • Annual VAT return • VAT groups of entities are possible • A Cash Register is necessary – exemption for very small enterprises • Compulsory receipt for every transaction	• Registration for VAT purposes, concerning supplies of goods and services in Austria • Austrian annual VAT return • Fiscal representation possible but, in many cases, not obligatory

	Residents	Non-residents
Real Property Tax	based on a special valuation (usually low)	
Real Property Transfer Tax	• 3.5% of the value of transaction if sold against payment • Between 0.5% and 3.5% on a calculated value for transaction for non-paid transactions and for all transactions of specific relatives, no matter if against payment or not • Specific rules for the calculated value for tax reasons	
Stamp Duty	Stamp duty is levied on a number of transactions (for example, assignment of receivables, rent and lease contracts). The stamp duty on mortgages has been abolished For example, the tax rate on a 3-year rent is about 1%	

Azerbaijan

(Hasan Hagverdiyev, Nexia EA LLC, hasan.hagverdiyev@nexia.az)

I MAIN LEGAL FORMS

Legal form / Characteristics	Limited Liability Company (LLC)	Open Joint Stock Company (OJSC) and Closed Joint Stock Company (CJSC)
Partners/shareholders • Number • Restrictions	• One or more • None	• One or more • None
Directors	Director as appointed by general meeting of founders	Director as appointed by general meeting of shareholders
Establishment	Can be founded as new or created through restructuring	
Registration	State Registration Body of Commercial Legal Entities	
Minimum capital	Unlimited	Minimum limit is appointed by the relevant government body (Azerbaijan Civil Code 103.5)
Liability	Limited to invested capital in business	
Governance	General Meeting of Members, Board of Directors	General Meeting of Shareholders, Board of Directors
Audit requirements	Audit is mandatory for LLC	Audit is mandatory
Taxation	Corporate taxation	

II   CORPORATION TAX

Legal Form / Description	Resident corporation	Permanent establishment (PE)
General description	Corporate income tax	Corporate income tax, Branch net profit remittance tax
Taxable entities	Any legal entity established in accordance with the legislation of the Azerbaijan Republic and performing entrepreneurial activity or the entity which is managed in Azerbaijan	PE located in Azerbaijan[1]
Taxable income	Worldwide income	A PE of a foreign legal entity is subject to taxation with respect to the income attributable to such PE
Calculation of taxable profits	Profit tax is computed on the basis of an enterprise's taxable profits. Profits are defined as the difference between the gross income and deductions allowed by the legislation	
Interest payments	Transfer pricing rules are in place that require funding arrangements to be at arm's length for interest payment to remain tax deductible	Transfer pricing rules are in place that require funding arrangements to be at arm's length for interest payment to remain tax deductible
Related party transactions	All related party transactions must take place on arm's length basis	
Tax year, return and payment	Tax year is calendar year Tax return should be submitted and final tax payments should be made no later than 31 March after the end of a tax year Advance tax payments are made within 15 days after the end of each calendar quarter	
Capital gains	There is no separate capital gains taxation in Azerbaijan. Proceeds from the disposal of capital assets are included in the ordinary taxable income	
Losses	Companies are allowed to carry forward their losses during a period of 5 years without limitation	
Tax group	No	No
Tax rate	20%[2]	20%[2]

---

1   A PE is an establishment of a foreign legal entity, through which it fully or partially performs commercial activity (for these purposes, a PE may be considered a management unit, office bureau, agency, construction site, etc) for more than 90 consecutive days within any 12-month period.
2   According to the changes to the Tax Code in June 2009, effective from 1 January 2010, the profit tax rate is reduced from 22% to 20%.

III   TAXES FOR INDIVIDUALS

<table>
<tr><td colspan="2"></td><th>Residents</th><th>Non-residents</th></tr>
<tr><td rowspan="14">Income Tax</td><td>General description</td><td colspan="2">Persons actually staying in the territory of Azerbaijan Republic for more than 182 days during a calendar year are considered as residents[3]</td></tr>
<tr><td rowspan="2">Taxable entities and taxable income</td><td>Taxable entity – physical person</td><td>Taxable entity – physical person</td></tr>
<tr><td>Taxable income – worldwide income (income generated in and outside of Azerbaijan Republic)</td><td>Taxable income – income generated from sources in Azerbaijan Republic</td></tr>
<tr><td rowspan="3">Types of taxable income</td><td colspan="2">Income from employment in Azerbaijan (salary, wage, etc)</td></tr>
<tr><td colspan="2">Income from activities not connected with employment (income from entrepreneurial activity)[4]</td></tr>
<tr><td colspan="2">All other kinds of income that are not tax exempt</td></tr>
<tr><td rowspan="4">Calculation of income</td><td colspan="2">Income is calculated as the difference between gross income for a tax year and expenses or deductions for this period</td></tr>
<tr><td colspan="2">Tax year is the calendar year</td></tr>
<tr><td colspan="2">Tax assessment – resident individual taxpayers (excluding employees) should prepare and file tax returns no later than 31 March of following year</td></tr>
<tr><td colspan="2">Tax payment – the above-mentioned taxpayer should pay all the taxes by 31 March considering the quarterly current tax payments which are due by the 15th day after the end of each quarter</td></tr>
<tr><td>Losses</td><td colspan="2">Losses can only be offset against taxable income from commercial activities of individual taxpayers. Such losses can be carried forward for 3 years</td></tr>
<tr><td rowspan="2">Tax rates</td><td>Monthly income: less than AZN 2,500 – 14% tax</td><td>Monthly income: less than AZN 2,500 – 14% tax</td></tr>
<tr><td>More than AZN 2,500 – AZN 350 + 25% of the amount exceeding AZN 2,500</td><td>More than AZN 2,500 – AZN 350 + 25% of the amount exceeding AZN 2,500</td></tr>
</table>

3   Residency of a physical person who stays either in the territory of the Azerbaijan Republic or in a foreign country for less than 182 days will be considered a resident of the Azerbaijan Republic according to the following criteria:
   • Place of permanent stay
   • Centre of vital interests
   • Regular place of residence
   • Citizenship of the Azerbaijan Republic.
4   From 2010 the business income for individual entrepreneurs is subject to taxation at 20%.
   The income of non-entrepreneurial persons is subject to ordinary personal income tax rates.

		Residents	Non-residents
Capital Gains Tax (CGT)	General description	There is no definition of capital gains of individuals in the tax legislation of Azerbaijan. However, income from the disposal of assets (as a difference between the purchase and sale value) is considered taxable income: • 14% to 25% of the income after expenses being deducted for non-residents with a permanent establishment (PE) • 10% at the source of payment for non-residents without a PE If tax treaties provide for lower rates, a credit or refund of the excess tax amount is possible	
	Taxable entities and chargeable assets		
	Tax year, tax assessment and tax payment		
	Losses		
	Tax rates		
		Domiciled	**Non-domiciled**
Inheritance Tax (IHT)	General description	There is no inheritance tax	
	Taxable entities and chargeable assets		
	Calculation of charge		
	Taxable events		
	Allowances		
	Tax rates		

IV WITHHOLDING TAXES

Under domestic law	Payments to residents	Payments to non-residents
Dividends	10%	10%
Interest	10%	10%
Royalties	14%	14%
On payments to artists and sportsmen	Prizes less than AZN 4,000 won in international competitions or AZN 200 won in national competitions are exempt from income tax	

Reduced rate available under the relevant Double Taxation Treaty			
Country	Dividends	Interest	Royalties
Austria	15%	10%	10%
Belarus	15%	10%	10%
Belgium	5%	10%	10%
Bulgaria	8%	7%	10%
Canada	15%	10%	10%
China	10%	10%	10%
Czech Republic	8%	10%	10%
Estonia	10%	10%	10%
Finland	10%	10%	10%
France	10%	10%	10%
Georgia	10%	10%	10%
Germany	15%	10%	10%
Hungary	8%	8%	8%
Iran	10%	10%	10%
Kazakhstan	10%	10%	10%
Latvia	10%	10%	10%
Lithuania	10%	10%	10%
Luxembourg	10%	10%	10%
Moldova	15%	10%	10%
Netherlands	10%	10%	10%
Norway	15%	10%	10%
Poland	10%	10%	10%
Qatar	7%	7%	5%
Republic of Korea	7%	10%	10%
Romania	10%	8%	10%
Russia	10%	10%	10%
Switzerland	15%	10%	10%
Tajikistan	10%	10%	10%

Note: the above rates are only available provided the specific Treaty criteria are satisfied. As treaties will not be identical, guidance should be sought in all cases. It is possible that lower rates than those shown above may be available provided that certain criteria are satisfied. If the treaty rate is higher than the domestic rate, the domestic rate will apply.

V   INDIRECT TAXES

<table>
<tr><th></th><th></th><th>Residents</th><th>Non-residents</th></tr>
<tr><td rowspan="10">Value Added Tax (VAT)</td><td>General description</td><td colspan="2">Value added tax (VAT) is levied on the supply of goods and services and on the import of goods</td></tr>
<tr><td>Entities obliged to levy VAT</td><td colspan="2">Any person who is or is to be registered as a VAT payer is regarded a taxable person. Companies are required to register for VAT if their taxable income exceeds AZN 200,000 for the previous 12 months</td></tr>
<tr><td>Taxable activities</td><td colspan="2">The supply of goods and services in Azerbaijan and imports to Azerbaijan are subject to taxation. Barter transactions are also subject to VAT. Such transactions are valued in accordance with normal prices</td></tr>
<tr><td>Taxable activities – zero-rated (examples)</td><td colspan="2">The zero rate applies to:

• exportation of goods and services
• operations under the Production Sharing Agreements regimes
• importation of goods, the supply of goods, and the implementation of works and provision of services to grant recipients on the expense of financial aid (grants) received from abroad
• international and transit cargo and passenger transportation, as well as the supply of works and services directly connected with international and transit flights; and
• the supply of gold and other valuables to the National Bank of Azerbaijan</td></tr>
<tr><td>Exemptions (examples)</td><td colspan="2">Some of the most important exemptions from VAT are the following:

• the supply and import of the national and foreign currencies (except for numismatic purposes) as well as of securities
• the import of gold and valuables to be deposited with the National Bank of Azerbaijan, as well as import of monetary means, anniversary coins and other similar valuables of Azerbaijan, manufactured abroad
• investment of property in the form of shares into the charter capital of a company, with the exception of imported property[5]</td></tr>
<tr><td>Refund of VAT</td><td colspan="2">The credited tax amount that exceeds the calculated tax amount in the accounting period shall be carried forward to the following 3 months and credited against the payments of that period. Any balance of the excess payment shall be refunded from the treasury within 45 days after filing a tax return for that period</td></tr>
<tr><td>Tax liability</td><td colspan="2">Supplier of goods and services and importer is responsible for charging VAT</td></tr>
<tr><td>Tax rates</td><td colspan="2">Tax rate is 18%</td></tr>
<tr><td>Administrative obligations</td><td colspan="2">Any person who is or is to be registered as a VAT payer is regarded as a taxable person. Companies are required to register for VAT if their taxable income exceeds AZN 200,000 for the previous 12 months</td></tr>
</table>

5   The Cabinet of Ministers is entitled to grant exemptions for the import of goods and equipment used for production purposes or to provide advanced technology know-how. Such exemptions are granted for a specific period and in a specific area, and can only be granted if it is impossible to satisfy the respective needs from local resources.

	Residents	Non-residents
Real Property Taxes	Property tax is levied on both movable and immovable tangible assets owned by individuals and companies. The tax base varies according to the identity of the taxpayer. Resident companies are subject to tax on their tangible assets recorded on their balance sheet. Non-resident companies carrying out a business activity by a PE in Azerbaijan are only subject to tax on their tangible assets connected with the permanent establishment	
Stamp Duty	None	

Bahrain

(Nabeel Al Saie, Nabeel Al-Saie – Public Accountants, nabilsai@batelco.com.bh)

I MAIN LEGAL FORMS

Legal form / Characteristics	Partnership, Limited Liability Partnership (WLL), Single Person Company (SPC)	BSC (Closed) and BSC (Public)
Partners/shareholders • Number • Restrictions	General partnership: minimum number – two WLL companies: partners should not exceed 50 SPC companies: fully owned by one person	BSC (Closed): number of persons not less than two BSC (Public): minimum number – seven
Directors	No minimum/maximum requirements	BSC (Public): minimum number of directors is five BSC (Closed): minimum number of directors is three
Establishment	In accordance with Bahrain Commercial Companies Law	
Registration	Registration through Bahrain Commercial Companies Law	
Minimum capital	WLL: BHD20,000 SPC: BHD50,000	BSC (Public): BHD1m BSC (Closed): BHD250,000
Liability	WLL: only liable to the extent of their respective share in the capital Partnership: partners are jointly liable to the extent of all their property of the company's obligations	BSC (Public): liable for the company's debts and obligations only to the extent of the value of their share BSC (Closed): N/A
Governance	As per Memorandum and Articles	Board of Directors and ultimately the equity shareholders in General Meeting
Audit requirements	As per Memorandum and Articles – audit is mandatory	Independent audit report to the shareholders as per the regulations
Taxation	No tax	No tax

II CORPORATION TAX

Legal form / Description	Partnership, Limited Liability Partnership WLL, Single Person Company (SPC)	BSC (Closed) and BSC (Public)
General description	No tax	No tax
Taxable entities		
Taxable income		
Calculation of taxable profits		
Interest payments	Interest is allowed on accrual basis	
Related party transactions	Transactions between related companies or persons are deemed to take place at market value	
Tax year, return and payment		
Capital gains		
Losses	As per the Articles of Association	
Tax group		
Tax rate		

III TAXES FOR INDIVIDUALS

		Residents	Non-residents
Income Tax	General description	There is no income tax for individuals	
	Taxable entities and taxable income		
	Types of taxable income		
	Calculation of income		
	Tax year, tax assessment and tax payment		
	Losses		
	Tax rates		
Capital Gains Tax (CGT)	General description	There is no capital gains tax	
	Taxable entities and chargeable assets		
	Calculation of gain		
	Tax year, tax assessment and tax payment		
	Losses		
	Tax rates		
		Domiciled	**Non-domiciled**
Inheritance Tax (IHT)	General description	There is no inheritance tax	
	Taxable entities and chargeable assets		
	Calculation of charge		
	Taxable events		
	Allowances		
	Tax rates		

IV   WITHHOLDING TAXES

Under domestic law	Payments to residents	Payments to non-residents
Dividends	Nil	Nil
Interest	Nil	Nil
Royalties	Nil	Nil
On payments to artists and sportsmen	Nil	Nil

Note: Bahrain has double tax treaties with a number of countries but these are of no relevance to the rate of withholding tax as there is none.

V INDIRECT TAXES

		Residents	Non-residents
Value Added Tax (VAT)	General description	There is no VAT in Bahrain	
	Entities obliged to levy VAT		
	Taxable activities		
	Taxable activities – zero-rated (examples)		
	Exemptions (examples)		
	Refund of VAT		
	Tax liability		
	Tax rates		
	Administrative obligations		
Real Property Taxes		There are no real property taxes in Bahrain	
Stamp Duty		There are no stamp duties in Bahrain	

Nexia International does not accept liability for any loss arising from any action taken, or omission, on the basis of this publication. Professional advice should be obtained before acting or refraining from acting on the contents of this publication. Membership of Nexia International, or associated umbrella organizations, does not constitute any partnership between members, and members do not accept any responsibility for the commission of any act, or omission to act by, or the liabilities of, other members.

Nexia International is the trading name of Nexia International Limited, a company registered in the Isle of Man. Company registration number: 53513C. Registered office: 2nd floor, Sixty Circular Road, Douglas, Isle of Man, IM1 1SA

© Nexia International 2017

Barbados

(Anthony Hobbs, Hobbs, Niles & Co, ahobbs@hobbsniles.bb)

I MAIN LEGAL FORMS

Legal form / Characteristics	Limited Partnership	• Regular Barbados Company/Corporation • International Business Company • International and Domestic Society with Restricted Liability • Exempt Insurance Company • Qualifying Insurance Company
Partners/ Shareholders/ Members • Number • Restrictions	One or more No restrictions	One or more No restrictions
Directors	General partner or limited partners	Resident and overseas directors/managers
Establishment	Partnership agreement	Articles of Incorporation (registered)
Registration	Corporate affairs and Intellectual property office	Corporate affairs and Intellectual property office
Minimum capital	None	None
Liability	General partner liable for all debts and obligations Limited liability for limited partners	Generally limited to shareholders and capital invested
Governance	General partner and general meeting	Board of Directors/ Managers Shareholders'/ Members' meetings
Audit requirements	None	Required for Companies or Societies whose assets/revenue exceeds Bds$4,000,000
Taxation	Partners' share of partnership income	– Subject to corporation tax rate on worldwide income – Dividends distributed to individuals are generally subject to withholding tax – Dividends distributed to corporations are not subject to withholding tax
Usage	Financial organizations and professional practices	Public corporation, small and medium-sized enterprises

II   CORPORATION TAX

Description / Legal form	Resident corporation	Permanent establishment (PE)
General description	Corporation Tax	
Taxable entities	Companies registered in Barbados and foreign companies with mind and management located in Barbados	PE located in Barbados
Taxable income	Worldwide income	Income derived by PE in Barbados
Calculation of taxable profits	Accounting income is adjusted for various tax add-backs and allowances to arrive at taxable income	
Interest payments	Interest payments deducted by an associated or a related company which do not take place at arm's length and are not paid within one year must be added back to assessable income Interest payments deducted by a non-associated or non-related company and not paid within two consecutive years after the income year in which the amount was deducted must be added back to the assessable income	
Related party transactions	Related party transactions should take place on an arm's length basis	
Tax year, return and payment	Tax year – Business year (Calendar or different year end) Tax returns must be filed on 15 March for companies with fiscal year ends between 1 January and 30 September, and 15 June for companies with fiscal year ends between 1 October and 31 December. Balance of taxes are due at 15 March and 15 June	
Capital gains	No capital gains taxes in Barbados	
Losses	Business losses can be carried forward for seven (7) years which became effective from the 2015 income year. No business losses can be carried back to prior income years	
Tax group	No filing of consolidated tax returns are permitted	
Tax rate	Regular Barbados Company – 25% Approved Small Business – 15% International Business Company – 2.5% up to Bds$10m and at reduced rates thereafter International Society with Restricted Liability – 2.5% up to Bds$10m and at reduced rates thereafter Qualifying Insurance Company – 25% and reduced by foreign currency tax credits to an effective tax rate of 1.7%	As for domestic entities but subject to the terms of relevant Double Taxation Agreement

III TAXES FOR INDIVIDUALS

		Residents	Non-residents
Income Tax	General description	Income tax on income for individuals	
	Taxable entities and taxable income	Resident individuals are subject to personal income tax on worldwide income from all sources	Non-resident individuals are taxable generally on income from Barbados sources
	Types of taxable income	Employment, business, rental, dividends, interest, royalties and other	Employment, business, rental, dividends and other
	Calculation of income	Aggregate of income minus certain deductions	Aggregate of income. Generally, no personal deductions
	Tax year, tax assessment and tax payment	Tax year – Calendar year Self assessment return and balance of taxes are due for filing on 30 April, following the end of year	
	Losses	No losses from business or property can be deducted against employment income. Losses from residential rental income can be carried forward for seven years	
	Tax rates	Basic personal amount tax-free: $25,000 Progressive tax rates: • 16% of taxable income up to and including $35,000 • 33.5% of taxable income above $35,000	Same as for residents except no personal deductions
		Residents	**Non-residents**
Capital Gains Tax (CGT)	General description	No capital gains taxes in Barbados	
	Taxable entities and chargeable assets	No capital gains taxes on entities or assets	
	Calculation of gain	None	None
	Tax year, tax assessment and tax payment	None	None
	Losses	None	None
	Tax rates	None	None
		Domiciled	**Non-domiciled**
Inheritance Tax (IHT)	General description	No inheritance taxes in Barbados	
	Taxable entities and chargeable assets	None	None
	Calculation of charge	None	None
	Taxable events	None	None
	Allowances	None	None
	Tax rates	Barbados has no inheritance estate taxes, duties or gift taxes	

IV   WITHHOLDING TAXES

Under domestic law	Payments to residents	Payments to non-residents
Dividends	12.5%	15%
Interest	12.5%	15%
Royalties	0%	15%
On payments to artists and sportsmen	0%	25%

Reduced rate available under the relevant Double Taxation Treaty			
Country	**Dividends**	**Interest**	**Royalties**
Austria	15%	0%	0%
Bahrain	0%	0%	0%
Botswana	12%	10%	10%
Canada	15%	15%	10%
Caricom	0%	15%	15%
China (PRC)	10%	10%	10%
Cuba	15%	10%	5%
Czech Republic	15%	5%	5%
Finland	15%	5%	5%
Ghana	Not yet in force	Not yet in force	Not yet in force
Italy	Not yet in force	Not yet in force	Not yet in force
Iceland	15%	10%	5%
Luxembourg	15%	0%	0%
Malta	15%	5%	5%
Mauritius	5%	5%	5%
Mexico	10%	10%	10%
Netherlands	15%	5%	5%
Norway	15%	5%	5%
Panama	5%	7.5%	7.5%
Portugal	Not yet in force	Not yet in force	Not yet in force
Qatar	0%	0%	5%
Rwanda	Not yet in force	Not yet in force	Not yet in force
San Marino	5%	5%	0%
Seychelles	5%	5%	5%
Singapore	0%	12%	8%
Spain	0%	0%	0%
Sweden	15%	5%	5%
Switzerland	0%	0%	0%
United Arab Emirates	Not yet in force	Not yet in force	Not yet in force
United Kingdom	0%	0%	0%
United States	15%	5%	5%
Venezuela	10%	15%	10%

Note: International Business Companies, International Societies with Restricted Liabilities, Exempt Insurance Companies and Qualifying Insurance Companies are exempt from withholding taxes on payments to non-resident persons or international business entities. Specific legislation applies.

Note: the above rates are only available provided the specific Treaty criteria are satisfied. It is possible that lower rates than those shown above may be available provided certain criteria are satisfied. As treaties will not be identical, guidance should be sought in all cases.

V INDIRECT TAXES

		Residents	Non-residents
Value Added Tax	General description	Goods and services are subject to Value Added Tax. Some goods and services are zero-rated or exempt	
	Entities obliged to levy VAT	Corporations, partnerships and proprietors who are registered with the Barbados Revenue Authority. Taxable supplies more than Bds$200,000	
	Taxable activities	Goods and services unless zero-rated or exempt	
	Taxable activities – zero-rated (examples)	Services and goods rendered to companies in the International Business sector regime. A basket of food items	
	Exemptions (examples)	Financial services, education, healthcare, certain real properties	
	Refund of VAT	Input tax credits if related to taxable or zero-rated supplies	Same rules as residents if registered for VAT
	Tax liability	Output tax	
	Tax rates	17.5%	17.5%
	Administrative obligations	Registration if more than Bds$200,000 of taxable supplies • Collection of VAT tax • Filing of VAT returns on a 2-month period and remitting balance due	Same requirements for residents if non-resident is carrying on business in Barbados

Real Property Taxes		Vacant Land Non Residential Residential
		    0.80% 0.70% 0% on first Bds$150,000
		                                 0.10% on the next $300,000
		                                 0.45% on the next $550,000
		                                 0.75% on amounts over $1,000,000
		Property transfer tax is payable by the vendor at a rate of 2.5% of the sale price	

Stamp Duty		1% of the sale price	

Belgium

(Edwin Vervoort, VGD, edwin.vervoort@vgd.eu; David Lornoy, VGD, david.lornoy@vgd.eu)

I MAIN LEGAL FORMS

Legal form / Characteristics	Partnership	Private corporation (Ltd) and Public corporation (Plc)
Partners/shareholders • Number • Restrictions	No restrictions. A partnership has no legal personality	Public limited liability company (NV/SA): at least two shareholders
		Private limited liability company (BVBA/SPRL): at least one shareholder (when this is a legal person, the company-subscriber of the whole capital of a BVBA is also jointly responsible for all engagements of the company, as long as the company-shareholder remains the only shareholder)
Directors	No specific requirements to register	NV: three directors at least or two in case of only two shareholders
		BVBA: at least one manager
Establishment	Notary deed or private contract	Notary deed
Registration	No specific requirement to register	• Deposit at the registry of the commercial court • Publication in the annexes of the Belgian Official Gazette • Inscription in the register of legal persons (Crossroads Bank for Enterprises)
Minimum capital	None	NV (SA): €61,500, fully subscribed and paid-in
		BVBA (SPRL): €18,550, fully subscribed, minimum €6,200 paid-in or €12,400 in case of only one shareholder
		'Starters' BVBA (SPRL): €1 capital
Liability	Unlimited	Limited liability
Governance	No specific rules apply	Board meetings
		Shareholders' meetings

Legal form / Characteristics	Partnership	Private corporation (Ltd) and Public corporation (Plc)
Audit requirements	None	Companies are subject to statutory audit if certain limits are exceeded (turnover, balance total, number of personnel)
Taxation	Transparent for tax purposes. Tax is levied on behalf of the partner's level	Resident companies are subject to corporation tax on their profits derived anywhere in the world

II CORPORATION TAX

Description \ Legal form	Resident corporation	Permanent establishment (PE)
General description	Corporation tax	
Taxable entities	Resident companies are subject to corporation tax on their worldwide income	Companies with a Belgian PE are taxable on all income derived from such establishment
Taxable income	Worldwide profits with some relief to avoid double taxation (DTTs)	All income derived from such establishment
Calculation of taxable profits	Accounting profit is adjusted for various tax add-backs and allowances to arrive to profits chargeable to corporation tax	
	Notional interest deduction (NID): up to 1.13% (1.63% for SMEs) for tax year 2017 calculated on the equity of the company (subject to certain deductions/restrictions). Excess of notional interest deduction cannot be carried forward (beginning from taxable period 2012)	
	A participation exemption of 95% applies to dividends received if the following conditions are met:	
	• The recipient company must own a minimum participation of 10% or a participation with an acquisition value of at least €2.5m	
	• The shares must be held for at least one year in full ownership	
	• The distributing company is subject to a common corporate tax regime (taxation test)	
	Patent income deduction regime: income from qualifying patents can be exempted from taxes for 80%. R&D department within the company is not required for SMEs. The current patent income deduction regime is abolished as of 30 June 2016 (but grandfathering period until 30 June 2021) and will be replaced by the deduction for innovation income. The new deduction reflects a broader scope of the qualifying income (eg breeder rights are eligible). In contrast to the previous regime, the qualifying income will be calculated on a net basis but the percentage of the deduction will be raised to 85%. Also new is the nexus approach to ensure that, in order to qualify for the benefits, a significant proportion of the actual R&D activities must have been undertaken by the taxpayer itself	
Interest payments	Interest expenses are tax deductible expenses when these are at arm's length. Thin capitalisation restrictions apply to loan if granted by shareholders or directors; 1:1 debt to equity ratio	
	For loans granted by a company enjoying an advantageous tax regime, the rate is 5:1 debt to equity ratio	
	For loans granted by some group companies, a 5:1 debt to equity ratio can apply	
Related party transactions	All related party transactions must take place on an arm's length basis, and transactions between related parties must be at fair market value	

Legal form / Description	Resident corporation	Permanent establishment (PE)
Tax year, return and payment	Usual tax year coincides with the calendar year, but the accounting year of a company can be fixed for any 12-month period	
	Legally the return must be filed not later than 6 months after the end of the accounting period. In practice a term of 8 or 9 months is allowed	
	Companies can make advance payments of taxes in four instalments:	
	• for the first quarter, no later than 10 April • for the second quarter, no later than 10 July • for the third quarter, no later than 10 October • for the fourth quarter, no later than 20 December	
	(if tax year does not coincide with the calendar year, other deadlines apply)	
	If the advance payments are too little compared to the final tax burden, there is an increase for insufficient prepayments. Small companies are exempted from making instalment payments during the first three tax years	
	Final notice of assessment will be issued no later than 18 months after the end of the tax year	
Capital gains	Capital gains are subject to the standard corporate income tax rate of 33.99%. Capital gains realised on tangible and intangible fixed assets can benefit from a deferred taxation regime	
	Capital gains on shares are exempted if certain conditions are met (hold period of at least 12 months and taxation test have to be satisfied). As from 2013 capital gains on shares are taxed at a rate of 0.412% for companies not qualifying as an SME	
	Capital gains on shares realised within 12 months after acquisition are taxed at a rate of 25.75% (applies to all companies)	
	Capital losses on shares are not deductible (exemption in case of liquidation of the company and to the extent of loss of the original paid-in capital)	
Losses	Tax losses can be carried forward (no time limit)	
Tax group	Not available	
Tax rate	General rate: 33.99% (if certain conditions are met, reduced tax rates apply: 24.98% and 31.93%)	
	For large companies (not SME companies) a fairness tax at a rate of 5.15% is also due if, for the same taxable period, the company distributes dividends *and* the taxable base is reduced with previous year tax losses and current year NID	

III TAXES FOR INDIVIDUALS

		Residents	Non-residents
Income Tax	General description	Tax levied on the taxable income a taxpayer receives during the preceding calendar year	
	Taxable entities and taxable income	Residents are taxed on their worldwide income with some relief to avoid double taxation (DTTs)	Non-residents are taxed on income arising from Belgian source
	Types of taxable income	• Property income (usually rent) • Income from capital investment (interests, dividends, royalties) • Income from independent business activities • Income from employment • Pensions • Capital gains • Miscellaneous income	
	Calculation of income	The taxable income equals the gross income minus expenses and minus certain allowances A specific tax regime for expats exists. Several allowances apply. Income that can be allocated to working days performed outside Belgium are exempt from taxes (travel exclusion)	
	Tax year, tax assessment and tax payment	• Tax year = calendar year • Tax assessment – issued by the Belgian tax authorities by the end of June of the second year following the calendar year • When no form is received by 30 June of the year following the calendar year during which the income is earned, the taxpayer must ask the authorities to send a form	
	Losses	Tax losses of professional activities can be carried forward (no time limit)	
	Tax rates	*Income (€)* *Tax rate (%) (for tax year 2017)* 0–10,860 25 10,860–12,470 30 12,470–20,780 40 20,780–38,080 45 > 38,080 50 Local taxes can apply from 0% to 10% (calculated on the taxes due) Interest, dividends, royalties are taxed separately at tax rates from 10% to 30% (see also section IV)	

		Residents	**Non-residents**
Capital Gains Tax (CGT)	General description	In general no capital gains tax for individuals	
		Capital gains tax on sale of land or buildings applies if transaction occurs within a period of 5 to 8 years after acquisition and varies from 16.50% to 33% + local taxes	
		Capital gains on shares: taxable at 33% + local tax unless the transaction can be considered as a normal management of the individual's private estate	
		Capital gains on shares: 16.5% + local tax if the transaction concerns a participation of at least 25% of the company and sold to a company outside the EEA (European Economic Area)	
		Belgian domiciled	**Non-Belgian domiciled**
Inheritance Tax (IHT)	Taxable entities and chargeable assets	In case of Belgian tax residency, Belgian inheritance taxes become due	Only real estate located in Belgium
	Calculation of charge	Based on value of estate, subject to exemptions	
	Allowances	Vary from region to region (Flanders, Brussels and Wallonie)	
	Tax rates	Tax rates may differ from region to region and vary between 3%–30% (direct line and husband-wife) but may reach up to 80% for non-related persons depending upon total value of assets and the kinship between the deceased and the beneficiary	
		Certain exemptions and reduced tax rates apply for family-owned businesses and family-owned companies	
		In most cases inheritance taxes can be avoided extremely by well-timed gifts	

IV WITHHOLDING TAXES

Under domestic law	Payments to residents (final taxation for individuals)	Payments to non-residents[1]
Dividends	General: 30%	Ditto
	15% for SMEs if certain conditions are met (only for dividends remunerating new capital paid in cash)	
	All SMEs are allowed to allocate part or all of their yearly 'profit after taxes' to a 'liquidation reserve'. This reserve needs to be recorded on an unavailable equity account (which cannot serve as a basis for any distribution or remuneration) and will be (immediately) subject to a separate 10% tax	
	No additional taxation (withholding or personal tax) will be due provided the 'liquidation reserve' is maintained until liquidation and hence distributed as a liquidation bonus	
	If the 'liquidation reserve' is distributed during the first 5 years, a 17% or 20%[2] withholding tax will be due	
	If the 'liquidation reserve' is distributed after 5 years and before liquidation, a 5% withholding tax will be due	
	The FIFO method will apply for any withdrawal from the 'liquidation reserve'	
Interest	General: 30%	General: 30%
	15% for some interest on deposit savings	15% for some interest on deposit savings
		0% in some cases
Royalties	30%	30%

Belgium has negotiated a range of tax treaties which provide an exemption or a reduction in withholding taxes on dividends, interest and royalties payable.

Reduced rate available under the relevant Double Taxation Treaty			
	Dividends	**Interest**	**Royalties**
Albania	15%	5%	5%
Algeria	15%	15%	15%
Argentina	15%	12%	15%
Armenia	15%	10%	8%

---

1 Reduced rates of withholding tax may apply where there is an appropriate double tax treaty.
2 Rate applicable for new reserves built up under this regime as of 1 January 2017.

Reduced rate available under the relevant Double Taxation Treaty			
	Dividends	**Interest**	**Royalties**
Australia	15%	10%	10%
Austria	15%	15%	Nil
Azerbaijan	15%	10%	10%
Bangladesh	15%	15%	10%
Belarus	15%	10%	5%
Brazil	15%	15%	15%
Bulgaria	10%	10%	5%
Canada	15%	15%	10%
China	10%	10%	10%
Croatia	15%	10%	Nil
Cyprus	15%	10%	Nil
Czech Republic	15%	10%	10%
Denmark	15%	10%	Nil
Ecuador	15%	10%	10%
Egypt	20%	15%	15%
Estonia	15%	10%	10%
Finland	15%	10%	5%
France	15%	15%	Nil
Gabon	15%	15%	10%
Georgia	15%	10%	10%
Germany	15%	15%	Nil
Greece	15%	10%	5%
Hong Kong	15%	10%	5%
Hungary	10%	15%	Nil
Iceland	15%	10%	Nil
India	15%	15%	10%
Indonesia	15%	10%	10%
Ireland	15%	15%	Nil
Israel	15%	15%	10%
Italy	15%	15%	5%
Ivory Coast	15%	15%	10%
Japan	15%	10%	10%
Kazakhstan	15%	10%	10%
Kuwait	10%	Nil	10%
Latvia	15%	10%	10%
Lithuania	15%	10%	10%
Luxembourg	15%	15%	Nil
Malaysia	15%	10%	10%
Malta	15%	10%	10%
Mauritius	10%	10%	Nil
Mexico	15%	15%	10%
Mongolia	15%	10%	5%
Morocco	10%	15%	10%
Netherlands	15%	10%	Nil
New Zealand	15%	10%	10%

Reduced rate available under the relevant Double Taxation Treaty			
	Dividends	Interest	Royalties
Nigeria	15%	12.5%	12.5%
Norway	15%	15%	Nil
Pakistan	15%	15%	15%
Philippines	15%	10%	15%
Poland	10%	5%	5%
Portugal	15%	15%	10%
Republic of Korea	15%	10%	10%
Romania	15%	15%	5%
Russian Federation	10%	10%	Nil
San Marino	15%	10%	5%
Senegal	15%	15%	10%
Singapore	15%	5%	5%
Slovakia	15%	10%	5%
Slovenia	15%	10%	5%
South Africa	15%	10%	Nil
Spain	15%	10%	5%
Sri Lanka	15%	10%	10%
Sweden	15%	10%	Nil
Switzerland	15%	10%	Nil
Taiwan	10%	10%	10%
Thailand	20%	25%	11%
Tunisia	15%	10%	15%
Turkey	20%	15%	10%
Ukraine	15%	10%	10%
United Arab Emirates	10%	5%	5%
United Kingdom	10%	15%	Nil
United States	15%	Nil	Nil
Uzbekistan	15%	10%	5%
Venezuela	15%	10%	5%
Vietnam	15%	10%	15%
Non-treaty countries	30%	30%	30%

It is possible that lower rates than those shown above may be available provided certain criteria are satisfied. EU Directives may also apply to reduce the rate of withholding tax.

V   INDIRECT TAXES

<table>
<tr><th></th><th></th><th>Residents</th><th>Non-residents</th></tr>
<tr><td rowspan="9">Value Added Tax (VAT)</td><td>General description</td><td colspan="2">Tax on the supply of goods and services (VAT)</td></tr>
<tr><td>Entities obliged to levy VAT</td><td colspan="2">Nature of entity is of no relevance. The kind of transaction triggers the VAT status</td></tr>
<tr><td>Taxable activities</td><td colspan="2">All goods and services excluding sales of (old) real property, education and cultural activities</td></tr>
<tr><td>Taxable activities – zero-rated (examples)</td><td colspan="2">Newspapers</td></tr>
<tr><td>Exemptions (examples)</td><td colspan="2">• Sales of real property
• Rent of real property
• Education and healthcare
• Cultural activities</td></tr>
<tr><td>Refund of VAT</td><td colspan="2">Companies dealing in the export of goods and services may receive a reimbursement of VAT on exports on a monthly basis</td></tr>
<tr><td>Tax liability</td><td colspan="2">Normally the supplier of goods and services is responsible for charging VAT</td></tr>
<tr><td>Tax rates</td><td colspan="2">Standard rate = 21%

Other rates: 6% and 12%</td></tr>
<tr><td colspan="2">Real Property Transfer Taxes</td><td colspan="2">10% (Flanders Region) or 12.5% in the other regions of Belgium</td></tr>
<tr><td colspan="2">Stamp Duty</td><td colspan="2">Transactions relating to public funds that are concluded or executed in Belgium are subject to stamp duty. Exemptions for non-residents are available</td></tr>
</table>

Nexia International is the trading name of Nexia International Limited, a company registered in the Isle of Man. Company registration number: 53513C. Registered office: 2nd floor, Sixty Circular Road, Douglas, Isle of Man, IM1 1SA

Bolivia

(Willy Tudela, Tudela & TH Consulting Group SRL, La Paz, willytudela@tudelanexia.com)

I MAIN LEGAL FORMS

Legal form / Characteristics	Partnership and Limited Liability Partnership (LLP)	Private corporation and Public corporation
Partners/shareholders • Number • Restrictions	• Minimum of two partners for LLPs and Partnerships • More for corporations	
Directors	Partnerships, LLPs: no restrictions	Minimum three directors
Establishment	Written agreement presented to a public notary which certifies its establishment	
Registration	Chamber of Commerce or Industry – Fundempresa – National Tax Service	
Minimum capital	None	
Liability	• Up to the amount of their equity • Limited to capital participation	Up to the amount of their shares
Audit requirements	Financial statements certified by public accountant	
Taxation	Taxable on worldwide income. Partnerships are transparent	
Usage	No restriction	

II CORPORATION TAX

Description \ Legal form	Resident corporation	Permanent establishment (PE)
General description	Corporation tax	
Taxable entities	Taxable entities are both resident and non-resident, except those companies that have services partially provided in Bolivia	Tax is applicable also to non-resident companies doing business in Bolivia
Taxable income	Profits derived in Bolivia	
Calculation of taxable profits	Accounting profit is adjusted for various tax add-backs and allowances to arrive to profits chargeable to corporation tax (PCTCT)	
Interest payments	Interest paid to an official financial institution is accounted as a business cost, interest paid to third persons should be paid with a deduction of 13% VAT and transaction tax of 3%. Interest paid to related parties cannot exceed 30% of the interest paid to third parties	
Related party transactions	All related party transactions must take place on arm's-length basis	
Tax year, return and payment	• Fiscal year • Manufacturing, oil and construction industries – 1 April to 31 March • Agricultural and agro-industrial companies – 1 July to 30 June • Mining industries – 1 October to 30 September • Trading, banking, insurance, general services and all other industries not specifically mentioned – 1 January to 31 December	
Capital gains	Taxed as business income	
Losses	Net total losses are accumulated and updated and can be carried forward for unlimited periods until fully utilised against profits	
Tax group	None	
Tax rate	25%	

III TAXES FOR INDIVIDUALS

		Residents	Non-residents
Income Tax	General description	Tax levied on the chargeable income of residents' and non-residents' income from Bolivian sources	
	Taxable entities and taxable income	Residents are taxed on their territorial income	Non-residents are taxed on income received from Bolivian sources through withholding when payment is made
	Types of taxable income	• Property income (usually rent) • Income from capital investment (interest, sale of goodwill, dividends, royalties, annuities) • Income from business activities • Employment from personal services or pensions	
	Calculation of income	Residents are charged with 13% complementary VAT when receiving salaries and 13% VAT and 3% transaction tax when receiving other kinds of income. Non-residents are charged with a 12.5% income tax on income received	
	Tax year, tax assessment and tax payment	Complementary VAT taxpayers, performing dependent personal services, are subject to a monthly withholding which the employer must apply on the salary payroll	
	Losses	For individuals, if deductions are more than taxable income, the balance is carried forward (compensated) against the next month filed	
	Tax rates	13% income tax	
Capital Gains Tax (CGT)	Taxable entities and chargeable assets	There are no capital gains taxes levied on individuals in Bolivia	

		Bolivia domiciled	Non-Bolivia domiciled
Inheritance Tax (IHT)	General description	Cost of goods transferred by inheritance	
	Taxable entities and chargeable assets	Individuals are levied with an inheritance tax when receiving and declaring the following chargeable assets: real estate property, vehicles, investments and all other assets subject to public registration	
	Calculation of charge	Levied on property received and value of goods subjected to property tax (real estate and vehicles)	
	Taxable events	When a relative dies	
	Allowances	No allowances exist	
	Tax rates	1% inheritance tax 3% transaction tax	

IV   WITHHOLDING TAXES

Under domestic law	Payments to residents	Payments to non-residents[1]
Dividends	0%	12.5%
Interest	0%	12.5%
Royalties	0%	12.5%
On payments to artists and sportsmen	0%	12.5%

Reduced rate available under the relevant Double Taxation Treaty			
Country	Dividends	Interest	Royalties
Argentina	12.5%	12.5%	12.5%
Colombia	12.5%	12.5%	12.5%
Ecuador	12.5%	12.5%	12.5%
France	12.5%	12.5%	12.5%
Germany	12.5%	12.5%	12.5%
Peru	12.5%	12.5%	12.5%
Spain	10%	12.5%	12.5%
Sweden	12.5%	12.5%	12.5%
United Kingdom	12.5%	12.5%	12.5%

Note: In all cases the upper limit of withholding tax is 15%. It is possible that lower rates than those shown above may be available provided certain criteria are satisfied. The above rates are only available provided the specific Treaty criteria are satisfied. As treaties will not be identical, guidance should be sought in all cases.

---

1   Reduced rates of withholding tax may apply where there is an appropriate double tax treaty.

V   INDIRECT TAXES

		Residents	Non-residents
Value Added Tax (VAT)	General description	Tax on the supply of goods and services (VAT)	
	Entities obliged to levy VAT	All entities selling goods and services are levied with VAT	
	Taxable activities	All goods and services; all phases of production and wholesale or retail selling of goods as well as services and leisure or entertainment activities	
	Taxable activities – zero-rated (examples)	None	
	Exemptions (examples)	Sale of shares, debentures, securities	
	Refund of VAT	VAT included in export costs is refunded at invoice (of costs) levied with VAT presentation	
	Tax liability	Normally the supplier of goods and services is responsible for charging VAT and paying it	
	Tax rates	Standard rate = 13%	
	Administrative obligations	VAT must be paid during the next month (day 13 through to day 22) depending on the last number of its tax registration number	
Real Property Taxes		There is no real property tax in Bolivia	
Stamp Duty		There is no stamp duty in Bolivia	

Brazil

*(Paulo José de Carvalho, PP&C Auditores Independentes,
pj.carvalho@ppc.com.br)*

I MAIN LEGAL FORMS

Legal form / Characteristics	Partnership and Limited Liability Partnership (LLP)	Private corporation (Ltd) and Public corporation (Plc)
Partners/shareholders • Number • Restrictions	• Two or more • No restrictions, except for certain activities, regarding foreign shareholders/partners (eg mining, telecommunications, postal services and nuclear power)	
Directors	No limitation It is mandatory to have a resident citizen as an attorney	
Establishment	Articles of Incorporation for LLP	By-laws for Corporations
Registration	Articles of Incorporation must be registered with the Board of Trade	By-laws for Corporations must be registered with the Board of Trade
Minimum capital	No minimum capital requirements	
Liability	Limited to capital subscribed	
Governance	No requirements	Representation of minority listed companies, banks and regulated sector with some specific requirements
Audit requirements	Not mandatory, in general Required for companies that have total assets higher than R$240m or annual gross revenue higher than R$300m	Mandatory for listed companies, banks, regulated entities and companies that have total assets higher than R$240m or annual gross revenue higher than R$300m
Taxation	Taxable on worldwide income	Taxable on worldwide income

II   CORPORATION TAX

Description \ Legal form	Resident corporation	Permanent establishment (PE)
General description	Corporation tax	
Taxable entities	All resident corporations or non-residents with PE in Brazil are subject to the Brazilian Income Tax rules	
Taxable income	Worldwide profits with consideration for double taxation treaties	Profits derived from PE in Brazil
Calculation of taxable profits	Companies have three Federal Taxation System Options **(a) Pretax Profit System** Mandatory for financial institutions, companies that receive income from outside Brazil or tax benefits or companies with gross income above R$78m *Basis of calculation* The company's net profit adjusted by various additions and exclusions determined by legislation The provisional measure MP-627, converted into Law No. 12,973 / 2014, lists exhaustively the operations in which the adjustment to exclude the effects of the new accounting standards (for example, leasing, depreciation of assets, impairment testing, present value adjustments and fair value adjustments) **(b) Presumed Profit System** Companies whose net income does not exceed R$78m the prior year, and with no restriction under Brazilian law (see **(a)** above) *Basis of calculation* A percentage of the company's gross income is the basis for the federal income tax: • manufacturing and commercial companies/8% • transportation services companies/16% • services companies/32% **(c) Unified System for the Payment of Taxes by Small Businesses/'SIMPLES'** Not eligible for this system, among many other exclusions, are companies with annual gross income above R$3.6m for customers domiciled in Brazil, *companies with partners outside Brazil* and companies engaged in the energy and automotive fields The company opting for 'SIMPLES' may have an additional billing for customers domiciled abroad amounting to R$3.6m, thereby reaching a total invoicing of up to R$7.2m *Basis of calculation* A percentage of the company's gross income is the basis for *all* revenue, sales and income taxes	
Interest payments	Interest paid to foreign companies is subject to a withholding tax of 15%. The interest paid to related parties is also subject to transfer pricing rules (thin capitalization basis is twice the invested capital)	
Related party transactions	All related party transactions should take place on an arm's length basis	

Legal form / Description	Resident corporation	Permanent establishment (PE)
Tax year, return and payment	The tax year corresponds to the calendar year / Payments are usually made during the year as advances and, after the return is filed, as final payments	
Capital gains	Capital gains and losses have no special treatment for corporate income tax purposes	
Losses	Carry forward for indefinite time; but offset limited to 30% of taxable income of each subsequent year	
Tax group	Not allowed	
Tax rate	15% of taxable income with the excess above R$240,000 subject to an additional 10%; plus a so-called 'social contribution' of 9% on taxable income, resulting in an effective rate of approximately 34%	

III   TAXES FOR INDIVIDUALS

		Residents	Non-residents
Income Tax	General description	The tax is levied on the chargeable income of a person on an annual basis	
	Taxable entities and taxable income	Residents are taxed on their worldwide income with some relief for double taxation	Non-residents are taxed on income arising in Brazil
	Types of taxable income	There are three kinds of taxation: (1) Employment from personal services or pensions (2) Capital gains (sales of tangible assets such as real estate, shares, vehicles) (3) Profits from financial investments that are subject to a withholding taxation directly by the banks and brokerages	
	Tax year, tax assessment and tax payment	Tax year/calendar year Tax assessment/up to 30 April of the following year Tax payment: 1–8 monthly instalments	
	Losses	Not allowed to be deducted or carried forward Only losses related to sale of listed shares and options can be recovered in the future operations	
	Tax rates	Progressive schedule to use on a monthly basis over income:	

Progressive schedule to use on a monthly basis over income:

Monthly income (R$)	%	Deduction (R$)
To 1,903.98	–	–
From 1,903.99 to 2,826.65	7.5	142.80
From 2,826.65 to 3,751.05	15.0	354.80
From 3,751.06 to 4,664.68	22.5	636.13
Over 4,664.68	27.5	869.36

Progressive schedule to use on an annual basis over income:

Annual income (R$)	%	Deduction (R$)
To 22,847.76	–	–
From 22,847.77 to 33,919.80	7.5	1,713.60
From 33,919.81 to 45,012.60	15.0	4,257.60
From 45,012.61 to 55,976.16	22.5	7,633.56
Over 55,976.16	27.5	10,432.32

Capital Gains Tax (CGT)	General description	Gains realised from the difference between the acquisition and disposal price of an asset
	Taxable entities and chargeable assets	An individual's capital gains are taxable, although capital losses are not deductible or in any way off-settable
	Calculation of gain	Sales value less cost = capital gain
	Tax year, tax assessment and tax payment	The income tax on capital gains must be paid by the last day of the month following the receipt of the value of the sale
	Losses	Individual cannot deduct losses, as each transaction is considered regardless of other operations
	Tax rates	15%

		Domiciled	Non-domiciled
Inheritance Tax (IHT)	Taxable entities and chargeable assets	Tax on the transfer of property. The individual who receives the property must pay tax regarding the value of the assets received	
	Calculation of charge	4% on amount, for example, in the State of São Paulo (each state may apply any % up to a maximum of 8%/Federal law)	
	Taxable events	Transfer by donations, legacies or inheritance	
	Allowances	Transactions up to approximately R$53,125.00 are exempt in São Paulo, but limits may vary from state to state	
	Tax rates	4% in São Paulo but this percentage may vary from state to state	

IV   WITHHOLDING TAXES

Under domestic law	Payments to residents	Payments to non-residents
Dividends	Nil	Nil, except if remitted to tax havens
Interest	Nil The interest paid in intercompany transactions is subject to a Tax Over Financial Transactions (IOF)/the rate is 0.0041% daily	15% on interest accrued or remitted
Royalties	Nil	Withheld income tax is due on royalties paid, credited, remitted, or delivered to non-residents, at the rate of 15% or 25% depending upon the beneficiary's country of residence and the nature of the royalties. It is also due a 'Contribution of Intervention in the Economic Domain' (CIDE), at the rate of 10%, upon remittances of royalties or compensation deriving from technology transfers, in cases where the withheld income tax rate is 15%
On payments to artists and sportsmen	Nil	25%

Brazil has treaties to avoid double taxation with the following countries.

Reduced rate available under relevant Double Taxation Agreement			
Country	Dividends	Interest	Royalties
Argentina	Domestic rates apply		
Austria	25%	25%	25%
Belgium	15%	15%	20%
Canada	25%	25%	25%
Chile	15%	15%	15%
China	15%	15%	25%
Czech Republic	15%	15%	25%
Denmark	25%	25%	25%
Ecuador	15%	15%	25%
Finland	10%	15%	25%
France	15%	25%	25%
Hungary	15%	15%	25%
India	15%	15%	25%
Israel	15%	15%	15%
Italy	25%	25%	25%
Japan	12.5%	12.5%	25%
Korea	15%	15%	15%
Luxembourg	25%	15%	25%
Mexico	15%	15%	15%
Netherlands	15%	15%	25%
Norway	15%	15%	25%

Reduced rate available under relevant Double Taxation Agreement			
Country	Dividends	Interest	Royalties
Peru	15%	15%	15%
Philippines	25%	15%	25%
Portugal	15%	15%	15%
Slovakia	15%	15%	25%
South Africa	15%	15%	15%
Spain	10%	15%	15%
Sweden	25%	25%	25%
Turkey	15%	15%	15%
Trinidad and Tobago	15%	15%	15%
Ukraine	15%	15%	15%
Venezuela	15%	15%	15%

Note: the above rates are only available if the specific Treaty criteria are satisfied. It is possible that lower rates than those shown above may be available provided certain criteria are satisfied. As treaties will not be identical, guidance should be sought in all cases.

V   INDIRECT TAXES

		Residents	Non-residents
Value Added Tax (VAT)	General description	Tax on the supply of goods and services:	
		Sales tax/IPI (VAT/excise tax): rates vary according to the Table of IPI incidence – Federal control. It occurs only on manufactured and imported products. In retail there is no incidence of IPI	
		Sales Tax/ICMS (VAT/sale of goods): rates vary from 4% to 25% – State control	
		PIS/Social Contribution of 0.65% or 1.65% (depending on the income tax option: Presumed Profit System/Pretax Profit System respectively) calculated over the gross revenue	
		COFINS/Social Contribution of 3% or 7.6% (depending on the Income tax option: Presumed Profit System/Pretax Profit System respectively) calculated over the gross revenue	
		Note: For the Pretax Profit System, the taxpayer is allowed to reduce the PIS and COFINS gross revenue by the purchase of products and services related to company's main purpose.	
	Entities obliged to levy VAT	Companies that manufacture, import and/or sell products and goods within the country	
	Taxable activities	Almost all domestic products as well as some services	
	Taxable activities/ zero-rated (examples)	Some basic food items	
	Exemptions (examples)	Exports	
	Refund of VAT	Usually, credits are negotiated with suppliers	
	Tax liability	Normally the supplier of goods and services is responsible for charging VAT. Some activities, such as breweries, pharmaceuticals, fuels and carmakers, should pay the amount for the whole chain when the product leaves the plant	
	Tax rates	Taxable rates vary according to the Table of IPI incidence – Federal Control	
		Taxable rates range from 0% to more than 300% for tax administered at federal level	
		Services Tax/ISS: rates vary from 2% to 5% – Municipality control	
	Administrative obligations	Monthly return filing	
		Special records kept	
Real Property Taxes		Progressive rates: this tax is calculated at a rate of 1.0% to 1.5% of market value (an undervalued price estimate for the municipal of the buildings). Tax is due annually	
Stamp Duty		None	

Nexia International does not accept liability for any loss arising from any action taken, or omission, on the basis of this publication. Professional advice should be obtained before acting or refraining from acting on the contents of this publication. Membership of Nexia International, or associated umbrella organizations, does not constitute any partnership between members, and members do not accept any responsibility for the commission of any act, or omission to act by, or the liabilities of, other members.

Nexia International is the trading name of Nexia International Limited, a company registered in the Isle of Man. Company registration number: 53513C. Registered office: 2nd floor, Sixty Circular Road, Douglas, Isle of Man, IM1 1SA

Bulgaria

(Anda Consulting OOD, abazlyankova@andaconsulting.bg)

I MAIN LEGAL FORMS

Legal form / Characteristics	General partnership (SD) Limited partnership (KD) Partnership limited by shares	Limited liability company/single person limited liability company (OOD/EOOD) Joint stock company/single person joint stock company (AD/EAD)
Partners/ shareholders • Number • Restrictions	Any natural person possessing capacity whose domicile is in the country may register as a sole proprietor (ET) A general partnership (SD) is a company formed by two or more persons for the purpose of effecting commercial activities by occupation under a common trade name. The partners are liable jointly and severally and their liability is unlimited A limited partnership (KD) is formed between two or more persons for carrying out commercial activities under a common trade name, whereby for the partnership's obligations one or more of the partners are liable jointly and severally and their liability is unlimited (general partners), and the remaining partners' liability does not exceed the amount of the agreed-upon contribution	A limited liability company (OOD) may be formed by one or more persons who are liable for the company's obligations to the amount of their contributions to the company's registered capital A joint stock company (AD) is a company the capital stock of which is divided into shares. The company is liable before its creditors with its assets

Legal form / Characteristics	General partnership (SD) Limited partnership (KD) Partnership limited by shares	Limited liability company/single person limited liability company (OOD/EOOD) Joint stock company/single person joint stock company (AD/EAD)
Directors	SD – each partner is entitled to manage the company, unless under the partnership agreement the management is entrusted to one or more partners, or any other party KD – the partners who are fully liable (general partners) manage the company. A partner with limited responsibility has no right to manage and cannot stop the decisions of the general partners	OOD – is managed by a General Meeting of the shareholders and a Managing Director/Directors. The Managing Director may also not be a partner AD – is managed by a General Meeting of the Shareholders and a Board of Directors (one-tier system) or a Supervisory Board and a Management Board (two-tier system). In the EOOD, the Sole shareholder takes the decisions on matters within the competence of the General Meeting The Board of Directors consists of at least 3 but not more than 9 persons. Board members are elected by the General Meeting of the Shareholders and their number can be from 3 to 7 persons. Board members are elected by the Supervisory Board, the number is 3 to 9 persons. Members of the Board of Directors, the Supervisory and Management Board are elected for a period of five years, unless the articles of association of the company provide a shorter period
Establishment	All types of merchants and branches of foreign merchants are registered in the Commercial Register, at the Registry Agency of the Ministry of Justice. Along with its registering, the company receives a Unified Identification Code serving for all commercial, taxation, social security, statistical and other public purposes The registration procedure varies depending on the type of company to be registered (eg the registration of a joint stock company (AD) or an OOD takes approximately five working days from the submission of the relevant documents). The registered company or branch becomes legally active within the meaning of the law after the date of its entry in the Commercial Register	
Registration	The registration requirements of each specific type of company or branch are defined in the Commerce Act. The registration procedure and the documents required for such registration are set out in the Commercial Register Act and the regulations for their implementation	

Legal form / Characteristics	General partnership (SD) Limited partnership (KD) Partnership limited by shares	Limited liability company/single person limited liability company (OOD/EOOD) Joint stock company/single person joint stock company (AD/EAD)
Minimum capital	ET, SD, KD – there are no requirements regarding capital	OOD – the capital of an OOD cannot be less than BGN 2 (EUR 1), and the shares of the partners cannot be less than BGN 1 (EUR 0.51) AD – the minimum capital amount of an AD is BGN 50,000 (EUR 25,565). For certain types of ADs a different minimum amount of capital may be provided by a separate law
Liability	According to Bulgarian law, sole proprietors, partners in a general partnership company and general partners in a limited partnership and in a partnership limited by shares have unlimited personal liability to creditors of the company Partners in a limited liability company and shareholders in joint stock companies are responsible to the value of their shares in the company	
Governance	SD – each partner has the right to manage the company, except when management has been assigned by the articles of association to one or several of the partners or to a third party KD – the general partners manage the company. A limited partner has no right to control and cannot stop decisions of the general partners	OOD – is managed by a General Meeting of the shareholders and a Managing Director/Directors. The Managing Director may also not be a partner AD – is managed by a General Meeting of the Shareholders and a Board of Directors (one-tier system) or a Supervisory Board and a Management Board (two-tier system). In the EOOD, the Sole shareholder takes the decisions on matters within the competence of the General Meeting The powers of the General Meeting, the Board of Directors, the Supervisory Board and the Managing Board are determined by the Commerce Act and the articles of association of the company

Legal form / Characteristics	General partnership (SD) Limited partnership (KD) Partnership limited by shares	Limited liability company/single person limited liability company (OOD/EOOD) Joint stock company/single person joint stock company (AD/EAD)
Audit requirements	Subject to annual independent financial audits by registered auditors are the financial statements of the following entities: 1. joint stock companies and partnerships limited by shares; 2. entities that are issuers under the Public Offering of Securities Act; 3. credit institutions, insurance and investment entities, companies for supplementary social insurance and the funds managed by them; 4. all companies not mentioned in items 1 to 3, except entities that apply a simplified form of financial reporting. Entities applying a 'simplified form of financial reporting' are companies that during the current or previous year do not exceed the parameters of two of the following criteria: 1. value of the assets as at 31 December – BGN 1,500,000 (EUR 767,000); 2. net revenue for the year – BGN 2,500,000 (EUR 1,278,000); 3. average number of employees for the year – 50 people For a newly established entity, the values of these criteria are taken into account only for the year of its establishment	
Taxation	ET – Personal income tax pursuant to the Personal Income Tax Act (PITA); SD and KD – Corporate income tax, defined pursuant to the Corporate Income Tax Act (CITA)	Corporate income tax, pursuant to the Corporate Income Tax Act (CITA)
Usage	In Bulgaria the most commonly used legal forms are companies such as a sole proprietor – a physical person (ET), a limited liability company (OOD), a joint stock company (AD)	

II CORPORATION TAX

Legal form / Description	Resident corporation	Permanent establishment (PE)
General description	Corporate income tax, pursuant to the Corporate Income Tax Act (CITA)	
Taxable entities	Taxable persons are the resident legal persons established under the Bulgarian law	Foreign legal persons are subject to tax pursuant to the CITA on their profit and income, as referred to in the CITA
Taxable income	Any resident legal persons are liable to taxes under the CITA in respect of the profits and income accruing thereto from all sources inside and outside the Republic of Bulgaria	Any non-resident legal persons are liable to taxes under the CITA in respect of the profits realized through a permanent establishment in the Republic of Bulgaria and of the income accruing from disposition of property of any such place of economic activity

Place of economic activity is a certain place (owned, rented or used on other grounds), whereby the non-resident legal person operates wholly or partially in the country (eg, branch, agency, office, studio, etc) |
Calculation of taxable profits	The taxable profit is defined as the accounting financial result converted pursuant to the CITA	
Interest payments	Under certain conditions, interest expenses on finance leases and bank loans are not recognized for tax purposes, when the parties to the transactions are related, or the lease/loan is guaranteed or secured by a related party. The unrecognized interest expenses are recognized for tax purposes in the next five years under certain conditions	
Related party transactions	When related parties perform their commerce and financial relations under conditions affecting the amount of the tax base, which are different from the conditions between unrelated parties, the tax base is determined and taxed under the conditions that would have been incurred between unrelated parties	
Tax year, return and payment	Annual tax return is filed for the annual corporate income tax and the tax year coincides with the calendar year - from 1 January to 31 December. The annual tax return is due by 31 March of the following year

The corporate income tax is paid until 31 March of the following year by deducting the advance contributions for the respective year. The advance contributions are monthly and quarterly depending on the estimated tax profit for the current year | |
Capital gains	Capital gains are included in the total amount of the income and are subject to corporate tax	
Losses	Tax losses can be consistently carried forward until depletion over the next five years	
Tax group	In Bulgaria, group taxation is not recognized. Any legal person is taxed as a separate person, subject to tax	
Tax rate	10%	

III   TAXES FOR INDIVIDUALS

<table>
<tr><th></th><th></th><th>Residents</th><th>Non-residents</th></tr>
<tr><td rowspan="8">Income Tax</td><td>General description</td><td colspan="2">Personal income tax of resident and non-resident individuals under the Personal Income Tax Act (PITA)</td></tr>
<tr><td>Taxable entities and taxable income</td><td>Resident individual, regardless of nationality is a person:

• With permanent address in Bulgaria, or
• Residing in the Republic of Bulgaria for more than 183 days in any 12-month period, or
• With a centre of vital interests in the Republic of Bulgaria

Resident individuals are liable to tax for their income from sources in Bulgaria and abroad</td><td>Non-resident individuals are liable to tax under the PITA for their income from sources in the Republic of Bulgaria</td></tr>
<tr><td>Types of taxable income</td><td>Under the PITA the main types of income depending on the source are:

• income from employment relations;
• income from economic activity as a sole proprietor (ET);
• rental income or other granting of use rights or property;
• income from transfer of rights or property;
• income from other business activity</td><td>Income from a source in the Republic of Bulgaria is:

• income from dividends and liquidation proceeds;
• rewards and remunerations for work carried out in the country by non-resident individuals (leaders in science, art, culture and sports, etc);
• income accrued by residents as interest, income from rent or other granting of use rights of property or chattels; royalties and licence fees, technical services fees, remunerations under management and control contracts, etc</td></tr>
<tr><td>Calculation of income</td><td colspan="2">Under the PITA taxable income and the tax base are determined separately for each source of income</td></tr>
<tr><td>Tax year, tax assessment and tax payment</td><td>Taxable is the income earned and received during the calendar year – from 1 January to 31 December. Annual tax return is due by 30 April of the year following the tax year</td><td>Personal income tax of non-resident individuals is withheld by the company – payer of the income, by the end of the month following the month in which the company has accrued the income. Where the payer of the income is not obliged to withhold and pay the income tax of non-residents, the tax is paid by the person, who has acquired the income, by the 15th day of the month following the 3-month period of acquisition of the income</td></tr>
<tr><td>Losses</td><td colspan="2">N/A</td></tr>
<tr><td>Tax rates</td><td>• The tax rate on the total annual tax base is 10%, with the exception of income tax from economic activity of sole proprietors (ET) – 15%</td><td>The tax rate is 10%, with the exception of income tax on dividends and liquidation proceeds – 5%</td></tr>
</table>

		Residents	**Non-residents**
Capital Gains Tax (CGT)	General description	Income from sale of rights and property are taxed under the PITA	
	Taxable entities and chargeable assets		
	Calculation of gain		
	Tax year, tax assessment and tax payment		
	Losses		
	Tax rates		
Inheritance Tax (IHT)	General description	Tax on inheritance is levied in respect of property inherited by Bulgarian citizens, by law or legacy, in the country or abroad, as well as in respect of property of foreign citizens inherited in the country, under the Local Taxes and Fees Act (LTFA)	
	Taxable entities and chargeable assets	Tax-liable persons are heirs-at-law or heirs under will, as well as devisees The inherited property includes that owned by the legator (property and chattels), as well as his/her other property rights, receivables and liabilities as at the moment of receiving the bequest	
	Calculation of charge	The taxable amount of the inherited property, specified in BGN at the moment of receiving the bequest, is divided into hereditary units/portions for each heir in accordance with the Succession Act	
	Taxable events	When receiving a bequest, the heirs-at-law or under will, devisees or their legal representatives within 6 months have to submit a declaration to the municipality where the legator was last resident The declaration submitted within time by one of the heirs also benefits the other heirs	
	Allowances	No tax on inheritance is due on inheritances received by the surviving spouse and lineal heirs Properties of Bulgarian citizens in other counties are exempt in circumstances where an inheritance tax is paid in the respective country	
	Tax rates	The tax rate on inheritance is determined by ordinance of the municipal council for each heir or legatee separately: • for brothers and sisters and their children – ranging from 0.4% to 0.8% for the portion in excess of BGN 250,000 (EUR 127,823); • for all other persons – from 3.3% to 6.6% on the portion in excess of BGN 250,000 (EUR 127,823)	

IV   WITHHOLDING TAXES

Under domestic law	Payments to residents	Payments to residents of EU Member states	Payments to non-residents[1]
Dividends	0 %	0%	5%
Interest	0 %	0%[3]	10%[2]
Royalties	0 %	10%[2]	10%[2]
On payments to artists and sportsmen	Normal income tax rates	10%[2]	10%[2]

Reduced rate available under the relevant Double Taxation Treaty			
Country	Dividends (%)	Interest (%)	Royalties (%)
Albania	5	10	10
Algeria	5	10	10
Armenia	5	10	10
Austria	0/5	5	5
Azerbaijan	5	7	10
Bahrain	5	5	5
Belarus	5	10	10
Belgium	5	10	5
Canada	5	10	10
China	5	10	10
Croatia	5	5	0
Cyprus	5	7	10
Czech Republic	5	10	10
Denmark	5	0	0
Egypt	5	10	10
Estonia	0	5	5
Finland	0	0	0
France	5	0	5
Georgia	5	10	10
Germany	5	5	5
Greece	5	10	10
Hungary	5	10	10
India	5	10	10
Indonesia	5	10	10
Iran	5	5	5

1   Reduced rate of withholding tax may apply where there is an appropriate double tax treaty.

2   The tax rate for the income from interest, royalties and licence fees may be reduced to 5% when a number of conditions are met, and some of them are: a) the owner of the income is a non-resident legal person in another Member State of the European Union; and b) resident legal person – the payer of the income is a related party of the non-resident legal person / owner of the income.

3   The interest revenue, copyright and licence remuneration shall not be taxed at source where the following conditions have been fulfilled:

- the owner of the income is a 'foreign legal person from a Member State of the European Union', as described in law,
- the local legal person who is a payer of the income is a related person, as described in law, to the foreign legal person who is the owner of the income, and
- the foreign legal person shall be treated as the owner of the income only if it receives this income for its own benefit and not as an intermediary or agent for some other person.

Reduced rate available under the relevant Double Taxation Treaty			
Country	Dividends (%)	Interest (%)	Royalties (%)
Ireland	5	5	10
Israel	5	10	7.5
Italy	5	0	5
Japan	5	10	10
Jordan	5	10	10
Kazakhstan	5	10	10
Kuwait	5	5	10
Latvia	5	5	5
Lebanon	5	7	5
Lithuania	5	10	10
Luxembourg	5	10	5
Macedonia	5	10	10
Malta	0	0	10
Moldova	5	10	10
Mongolia	5	10	10
Montenegro	5	10	10
Morocco	5	10	10
Netherlands	5	0	0
North Korea	5	10	10
Norway	5	0	0
Poland	5	10	5
Portugal	5	10	10
Qatar	0	3	5
Romania	5	10	10
Russia	5	10	10
Serbia	5	10	10
Singapore	5	5	5
Slovakia	5	10	10
Slovenia	5	5	10
South Africa	5	5	10
South Korea	5	10	5
Spain	5	0	0
Sweden	5	0	5
Switzerland	5	10	0
Syria	5	10	10
Thailand	5	10	10
Turkey	5	10	10
Ukraine	5	10	10
United Arab Emirates	5	2	5
United Kingdom	5	0	0
USA	5	5	5
Uzbekistan	5	10	10
Vietnam	5	10	10
Zimbabwe	5	10	10

Note: the above rates are only available provided the specific Treaty criteria are satisfied. It is possible that lower rates than those shown above may be available provided certain criteria are satisfied. As treaties will not be identical, guidance should be sought in all cases.

V   INDIRECT TAXES

		Residents	Non-residents
Value Added Tax	General description	The Value Added Tax Act (VAT Act) regulates the levying of value added tax (VAT) of residents (physical, legal and unpersonified, performing an independent economic activity), as well as non-resident indivuduals, where it is provided for by the law	
	Entities obliged to levy VAT	Taxable person is any person who carries out an independent economic activity, whatever its purpose and results, as well as any person who casually carries out an intra-Community supply of a new vehicle for consideration	
	Taxable activities	VAT is levied on: – any taxable supply of goods or services for consideration; – any inter-Community acquisition (ICA) for consideration with the place of performance in the country, made by a person registered under the VAT Act, or by any person who should be registered; – any ICA for consideration of new vehicles where the place of performance is within the country; – any ICA for consideration of excise goods where the place of performance is within the country, when the recipient is a taxable person or non-taxable legal person, who is not registered under this Act; – import of goods	
	Taxable activities – zero-rated (examples)	Zero rate is applied to intra-Community supplies (ICS), export of goods outside the EU, international transport and others	
	Exemptions (examples)	VAT is not charged for an exempt supply, a free-of-tax intra-Community acquisition (ICA), as well as for a supply where the place of performance is outside the country Other examples of exempt supplies, under certain conditions, are: • supplies regarding healthcare, education, sports • supplies related to land and buildings • delivery of financial and insurance services	
	Refund of VAT	The VAT Act entitles a tax credit to be taken in respect of goods or services acquired which will be used for the performance of taxable supplies (including at 0% rate) both in the country and also with a place of performance outside Bulgaria Right of deduction of tax credit is not available when the goods and services are related to: • exempt supplies • gratuitous supplies or activities, other than those of the economic activity of the person – eg donations, personal use of goods and others • representation and entertainment purposes – eg business lunches and dinners, gifts and more • purchase, rental and operating costs of cars (ie cars where the number of seats, excluding the driver, does not exceed 5). This group does not include cars for freight (ie 1 driver + 1 other). Operating costs for which a tax credit is not available include fuel, repairs, maintenance, parking and others of a similar nature Right to a partial tax credit is available for purchases that are related to both exempt and taxable supplies. The amount of the partial tax credit is determined as the amount of the tax credit multiplied by the coefficient obtained as the ratio between the turnover for supplies for which the person is entitled to a tax credit, and the turnover of all supplies made by the person	

		Residents	Non-residents
Value Added Tax – *contd*	Tax liability	VAT registration is obligatory for persons with taxable turnover over BGN 50,000 (EUR 25,565) for the last 12 consecutive months, and for those who for the current calendar year have total amount of ICA over BGN 20,000 (EUR 10,226)	
		Taxable persons who receive services from foreign suppliers (from the EU or outside the EU) with a place of performance in Bulgaria, or who provide services with a place of performance in the EU, are obliged to register for VAT, regardless of the accumulated taxable turnover	
		All tax-liable persons also have the right to a voluntary registration under the VAT Act	
		Non-resident persons from countries outside the European Union, with the exception of those who have a branch in Bulgaria, are registered under the VAT Act through an accredited representative. Non-resident persons in the European Union can register under the VAT Act without an accredited representative	
	Tax rates	20% – for taxable supplies with the place of performance in Bulgaria, ICA and imports	
		9% – for accommodation services provided in hotels and similar establishments, including the provision of holiday accommodation and the letting of places for camping or caravans	
		0% – for intra-Community supplies (ICS), export of goods outside the EU, international transport, etc	
	Administrative obligations	The tax period pursuant to the VAT Act is a calendar month. VAT-registered persons are required to submit each month, by the 14th of the next month, a declaration form presenting summarized information on the supplies performed and received during the month and the result for the month – VAT liability or VAT refundable. When performing supplies for which recipients were companies from the EU, a VIES declaration (being the equivalent of the European Sales List) should also be filed	
		The VAT Act has certain requirements regarding the content and issuance of tax documents under the VAT Act (invoice, notice to invoices, protocols and others)	
Real Property Taxes		Under the Local Taxes and Fees Act (LTFA) a tax is levied on the acquisition of real estate including any limited property rights	
		Basis for determining the tax is the higher of the negotiated price and the tax valuation of the property and property rights	
		The amount of tax is determined by the municipal council at the rate of 0.1% to 3% of the valuation of the property	
Stamp Duty		Notary deeds to transfer real estate, legitimate mortgages and other legal acts are subject to entry in a common public register pursuant to the Ownership Act. The amount of the notary fees depends on the evidenced material interest and is within the range of BGN 30 to BGN 6,000 (EUR 15 to EUR 3,068)	

Cambodia

(Henry Tan, Nexia TS, henrytan@nexiats.com.sg)

I   MAIN LEGAL FORMS

Legal form / Characteristics	Partnership and Limited Partnership	Private corporation (Private Limited Company) and Public corporation (Public Limited Company)
Partners/shareholders • Number • Restrictions	**Partnership:** • Between two or more partners • Restriction on transferability of ownership **Limited Partnership:** • Between one or more general partners and one or more limited partners • Limited partner may transfer his interest without unanimous consent of other partners **Foreign Direct Investment (FDI) restrictions:** • Although there are no specific FDI restrictions, in practice no partnership has been registered in Cambodia	**Private Corporation:** • Minimum 2 shareholders and not more than 30 shareholders • A private corporation can also be established by one person and it is called a 'Single Member Limited Company' • Restriction on right to transfer shares **Public Corporation:** • A public corporation can issue securities to the public • In practice, very few public corporations exist in Cambodia **Foreign Direct Investment (FDI) restrictions:** • Cambodia has few restrictions on FDI • The Cambodian Law on Investment encourages both local and foreign investors without discrimination
Directors	**Partnership and Limited Partnership:** • Management by general partners	**Private Corporation:** Minimum – 1 director **Public Corporation:** Minimum – 3 directors
Establishment	**Partnership and Limited Partnership:** • Partnership Deed/ Agreement	**Private and Public Corporations:** • Memorandum and Articles of Association

Legal form / Characteristics	Partnership and Limited Partnership	Private corporation (Private Limited Company) and Public corporation (Public Limited Company)
Registration	**Partnership:** • Registration is optional **Limited Partnership:** • If the limited partnership is not registered, it is deemed to be a general partnership	**Private and Public Corporations:** • Cambodian Ministry of Commerce **Qualified investment projects (QIPs):** • Investors may apply for QIP status by registering their projects with the Council for Development of Cambodia • A project with investment capital less than US$2 million shall be registered with the provincial/municipal investment sub-committee
Minimum capital	**Partnership and Limited Partnership:** • No Minimum Capital	**Private Corporations:** Minimum 1,000 shares with a par value of at least KHR 4,000
Liability	**Partnership:** • Unlimited • Partners are jointly and severally liable for all debts and obligations **Limited Partnership:** • General partners are jointly and severally liable for debts of partnership, whereas limited partner is liable only to the extent of his contribution	**Private and Public Corporations:** • Limited
Governance	**Partnership and Limited Partnership:** • Partners' meetings	**Private and Public Corporations:** • Directors' meetings • Shareholders' meetings - A general meeting shall be held within 12 months from the date of incorporation and thereafter at least once every year
Audit requirements	• All enterprises that meet at least two of the following criteria are required to have their accounts audited by an independent auditor: ➢ Annual turnover above KHR 3 billion ➢ Total assets above KHR 2 billion ➢ More than 100 employees • For QIPS registered with Council for Development of Cambodia, audit of financial statements is compulsory	
Taxation	All enterprises are taxed on their profits as separate entities at the corporation tax rates discussed in the next segment	

II CORPORATION TAX

Legal form / Description	Resident corporation
General description	• From 2016, corporate tax in Cambodia is determined in accordance with the Real Regime Tax System (RRTS)[1] • RRTS is comprised of three categories of taxpayer: small, medium and large. These categories are determined on the basis of the turnover of the business
Taxable entities	• Corporate taxpayers in Cambodia are classified as either resident taxpayers or non-resident taxpayers • A **resident** taxpayer is an enterprise that has a place of management and carries on business in Cambodia • A **non-resident** taxpayer is an enterprise that derives Cambodian source income, but does not have a place of management or permanent establishment[2] (PE) in Cambodia • A non-resident taxpayer is deemed to be a Cambodian resident for tax purposes, if it is found to have a PE in Cambodia. A PE is subject to tax in Cambodia in respect of its Cambodian-sourced income. However, in practice, the tax authority has no mechanism to tax foreign enterprises that derive income from Cambodian sources other than through the use of the withholding tax (WHT) system
Taxable income	• Resident taxpayers are taxed on a worldwide basis, whereas non-resident taxpayers are taxed only on Cambodian source income
Calculation of taxable profits	• Taxable income is the net profit obtained from all types of business operations and also includes capital gains, interest, rental and royalty income as well as income from financial or investment assets including immovable assets • Tax is levied on total income, after deduction of allowable expenditure and depreciation
Interest payments	• There are no specific thin capitalisation rules • The maximum interest deduction is capped at an amount equal to total interest income and 50% of net non-interest income earned during the year
Related party transactions	• There are no comprehensive transfer pricing regulations in Cambodia for related party transactions • However, General Department of Taxation has broad powers to re-determine related party transactions to impose pricing at arm's length. A related party relationship is one where there is a 20% or more shareholding relationship
Tax year, return and payment	• The default tax year and the accounting year is the calendar year • If the tax payer wishes to use a different tax year, an approval letter from General Department of Taxation is required • The company is subject to monthly prepayment of tax on profit which becomes due by the 15th day of the following month • The annual tax return must be filed and the balance tax (if any) must be paid within 3 months from the year end. A minimum tax @ 1% of the annual turnover (inclusive of all taxes, except VAT) is payable by the companies, regardless of whether the company is in a profit or loss situation. However, QIPs are not subjected to the minimum tax
Capital gains	• There is no separate capital gains tax • Any gain on the sale of fixed assets/shares is subject to the tax on profits at a rate of 20% on the higher of the contract price or the market value. The proceeds also are subject to minimum tax

Legal form / Description	Resident corporation
Losses	• Tax losses can be carried forward for a maximum period of 5 years provided there is no change in the ownership of business or business activity and the company is not subject to any unilateral tax assessment • Tax losses cannot be carried back
Tax group	There are no provisions that allow for group taxation
Tax rate	• The tax rate on profits ranges from 0% to 30%, based on the business activity. The standard rate is 20% • Enterprises operating in certain industries, such as oil and natural gas production or exploitation of natural resources including timber, ore, gold and precious stones, are taxable at a 30% rate • QIPs may enjoy a tax holiday period for up to 9 years • Insurance companies are subject to a 5% tax rate on gross premiums

1 The Law on Financial Management 2016 abolished the Simplified and Estimated tax regimes in Cambodia. The only remaining tax regime in Cambodia is the Real Regime Tax System (RRTS). Taxpayers under the RRTS are classified into three categories:
Small taxpayers are Sole Proprietorships or Partnerships that:
   • have annual taxable turnover from KHR 250 million (approx US$62,500) to KHR 700 million (US$175,000);
   • have taxable turnover, in any period of three consecutive calendar months (within the tax year), exceeding KHR 60 million (US$15,000);
   • have expected taxable turnover of KHR 60 million (US$15,000) or more in the next three consecutive months; and
   • participate in any bidding, quotation or survey for the supply of goods and services including duties.
Medium taxpayers include:
   • enterprises that have annual turnover from KHR 700 million (US$175,000) to KHR 2,000 million (US$500,000);
   • enterprises that have been incorporated as legal entities; and
   • sub-national government institutions, associations, and non-governmental organizations.
Large taxpayers include:
   • enterprises that have annual turnover over KHR 2,000 million (US$500,000);
   • branch of a foreign company;
   • enterprises registered as a Qualified Investment Project ('QIP') as approved by the Council for the Development of Cambodia; and
   • government institutions, foreign diplomatic and consular missions, international organizations and agencies.
2 A PE is defined as 'a fixed place of business, the branch of a foreign company or an agent resident in Cambodia, through which a non-resident person carries on their business'. The term also includes any other association or connection through which a non-resident person engages in economic activity in Cambodia.

III TAXES FOR INDIVIDUALS

		Residents	Non-residents
Income Tax	General description	• Cambodian resident and non-resident individuals are subject to tax on salary (TOS) on income from their employment activities and withholding tax on certain types of income • The TOS is imposed through withholding tax mechanism, and taxes so deducted and paid by the employer are deemed to be final tax • Sole proprietors falling under RRTS are required to adhere to all the requirements listed under Section II (Corporation Tax), depending on the category in which they fall into, ie small tax payer or medium tax payer	
	Taxable entities and taxable income	• A person who is 'domiciled in' or has a 'principal place of abode in' or who is present in Cambodia for more than 182 days during any 12-month period ending in the current tax year is considered to be a resident in Cambodia • Resident individuals are liable to tax on salary (TOS) on Cambodian as well as foreign source employment income	• Non-residents are subject to income tax only on Cambodian source employment income
	Types of taxable income	• The TOS is imposed on salaries received as compensation for employment activities • The term 'salary' is defined broadly to include wages, remuneration, bonuses, overtime, compensation and fringe benefits. Fringe benefits (either in cash or in kind) include the private use of motor vehicles, the provision of meals and/ or accommodation, pension fund contributions that are more than 10% of salary, etc	
	Calculation of income	Taxable income, after deducting any allowances and/ or income specifically exempted, is assessed to tax	
		Tax relief for dependent spouse and minor children available	Tax relief for dependent spouse and minor children not available
	Tax year, tax assessment and tax payment	• The tax year is the calendar year • Employers are responsible for withholding and remitting the TOS to the tax authority by the 15th day of the following month • Employees are not required to file personal tax returns	
	Losses	Not Applicable	
	Tax rates	Resident individuals earning employment income are taxed at progressive tax rates from 0% to 20%. Fringe benefits are taxed at the rate of 20%	Non-resident individuals are taxed at a flat rate of 20% on their employment income including fringe benefits
Capital Gains Tax (CGT)	General description	No CGT	

		Domiciled	Non-domiciled
Inheritance Tax (IHT)	General description	No IHT	

IV   WITHHOLDING TAXES

Under domestic law[3]	Payments to residents	Payments to non-residents
Dividends	Nil	14%
Interest	15%[4] (except domestic bank and saving institution)	14%
Royalties and fees for technical services	15%	14%
Rent	10%	14%[5]

---

3   Cambodia has not entered into any Double Tax Agreements (DTA) with any countries. Thus, the benefit of a lower rate as per DTA is not available. Cambodia signed its first DTA with Singapore on 20 May 2016, which is pending ratification.
4   The withholding tax rates for certain interest payments are:
 – on fixed deposits made by local banks to residents – 6%
 – on savings accounts made by local banks to residents – 4%.
5   Rental income includes other income connected with the use of property.

V INDIRECT AND OTHER TAXES

		Overview
Value Added Tax (VAT)	General description	VAT is levied on taxable supplies, which include a wide range of goods and services supplied in Cambodia, and on the importation of goods
	Entities obliged to levy VAT	All taxpayers under RRTS making supplies of taxable goods and services in Cambodia must register for VAT before making taxable supplies

	Taxable activities	• 'Taxable supplies' are defined as all supplies excluding non-taxable/exempt supplies. These include:
		  • supply of goods or services by a taxable person in the Kingdom of Cambodia
		  • appropriation of goods for his/her own use by the taxable person
		  • making of a gift or supply at below cost of goods or services by the taxable person
		  • import of goods into the customs territory of the Kingdom of Cambodia

	Taxable activities – zero-rated (examples)	The zero rate applies to export of goods and services and certain charges in relation to international transport of people and goods

	Exemptions (examples)	• Non-taxable/exempt supplies are as follows:
		  • public postal service
		  • hospital, clinic, medical and dental services, and the sale of medical and dental goods incidental to the performance of such services
		  • transportation of passengers by a wholly state-owned public transportation system
		  • insurance services
		  • primary financial services
		  • importation of articles for personal use that are exempt from customs duties
		  • non-profit activities in the public interest that have been recognised by the Ministry of Economy and Finance
		  • supply of electricity and water

	Refund of VAT	Refund of input credit is granted to exporters and in cases where excess credit continue for three months or more, subject to fulfilment of certain conditions
	Tax liability	Entities that are registered for VAT and importers
	Tax rate	10%
	Administrative obligations	VAT returns and payment are due to be filed and paid by the 20th day of the following month
Customs Duty		• Import duties are levied on certain goods entering Cambodia • The duty rates are 0%, 7%, 15% and 35% • The customs duty for most goods is from 0% to 5% • Exemptions may be granted to QIPs and specific industries, eg telecommunication services, exploration for oil, gas and mining activities

	Overview
Specific tax on certain merchandise and services (STCMS)	• STCMS is a form of excise duty which is levied on certain imports in addition to import duties and on certain locally manufactured goods and services. The rates of STCMS vary from 3% to 45% depending on the goods and services in question. For example:<table><tr><td>**Item**</td><td>**Tax rate**</td></tr><tr><td>Domestic and international air ticket</td><td>10%</td></tr><tr><td>Domestic and international telephone services</td><td>3%</td></tr><tr><td>Entertainment services and all types of beverages</td><td>10%</td></tr><tr><td>Selling of domestic beer and import of beer</td><td>25%</td></tr><tr><td>All petroleum products, and automobile under 2000 cc</td><td>20%</td></tr><tr><td>Automobile over 2000 cc</td><td>45%</td></tr></table>• STCMS on imported goods is collected by the customs authority upon entry of the goods into Cambodia. STCMS on services and locally manufactured goods is required to be filed and paid by the 15th day of the following month
Tax on Public Lighting (TPL)	• TPL is imposed on the sale of alcohol and cigarette products, both imported and domestically manufactured, at each stage of supply • The tax rate is 3% of the selling price is inclusive of all applicable taxes, but exclusive of TPL and VAT • Payment of TPL is due on the 15th day of the following month
Accommodation tax (AT)	• AT is imposed on the provision of hotel accommodation services • AT is levied at the rate of 2% on the accommodation services fees, inclusive of other service charges and all kinds of taxes except AT and VAT • AT is payable by the 15th day of the month following the month in which the service was provided
Stamp Duty or Registration tax	Stamp duty is imposed on the following: • Transfer of ownership or right of possession of immovable property and the contribution of immovable property as capital in a company – 4% of the value of the immovable property • Transfer of ownership or right of possession of vehicles – 4% of the value of the vehicle • Transfer of any or all parts of the company's shares – 0.1% of the value of shares transferred • Registration of contracts to supply goods or service to the Government – 0.1% of the contract price • Registration of legal documents such as certificates of incorporation, certificates of merger and letter evidencing the winding up of the company – KHR 1,000,000 (US$250)
Tax on Unused Land	• Unused land is subject to 2% unused land tax which must be paid by the registered owner of the property • The unused land tax is based on the market value of the land per square metre, which is determined by the Committee for Evaluation of Undeveloped Land by June 30 of the relevant year. The property owner must pay this tax prior to 30 September of the relevant year

	Overview
Tax on Immovable Property (TIP)	• Immovable property is defined as including land, houses, buildings and other constructions built on the land. Agricultural land, immovable properties located in a Special Economic Zone that directly serves production activities and a few other immovable properties are exempted from TIP • TIP is imposed at the rate of 0.1% on the value of the immovable property exceeding the threshold of KHR 100,000,000 (US$25,000) • The value of the immovable property is determined by the Immovable Property Assessment Committee. The property tax return must be filed and the taxes must be paid by 30 September each year
Patent Tax	• All taxpayers operating in Cambodia are required to register and pay Patent Tax by 31 March each year for each business activity that they carry out • The amount of Patent Tax payable is dependent on what class a taxpayer is classified as under the RRTS. The Patent Tax fees for 2016 are: • Small Taxpayers – KHR 400,000 (US$100) • Medium Taxpayers – KHR 1,200,000 (US$300) • Large Taxpayers – KHR 3,000,000 (US$750) if annual turnover is between KHR 2,000 million and KHR 10,000 million, and KHR 5,000,000 (US$1,250) if annual turnover exceeds KHR 10,000 million
Additional tax on dividend distribution	• Additional tax on dividend distribution applies to the distribution of profits that has not previously been taxed at the full rate of 20% (such as those distributed by QIPs) • Profits realised when a company is exempt from tax on profit are not subject to the additional tax on dividend distribution, until the retained earnings are distributed, either during or after the tax holiday period

Cameroon

(CLS Audit Conseil, contact@clsauditconseil.com)

I MAIN LEGAL FORMS

Legal form / Characteristics	Partnership and Limited Liability Partnership (LLP)	Ltd (private corporation) and Plc (public corporation)
Partners /shareholders • Number • Restrictions	*Société en nom collectif (SNC):* • at least one partner *Société en Commandite Simple (SCS):* • at least one partner *Société civile (SC):* • at least one partner	*Société à responsabilité limitée (SARL) / société à responsabilité limitée unipersonnelle (SARLU):* • between one or many shareholders *Société anonyme (SA):* • between one or many shareholders • *Société par Actions Simplifié (SAS):* • between one or many shareholders
Directors	*SNC:* One or more managers *SCS:* Unless otherwise stipulated in the company's articles, all the 'commandités' are managers It is possible to choose one or more managers, who can be a partner or not	*SARL:* One or more manager or partner *SA:* • *Classic system* – 'conseil d'administration' (CA): – between 3 and 12 members – management of the company by the President of the CA or a 'general director' – management of the company by an 'administrateur directeur général'[1]

---

1 Public limited liability companies with not more than three shareholders may not form a board of directors and may appoint a managing director who shall be responsible for administering and managing the company. In this case, the provisions of the first paragraph of Art 417 shall not apply.

Legal form / Characteristics	Partnership and Limited Liability Partnership (LLP)	Ltd (private corporation) and Plc (public corporation)
	SC: One or more manager or partner	• *Dualistic system*: – 'directeur général' and 'conseil d'administration': – the 'directeur général' manages the company – 'conseil d'administration': between 3 and 12 members (checks the 'directeur général') SAS: one president
Establishment	Partnership deed	By-laws of company
Registration	All entities to be registered at the Commercial Court and publication of by-laws. But the legislator, through the 2010 finance law, has imposed free registration of instruments of incorporation, extension of company and capital increase	
Minimum capital	*SNC, SCS and SC:* No minimum	*SARL:* Minimum capital: F CFA1m *SA:* Minimum capital: F CFA10m SAS: Defined by laws of company
Liability	*SNC:* Jointly and unlimited liability of all debts *SCS:* • 'commandités': joint and unlimited liability of all debts • 'commanditaires': liability limited to their contribution *SC:* Unlimited liability of all debts	*SARL, SA, SAS:* Liability limited to contribution
Governance	Partnership deed	*SARL, SA:* Defined by the commercial law *SAS:* Freedom of governance, defined by the law of company
Audit requirements	*SNC, SC and SCS:* No obligation for audit	*SARL, SAS:* No obligation, unless the company exceeds one of the three following ceilings: • total assets ≥ F CFA125m • annual turnover > F CFA250m • employees > 50 *SA:* The legal auditor has to certify the corporate accounts annually

Legal form / Characteristics	Partnership and Limited Liability Partnership (LLP)	Ltd (private corporation) and Plc (public corporation)
Taxation	*SNC, SCS and SC:* Each partner subject to personal income tax. From January 2009, taxes should be withheld by the entity	*SARL, SAS and SA:* Corporate income tax
Usage	*SNC/SCS:* Used for small businesses *SC:* Used for patrimonial operations or civil/professional activity or real estate operations	*SARL:* Start-ups and small or medium-sized companies *SA, SAS:* Listed companies and medium-sized companies

II   CORPORATION TAX

Legal form / Description	Resident corporation	Non-resident corporation
General description	Corporation tax	
Taxable entities	The company	Foreign entity
Taxable income	Territoriality principle: tax is only due on business income generated by enterprises operating in Cameroon	
Calculation of taxable profits	Taxable profits result from accountable benefits plus reinstatement less deduction; expenses equal to or greater than F CFA500,000 are not admitted in tax deduction when they are paid in cash	
Interest payments	Deductible unless paid to shareholders. Certain other restrictions apply	
Related party transactions	All related party transactions must take place on an arm's length basis	
Tax year, return and payment	• Calendar year, or if the taxpayer's financial year does not coincide, the financial year of 12 months closed during the relevant calendar year • Returns to be filed within 2½ months of financial year end • Advance payments required each month. Each corporation submits a tax return to the tax administration for the payment in advance of a part of the corporation tax. The amount of this partial payment is equal to 2.2%, and 5.5% applied to monthly turnover without VAT	
Capital gains and dividends	• Generally deemed as ordinary income and subject to standard corporate tax rate • Dividends: 10% exempt, 90% of dividends received plus tax credit are subject to corporate income tax • Capital gains: subject to corporate income tax • Capital gains of real estate company are subject to corporate income tax	
Losses	Carried forward for 4 years. It is extended to 5 years for firms with a special statute	
Tax rate	• Standard rate: 33% with a minimum of 2.2%, and 5.5% of turnover without VAT • Reduced rate for firms with a special statute: 19.25%, 30%	

III   TAXES FOR INDIVIDUALS

		Residents	Non-residents
Income Tax	General description	Income tax	
	Taxable entities and taxable income	Worldwide	Cameroon source income only
	Types of taxable income	• Real estate income • Commercial and non-commercial income (BIC, BNC, BA etc) • Salary • Investment income	
	Calculation of income	• Net salary: gross salary less rebate of 30% represents families' charges and F CFA500,000 for professional charges • Since the 2015 Finance Law, the tax regime for professional incomes of individual (real estate rental income, income from BIC, BC, BNC, BA) is identical to the one for corporations	Net global income
	Tax year, tax assessment and tax payment	• Generally the calendar year • Individuals with business income may be assessed on the basis of an accounting period • One instalment is required on 15 March	
	Losses	A loss in one category of professional income cannot be offset against income of another category	
	Tax rates	• Dependent upon income • Progressive tax brackets from 10%–38%	
	Dividends	Taxation to the income progressive tax brackets or optional withholding tax of 16.5%, 15% if the beneficiary is French and 12% if Tunisian	
		Residents	**Non-residents**
Capital Gains Tax (CGT)	General description	Capital gains tax (the products of shares, bonds, income of indebtedness, deposits)	
	Taxable entities and chargeable assets	Disposal of business assets/immovable properties	
	Calculation of gain	*Shares:* proceeds less acquisition costs *Immovable property:* Difference between actual value and the value at the precedent transfer	
	Tax year, tax assessment and tax payment	*Shares:* with tax return *Immovable property:* within 1 month of disposal	
	Exceptions	• Interest on saving account • Interest on certificate of deposit	
	Tax rates	*Shares:* 16.5% *Immovable property:* 10%–30%	

		Resident	Non-resident
Inheritance Tax (IHT)	General description	Registration fees	
	Taxable entities and chargeable assets	Each beneficiary is subject to tax	
	Calculation of charge	Levied on the value of all transferred assets less related liabilities. In the case of gifts liabilities are usually not deductible	
	Taxable events	On death and all gifts made prior to death	
	Allowances	None	
	Tax rates	Dependent upon the proximity of the relationship between the donor and the recipient and upon the value of the elements transferred: from 2%–10%	

IV   WITHHOLDING TAXES

Under domestic law	Payments to residents[2]	Payments to non-residents[2]
Dividends	16.5%	12%, 15%, 16.5%
Interest	Income of claims, deposits and cautionnements, income of obligations are subject to taxes at 16.5%. While the interest on negotiable loans emitted by the State, the interests of receipts, the interest of home savings accounts are not subject to taxes	16.5%
Royalties	Nil	Depending on the treaty
On payments to artists and sportsmen	Nil	12%, 15%, 16.5%

Reduced rate available under the relevant Double Taxation Treaty			
Country	Dividends	Interest	Royalties
France	Reduced rate available	No reduction	Depends on treaty
Tunisia	Reduced rate available	No reduction	Depends on treaty

Note: the above rates are only available provided the specific Treaty criteria are satisfied. As treaties will not be identical, guidance should be sought in all cases.

---

2   Reduced rates of withholding tax may apply where there is an appropriate double tax treaty.

V INDIRECT TAXES

		Residents	Non-residents
Value Added Tax (VAT)	Entities being obliged to levy VAT	Persons making taxable supplies of goods and services in the course of a business	
	Taxable activities	Unless expressly exempt, all goods and services are taxable activities	
	Taxable activities – zero-rated (examples)	Exports	
	Exemptions (examples)	• Former necessity product • Commission for health insurance	
	Refund of VAT	Quarter reimbursement if VAT refund is greater than F CFA50m for an entity which is a large company with an annual turnover greater than F CFA3bn, and F CFA20m for others	
	Tax liability	Supplier or provider of services established in Cameroon	
	Tax rates	• 0% exports • 19.25% standard	
	Administrative obligations	VAT return	
Stamp Duty Land Tax		0.11% of the land value	
Stamp Duty		Paid for registration and administrative documents	

Nexia International does not accept liability for any loss arising from any action taken, or omission, on the basis of this publication. Professional advice should be obtained before acting or refraining from acting on the contents of this publication. Membership of Nexia International, or associated umbrella organizations, does not constitute any partnership between members, and members do not accept any responsibility for the commission of any act, or omission to act by, or the liabilities of, other members.

Nexia International is the trading name of Nexia International Limited, a company registered in the Isle of Man. Company registration number: 53513C. Registered office: 2nd floor, Sixty Circular Road, Douglas, Isle of Man, IM1 1SA

Canada

(Jonathan Bicher, Nexia Friedman LLP, bicher@nexiafriedman.ca)

I   MAIN LEGAL FORMS

Legal form / Characteristics	Partnership and Limited Liability Partnership (LLP)	Corporation
Partners /shareholders • Number • Restrictions	• Two or more • No restrictions	• One or more • No restrictions
Directors	Management by partners	Depending on jurisdiction, may need resident directors
Establishment	Partnership agreement (unregistered)	Articles of Incorporation (registered)
Registration	None	Federal or provincial authorities
Minimum capital	None	
Liability	Unlimited for all partners in a general partnership, unlimited for general partners and limited for limited partners in a limited partnership, limited to capital and clients involved with for LLP	Generally limited to share capital for all shareholders
Governance	• Partners • General meeting	• Board of Directors • Shareholders' meetings
Audit requirements	Not required	Not required for private companies, required for public companies
Taxation	• Not subject to income taxes (pass-through entity) • Partners subject to income tax or corporate tax on their profit share	• Subject to corporate tax and rarely capital tax • Dividends distributed to individuals subject to reduced income tax rate • Dividends distributed to Canadian corporations generally tax-free; portfolio dividends may be subject to refundable tax

II   CORPORATION TAX

Description \ Legal form	Resident corporation	Permanent establishment (PE)
General description	Corporation tax	
Taxable entities	Companies incorporated in Canada and foreign companies with management and control located in Canada	PE located in Canada
Taxable income	Worldwide profits	Profits derived by PE in Canada
Calculation of taxable profits	Accounting profit is adjusted for various tax add-backs and allowances to arrive at taxable income	
Interest payments	Thin capitalisation rules on payments to non-arm's length non-residents: • maximum debt/equity ratio of Canadian subsidiaries is 1.5:1 • excess interest not deductible and subject to withholding tax Back-to-back loans may be caught as well	
Related party transactions	All related party transactions must take place on arm's length basis	
Tax year, return and payment	• Tax year – business year (calendar or different) • Tax return has to be filed within 6 months after end of the financial year of the company • Monthly or quarterly prepayments, final payment generally 2 months after year end	
Capital gains	50% of amount of all realised worldwide capital gains are taxable	50% of amount of certain capital gains on taxable Canadian properties are taxable
Losses	• Business losses must be fully deducted against any income arising in the same year • Losses may be carried back for up to 3 years • Losses may be carried forward for up to 20 years	
Tax group	• Special rules allow groups of commonly controlled Canadian corporations to reorganise on a tax-free basis. This includes the movement of shares and assets and in some cases, capital losses and business losses • Certain reorganisations of company's own debt and share capital can also be done on a tax-free basis • However, consolidated tax returns are not permitted • Associated groups consider group tax attributes to determine limits on tax incentives	No
Tax rate	12%–54.67%	25%–31%

III TAXES FOR INDIVIDUALS

		Residents	Non-residents
Income Tax	General description	Federal and provincial income tax on income for individuals	
	Taxable entities and taxable income	Resident individuals are subject to personal income tax on their worldwide income from all sources	Non-resident individuals are taxable generally on income from Canadian sources
	Types of taxable income	• Employment and business • Capital gains • Investment income (eg rental, dividends, interest) • Certain other income	• Employment and business • Capital gains on certain taxable Canadian property (see below) • Rental, if election made • Pension, if election made
	Calculation of income	Aggregate of incomes listed above minus certain tax deductions	
	Tax year, tax assessment and tax payment	• Tax year – calendar year • Self-assessment return is due for filing on 30 April following the end of the tax year • No joint tax return for spouses • Quarterly prepayments, final payment generally due 30 April of following year	• Normally, no tax assessment in case of withholding taxes • Can file Canadian tax returns in certain cases to claim back some withholding taxes • Canadian tax returns may be required if have employment or business income in Canada
	Losses	Non-capital losses can be carried back for 3 years and carried forward for 20 years	
	Tax rates	• Basic personal amount (tax-free earnings): – Federal: $11,474 – Provincial: $8,000–$18,451 • Progressive tax rates • Highest marginal tax rates: 47.70%–58.75% (depending on province)	Same as for residents except no personal amounts

		Residents	Non-residents
Capital Gains Tax (CGT)	General description	Only 50% of realised capital gains are taxable	
	Taxable entities and chargeable assets	Capital gains on worldwide investments	Capital gains generally on Canadian real estate or shares of corporation deriving its value primarily from real estate in Canada and certain other situations
	Calculation of gain	• The excess of the disposal proceeds over the original cost, improvement costs and disposal expenses such as commission and fees • One half of a realised capital gain is taxable, the other half is tax-free	
	Tax year, tax assessment and tax payment	Same tax return as that for all other types of income	
	Losses	Capital losses can be carried back 3 years and forward indefinitely	
	Tax rates	50% of applicable income tax on personal tax rates	

		Domiciled	Non-domiciled
Inheritance Tax (IHT)	General description	No inheritance taxes in Canada	
	Tax rates	Canada has no inheritance duties, estate taxes, or gift taxes but there is a deemed disposition of assets at their fair market value upon death, and any gains or losses are realised for tax purposes. Heirs receive a stepped-up tax cost	

IV WITHHOLDING TAXES

Under domestic law	Payments to residents	Payments to non-residents[1]
Dividends	Nil	Up to 25%
Interest[2]	Nil	Up to 25%
Royalties	Nil	Up to 25%
On payments to artists and sportsmen	Nil	Up to 24% if service performed in Canada

Reduced rate available under the relevant Double Taxation Treaty			
Country	Dividends[3]	Interest[2,3]	Royalties[3]
Algeria	15%	15%	15%
Argentina	15%	12.5%	15%
Armenia	15%	10%	10%
Australia	15%	10%	10%
Austria	15%	10%	10%
Azerbaijan	15%	10%	10%
Bangladesh	15%	15%	10%
Barbados	15%	15%	10%
Belgium	15%	10%	10%
Brazil	25%	15%	25%
Bulgaria	15%	10%	10%
Cameroon	15%	15%	15%
Chile	15%	15%	15%
China	15%	10%	10%
Colombia	15%	10%	10%
Croatia	15%	10%	10%
Cyprus	15%	15%	10%
Czech Republic	15%	10%	10%
Denmark	15%	10%	10%
Dominican Republic	18%	18%	18%
Ecuador	15%	15%	15%
Egypt	15%	15%	15%
Estonia	15%	10%	10%
Finland	15%	10%	10%
France	15%	10%	10%
Gabon	15%	10%	10%
Germany	15%	10%	10%

1 Reduced rates of withholding tax may apply where there is an appropriate double tax treaty.
2 Pursuant to Canadian domestic law, interest paid to arm's length parties is no longer subject to withholding tax.
3 The rates provided are the highest possible rates under the applicable Treaty. Lower rates may be available on certain types of payments and/or to certain categories of payees. Guidance should be sought in all cases.

Reduced rate available under the relevant Double Taxation Treaty			
Country	Dividends[3]	Interest[2,3]	Royalties[3]
Greece	15%	10%	10%
Guyana	15%	15%	10%
Hong Kong	15%	10%	10%
Hungary	15%	10%	10%
Iceland	15%	10%	10%
India	25%	15%	20%
Indonesia	15%	10%	10%
Ireland	15%	10%	10%
Israel	15%	15%	15%
Italy	15%	10%	10%
Ivory Coast	15%	15%	10%
Jamaica	15%	15%	10%
Japan	15%	10%	10%
Jordan	15%	10%	10%
Kazakhstan	15%	10%	10%
Kenya	25%	15%	15%
Korea	15%	10%	10%
Kuwait	15%	10%	10%
Kyrgyzstan	15%	15%	10%
Latvia	15%	10%	10%
Lebanon[4]	15%	10%	10%
Lithuania	15%	10%	10%
Luxembourg	15%	10%	10%
Malaysia	15%	15%	15%
Malta	15%	15%	10%
Mexico	15%	10%	10%
Moldova	15%	10%	10%
Mongolia	15%	10%	10%
Morocco	15%	15%	10%
Namibia[4]	15%	10%	10%
Netherlands	15%	10%	10%
New Zealand	15%	10%	10%
Nigeria	15%	12.5%	12.5%
Norway	15%	10%	10%
Oman	15%	10%	10%
Pakistan	15%	15%	15%
Papua New Guinea	15%	10%	10%
Peru	15%	15%	15%
Philippines	15%	15%	10%
Poland	15%	10%	10%
Portugal	15%	10%	10%

4   Signed but not yet in force. Until in force, 25% rate applies.

Reduced rate available under the relevant Double Taxation Treaty			
Country	Dividends[3]	Interest[2,3]	Royalties[3]
Romania	15%	10%	10%
Russia	15%	10%	10%
Senegal	15%	15%	15%
Serbia	15%	10%	10%
Singapore	15%	15%	15%
Slovakia	15%	10%	10%
Slovenia	15%	10%	10%
South Africa	15%	10%	10%
Spain	15%	10%	10%
Sri Lanka	15%	15%	10%
Sweden	15%	10%	10%
Switzerland	15%	10%	10%
Taiwan[4]	15%	10%	10%
Tanzania	25%	15%	20%
Thailand	15%	15%	15%
Trinidad and Tobago	15%	10%	10%
Tunisia	15%	15%	20%
Turkey	20%	15%	10%
Ukraine	15%	10%	10%
United Arab Emirates	15%	10%	10%
United Kingdom	15%	10%	10%
United States	15%	Nil	10%
Uzbekistan	15%	10%	10%
Venezuela	15%	10%	10%
Socialist Republic of Vietnam	15%	10%	10%
Zambia	15%	15%	15%
Zimbabwe	15%	15%	10%

Note: the above rates are only available if the specific Treaty criteria are satisfied. It is possible that lower rates than those shown above may be available provided certain criteria are satisfied. As treaties will not be identical, guidance should be sought in all cases.

V   INDIRECT TAXES

		Residents	Non-residents
Value Added Tax (VAT)	General description	Goods and services tax (GST) and harmonised sales tax (HST) are VATs, some provincial sales taxes (PSTs) are VATs whereas others are charged to the end consumers only	
	Entities obliged to levy VAT	Corporations, partnerships and individuals with more than $30,000 of taxable supplies	
	Taxable activities	Goods and services, unless exempt or zero-rated	
	Taxable activities – zero-rated (examples)	For GST/HST, includes prescription drugs and biologicals, medical devices, basic groceries, agricultural and fishing, exports, international travel and transportation	
	Exemptions (reduced rate examples)	For GST/HST, includes certain real properties, healthcare, education, legal aid, supplies by charities, financial services	
	Refund of VAT	Input tax credits if related to taxable or zero-rated supplies	If registered for GST/HST, same rules as residents
	Tax rates	• GST/HST at 5%–15% • PST 0%–9.975%	
	Administrative obligations	• Registration if more than $30,000 of taxable supplies ($50,000 for public sector bodies) • Collecting sales tax • Filing periodic sales tax returns and remitting balance due	• Same requirements for residents if non-resident is carrying on business in Canada • Security may be required if no PE in Canada
Real Property Taxes		Levied by each province or municipality at varying rates	
Land Transfer Tax		Levied by each province or municipality at varying rates	

Cayman Islands

(Matthew Wright, RHSW (CAYMAN) Limited, MWright@RHSWCaribbean.com)

I   MAIN LEGAL FORMS

Legal form / Characteristics	Limited Partnership (LP) and Exempt Limited Partnership (ELP)	Exempted Company (EC)/Exempted Limited Duration Company (ELDC)	Foreign Company	Ordinary resident company (Ltd) and non-resident company (NRC)
Nature of entity	LP: established for any business ELP: must not do business with public in Cayman other than for carrying on business outside Cayman	EC: must carry on business mainly outside Cayman ELDC: the company documents must limit the life of the company to 30 years or less	A Company incorporated outside Cayman carrying on business or having a place of business in Cayman or being a General Partner of an ELP. May not own land	Ltd: can conduct business in the Cayman Islands NRC: must not do business with public in Cayman other than for carrying on business outside Cayman
Partners/shareholders • Number • Restrictions	LP: one or more General Partners and one or more Limited Partners ELP: one or more Cayman General Partners and one or more Limited Partners	EC: one or more members ELDC: two or more members Both types of company may issue bearer shares	Subject to the provisions of the jurisdiction in which it is incorporated	Ltd & NRC: one or more Ordinary companies must be 60% Caymanian owned
Directors	Management by partners	One or more directors	Subject to the provisions of the jurisdiction in which it is incorporated	Ltd & NRC: One or more directors
Establishment	Registration with Registrar	It can be transferred in and transferred out	Must file documents with Registrar within one month	Ltd: requires licence and registration with Registrar NRC: registration with Registrar
Minimum capital	None	None	Subject to the provisions of the jurisdiction in which it is incorporated	Ltd & NRC: none

Legal form / Characteristics	Limited Partnership (LP) and Exempt Limited Partnership (ELP)	Exempted Company (EC)/Exempted Limited Duration Company (ELDC)	Foreign Company	Ordinary resident company (Ltd) and non-resident company (NRC)
Liability	Limited Partners liable to extent of contribution General Partners have unlimited liability	Limited to amount unpaid on capital	Subject to the provisions of the jurisdiction in which it is incorporated	Ltd & NRC: limited to amount unpaid on capital
Governance	No requirement for meetings unless stated in the partnership agreement	Unless company is a Segregated Portfolio Company (SPC), no requirement to hold annual meetings unless required by company documents	Subject to the provisions of the jurisdiction in which it is incorporated. If capital divided by shares, annual meeting required	Ltd & NRC: if capital divided by shares, annual meeting required
Audit requirements	No audit requirements for partnerships	Annual declaration filed with Registrar. An audit is required if the company is CIMA registered or holds a licence Details of ownership, shareholders, directors, accounts are not on the public record	Annual report filed with Registrar	Ltd & NRC: annual report to Registrar giving details of members, directors and paid-up capital
Taxation	No corporation, profits, income or capital gains tax			
Usage		ELDC has some characteristics of a partnership (eg limited duration and non-transferability of interests without the consent of all members) which may lead to a favourable tax treatment for its members in certain foreign jurisdictions where it may be treated as a partnership		

II   CORPORATION TAX

Legal form / Description	UK resident corporation	Permanent establishment (PE)
General description	There is no corporation tax	

III TAXES FOR INDIVIDUALS

		Residents	Non-residents
Income Tax	General description	There is no income tax	
		Residents	**Non-residents**
Capital Gains Tax (CGT)	General description	There is no Capital Gains Tax	
		Residents	**Non-residents**
Inheritance Tax (IHT)	General description	There is no Inheritance tax	

IV   WITHHOLDING TAXES

Under domestic law	Payments to residents	Payments to non-residents
Dividends	Nil	Nil
Interest	Nil	Nil
Royalties	Nil	Nil
On payments to artists and sportsmen	Nil	Nil

The above rates are not affected by the Double Taxation Treaties that the Cayman Islands have with other countries.

V   INDIRECT TAXES

		Residents	Non-residents
Value Added Tax	General description	There is no tax on the supply of goods and services	
Import Duties		Import duties range from 5% to 25% subject to exemptions and higher duties for luxury items	
Stamp Duty		A range of fixed and variable duties apply to documents where the original is in the Cayman Islands	
Work Permit fees		Work permit fees are due on foreign labour	

Nexia International is the trading name of Nexia International Limited, a company registered in the Isle of Man. Company registration number: 53513C. Registered office: 2nd floor, Sixty Circular Road, Douglas, Isle of Man, IM1 1SA

Channel Islands, Guernsey

(Mark Le Ray, Saffery Champness, mark.leray@saffery.gg)

I MAIN LEGAL FORMS

Characteristics \ Legal form	Partnership and Limited Partnership (LP)	Private corporation (Ltd) and Public corporation (Plc)
Partners/shareholders • Number • Restrictions	• Two or more • None	• Private company: one or more, but generally less than 30 • Public company: two or more
Directors	Management by partners	Management by directors
Establishment	Partnership Deed	Articles of Association
Registration	Registration with Registrar of Companies, Guernsey Financial Services Commission	Registration with Registrar of Companies, Guernsey Financial Services Commission
Minimum capital	None	£1
Liability	Partners liable either jointly or jointly and severally for debts	Limited to capital
Governance	Partners	Directors' meetings, shareholders' meetings
Audit requirements	No audit requirements for partnership or LP	Required unless certain qualifying conditions are met and company is not regulated
Taxation	Tax transparent partners assessed on share of profits	Guernsey resident companies are usually taxed at the standard rate of 0% on worldwide profits (10% or 20% on certain sources on income). For non-Guernsey resident beneficial members, distributions to them suffer no further liability to Guernsey tax

II CORPORATION TAX

Legal form / Description	Resident corporation	Permanent establishment (PE)
General description	Liability to Guernsey Income tax, usually at the standard rate of 0%	Only liable to Guernsey income tax on Guernsey source income, unless tax resident in Guernsey
Taxable entities	Resident companies are subject to income tax on their worldwide income, at 0%, 10% or 20% (depending upon the source of income), unless also resident, managed and controlled in the UK, when only Guernsey source income (except bank interest) is taxable in Guernsey 20% tax must have been paid on any distributions paid to Guernsey resident beneficial members (credit is given for tax already suffered) – this is tax paid by the company on the member's behalf, not a tax liability of the company. This also applies to outstanding loans. There is no additional tax payable on distributions to non-resident beneficial members	Companies incorporated in other jurisdictions are only subject to Guernsey tax on their Guernsey source income (except bank interest), unless they have Guernsey resident beneficial members (shareholders and/or loan creditors), in which case they are taxed as a resident company
Taxable income	Worldwide profits, unless also tax resident in the UK (see above)	Worldwide profits if company is Guernsey resident, otherwise only Guernsey source income (except bank interest)
Calculation of taxable profits	Accounting profit is adjusted for various tax add-backs and allowances to arrive at profits chargeable to income tax	
Interest payments	Relevant interest payments allowed	
Related party transactions	All related party transactions must take place on arm's length basis and transactions between related parties must be at fair market value	
Tax year, return and payment	The tax year is the calendar year Profits from trade are assessed on the accounting period ending in the year of assessment Tax is due, in equal instalments, at the end of June and December (or 30 days after an assessment is issued, if not previously assessed)	
Capital gains	Capital gains are not subject to tax	
Losses	Loss relief available	
Tax group	Group loss relief is available	

Description \ Legal form	Resident corporation	Permanent establishment (PE)
Tax rate	There are three rates for companies, depending on the source of income: Company Standard Rate – 0% Company Intermediate Rate – 10%, which applies to: • certain banking activities and domestic insurance business, fiduciary business, insurance intermediary and insurance manager business, fund administration business and provision of custody services by banks Company Higher Rate – 20%, which applies to: • activities regulated by the Office of Utility Regulation • Guernsey property income • Importation and/or supply of hydrocarbon oil or gas in Guernsey • Large retail business in Guernsey where the company has a taxable profit of more than £500,000 Certain investment fund vehicles may apply for exemption from Guernsey tax	Where taxed on Guernsey source income only (except bank interest), rates as per Guernsey resident companies

III   TAXES FOR INDIVIDUALS

		Residents	Non-residents
Income Tax	General description	Tax levied on the chargeable income of a chargeable person for a year of assessment	
	Taxable entities and taxable income	Residents are taxed on their worldwide income with some relief for double taxation	Generally not taxable apart from on certain income arising in Guernsey
	Types of taxable income	• Employment, bonuses, casual earnings • Income from business activities • State/occupational pensions • Property income (usually rent) • Investment income (eg interest, dividends, bonds, government stock, settlements, royalties, annuities, actual distributions)	
	Calculation of income	All income is taxable on a current year basis	
	Tax year, tax assessment and tax payment	• Tax year – calendar year • Tax assessment – individual returns for each taxpayer (unless Tax Office confirms not required) • Income tax is finalised after the year end by the issue of a final assessment once the tax return is processed • Tax is collected throughout the year on employed persons under the Employee Tax Instalment (ETI) scheme • Interim assessments may be issued with tax payable, in June and December (ie payments on account), on income which does not have tax deducted at source	
	Losses	Business losses may be offset against other income of the individual	
	Tax rates	20% income tax	

		Residents	Non-residents
Capital Gains Tax (CGT)	General description	Capital gains are not subject to tax in Guernsey	
	Taxable entities and chargeable assets		
	Calculation of gain		
	Tax year, tax assessment and tax payment		
	Losses		
	Tax rates		

		Domiciled	Non-domiciled
Inheritance Tax (IHT)	General description	There is no estate or inheritance tax in Guernsey	
	Taxable entities and chargeable assets		
	Calculation of charge		
	Taxable events		
	Allowances		
	Tax rates		

IV WITHHOLDING TAXES

Under Domestic Law	Payments to residents	Payments to non-residents
Dividends	Nil	Nil
Interest	Nil	Nil
Royalties	Nil	Nil
On payments to artists and sportsmen	Nil	First £2,500 = 0% Thereafter 20%

Reduced rate available under the relevant Double Taxation Treaty			
Country	Dividends	Interest	Royalties
See below[1]	See below[1]	See below[1]	See below[1]

Note: the above rates are only available provided the specific Treaty criteria are satisfied. As treaties will not be identical, guidance should be sought in all cases.

---

1 Guernsey has several full and partial Double Tax Arrangements in force, details of which are available at www.gov.gg/dta.

V   INDIRECT TAXES

		Residents	Non-residents
Value Added Tax (VAT)	General description	There is no VAT, or sales tax, in Guernsey	
	Entities obliged to levy VAT		
	Taxable activities		
	Taxable activities – zero-rated (examples)		
	Exemptions (examples)		
	Refund of VAT		
	Tax liability		
	Tax rates		
	Administrative obligations		
Real Property Taxes		• Tax on real property: an annual charge of between 5p and £37.55 per unit of footage (depending on category)	
Stamp Duty		• Document duty between 2% and 3% on most property purchases	

Nexia International does not accept liability for any loss arising from any action taken, or omission, on the basis of this publication. Professional advice should be obtained before acting or refraining from acting on the contents of this publication. Membership of Nexia International, or associated umbrella organizations, does not constitute any partnership between members, and members do not accept any responsibility for the commission of any act, or omission to act by, or the liabilities of, other members.

Nexia International is the trading name of Nexia International Limited, a company registered in the Isle of Man. Company registration number: 53513C. Registered office: 2nd floor, Sixty Circular Road, Douglas, Isle of Man, IM1 1SA

Channel Islands, Jersey

*(Andrew Shaw, Smith & Williamson (Channel Islands) Limited, andrew.shaw@
smithandwilliamson.com)*

I MAIN LEGAL FORMS

Legal form / Characteristics	Partnership and Limited Liability Partnership (LLP)	Corporations (Ltd)
Partners/shareholders • Number • Restrictions	• Two or more • One or more general partners • One or more limited partners • None	• Registered Private company: one or more, but generally less than 30 • Registered Public company: two or more
Directors	Management by partners	Management by directors
Establishment	Partnership deed	Articles of Association
Registration	Registration with Registrar of Companies, Jersey Financial Services Commission	
Minimum capital	None	£1
Liability	• Partners liable either jointly or jointly and severally for debts • LLP: general partners; unlimited liability but liability of partners limited	Limited to capital
Governance	Partners	Directors' meetings, shareholders' meetings
Audit requirements	No audit requirements for partnership or LLP	Not required unless stated in articles
Taxation	Tax transparent partners assessed on share of profits Jersey resident parties taxed on all profits regardless of where they are derived. Non-resident parties only liable to tax on profits arising from income sourced or arising in Jersey	Under Jersey Law, Jersey Companies residing in the island are generally taxed at the standard rate of 0% (10% or 20% if undertaking specific prescribed activities). For non-Jersey resident beneficial owners, profits, dividends or otherwise attributed to them from the Jersey Company suffer no further liability to Jersey tax

Legend form / Characteristics	Partnership and Limited Liability Partnership (LLP)	Corporations (Ltd)
Usage	• Partnerships: professional firms • LLPs – non-residents	• Small and medium-sized enterprises • Personal Investment Companies • Registered Public companies used by larger entities generally seeking a listing on Stock Exchange or AIM

II INCOME TAX

Description \ Legal form	Resident corporation	Permanent establishment (PE)
General description	Income tax	
Taxable entities	Resident companies are subject to income tax on their worldwide income. Jersey resident companies are taxed at 0%, 10% or 20% (depending upon the activity of the company) Jersey resident shareholders of these companies can be taxable when funds are extracted from the company. Non-resident shareholders are not taxed on cash dividends or interest paid by such companies	Companies incorporated in other jurisdictions that are managed and controlled in Jersey are taxable in Jersey albeit normally at a rate of 0%
Taxable income	Worldwide profits	All income derived from such establishment, including foreign source income
Calculation of taxable profits	Accounting profit is adjusted for various tax add-backs and allowances to arrive at profits chargeable to income tax	
Interest payments	Qualifying interest payments allowed	
Related party transactions	All related party transactions must take place on arm's length basis and transactions between related parties must be at fair market value There is no transfer pricing or related party legislation in Jersey	
Tax year, return and payment	• The year of assessment for income tax is the calendar year, although companies may adopt an accounting year end of their choice • Profits from trade are normally assessed on a preceding year basis • Taxpayers are issued with assessments in the year following the year of assessment and tax is payable the day following the issue of an assessment	
Capital gains	Capital gains are not subject to tax	
Losses	Loss relief available	
Tax group	Group relief for losses available for qualifying financial services companies. Companies taxed at 0% and which are part of a group allowed to pass on losses so as to offset the profits of another company in the group	
Tax rate	Jersey resident companies are taxed at either 0%, 10% or 20% depending upon activities	Companies incorporated in other jurisdictions that are managed and controlled in Jersey are taxable in Jersey albeit normally at a rate of 0%

III   TAXES FOR INDIVIDUALS

<table>
<tr><th colspan="2"></th><th>Residents</th><th>Non-residents</th></tr>
<tr><td rowspan="8">Income Tax</td><td>General description</td><td colspan="2">Tax levied on the chargeable income of a chargeable person for a year of assessment</td></tr>
<tr><td>Taxable entities and taxable income</td><td>Residents are taxed on their worldwide income with some relief for double taxation</td><td>Not taxable</td></tr>
<tr><td>Types of taxable income</td><td colspan="2">• Property income (usually rent)
• Income from capital investment (interest, sale of goodwill, dividends, royalties, annuities)
• Income from business activities
• Employment from personal services or pensions</td></tr>
<tr><td>Calculation of income</td><td colspan="2">• Property – current year basis
• Trading – current year basis
• Investment – current year basis
• Employment – current year basis</td></tr>
<tr><td>Tax year, tax assessment and tax payment</td><td colspan="2">• Tax year – calendar year
• Tax assessment – individual self-assessment returns for each taxpayer
• Income tax is assessed about 6 months following the year of assessment
• Employees pay income tax as a deduction from their earnings throughout the year under the Income Tax Instalment Scheme (ITIS). Any balance remaining when the assessment is issued then requires settlement on or by 1 December following the end of the year of assessment</td></tr>
<tr><td>Losses</td><td colspan="2">None</td></tr>
<tr><td>Tax rates</td><td colspan="2">20% income tax (income less specific deductions and some limited personal allowances)</td></tr>
<tr><td rowspan="2">Capital Gains Tax (CGT)</td><td>General description</td><td colspan="2">Tax on increase in the value of asset between acquisition and disposal, not chargeable to income or corporate tax</td></tr>
<tr><td>Taxable entities and chargeable assets</td><td colspan="2">There is no capital gains tax in Jersey</td></tr>
<tr><td></td><td></td><th>Domiciled</th><th>Non-domiciled</th></tr>
<tr><td>Inheritance Tax (IHT)</td><td>Taxable entities and chargeable assets</td><td colspan="2">There is no estate or inheritance tax in Jersey</td></tr>
</table>

IV WITHHOLDING TAXES

There are no withholding taxes under Jersey Law.

V   INDIRECT TAXES

		Residents	Non-residents
Goods and Services Tax (GST)	General description	Tax on the supply of goods and services (GST)	
	Entities obliged to levy GST	Registered businesses are required to apply GST at standard rate of 5% on consumption of imported and locally produced goods/services. GST Returns are due quarterly in respect of GST charged on supplies less GST imposed on costs incurred. International Services Entities, which are mainly financial service entities, may apply for an alternative to the GST registration whereby the GST provisions do not apply but an annual fee is paid. This alternative to GST registration primarily serves non-residents	
Real Property Taxes		Land transaction tax, equivalent to stamp duty, collects tax on some property transactions not previously caught by the stamp duty legislation. This relates to share transfer transactions	
Stamp Duty		Stamp duty on some property transactions	

Nexia International is the trading name of Nexia International Limited, a company registered in the Isle of Man. Company registration number: 53513C. Registered office: 2nd floor, Sixty Circular Road, Douglas, Isle of Man, IM1 1SA

Chile

(David Barros, Humphreys & Cia, david.barros@humphreysycia.cl)

I MAIN LEGAL FORMS

Legal form Characteristics	General Partnership and Limited Liability Partnership (LTD)	Stock Corporation (SA) (private or public)
Partners/shareholders • Number • Restrictions	• From 2–50 partners, who have property rights • Changes to the by-laws must be approved unanimously	• More than two stock holders (SpA or Single Shareholder Company is a special type of stock corporation but more flexible. It can be transformed into a common stock corporation with two or more shareholders at any time) • Both kinds of companies are subject to the Corporations Act of 1981
Directors	N/A	Minimum: three directors
Registration	By-laws in public deed, registered and published Public Corporations must register with the Superintendence of Corporations and file periodic information	
Minimum capital	None	
Liability	Limited to rights ownership for LTDs General partnerships unlimited	Limited to capital ownership
Governance	Partners Legal representative	Assembly of Shareholders Board of Directors General manager
Audit requirements	None (IFRS applicable from 2013)	Private corporations: None (IFRS applicable from 2013) Listed corporations: Yes (IFRS applicable from 2009)

Legal form / Characteristics	General Partnership and Limited Liability Partnership (LTD)	Stock Corporation (SA) (private or public)
Taxation	Resident companies taxable on worldwide profits Partnerships are transparent From 2017, partnerships with individuals as partners and sole proprietor entities may opt between the partially integrated and the attributed income systems (see definitions below). Stock companies will be under the partially integrated system	
Usage	Small businesses; family-owned businesses; wholly owned subsidiaries	Joint ventures; medium-sized and large companies. By law, banks, insurance companies, pension fund managing companies, etc

II CORPORATION TAX

Description ╲ Legal Form	Resident corporation	Permanent establishment (PE)
General description	Company or 'first category' tax	
	An important tax reform was enacted in September 2014	
	1. Two Corporate Income Tax systems are established:	
	From 2017 onwards, two optional company tax systems will exist:	
	Attributed Income System Under this system, all of the taxable basis will be apportioned for corporate purposes to each partner/shareholder, down to the final taxpayer who will be subject to taxation, whether dividends have been distributed or not. The attributed income will have a 100% tax credit for the corporate tax paid	
	Partially Integrated System This system will be the default option for stock corporations and any other entity not mentioned under the 'attributed' option. Similarly, as in the old system, this option taxes at individual level only dividends and withdrawals paid to final taxpayers; however, the credit for the corporate tax paid will no longer be 100% but only 65%	
	The 65% limit on the credit shall not apply to investors residing in countries where Chile has a double taxation treaty in force. These investors will, therefore, maintain the current full credit	
	The taxpayers will be subject to the above systems for five years; afterwards, they may opt for one system or the other	
	2. Increase in the Corporate Income Tax rate:	
	The tax rate is gradually increasing from 20% in 2013 to:	
	• 21% in 2014 • 22.5% in 2015 • 24% in 2016 • 25% in 2017 for companies subject to the 'attributed income system', and to 25.5% for companies subject to the 'partially integrated system' • 27% in 2018 for companies subject to the 'partially integrated system'	
Taxable entities	Basic entities are deemed to be resident, for tax purposes, if they are incorporated or indentured in the country	Income derived by PE in Chile
Taxable income	Chilean income on accrued basis and income from foreign sources received by Chilean residents (see double taxation treaties below)	
Calculation of taxable profits	All operating and non-operating income is treated as taxable income with relief for all operating and non-operating expenses incurred in producing this income	
Interest payments	Transfer pricing rules are in place that require funding arrangements to be at arm's length for interest payments to remain tax deductible	
Related party transactions	All related party transactions must take place on arm's-length basis	
Tax year, return and payment	• Tax period coincides with calendar year • Annual tax return must be filed by the following 30 April • Business entities are required to make monthly provisional payments against their annual tax liabilities. The annual net balance of the tax liability accrued after deductions of provisional payments is due, or recoverable, with the filing of the return in April	

Description＼Legal Form	Resident corporation	Permanent establishment (PE)
Capital gains	Capital gains are tax exempt if derived from transactions of first public offerings and listed corporations, with qualified market presence	
Losses	Losses may be carried forward indefinitely	
Tax group	None	
Tax rate	See above	
Double taxation treaties	See www.sii.cl/pagina/jurisprudencia/convenios.htm	
Free trade agreements	See www.aduana.cl/prontus_aduana_eng/site/edic/base/port/international_agree.html	

III   TAXES FOR INDIVIDUALS

		Residents	Non-residents
Income Tax	Taxable entities and taxable income	Any individual becomes tax resident if he stays continuously in the country for 6 months or more in one year, or more than 6 months in total in 2 consecutive years Any person resident or domiciled in Chile must pay tax on their worldwide income	Foreign individual who becomes resident is subject to tax only on income arising in Chile, during the first 3 years of residence. After that, the tax is applied on worldwide income
	Types of taxable income	• Property income (usually rent) • Income from capital investment (interest, sale of goodwill, dividends, royalties, annuities) • Income from business activities • Employment from personal services or pensions	
	Taxable income	• Gross earnings less social security payments (with limits) • Individuals are also covered by the double taxation treaties	
	Tax year, tax assessment and tax payment	• Tax year – calendar year • Employees pay a withholding scaled tax rate monthly as sole requirement, without further filings • Persons receiving income from more than one source and independent service providers must file an annual tax return	
	Losses	Losses can be carried forward indefinitely	
	Tax rates	Tax rate computed on a progressive marginal scale, exempt up to US$11,000 p.a. and increasing from 4% marginal to 40% (35% in 2017) marginal for income equivalent to US$118,000 or more per year (all dollar amounts are approximate)	See Withholding Taxes below
Capital Gains Tax (CGT)	General description	Investments in shares of listed companies that comply with stock exchange IPOs and general public offerings, are exempt from capital gains tax	

		Domiciled	Non-domiciled
Inheritance Tax (IHT)	General description	Tax is applied to assessed inheritable estate	
	Taxable entities and chargeable assets	All legal inheritors	

		Domiciled	Non-domiciled
Inheritance Tax (IHT) – *contd*	Calculation of charge	The tax base includes the whole inventory of assets and liabilities in the estate: property, securities, funds in every form, vehicles, participations in businesses, etc, less debts, each one valued according to the specifications in the law. If the originator was married under a connubial society regime only 50% of the estate is subject to this procedure	
	Taxable events	Death	
	Allowances	Equivalent to (approx.) US$43,000 per inheritor	
	Tax rates	Gifts and inheritances are subject to a progressive tax that goes up to 25% on the net amount, after deducting expenses and allowances	

IV WITHHOLDING TAXES

Under domestic law	Payments to residents	Payments to non-residents[1]
Dividends	Nil	35% The corporate income tax paid is credited to this tax with a limit of 65%, unless the foreign investor is covered by a Double Taxation Treaty, where the credit is 100%
Interest	Nil	4% when paid to a bank, otherwise can go up to 35%
Royalties	Nil	30%
On payments to artists and sportspeople	Nil	20%
On payments to service providers who perform work of a technical or engineering nature	Nil	15%

Reduced rate available under the relevant Double Taxation Treaty			
Countries	Dividends[2]	Interest[3]	Royalties
Belgium	35%	15%	10%
Brazil	35%	15%	15%
Canada	35%	15%	15%
Columbia	35%	15%	10%
Croatia	35%	15%	10%
Denmark	35%	15%	15%
Ecuador	35%	15%	15%
France	35%	15%	10%
Ireland	35%	15%	10%
Korea, Republic of	35%	15%	15%
Malaysia	35%	15%	10%
Mexico	35%	15%	15%
New Zealand	35%	15%	10%
Norway	35%	15%	15%
Paraguay	35%	15%	15%
Peru	35%	15%	15%
Poland	35%	15%	15%
Portugal	35%	15%	10%

1　Reduced rates of withholding tax may apply where there is an appropriate double tax treaty.
2　Dividends paid from Chile to a non-resident investor are subject to 35% withholding tax in Chile with a 65% credit of the Corporate Tax paid, unless the investor resides in a country with a DTT with Chile, where the credit will be 100% of the Corporate Tax.
3　Interest paid to foreign banks has a 4% tax rate.

Reduced rate available under the relevant Double Taxation Treaty			
Countries	**Dividends[2]**	**Interest[3]**	**Royalties**
Spain	35%	15%	10%
Sweden	35%	15%	10%
Switzerland	35%	15%	10%
Thailand	35%	15%	15%
United Kingdom	35%	15%	10%

Note: The above rates are only available provided the specific treaty criteria are satisfied. It is possible that lower rates than those shown above may be available provided that certain special criteria are satisfied. As treaties will not be identical, guidance should be sought in all cases. Treaties provide a reference framework for the signatory countries, which have the power to use lower rates if they are already in use or if there are most favoured nation clauses that permit adjusting the rates to the reduced amounts agreed to in other treaties.

V INDIRECT TAXES

		Residents	Non-residents
Value Added Tax (VAT)	Entities obliged to levy VAT	• All entities that transfer title of a new good on a recurring basis • All entities that sell commercial services	
	Taxable activities	Supply of goods and services, imports of goods, etc	
	Taxable activities – zero-rated (examples)	None	
	Exemptions (examples)	• Life insurance • Exports and insurance relating to exports • Property • Sale of used fixed assets • Personal services rendered by employees or by independent contractors, whether resident or not	
	Refund of VAT	If in a given month credit exceeds debit, the difference may be carried forward and added to the credit of the next month	
	Tax liability	Normally the seller of goods and services is responsible for charging VAT on the invoice	
	Tax rates	19% flat and uniform rate	
	Administrative obligations	Tax payable monthly	
Real Property Taxes		Land and buildings, including housing that exceeds a certain value, are taxed at 2% each year on the taxable valuation of the property. This annual tax is paid in four quarterly instalments	
Stamp Duty		• Applicable to transactions related to credit operations, cheques, ATM withdrawals, etc • 0.066% per month with a maximum of 0.8% p.a., calculated on the par value of the document, or 0.332% if the document is payable on sight, is applied to bills of exchange, promissory notes, import letters of credit, IOUs and in general to any document representative of a loan or credit operation (rates valid from 1 January 2015)	

China

(Flora Luo and Scott Heidecke, Nexia TS (Shanghai) Co. Ltd., floraluo@nexiats.com.cn, scott@nexiats.com.cn)

I MAIN LEGAL FORMS

Legal form / Characteristics	Partnership and Limited Liability Partnership (LLP)	Private Limited corporation (Ltd) and Public corporation(Plc)
Partners/shareholders • Number • Restrictions	• Minimum: two persons • Unlimited liability	Ltd: 1–50 persons Plc: Minimum: two persons
Directors	No appointment of directors is required	Ltd: A Board of Directors of 3–13 persons is mandatory for Joint Ventures. WFOEs may have either a Board of Directors or a single Executive Director. A Supervisory Board is also required Plc: Mandatory to have a Board of Directors of 5–19 persons
Establishment	Registered business name, registered address and partnership deed	Ltd: Registered business name and address; Articles of Association, feasibility study; legal representative and supervisor appointments. Joint Ventures must also register a JV contract Plc: registered business name, registered address Founders number: 2–200 Founders share: no less than 35%
Registration	Except for certain restricted industries or businesses that are listed on a published 'negative list', foreign invested companies no longer need pre-approval before registration. Allowed companies may register with the appropriate local registration authority to obtain a business licence and then proceed to register with up to 10 other government agencies, including tax, customs and statistics bureaux	

Legal form / Characteristics	Partnership and Limited Liability Partnership (LLP)	Private Limited corporation (Ltd) and Public corporation(Plc)
Minimum capital	No restriction for Partnership LLP: RMB 100,000 for a one-person company and RMB 30,000 for a more than two-person company	Ltd: Private corporations in encouraged industries no longer have minimum registered capital requirements. However, local registration authorities reserve the right to refuse registration if the registered capital amount is deemed to be unreasonably low. Certain restricted industries, such as medical institutions, must satisfy minimum registered capital requirements Plc: not less than RMB 5m
Liability	Unlimited liability for partners and general partners	Generally limited to invested registered capital
Governance	By partners	Ltd: Board of Directors or Executive Director; Managing Director; Legal Representative; Supervisory Board or Supervisor Plc: governance consists of: • Board of Shareholders • Board of Directors • Audit Committee
Audit requirements	Annual statutory audit required – performed by certified public accountant (CPA)	Ltd: Annual statutory audits are required for all companies and must be performed by a CPA licensed in China
Taxation	Enterprise income tax on worldwide revenue Partnerships are transparent	
Usage	Rarely used other than for law firms or accounting firms	Commonly used for local or foreign invested businesses and for all public companies

II CORPORATION TAX

Legal Form / Description	Non-resident enterprise	Resident enterprise
General description	Enterprise income tax (EIT)	
Taxable entities	Enterprises established outside China with effective management not in China, and either have an establishment in China or no establishment in China but have income derived from sources inside China	Any enterprise that is formally registered as a company in China, and also foreign enterprises established outside China but with effective management based in China
Taxable income	China-related income only	Worldwide income
Calculation of taxable profits	Taxable income is gross revenue minus non-taxable income, exempt income, allowable deductions and permitted loss carry-overs	
Interest payments	Interest paid on loans from financial institutions is fully deductible, whereas interest on loans from non-financial institutions is deductible to the extent that the interest accrued or actually paid is no higher than that on similar loans from financial institutions. Interest paid between associated enterprises is subject to thin capitalisation and transfer pricing rules	
Related party transactions	All related party transactions must take place on an arm's length basis. Substantial related party/transfer pricing documentation required during year-end tax filing	
Tax year, return and payment	• Tax year normally coincides with calendar year • EIT is declared and paid monthly or quarterly (as registered) using provisional corporate tax returns, which must be filed within 15 days after the end of each term • A final annual tax declaration and settlement is required within 5 months after the end of a tax year. The annual filing includes mandatory submission of 9 related party transaction disclosure forms	
Capital gains	No separate Capital Gains Tax for companies. Gains on the disposal of property, including gains from transactions involving securities instruments (eg stocks, bonds, etc), are subject to EIT of 25%. Also applies to gains obtained from corporate reorganizations, such as equity and share transfers. Such gains are subject to withholding tax (10%) if they are derived by a non-resident enterprise	
Losses	Tax losses may be carried forward to offset future income for a period of 5 years No losses can be carried back	
Tax group	None	
Tax rate	25% is the standard EIT rate for all companies, domestic and foreign-held. Encouraged industry companies set up in certain western provinces and earning at least 75% of profits in those provinces may be granted a rate of 15%. Countrywide, those companies that can meet criteria as high or new technology companies, and certain others engaged in infrastructure or environmental businesses, as well as some agricultural companies, may enjoy rates as low as 15%. Thin-profit enterprises are subject to EIT at a 20% rate	

III   TAXES FOR INDIVIDUALS

		Residents	Non-residents
Income Tax	General description	Individual income tax (IIT)	
	Taxable persons and taxable income	Tax is levied on the worldwide income of Chinese nationals, as well as foreign individuals who have been domiciled or resident in China for more than five years	Tax is levied on China-sourced income (regardless of whether paid in China or overseas) of foreign workers who are present in China longer than 90 days (183 days if from a treaty country). Legal Representatives, Chief Representatives and other high-level managers are liable for IIT without regard to the 90/183-day rules, but do qualify for time apportionment of tax
	Types of taxable income	• wages and salaries derived from a position or contract of employment • production and business income derived by industrial and commercial households/entrepreneurs • income derived from contracting for or leasing operations of enterprises or institutions • remuneration for personal services performed by an independent contractor • remuneration for manuscripts • royalty income • interest income, dividends and bonuses • income derived from leasing properties • income derived from assignment or transfer of properties • contingency income • other income specified to be taxable by the finance department of the State Council	
	Calculation of income	For wages and salaries, a monthly standard allowance (deduction) of RMB 3,500 is granted to all individuals. Foreign individuals working in China are entitled to a monthly standard allowance of RMB 4,800. Social Security contributions are also deductible. No other deductions allowed	
	Tax year, tax assessment and tax payment	• Tax year normally coincides with the calendar year • IIT is in most cases deducted and filed monthly by the employer or other withholding agent. If no withholding agent is available, the individual is responsible for monthly IIT filing • The tax withholding agent or individual must declare and pay IIT to the State treasury within 15 days following each month of tax liability • For any individual with annual income in excess of RMB 120,000, an annual tax return must be filed within three months following the end of a calendar year (by 31 March of each calendar year)	
	Losses	Losses incurred by an individual deriving income from production and business income in a tax year may be carried forward for a period of 5 years to be offset against future taxable income. There is no loss relief for other types of income. Losses cannot be carried back	
	Tax rates	There is no difference in IIT rates for income of residents and non-residents. Tax on wages and salary is computed as a percentage of the income based on a 7-tier progressive scale ranging from 5% up to 45%. Tax on income from production and business operations (or leasing operations) by self-employed individuals is taxed at progressive rates ranging from 5% to 35%. Tax on income for independent contractors is generally 20% but may range as high as 40%. Income from other sources is generally taxable at a flat rate of 20%	

		Residents	Non-residents
Capital Gains Tax (CGT)	General description	Individual income tax capital gains	
	Taxable entities and chargeable assets	Resident and non-resident individuals	
	Calculation of gain	Selling price minus deductible expenses (including cost and other reasonable expenses)	
	Tax year, tax assessment and tax payment	Tax year – N/A Capital gains tax is generally due at the close of relevant transactions	
	Losses	N/A	
	Tax rates	Usually 20% of the gains	
		Domiciled	**Non-domiciled**
Inheritance Tax (IHT)	Taxable entities and chargeable assets	Currently there is no inheritance tax	

IV   WITHHOLDING TAXES

Under Domestic Law	Payments to residents	Payments to non-residents[1,2]
Dividends	No withholding. Tax is paid during EIT filing	10%
Interest	No withholding. Tax is paid during EIT filing	10%
Royalties	No withholding. Tax is paid during EIT filing	10%
Lease Income	No withholding. Tax is paid during EIT filing	10%
Equity or share transfers of China registered companies	Paid at time of transaction	10%
On payments to artists and sportsmen	Must be withheld by employer if applicable, otherwise filed and paid by the individual on a monthly basis	20%

China has negotiated a range of tax treaties which provide an exemption or a reduction in withholding taxes on dividends, interest and royalties payable.

Reduced rate available under the relevant Double Taxation Treaty			
Country	Dividends	Interest	Royalties
Australia	15%	10%	10%
Germany	5%	10%	10%
Hong Kong	5%	7%	7%
Jamaica	5%	7.5%	10%
Korea	5%	10%	10%
New Zealand	15%	10%	10%
Singapore	5%	7%	6%
USA	10%	10%	7%

Note: The above rates are only available provided the specific Treaty criteria are satisfied. As treaties are not identical, guidance should be sought in all cases.

1   Reduced (or increased) rates of withholding may apply where there is an appropriate double tax treaty and certain conditions are met. Examples are shown in the following table.
2   Note that VAT also applies to interest, royalty and leasing income.

V INDIRECT TAXES

		Residents	Non-residents
Value Added Tax (VAT)	Entities obliged to levy VAT	All enterprises, organisations or individuals that sell goods, provide services or import goods and services. This includes non-resident companies or individuals, although non-residents are generally not able to register for VAT and thus must use the services of an approved withholding agent. Guidance must be sought for specific application of the latest rules related to specific cross-border services transactions	
	Taxable activities	Sale of goods and services, including imported goods and services	
	Taxable activities – zero-rated (examples)	Export of goods and some services (if the services are entirely consumed offshore) is exempt or zero-rated	
	Exemptions (examples)	• Self-produced agricultural products sold by agricultural producers • Contraceptive drugs and devices • Antique books • Imported instruments and equipment used directly in scientific research, experiments and education • Materials and equipment imported free of charge from foreign governments and international organisations • Equipment and machinery required to be imported under contract processing, contract assembly and compensation trade • Articles imported directly by organisations for the disabled for special use by the disabled • Certain exported services, such as design or advertising, where the service is entirely consumed offshore	
	Refund of VAT	A percentage of VAT paid during manufacture of exported products can be refunded where certain conditions are met	
	Tax liability	Normally the supplier of goods and services is responsible for the collection and subsequent payment of VAT during sales. For imported goods or services, the buyer must act as withholding agent and ensure payment of VAT	
	Tax rates	• General taxpayer = 17% (13% for some agricultural and textile goods) on goods and 6%–17% for services. Input VAT is creditable against output VAT • Small-scale taxpayer = 3% of total sales turnover	
	Administrative obligations	All enterprises or individuals selling goods and services in China must register for VAT with the local tax authority (although foreign entities are generally not allowed to register and thus must rely on an approved withholding agent in China). VAT taxpayers are generally classified into two categories: the general VAT payer or the small-scale VAT payer. All entities with revenues in excess of RMB 5 million are automatically considered as general VAT taxpayers and shall be registered as such. Others must meet certain accounting requirements in order to register as general taxpayers. General taxpayers must issue special VAT invoices upon request of the buyer and must obtain special VAT invoices in order to claim input VAT credit	
Business Tax (BT)		Since the latest VAT laws have taken effect, BT is no longer collected for most transactions, although there is some regional variation. Where BT is collected, the rates range from 3% to 20% of the transaction	
		Representative Offices of foreign entities continue to pay BT in addition to EIT, usually 5% of the total expenses of the office	

Consumption Tax (CT)	CT applies to the manufacture, import, commissioning of processing, and sale of CT liable goods in China. Tax collected from the consumer (buyer) is based on the sales value or sales volume of the goods, or a composite of both
	CT liable goods fall into more than 10 general categories and include tobacco, alcohol, some motor vehicle-related goods, luxury watches and jewellery. CT has recently been eliminated for cosmetics, but remains subject to change. Tax rates vary widely, in some cases as a percentage of the sales value and in other cases as a fixed amount per item
Real Property Taxes	Deed tax is between 3% and 5% on the total value of land use rights or building ownership rights transferred, and is payable by the transferee
	Land value-added tax is a tax on the gain realised on the transfer of land-use rights of state-owned land, including the buildings and associated structures on it. Tax is charged in four bands ranging from 30% to 60% depending on the percentage gain versus deductions. Some exemptions for residences, or other special situations, may apply
Stamp Duty	• Stamp tax stamps must be purchased and affixed to contractual and other similar legal documents (such as purchase agreements)
	• The amount of tax ranges from 0.003% to 0.1% of the contract value

Nexia International does not accept liability for any loss arising from any action taken, or omission, on the basis of this publication. Professional advice should be obtained before acting or refraining from acting on the contents of this publication. Membership of Nexia International, or associated umbrella organizations, does not constitute any partnership between members, and members do not accept any responsibility for the commission of any act, or omission to act by, or the liabilities of, other members.

Nexia International is the trading name of Nexia International Limited, a company registered in the Isle of Man. Company registration number: 53513C. Registered office: 2nd floor, Sixty Circular Road, Douglas, Isle of Man, IM1 1SA

Colombia

(Roberto Montes Marin, Montes y Asociados SAS, montesyasociados@nexiamya. com.co and gerencia@nexiamya.com.co)

I MAIN LEGAL FORMS

Legal form / Characteristics	Partnership and Limited Liability Partnership (LLP)	Private corporation (Ltd) and Public corporation (Plc)
Partners/shareholders • Number • Restrictions	Minimum of two partners to begin	Minimum of five partners to begin
Directors	As a minimum a general manager and Board of Directors for companies	
Establishment	Written agreement presented to notary public which certifies legality	
Registration	Chamber of Commerce National Tax Administration	
Minimum capital	None	No less than authorised amount and no less than one-third of the shares to be paid upfront
Liability	Unlimited responsibility	Up to the full amount of their shares
Governance	Optional external auditor (fiscal revisor)	External auditor (fiscal revisor)
Audit requirements	Financial statement must be certified by public accountant	Financial statement must be certified by public accountant and audited by fiscal revisor
Taxation	Corporate taxes on worldwide profits Partnerships are transparent	
Usage	No restrictions	

II   CORPORATION TAX

Legal form Description	Resident corporation	Foreign corporation with permanent establishment (PE)
General description	Corporate tax	
Taxable entities	Colombian companies, regardless of whether ownership is in the hands of non-Colombian residents, pay tax on income derived from all sources, with some activities and services performed outside Colombia being taxable	PE located in Colombia
Taxable income	Worldwide profits	Profits derived by PE in Colombia
Calculation of taxable profits	Accounting profit is adjusted for various tax add-backs and allowances to arrive to chargeable profits	
Interest payments	Interest paid to authorised local banks or other authorised financial institutions is deductible in full, if certified by the recipient	
Related party transactions	All related party transactions must take place on arm's-length basis	
Tax year, return and payment	Tax period coincides with calendar year The return should be filed within 2 years after the financial year end Tax payable in two or five instalments depending on how the National Tax Administration has classified the taxpayer	
Capital gains	Capital gains are subject to corporation tax at normal rates	
Losses	Companies may offset current year losses against the income earned over the following 5 years	
Tax group	None	
Tax rate	33% for income tax equality	

III TAXES FOR INDIVIDUALS

		Residents	Non-residents
Income Tax	Taxable entities and taxable income	Taxed on worldwide income	Taxed on Colombian source income
	Types of taxable income	• Property income (usually rent) • Income from capital investment (interest, sale of goodwill, dividends, royalties, annuities) • Income from business activities • Employment from personal services or pensions	
	Calculation of income	Determined according to table established by the National Tax Administration	
	Tax year, tax assessment and tax payment	Tax year – calendar year Self-assessment returns should be filed by August of the following year	
	Losses	No specific rules	
	Tax rates	Income tax based on a progressive rate schedule, with 33% being the highest marginal rate applicable to earnings	
Capital Gains Tax (CGT)	General description	Not taxable	
		Domiciled	**Non-domiciled**
Inheritance Tax (IHT)	General description	No inheritance or gift taxes	

IV   WITHHOLDING TAXES

Under domestic law	Payments to residents	Payments to non-residents[1]
Dividends	20%	33%
Interest	Income tax at progressive rates up to 33%	33%
Royalties	Income tax at progressive rates up to 33%	33%
On payments to artists and sportsmen	Income tax at progressive rates up to 33%	33%

1   Residence for tax purposes. The individuals who meet the following conditions are considered residents for tax purposes:
   a) Continuous or discontinuous stay in the country for more than 183 calendar days including days of arrival and departure to/from the country, during a taxable year (1 January to 31 December). When continuous or discontinuous stay in the country falls in more than one year or taxable period, the individual is considered resident from the second year or period.
   b) If the individual lives abroad providing service to the country under the Vienna Convention on diplomatic or consular service and is exempt from taxation where he is with respect to all or part of his income and capital gains during the taxable year or period.
   c) Nationals who during the relevant taxable year or period meet one of the following:
      • The spouse or partner (not legally separated) or minor dependent children have tax residence in the country.
      • Fifty per cent (50%) or more of the income is from domestic sources.
      • Fifty per cent (50%) or more of the assets are managed in the country.
      • Fifty per cent (50%) of more of the assets are owned in the country.
      • Being required by the tax authorities, the person does not prove the status of residence abroad for tax purposes.
      • Have residence in a jurisdiction classified by the Government as a tax haven.

Reduced rate available under the relevant Double Taxation Treaty			
Country	Dividends	Interest	Royalties
Chile	7%[2]	15%	10%
Spain	Nil	10%	10%
Switzerland	10%	15%	10%

Note: the above rates are only available provided the specific Treaty criteria are satisfied. It is possible that lower rates than those shown above may be available provided that certain criteria are satisfied. As treaties will not be identical, guidance should be sought in all cases.

2 If the dividend income is derived from an exempt activity (if it is invested in productive activity in Colombia for a term of not less than three years).

V INDIRECT TAXES

		Residents	Non-residents
Value Added Tax (VAT)	Entities obliged to levy VAT	ALL	
	Taxable activities	Supply of goods and services, imports of goods, etc	
	Taxable activities – zero-rated (examples)	Responsibility of suppliers of taxable goods or taxable services	
	Exemptions (examples)	• Export of moveable goods • Scientific and cultural books and magazines • Services rendered in Colombia and used exclusively abroad	
	Refund of VAT	For exempt goods	
	Tax liability	Normally the supplier of goods and services is responsible for charging VAT	
	Tax rates	Standard rate = 19% Differential rates of 0%, 5%, 10% on various goods depending on circumstances described in the Tax Code	
	Administrative obligations	Charging, filing and payment of taxes	
Real Property Taxes		Determined by Municipal Government	
Consumption Tax		Generated by the supply or sale to the final consumer, or importation by the user, of the following goods and services: • The provision of mobile services. Rate 4% • The sale, production or import of any tangible moveable property (vehicles, boats and aircraft). Rate 16% • The sale of prepared food and drinks. Rate 8%	
Patrimony Tax		The Equity tax is levied on the value of the total patrimony exceeding $1 million of the legal person or individual on 1 January 2015, 2016 and 2017 The rate for legal persons is between 0.20% and 1.15% for the first year. In the following years the rate decreases The rate for individuals is between 0.125% and 1.50% for each year	

Croatia

(Dubravka Kopun, KOPUN Group, info@kopun.hr)

I MAIN LEGAL FORMS

Characteristics / Legal form	Partnership and Limited Partnership	Private Corporation (d.o.o.) and Public Corporation (d.d.)
Partners/ shareholders • Number • Restrictions	Two or more No restrictions	One or more No restrictions
Directors	Management by partners (partnership) LLP – only general partner(s) Limited partner shall not have the authority to manage business activities of the company, but he can be appointed as a procurator or proxy	Management by directors (One or more)
Establishment	Partnership agreement[1]	Notarial deed of incorporation
Registration	Trade register, tax authorities, State Bureau of statistics	Trade register, tax authorities, State Bureau of statistics
Minimum capital	None	Private: HRK 20,000 (approx EUR 2,700) Public: HRK 200,000 (approx EUR 27,000)
Liability	Unlimited – partnership LLP – limited partner's liability – up to his share[2]	Unlimited[2]

---

1 Verification of signatures by public notary.
2 However, anyone who abuses his position as a shareholder or partner could be liable:
   (a) if he uses the company to achieve a goal that is otherwise prohibited to him,
   (b) if used by the company to prevent damage to creditors,
   (c) if, contrary to the law, he manages the assets of the company as if they were his property,
   (d) if, in his favour or in favour of any other person, he reduces the company's assets, even though he knew or should have known that the company would not be able to meet its obligations.

Legal form / Characteristics	Partnership and Limited Partnership	Private Corporation (d.o.o.) and Public Corporation (d.d.)
Governance	Partners[3]	General meeting, Supervisory Board,[4] Board of directors
Audit requirements	Normally, no audit requirements	No audit requirements if in previous year at least 2 out of 3 conditions were not exceeded: • Total income = approx EUR 4,000,000 • Total assets = approx EUR 2,000,000 • Number of employees = 25
Taxation	Income tax or corporate tax	Corporate tax
Usage	Mostly because specific law requires such type	Public: mostly companies transformed in the privatization process of 'social owned companies' Private: the remainder

---

3   Partners of an LLP could establish bodies in accordance with company agreement.
4   A supervisory board of a Private Corporation is required where:
   (a)   the average number of employees exceeds 200 per year,
   (b)   it is regulated by a special law,
   (c)   share capital exceeds HRK 600,000 and the company has more than 50 shareholders,
   (d)   the company is a general partner in an LLP and the number of employees in the company and in the LLP jointly exceeds 200.

II CORPORATION TAX

Legal form / Description	Resident corporation	Permanent establishment (PE)
General description	Tax on income of corporations	
Taxable entities	A company or another legal or natural person resident in the Republic of Croatia, who is permanently and independently engaged in an economic activity for the purpose of deriving a profit, an income or a revenue or other assessable economic benefits	A resident permanent establishment (an inland business unit) of a non-resident entrepreneur
Taxable income	Residents are taxed on their worldwide income	Income derived by PE in Croatia
Calculation of taxable profits	Profit determined pursuant to the accounting regulations as the difference between revenues and expenditures before the profit tax assessment, increased and reduced in accordance with the provisions of the Croatian Profit Tax Law	
Interest payments	For the determination of interest income from loans granted to associated persons, the minimum calculated interest rate must be the rate which would apply to non-associated persons at the time of granting a loan	
	For the determination of interest expense on loans received from associated persons, the maximum interest accrued must be recognised at the interest rate which would apply to non-associated persons at the time of granting a loan	
	This interest rate is determined and published by the finance minister, prior to the beginning of the tax period in which it will be applied, taking into account that this interest rate is realised under comparable circumstances or would be realised in the transactions between non-associated persons	
Related party transactions	All related party transactions must take place on an arm's length basis	
Tax year, return and payment	Tax year generally coincides with the business year, but may also differ from business year	
	Corporate income tax return must be submitted to tax authorities within 4 months after the end of the year	
	During the tax year, the corporate income tax is prepaid on a monthly basis	
Capital gains	Capital gains are included in taxable income and taxed at the standard rate of 18% / 12%	
Losses	Tax losses may be carried forward for up to five consecutive years. The carry back of losses is not permitted	
Tax group	Consolidated tax returns are not allowed	
Tax rate	18% for companies having an income of HRK 3,000,000 (approx EUR 400,000) or more. Companies having an income below HRK 3,000,000 are taxed with 12% corporate tax	

III   TAXES FOR INDIVIDUALS

<table>
<tr><th></th><th></th><th>Residents</th><th>Non-residents</th></tr>
<tr><td rowspan="8">Income Tax</td><td>General description</td><td colspan="2">Personal income tax that is levied and paid for the calendar year (the taxable period)</td></tr>
<tr><td>Taxable entities and taxable income</td><td>Resident taxable person is a natural person who in the Republic of Croatia:

– has domicile or habitual residence,

– has neither domicile nor habitual residence, but is employed in the civil service of the Republic of Croatia and receives a salary on that basis</td><td>Non-resident taxable person is a natural person who has neither domicile nor habitual residence in the Republic of Croatia, but acquires an income in the Republic of Croatia which is subject to taxation provided by The Income Tax Law</td></tr>
<tr><td>Types of taxable income</td><td colspan="2">1. Income from employment
2. Income from independent personal activities (small business, self-employment and professional income)
3. Income from property and property rights
4. Income from capital
5. Income from insurance
6. Other income</td></tr>
<tr><td>Calculation of income</td><td>Taxable base of a resident is the total amount of income that the taxable person obtains inland and abroad, decreased for personal allowance</td><td>Taxable base of a non-resident is the total amount of income that the taxable person obtains in the Republic of Croatia, decreased for personal allowance</td></tr>
<tr><td>Tax year, tax assessment and tax payment</td><td colspan="2">Income tax is levied and paid for the calendar year (the taxable period). The taxable period may be shorter than the calendar year in the following cases:

1. if a resident becomes a non-resident during a single calendar year, or vice versa
2. on the birth or death of the taxable person

All payers of the income are required to report income paid to individuals by the end of January for the previous calendar year

Depending on type of income, tax payments are made at the same time as the payment of income, up to the last day in the month for the current month, up to the last day in the month for the preceding month, according to a ruling from the Tax Administration or 15 days from the receipt of the ruling</td></tr>
<tr><td>Losses</td><td colspan="2">Professional income: Tax losses may be carried forward for five years</td></tr>
<tr><td>Tax rates</td><td colspan="2">Annual Personal allowance (tax-free earnings): HRK 45,600 (approx EUR 6,100)

Annual taxable base for income from employment:

Up to HRK 210,000 (approx EUR 28,000) – 24%

Over HRK 210,000 – 36%</td></tr>
</table>

		Residents	Non-residents
Capital Gains Tax (CGT)	General description	Taxes are charged by the state over transactions, dividends and capital gains	
	Taxable entities and chargeable assets	Natural persons who obtain an income from capital gains are subject to capital gains tax	
		Income from dividends, shares, interest and withdrawals are considered as a capital gain	
	Calculation of gain	**Dividends** – Sum paid out	
		Shares – Market value of the shares in corporate income (profit) realised through the allocation of own shares, or the difference between the market value of allocated shares and consideration paid, if shares are acquired for a partial consideration	
		Withdrawals – The market value of withdrawals of assets and the use of services at the expense of the corporate income (profit) realised in the current period	
		Interest – Receipts acquired by a natural person (individual) on account of claims arising from loans and credit granted, including the receipts from commission loans realised through banks	
	Tax year, tax assessment and tax payment	Tax year – calendar year	
		A reduction for a non-taxable portion of receipts of up to HRK 12,000 (approx EUR 1,600) per year shall be recognized in the income tax annual assessment on the basis of the annual tax return filed	
		Depending on the type of capital gain, tax payments are made at the same time as the payment or within 8 days from the date of payment	
	Losses	There is no relief for tax losses	
	Tax rates	Dividends and shares in corporate income (profit) – 12% + surtax	Dividends and shares in corporate income (profit) – 12%
		Income from allocation or purchase of own shares – 24% + surtax	Income from allocation or purchase of own shares – 24%
		Withdrawals and interest – 36% + surtax	Withdrawals and interest – 36%
			This is also dependent on double taxation agreement
		Domiciled	**Non-domiciled**
Inheritance Tax (IHT)	General description	Tax for recipients of inheritances	
	Taxable entities and chargeable assets	The taxpayer is the legal or natural person in Croatia that inherits or accepts a gift or acquires on another basis, without compensation, property on which tax is paid	
		The chargeable assets are the amount of cash and the market value of financial and other assets on the day of the transaction, after deduction of debts and costs that relate to the property on which the tax is paid	
	Calculation of charge	5% of market value	
	Taxable events	Inherited or donated money and other assets, if not received from immediate family members	
	Allowances	○ former spouses when they settle their property relations in connection with a divorce	
		○ spouse, descendants and forebears and adopted children and adoptive parents of the deceased	
	Tax rates	Up to 5%	

IV   WITHHOLDING TAXES

Under domestic law	Payments to residents	Payments to non-residents
Dividends	12%	12%
Interest	12% – Applies surtax on income tax	12%
Royalties	24% – Applies surtax (30% of total income is tax deductible)	24% – (30% of total income is tax deductible)
On payments to artists and sportsmen	24% – Applies surtax	Applies the tax rate in accordance with the double taxation agreement

Reduced rate available under the relevant Double Taxation Treaty (%)				
Country	Dividends, provided criteria satisfied	Dividends in all other circumstances	Interest	Royalties
Albania	10	10	10	10
Armenia	0[2]	10	10	5
Austria	0[3]	15	5	0
Azerbaijan	5[10]	10	10	10
Belgium	5	15	10	0
Belarus	5[1]	15	10	10
Bosnia and Herzegovina	5	10	10	10
Bulgaria	5	5	5	0
Canada	5	15	10	10
Chile	5[7]	15	5–15	5–10
China	5	5	10	10
Czech Republic	5	5	0	10
Denmark	5	10	5	10
Estonia	5	15	10	10
Finland	5	15	0	10
France	0	15	0	0
Georgia	5	5	5	5
Germany	5	15	0	0
Greece	5	10	10	10
Hungary	5	10	0	0
Iceland	5	10	10	10
India	5	15	10	10
Indonesia	10	10	10	10
Iran	5	10	5	5
Ireland	5[5]	10	0	10
Israel	5–10[9]	15	5	5
Italy	15	15	10	5
Jordan	5	10	10	10
Korea, South	5	10	5	0
Kuwait	0	0	0	10
Latvia	5	15	10	10

Reduced rate available under the relevant Double Taxation Treaty (%)				
Country	Dividends, provided criteria satisfied	Dividends in all other circumstances	Interest	Royalties
Lithuania	5	10	10	10
Macedonia	5	15	10	10
Malaysia	5	10	10	10
Malta	5[4]	5	0	0
Mauritius	0	0	0	0
Moldova	5	10	5	10
Montenegro	5	10	10	10
Morocco	8	10	10	10
Netherlands	0	15	0	0
Norway	15	15	0	10
Oman	5	10	0	0
Poland	5	15	10	10
Portugal	5	10	10	10
Qatar	0	0	0	10
Romania	5	5	10	10
Russia	5[6]	10	10	10
San Marino	5	10	10	5
Serbia	5	10	10	10
Slovakia	5	10	10	10
Slovenia	5	5	5	5
South Africa	5	10	0	5
Spain	8[8]	15	0	0
Sweden	5	15	0	0
Switzerland	5	15	5	0
Syria	5	10	10	12
Turkey	10	10	10	10
Turkmenistan	10	10	10	10
Ukraine	5	10	10	10
United Kingdom (UK)	5[11]–15[12]	10	5	5

Note: the above rates are only available provided the specific Treaty criteria are satisfied. It is possible that lower rates than those shown above may be available provided certain criteria are satisfied. As treaties will not be identical, guidance should be sought in all cases.

Notes:

1   If the beneficial owner is a company which holds at least 25% of the capital of the company paying the dividends.

2   If the beneficial owner is a company (other than a partnership) which holds directly at least 25% of the capital of the company paying the dividends.

3   If the beneficial owner is a company which directly or indirectly owns at least 10% of the capital of the company paying the dividends.

4   If the dividends paid by a company which is a resident of Croatia to a resident of Malta who is the beneficial owner thereof. (If the dividends were paid by a company which is a resident of Malta to a resident of Croatia, which is the beneficial owner of the same, the Malta tax on the gross amount of dividends shall not exceed the corporate income tax which is levied on the income from which the dividends are paid.)

5   If the beneficial owner is a company (other than a partnership) which directly has at least 10% of voting rights in the company paying the dividends.

6   If the beneficial owner is a company which holds directly at least 25% of the capital of the company paying the dividends, and this share must be at least $100,000.

7   If the beneficial owner is a company which holds directly at least 20% of the capital of the company paying the dividends.

8   If the dividends are paid to a company whose assets are wholly or partly divided into shares, as long as it holds directly at least 25% of the assets of the company paying the dividends.

9   When the beneficial owner of the dividends is a company which holds at least 10% of the capital of the company paying the dividends in the case when the latter firm is a resident of Israel, and the dividends are paid out of profits that are subject to tax in Israel at a rate lower than the normal rate of Israeli tax on profits.

10 When the beneficial owner is a company which holds 25% of the capital of the company paying the dividends and has invested in the equity of the company the amount of at least EUR 150,000.

11 If the beneficial owner is a company which is a resident of the other Contracting State and controls, directly or indirectly, at least 25% of the capital of the company paying the dividends (except dividends paid to the subject of investments, as mentioned in note 12 below).

12 When dividends are paid out of income (including profits) arising directly or indirectly from real estate, within the meaning of Article 6 of the Treaty, by an investor which distributes most of this income on an annual basis and whose income from such property is exempt from tax.

V INDIRECT TAXES

		Residents	Non-residents
Value Added Tax	General description	Tax on the supply of goods and services (VAT)	
	Entities obliged to levy VAT	Sales tax at all levels of the production / service chain with right to tax credit	The same as applies to residents
	Taxable activities	Delivery of goods and services within Croatia	
	Taxable activities – zero-rated (examples)	A zero rate applies to the export of goods and services, including transportation	
	Exemptions (examples)	o Banking and insurance services o Small business entrepreneurs (limit up to approx EUR 30,000; from 1 January 2018, limit up to approx EUR 40,000) o Exports and supply of services in EU member state	
	Refund of VAT	VAT on supplies and services paid by an entrepreneur is deductible as input tax, if supplies or services were taxable supplies and services of his enterprise No tax credit for input tax paid on tax-exempt supplies and services (does not include input tax for exports and delivery of goods within the EU)	VAT refund procedure
	Tax liability	Normally, a supplier of goods and services is liable to charge VAT Reverse charge for imports and intra-Community acquisitions of goods and services if those transactions are deemed to take place in Croatia Reverse charge in case of supply of: o Construction services o Supply of waste materials and related services	
	Tax rates	Standard rate = 25% Reduced rate I = 13% for hotel services, newspapers and magazines, tickets for concerts, water, electrical energy, baby foods, edible oils and fats Reduced rate II = 5% for milk, bread, books, medicines and medical equipment, cinema tickets, scientific journals	
	Administrative obligations	o Formal requirements concerning business records and invoices o Monthly tax self-assessments (for smaller companies quarterly) o VAT identification number	o Registration for VAT purposes, if rendering supplies and services in Croatia o Fiscal representation possible but not obligatory for EU member states o Fiscal representation obligatory for non-EU member states
Real Property Taxes		Tax rate is 4% on the value of transaction	
Stamp Duty		The calculation is complex but the liability is relatively small	

Nexia International does not accept liability for any loss arising from any action taken, or omission, on the basis of this publication. Professional advice should be obtained before acting or refraining from acting on the contents of this publication. Membership of Nexia International, or associated umbrella organizations, does not constitute any partnership between members, and members do not accept any responsibility for the commission of any act, or omission to act by, or the liabilities of, other members.

Nexia International is the trading name of Nexia International Limited, a company registered in the Isle of Man. Company registration number: 53513C. Registered office: 2nd floor, Sixty Circular Road, Douglas, Isle of Man, IM1 1SA

Cyprus

(Michael Mavrommatis, Nexia Poyiadjis, michael.mavrommatis@nexia.com.cy, np@nexia.com.cy)

I MAIN LEGAL FORMS

Legal form / Characteristics	General partnerships and Limited partnerships	Private Company Limited by Shares (Ltd) and Public Company Limited by Shares (Plc)
Partners/shareholders • Number • Restrictions	General partnership: not more than 20 partners Limited partnership: at least one general partner	Ltd: minimum one shareholder – not more than 50 shareholders Plc: minimum number of shareholders required is seven
Composition of Board and Management	Management by Partners in accordance with Partnership Agreement	The Directors of the Company manage and effect the decisions taken by the Company that must comply with the Company's Articles Ltd: no restrictions. Regulated by the Articles of Association. Alternate directors are permitted
Establishment	By Partnership Deed	By Articles of Association
Registration	The registration of partnerships, whether general or limited, shall be effected by submitting a statement in writing signed by all of the partners to the Registrar of Companies, within one month of the date of its establishment A general partnership is defined as a relationship which subsists between persons carrying on a business in common with the view to profit	Registrar of Companies Companies are legal entities registered with the Registrar of Companies

Legal form / Characteristics	General partnerships and Limited partnerships	Private Company Limited by Shares (Ltd) and Public Company Limited by Shares (Plc)
Directors		Ltd: minimum of one Director. Directors and Secretary must be separate (except where there is one sole shareholder who can be sole shareholder, sole director and secretary) Plc: minimum of two Directors required
Partners in a partnership	The minimum number of Partners required for partnerships (whether general or limited) is 2 and the maximum is 20	
Minimum capital	None	Ltd: No minimum Plc: Minimum €25,650
Liability	General Partners: Unlimited liability Limited Partners: Limited to capital contribution	Capital subscribed
Governance	Partnership Agreement and the Partnership & Business Names Act of Cyprus (CAP 116) as amended	Articles of Association and the Cyprus Companies Law (CAP 113) as amended
Audit requirements	Audit required Partnerships with a turnover above €70,000 should prepare audited financial statements	Audit required All companies require audit by law, except for exemptions stated in the Companies Act
Taxation	Transparent	Worldwide income
Usage	Professionals	SMEs, listed companies

II CORPORATION TAX

Legal form / Description	Resident corporation	Permanent establishment (PE)
General description	Corporation tax	
Taxable entities	Resident companies	PE located in Cyprus and activities relating to the extraction, exploration and use of Cyprus' continental shelf, of the subsoil or the natural resources, and also the construction and exploitation of pipelines and other constructions in the bottom of the sea of Cyprus
Taxable income	Worldwide profits	Profits derived by PE in Cyprus
Calculation of taxable profits	Accounting profits as adjusted for non-tax deductible expenses, allowances and exempt income • Foreign dividend income is generally tax exempt • Profit on the sale of 'titles' (ie shares, bonds, options, REPOs, units in funds, participations in various types of foreign companies and many other financial instruments) is unconditionally tax exempt • Foreign PE profits are, in general, tax exempt. As from 1 July 2016, taxpayers may elect for the taxation of profits earned by foreign PEs, with a tax credit for foreign taxes incurred on the foreign PE profits. In the absence of such an election, the exemption method will remain the default position • 80% of the net royalty income/gain on disposal of IPs (both net of any direct expenses) is tax exempt – effective tax rate as low as 2.5%	
Interest payments	• Notional Interest Deduction (NID) – The NID is an annual tax-allowable deduction for corporate equity. New equity introduced to a company as from 1 January 2015 in the form of paid-up share capital or share premium is eligible for the annual NID deduction. The NID granted on new equity cannot exceed 80% of the taxable profit as calculated before allowing the NID • Interest deduction may not be allowed in cases where the loan is used to finance assets which are not used in the business • Interest expense incurred in relation to the direct or indirect acquisition of 100% of the share capital of a subsidiary company is tax deductible provided that the subsidiary company does not own any assets that are not used in the business, eg loans granted by the subsidiary company should be considered as assets used in the business	

Related party transactions	• Arm's length basis, but no formal documentation requirements
	 • Spread/net margin on finance income between related parties is as follows:
	   – Loans up to €50m – net margin of 0.35%
	   – Loans from €50m to €200m – net margin of 0.25%
	   – Loans over €200m – net margin of 0.125%
	
	 The above spread/net margin is taxable at 12.5% corporation tax	

Legal form / Description	Resident corporation	Permanent establishment (PE)
Tax year, return and payment	• Tax year = calendar year • Normally the financial year of a company is the same as the tax year • A company's income tax return must be submitted to the tax authorities by the end of the following tax year • Provisional tax payment should be made via the provisional tax declaration that is due on the 31 July of the same tax year. Via this declaration, provisional tax should be paid to the tax authorities in two equal instalment payments, ie on 31 July and 31 December of the same tax year • The balance of the tax due (if any) should be paid to the tax authorities by 1 August of the following tax year	
Capital gains	• Gains on qualifying disposals (ie shares, bonds, options, REPOs, units in funds, participations in various types of foreign companies and many other financial instruments) are unconditionally exempt from any Cyprus taxes, unless related to real estate located in Cyprus	
Losses	May be carried forward and set off against future profits of the next five years	
Tax group	Group losses can only be offset against profits of the corresponding year of assessment. Both companies should be members of the same group for the whole year of assessment If a company is incorporated by its parent company during a specific tax year, then this subsidiary company is considered to be a member of the 'group' for the whole tax year and thus eligible for group loss relief Two companies shall be deemed to be members of a group if: • one is a 75% subsidiary of the other or • each one separately is a 75% subsidiary of a third company As from 1 January 2015, a Cyprus tax-resident company can include, in the calculation of its taxable profits, tax losses (as computed under Cyprus tax law) of a company which is a tax resident of another EU country, as long as both companies are part of the same group according to Cyprus group relief provisions	Tax losses incurred by a business carried on <u>outside</u> Cyprus, whether through a PE or not, can be used as a deduction against income from other sources of the same person for the same year Any remaining/unutilised PE loss may only be c/f for future offsetting against the same company's income for subsequent years (ie unutilised PE tax losses may not be used in group relief) PE losses deducted in previous years against taxable income are recaptured when the PE returns to profitability
Tax rate	12.5%	12.5%
Tax rate in relation to natural resources	As from 1 January 2016, income earned by persons who are not Cyprus tax residents and do not have a permanent establishment in Cyprus, from services which are carried out in Cyprus in relation to the extraction, exploration or use of the continental shelf, as well as the establishment and use of pipelines and other installations on the ground, on the seabed and on the surface of the sea, is subject to taxation at the rate of five per cent (5%), which is withheld in the case of direct or indirect payment by a Cyprus tax resident	

III TAXES FOR INDIVIDUALS

<table>
<tr><td></td><td></td><td colspan="1">Residents</td><td>Non-residents</td></tr>
<tr>
<td rowspan="9" style="writing-mode: vertical-lr;">Income Tax</td>
<td>General description</td>
<td colspan="2">Tax is levied on the chargeable income of a chargeable person for a year of assessment</td>
</tr>
<tr>
<td>Taxable entities and taxable income</td>
<td>Individuals resident for a period or periods exceeding in aggregate 183 days in the year of assessment (tax year)</td>
<td>Non-residents only liable to income tax on income derived from sources within Cyprus</td>
</tr>
<tr>
<td>Types of taxable income</td>
<td colspan="2">• Trading income of a trade, profession (business activities)
• Employment, pension income
• Property and royalty income</td>
</tr>
<tr>
<td>Calculation of income</td>
<td colspan="2">Gross income less any exempt sources of income, less any tax deductions and allowances</td>
</tr>
<tr>
<td>Tax year, tax assessment and tax payment</td>
<td colspan="2">• Tax year = calendar year
• Individuals submit personal income tax returns by 30 April, 30 June or 31 December of the following tax year
• PAYE system for employees
• Self-employed individuals pay their tax due via self-assessment by 30 June and 1 August of the following tax year (depending on their gross turnover)</td>
</tr>
<tr>
<td>Losses</td>
<td colspan="2">May be carried forward and set off against future profits of the next five years</td>
</tr>
<tr>
<td>Tax rates</td>
<td colspan="2">Nil tax rate up until €19,500

Income (€)	Tax rate (%)
0–19,500	0
19,501–28,000	20
28,001–36,300	25
36,300–60,000	30
Over 60,000	35

• Income from pension from abroad is subject to income tax as follows (irrespective of whether it is remitted to Cyprus or not):
 – At 5% (flat rate) on any amount in excess of €3,420 (ie annual exemption) or
 – At the above normal income tax rates
• 50% of the remuneration from any office or employment exercised in Cyprus by an individual who was a resident outside Cyprus before the commencement of his/her employment is exempt from income tax for a period of 10 years of employment. This provision applies when annual remuneration exceeds €100,000 and subject to certain conditions
• 20% or €8,550, whichever is the lower, of the remuneration from any office or employment exercised in Cyprus by an individual who was resident outside Cyprus before the commencement of his employment. This exemption applies for a period of 5 years commencing from 1 January following the year of commencement of employment. This exemption will be available up to year 2020</td>
</tr>
</table>

		Residents	Non-residents	
Capital Gains Tax (CGT)	General description		CGT is imposed on the increase of the value of the property from its date of acquisition to the date of its disposal/transfer (if applicable)	
	Taxable entities and chargeable assets		Gains of any person accruing from the disposal of immovable property or shares in a company that owns immovable property located in Cyprus. Land and land with buildings acquired at market value from unrelated parties from 16 July 2015 until 31 December 2016 will be exempt from Capital Gains Tax upon future disposal	
	Calculation of gain		Disposal proceeds less the greater of the cost or market value of the property on 1 January 1980 adjusted for inflation, less • expenditure wholly and exclusively incurred in relation to the acquisition of such gains, • improvements on the building, • losses from previous disposals	
	Tax year, tax assessment and tax payment		Declaration of disposal of property • needs to be filed within 30 days from the date of disposal, or • in any case before the transfer of the property Payment of the resulting CGT needs to be effected with the submission of the above declaration	
	Losses		Capital losses are set off against chargeable gains made on the same date. Any unrelieved loss is carried forward and is set off against future chargeable gains No carry back of losses	
	Tax rates		The CGT rate is 20%	
			Cyprus domiciled	**Non-Cyprus domiciled**
Inheritance Tax (IHT)	General description		No inheritance tax in Cyprus	

IV WITHHOLDING TAXES

Under domestic law	Payments to residents	Payments to non-residents
Dividends	17% (not applicable if the ultimate beneficial owner of the group of companies is a non-Cyprus tax resident or a Cyprus tax resident who is a non-Cyprus domicile)	Nil – Also applies to Cyprus tax residents who are non-Cyprus domiciles
Interest	30% (not applicable to Cyprus tax residents who are non-Cyprus domiciles)	Nil – Also applies to Cyprus tax residents who are non-Cyprus domiciles
Royalties	10%	Nil, but 10% if the right for which such royalty payment is made is used within Cyprus
On payments to artists and sportsmen	None	10%

Reduced rate available under the relevant Double Taxation Treaty in relation to inbound payments only, as Cyprus does not impose any withholding taxes for outbound payments as indicated above			
Country	Dividends	Interest	Royalties
Armenia	Nil	5%	5%
Austria	10%	Nil	Nil
Bahrain	Nil	Nil	Nil
Belarus	5%	5%	5%
Belgium	10%	0/10%	Nil
Bosnia	10%	10%	10%
Bulgaria	5%	0/7%	10%
Canada	15%	0/15%	0/10%
China	10%	10%	10%
Czech Republic	Nil	Nil	Nil
Denmark	Nil	Nil	Nil
Egypt	15%	15%	10%
Estonia	Nil	Nil	Nil
Ethiopia	5%	5%	5%
Finland	5%	Nil	Nil
France	10%	0/10%	0/5%
Georgia	Nil	Nil	Nil
Germany	5%	Nil	Nil
Greece	25%	10%	Nil
Guernsey	Nil	Nil	Nil
Hungary	5%	0/10%	Nil
Iceland	5%	Nil	5%
India	10%	0/10%	15%
Iran	5/10%	5%	6%
Ireland	Nil	Nil	Nil
Italy	15%	10%	Nil
Jersey	Nil	Nil	Nil

Reduced rate available under the relevant Double Taxation Treaty in relation to inbound payments only, as Cyprus does not impose any withholding taxes for outbound payments as indicated above			
Country	Dividends	Interest	Royalties
Kuwait	Nil	Nil	5%
Kyrgyzstan	Nil	Nil	Nil
Latvia	Nil	Nil	Nil
Lebanon	5%	5%	Nil
Lithuania	Nil	Nil	5%
Malta	Nil	10%	10%
Mauritius	Nil	Nil	Nil
Moldova	5%	5%	5%
Montenegro	10%	10%	10%
Norway	Nil	Nil	Nil
Poland	Nil	0/5%	5%
Portugal	10%	10%	10%
Qatar	Nil	Nil	5%
Romania	10%	0/10%	0/5%
Russia	5%	Nil	Nil
San Marino	Nil	Nil	Nil
Serbia	10%	10%	10%
Seychelles	Nil	Nil	5%
Singapore	Nil	0/7/10%	10%
Slovakia	10%	0/10%	0/5%
Slovenia	5%	5%	5%
South Africa	5/10%	Nil	Nil
Spain	0/5%	Nil	Nil
Sweden	5/15%	0/10%	Nil
Switzerland	0/15%	Nil	Nil
Syria	0/15%	10%	15%
Tajikistan	Nil	Nil	Nil
Thailand	10%	10/15%	5/10/15%
Ukraine	5/15%	2%	5/10%
United Arab Emirates	Nil	Nil	Nil
United Kingdom	0/15%	10%	0/5%
United States	5/15%	0/10%	Nil
Uzbekistan	Nil	Nil	Nil

Note: the above rates are only available provided the specific Treaty criteria are satisfied. It is possible that lower rates than those shown above may be available provided that certain criteria are satisfied. As treaties will not be identical, guidance should be sought in all cases.

V INDIRECT TAXES

<table>
<tr><td colspan="2"></td><th>Residents</th><th>Non-residents</th></tr>
<tr><td rowspan="11">Value Added Tax (VAT)</td><td>General description</td><td colspan="2">Tax on the supply of goods and services (VAT)</td></tr>
<tr><td>Entities obliged to levy VAT</td><td colspan="2">• Self-employed persons
• Companies
• Informal bodies of persons, such as joint ventures, deemed partnerships, associations
• Partnerships
• Clubs, charities, institutions, societies, trade unions
• Registration threshold: if turnover is in excess of €15,600</td></tr>
<tr><td>Taxable activities</td><td colspan="2">VAT is imposed on the provision of goods and services in Cyprus, on the importation of goods into Cyprus and on the acquisition of goods from the European Union (EU)</td></tr>
<tr><td>Taxable activities – zero-rated (examples)</td><td colspan="2">• Examples of zero-rated supplies are exports, leasing of aircrafts, ship management services, etc
• Supply of services and goods with another EU / non-EU Member State</td></tr>
<tr><td>Exemptions (examples)</td><td colspan="2">Post office services, most of the hospital, medical and dental care services, social providence and insurance, education, sports, certain cultural services, financial services, lottery tickets, the rental of immovable property</td></tr>
<tr><td>Refund of VAT</td><td colspan="2">If there is a balance in favour of the taxpayer (a VAT credit), then this is refundable by the VAT Commissioner. The VAT Commissioner may direct that the VAT credit be carried forward to a later VAT return or postpone the refund in case a trader failed to submit a VAT return of any previous VAT period</td></tr>
<tr><td>Tax liability</td><td colspan="2">• Normally the supplier of goods and services is responsible for charging VAT
• Reverse charge for certain supplies of goods and services, eg consulting services received from a business established outside Cyprus</td></tr>
<tr><td>Tax rates</td><td colspan="2">• Standard rate = 19%
• Reduced rate (eg restaurants, accommodation, taxi and bus fares, etc) = 9%
• Reduced rate (eg food, medicine, acquisition of property) = 5%
• Zero rate (eg exports, leasing of aircrafts, ship management services etc) = 0%
• Yacht registration – VAT rate can be as low as 3.4%</td></tr>
<tr><td>Administrative obligations</td><td colspan="2">• VAT returns must be completed and submitted to the VAT Commissioner together with any VAT payable due within 40 days from the end of each quarter for which the company is obliged to file a VAT return
• VAT groups are allowed, subject to certain conditions</td></tr>
<tr><td colspan="2">Real Property Taxes</td><td colspan="2">Immovable property tax (IPT): The rate of IPT depends on the market value of the property as at 1 January 1980 and ranges from 0.6% to 1.9% on annual basis</td></tr>
</table>

	Residents	Non-residents
Real Property Transfer Taxes	Transfer fees are imposed by the Department of Land and Surveys and apply on transfers of immovable property situated in Cyprus. These transfer fees depend on the value of the plot of land: €0–€85,000 – 3% €85,000–€170,000 – 5% Over €170,000 – 8% Exemptions and/or reduced rates are available, subject to certain criteria	
Stamp Duty	Cyprus Stamp Duty is only imposed on written contracts relating to assets located in Cyprus or to things/matters that will take place in Cyprus The applicable rates are generally low and capped at a maximum of €20,000	

Nexia International does not accept liability for any loss arising from any action taken, or omission, on the basis of this publication. Professional advice should be obtained before acting or refraining from acting on the contents of this publication. Membership of Nexia International, or associated umbrella organizations, does not constitute any partnership between members, and members do not accept any responsibility for the commission of any act, or omission to act by, or the liabilities of, other members.

Nexia International is the trading name of Nexia International Limited, a company registered in the Isle of Man. Company registration number: 53513C. Registered office: 2nd floor, Sixty Circular Road, Douglas, Isle of Man, IM1 1SA

Czech Republic

(Marek Votlučka, NEXIA AP a.s., votlucka@nexiaprague.cz and Pavel Zachariáš, NEXIA AP a.s., zacharias@nexiaprague.cz)

I MAIN LEGAL FORMS

Legal form / Characteristics	Partnership (vos) and Limited Liability Partnership (ks)	Private corporation (sro) and Public corporation (as)
Partners/shareholders • Number • Restrictions	VOS: at least two natural persons KS: at least one unlimited partner and at least one limited partner No restrictions	SRO: one or more, maximum 50 partners AS: one or more No restrictions
Directors	VOS: Managed by partners KS: unlimited partner	SRO: at least one executive AS: Board of Directors – at least three, except when one shareholder owns 100%, then there must be at least one director
Establishment	Notarial deed – Partnership agreement	Notarial deed – Memorandum of Association
Registration	The request for registration in the Commercial Register must be placed within 90 days from the establishment of company	
Minimum capital	VOS: No requirements KS: No requirements, except CZK5,000 for limited partners	SRO: CZK200,000 AS: CZK2m when established without public bid, CZK20m with public bid
Liability	Unlimited for all partners of VOS and general partner of KS, limited for limited partner; with effect from 2014, significant for statutory and supervisory bodies	Limited for all shareholders; with effect from 2014, significant for statutory and supervisory bodies
Governance	• Partner • Unlimited Partner	Managing director General meeting Supervisory board additionally for AS

Legal form / Characteristics	Partnership (vos) and Limited Liability Partnership (ks)	Private corporation (sro) and Public corporation (as)
Audit requirements	Audit is obligatory for: • Big-sized units • Medium-sized units • Small-sized units – when they are AS and when they exceed one of the criteria below • Other units – when they exceed two of the criteria below Criteria for audit are the following: • total assets more than CZK40m • turnover more than CZK80m • more than 50 employees	
Taxation	VOS: tax resident KS: share on profit of unlimited partners, tax transparent, share on profit of limited partners subject to corporate income tax	Non-transparent – profit is subject to corporate income tax

II CORPORATE TAX

Description / Legal form	Resident corporation	Permanent establishment (PE)
General description	Tax on corporate income	
Taxable entities	Corporations incorporated in the Czech Republic and/or foreign companies with central management and control located in the Czech Republic	PE located in the Czech Republic
Taxable income	Worldwide income	Business income of PEs generated in the Czech Republic
Calculation of taxable profits	Taxable profit is based on accounting profit adjusted under the tax law	
Interest payments	Generally, interest payments are considered to be operational expenditures and are under certain conditions deductible; thin capitalisation rules apply to related parties	
Related party transactions	All related party transactions must take place on arm's-length basis	
Tax year, return and payment	Tax year – calendar year or business year A tax return must be filed within 3 months after the end of the tax year or within 6 months if a chartered tax advisor is acting on behalf of the company, or if mandatory statutory audit is performed	
Capital gains	Capital gains are subject to corporate tax at standard rates; dividends and profits from shareholding received from abroad companies are included in a separate income tax base	
Losses	Incurred losses may be offset against the profits of the five subsequent tax periods	
Tax group	None	
Tax rate	Flat tax rate 19%	

III   TAXES FOR INDIVIDUALS

<table>
<tr><th></th><th></th><th>Residents</th><th>Non-residents</th></tr>
<tr><td rowspan="8">Income Tax</td><td>General description</td><td colspan="2">Individuals' monetary and non-monetary income is subject to individual income tax</td></tr>
<tr><td>Taxable entities and taxable income</td><td>Resident individuals are taxed on their income from worldwide sources</td><td>Non-resident individuals are subject to income tax solely on income arising in the Czech Republic</td></tr>
<tr><td>Types of taxable income</td><td colspan="2">• Employment income
• Income tax on entrepreneurs
• Capital gains
• Rental income
• Other income</td></tr>
<tr><td>Calculation of income</td><td colspan="2">• Employment income
• Business income – sole proprietor, share of income from a partnership
• Capital income – dividends, interest and other income from bonds, securities, certificates of deposit, deposits in a bank, etc
• Rental income</td></tr>
<tr><td>Tax year, tax assessment and tax payment</td><td colspan="2">Tax year – calendar year

Tax assessment: individual self-assessment returns for each taxpayer

Advanced payments based on tax paid in previous year

Payroll deductions: monthly by the employer, tax deducted can be offset against the final income tax</td></tr>
<tr><td>Losses</td><td colspan="2">Losses can be offset against income from other sources in the current year with the exception of employment income. Excess losses can be carried forward for 5 years, but only against the same type of income</td></tr>
<tr><td>Tax rates</td><td colspan="2">flat tax rate 15%</td></tr>
<tr><td rowspan="1"></td><td colspan="2"></td></tr>
<tr><td>Capital Gains Tax (CGT)</td><td>General description</td><td colspan="2">• No special tax
• Capital gains may be subject to income tax (see above)</td></tr>
<tr><td></td><td></td><th>Domiciled</th><th>Non-domiciled</th></tr>
<tr><td rowspan="4">Inheritance Tax (IHT)</td><td>General description</td><td colspan="2">• No special tax
• Applies to the transfer of assets by inheritance which are subject to income tax</td></tr>
<tr><td>Taxable entities and chargeable assets</td><td colspan="2">Taxable entities: legal entities and individuals except the so-called first group of relatives (parents, children and husband or wife) and also except the second group of relatives (siblings, nephews, nieces, aunts, uncles, husbands, husband's children, husband's parents, parent's husbands and cohabiting partners)

Chargeable assets: real estate, movable assets, cash, securities, receivables, rights in property and other assets</td></tr>
<tr><td>Taxable events</td><td colspan="2">The probate in inheritance procedure</td></tr>
<tr><td>Allowances</td><td colspan="2">• Proved decedent's debts passed to the heritor
• Assets exempt from inheritance tax
• Appropriate funeral cost
• Notary's remuneration and cost certified by court
• Inheritance charge paid to foreign country</td></tr>
</table>

IV WITHHOLDING TAXES

Under domestic law	Payments to residents	Payments to non-residents[1]
Dividends	15%	35% or 0%[2]
Interest	0%	35% or 0%[2]
Royalties	0%	35% or 0%[3]
On payments to artists and sportsmen	0%	35%

The Czech Republic has negotiated a range of tax treaties which provide an exemption or a reduction in withholding taxes on dividends, interest and royalties payable.

Reduced rate available under the relevant Double Taxation Treaty					
	Dividends		Interest	Royalties	
Country	Intercompany	Personal		Industrial	Cultural
Albania	5%	15%	5%	10%	10%
Armenia	10%	10%	10%	10%	5%
Australia	5%	15%	10%	10%	10%
Austria	0%	10%	0%	5%	0%
Azerbaijan	8%	8%	10%	10%	10%
Bahrain	5%	5%	0%	10%	10%
Barbados	5%	15%	5%	10%	5%
Belarus	5%	10%	5%	5%	5%
Belgium	5%	15%	10%	5%	0%
Bosnia and Herzegovina	5%	5%	0%	10%	0%
Brazil	15%	15%	15%	15%	15%
Bulgaria	10%	10%	10%	10%	10%
Canada	5%	15%	10%	10%	10%
China	5%	10%	7%	10%	10%
Croatia	5%	5%	0%	10%	10%
Cyprus	0%	5%	0%	10%	0%
Denmark	0%	15%	0%	10%	0%
Egypt	5%	15%	15%	15%	15%
Estonia	5%	15%	10%	10%	10%
Ethiopia	10%	10%	10%	10%	10%
Finland	5%	15%	0%	10%	0%
France	0%	10%	0%	10%	0%
Georgia	5%	10%	8%	10%	0%
Germany	5%	15%	0%	5%	5%
Greece	15%	15%	10%	10%	0%
Hong Kong	5%	5%	0%	10%	10%
Hungary	5%	15%	0%	10%	10%

1 Reduced rates of withholding tax may apply to EU residents or where there is an appropriate tax treaty. From 2015 these will be income tax exempt under specific conditions.
2 Exemptions apply on payments made by a subsidiary to parent company (under certain conditions).
3 As of 1 January 2011, exemption applies on payments made to an EU-resident company by a Czech tax resident or Czech PE of an EU-resident company.

Reduced rate available under the relevant Double Taxation Treaty					
	Dividends		Interest	Royalties	
Country	Intercompany	Personal		Industrial	Cultural
Iceland	5%	15%	0%	10%	10%
India	10%	10%	10%	10%	10%
Indonesia	10%	15%	12.5%	12.5%	12.5%
Ireland, Republic of	5%	15%	0%	10%	10%
Israel	5%	15%	10%	5%	5%
Italy	15%	15%	0%	5%	0%
Japan	10%	15%	10%	10%	0%
Jordan	10%	10%	10%	10%	10%
Kazakhstan	10%	10%	10%	10%	10%
Kuwait	5%	5%	0%	10%	10%
Latvia	5%	15%	10%	10%	10%
Lebanon	5%	5%	0%	10%	10%
Lithuania	5%	15%	10%	10%	10%
Luxembourg	5%	15%	0%	10%	0%
Macedonia	5%	15%	0%	10%	10%
Malaysia	10%	10%	12%	12%	12%
Malta	5%	5%	0%	5%	5%
Morocco	10%	10%	10%	10%	10%
Mexico	10%	10%	10%	10%	10%
Moldova	5%	15%	5%	10%	10%
Mongolia	10%	10%	10%	10%	10%
Netherlands	0%	10%	0%	5%	5%
New Zealand	15%	15%	10%	10%	10%
Nigeria	12,5%	15%	15%	15%	15%
Northern Korea	10%	10%	10%	10%	10%
Norway	0%	15%	0%	10%	0%
Philippines	10%	15%	10%	10%	10%
Poland	5%	5%	5%	10%	10%
Portugal	10%	15%	10%	10%	10%
Romania	10%	10%	7%	10%	10%
Russia	10%	10%	0%	10%	10%
Saudi Arabia	5%	5%	0%	10%	10%
Serbia and Montenegro	10%	10%	10%	10%	5%
Singapore	5%	5%	0%	10%	10%
Slovakia	5%	15%	0%	10%	0%
Slovenia	5%	15%	5%	10%	10%
South Africa	5%	15%	0%	10%	10%
South Korea	5%	10%	10%	10%	0%
Spain	5%	15%	0%	5%	0%
Sri Lanka	15%	15%	10%	10%	0%
Sweden	0%	10%	0%	5%	0%

Reduced rate available under the relevant Double Taxation Treaty					
	Dividends		Interest	Royalties	
Country	Intercompany	Personal		Industrial	Cultural
Switzerland	5%	15%	0%	5%	5%
Syria	10%	10%	10%	12%	12%
Tajikistan	5%	5%	7%	10%	10%
Thailand	10%	10%	10%	15%	5%
Tunisia	10%	15%	12%	15%	5%
Turkey	10%	10%	10%	10%	10%
Ukraine	5%	15%	5%	10%	10%
United Arab Emirates	0%	5%	0%	10%	10%
United Kingdom	5%	15%	0%	10%	0%
USA	5%	15%	0%	10%	0%
Uzbekistan	5%	10%	5%	10%	10%
Venezuela	5%	10%	10%	12%	12%
Vietnam	10%	10%	10%	10%	10%

Note: the above rates are only available provided the specific Treaty criteria are satisfied. It is possible that lower rates than those shown above may be available provided that certain criteria are satisfied. As treaties will not be identical, guidance should be sought in all cases.

V   INDIRECT TAXES

		Residents	Non-residents
Value Added Tax (VAT)	General description	Tax on the supply of goods and services, imports and others	
	Entities obliged to levy VAT	Any individual, partnership, corporation or other body, which carries out economic activities	
		Those with a turnover exceeding CZK1m in the preceding 12 months. From 2015, the minimum turnover is CZK750,000	
	Taxable activities	Supplies of goods and services, imports of goods, etc	
	Tax exempt activities (generally)	Export of goods and services, financial and insurance services, postal services, education, health care services, etc	
	Exemptions (examples)	• Disposal of company or contribution of company or of its part, integral organisational branch of company • Free supply of advertising articles which are related to the business activity, acquisition cost does not exceed CZK500 excl. VAT apiece and trade samples provided it is supplied free of charge	
	Refund of VAT	Refund of VAT is possible on a taxable supply made by the registered entity who settles this supply from the resources of international help in accordance with an international treaty which is part of the Czech legislation	• Entity registered for VAT in an EU country or third county which did not make any taxable supply in the Czech Republic in the calendar year • Persons enjoying privilege and immunity and related persons
	Tax liability	VAT is calculated over and paid to the local tax authority monthly on the difference between the VAT charged on sales and the VAT incurred on expenditure. If the turnover did not exceed CZK10m in the previous calendar year, the VAT can be paid quarterly	
	Tax rates	• Standard rate = 21% (most goods and services) • Reduced rate = 15% (specified goods and services, eg food, books, health and social care)	
	Administrative obligations	Any business making taxable supplies may register for VAT voluntarily. However, registration is compulsory if taxable income exceeds the registration limit, currently CZK1m within 12 successive months. From 2015, the limit is CZK750,000	Entities registered to VAT in an EU country or third country and having PE in the Czech Republic, apply the same rules as the Czech entities. Entities registered to VAT in an EU country or third country and having no PE in the Czech Republic, are liable to VAT as from the day of making certain types of taxable supplies
Real Property Transfer Tax		The rate is 4% of the higher of the sale price and the value of the property. The real estate transfer tax is payable by the buyer and is deductible for income tax purposes	
Real Estate Tax		At varying rates; special tax exemptions apply; building is considered as a part of land	

Denmark

(Iver Haugsted, Christensen Kjaerulff, ih@ck.dk)

I MAIN LEGAL FORMS

Legal form Characteristics	Partnership (I/S) and Limited Liability Partnership (LLP, K/S)	Private corporation (Ltd: ApS, IVS) and Public corporation (Plc: A/S)
Partners/ shareholders • Number • Restrictions	• One or more • None	• One or more • None
Directors	No minimum	One or more
Establishment	Deeds Registration of LLP	• Deeds • Registration
Registration	Registration takes place at the Danish Commerce and Companies Agency (Erhvervsstyrelsen). Only companies with limited liability must register	
Minimum capital		• DKK 50,000 for ApS • DKK 1 for IVS • DKK 500,000 for A/S
Liability	• Unlimited for partnership • Limited to capital for LLP	Limited to share capital
Governance	Deeds	Corporate law
Audit requirements	None	Yes (micro-entities are exempt)
Taxation	Partnerships are transparent, ie individual partners are assessed on their share of profits	Resident companies are subject to corporation tax on their profits derived in Denmark
Usage	No general restrictions exist, ie any business activity conducted by the entity	

II   CORPORATION TAX

Legal form / Description	Resident corporation	Permanent establishment (PE)
General description	Corporation tax – 22%	
Taxable entities	Corporations incorporated in Denmark and/or overseas companies with central management and control located in Denmark	PE located in Denmark
Taxable income	Since 2006 a Danish company is only taxed on profit from Danish activity, and not on profit from PE or immovable property in a foreign jurisdiction. However the Danish company can select international group taxation, which includes taxation of all foreign group companies and PEs in foreign jurisdictions (including immovable property)[1]	Profits derived by PE in Denmark
Calculation of taxable profits	Accounting profit is adjusted for various tax add-backs and allowances to arrive at profits chargeable to corporation tax	
Interest payments	Deductible. Limitation on interest charges of DKK 21.3m on group level	
Related party transactions	All related party transactions must take place on arm's length basis	
Tax year, return and payment	• Company can choose any period as its financial year as long as it runs to the end of the month • Company must file its tax return no later than 6 months after the end of the financial year. If the financial year ends between 1 February and 31 March, the tax return must be filed by 1 August in the same calendar year. Preliminary tax is payable in two equal instalments on 20 March and 20 November	A PE may use the same period as foreign corporation, or calendar year is used
Capital gains	Certain types of realised capital gains are included in the ordinary taxable income	
Losses	Tax losses may be carried forward indefinitely and offset against future taxable profits. No carry back is permitted	
	Taxable income on group level can only be reduced to 40% of the income exceeding DKK 8,025m (2017) by carrying forward tax losses	

Description \ Legal form	Resident corporation	Permanent establishment (PE)
Tax group	Danish Group entities must be jointly taxed. A subsidiary[1] in Denmark or a PE in Denmark must be included in the joint taxation regime All subsidiaries or PEs – including non-resident companies may also apply for international joint taxation regime where all group entities (resident and non-resident) are included in a Danish tax consolidation scheme. The decision is binding for a period of 10 years	A PE is taxed on its Danish income. However, the PE must be included in the Danish joint taxation regime provided there are other group entities that are registered in Denmark
Tax rate	22%	

---

1 A majority of the voting rights.

III   TAXES FOR INDIVIDUALS

<table>
<tr><td></td><td></td><td>Residents</td><td>Non-residents</td></tr>
<tr><td rowspan="9">Income Tax</td><td>General description</td><td colspan="2">Tax levied on the chargeable income of a chargeable person for a year of assessment</td></tr>
<tr><td>Taxable entities and taxable income</td><td>Residents are taxed on their worldwide income, with some relief for double taxation</td><td>Non-residents are taxed on income from personal services performed in Denmark for Danish employers or on income from Danish immovable property or as self-employed with a PE in Denmark on all income derived from Danish sources</td></tr>
<tr><td>Types of taxable income</td><td colspan="2"><ul><li>Personal income (employment income and income from business activity)</li><li>Income from capital investment (interest, sale of goodwill, dividends, royalties, annuities, etc), property income</li><li>Pensions, distribution from trusts</li><li>Dividend and capital gains on shares</li></ul></td></tr>
<tr><td>Calculation of income</td><td colspan="2">In general, taxable income is calculated as gross income less deductible costs</td></tr>
<tr><td>Tax year, tax assessment and tax payment</td><td colspan="2"><ul><li>Tax year – calendar year</li><li>Each individual has to complete a self-assessment (tax return) for each year</li><li>Returns must be filed by 1 May in the year following the taxable period (or 1 July for individuals engaged in business activities), or accepted the proposal for the tax return proposed by SKAT (Danish tax authority) in March based on the information from employer and banks, etc</li><li>Payment of preliminary tax on an accrual basis, ie deductions from employment income (at source)</li></ul></td></tr>
<tr><td>Losses</td><td colspan="2">Losses can be carried forward indefinitely and offset against future income</td></tr>
<tr><td>Tax rates</td><td><ul><li>Labour market contribution 8% of the total personal income (wages and income from business activity). This labour market contribution is deductible when calculating income tax</li><li>Local tax of approx 26–28% (2017) according to local municipality</li><li>State tax of 10.08% (2017)</li><li>State tax of 15% on personal income, pension and positive capital income with a deduction of DKK 479,600 (2017)</li><li>Income of dividend and capital gain on shares 42%, but only 27% of the first DKK 51,700 (2017)</li></ul></td><td>In principle, the tax calculation is similar to residents' assessment</td></tr>
</table>

		Residents	Non-residents
Capital Gains Tax (CGT)	General description	Tax on increase in the value of asset between acquisition and disposal	
	Taxable entities and chargeable assets	• Shares • Investments • Immovable property (private homes and holiday homes may be exempt under certain conditions)	Immovable property located in Denmark (private homes and holiday homes may be exempt under certain conditions)
	Calculation of gain	The difference between disposal price reduced by incidental expenses and the acquisition cost including incidental expenses and capital refurbishment costs, etc	
	Tax year, tax assessment and tax payment	• Gains are included each year in the self-assessment return • Returns must be filed by 1 May in the year following the taxable period (or 1 July for individuals engaged in business activities)	
	Losses	Losses are normally deductible and may be carried forward indefinitely	
		Some sort of realised capital losses can only be offset against gains arising on assets of a similar type (Losses on public traded shares and losses on immovable property)	
	Tax rates	Normal income tax rate, but without the labour market contribution	

		DK Domiciled	Non-DK domiciled
Inheritance Tax (IHT)	General description	Inheritance tax comprises an estate duty on the net value of the estate of a deceased person	
	Taxable entities and chargeable assets	The worldwide net estate is subject to tax in Denmark	Only immovable property in Denmark and assets of PE in Denmark are subject to Danish tax
	Calculation of charge	Net assets (market value)	
	Taxable events	• Death • Gift	
	Allowances	Transfers at death to surviving spouse are exempt from inheritance tax	
	Tax rates	• Flat rate of 15% on the net value of the estate exceeding DKK 282,600 (2017) • 36.25% for beneficiaries other than close relatives	

IV   WITHHOLDING TAXES

Under domestic law	Payments to residents	Payments to non-residents[2]
Dividends	27%	27%
Interest	Nil	Nil
Royalties	Nil	25%
On payments to artists and sportsmen	Nil	Nil

Reduced rate available under the relevant Double Taxation Treaty			
Country	Dividends	Interest	Royalties
Argentina	15%	12%	15%
Armenia	15%	Nil	Nil
Australia	15%	10%	10%
Austria	15%	Nil	Nil
Bangladesh	15%	10%	10%
Belarus	15%	Nil	Nil
Belgium	15%	10%	Nil
Brazil	25%	15%	25%
Bulgaria	15%	Nil	Nil
Canada	15%	15%	10%
Chile	15%	15%	10%
China	10%	10%	10%
Croatia	10%	5%	10%
Cyprus	15%	Nil	Nil
Czech Republic	15%	Nil	5%
Egypt	20%	15%	20%
Estonia	15%	10%	10%
Faroe Islands	15%	Nil	Nil
Finland	15%	Nil	Nil
Georgia	10%	Nil	Nil
Germany	15%	Nil	Nil
Greece	18%	8%	5%
Greenland	Nil	Nil	10%
Hungary	15%	Nil	Nil
Iceland	15%	Nil	Nil
India	25%	15%	20%
Indonesia	20%	10%	15%
Ireland	15%	Nil	Nil
Israel	10%	5%	Nil
Italy	15%	10%	5%
Jamaica	15%	12.5%	10%
Japan	15%	10%	10%
Kenya	30%	20%	20%
Kuwait	15%	Nil	10%

2   Other rates of withholding tax may apply where there is an appropriate double tax treaty.

Reduced rate available under the relevant Double Taxation Treaty			
Country	Dividends	Interest	Royalties
Kyrgyzstan	15%	Nil	Nil
Latvia	15%	10%	10%
Lithuania	15%	10%	10%
Luxembourg	15%	Nil	Nil
Macedonia (FYR)	15%	Nil	10%
Malaysia	Nil	Nil	10%
Malta	15%	Nil	Nil
Mexico	15%	15%	10%
Montenegro	15%	Nil	10%
Morocco	25%	10%	10%
Netherlands	15%	Nil	Nil
New Zealand	15%	10%	10%
Norway	15%	Nil	Nil
Pakistan	15%	15%	12%
Philippines	15%	10%	15%
Poland	15%	5%	5%
Portugal	10%	10%	10%
Republic of Korea	15%	15%	15%
Romania	15%	10%	10%
Russia	10%	Nil	Nil
Serbia	15%	10%	10%
Singapore	10%	10%	10%
Slovakia	15%	Nil	5%
Slovenia	15%	5%	5%
South Africa	15%	Nil	Nil
Sri Lanka	15%	10%	10%
Sweden	15%	Nil	Nil
Switzerland	15%	Nil	Nil
Taiwan	10%	10%	10%
Tanzania	15%	12.5%	20%
Thailand	10%	15%	15%
Trinidad and Tobago	20%	15%	15%
Tunisia	15%	12%	15%
Turkey	20%	15%	10%
Uganda	15%	10%	10%
Ukraine	15%	10%	10%
United Kingdom	15%	Nil	Nil
United States	15%	Nil	Nil
Venezuela	15%	5%	10%
Vietnam	15%	10%	15%
Zambia	15%	10%	15%

Note: the above rates are only available provided the specific Treaty criteria are satisfied. It is possible that lower rates than those shown above may be available provided that certain criteria are satisfied. As treaties will not be identical, guidance should be sought in all cases.

V   INDIRECT TAXES

		Residents	Non-residents
Value Added Tax (VAT)	General description	Tax on the supply of goods and services	
	Entities obliged to levy VAT	Suppliers of goods and services with annual turnover of more than DKK 50,000	
	Taxable activities	All goods and services, excluding personal transport, education and cultural activities. VAT applies on sales of land and sales of new real estate. Sales by foreign companies to private individuals in Denmark exceeding the threshold of EUR 35,000 per year	
	Taxable activities – zero-rated (examples)	Goods and services supplied to registered businesses within the EU, and export sales to non-EU countries	
	Exemptions (examples)	• Sales of existing real estate more than 5 years old • Financial services • Personal transport • Education • Cultural activities	
	Refund of VAT	Yes Companies dealing in the export of goods and services may receive a reimbursement of VAT on exports on a monthly or weekly basis and export companies may receive the reimbursement in advance	Foreign companies with taxable activities in Denmark may receive a reimbursement of VAT similar to Danish companies
	Tax liability	Normally the supplier of goods and services is responsible for charging VAT, according to the EU VAT Directive	
	Tax rates	Standard rate of 25%	
	Administrative obligations	• Formal requirements concerning business records and invoices • Quarterly selfassessment VAT return plus quarterly payment of any VAT liability to SKAT (special arrangements and schemes available for smaller businesses and repayment traders where monthly returns are possible) • VAT groups are allowed subject to certain requirements • Certain arrangements may need to be disclosed • VAT identification number must be shown on all invoices issued • EU Invoicing Directive must be adhered to	• Registration for VAT purposes, if making supplies of goods and services in Denmark • Appointment of fiscal tax representative possible but not obligatory
Real Property Taxes		DKK 1,660 + 0.6% (transfer of immovable property)	
Stamp Duty		DKK 1,660 + 1.5% (loans against immovable property, mortgage loans)	

Nexia International does not accept liability for any loss arising from any action taken, or omission, on the basis of this publication. Professional advice should be obtained before acting or refraining from acting on the contents of this publication. Membership of Nexia International, or associated umbrella organizations, does not constitute any partnership between members, and members do not accept any responsibility for the commission of any act, or omission to act by, or the liabilities of, other members.

Nexia International is the trading name of Nexia International Limited, a company registered in the Isle of Man. Company registration number: 53513C. Registered office: 2nd floor, Sixty Circular Road, Douglas, Isle of Man, IM1 1SA

Dominican Republic

(Elvis Brens, Francisco & Asociados, ebrens@franciscoyasociados.com)

I MAIN LEGAL FORMS

Legal form / Characteristics	Partnership and Limited Liability Partnership (LLP)	Private corporation (Ltd) and Public corporation (Plc)
Partners/shareholders • Number • Restrictions	• Two or more • LLPs, with 50 partners or more, have 2 years to formally become a private corporation	• Two or more
Directors	Managed by partners or directors	Managed by at least 3 directors
Establishment	Trade name registration with the National Office of Industrial Property ('ONAPI'), Commercial Registration with the Internal Revenue Authority ('DGII'), Ministry of Labour, Social Security Treasury ('TSS')	
Registration	• Santo Domingo Chamber of Commerce and Production • National Office of Industrial Property ('ONAPI') • Superintendent of Insurance (for public corporations)	
Minimum capital	LLPs: RD$100,000 SASs: RD$3,000,000	RD$30,000,000 (10% paid-in of minimum capital) For public corporations, the Superintendent of Securities determines the minimum capital
Liability	Partnerships: unlimited LLPs: limited to start-up capital	Limited to start-up capital
Governance	For LLPs a legal representative needs to be appointed and is known as the manager	By a President or by a Board of Directors with at least 3 members (President, a Vice President and a Secretary)

Legal form / Characteristics	Partnership and Limited Liability Partnership (LLP)	Private corporation (Ltd) and Public corporation (Plc)
Audit requirements		• Companies that acquire loans from financial institutions • Companies that issue debt of any kind • Companies with annual incomes of one hundred (100) minimum wages
Taxation	Corporate taxes on the local income and income from Dominican sources. See also Section II (Corporation Tax)	

II CORPORATION TAX

Legal Form / Description	Resident corporation	Permanent Establishment (PE)
General description	Resident corporations are taxed on Dominican-source income and on foreign investment income, such as dividends, interest and capital gains	Non-resident corporations are taxed on Dominican-source income only
Taxable entities	All legal entities excluding non-governmental organisations (NGOs) and those which benefit from special tax regimes (eg FTZ)	
Taxable income	All profits	Dominican-source income only
Calculation of taxable profits	Accounting profits plus (or minus), permanent or temporary differences, minus compensable losses available for carry forward, minus advances in income tax payments	
Interest payments	Interest is tax deductible	
Related party transactions	All related party transactions should be reported to the tax administration in a special report	
Tax year, return and payment	• Companies may adopt a fiscal year ending on 31 March, 30 June, 30 September and 31 December • Income tax returns must be filed with 120 days after the end of the fiscal year	
Capital gains	All types are taxable	
Losses	Net operating losses may be carried forward for 5 years. Carryback is not allowed	
Tax group	Groups are taxed individually	
Tax rate	• Income tax: 27% • Asset tax: 1% of total assets (minus) exempt assets (only if the company declares a loss in the period or if the payable asset tax is higher than the income tax) • Dividends: 10% • VAT (ITBIS): 18% • Other products: 16% • Excise tax: variable • Payments abroad: 27% • Fringe benefits: 27% (on expenses) • Telecommunications tax: 10% (cable TV, land lines and wireless communications) • Free-Zone tax: 3.5% (on gross sales to local individuals and legal entities)	

III   TAXES FOR INDIVIDUALS

<table>
<tr><td rowspan="10" style="writing-mode:vertical-rl">Income Tax</td><td></td><td>Residents</td><td>Non-residents</td></tr>
<tr><td>General description</td><td colspan="2">All individuals, resident in the Dominican Republic, are subject to tax on their Dominican Republic-source income as well as on their foreign-source income from investments and financial gains</td></tr>
<tr><td>Taxable entities and taxable income</td><td>All income generated by an individual is taxed</td><td>There is an exception for the first 182 days of stay – all income generated after that is taxed</td></tr>
<tr><td>Types of taxable income</td><td>• Salaries
• Commissions
• Any amount received in cash or in goods</td><td></td></tr>
<tr><td>Calculation of income</td><td>Based on total income, with a monthly exemption of up to RD$34,106.75 or RD$409,281 yearly

For individual service providers the withholding tax is calculated based on 10% or 2% of the income (based on the service)</td><td></td></tr>
<tr><td>Tax year, tax Assessment and tax payment</td><td>• Monthly deductions, including an annual declaration (March), for full-time employees
• Annual tax based on declared profits by individual service providers</td><td></td></tr>
<tr><td>Losses</td><td colspan="2">Can carry forward. The excess income tax payment is refunded or compensated</td></tr>
<tr><td>Tax rates</td><td>For full-time employees:

• Income up to RD$409,281: exempt
• Income from RD$409,281.01 to RD$613,921.00: 15%
• Income from RD$613,921.01 to RD$852,667.00: RD$30,696.00 plus 20% on surplus over RD$613,921.01
• Income over RD$852,667.01: RD$78,446.00 plus 25% on surplus over RD$852,667.01

For individual service providers:

Withholdings of 10% and 2% of all income (depending on the service provided)
• 1% on all property values (IPI) of or over RD$6,858,885 based on DGII appraisal
• For retailers, including bars and restaurants with purchases totalling over RD$50,000, a fixed tax of RD$12,000 will be imposed yearly</td><td></td></tr>
</table>

		Residents	Non-residents
Capital Gains Tax (CGT)	General description	Gains derived from direct and indirect transfers of Dominican assets or rights located or economically used in the Dominican Republic are taxable and subject to the capital gains tax rate of 27%	
	Taxable entities and chargeable assets	• Shares • Fixed assets • Investment in shares	
	Calculation of gain	The tax cost for such assets equals the original cost plus indexation adjustments minus the selling price	
	Tax year, tax assessment and tax payment	Tax year – the current fiscal year Tax assessment – individual self-assessment returns for each taxpayer Tax payment – 120 days after year-end	
	Losses	Can carry forward and applied only against capital gains	
	Tax rates	27%	

		Domiciled	Non-domiciled
Inheritance Tax (IHT)	General description	Taxes paid by a person who inherits money or property, or a tax on the estate (total value of the money and property) of a person who has died, or a tax charge on the transfer of value made during the person's lifetime	
	Taxable entities and chargeable assets	Domiciled and non-domiciled (Inheritors, successors and beneficiaries of wills) On all net assets	
	Calculation of charge	Based on valuation of the estate or gift upon transfer	
	Taxable events	Any inheritance or gifts received from a Dominican or person who has had his last domicile in the Dominican Republic, with or without the existence of a will, of personal property located within or outside of the Dominican Republic	
	Allowances	None	
	Tax rates	3% (if paid late, this tax rate will increase up to 50%)	

IV   WITHHOLDING TAXES

Under domestic law	Payments to residents	Payments to non-residents
Dividends	10% of the declared dividend amount	10% of the declared dividend amount
Interest	10% (levied only on individuals)	10% (levied on individuals or non-resident legal entities)
Royalties	27%	27%
On payments to artists and sportsmen	Nil	For artists, dependent on the market value See also Section III Taxes for Individuals – non-residents

Reduced rate available under the relevant Double Taxation Treaty			
Country	Dividends	Interest	Royalties
Canada	No more than 18%	No more than 18%	No more than 18%
Spain	No more than 10%	No more than 10%	No more than 10%
Non-treaty countries	10%	10%*	27%
* A 10% rate applies to interest paid to foreign financial institutions.			

Note: the above rates are only available provided the specific Treaty criteria are satisfied. It is possible that lower rates than those shown above may be available provided that certain criteria are satisfied. As treaties will not be identical, guidance should be sought in all cases.

V INDIRECT TAXES

		Residents	Non-residents
Value Added Tax (VAT)	General description	Tax on the transfer of industrialized goods and services ('ITBIS')	
	Entities obliged to levy VAT	• Individuals or business entities, whether domestic or foreign, that transfer industrialized goods as part of their industrial or commercial activities • Individuals or business entities engaged in the importation of goods subject to ITBIS • Individuals or business entities that render services subject to ITBIS	
	Taxable activities	• The sale or transfer of all goods and services, with a few exceptions specified by law • Imports of industrialized goods • Leasing and rendering of services	
	Taxable activities – zero-rated (examples)	Exported goods are zero-rated for ITBIS purposes. Under the ITBIS law, a compensation and reimbursement procedure is provided for exporters and producers of ITBIS-exempt goods	
	Exemptions (examples)	• Education services, including theatre, ballet, opera, and dance • Health services • Electricity, water, and garbage collection services • Financial services, including insurance, pension and retirement planning services • Transportation services, including cargo and taxi services • Hairdressing services • Funeral home services • Private property rental (non-commercial use)	
	Refund of VAT	If the total deductible taxes in a period are greater than the gross tax payable, the difference may be carried forward by the taxpayer as a deduction in the following months Exporters that have excess credits for advance taxes paid on the purchase of raw materials may request a refund for the advance tax over a six-month period. The same treatment is granted to producers of goods exempt from ITBIS An ITBIS refund may be requested if the invoice is voided within 30 days after the issuance of the invoice. The law provides a refund when the VAT paid from supplies and services provided is higher than the one collected from the sales of goods and services	
	Tax liability	All legal entities are tax retention agents. Private and public companies, whether or not they perform taxable activities, are obliged to withhold VAT from the transference of any service (including professional services), goods or leasing of property received from individuals, residents or non-residents	
	Tax rates	18%	
	Administrative obligations	ITBIS returns are submitted monthly. Returns must be submitted by the 20th day of the month following the end of the return period. Payment in full is due on the same date. A return must be filed, even if no ITBIS is due for the period	
Real Property Taxes		None	
Stamp Duty		Law 243 for liquor and similar products	
		Laws 84–71 for cigars and similar products	

Nexia International does not accept liability for any loss arising from any action taken, or omission, on the basis of this publication. Professional advice should be obtained before acting or refraining from acting on the contents of this publication. Membership of Nexia International, or associated umbrella organizations, does not constitute any partnership between members, and members do not accept any responsibility for the commission of any act, or omission to act by, or the liabilities of, other members.

Nexia International is the trading name of Nexia International Limited, a company registered in the Isle of Man. Company registration number: 53513C. Registered office: 2nd floor, Sixty Circular Road, Douglas, Isle of Man, IM1 1SA

Ecuador

(Cristina Trujillo, ASTRILEG CIA. LTDA., cristina.trujillo@astrileg.com.ec)

I   MAIN LEGAL FORMS

Legal form		Partnerships			TRADING COMPANIES		
Characteristics		General partnership (sociedad colectiva)	Limited partnership (sociedad en comandita)	Limited Liability Company (Cia. Ltda.)	Corporation (compañía anónima or sociedad anónima)	Mixed Economy Company (compañías de economía mixta)
Fiscal Year		From 1 January to 31 December				
Partners or shareholders	Overview	May examine the books and documents related to the management of the partnership twice a year		May review books and records of the business	May examine the books and documents related to the management of the company during 15 days prior to general meetings held to review and approve financial statements	The state, local government or a semi-public entity may hold stock and participate in management May examine the books and documents related to the management of the company during 15 days prior to general meetings to review and approve financial statements
	Number	2 or more		3–15 shareholders	2 or more (public), 1 or more (private)	2 or more
Attorney or Legal Representative				• Required for any domestic or foreign company which negotiates or gets obligations in Ecuador • A specific number of Directors is not required		
Registered office		• Primary residence in the country		• Primary location within the country • For branches or establishments operated by an agent, the places where they work will be considered to be the location of the entity		

Establishment	By public deed or partnership agreement approved by a civil provincial judge Sociedad en Comandita may also be formed by issuing shares		3 or more people/ entities execute a public deed	Private: 2 or more people/ entities execute a public deed and have it notarized. Once established, the shares can be sold so that all can be owned by one person Public: subscription of stock under company law May take as long as 90 days	Private: 2 or more people/ entities execute a public deed and have it notarized. Once established, the shares can be sold so that all can be owned by one person Public: subscription of stock under company law May take as long as 90 days
Registration	Mercantile Register		Superintendency of Companies and Internal Revenue Service		
Capital	Subscribed contributions by partners. At least 50% must be paid up on incorporation		Not less than USD400.00 fully subscribed with at least 50% paid up, the balance payable within 12 months	Not less than USD800, fully subscribed with at least 25% paid up	
Liability	Unlimited joint liability	At least two partners must have unlimited joint liability. Other partners are liable up to the amount of their contributed capital	Stockholder's liability limited to amount of stock owned		
Responsibility	Administrative, Civil and Criminal				
Government	All partners have the right to participate in the management of the business, or as stated in the partnership agreement		Company's deed must name shareholders entrusted with management. Annual general meetings are obligatory	Stockholders in ordinary and extraordinary meeting (General Assembly)	Stockholders in ordinary and extraordinary meeting (General Assembly). Board of Directors must include government representatives in proportion to stock owned

Audit requirements	No statutory audit required. Non-managing partners may designate an auditor or inspector	Statutory auditors not required. Vigilance committee may be named if there are more than 10 shareholders. An independent external audit may be required	Two statutory auditors, who may be stockholders, are required. An independent external audit may also be required
Taxation	Direct and Indirect Tax. Partnerships are not tax transparent	Direct and Indirect Tax	Direct and Indirect Tax. Exempt from taxes in proportion to Government participation
Usage	Any commercial or professional operation except banking, insurance or finance	Any commercial or professional operation	Public services or a development project

II CORPORATION TAX

Legal form / Description	Resident company	Permanent Establishment (PE)
General Description	Corporation Tax	
Taxable entities	Companies, corporations, partnerships, trusts and undivided estates that are legally constituted in Ecuador	Branches or permanent establishments of foreign companies, who obtain taxable income in Ecuador
Tax Base	ACCOUNTING PROFIT OR LOSS (-) Less 15% of Labor Force Participation (+) Non-deductible Expenses (-) Exempt income (+) Autoglosa by exempt income (+) Autoglosa for labor participation in exempt income (-) Special Deduction • Net Increase in Jobs • Recruiting Employees with Disabilities • Special deductions for Organic Production Code (-) Amortization of Tax Losses (+) Transfer Pricing Adjustments (=) TAX BASE	As for resident companies but applied to the PE
Calculation of taxable profits	• Exclusion of expenses incurred to generate exempt income: (exempt income / Total Income) * Total Costs and Expenses 15% Labor Participation in Exempt Dividends and Other Income Earned Autoglosas: (exempt income – Previous Autoglosa) • Deduction for net increase in jobs: • Net increase in jobs * Average values of wages and benefits paid to IESS	As for resident companies but applied to the PE

Legal form / Description	Resident company	Permanent Establishment (PE)
	• Deduction for employees with disabilities: • Value of wages and benefits paid to disabled employees IESS and employees with spouses or children with disabilities * 150% • Tax credit for hiring workers living in economically depressed areas: In the case of new investment in economically depressed areas and the border area, an additional deduction may be considered during the first 5 fiscal years after the start of the new investment. The deduction is calculated based on wages and salaries which during this period have been paid to resident workers in these areas, the deduction will be the same each year for the period of 5 years DAE: • There will be 100% additional depreciation and amortization applicable to the acquisition of machinery, equipment and technologies, and other expenses, for the implementation of cleaner production mechanisms to mechanisms of power generation from renewable sources (solar, wind or similar) or reducing the environmental impact of production activities. The maximum claim will not exceed 5% of total revenues	
Interest payments	Interest payments are limited to an annual rate which is equivalent to 1.5 times the benchmark lending rate for ninety (90) days as established by the Central Bank Ecuador, from the date of the debt until its extinction	
Related party transactions	Transactions between related parties will be subject to the arm's length provisions. The following are examples of related parties: 1. When an individual or corporation directly or indirectly holds 25% or more of the equity or equity in another company 2. Companies in which the same members, shareholders or their spouses or relatives up to and including the fourth degree of consanguinity (i) are directly or indirectly involved in at least 25% of the equity or equity transactions or (ii) have a continuing business relationship, or (iii) are employed 3. When an individual or corporation directly or indirectly holds 25% or more of the capital or equity in two or more companies 4. When an individual or company, whether or not living in Ecuador, make 50% or more of their sales or purchases of goods, services or other operations, with an individual or society, whether or not living in the country	

Legal form / Description	Resident company	Permanent Establishment (PE)
Tax year, return and payment	Year: 1 January to 31 December	
	Payment: In April following the tax year, with two prepayments being made in June and September during the tax year	
	Return: Filed between February and April following the tax year	
Capital Gains	N/A	N/A
Losses	These are losses resulting from differences between taxable income that is not exempt less costs and deductible expenses	
	Companies and corporations can offset losses against taxable income arising within the next five tax years, without exceeding in each period 25% of the earned profits	
	In case of liquidation of the company or termination of its activities in the country, the balance of the cumulative loss over the past five years will be deductible in full in the tax year in which it completes its liquidation or terminates its activities	
	No deduction will be accepted for losses on disposal of fixed assets or current assets when the transaction takes place between related parties or between the company and a member or his/her spouse or relatives within the fourth degree of consanguinity or second degree, or between the subject person and his spouse or relatives within the fourth degree of consanguinity or second degree	
Tax group	No tax grouping available	
Tax rate	– During fiscal 2011, the tax rate is 24% – During fiscal 2012, the tax rate is 23% – From fiscal 2013 onwards, the tax rate is 22%	

III   TAXES FOR INDIVIDUALS

<table>
<tr><td colspan="2"></td><th>Residents</th><th>Non Residents</th></tr>
<tr><td rowspan="9" style="writing-mode: vertical">Income Tax</td><td>**General Description**</td><td colspan="2">An individual is domiciled or habitually resident in Ecuador when they remain in the country one hundred and eighty-three (183) calendar days or more, consecutive or not, in the same tax year</td></tr>
<tr><td>**Taxable entities and taxable income**</td><td>Taxpayers are required to keep accounts, and pay income tax on the basis of the results produced

The total income of Ecuador residents is taxable whether from an Ecuadorian source or not</td><td>Foreigners are taxed on income derived from activities undertaken in Ecuador and from income sourced in Ecuador</td></tr>
<tr><td>**Types of tax base**</td><td colspan="2">***Labor taxable income/employment income:***
Relationship of dependency: Income less Personal Contributions IESS
Independent: Income less Direct Costs
Non-trading gains from sales/transfers of shares and real estate are exempt</td></tr>
<tr><td>**Calculation of Income**</td><td>Ecuador residents' total income is taxable whether from an Ecuadorian source or not. Dividends from Ecuador companies are exempt</td><td>Similar rules to those for residents are applied to taxable income</td></tr>
<tr><td>**Tax year, tax assessment and tax payment**</td><td colspan="2">1 January to 31 December
When the income-generating activity is initiated at a date later than 1 January, the mandatory tax year closes at the next 31 December</td></tr>
<tr><td>**Losses**</td><td colspan="2">Societies, individuals required to maintain accounting records and undivided estates required to keep accounting records can offset losses against taxable income arising within the following five tax years, without exceeding in each period 25% of the profits obtained. To this effect it will be understood as gains or losses resulting in differences between taxable income that is not exempt less costs and deductible expenses

Earnings from employment may not be reduced by losses, whatever their origin</td></tr>
<tr><td>**Tax rate**</td><td colspan="2">The following rates shall apply to the taxable income of individuals and undivided estates:</td></tr>
</table>

IR 2013			
BASIC FRACTION	**EXCESS TO**	**TAX FRACTION**	**% TAX**
-	10,180.00	0	0%
10,180.00	12,970.00	0	5%
12,970.00	16,220.00	140	10%
16,220.00	19,470.00	465	12%
19,470.00	38,930.00	855	15%
38,930.00	58,390.00	3,774	20%
58,390.00	77,870.00	7,666	25%
77,870.00	103,810.00	12,536	30%
103,810.00	onwards	20,318	35%

		Residents	Non-Residents
Capital Gains Tax (CGT)	**General Description**	N/A	
	Taxable entities and chargeable assets	N/A	
	Profit Calculation	N/A	
	Tax year, tax assessment and tax payment	N/A	
	Losses	N/A	
	Tax rate	N/A	
		Residents	Non Residents
Inheritance Tax (IHT)	**General Description**	N/A	
	Taxable entities and chargeable assets	N/A	
	Calculation of charge		
	Taxable events	N/A	
	Allowances	N/A	
	Tax rates	N/A	

IV   WITHHOLDING TAXES

Under domestic law	Payments to residents	Payments to Non residents
Dividends	Distributed to individuals residing in Ecuador: |			% | **Basic fraction**	**Excess up to**	**Tax to basic fraction**	**Percentage of retention on excess**
-	100,000	0	1%
100,000	200,000	1,000	5%
200,000	onwards	6,000	10%	 Dividend payments to companies: 0%	Distributions to entities other than those entities domiciled in tax havens or jurisdictions with lower tax rates and individuals not resident in Ecuador: 0% When dividends or profits are distributed to companies based in tax havens or jurisdictions with lower tax rates there shall be the appropriate withholding of income tax. The rate of this withholding tax will equal the difference between the maximum rate of income tax for individuals and the general rate of income tax provided for companies
Interest	1% on: • Interest and commissions incurred in credit transactions among financial system institutions 2% on: • Income from interest, discounts and any other kind of financial returns • Interest that any public sector entity reports for taxable persons 0%–8% • interest payable by companies, other than as above	22%
Royalties	8%	22%
On payments to artists and sportsmen	8% to: • Those made to athletes, coaches, referees and members of the coaching staff as well as in the case of residents and foreign artists, who are not independent • Those made to both local and foreign artists resident in the country for more than six months	22%

Reduced rate available under the relevant double taxation treaty			
Country	Dividends	Interest	Royalties
Andean community	The dividends and participations will only be taxable for the member country where the company that distributes them will be domiciled	22%. Unless proven otherwise, it is assumed that the credit is used in the country from which interest is paid	22%
Belgium	15%	10%	10%
Canada	5%, 15%, 25%	15%	15%
Chile	5%, 15%, 25%	15%	15%
France	15%	10%, 15%	15%
Germany	15%	10%, 15%	15%
Italy	15%	10%	5%
Mexico	5%	15%	10%
Romania	15%	10%	10%
Spain	15%	10%	10%
Swiss federation	15%	10%	10%
Uruguay	15%, 25%	15%	15%
Decision 578 **Regime for the avoidance of double taxation and the prevention of fiscal evasion**	Dividends and shares shall be taxable only by the member country where the company that distributes them is domiciled The member country where the company is domiciled or recipient or beneficiary individual of the dividends or shares cannot tax the receiving company or investor, or those who in turn are shareholders or partners of the receiving or investment company	Interest and other financial income shall be taxable only in the member country where it is charged and the payment is registered	Royalties shall be taxable only in the member country where it is charged and the payment is registered

Note: the above rates are only available provided the specific Treaty criteria are satisfied. It is possible that lower rates than those shown above may be available provided certain criteria are satisfied. As treaties will not be identical, guidance should be sought in all cases.

V   INDIRECT TAXES

	General description	Residents	Non-residents
Value Added Tax (VAT)		Levied on the value of the transfer of ownership or import of movable corporeal nature, in all stages of manufacturing, as well as copyrights, related industrial property rights, and the value of services provided	
	Entities being obliged to levy vat	**As taxpayers:** Those who would carry a fee levied on imports, either by themselves or others **a) As agents of perception:** Private citizens and companies that usually make transfers of assets subject to a fee and / or provide services usually taxed at a rate **b) As withholding agents:** 1. Special contributors 2. Issuers of credit cards 3. The insurance and reinsurance industries 4. Exporters 5. Tourism Operators 6. The natural persons, undivided successions or companies, which import taxed services 7. Petrochemical and fuel marketers presumptive VAT on fuel sales	
	Taxable activities	Examples are: 1. transfers of goods in Ecuador 2. Services provided in Ecuador 3. For services to advance work or stages 4. Purchases for personal use or consumption 5. Imports of goods	
	Taxable activities – zero-rated (examples)	• Milk in natural condition of national production • Bond paper • Hybrid Vehicles to USD35,000	
	Exemptions (examples)	• With the enactment of the Environmental Development and Optimization of State revenues law, exemptions from VAT include, for example, importation of household goods and work equipment imported as the personal effects of passengers on the dictated terms by the SENAE	
	Refund vat	• Exporter of Goods • Exporters' Direct Suppliers • Passengers' terrestrial public transport in buses • People with disabilities • Diplomatic missions, consular posts, international organizations and their paid officials of foreign nationality • Tourists • Plane fuel used in the provision of freight service abroad • Administrators and Operators of Special Economic Development Zones • Tour operators • Senior citizens	
	Tax liabilities	VAT charged less tax creditable	
	Tax rates	12% Value Added Tax	

		Residents	Non-residents
Value added tax (VAT) – contd	**Administrative obligations**	Monthly returns are required to be filed on the dates set by the tax administration	
Real Property Taxes		N/A	
Stamp Duty		N/A	

Nexia International does not accept liability for any loss arising from any action taken, or omission, on the basis of this publication. Professional advice should be obtained before acting or refraining from acting on the contents of this publication. Membership of Nexia International, or associated umbrella organizations, does not constitute any partnership between members, and members do not accept any responsibility for the commission of any act, or omission to act by, or the liabilities of, other members.

Nexia International is the trading name of Nexia International Limited, a company registered in the Isle of Man. Company registration number: 53513C. Registered office: 2nd floor, Sixty Circular Road, Douglas, Isle of Man, IM1 1SA

© Nexia International 2017

Egypt

(Sherif William, Adel Saad & Co, sherif.william@adelsaadandco.com)

I MAIN LEGAL FORMS

Legal form / Characteristics	Partnership and Limited Liability Partnership (LLP)	Private corporation (Ltd) and Public corporation (Plc)
Partners/shareholders • Number • Restrictions	Partnership: Unlimited number of partners LLP: One general partner, unlimited number of limited partners	Ltd: At least two shareholders (partners) Joint Stock Co: At least three shareholders
Directors	Partnership: At least one partner LLP: At least one general partner	Ltd: One or more managing director(s) Joint Stock Co: Board of directors of at least three persons (including the chairman)
Establishment	Partnership deed	Legalised, approved contract by the investment authority
Registration	• Commercial register • Tax department	• Authority of Investment • Commercial register • Tax department
Minimum capital	Partnership: 5,000 EG P LLP: 5,000 EG P	Ltd: No minimum Joint Stock Co: 250,000 EG P
Liability	• General partner liability is unlimited • Limited partner liability is limited to the extent of his share	Shareholders' liability is limited to the extent of their shares
Governance	• Commercial register • Tax department	• Authority of Investment • Commercial register • Tax department
Audit requirements	• Not generally required • For companies with a revenue higher than 2m EG P the tax department require that the FS must be audited by a chartered accountant	Yes
Taxation	Corporate income tax (no tax on partners share)	Corporate income tax

II   CORPORATION TAX

Description \ Legal form	Resident corporation	Permanent establishment (PE)
General description	In June 2005, the Egyptian Ministry of Finance issued a new tax law which mainly changed and reformed the following: • Decreased tax rates to encourage investment • Simplified the rules and procedures • Changed the tax return inspection system. Currently tax departments inspect tax returns, taxpayer's accounts on a random basis, once every 3–5 years. Previously, inspection was on a yearly basis	
Taxable entities	Joint Stock Co (corporation), Ltd, Partnership, LLP: • Tax applies to entities residing in Egypt, with respect to all profits realised in Egypt or abroad • Tax applies to non-resident entities with respect to the profits realised in Egypt	
Taxable income	Profits of a business activity are determined based on the revenues resulting from all the business operations, including capital gains, and after deducting all allowable costs Taxable profit is determined based on net profit as per the income statement prepared according to the Egyptian Accounting Standards, adjusted by taxable bases	
Calculation of taxable profits	The taxable profit is calculated based on net income adjusted by (for example): • taxable depreciation bases • taxable bases for capital gain and losses • deductible donations limited to 10% from annual net profit • reserves and provisions as per FS are not tax deductible • bad debts and interest paid shall be in accordance with tax bases and law provisions • losses can be carried forward for 5 years	
Interest payments	Debt to equity ratio of 4:1. Any excess amounts of interest are not deductible	
Related party transactions	Arm's length rates apply	
Tax year, return and payment	Tax year: 31 December Return and payment: 30 April	
Capital gains	Treated as ordinary income	
Losses	Carried forward for 5 years	
Tax group	Not available	
Tax rate	22.5% on net taxable profit	

III   TAXES FOR INDIVIDUALS

		Residents	Non-residents
Income Tax	General description	An annual tax shall be imposed on the total net income of resident and non-resident Egyptian persons in respect to their revenues earned in Egypt	
		Resident individuals consist of Egyptians and non-Egyptians having a permanent residence in Egypt, who reside more than 183 days within 12 months	
	Taxable entities and taxable income	Sole practitioner	
	Types of taxable income	• Employment revenues (individuals with employment revenues do not need to submit a tax return. Tax is deducted and remitted by employer) • Commercial or manufacturing business • Professional income (activity) • Real estate income (activity) • Profits of a business activity shall be determined based on the revenues resulting from all the business operations, including capital gains, and after deducting all allowable costs	
	Calculation of income	*Employee:* The following deductions are allowed on gross salary, in order to calculate the payroll taxable income: • employee social insurance share deducted according to social insurance laws; employee subscription in private insurance/pension funds • life and health insurance premiums paid by the employee in his favour, for his/her spouse or minor children • employee's profit sharing	No allowed deduction
		Sole practitioner: The taxable profit is calculated based on net income adjusted by (for example): • taxable depreciation bases • taxable bases for capital gain and losses • deductible donations limited to 10% from annual net profit • reserves and provisions as per FS are not tax deductible • losses can be carried forward for 5 years	
	Tax year, tax assessment and tax payment	*Employee:* Employer submits a tax declaration on a quarterly basis, remits the tax deducted from his employee on a monthly basis *Sole practitioner:* Tax year: 31 December Return and payment: 31 March	
	Losses	*Sole practitioner:* Carried forward for 5 years	

		Residents		Non-residents
Income Tax – *Contd*	Tax rates	*Sole practitioner:*		10%
		Tax Bracket in EG P	*%*	
		0–13,500	0	
		13,501–30,000	10	
		30,001–45,000	15	
		45,001–200,000	20	
		200,000+	22.5	
		Employee:		
		Tax Bracket in EG P	*%*	
		0–13,500	0	
		13,501–30,000	10	
		30,001–45,000	15	
		45,001–250,000	20	
		200,000+	22.5	

		Residents	Non-residents
Capital Gains Tax (CGT)	General description	No capital gains tax	
	Taxable entities and chargeable assets		
	Calculation of gain		
	Tax year, tax assessment and tax payment		
	Losses		
	Tax rates		

		Domiciled	Non-domiciled
Inheritance Tax (IHT)	General description	No inheritance tax	
	Taxable entities and chargeable assets		
	Calculation of charge		
	Taxable events		
	Allowances		
	Tax rates		

IV WITHHOLDING TAXES

Under domestic law	Payments to residents	Payments to non-residents
Dividends	Exempt	Exempt
Interest	• Interest received on deposits, saving accounts from banks registered in Egypt are exempt • Interest received from other sources are taxable at 20%	• Interest received on deposits, saving accounts from banks registered in Egypt are exempt • Interest received from other sources are taxable at 20%
Royalties	20%	20%
On payments to artists and sportsmen	20%	20%

Reduced rate available under the relevant Double Taxation Treaty			
Country	Dividends	Interest	Royalties
Albania	Nil	10%	10%
Algeria	Nil	5%	10%
Austria	Nil	15%	Nil
Bahrain	Nil	Nil	Nil
Belarus	Nil	10%	15%
Belgium[1]	Nil	15%	25%
Canada	Nil	15%	15%
China	Nil	10%	8%
Cyprus	Nil	15%	10%
Czech Republic	Nil	15%	15%
Denmark[2]	Nil	15%	20%
Finland[3]	Nil	15%	20%
France	Nil	15%	15%
Germany[4]	Nil	15%	25%
Hungary	Nil	15%	15%
Indonesia	Nil	15%	15%
Iraq[5]	Nil	10%	10%
Italy[6]	Nil	20%	15%
Japan	Nil	L	15%
Republic of Korea[7]	Nil	15%	15%
Libya[8]	Nil	L	L
Malaysia	Nil	15%	15%
Malta	Nil	10%	12%

1 Royalties paid for trademarks subject to 25%, all other cases 15%.
2 The authorities in both countries shall mutually agree on the mode of rate application.
3 The treaty was providing 25% on royalties, but since the local rate decreased to 20%, lower rate applies.
4 Royalties paid for trademarks subject to 25%, all other cases 15%.
5 Treaty provides that royalties rate shall be 50% of local rate.
6 The treaty was providing 25% on royalties, but since the local rate decreased to 20%, lower rate applies.
7 Interest paid for a loan or debt exceeding 3 years – 10%, all other cases 15%.
8 Treaty provides that local rate applies.

Morocco	Nil	10%	10%
Netherlands	Nil	12%	12%
Norway	Nil	15%	15%
Pakistan	Nil	15%	15%
Poland	Nil	12%	12%
Romania	Nil	15%	15%
Russia	Nil	15%	15%
Serbia[9]	Nil	15%	15%
Singapore	Nil	15%	15%
Slovak Republic[10]	Nil	12%	15%
South Africa	Nil	12%	15%
Spain	Nil	10%	12%
Sudan[11]	Nil	L	10%
Sweden[12]	Nil	L	Nil
Switzerland	Nil	15%	12.5%
Syria	Nil	15%	20%
Tunisia	Nil	10%	15%
Turkey	Nil	10%	10%
Ukraine	Nil	12%	12%
United Arab Emirates	Nil	10%	10%
United Kingdom	Nil	15%	15%
United States	Nil	15%	15%

Note: L: Local – Dividends 0%, Interest 20%, Royalties 20%

It is possible that lower rates than those shown above may be available provided that certain criteria are satisfied. As treaties are not identical, guidance is recommended to be sought in all cases.

9 Treaty with Serbia & Montenegro applies.
10 The authorities in both countries shall mutually agree on the mode of rate application.
11 Interest provides local rate to be applied. Royalties, rent and film making subject to 3%, all other cases 10%.
12 Royalties are exempted.

V   INDIRECT TAXES

		Residents	Non-residents
Value Added Tax (VAT)	General description	Tax on the supply of goods and services	
	Entities obliged to levy VAT	• Manufacturing entities with turnover higher than 54,000 EG P • Commercial, trading entities with turnover higher than 150,000 EG P	
	Taxable activities	All activities except: agricultural, professional	
	Taxable activities – zero-rated (examples)	All exporting activities	
	Exemptions (examples)	• All activities within some important governmental sector (ministry of defence, interior ministry, petroleum sector) • All activities within the free zone areas	
	Refund of VAT	Yes	
	Tax liability	Goods and services provided in Egypt	
	Tax rates	The general tax rate is 13% until 2016/2017 (from July 2017: 14%) Some exceptions exist: • 5% for machinery and equipment • 8% will be added to some items such as air conditioners and TVs • 1% to 30% will be added to some items such as motor vehicles • 10% for professional and consulting services	
	Administrative obligations		
Real Property Taxes		Property tax is 10%	
Stamp Duty		• Stamp duty per signed document 0.40 EG P • Newspaper advertisement stamp duty is 15% • Stamp duty on other advertisements is calculated based on length/space of the advertisement	

El Salvador

(Carlos Lopez, LATINCO, LTDA DE C.V, carlos.lopez@latincoltda.com)

I MAIN LEGAL FORMS

Legal form / Characteristics	Types of partnership	Types of company
Partners/ shareholders • Number • Restrictions	Minimum 2 shareholders or partners, which depends on the type of company being formed	All the societies that are of person or of capital
Directors	In accordance with the deed of incorporation of the company, the number of directors is defined The minimum number of Directors is three, which correspond to President, secretary and a director proprietary	The number of substitutes must be named, as many directors establish the deed of incorporation
Establishment	It is considered that there is permanent establishment, when there are facilities where the public is served and services are provided within the territory	This includes branches of foreign companies
Registration	According to the date of constitution, this is done in all government institutions. The process starts with the Trade Register, to obtain registration of the company and its respective commercial registration and tax registration	It is required for all companies, including branches of foreign companies
Minimum capital	US$2,000, which must be provided with a minimum of 5% in cash, and the remaining balance must be provided as soon as possible	It is applicable to all types of companies
Liability	There are no borrowing requirements	There are no borrowing requirements

Legal form / Characteristics	Types of partnership	Types of company
Governance	Partners	Board of Directors
Audit requirements	Statutory annual	Statutory annual
Taxation	Statutory annual In El Salvador, there is an obligation to conduct a tax audit and issue an opinion on compliance with tax obligations annually	Statutory annual In El Salvador, there is an obligation to conduct a tax audit and issue an opinion on compliance with tax obligations annually
Usage	Many uses	Many uses

II CORPORATION TAX

Description \ Legal form	Resident corporation	Permanent establishment (PE)
General description	Every organization, to be considered an entity domiciled or not and with the obligations that the law establishes, must show operations in El Salvador, to say that it performs acts of commerce and therefore is understood that it produces rents	
Taxable entities	yes	yes
Taxable income	yes	yes
Calculation of taxable profits	30% 25% if income is less than US$150,000	30% 25% if income is less than US$150,000
Interest payments	They are subject to 20% withholding	They are subject to 20% withholding
Related party transactions	Transfer pricing should be reviewed annually	Transfer pricing should be reviewed annually
Tax year, return and payment	31 December is the fiscal year end, but return must be submitted no later than 30 April of each year	31 December is the fiscal year end, but return must be submitted no later than 30 April of each year
Capital gains	Yes 10%	
Losses	n/a	
Tax group	n/a	
Tax rate	30%	30%

III   TAXES FOR INDIVIDUALS

		Residents	Non-residents
Income Tax	General description	The operative event is the obtaining of income by taxpayers in the tax period	
	Taxable entities and taxable income	Individuals, artists, athletes	Individuals, artists, athletes
	Types of taxable income	Wages, fees, commissions, rents, dividends, interest and all income from whatever source	Wages, fees, commissions, rents, dividends, interest and all income from whatever source
	Calculation of income	Natural persons domiciled with different incomes calculate their taxable income by deducting all expenses necessary for the production of income and preservation of its source (Art. 28 Income Tax Law). Additionally they may deduct $800 in respect of expenditure on health and education (Art. 33 Income Tax Law) Natural persons whose income comes solely from wages may deduct only the $800 in respect of health and education expenditure (Art. 33 Income Tax Law)	Income is calculated on the amount charged in respect of fees, commissions, rents, dividends and interest, because these are considered to be final payments
	Tax year, tax assessment and tax payment	The fiscal year is the calendar year (Art. 13 Income Tax Law) Tax payment must be made within four months following the expiration of the period of taxation (Art. 51)	same
	Losses	There is no relief for tax losses	
	Tax rates	5% to 30%	30% of net or taxable income (Art. 37)
		Residents	**Non-residents**
Capital Gains Tax (CGT)	General description	It corresponds to transactions that are unusual and are not in the ordinary course of business	
	Taxable entities and chargeable assets	Mainly from sales of fixed assets and shares and intangible assets, as they are not in the ordinary course	same
	Calculation of gain	Sale proceeds less direct costs	same
	Tax year, tax assessment and tax payment	The fiscal year is the calendar year (Art. 13 Income Tax Law)	same
	Losses	Losses may be carried forward for a period of 5 years, to be written off only against capital gains	same
	Tax rates	10%	same

		Domiciled	Non-domiciled
Inheritance Tax (IHT)	General description	There is no death tax, but registration fees are payable on successions, especially in real estate	
	Taxable entities and chargeable assets	Individuals All property is chargeable	same
	Calculation of charge	Tax is based on the value of the property	same
	Taxable events	The succession	same
	Allowances	None	same
	Tax rates	Progressive rates for registration fees	same

IV   WITHHOLDING TAXES

Under domestic law	Payments to residents	Payments to non-residents
Dividends	5% of ISR (Art. 72 Income Tax Law)	5% of ISR (Art. 73 Income Tax Law)
Interest	None	10% on amounts paid on financial services provided by financial institutions supervised by a body of regulation financier (Art. 158 Código Tributario (CT)) 25% when paid to a natural or juridical person that is domiciled in a country or state with a preferential tax regime (Art. 158-A CT) 20% on amounts paid to an entity not domiciled in El Salvador (Art. 158 CT)
Royalties	10% to individuals without labour dependency (Art. 156 CT) With labour dependency applies as wage withholding table	20% (Art. 158 CT)
On payments to artists and sportsmen	10% income tax for professional services	20% of ISR

Reduced rate available under the relevant Double Taxation Treaty			
Country	Dividends	Interest	Royalties
n/a	n/a	n/a	n/a

V   INDIRECT TAXES

		Residents	Non-residents
Value Added Tax	General description	Indirect taxes levied on all kinds of economic transactions for transfer of goods or providing services	
	Entities obliged to levy VAT	Individuals or corporations, estates, trusts, cooperative associations, unions of persons, partnerships and consortia	same
	Taxable activities	Goods or providing services	
	Taxable activities – zero-rated (examples)	Transfer of goods, provision of services, self-consumption of goods and services, importation The export of goods and services is taxed at zero rate	
	Exemptions (examples)	None	
	Refund of VAT	Only an exporter is unable to deduct in full the tax credits	
	Tax liability	On value transferred	
	Tax rates	0% on exports and 13% on local operations and imports	
	Administrative obligations		
Real Property Taxes		According to the value	
Stamp Duty		N/A	N/A

Nexia International does not accept liability for any loss arising from any action taken, or omission, on the basis of this publication. Professional advice should be obtained before acting or refraining from acting on the contents of this publication. Membership of Nexia International, or associated umbrella organizations, does not constitute any partnership between members, and members do not accept any responsibility for the commission of any act, or omission to act by, or the liabilities of, other members.

Nexia International is the trading name of Nexia International Limited, a company registered in the Isle of Man. Company registration number: 53513C. Registered office: 2nd floor, Sixty Circular Road, Douglas, Isle of Man, IM1 1SA

© Nexia International 2017

Estonia

(Evald Veldemann, Audiitorbüroo ELSS AS, evald.veldemann@elss.ee)

I MAIN LEGAL FORMS

Characteristics \ Legal form	Partnership and Limited Partnership (LP)	Private corporation (Ltd) and Public corporation (Plc)
Partners/shareholders • Number • Restrictions	Two or more persons	One or more shareholders
Directors	Management by partners	At least one director
Establishment	Partnership Deed	Memorandum of Association
Registration	Notarised agreements filed on the commercial register	
Minimum capital	No formal requirements	Ltd: €2,500 Plc: €25,000
Liability	Unlimited liability for general partner, limited liability for limited partner	Limited to capital
Governance	Partners	Annual general meeting Ltd: meeting of shareholders, management board, and supervisory board required if it is set forth in the Articles of Association Plc: general meeting, supervisory board, management board
Audit requirements	Required if two of the following three limits are exceeded: • turnover more than €4,000,000 • balance sheet total more than €2,000,000 • number of employees more than 60 And one of the three following criteria: • turnover more than €12,000,000 • balance sheet total more than €6,000,000 • number of employees more than 180	

Characteristics \ Legal form	Partnership and Limited Partnership (LP)	Private corporation (Ltd) and Public corporation (Plc)
Review requirements	Required if two of the following three limits are exceeded: • turnover more than €1,600,000 • balance sheet total more than €800,000 • number of employees more than 24 And one of the three following criteria: • turnover more than €4,800,000 • balance sheet total more than €2,400,000 • number of employees more than 72 Plc: audit is compulsory	
Taxation	Corporate taxes on worldwide income	Corporate taxes on worldwide income
Usage	Rare	Common

II CORPORATION TAX (CORPORATE INCOME TAX)

Description \ Legal form	Resident corporation	Permanent establishment (PE)
General description	Distribution tax on distributed profits	Non-residents subject to tax on Estonian-source income, which has been taken out the permanent establishment
Taxable entities	Corporations registered and/or place of effective management and control in Estonia	Foreign corporations with PE in Estonia
Taxable income	Worldwide profits	Estonian-source income
Calculation of taxable profits	Distributed profit for the period	
Interest payments	No thin cap rules	
Related party transactions	Arm's length prices should be applied	
Tax year, return and payment	The taxable period is the calendar month	
	Tax must be paid on the 10th day of the next month	
Capital gains	Included in taxable profits	
Losses	No relief	
Tax group	No group taxation	
Tax rate	20% on distributed profit	

III TAXES FOR INDIVIDUALS

		Residents	Non-residents
Income Tax	General description	Federal tax on income of individuals	
	Taxable entities and taxable income	A natural person is a resident if their place of residence is in Estonia or if they stay in Estonia for at least 183 days over the course of 12 consecutive calendar months. All income is taxable, whether derived in Estonia or outside Estonia	Income tax on income derived from Estonian sources
	Types of taxable income	• Employment income • Property income • Trading income from a trade or vocation • Savings and investment income	
	Calculation of income	Generally on a cash basis	
	Tax year, tax assessment and tax payment	The tax year is the calendar year and declaration of income must be presented on 31 March of the next calendar year	Taxes are mainly collected through withholding of tax
	Losses	Business-related loss may be carried forward for 7 years	
	Tax rates	20%	
Capital Gains Tax (CGT)	General description	There is no special capital gains taxation	
		Capital gains are taxed alongside taxable income	
	Taxable entities and chargeable assets	Disposal of securities	Disposal of shares in Estonian companies and of shares in companies, where assets are constituted more than 50% from immoveable property located in Estonia
	Calculation of gain	Difference between selling price and acquisition costs	
	Tax year, tax assessment and tax payment	Declaration is the same as for other income	
	Losses	Losses can be carried forward indefinitely against future capital gains	Losses not deductible
	Tax rates	20%	
		Estonia domiciled	Non-Estonia domiciled
Inheritance Tax (IHT)	General description	No inheritance tax is levied	

IV WITHHOLDING TAXES

Under domestic law	Payments to residents	Payments to non-residents
Dividends	Nil	According to Estonian Income Tax Act there is no withholding of taxes, so tax treaties have no importance
Interest	20% As an exception, income tax is not charged on interest received from credit institutions	Generally non-taxable. Exception includes transactions with investment funds, which own immovables in Estonia
Royalties	20%	10%
On payments to artists and sportsmen	20%	10%

Estonia has negotiated a range of tax treaties which provide an exemption or a reduction in withholding taxes on dividends, interest and royalties payable.

Reduced rate available under the relevant Double Taxation Treaty			
Country	Dividends	Interest[1]	Royalties[2]
Albania	Nil	5%	5%
Armenia	Nil	10%	10%
Austria	Nil	10%	5%/10%
Azerbaijan	Nil	10%	10%
Bahrain (Kingdom of)	Nil	Nil	Nil
Belarus	Nil	10%	10%
Belgium	Nil	10%	5%/10%
Bulgaria	Nil	5%	5%
Canada	Nil	10%	10%
China	Nil	10%	10%
Croatia	Nil	10%	10%
Cyprus	Nil	Nil	Nil
Czech Republic	Nil	10%	10%
Denmark	Nil	10%	5%/10%
Finland	Nil	10%	5%/10%
France	Nil	10%	5%/10%
Germany	Nil	10%	5%/10%
Greece	Nil	10%	5%/10%
Hungary	Nil	10%	5%/10%
Iceland	Nil	10%	5%/10%
India	Nil	10%	10%
Ireland (Republic of)	Nil	10%	5%/10%
Isle of Man	Nil	Nil	Nil
Israel	Nil	5%	0%

1 Interest in Estonia is generally not taxable as income of a non-resident, so the tax rate provided in the Tax Treaty has no practical effect.
2 The more favourable tax rate is applied to the right to use industrial, commercial or scientific equipment.

Reduced rate available under the relevant Double Taxation Treaty			
Country	Dividends	Interest[1]	Royalties[2]
Italy	Nil	10%	5%/10%
Jersey	Nil	Nil	Nil
Kazakhstan	Nil	10%	15%
Latvia	Nil	10%	5%/10%
Lithuania	Nil	10%	0%/10%
Luxembourg	Nil	10%	5%/10%
Macedonia	Nil	5%	0%/5%
Malta	Nil	10%	10%
Mexico	Nil	10%	10%
Moldova	Nil	10%	10%
Netherlands	Nil	10%	5%/10%
Norway	Nil	10%	5%/10%
Poland	Nil	10%	10%
Portugal	Nil	10%	10%
Romania	Nil	10%	10%
Serbia	Nil	10%	10%
Singapore	Nil	10%	7.5%
Slovakia	Nil	10%	10%
Slovenia	Nil	10%	10%
South Korea	Nil	10%	5%/10%
Spain	Nil	10%	5%/10%
Sweden	Nil	10%	5%/10%
Switzerland	Nil	10%	5%/10%
Thailand	Nil	10%	8%/10%
Turkey	Nil	10%	5%/10%
Turkmenistan	Nil	10%	0%/10%
Ukraine	Nil	10%	10%
United Kingdom	Nil	10%	5%/10%
Uzbekistan	Nil	5%	0%/10%
United States	Nil	10%	5%/10%

Note: the above rates are only available provided the specific Treaty criteria are satisfied. It is possible that lower rates than those shown above may be available provided that certain criteria are satisfied. As treaties will not be identical, guidance should be sought in all cases.

Where the domestic rate is lower than the treaty rate, the domestic rate will apply.

V INDIRECT TAXES

		Residents	Non-residents
Value Added Tax (VAT)	General description	Tax on the supply of goods and services, imports and others	
	Entities obliged to levy VAT	• Those with taxable turnover exceeding €16,000 in a calendar year (this will increase to €40,000 from 1 January 2018) • Entities who import from the EU	
	Taxable activities	• The supply of goods and services in Estonia • Imports • Acquiring goods or services from a non-resident taxpayer, who is not registered as an Estonian taxpayer (if the location of creation of turnover is in Estonia)	
	Taxable activities – zero-rated (examples)	• Exports • Intra-Community supply of goods • Services, where the place of service is not Estonia	
	Exemptions (examples)	The following are exempt: • medical services • certain educational services • insurance services • leasing of dwellings	
	Refund of VAT	The excess VAT will be refunded within 30 days starting from the day the application is received	
	Tax liability	Taxable period is calendar month. Deadline for submission of return and payment is 20th day of the following month	
	Tax rates	Standard rate of 20%, 14%, 9% or 0% for certain other activities	
	Administrative obligations	• Invoice has to be issued within 7 days • Special requirements for details of invoices • In some cases invoice can be issued by the acquirers of goods or the recipients of services	
Real Property Taxes		Land is the object of taxation, other real property is not. Different rates apply depending on the region where the land is located	
Stamp Duty		Depending on the document stamped, the duty can be a flat levy or a percentage of the transaction amount	

Nexia International is the trading name of Nexia International Limited, a company registered in the Isle of Man. Company registration number: 53513C. Registered office: 2nd floor, Sixty Circular Road, Douglas, Isle of Man, IM1 1SA

Finland

(Karri Nieminen, Fiscales Ltd, Tax Advisers, karri.nieminen@fiscales.fi)

I   MAIN LEGAL FORMS

Legal form / Characteristics	Partnership and Limited Partnership (LP)	Private corporation (Ltd) and Public corporation (Plc)
Partners/shareholders • Number • Restrictions	Partnership: minimum two partners – general partners LP: at least one general partner and one limited partner	Minimum one shareholder
Directors	Management by partners	Minimum one director and one deputy
Establishment	Deed	Notarial deed
Registration	Trade register; registration usually takes less than a month	
Minimum capital	Partnership: no minimum capital	Ltd: €2,500
	LP: at least one limited partner with financial input	Plc: €80,000
Liability	Unlimited for general partner Limited for limited partner	Limited
Governance	No formal requirements	Shareholder and director meetings
Audit requirements	Audit mandatory if two out of three conditions are satisfied for consecutive years: • turnover of at least €200,000 • balance sheet of at least €100,000 • employs at least three people The new Auditing Act came into operation on 1 January 2016. It contains implementing provisions concerning audit requirements	
Taxation	All income is assessed on individual partners; part of the income is taxed as capital income depending on the net assets of the partnership and the rest is taxed at progressive rates	Subject to corporation tax, 2017: 20% flat
Usage	Uncommon due to unlimited liability and higher rates of tax	More common, especially with higher incomes

II CORPORATION TAX

Legal form / Description	Resident corporation	Permanent establishment (PE)
General description	Corporation tax	
Taxable entities	Corporations resident in Finland	PE located in Finland
Taxable income	Worldwide profits	All income attributable to PE, whether derived from Finland or abroad
Calculation of taxable profits	Accounting profit is adjusted for various tax add-backs and allowances to arrive at chargeable profits	
Dividends	Dividend income from unlisted companies is tax exempt if the distributing company is a resident company **or** a company which is mentioned in the Parent-Subsidiary Directive **or** a company resident in a EEA country and which is liable to pay at least 10% tax on its income	
	However, dividend income is 100% subject to corporate tax if the distributing company is a listed company and the recipient is an unlisted company owning less than 10% of the share capital of the distributing listed company. If the ownership exceeds 10%, the dividend income is tax exempt	
	Dividend income from outside of EU and EEA is 100% subject to corporate tax. However, if there is a tax treaty, the tax treaty provisions have to be taken into account. Tax treaties usually prevent taxation of dividends if the recipient's ownership exceeds 10% or 25%	
	According to the new rules, the dividend income would not be tax exempt for the parent company in Finland if the dividends were tax deductible as a payment for the subsidiary	
Interest payments	Interest paid on borrowed capital is generally deductible. Dividend paid on equity capital is not deductible	
	There is a regulation limiting the deductibility of interest payments when these payments have been made to group companies	
	According to the provisions, interest expenses are fully deductible up to the amount equal to the interest income accrued during the same tax year. Interest expenses are also always deductible if the net interest expenses are at most €500,000 (so-called 'safe haven'). If the interest expenses exceed the accrued interest income by more than €500,000, the net interest expenses are not deductible for the part that the net interest expenses 1) exceed an amount corresponding to 25% of EBITDA and 2) the amount of net interest expenses exceeding the 25% limit is equal to or less than the amount of net interest expenses of any debts between related parties	
	The regulation has been applicable from the beginning of the tax year 2014	
Related party transactions	All related party transactions must take place on an arm's length basis	
	Transfer pricing rules have been in effect from 1 January 2007 onwards which are in line with EU regulations	
Tax year, return and payment	• The financial year of a company may be any 12-month period • Companies must file the tax return no later than 4 months after the end of their financial year • Companies are required to settle tax on account during the course of the year	

Legal form / Description	Resident corporation	Permanent establishment (PE)
Capital gains	Capital gains and losses are usually assessed as part of company's profits subject to corporation tax (20%)	
	Sale of shares in associated companies can, under certain conditions, be tax-free	
Losses	Losses can be carried forward and set off against profits of the subsequent 10 years. Losses are utilised on a first-in, first-out basis. Capital losses may have a set-off period of 5 years	
Tax group	There is no group taxation in Finland. All group companies are taxed separately. Moreover, some kind of group taxation may be achieved by tax deductible contributions which are taxed at the other company	There is no group taxation in Finland. All group companies are taxed separately
Tax rate	2017: 20%	

III TAXES FOR INDIVIDUALS

<table>
<tr><th></th><th></th><th>Residents</th><th>Non-residents</th></tr>
<tr><td rowspan="9">Income Tax</td><td>General description</td><td colspan="2">Tax levied on the chargeable income of a chargeable person for a year of assessment</td></tr>
<tr><td>Taxable entities and taxable income</td><td>Residents are taxed on their worldwide income with some relief for double taxation

There is an expatriate regime for a flat tax of 35% for a period of 48 months if certain conditions are met (eg the expatriate becomes tax resident in Finland)</td><td>Non-residents are taxed on income derived in Finland including investments. However, if there is a tax treaty, the tax treaty provisions have to be taken into account</td></tr>
<tr><td>Types of taxable income</td><td colspan="2">Capital income:
• property income
• income from capital investment (interest, sale of goodwill, dividends (partly), royalties, annuities)
• income from business activities (partly)

Earned income:
• income from business activities (partly)
• dividends (partly)
• employment income including benefits in kind stock options</td></tr>
<tr><td>Calculation of income</td><td colspan="2">Dividends to residents:
From listed companies 15% of dividend income is exempt and 85% is taxed as capital income with a tax rate of 30%/34%

Dividends from non-listed companies are divided into capital income and earned income. 8% of shares' mathematical (corrected net asset) or market value (foreign shares) at the end of the fiscal year preceding the tax year is regarded as capital income, of which 75% is tax exempt and 25% is taxed as capital income with a tax rate of 30%/33%

If the dividend exceeds €150,000 but stays within the 8% threshold, 15% of it is tax exempt and 85% is taxed as capital income with a tax rate of 30%/34%

If the dividend exceeds the 8% threshold, 25% of it is tax exempt and 75% is taxed as earned income with progressive tax rates</td></tr>
<tr><td>Tax year, tax assessment and tax payment</td><td colspan="2">• Tax year – calendar year
• Individual self-assessment returns (pre-completed tax returns) should be completed and filed by mid-May
• Tax is deducted at source on employment income</td></tr>
<tr><td>Losses</td><td colspan="2">Losses can be deducted from other income. Some restrictions</td></tr>
<tr><td>Tax rate</td><td colspan="2">

(€)	Rate
16,900–25,300	6.25% + €8[1]
25,300–41,200	17.5% + €533
41,200–73,100	21.5% + €3,315.50
73,100–	31.75% + €10,174

In addition there is a municipality tax, sickness insurance and church tax. The highest marginal tax rate can go up to around 60%
These are the tax rates for 2017
Tax rate for capital income is 30%/34%
Tax rate for capital income exceeding €30,000 is 34%</td></tr>
</table>

1   This represents the amount of tax that has to be paid at the lower end of the bracket, ie tax of €8 has to be paid on €16,900. Tax at a rate of 6.25% will be levied on amounts in excess of €16,900 on top of the €8.

		Residents	**Non-residents**
Capital Gains Tax (CGT)	General description	Tax on increase in the value of the asset between acquisition and disposal	
	Taxable entities and chargeable assets	Capital gain arising on the sale of a private residence is tax exempt if the person has lived in this property for a continuous period of at least 2 years during the period of ownership. Sale of a business can also be tax exempt if sold under strict conditions to members of immediate family	
	Calculation of gain	Capital gain is calculated by deducting the acquisition and sale costs from the disposal proceeds	
		A minimum deduction of 20% of the sale price is applied. If the asset has been owned for at least 10 years, the minimum deduction is 40%	
	Tax year, tax assessment and tax payment	• Tax year – calendar year • Tax return has to be filed at the latest in early May (dates vary). Tax can be paid interest-free up until the end of January and must be paid at the latest by November of the following year and February the year after (eg tax for 2016 will have to be paid at the latest by 29 November 2017 (first half) and 1 February 2018 (second half))	
	Losses	Capital losses realized before 2015 can be deducted from capital gains arising in the same year or the following 5 years. No possibility of carry back	
		Capital losses realized in 2016 or after are deducted first from capital gains arising in the same year. If capital losses exceed the amount of capital gains, the 'net capital loss' can be deducted from other capital income (eg dividend income, rent income). If there is no other capital income or the 'net capital loss' exceeds the amount of other capital income, the left-over amount can be deducted during the following 5 years. No possibility of carry back	
	Tax rates	30%/34%	

		Domiciled	**Non-domiciled**
Inheritance Tax (IHT)	General description	Chargeable on estates and beneficiaries resident in Finland. Transfer of a business or a farm to a descendant is partially exempt from taxes	
	Taxable entities and chargeable assets	All assets	
	Calculation of charge	Calculation based on the market value of the assets	
	Taxable events	Death	
	Allowances	• Allowance for household belongings of €4,000 • Spouse allowance of €90,000 • Minor allowance of €60,000	

		Domiciled	Non-domiciled
Inheritance Tax (IHT) – contd	Tax rates	There are two different classes of recipients for inheritance tax purposes A spouse, children and parents of the deceased and spouse's children belong to the first class. The remainder belong to the second class • The tax rates in first class are as follows: *(€)* *Rate* 20,000–40,000 7% + €100 40,000–60,000 10% + €1,500 60,000–200,000 13% + €3,500 200,000–1,000,000 16% + €21,700 1,000,000– 19% + €149,700 • The tax rates in second class are as follows: *(€)* *Rate* 20,000–40,000 19% + €100 40,000–60,000 25% + €3,900 60,000–200,000 29% + €8,900 200,000–1,000,000 31% + €49,500 1,000,000– 33% + €297,500	

IV   WITHHOLDING TAXES

Under domestic law	Payments to residents	Payments to non-residents[2]
Dividends	25.5% or 7.5%/27%[3]	20%/30.0%
Interest	30%	20%/30.0%
Royalties	30%/progressive[4]	20%/30.0%
On payments to artists and sportsmen	Progressive	15%

Reduced rate available under the relevant Double Taxation Treaty			
Country	Dividends	Interest[5]	Royalties
Argentina	15%	Nil	15%[6]
Armenia	15%	Nil	10%
Australia	15%	Nil	5%
Austria	10%	Nil	5%
Azerbaijan	10%	Nil	5%[7]
Barbados	15%[8]	Nil	5%[9]
Belarus	15%	Nil	5%
Belgium	15%	Nil	5%[9]
Bosnia-Herzegovina	15%	Nil	10%
Brazil	20/30%	Nil	20/30%
Bulgaria	10%	Nil	5%[9]
Canada	15%	Nil	10%[9]
China	10%	Nil	10%
Czech Republic	15%	Nil	10%[9,10]
Croatia	15%	Nil	10%
Cyprus	15%	Nil	Nil
Denmark	15%	Nil	Nil
Egypt	10%	Nil	25%
Estonia	15%	Nil	10%
France	Nil	Nil	Nil
Georgia	10%	Nil	Nil
Germany	15%	Nil	5%[9]
Greece	13%	Nil	10%[9]

2   Reduced rates of withholding tax (WHT) may apply where there is an appropriate double tax treaty.
3   WHT for dividends received from listed companies is 25.5%. WHT for dividends received from non-listed companies is 7.5% up to €150,000 and 27% for dividends exceeding the €150,000 threshold.
4   WHT for corporate entities 20% and for others 30%.
5   According to the national law of Finland, interest paid to a non-resident is usually exempt from taxation in Finland.
6   Tax 10% on industrial royalty, 3% on royalties to news agency, and 5% on artistic royalty to the author or his mortis causa successor.
7   Tax 10% on literary, scientific, artistic and film royalties.
8   Tax for an individual is 30% if income is tax-exempt in the country of residence.
9   Tax is not levied on literary, scientific or artistic royalties.
10 Tax 1% for finance lease of equipment, 5% for operating lease of equipment and computer software.

Reduced rate available under the relevant Double Taxation Treaty			
Country	Dividends	Interest[5]	Royalties
Hungary	15%	Nil	5%[9]
Indonesia	15%	Nil	15%[7]
India	10%	Nil	10%
Ireland	Nil[8]	Nil[8]	Nil[8]
Iceland	15%	Nil	Nil
Israel	15%	Nil	10%
Italy	15%	Nil	5%
Japan	15%	Nil	10%
Kazakhstan	15%	Nil	10%
Kyrgyzstan	15%	Nil	5%
Latvia	15%	Nil	10%[12]
Liechtenstein	20/30%	Nil	20/30%
Lithuania	15%	Nil	10%
Luxembourg	15%	Nil	5%[9]
Macedonia	15%	Nil	Nil
Malaysia	15%	Nil	5%
Malta	15%	Nil	Nil
Mexico	Nil	Nil	10%
Moldova	15%	Nil	7%
Morocco	10%	Nil	10%
Netherlands	15%	Nil	Nil
New Zealand	15%	Nil	10%
Norway	15%	Nil	Nil
Pakistan	20%[13]	Nil	10%
The Philippines	20/30%	Nil	25%[11]
Portugal	15%	Nil	10%
Poland	15%	Nil	5%
Republic of Korea	15%	Nil	10%
Romania	5%	Nil	5%[14]
Russia	12%	Nil	Nil
Serbia and Montenegro	15%	Nil	10%
Singapore	10%	Nil	5%
Slovakia	15%	Nil	10%
Slovenia	15%	Nil	5%
South Africa	15%	Nil	Nil
Spain	15%	Nil	5%
Sri Lanka	15%	Nil	10%
Sweden	15%	Nil	Nil

11 Tax 15% on films, tapes used in television or radio broadcasts, use of copyright of literary, artistic or scientific works or royalty paid for usufruct.

12 Tax 5% on royalties paid for the use of industrial, commercial or scientific equipment.

13 Tax 15% if the recipient is a company.

14 Tax 2.5% on royalties paid for the use of industrial, commercial or scientific equipment or computer software.

Reduced rate available under the relevant Double Taxation Treaty			
Country	Dividends	Interest[5]	Royalties
Switzerland	10%	Nil	Nil
Tadzhikistan	15%	Nil	5%
Tanzania	20%	Nil	20%
Thailand	20/30%	Nil	15%
Turkey	15%	Nil	10%
Ukraine	15%	Nil	10%[16]
United Arab Emirates	20/30%[8]	20/30%[8]	20/30%[17]
United Kingdom	Nil	Nil	Nil
United States	15%	Nil	Nil
Uruguay	15%	Nil	10%[18]
Uzbekistan	15%	Nil	10%
Vietnam	15%	Nil	10%
Zambia	15%	Nil	15%[9,15]

Note: The above rates are only available provided the specific Treaty criteria are satisfied. It is possible that lower rates than those shown above may be available provided that certain criteria are satisfied. As treaties will not be identical, guidance should be sought in all cases.

EU countries:

- No tax if dividends were tax free under the Finnish Business Tax Act § 6 a if paid to a Finnish corporate entity, and if the recipient does not receive a full credit for the Finnish tax in the country of residence.
- No tax on dividend paid to a company as defined in the EU Parent-Subsidiary Directive owning at least 10% of the capital of the paying company.
- No tax on royalties between associated companies as defined in EU Directives (2003/49/EC, 2013/13/EU).

15 Tax 5% on royalties from films and tapes.
16 Tax 5% for the use of secret process or know-how, no tax for computer software or patent.
17 No tax if the recipient proves that he has domicile (individual) or is incorporated in the United Arab Emirates.
18 Tax 5% on royalties paid for the use or the right to use of industrial, commercial or scientific equipment or software.

V INDIRECT TAXES

		Residents	Non-residents
Value Added Tax (VAT)	General description	Tax on the supply of goods and services	
	Entities obliged to levy VAT	Minimum turnover €10,000 (obligatory); if turnover is less than €10,000, entity is allowed to register	
	Taxable activities	Broad-based tax on most goods and services	
	Taxable activities – zero-rated (examples)	• Sale of gold to the Bank of Finland • Goods and services sold in connection with the sale of a business	
	Exemptions (examples)	• Healthcare, certain education, sale of properties (usually) • Certain financial services, gold bullions, insurance services	
	Refund of VAT	Yes (if overpaid or if taxpayer is in export business and makes VAT purchases in Finland)	
	Tax liability	Normally the supplier of goods and services is responsible for charging VAT	
	Tax rates	• Standard rate = 24% • Reduced tax rates for certain commodities and services are 14%, 10% and 0%	
	Administrative obligations	Normally monthly tax returns (in some cases quarterly or yearly)	
Transfer taxes		• 4% real properties • 2% housing companies' shares • 1,6% corporate stocks	

Nexia International does not accept liability for any loss arising from any action taken, or omission, on the basis of this publication. Professional advice should be obtained before acting or refraining from acting on the contents of this publication. Membership of Nexia International, or associated umbrella organizations, does not constitute any partnership between members, and members do not accept any responsibility for the commission of any act, or omission to act by, or the liabilities of, other members.

Nexia International is the trading name of Nexia International Limited, a company registered in the Isle of Man. Company registration number: 53513C. Registered office: 2nd floor, Sixty Circular Road, Douglas, Isle of Man, IM1 1SA

France

(Yves Sevestre, Cabinet SEVESTRE ET ASSOCIES, y.sevestre@sevestre-associes.com)

I MAIN LEGAL FORMS

Legal form / Characteristics	Partnership and Limited Liability Partnership (LLP)	Private corporation (Ltd) and Public corporation (Plc)
Partners/shareholders • Number • Restrictions	*Société en nom collectif (SNC):* • at least 2 partners. No maximum number of partners *Société en Commandite Simple (SCS) and Société en Commandite par Actions (SCA):* • at least 2 partners: – one of whom is a 'commandités': joint and unlimited liability of all debts – and the other one, a 'commanditaires': liability limited to their contribution *Société civile (SC):* • at least 2 partners	*Société à responsabilité limitée (SARL) or entreprise unipersonnelle à responsabilité limitée (EURL):* • between 1 and 100 *Société anonyme (SA):* • at least 2 shareholders • at least 7 shareholders if listed company No maximum number of shareholders *Société par actions simplifiée (SAS):* • at least 1 partner
Directors	*SNC:* One or more manager, partner or not. If partner, he must be registered at the Commercial Court and have ability to trade *SCS and SCA:* Unless otherwise stipulated in the company's articles, all the 'commandités' are managers It is possible to choose one or more managers, who can be a partner or not *SC:* One or more manager, partner or not	*SARL:* One or more manager, partner or not *SA:* • *Classic system* – 'conseil d'administration' (Board of Directors): – between 3 and 18 members – management of the company by the President of the Board of Directors which is also the Chief Executive (CEO) or by a Chief Executive other than the President of the Board of Directors

Legal form \ Characteristics	Partnership and Limited Liability Partnership (LLP)	Private corporation (Ltd) and Public corporation (Plc)
		• *Dualistic system:* – 'directoire' (Management Board) and 'conseil de surveillance' (Supervisory Board): – Management Board: maximum 5 members – Management Board manages the company – Supervisory Board: between 3 and 18 members (checks the Management Board) *SAS:* One President and Chief Executive if any
Establishment	By-laws of company	By-laws of company
Registration	All entities have to be registered at the Commercial Court and publication of by-laws	
Minimum capital	*SNC:* No minimum *SCS:* No minimum *SCA:* €37,000 *SC:* No minimum, except SC which offers its shares to the public	*SARL:* Minimum capital: €1 *SA:* Minimum capital: • €37,000 • €225,000 for listed public companies *SAS:* Minimum capital: €1
Liability	*SNC:* Jointly and unlimited liability of all debts *SCS/SCA:* • 'commandités': joint and unlimited liability of all debts • 'commanditaires': liability limited to their contribution *SC:* Unlimited liability of all debts	*SARL, SA, SAS:* Liability limited to contribution
Governance	Partners	*SARL and SA:* Defined by the commercial law *SAS:* Freedom of governance, defined in the by-laws

Legal form \ Characteristics	Partnership and Limited Liability Partnership (LLP)	Private corporation (Ltd) and Public corporation (Plc)
Audit requirements	*SNC and SCS:* No obligation for audit Except if the company exceeds two of the three following thresholds: • balance sheet >€1.55m • turnover > €3.1m • employees > 50 *SCA:* An auditor must be appointed at the moment of the registration of the company *SC:* No obligation for audit except for particular cases	*SARL:* No obligation Except if the company exceeds two of the three following thresholds: • balance sheet > €1.55m • turnover > €3.1m • employees > 50 *SA:* The legal auditor has to certify the corporate accounts annually and must be appointed at the moment of the registration of the company *SAS:* Audit mandatory: • if the company exceeds two of the three following thresholds: – balance sheet > €1m – turnover > €2m – employees > 20 • if the company belongs to a group SAS which already has legal auditor and which has no obligation for audit has to wait until the end of the legal auditor mandate before stopping the obligation of audit
Taxation	*SNC:* Each partner is subject to personal income tax in proportion of their share in the company unless the company elected for corporate income tax *SCS/SCA:* Each partner 'commandités' is subject to personal income tax unless the company elected for corporate income tax Profits corresponding to share of 'commanditaire' are taxable to corporate income tax *SC:* Each partner is subject to personal income tax unless the company is subject to corporate income tax (in case of election or activity)	*SARL:* Corporate income tax, unless election for personal income tax *SA and SAS:* Corporate income tax

Legal form Characteristics	Partnership and Limited Liability Partnership (LLP)	Private corporation (Ltd) and Public corporation (Plc)
Usage	*SNC/SCS:* Used for small businesses *SCA:* Used to prevent takeover and to secure the company capital structure controlled by a family (such as Michelin, Hermès) *SC:* Used for patrimonial operations or civil/professional activity or real estate operations	*SARL:* Start-ups and small or medium-sized companies *SA:* Often listed companies, but not exclusively *SAS:* As SARLs and not SAs

II   CORPORATION TAX

Description \ Legal form	Resident corporation	Permanent establishment (PE)
General description	Corporation tax	
Taxable entities	The company	Foreign entity
Taxable income	Territoriality principle: tax is only due on business income generated by enterprises operating in France	Territoriality principle: tax is only due on business income generated by the French PE
Calculation of taxable profits	• Net taxable benefits less tax losses: carry forward within the limit of (€1m + 50% (taxable result – €1m)) each year • Losses can be carried back over 1 year within the limit of €1m • Accruals method of accounting	
Interest payments	Deductible under conditions	
Related party transactions	All related party transactions must take place on an arm's length basis	
Tax year, return and payment	• Calendar year, or if the taxpayer's financial year does not coincide, the financial year of 12 months ending during the relevant calendar year • Returns to be filed within 3 months of financial year end • Advance payments required each quarter	
Capital gains and dividends	• Generally deemed as ordinary income and subject to standard corporate tax rate *Dividends* 95% exempt, 5% of dividends received plus tax credit are subject to corporate income tax. As from the tax years opening 1 January 2015, the parent/subsidiary regime will no longer apply to income distributed by a subsidiary to its parent company (mainly dividends) if such distributed income is deductible from the subsidiary's taxable result or if it is leading to an abuse of the parent/subsidiary regime Following the *Steria* decision (Case C-386/14), dividends paid within a tax consolidated group are no longer exempted from taxable fraction. For tax year starting on or after 1 January 2016, 1% will be subject to corporate income tax. It applies to distributions received by a company member of a French tax consolidated group or from subsidiaries held at 95% or more within the European Union (EU) or European Economic Area (EEA) and who should qualify if they were French entities to the French tax consolidation regime According to Council Directive (EU) 2015/121 of 27 January 2015 and article 145, 6., k) of FTC, parent/subsidiary regime is not applicable since 1 January 2016 to dividends paid inside an artificial arrangement if one of the main purposes of this arrangement is to obtain a tax advantage which defeats the purpose or object of parent/subsidiary regime, and if the arrangement is not authentic because there is no economic reason Henceforth, since 3 February 2016, shares without voting right are also taken into account to benefit of parent/subsidiary regime *Capital gains on participations* 88% exempt, 12% subject to corporate income tax Capital gains of listed real estate companies are taxed at reduced rate of 19%. If not, the standard corporate rate applies (33.33%)	
Losses	Carried forward indefinitely (within the limit of (€1m + 50% (taxable result – €1m))) or option for carry back for the previous year only within the limit of €1m	

Description \ Legal form	Resident corporation	Permanent establishment (PE)
Tax group	A group of companies can opt for a consolidated tax regime. The income and losses of resident companies within a 95% group may be aggregated and dealt with in the hands of the parent corporation. The full exemption for dividends paid within a tax group no longer applies (see above)	Possibility of a consolidated tax regime: the foreign PE can be the head of the group or can be a tax member
	The amended Finance Bill for 2014 allows the creation of a so-called 'horizontal' consolidation tax group. Thus, as from the tax years ending 31 December 2014, a tax group can be created between sister companies which are subsidiaries of a company holding at least 95% of their share capital and established in an European Union member State or a European Economic Area member State which has entered into a double taxation agreement covering administrative assistance against tax evasion and fraud with France	
Tax rate	• Standard rate: 33.33% (28% in 2020)	
	Finance Bill for 2017 introduces a gradual reduction of CIT tax rate to reach 28% in 2020 for all companies. In 2017, profits under €75,000 will be taxed at the rate of 28% as long as the turnover is lower than €50 million. In 2018, profits under €500,000 will be taxed at the rate of 28%. In 2019, the 28% will apply to all companies with a turnover lower than €1 billion (if higher, limited to a €500,000 profit)	
	Plus further 3.3% of the CIT, less €763,000 (ie an effective rate of 34.43% on the basis of a 33.33% rate) • Small and medium-sized enterprises: 15% on first €38,120 of profits, standard rate above €38,120 • 3% contribution on profit distributions in some circumstances. Profits distributions are not subject to the 3% contribution if the company fulfils the conditions of the French tax consolidation regime (located in France, in Europe or in state which signed with France a convention on mutual administrative assistance in tax matters)	
	If companies are located in a non-cooperative state or territory, the exemption applies if the company proves that its activities do not have the effect or purpose of localising the benefits in a non-cooperative state or territory with the aim of tax evasion	

III TAXES FOR INDIVIDUALS

		Residents	**Non-residents**
Income Tax	General description	Income tax	
	Taxable entities and taxable income	Worldwide	French source income only if no permanent dwelling held in France
	Types of taxable income	• Employment and business income • Capital gains • Income from immovable property • Investment income	• Real estate income • Certain income subject to tax at source • Income linked to an activity located in France
	Calculation of income	• Net salary: gross salary less compulsory social charges and less rebate of 10% on salaries or effective expenses • Net capital gains: gross capital gains less acquisition costs • Net rental income	Net real estate income Net French professional income Other net French income
	Tax year, tax assessment and tax payment	• Generally the calendar year • Individuals with business income may be assessed on the basis of an accounting period • Income tax computed on the income of the preceding year • Tax form sent in May by electronic tax assessment except in particular cases • Two instalments are required on 15 February and 15 May • Final liability due on 15 September • As from 2018, a general income tax withholding system will be implemented • As from 2019, online platform should communicate to the French Tax Authorities, every year, information concerning the income of the users earned via the platform	
	Losses	A loss in one category of professional income can be offset against income of another category. Excess losses that cannot be offset against the income of a given year may be carried forward for 6 years	
	Tax rates	• Dependent upon family situation (ie marital status and number of children) • Progressive tax brackets from 14%–45%	
	Dividends	• Taxation to the income progressive tax bands after withholding tax of 21% and tax-free allowance of 40% • Mandatory social charges are paid at the standard taxation rate of 15.5% within the first 15 days of the month, which follows the payment of dividends, whatever is the taxation regime of dividends	

		Residents	**Non-residents**
Capital Gains Tax (CGT)	General description	Capital gains tax	
	Taxable entities and chargeable assets	• Disposal of business assets • Immovable property	• Disposal of business assets • Immovable property
	Calculation of gain	*Shares:* Proceeds less acquisition costs. Rebate according to length of ownership: 50% for holding period between 2 and 8 years, 65% for holding period exceeding 8 years. Possibility to have higher tax rebates in some cases *Capital gains on real estate:* Net gains less a rebate of 6% per year as from the fifth year of ownership and 4% per year as from the 22nd year of ownership. Concerning social contributions, application of a rebate of 1.65% per year as from the fifth year, 1.60% for the 22nd and 9% per year as from the 22nd year of ownership Additional taxation if the net real estate capital gain exceeds €50,000 (capital gains realised on sale of building plots or exempted sales are excluded from this additional taxation) An exceptional 30% rebate applies for the calculation of a capital gain realised on the sale of a building plot for agreement to sell signed before 31 December 2015 and performed between 1 January 2015 and 31 December 2017	
	Tax year, tax assessment and tax payment	*Shares:* With tax return *Immovable property:* Within 2 months of disposal	*Immovable property:* At the moment of the registration formality or within a month of the sale
	Tax rates	*Shares for France domiciled:* Income tax bracket + 15.5% (social security) *Immovable property, furniture and racehorses:* Rate of 19% + 15.5% (social security) = 34.5% *Furniture and racehorses:* Rate of 19% + 15.5% (social security) = 34.5% for French tax residents	

		France domiciled	**Non-France domiciled**
Inheritance Tax (IHT)	General description	Registration fees	
	Taxable entities and chargeable assets	Each beneficiary is a taxable person	Taxation on French assets if the beneficiary is not French domiciled or on worldwide assets if the deceased was French tax resident
	Calculation of charge	Levied on the value of all transferred assets less related liabilities. In the case of gifts, liabilities are usually not deductible	
	Taxable events	On death and all gifts made prior to death	
	Allowances	No inheritance tax between spouses and persons liable to PACS (*Pacte civil de solidarité*), which is a civil contract binding non-married partners €100,000 direct line for each parent to each child	
	Tax rates	Dependent upon the proximity of the relationship between the donor and the recipient and upon the value of the elements transferred: from 0%–60%	
Wealth tax		On worldwide net assets of more than €1,300,000	On French assets whose net value exceeds €1,300,000 (financial investments are wealth tax exempt except substantial participation)

IV WITHHOLDING TAXES

Under domestic law	Payments to residents	Payments to non-residents[1]
Dividends	21%	15%–75%
Interest	24%	See schedule below
Royalties	Nil	33.33% subject to Treaty or Royalty Directive – 75%
Capital gain	Nil	45% when participation exceeds 25% of the profit rights
On payments to artists and sportsmen	Nil	15%

Reduced rate available under the relevant Double Taxation Treaty			
Country	Dividends	Interest	Royalties
Albania	15%	10%	5%
Algeria	15%	10%	10%
Andorra	15%	5%	5%
Argentina	15%	20%	18%
Armenia	15%	10%	10%
Australia	15%	10%	5%
Austria	15%	Nil	Nil
Azerbaijan	10%	10%	10%
Bahrain	Nil	Nil	Nil
Bangladesh	15%	10%	10%
Belgium	15%	15%	Nil
Benin	Nil	Nil	Nil
Bolivia	15%	15%	15%
Botswana	12%	10%	10%
Brazil	15%	15%	25% for brands; 15% others
Bulgaria	15%	Nil	5%
Burkina Faso	Nil	Nil	Nil
Cameroon	15%	15%	15%
Canada	15%	10%	10%
Central African Republic	Nil	Nil	Nil
Chile	15%	15%	10%
China	10%	10%	10%
Congo	20%	Nil	15%
Croatia	15%	Nil	Nil
Cyprus	15%	10%	Nil
Czech Republic	10%	Nil	10%
Ecuador	15%	15%	15%
Egypt	Nil	15%	15%
Estonia	15%	10%	10%
Ethiopia	10%	5%	7.5%
Finland	Nil	10%	Nil

---

1   Reduced rates of withholding tax may apply where there is an appropriate double tax treaty or the EU Parent Subsidiary Directive.

Reduced rate available under the relevant Double Taxation Treaty			
Country	Dividends	Interest	Royalties
French Polynesia	Nil	Nil	Nil
Gabon	15%	10%	10%
Georgia	10%	Nil	Nil
Germany	15% or Nil if dividends issued of immovable property gains (profit or capital gain) – internal rate is then applicable	Nil	Nil
Ghana	15%	12.5%	10%
Greece	Nil	10%	5%
Guinea	15%	10%	10%
Hong Kong	10%	10%	10%
Hungary	15%	Nil	Nil
Iceland	15%	Nil	Nil
India	15%	15%	Nil
Indonesia	15%	15%	10%
Iran	20%	15%	10%
Ireland	15%	Nil	Nil
Israel	15%	10%	10%
Italy	15%	10%	5%
Ivory Coast	15%	15%	10%
Jamaica	15%	10%	10%
Japan	10%	10%	Nil
Jordan	15%	15%	25% for brands; 15% others
Kazakhstan	15%	10%	10%
Kenya	10%	12%	10%
Kuwait	Nil	Nil	Nil
Latvia	15%	10%	10%
Lebanon	Nil	Nil	Nil
Libya	10%	Nil	10%
Lithuania	15%	10%	10%
Luxembourg	15%	10%	Nil
Macedonia	15%	Nil	Nil
Madagascar	25%	15%	15%
Malawi	Nil	Nil	Nil
Malaysia	15%	15%	10%
Mali	Nil	Nil	Nil
Malta	15%	5%	10%
Morocco	15%	10%	10%
Mauritania	Nil	Nil	Nil
Mauritius	15%	Nil	15%
Mayotte	Nil	Nil	Nil
Mexico	15%	15%	15%
Mongolia	15%	10%	5%
Namibia	15%	10%	10%
Netherlands	15%	Nil	Nil

Reduced rate available under the relevant Double Taxation Treaty			
Country	Dividends	Interest	Royalties
New Caledonia	15%	Nil	10%
New Zealand	15%	10%	10%
Niger	Nil	Nil	Nil
Nigeria	15%	12.5%	12.5%
Norway	15%	Nil	Nil
Oman	Nil	Nil	Nil
Pakistan	15%	10%	10%
Panama	15%	5%	5%
Philippines	15%	15%	15%
Poland	15%	Nil	10%
Portugal	15%	12%	5%
Qatar	Nil	Nil	Nil
Republic of Korea	15%	10%	10%
Romania	10%	10%	10%
Russia	15%	Nil	Nil
Saint Martin	15%	10%	Nil
Saint-Pierre et Miquelon	15%	Nil	10%
Saudi Arabia	Nil	Nil	Nil
Senegal	15%	15%	15%
Singapore	15%	10%	Nil
Slovakia	10%	Nil	5%
Slovenia	15%	5%	5%
South Africa	15%	Nil	Nil
Spain	15%	10%	5%
Sri Lanka	Nil	10%	10%
Sweden	15%	Nil	Nil
Switzerland	15%	Nil	5%
Syria	15%	10%	15%
Taiwan	10%	10%	10%
Thailand	Nil	Nil	15%
Togo	Nil	Nil	Nil
Trinidad and Tobago	15%	10%	10%
Tunisia	Nil	12%	20% for brands; 15% others
Turkey	20%	15%	10%
Ukraine	15%	10%	10%
United Emirates Arab	Nil	Nil	Nil
United Kingdom	15%	Nil	Nil
United States	15%	Nil	Nil
USSR (ex-) (Tadjikistan, Kyrgyzstan, Belarus, Turkménistan)	15%	10%	Nil
Uzbekistan	10%	5%	Nil
Venezuela	5%	5%	5%
Vietnam	15%	Nil	10%

Reduced rate available under the relevant Double Taxation Treaty			
Country	Dividends	Interest	Royalties
Yugoslavia (ex-) (Serbia, Montenegro, Bosnia-Herzegovina, Kosovo)	15%	Nil	Nil
Zambia	Nil	Nil	Nil
Zimbabwe	15%	10%	10%

Note: the above rates are only available provided the specific Treaty criteria are satisfied. It is possible that lower rates than those shown above may be available provided that certain criteria are satisfied. As treaties will not be identical, guidance should be sought in all cases.

V INDIRECT TAXES

<table>
<tr><th colspan="2"></th><th>Residents</th><th>Non-residents</th></tr>
<tr><td rowspan="11">Value Added Tax (VAT)</td><td>Entities obliged to levy VAT</td><td colspan="2">Persons making taxable supplies of goods and delivery of services in the course of a business</td></tr>
<tr><td>Taxable activities</td><td colspan="2">Unless expressly exempt, all goods and services are taxable activities</td></tr>
<tr><td>Taxable activities – zero-rated (examples)</td><td colspan="2">Exports</td></tr>
<tr><td>Exemptions (examples)</td><td colspan="2">• Financing and banking
• Insurance
• Commission
• Interest</td></tr>
<tr><td>Refund of VAT</td><td colspan="2">• Annual reimbursement if VAT refund is greater than €150
• Possible quarterly reimbursement if conditions are fulfilled
• As from 1 January 2017, the FTA will audit all the VAT refund claims</td></tr>
<tr><td>Tax liability</td><td>Supplier or provider of services established in France</td><td>Regime of reverse charge system: payment of the VAT by the French client subject to VAT for a supplier or a provider of service not established in France</td></tr>
<tr><td>Tax rates</td><td colspan="2">2.1% (for example, on medicines eligible for reimbursement, online press since 1 February 2014)</td></tr>
<tr><td></td><td colspan="2">5.5% (for example, on water, books, hygienic products since 1 January 2016)</td></tr>
<tr><td></td><td colspan="2">10% (for example, on passenger transport, hotels, goods for consumption on site or to take away if for immediate consumption)</td></tr>
<tr><td></td><td colspan="2">20% standard (including farming raw product not used for producing human or animal food since 1 January 2016)</td></tr>
<tr><td>Administrative obligations</td><td colspan="2">VAT registration</td></tr>
<tr><td colspan="2">Real Property Taxes</td><td colspan="2">None but registration duty of 5.09006% or 5.80665% according to the department</td></tr>
<tr><td colspan="2">Stamp Duty</td><td colspan="2">None</td></tr>
</table>

French Polynesia

(Veronique Morin, EDEC Sarl, Veronique.morin@edec-tahiti.com)

I MAIN LEGAL FORMS

Legal form — Characteristics	Partnership	Private corporation (Ltd) and Limited Liability Partnership (LLP)
Partners/shareholders • Number • Restrictions	*Société en nom collectif* (SNC): At least two partners *Société en commandite simple* (SCS): At least two partners *Société civile* (SC): At least two partners	*Société à responsabilité limitée* (SARL) or *entreprise unipersonnelle à responsabilité limitée* (EURL): Between 1 and 100 *Société anonyme* (SA): At least 7 shareholders *Société par actions simplifiée* (SAS): At least one partner
Directors	SNC: One or more manager registered at the Registrar of companies SCS: Unless otherwise stipulated in the company's articles, all the 'commandités' are managers. It is possible to choose one or more managers, who can be a partner or not SC: One or more manager or partner	SARL: One or more manager or partner SA: Classic system – Board of directors (*conseil d'administration*, CA): • Between 3 and 18 members • Management of the company by the President of the CA or a general director Dualistic system: *directoire* and *conseil de surveillance*: • Executive board (*directoire*): maximum five members • Supervisory board (*conseil de surveillance*): between 3 and 18 members (supervises the executive board) SAS: One President
Establishment	Partnership deed	By-laws of company
Registration	All entities to be registered at the Registrar of companies and publication of by-laws	

Legend form / Characteristics	Partnership	Private corporation (Ltd) and Limited Liability Partnership (LLP)
Minimum capital	SNC: No minimum SCS: No minimum	SARL: Minimum capital: €1 SA, SAS: €37,000
Liability	SNC: Jointly and unlimited liability of all debts SCS: '*Commandités*': joint and unlimited liability of all debts '*Commanditaires*': liability limited to their capital contribution SC: Unlimited liability of all debts	SARL, SA, SAS: Liability limited to capital contribution
Governance	Partners	SARL and SA: Defined by the commercial law SAS: Freedom of governance, defined in the by-laws
Audit requirements	SNC and SCS: May qualify for an audit exemption if it has at least 2 of the following thresholds: – Balance sheet > €0.838m – Turnover > €1.676m – Employees > 20 SC: No audit requirement	SARL: May qualify for an audit exemption if it has at least 2 of the following thresholds: – Balance sheet > €0.838m – Turnover > €1.676m – Employees > 20 SA and SAS: The legal auditor has to certify the corporate accounts annually
Taxation	Corporation tax: Income tax (IS) or Transaction tax (IT), depending on company legal form and option by partners when available SARL, SA, SAS: IS regime EURL (solely owned SARL): IS and it can elect for IT regime SCS, SC: IT regime SC is subject to IS when its activity is actually commercial (rental of fully equipped premises) SNC: IT and it can elect for IS regime	

II CORPORATION TAX

Legal Form / Description		Resident corporation	Permanent Establishment (PE)
General description		Corporate income tax (IS) or 'Transaction Tax' (IT) It depends on the legal form of the company or on the local entity's activity	Corporate income tax (IS)
Taxable entities		The company except companies with professional members	Local entity
Taxable income		Territoriality principle: tax is only due on business generated by enterprises registered and operating in French Polynesia	Territoriality principle: tax is only due on business generated by the French Polynesia PE
Calculation of taxable profits	IS	Net taxable benefits less tax losses carried forward. The corporate tax cannot be lower than a fixed minimum tax (IMF) based on the Turnover + other operating income + financial income	
		For the tax result higher than 50 MF CFP, an additional tax (CSIS) must be paid + an exceptional increase (MCSIS) of 7% for the year ended as of 31 December 2013 until fiscal years ending on 31 December 2015	
		New companies are exempted from IS or IMF for the two first fiscal years until 24 months	
		→ Updated by the law on 15 July 2014: The Polynesian government redefined the scope of the 24 months: 'For the fiscal year open from 16 July 2014, the tax exemption will concern the two first fiscal years for a cumulative maximum of 24 months'. So the tax exemptions for the second fiscal year will be prorated in case of the two first fiscal years' duration exceeding 24 months	
	IT	Turnover + others operating income + financial income with some specific rebates according to activity or on sale of assets	
		The new activities are exempted from IT for the two first fiscal years until 24 months, updated on 15 July 2014 (same as IS)	
Interest payments		Deductible within the following 2 thresholds: • Interest rate of 4% • The basis must not exceed four times the amount of the share capital for individual's shareholders loans Tax on revenue distributed (IRCM Tax) and Solidarity Tax (CST) on gross interest with a tax rate of 15%	
Related party transactions		All related party transactions must take place on an arm's length basis	
Tax year, return and payment		Calendar year or, if the taxpayer's financial year does not coincide, the financial year of 12 months ending during the relevant calendar year Returns to be filed within 3 months of financial year end This tax is paid in three payments (two instalments and the balance)	
Capital gains		Generally subject to standard corporate tax rate Calculation of capital gains on assets: net gains less a rebate of 33% if posted in fixed asset account over 5 years, and a rebate of 60% if posted in fixed asset account over 10 years	

Description \ Legal Form	Resident corporation	Permanent Establishment (PE)
Dividends	Dividends : 85% exemption if the dividends are distributed by a company subject to French Polynesian income tax (IS); 15% subject to corporate income tax (IS)	
	Dividends are subject to a Tax on distributed revenue (IRCM) of 10% and a Solidarity Tax (CST) of 5%. Paid by the distributing company	
Losses	Tax losses can be carried forward five years only	
	Amortization recorded in tax losses period can be carried forward indefinitely	
Tax group	Not applied in French Polynesia	

Tax rate	IS CSIS MCSIS	Standard rate between 25% and 35% according to the following ratio: C = (I + P) / R, where:
		  – I is the net value of intangible and tangible amortizable assets,
		  – P is personal cost deductible except personal cost for directors,
		  – R is taxable income,
		when:
		  – C > 5.5 tax rate is 25%
		  – 5 < C ≤ 5.5 tax rate is 26%
		  – 4.5 < C ≤ 5 tax rate is 27%
		  – 4 < C ≤ 4.5 tax rate is 28%
		  – 3.5 < C ≤ 4 tax rate is 29%
		  – 3 < C ≤ 3.5 tax rate is 30%
		  – 2.5 < C ≤ 3 tax rate is 31%
		  – 2 < C ≤ 2.5 tax rate is 32%
		  – 1.5 < C ≤ 2 tax rate is 33%
		  – 1 < C ≤ 1.5 tax rate is 34%
		  – C ≤ 1 tax rate is 35%
		The corporate tax cannot be lower than a fixed minimum tax (IMF) equal to 0.5% of the operating and financial revenue. In case of tax losses, IMF is equal to 0.25% of the operating and financial revenue
		The standard rate of the CSIS is:

Basis: taxable income	Rate
When tax income exceeds 50 MF CFP between FCFP0 and FCFP100,000,000	7%
Between FCFP100,000,001 and FCFP200,000,000	10%
Between FCFP200,000,001 and FCFP400,000,000	12%
> FCFP400,000,001	15%

During fiscal years as from ending 31 December 2013 until 31 December 2015

Additional contribution to the income tax (MCSIS): application of a single rate of 7% on the taxable income

Legal Form / Description		Resident corporation	Permanent Establishment (PE)
	IT	The standard rate varies as follows:	

The standard rate varies as follows:

- Service providers and professionals:

Basis	Rate
< FCFP5,500,000	1.5%
Between FCFP 5,500,001 and FCFP11,000,000	4%
Between FCFP 11,000,001 and FCFP 22,000,000	5%
Between FCFP 22,000,001 and FCFP 55,000,000	6%
Between FCFP 55,000,001 and FCFP 82,500,000	8%
> FCFP 82,500,000	11%

There are rebates for certain activities or when expenses, except management or directors' indemnity and transaction tax, amount to at least half (50%) of the revenue

- Traders:

Basis	Rate
< FCFP22,000,000	0.5%
between FCFP22,000,001 and FCFP44,000,000	1.5%
Between FCFP44,000,001 and FCFP88,000,000	2.5%
Between FCFP88,000,001 and FCFP220,000,000	3.5%
Between FCFP220,000,001 and FCFP330,000,000	4.5%
Between FCFP330,000,001 and FCFP550,000,000	6%
Between FCFP550,000,001 and FCFP825,000,000	7%
Between FCFP825,000,001 and FCFP990,000,000	8%
> FCFP990,000,000	9%

Legal Form / Description	Resident corporation	Permanent Establishment (PE)
Tax Shelter for investments	Firms which are liable to IS or IT and participate in investment programs in business sectors which are defined and agreed by the French Polynesian Government receive, under condition, a tax exemption The main conditions include the following: - Headquarters has to be based in French Polynesia - Business sectors are restricted - The agreement has to be delivered before beginning the investments - The investments have to be new 'property and equipment' - Investment amount requirement: defined by government and varies according to business sector - Delay: 12 months from the government's notification to begin the program and 36 months to finish the program from the government's notification - 2 tax schemes: directly by the firm or by indirect investor (the tax exemption will then be transferred back to the firm in a proportionate share) - Tax exemption imputation: tax credit is deducted from the tax IS or IT of the fiscal year with a limit of 50% of the tax due and following three years with the same limit of 50% → Updated by the law on 15 July 2014: Housing sector is no longer eligible for the tax shelter for investments for any agreement registered after 16 July	

III TAXES FOR INDIVIDUALS

<table>
<tr><td></td><td></td><td>**Residents**</td><td>**Non-residents**</td></tr>
<tr><td rowspan="9">Income Tax</td><td>General description</td><td colspan="2">No individual Income Tax but a Solidarity Tax: *Contribution sociale territoriale* (CST)</td></tr>
<tr><td>Taxable entities and taxable income</td><td colspan="2">French Polynesian income source only</td></tr>
<tr><td>Types of taxable income</td><td colspan="2">– Employment income
– Revenue providing from companies under IS scheme: Management income
– Revenue providing from companies under IT scheme: Turnover
– Dividends distributed by a company subject to French Polynesian income tax (IS)</td></tr>
<tr><td>Calculation of income</td><td colspan="2">Employment and management income : gross salary
Business income (turnover): same basis as IT
Dividends: Gross dividends</td></tr>
<tr><td>Tax return</td><td colspan="2">Monthly or quarterly on employment and management income
Yearly on turnover
Quarterly on dividends</td></tr>
<tr><td>Losses</td><td colspan="2">It is not possible to impute any losses on the calculation of income</td></tr>
<tr><td>Tax rates</td><td colspan="2">On employment and management income:</td></tr>
</table>

Basis	Rate
From FCFP0 to FCFP150,000	0.5%
From FCFP150,001 to FCFP250,000	3%
From FCFP250,001 to FCFP400,000	5%
From FCFP400,001 to FCFP700,000	7%
From FCFP700,001 to FCFP1,000,000	9%
From FCFP1,000,001 to FCFP1,250,000	12%
From FCFP1,250,001 to FCFP1,500,000	15%
From FCFP1,500,001 to FCFP1,750,000	18%
From FCFP1,750,001 to FCFP2,000,000	21%
From FCFP2,000,001 to FCFP2,500,000	23%
over FCFP2,500,000	25%

		Residents	**Non-residents**

Income Tax - *contd*		On business income:
		The standard rate varies for:
		  - Service providers and professionals:
		
		Basis — Rate
		< FCFP5,000,000 — 0.75%
		between FCFP5,000,001 and FCFP10,000,000 — 1.75%
		Between FCFP10,000,001 and FCFP20,000,000 — 2.25%
		Between FCFP20,000,001 and FCFP50,000,000 — 2.75%
		Between FCFP50,000,001 and FCFP75,000,000 — 3.5%
		> FCFP75,000,000 — 4%
		
		  - Traders:
		
		Basis — *Rate*
		< FCFP20,000,000 — 0.4%
		between FCFP20,000,001 and FCFP40,000,000 — 0.75%
		Between FCFP40,000,001and FCFP80,000,000 — 1%
		Between FCFP80,000,001 and FCFP200,000,000 — 1.25%
		Between FCFP200,000,001 and FCFP300,000,000 — 1.75%
		> FCFP300,000,000 — 2.25%
		On dividends: 5%	

		Residents	**Non-residents**
Capital Gains Tax (CGT)	General description	Capital gains tax	
	Taxable entities and chargeable assets	Immovable property or shares in property investment company (SCI) only Individuals only when not subject to IT taxation (property allocated to its activities)	
	Calculation of gain	Capital gains on immovable property or SCI shares: net gains less a rebate of 20% per year as from the fifth year of ownership	
	Tax return	Immovable property: on disposal	
	Losses	Not applied	
	Tax rates	Immovable property: rate of 20%	
	Others	Government intention to implement a distribution tax on capital gains on company shares but not in place yet	

		Domiciled	**Non-domiciled**
Inheritance Tax (IHT)		There is no inheritance tax Lifetime gifts tax when amount exceeds MFCP 50 Government intention to implement inheritance tax	

IV WITHHOLDING TAXES

Under domestic law	Payments to residents	Payments to non-residents
Dividends	IRCM + CST = 15%	IRCM + CST = 15%
Interest	IRCM + CST = 15%	IRCM + CST = 15%
Royalties and several disclosed activities and services such as management fees, technical fees	Nil	20%
On payments to artists and sportsmen	Nil	Nil

Reduced rate available under the relevant Double Taxation Treaty			
Country	Dividend	Interest	Royalties
France	The basis is split between both countries	Nil	Nil

V   INDIRECT TAXES

		Residents	Non-residents
Value Added Tax (VAT)	General description	Value added tax or TVA	
	Entities being obliged to levy VAT	Persons making taxable supplies of goods and services in the course of a business	
	Taxable activities	Unless expressly exempted, all sales of goods and services are taxable activities	
	Taxable activities – zero-rated (examples)	Exportations of goods and services	
	Exemptions (examples)	Banking and insurance services Building rental Medical supplies Some educational activities	
	Refund of VAT	Quarterly reimbursement possible if conditions are fulfilled	
	Tax liability	Supplier or provider of services established in French Polynesia	Payment of the VAT by the French Polynesian client for a supplier or a provider of service not established, nor registered in French Polynesia Otherwise by tax representative
	Tax rates	13% on services (10% before 1 October 2013) 16% on goods 5% reduced rate on specific goods and services listed	
	Administrative obligations	VAT registration directly by company	VAT registration directly by PE or tax representative
Real Property Taxes		10% of the rental value	
Stamp Duty		Various rates apply	
		Disposal on property average rate: 12%	

		Residents	Non-residents
Trading Licence	General description	Trading Licence (Patente)	
	Entities being subject to trading licence	Persons who exercise permanently or temporarily a non-salaried professional activity Apply to companies as well	
	Taxable activities	Unless expressly exempt, all non-salaried professional activities	
	Calculation	It consists of a fixed right and a proportional right. The amounts of the rights depend on the activity The standard right is around €250 but it can vary between €42 and €4,200 (Average is €840) The amount of the proportional right depends on the rental value of the premises and operating assets used for the business, and the value of the imported goods. The standard rate varies between 10% and 20% Plus €42 per staff member employed	
	Administrative obligations	Yearly basis statement	

Nexia International does not accept liability for any loss arising from any action taken, or omission, on the basis of this publication. Professional advice should be obtained before acting or refraining from acting on the contents of this publication. Membership of Nexia International, or associated umbrella organizations, does not constitute any partnership between members, and members do not accept any responsibility for the commission of any act, or omission to act by, or the liabilities of, other members.

Nexia International is the trading name of Nexia International Limited, a company registered in the Isle of Man. Company registration number: 53513C. Registered office: 2nd floor, Sixty Circular Road, Douglas, Isle of Man, IM1 1SA

Georgia

(Gela Mghebrishvili, Nexia TA LLC, gela.mghebrishvili@nexia.ge; info@nexia.ge)

I MAIN LEGAL FORMS

Legal form / Characteristics	Individual entrepreneur	General partnership (GP)	Limited partnership (LP)	Limited liability company (LLC)	Joint-stock company (JSC, corporation)	Cooperative
Partners/ shareholders	One	Two or more	Two or more	One or more	One or more	Two or more
• Restrictions	None	None	None	None	None	None
Directors	Private person	Director as appointed by general meeting of founders	Director as appointed by general meeting of founders	Director as appointed by general meeting of founders	Director as appointed by general meeting of founders	Director as appointed by general meeting of members
Establishment	Private person	Can be founded as new or created through restructuring				
Registration	National Agency of Public Registry of Ministry for Justice of Georgia ('the registration authority')					
Minimum capital	None	None	None	None	None	None

Legal form / Characteristics	Individual entrepreneur	General partnership (GP)	Limited partnership (LP)	Limited liability company (LLC)	Joint-stock company (JSC, corporation)	Cooperative
Liability	With all their assets for all obligations	Partners of a general partnership shall be jointly liable to creditors for the obligations of the company, ie each partner with all of its assets shall be directly and immediately liable. Any agreement between the partners to the contrary shall be void as to any third person	Personally liable partners ie the general partners (komplementars) of a limited partnership shall be jointly liable to creditors for the obligations of the company, ie each partner with all of its assets shall be directly and immediately liable. Any agreement between the partners to the contrary shall be void as to any third person Limited partners (komandits) of a limited partnership shall not be liable to creditors for the obligations of the company. Limited partners of a limited partnership shall be liable to creditors up to the full amount of their pledged contribution if such liability arises before having made the full contribution agreed upon among the partners	Partners of a limited liability company, and partners of a joint-stock company or cooperative shall not be liable to creditors for the obligations of the company. Partners of a limited liability company, and partners of a joint-stock company or cooperative shall be liable to creditors up to the full amount of their pledged contribution if such liability arises before having made the full contribution agreed upon among the partners		
Governance	Private person	General Meeting of Members, shareholders, Board of Directors			General Meeting of Members, shareholders, Board of Directors	General Meeting of Members, Board of Directors
Audit requirements	It is not mandatory	It shall be mandatory to perform an audit in an enterprise which, according to the Law of Georgia on Securities Markets, is publicly accountable, and the securities of which are able to be traded on a securities market, or in an enterprise licensed by the National Bank of Georgia, or in an enterprise whose number of partners exceeds 100				
Taxation	Private taxation	Corporate Taxation				

II   CORPORATION TAX

Legal form / Description	Resident corporation	Permanent establishment (PE)
General description	Corporate income tax	
Taxable entities	Any legal entity established in accordance with the legislation of Georgia and performing entrepreneurial activity or the entity which is managed in Georgia	PE located in Georgia
Taxable income	Worldwide income ONLY distributed as a dividend	Income from Georgian source, distributed to 'mother company'
Calculation of taxable profits	Taxable profit is a profit distributed as a dividend (except dividends distributed to Georgian legal entities). Taxable expenses are also expenses which are not related to economic activities OR are not documented	
Interest payments	No thin capitalization rule applies (3:1). Interest paid more than 24% a year will be treated as distribution of dividend and will be taxed accordingly (see above)	
Related party transactions	All related party transactions must take place on arm's length basis (except transactions between legal entities)	
Tax period, return and payment	Tax period is calendar month Tax return should be submitted and final tax payments should be made no later than the 15th of the following month after the end of a month	
Capital gains	There is no separate capital gains taxation in Georgia. Proceeds from the disposal of capital assets are included in the ordinary taxable income	
Losses	Losses generated before 1 January 2017 cannot be carried forward in 2017 or after	
Tax group	No	No
Tax rate	15%	15%

III TAXES FOR INDIVIDUALS

		Residents	Non-residents
Income Tax	General description	Natural persons shall be: a) citizens of Georgia b) foreign citizens c) Stateless persons A Georgian resident for the entire current tax year shall be a natural person who has actually stayed in the territory of Georgia for 183 or more days in any continuous 12-calendar-month period ending in that tax year, or a natural person who was in a foreign country in the public service of Georgia during that tax year. Georgian residency can be accorded to a high net worth individual under the procedure and conditions determined by the Minister for Finance and the Minister for Justice of Georgia, subject to exceptions. A high net worth individual shall be a person as defined by the Law of Georgia on Securities Market	
	Taxable entities and taxable income	Taxable entity – physical person Taxable income – worldwide income (NOTE: income not from Georgian source is tax exempt)	Taxable entity – physical person Taxable income – income generated from Georgian sources
	Types of taxable income	Gross income shall be income earned in any form and/or through any activity, namely: a) salary income b) income earned from economic activity, which is not related to employment c) other income not related to employment and economic activity	A non-resident's gross income shall consist of the income earned from a Georgian source
	Calculation of income	A resident natural person shall be subject to income tax with respect to his/her taxable income, which is the difference between the total income earned during a calendar year and deductions under the Code for that period	A non-resident natural person conducting business through a permanent establishment in Georgia shall be subject to income tax with respect to his/her taxable income, which is the difference between the total income earned during a calendar year from a Georgian source related to the permanent establishment and deductions under this Code for that period. The gross income of a non-resident natural person that is not related to his/her permanent establishment in Georgia shall be taxed under Article 134 of this Code at source without deductions, subject to exceptions

		Residents	**Non-residents**
Income Tax – *contd*	Tax year, tax assessment and tax payment	Tax return should be submitted and final tax payments should be made no later than 31 March after the end of a tax year. Enterprises and entrepreneur natural persons conducting economic activity shall transfer the amount of current taxes to the budget according to the annual tax of the last tax year, in the following amounts: a) by not later than 15 May – 25% b) by not later than 15 July – 25% c) by not later than 15 September – 25% d) by not later than 15 December – 25%	
	Losses	The excess of deductions over the gross income from economic activity not related to employment, received by an entrepreneur natural person shall not be deducted from the salary received by such person. It shall be carried forward for up to five years and shall be covered by the excess of gross income of future periods over deductions not related to employment	
	Tax rates	A natural person's taxable income shall be taxed at the rate of 20%	Income earned by a non-resident from a Georgian-based source that is not attributed to the non-resident's permanent establishment registered for tax purposes in Georgia shall be taxed at source without deductions at the following rates: a) dividends – 5% b) interest – 5% c) amounts paid by an enterprise, organization and/or entrepreneur natural person for international telecommunication services and international transport services – 10% d) income earned by non-resident subcontractors in conducting the oil and gas operations provided for by the Law of Georgia on Oil and Gas – 4% e) salary income – 20% f) lease service charges paid to a natural person – 20%
Capital Gains Tax (CGT)	General description	Assessed as part of ordinary income	
	Taxable entities and chargeable assets		
	Calculation of gain		
	Tax year, tax assessment and tax payment		
	Losses		
	Tax rates		

		Domiciled	Non-domiciled
Inheritance Tax (IHT)	General description	There is no inheritance tax	
	Taxable entities and chargeable assets		
	Calculation of charge		
	Taxable events		
	Allowances		
	Tax rates		

IV   WITHHOLDING TAXES

Under domestic law	Payments to residents	Payments to non-residents
Dividends	5%	5%
Interest	5%	5%
Royalties	No separate tax on Royalties	No separate tax on Royalties
On payments to artists and sportsmen	Monetary and other awards to sportsmen and their coaches for winning and/or taking podium places in Olympic Games, World and/or European Championships are tax exempt	

Reduced rate available under the relevant Double Taxation Treaty			
Country	Dividends	Interest	Royalties
Armenia	5%/10%	10%	5%
Austria	0%/5%/10%	0%	0%
Azerbaijan	10%	10%	10%
Belgium	5%/15%	10%	5%/10%
Bahrain	0%	0%	0%
Bulgaria	10%	10%	10%
China	0%/5%/10%	10%	5%
Croatia	5%	5%	5%
Czech Republic	5%/10%	0%	0%/5%/10%
Denmark	0%/5%/10%	0%	0%
Egypt	10%	10%	10%
Estonia	0%	0%	0%
Finland	0%/5%/10%	0%	0%
France	0%/5%/10%	0%	0%
Germany	0%/5%/10%	0%	0%
Greece	8%	8%	5%
Hungary	0%/5%	0%	0%
India	10%	10%	10%
Iran	5%/10%	10%	5%
Ireland	0%/5%/10%	0%	0%
Israel	5%	15%	0%
Italy	5%/10%	0%	0%
Kazakhstan	15%	10%	10%
Kuwait	0%/5%	0%	10%
Latvia	5%	5%	10%
Lithuania	5%/15%	10%	10%
Luxembourg	0%/5%/10%	0%	0%
Malta	0%	0%	0%
Netherlands	0%/5%/15%	0%	0%
Norway	5%/10%	0%	0%
Poland	10%	10%	10%
Qatar	0%	0%	0%
Romania	8%	10%	5%

Reduced rate available under the relevant Double Taxation Treaty			
Country	Dividends	Interest	Royalties
San Marino	0%	0%	0%
Serbia	5%/10%	10%	10%
Singapore	0%	0%	0%
Slovakia	0%	5%	5%
Slovenia	5%	5%	5%
Spain	0%/10%	0%	0%
Sweden	0%/10%	0%	0%
Switzerland	10%	0%	0%
Turkey	10%	10%	10%
Turkmenistan	10%	10%	10%
Ukraine	5%/10%	10%	10%
United Arab Emirates	0%	0%	0%
United Kingdom	0%/15%	0%	0%
Uzbekistan	5%/15%	10%	10%

Note: the above rates are only available provided the specific Treaty criteria are satisfied. It is possible that lower rates than those shown above may be available provided certain criteria are satisfied. As treaties will not be identical, guidance should be sought in all cases.

V   INDIRECT TAXES

		Residents	Non-residents
Value Added Tax	General description	Value added tax (VAT) is levied on the supply of goods and services and on the import of goods	
	Entities obliged to levy VAT	Any person who is or is to be registered as a VAT payer is regarded a taxable person. Companies and individuals are required to register for VAT if their taxable income exceeds GEL 100,000 for the previous 12 months	
	Taxable activities	• Supply of goods and/or services in the territory of Georgia within the scope of economic activity • If VAT registration is revoked – the balance of goods, for which the taxpayer has obtained a deduction • The use of buildings or structures of one's own production as a fixed asset • Receipt into individual ownership of goods or services from an enterprise and/or a partnership in return for an interest in property and/or registration of property shall be regarded as the supply of property by the partnership	
	Taxable activities – zero-rated (examples)	• Re-export or export of goods • Supply of goods and/or services intended for official use of foreign diplomatic and other equivalent missions, for the personal use of the diplomatic and administrative-technical personnel (including family members living with them) of such missions and the procedure for the use of which is determined by the Minister for Finance of Georgia • Carriage of goods placed under the export, re-export, outward processing or transit procedure and delivery of the services directly related to such carriage • Delivery of passenger and cargo transportation services and the services directly related to such transportation, provided that the point of departure or destination is located outside Georgia and a single transport document is drawn up in respect of such transportation	
	Exemptions (examples)	• supply of a land parcel • executing financial transactions and/or delivering financial services • delivery of medical services • educational services delivered by educational institutions	
	Refund of VAT	Usually within 3 months after deposit declaration (in some cases within one month)	
	Tax liability	Supplier of goods and services and importer are responsible for charging VAT	
	Tax rates	18%	
	Administrative obligations	Monthly declaration	

	Residents	Non-residents
Real Property Taxes	Annual tax rates are determined by resolutions of the local government and may be different in each administrative area A property tax payer shall be: – a resident enterprise/organization – on assets, uninstalled equipment, and unfinished construction registered on its balance sheet as fixed assets, as well as its leased property – non-resident enterprise – on property based in the territory of Georgia (including property based in the territory of Georgian transferred under a lease, rent, usufruct or any similar agreement) – a natural person: a) on any real estate (including unfinished construction, buildings or their parts), yachts (cutters), helicopters and airplanes owned by him/her b) on property received by him/her from a non-resident under a lease agreement c) in the case of carrying out economic activities, on assets, uninstalled equipment, and unfinished construction registered on his/her balance sheet as fixed assets, as well as his/her leased property	
Stamp Duty	none	

Germany

*(Heinrich Watermeyer, DHPG, Bonn, heinrich.watermeyer@dhpg.de;
Sten Guensel, EbnerStolz, Stuttgart, sten.guensel@ebnerstolz.de)*

I MAIN LEGAL FORMS

Legal form / Characteristics	Partnership (OHG) and Limited partnership (KG)	Private corporation (GmbH) and Public corporation (AG)
Partners/share-holders		
• Number	• Two or more	• One or more
• Restrictions	• No restrictions	• No restrictions
Directors	Management by partners	No restrictions
Establishment	No formal requirements	Notarial deed
Registration	Commercial Register	
Minimum capital	None, except some €500 for limited partners	€25,000 for GmbH[1] and €50,000 for AG
Liability	Unlimited for all partners of OHG and general partner of KG, limited for limited partner	Limited for all shareholders
Governance	• Partner • General meeting	• Managing director • Shareholders' (stockholders') meeting • Supervisory board additionally for AG
Audit requirements	Only if all general partners are corporations, especially in the case of GmbH (AG) & Co KG,[2] if two of the following criteria are met: • turnover more than €12.0m • total assets more than €6.0m • more than 50 employees	Yes, if two of the following criteria are met: • turnover more than €12.0m • total assets more than €6.0m • more than 50 employees

---

1 Foundation with €1 possible; several restrictions to be observed in that case.
2 A 'GmbH & Co KG' is a Limited Partnership, where the general partner is a GmbH; the limited partners may be individuals or corporations as well. A very common structure is the GmbH & Co KG with individuals as limited partners or even with only one limited partner being the only shareholder of GmbH. A variation is the 'AG & Co KG'.

Legal form \ Characteristics	Partnership (OHG) and Limited partnership (KG)	Private corporation (GmbH) and Public corporation (AG)
Taxation	Subject to trade tax, but not subject to income tax or corporate tax (transparent entity)[3]	Subject to trade tax and to corporate tax[4]
Usage	OHG not popular, KG popular as GmbH + Co KG, especially for SMEs	GmbH popular, especially for SMEs, AG legal form for listed companies; not popular for others

---

3 Partners are subject to income tax or corporate tax on their profit shares.
4 Dividends distributed to individuals subject to a flat tax of 25% plus solidarity surcharge of 5.5% or to income tax (if shares are, eg, trade assets) on 60% of dividends (part-income-system); dividends distributed to corporations 95% tax-free if participation at least 10% at the beginning of the calendar year; some special rules for deemed retroactive acquisition in place, see also footnote 6.

II CORPORATION TAX

	Resident corporations		Special rules for non-resident corporations
	Corporate tax	**Trade tax**	
General description	Federal tax on income of corporations	Municipal tax on business income	No special rules
Taxable entities and taxable income	Corporations with seat and/or place of management and control in Germany: worldwide income	Business income of PEs located in Germany	Corporations with German income (especially from German PE)
Calculation of income	Profit of commercial accounts +/– results deriving from different rules for tax balance sheet[5] +/– other differences[6] = income for corporate tax purposes	Income for corporate tax purposes +/– adjustments[7] = income for trade tax purposes	AOA (Authorized OECD Approach) to be observed for PE profit-calculation; tax treaty rules overriding AOA depending on double taxation treaty; special proofs of taxpayer necessary to avoid double taxation
Interest payments	Restrictions by so-called 'Zinsschranke'. Generally, only 30% of tax EBITDA (Earnings Before Interest, Taxes, Depreciation and Amortisation) is deductible if interest payments minus interest earnings exceed €3m (not only the exceeding amount). Certain exceptions apply. Non-utilized positive EBITDA can be carried forward for five years; non-deductible interest can be carried forward for an unlimited period of time. Restrictions may apply, eg in case of reorganisation	So-called 'Zinsschranke' as in case of corporate tax applicable. If no restrictions by 'Zinsschranke', only 75% interest on all kinds of debt financing deductible	No special rules
Related party restrictions	To be at arm's length; special documentation requirements for cross-border transactions; AOA to be observed for PE profit calculation inbound and outbound		No special rules
Tax year and tax payment	Tax year – calendar year or different business year Tax return Quarterly prepayments, final payment or refund after tax assessment		No special rules in case of a PE; flat tax in some other cases (sec 2 no 2 CTA)

Taxes on Income

5 Examples: special liabilities/accruals, see s 5 para 2a subs. Income Tax Code.
6 Examples: 95% exemption for dividends (minimum participation of 10% at beginning of the calendar year required, some special rules for deemed retroactive acquisition in place) and capital gains, no deductibility of losses deriving from the sale and write down of shares. Gifts and entertaining expenses are only partly deductible.
7 Examples: part of interest, rental, lease, licence and fee payments; 95% dividend exemption (minimum participation of 15% [domestic and non-EU] or 10% [EU] at the beginning of the calendar year required).

Taxes on Income – contd			
Capital gains	Taxable at regular rates (no special capital gains tax) Capital gains on disposal of shares normally 95% tax-free		No special rules
Losses	• One year carry back (maximum €1.0m) • Carry forward may be offset against profits up to €1.0m, exceeding amount by 60%[8]	• No carry back • Carry forward may be offset against profits up to €1.0m, exceeding amount by 60%	No special rules
	Carry forward lost in case of direct or indirect share transfer: • of more than 25% during a 5-year period – lost quotally • of more than 50% during a 5-year period – lost completely[9]		No special rules
Tax group • Prerequisites • Consequences	• More than 50% shareholding of business company in corporation plus profit and loss absorption agreement • Consolidation of profits and/or losses; special rules in case of (double) utilization of German losses (domestic and in foreign state) to be observed		No cross-border tax consolidation; consolidation possible with German PE of non-resident corporation if shareholding in German corporation is allocated to German PE and profit taxable in Germany; special rules in case of losses
Tax rate	15% + 5.5% solidarity surcharge = 15.83% Overall tax rate (%): – trade tax (levy rate = 400%) 14.00 – corporate tax/solidarity surcharge 15.83 = 29.83	Normally 14%–17%, depending on levy rate of municipality	None, except in case of sec 2 no 2 CTA
Solidarity surcharge	Federal tax of 5.5% of corporate tax (included above)		
Wealth tax	No wealth tax is levied		
Real property tax	• Local tax, paid by the owner of real estate • Approximately 1% per year of value of real estate as per 1964, final tax burden depending on levy rate of respective municipality		No special rules

8   No time limit for loss carry forward.

9   Preservation of losses under special circumstances (i) in the case of intra-group transactions (holding privilege), and (ii) as far as hidden reserves in assets of the loss corporation would be subject to tax in Germany; special restructuring clause not applicable due to EU challenge. Loss preservation rules in special cases for venture capital participation.

III   TAXES FOR INDIVIDUALS

Individuals pay trade tax on their business income. The rules are nearly the same as for corporations (see II above).

		Residents	**Non-residents**
Income Tax	General description	Federal tax on income of individuals	
	Taxable entities and taxable income	Individuals with residence or habitual abode in Germany: worldwide income	Individuals with neither residence nor habitual abode in Germany: domestic income (eg from real estate or PE located in Germany)
	Types of taxable income	• Trade income • Professional income • Rural income • Employment income • Capital income • Rental income • Certain other income	
	Calculation of income	• Trade income: accrual basis (AOA as in case of corporations applicable for inbound and outbound PE); small businesses: cash basis • Rural income: special method • Other types of income: cash basis	
	Tax year, tax assessment and tax payment	Tax year = calendar year (business year for business income) Tax return; joint tax return for spouses possible Quarterly prepayments, final payment or refund after tax assessment	Normally no tax assessment in case of withholding taxes (eg on dividends, on employment income) No joint tax return for spouses (exceptions for EU nationals)
	Capital gains	• No special capital gains tax but included in income tax	
		• Taxable: capital gains on shares	• Taxable: capital gains on shares (seat and or place of management/control is in Germany)
		• 60% tax exempt (part-income system), regular tax rate • If shareholding does not reach 1% during any point of time of 5 years before disposal: 100% taxable but flat tax of 25% plus solidarity surcharge of 5.5% leading to 26.38%	
	Losses	See I above (corporate tax) In case of joint assessment of spouses: loss carry back and loss carry forward may be offset against profits up to €2.0m, exceeding amount in case of loss carry-forward by 60%	Usually no joint assessment of spouses
	Tax rates	• Personal allowance (tax-free earnings): €8,820 (€17,640 for spouses)	• Usually no joint assessment of spouses • No personal allowance (tax-free earnings)
		Progressive tax rate from 14% to 45%[10]	
		Flat tax of 25% for capital income	

10 Highest marginal tax rate for business, rural and professional income: 42% + 5.5% × 42% solidarity surcharge = 44% for income exceeding €53,665 (€107,330 for spouses); highest marginal tax rate for income exceeding €254,446 (€508,892 for spouses): 45% + 5.5% × 45% = 48%; special tax rate of 28.25% for retained earnings derived from agriculture/forestry, business and self-employment with a deferred taxation of 25% in case of distribution/withdrawal.

Solidarity surcharge		Federal tax of 5.5% of income tax	
Capital Gains Tax	General description	No special tax Capital gains may be subject to income tax (see above)	
		Residents	**Non-residents**
Inheritance Tax and Gift Tax	General description	Federal tax for recipients of inheritances and lifetime gratis conveyances	
	Taxable events	Inheritances or lifetime gifts of net assets located worldwide	Inheritances or lifetime gifts of assets located in Germany (real estate, PE, shares in German corporations with minimum quota of 10%). If the successor or donor is resident in Germany: assets located worldwide
	Valuation	• Normally market value • Special valuations for real estate, businesses and non-quoted shares[11]	
	Allowances	• €500,000 for spouse • €400,000 per child • Minor amounts for others	• €2,000 in any case[12]
	Tax rates	7%–30% for children and spouses (higher rates for others)	
Wealth tax		No wealth tax is levied	
Real property tax		See II above	
Church tax		For members of catholic or protestant church 8%–9% of income tax, deductible for income tax purposes	

11 Special discount for business assets in place but challenged by Federal Tax Court and the Federal Constitutional Court. This remained applicable until 30 June 2016. Revised rules apply as of 1 July 2016.
12 For EU inhabitants, election to be taxed as unlimited tax liable person, despite this not being in line with EU law (see Tax Court Düsseldorf, 4 K 488/14 Erb).

IV WITHHOLDING TAXES

Under Domestic Law	Payments to residents	Payments to non-residents
On employment income (wage tax)	Wage tax bracket only for singles; for married special wage tax bracket (upon choice)	Only wage tax bracket for singles[13]
On dividends	25% + 5.5% solidarity surcharge of 25% = 26.38%	• 25% + 5.5% solidarity surcharge of 25% = 26.38%[14] • 15% + 5.5% solidarity surcharge of 15% = 15.83% in case of a foreign corporate entity (s 44, para 9, Income Tax Act)
On interest paid by banks	25% + 5.5% solidarity surcharge of 25% = 26.38%[15]	Usually n/a
On royalties	n/a	15% + 5.5% solidarity surcharge of 15% = 15.83%[15]
On payments to artists and sportsmen	n/a	15% + 5.5% solidarity surcharge of 15% = 15.83%[16]

Reduced rate available under the relevant Double Taxation Treaty			
Country	Dividends (%)	Interest (%)	Royalties (%)
Algeria	15/5	10	10
Armenia	15/15	5	0
Argentina	15/15	15	15[17]
Albania	15/5	5	5
Australia[18]	15/5	10	5
Austria	15/5	0	0
Azerbaijan	15/5	10	10[19]
Bangladesh	15/15	0	10
Belarus	15/5	5	3
Belgium	15/15	15	0
Bolivia	10/10[20]	15	15
Bosnia-Herzegovina[21]	15/15[22]	0	10
Bulgaria	15/5	5	5
Canada	15/5	10	10[23]
China	10/5	10	10[24]

13 Exceptions for EU residents.
14 Possibly reduced by Tax Treaty or Parent-Subsidiary Directive within the EU.
15 Possibly reduced by Tax Treaty or Interest and Royalty Directive within the EU.
16 Possibly reduced by Tax Treaty.
17 Government approval of the respective contract required; if not: unlimited (national) withholding in Argentina.
18 Decrease of withholding tax on dividends to 0% if special circumstances are met.
19 For Know-how, patents, trademarks etc 5%.
20 From Germany to Bolivia; from Bolivia: 15%.
21 Tax treaty with former Yugoslavia is applicable.
22 No treaty provision for dividends from Bosnia-Herzegovina to Germany.
23 Decrease to 0% for copyright (not incl films for cinema and television), computer software, industrial, commercial or scientific experience.
24 7% for commercial, technical or scientific equipment.

Reduced rate available under the relevant Double Taxation Treaty			
Country	Dividends (%)	Interest (%)	Royalties (%)
Croatia	15/5	0	0
Cyprus	15/5	0	0
Czech Republic	15/5	0	5
Denmark	15/5	0	0
Ecuador	15/15	15[25]	15
Egypt	15/15	15	25[26]
Estonia	15/5	10	10[27]
Finland	15/5	0	5[28]
France	15/5[29]	0	0
Georgia	10/10[30]	0	0
Ghana	15/5	10	8
Greece	25/25	10	0
Hungary	15/5	0	0
Iceland	15/5	0	0
India	10/10	10	10
Indonesia	15/10	10[31]	15[32]
Iran	20/15	15	10
Ireland	15/5	0	0
Israel	25/25	15	0[33]
Italy	15/15	10[34]	5[28]
Ivory Coast	15/15	15	10
Jamaica	15/10	12.5[35]	10
Japan	15/15[36]	10	10
Kazakhstan	15/5	10	10
Kenya	15/15	15	15
Korea	15/5	10	10[37]
Kuwait	15/5	0	10
Kyrgyzstan	15/5	5	10
Latvia	15/5	10	10[37]
Liberia	10/15	20[38]	20[39]

25 10% in special cases, eg bank loan.
26 For trademarks, others: 15%.
27 5% for commercial, technical or scientific equipment.
28 0% for copyright (incl. television and broadcasting).
29 Dividends from Germany to France; from France to Germany: 0%.
30 Decrease to 5% or 0% depending on percentage of shareholding and amount of investment.
31 For special public loans: 0%.
32 Decrease to 10% for commercial, trade or scientific equipment, to 7.5% for technical services.
33 5% for patents, trademarks, know-how, films for cinema and television, commercial, trade or scientific equipment.
34 Special exemptions (to 0%) applicable.
35 Payments to banks: 10%.
36 From Japan to Germany: 15/10%.
37 Decreased rate in case of trade, commercial or scientific equipment.
38 Payments to a bank: 10%.
39 In special cases, 10% applicable.

Reduced rate available under the relevant Double Taxation Treaty			
Country	Dividends (%)	Interest (%)	Royalties (%)
Liechtenstein	10/0	0	0
Lithuania	15/5	10	10^{40}
Luxembourg	15/5	0	5
Macedonia	15/5	5	5
Malaysia	15/5	10	0^{41}
Malta	15/5	0	0
Mauritius	15/5	0	10
Mexico	15/5	10^{42}	10
Moldova	15/15	5	0
Mongolia	10/5	10	10
Morocco	15/5	10	10
Namibia	15/10	0	10
Netherlands	15/5	0	0
New Zealand	15/15	10	10
Norway	15/0	0	0
Pakistan	15/10	20^{43}	10
Philippines	15/10	15^{44}	10
Poland	15/5	5	5
Portugal	15/15	15^{45}	10
Romania	15/5	3	3
Russian Federation	15/5	0	0
Serbia & Montenegro[46]	$15/15^{47}$	0	10
Singapore	15/5	8	8
Slovakia[48]	15/15	0	5
Slovenia	15/5	5	5
South Africa	15/7.5	10	0
Spain	15/5	0	0
Sri Lanka	15/15	10	10
Sweden	15/0	0	0
Switzerland	15/0	0	0
Syria	10/5	10	12
Taiwan[49]	10/10	10	10
Tajikistan	15/5	0	5
Thailand	20/15	25^{50}	15^{51}

40 Decreased rate in case of trade, commercial or scientific equipment.
41 7% for technical services.
42 Bank loan: 5%.
43 Payments to a bank: 10%.
44 Decrease to 10% in special cases, eg public loans.
45 Payments to a bank: 10%.
46 Tax treaty with former Yugoslavia is applicable.
47 No treaty provisions for dividends from Serbia and Montenegro to Germany.
48 Tax treaty with Czech Republic (as identical) applicable.
49 Tax treaty concluded by Taipei, applicable since 2013.
50 Payments to a bank: 10%.
51 Decrease to 10% in case of literature, artist or science.

Reduced rate available under the relevant Double Taxation Treaty			
Country	Dividends (%)	Interest (%)	Royalties (%)
Trinidad and Tobago	20/10	15[52]	10[53]
Tunisia	15/10	10	15[54]
Turkey	15/5	10	10
Turkmenistan	15/15	5	0
Ukraine	15/5	5[55]	5[56]
United Kingdom	15/5	0	0
Uruguay	15/5	10	10
United Arab Emirates	10/5	0	10
United States of America	15/5[57]	0	0
Uzbekistan	15/5	5	3
Venezuela	15/5	5	5
Vietnam	15/10/5	10	10
Zambia	15/5	10	10
Zimbabwe	20/10	10	7.5

Note: the above rates are only available provided the specific treaty criteria are satisfied. As treaties will not be identical, guidance should be sought in all cases.

• Different treaty tax rates for: dividends from intercorporate capital holdings/ dividends from diversified holdings.
• Different rates may apply for copyright royalties for literary, dramatic, musical and artistic work.

There are several rules and exemptions regarding the levels of these withholding taxes.

52 Payments to a bank: 10%.
53 0% for copyright (excl. cinema, television and broadcasting).
54 Decrease to 5% in case of literature, artist or science.
55 Decrease to 2% in special cases, eg payments to banks.
56 Decrease to 0% for rights in literature, patents, brands, know-how, trade/ commercial and scientific experience.
57 Decrease to 0% if special preconditions are met.

V INDIRECT TAXES

		Residents	Non-residents
Value Added Tax (VAT)	General description	Tax on the supply of goods and services, imports and others	
	Entities obliged to levy VAT	• Any individual, partnership, corporation or other body, which carries out economic activities • On request no VAT, if turnover does not exceed €17,500 in the preceding year and €50,000 in the current year	
		• Fiscal unity, if entrepreneur owns more than 50% of shares in subsidiary and if certain other conditions are met[58]	• No fiscal unity
	Taxable activities	Supply of goods and services, import of goods, intra-Community acquisition of goods, use of goods and services by entrepreneur or staff Place of delivery or rendering of service must be in Germany	
	Exemptions (examples)	• Lease of premises (in certain cases allowed to opt for VAT) • Bank and insurance services • Exports and supply of services in EU member state • Certain hospital and medical care services	
	Refund of VAT	VAT on supplies and services paid by an entrepreneur is deductible as input tax, if supply or service was for taxable supplies and services of his enterprise No credit for input tax paid on tax-exempt supplies and services (main exceptions: input tax for exports and delivery of goods within the EU)	Special refund system for non-resident enterprises with no taxable supplies in Germany
	Tax liability	• Normally supplier of goods and services • Reverse charge for certain supplies of goods and services (eg real estate)	
	Tax rates	• Regular rate = 19% • Reduced rate = 7%[59]	
	Administrative obligations	• Formal requirements concerning business records and invoices • Monthly tax self-assessments plus annual tax return (smaller companies quarterly or no self-assessments) • VAT identification number	• Registration for VAT purposes, if rendering of supplies and services in Germany • Fiscal representation possible but not obligatory
Real Property Tax		• Levied by cities at varying rates; special tax exemptions apply	
Real Property Transfer Tax		• Transfer of real estate located in Germany; transfers of shares in corporations as well as participations in partnerships owning real estate, if at least 95% of shares are transferred (certain exemptions apply; for group structures, holding privilege available) • Regular tax rate = 3.5%, but effective tax rate varies from state to state[60]	

58 Due to EU jurisdiction and subsequent jurisdiction of the Federal Tax Court, a partnership can be a controlled entity in a VAT fiscal unity under special circumstances (Federal Tax Court, 2.12.2015, V R 67/14, V R 15/15 and V R 25/15).

59 For food, books, certain medical and cultural goods, etc.

60 4.5% in Hamburg; 5% in Baden-Württemberg, Brandenburg, Bremen, Mecklenburg-Vorpommern, Lower-Saxony, Rheinland-Pfalz, Saxony-Anhalt, Thüringen; 6% Berlin and Hessen; 6.5% Northrhine-Westfalia, Saarland and Schleswig-Holstein.

Nexia International does not accept liability for any loss arising from any action taken, or omission, on the basis of this publication. Professional advice should be obtained before acting or refraining from acting on the contents of this publication. Membership of Nexia International, or associated umbrella organizations, does not constitute any partnership between members, and members do not accept any responsibility for the commission of any act, or omission to act by, or the liabilities of, other members.

Nexia International is the trading name of Nexia International Limited, a company registered in the Isle of Man. Company registration number: 53513C. Registered office: 2nd floor, Sixty Circular Road, Douglas, Isle of Man, IM1 1SA

Ghana

(K Manu-Debrah, Nexia Debrah & Co, debrah@nexiadebrah.com)

I MAIN LEGAL FORMS

Legal form / Characteristics	Partnership[1] and Limited Liability Partnership (LLP)	Private corporation (Ltd) and Public corporation (Plc)
Partners/shareholders • Number • Restrictions	A minimum of two and maximum of 20 partners No LLP under Ghana law[1]	• A minimum of one shareholder for Ltd and Plc • Maximum of 50 shareholders for Ltd • No restriction for Plc
Directors	N/A	A minimum of two directors for Ltd and Plc
Establishment	Partnership agreement or deed	Company Regulations (ie Memorandum or Articles of Association)
Registration	The Registrar General of Ghana is responsible for the registration of all partnerships and companies	
Minimum capital	None required by law	GH¢ 500
Liability	Unlimited liability and every partner is jointly and severally responsible for them	Liability limited to the value of any unpaid liability on issued shares
Governance	The Board (or Council) of Partners	The Board of Directors
Audit requirements	Audit not required by law	Audited accounts due by law not later than 6 months after every accounting year
Taxation	Transparent	Corporate income tax on worldwide profits

---

1   Under Ghanaian law, partnership firms are registered under the Incorporated Private Partnership Act 1962 (Act 152). The law considers partnership firms as a separate legal personality distinct from its owners. A change in the composition of partners does not therefore lead to the automatic dissolution of the firm, as is the case in some jurisdictions. Notwithstanding this, each and every partner of the firm is jointly and severally responsible for the liabilities of the firm.

II   CORPORATION TAX

Legal form / Description	Resident corporation	Permanent establishment (PE)
General description	Corporate income tax	
Taxable entities	Incorporated in the Republic of Ghana, or having its management and control exercised from within Ghana at any time during the year of assessment	PE located in Ghana, includes: • a business carried on through an agent or any such representative of independent status acting in the ordinary course of business in Ghana • a business having installed substantial equipment or machinery • having business operations in Ghana requiring more than 90 days to complete
Taxable income	Worldwide profits	Profits derived by a PE in Ghana
Calculation of taxable profits	All incomes/revenues accruing to the business less deductions allowable by law	
Interest payments	Debt-to-equity ratio should not exceed 3:1 Payment of interest to both resident and non-residents attracts 8% withholding tax on the gross amount	
Related party transactions	Related party transactions should be at arm's length rates	
Tax year, return and payment	The fiscal year in Ghana is January to December. Companies are expected to file their tax returns by the end of the fourth month after the end of their financial year, or by 30 April each year, whichever is earlier The filing requirements include a full set of audited financial statements together with the necessary forms disclosing relevant details about the earnings of the company for the tax year involved Tax payments are made on an advance quarterly instalment basis within the year based on a self-assessement estimate submitted by the tapayer to the Commissioner-General before the date of payment of the first instalment A final assessment is prepared after the filing of the audited accounts with the Ghana Revenue Authority, and any difference is either paid by, or refunded to, the tax payer	
Capital gains	Capital gains tax is now known as 'gain or loss from realisation of assets and liabilities' and is added to business income or investment income, as the case may be, and is taxed at the normal corporate tax rate	
Losses	All taxpayers can carry forward losses for a period of 3 years. Taxpayers within priority areas can carry forward losses for 5 years	
Tax group	N/A	
Tax rate	• General corporate tax rate – 25% • Companies engaged in mineral or petroleum operations – tax rate of 35% on chargeable income from such operations • Companies principally engaged in the hotel industry – tax rate of 22% • Company income from the export of non-traditional goods – tax rate of 8% • Manufacturing businesses located in regional capitals (except Accra and Tema) – tax rate equivalent to 75% of the corporate tax rate • Manufacturing businesses located outside the regional capitals – tax rate equivalent to 50% of the corporate tax rate	

III TAXES FOR INDIVIDUALS

		Residents	Non-residents
Income Tax	General description	Income tax is levied on the chargeable income of every chargeable person residing in Ghana in a year of assessment	
	Taxable entities and taxable income	Income derived from business, employment, or investments regardless of the source	Income derived from business, employment, or investments accruing in, derived from Ghana
	Types of taxable income	• Employment income • Income from business activities • Income from investments (eg interest, dividends, rent and royalties)	
	Calculation of income	All gains and receipts less standard deductions and personal reliefs applicable under the law	
	Tax year, tax assessment and tax payment	• Year of assessment is the calendar year from 1 January to 31 December • A return of income must be filed no later than 4 months after the end of a basis period. For employment income a fixed monthly Pay As You Earn (PAYE) regime is in place	
	Losses	None	
	Tax rates	*Income (Monthly)* *Rate (%)* First GH¢216.00 Nil Next GH¢108.00 5 Next GH¢151.00 10 Next GH¢2,775.00 17.5 Exceeding GH¢3,240.00 25.0	Flat rate of 20%

		Residents	Non-residents
Capital Gains Tax (CGT)	General description	Capital gains tax is now known as 'gain or loss from realisation of assets and liabilities' and is added to business income or investment income, as the case may be, and is taxed at the normal corporate tax rate Individuals can opt to pay at 15%	
	Taxable entities and chargeable assets	*Resident individuals* Chargeable assets: land and buildings in Ghana, businesses and business assets including goodwill, shares in companies, etc. Income derived from the realisation of assets brought into or received in Ghana	
	Calculation of gain	Gains and losses are calculated by deducting the net book value of the assets disposed off from the sales proceeds realised at the date of disposal	
	Tax year, tax assessment and tax payment	To file with returns	
	Losses	Losses can be carried forward for 3 years	
	Tax rates	15% on the capital gain (optional)	

		Domiciled	Non-domiciled
Inheritance Tax (IHT)	General description	Inheritance tax is not applicable in Ghana. However, a regime of gift tax is in operation in Ghana under which the value of gifts given beyond a certain limit is subject to gift tax at the rate of 15%. Exchange of gift between spouses, father and child or mother and child and vice versa is exempt from gift tax	

IV   WITHHOLDING TAXES

Under domestic law	Payments to residents	Payments to non-residents[2]
Dividends	8%	8%
Interest	8%	8%
Royalties	10%	15%
On payments to artists and sportsmen	7.5%	20% Subject to applicable international protocols

Reduced rate available under the relevant Double Taxation Treaty			
Country	Dividends	Interest	Royalties
Belgium	8%	8%	10%
France	8%	8%	12.5%
Italy	8%	Nil	Nil
South Africa	8%	8%	10%
United Kingdom	8%	8%	12.5%

Note: the above rates are only available provided the specific Treaty criteria are satisfied. It is possible that lower rates than those shown above may be available provided that certain criteria are satisfied. As treaties will not be identical, guidance should be sought in all cases.

---

2   Reduced rates of withholding tax may apply where there is an appropriate double tax treaty.

V INDIRECT TAXES

		Residents	Non-residents
Value Added Tax (VAT)	General description	VAT is imposed on every supply of goods and services and the supply of any imported service, other than exempt goods and services	
	Entities obliged to levy VAT	All registered businesses	
	Taxable activities	Any activity that terminates in the exchange of goods and services for valuable consideration and profit in the course of, or as part of, any business activity including without limitation the following: • processing of data or supply of information or similar service • delivery of accounting, legal, or other professional services given in an advisory capacity but excluding banking and insurance • leasing or letting of goods on hire	
	Taxable activities – zero-rated (examples)	Exports of taxable goods and services Exports of goods shipped as stores on aircraft and vessels leaving the territories of Ghana	
	Exemptions (examples)	Goods or services with exempt status include imports of commodities such as musical instruments, agricultural inputs like fertilisers, books, medical/surgical instruments and pharmaceutical products and related raw materials	
	Refund of VAT	Subject to certain conditions, VAT refunds may be paid by the commissioner of domestic tax revenue upon receipt of an application from a VATable entity within 30 days of the refund claim arising	
	Tax liability	The tax liability is the excess of output VAT over input VAT in any reporting period (ie a 30-day reporting cycle period)	
	Tax rates	VAT rate is 15% and a National Health Insurance Levy of 2.5% making a total of 17.5%	
	Administrative obligations	Returns should be filed on or before the last working day of the month following the month of transaction	
Real Property Taxes		This generally varies with the value and location of the property, as well as the local government authority involved	
Stamp Duty		It is levied at 0.5% of the face value of the transaction and payable on items such as stated capital on the incorporation of a company, as well as on the transfer of landed property	

Gibraltar

(Mark Benady, Benady Cohen & Co, mbenady@benadycohen.com)

I MAIN LEGAL FORMS

Legal form / Characteristics	Partnership and Limited Partnership (LP)	Private corporation (Ltd) and Public corporation (Plc)	Protected cell companies (PCC)	Experienced Investor Funds (EIF)
Partners/ shareholders • Number • Restrictions	• Two or more • Only LPs are restricted to no more than 20 partners	• One or more • Private corporations restricted to no more than 50 shareholders		• One or more • None
Directors	Management by partners or general partner for an LP	Management by directors		
Establishment	Partnership deed	Articles of Association	Articles of Association for insurance companies and collective investment schemes; consent and approval is required from the Financial Services Commission	
Registration	Gibraltar Companies House (and the Financial Services Commission for PCCs and EIFs)			
Minimum capital	None	None except £20,500 for Plcs		
		A European Public Liability Company (EPLC) or Societas Europaea (SE) requires issued share capital of €120,000		
Liability	Unlimited but limited partners of LP are limited to capital	Limited to capital	Limited to net assets of the cell and any non-cellular assets	Limited to capital
Governance	Partners, general meeting	Managing director/Board of Directors, secretary, shareholders' meeting		
Audit requirements	None	No audit required unless medium/ large-sized enterprise or if it is subject to taxation	Required	

Legal form / Characteristics	Partnership and Limited Partnership (LP)	Private corporation (Ltd) and Public corporation (Plc)	Protected cell companies (PCC)	Experienced Investor Funds (EIF)
Taxation	Partners are subject to Gibraltar income tax on their share of the profits Non-Gibraltarian resident partners are only taxed on Gibraltar sourced income	Only corporation tax is charged and only on Gibraltar sourced income Most investment income and capital gains are exempt		Tax transparent
Uses	Varied including professional and financial organisations	Small and medium-sized enterprises. Plc used for larger companies EPLCs allow EU companies to merge into one entity while avoiding legal and practical constraints	Insurance companies and collective investment schemes	

II CORPORATION TAX

Description \ Legal form	Resident corporation	Permanent establishment (PE)
General description	Gibraltar companies are subject to corporation tax only (see IV Withholding Taxes below)	
Taxable entities	• Companies are subject to corporation tax on Gibraltar sourced income • Investment income and capital gains are exempt subject to tax on intercompany loan interest in certain circumstances (see below)	
Taxable income	• Profits from Gibraltar activities after deduction of all expenses which are wholly and exclusively incurred in the production of income • As from 1 July 2013, loan interest in excess of £100,000 per annum received from a particular company (or connected companies) will also be subject to tax	
Calculation of taxable profits	Accounting profit is adjusted for various tax add-backs and allowances to arrive at profits chargeable to income tax	
Interest payments	Interest expenses for trading companies are fully tax deductible assuming they are at arm's length	
Related party transactions	All related party transactions must take place on arm's length basis	

Tax year, return and payment	• The tax year or the year of assessment for corporation tax purposes follows the financial year end
	• A tax return should be completed and submitted by nine months following the year end. The filing requirements are as follows:
	  ○ For a 'Large Sized Company' with no Assessable Income – Tax Return and Audited accounts
	  ○ For a 'Medium Sized Company' with no Assessable Income – Tax Return and Audited accounts, but P&L can be in abridged form
	  ○ For a 'Small Sized Company' with no Assessable Income – Tax Return and an abridged Balance Sheet only
	  ○ For any Company with Assessable Income up to £1,249,999 – Tax Return and unaudited accounts containing Independent Accountant's report
	  ○ For any Company with Assessable Income over £1,250,000 – Tax Return & Audited accounts
	• Payments on account due by 28 February and 30 September, with balancing payments due nine months after accounting year end	

Capital gains	There is no capital gains tax	
Losses	Trading losses of a company may be offset against any other income in the tax year of the loss or carried forward and offset against future income of the same trade	
Tax rate	• The standard rate of corporation tax is 10% • Certain utility and energy providers and companies that abuse a dominant position pay at a rate of 20%	
Gaming tax	Levied at 1% of the relevant income on online gaming activities. Capped at £425,000 and a minimum of £85,000 per annum	

III   TAXES FOR INDIVIDUALS

<table>
<tr><td colspan="2"></td><th>Residents</th><th>Non-residents</th></tr>
<tr><td rowspan="7">Income Tax</td><td>General description</td><td colspan="2">Tax levied on the chargeable income of a chargeable person for a year of assessment</td></tr>
<tr><td>Taxable income</td><td>Gibraltar residents are taxed on their worldwide income with relief for double taxation

There are special categories of individuals who have the tax capped, eg Category 2 (High Net Worth Individuals) pay a maximum tax of £27,560 and a minimum of £22,000 on worldwide income and similarly High Executives Possessing Specialist Skills (HEPPS) who are capped at £29,940 per annum</td><td>Permitted individuals (non-residents who work in Gibraltar) are liable to taxation on their Gibraltar income only</td></tr>
<tr><td>Types of taxable income</td><td colspan="2">• Gibraltar Property income (overseas property income not taxable)
• Savings and investment income are not taxable
• Income from business activities
• Employment from personal services or pensions
• Income from trusts and estates received in Gibraltar
• Taxable income generated by a pension imported from another country (eg QROPS) will be taxable at a special rate of 2.5%</td></tr>
<tr><td>Calculation of income</td><td colspan="2">Generally, that received in the year less applicable personal allowances</td></tr>
<tr><td>Tax year, tax assessment and tax payment</td><td colspan="2">• Tax year – runs from 1 July to the following 30 June
• Tax assessment – individual returns and assessments for each taxpayer
• Returns must be filed by 30 November following the year of assessment
• Wages and salaries paid to employees are subject to tax deduction at source
• Payments on account (if applicable) due by 31 January and 30 June with balancing payment due by 30 November following tax year</td></tr>
<tr><td>Losses</td><td colspan="2">Losses created by trading activities can be offset against other income or carried forward against future profits</td></tr>
</table>

		Residents	Non-residents
Income Tax – *contd*	Tax rates	Income is either taxed using the Allowance Based System or the Gross Income Based Method *Allowance Based System* • 14% on first £4,000 (reduced rate) • 17% on next £12,000 (standard rate) • 39% thereafter (higher rate) Personal allowances are a minimum of £4,088 and include numerous allowances, such as mortgage interest and life insurance A tax credit of £300 minimum, or 2% of the tax payable *Gross Income Based Method* • 16% on first £17,000 • 19% on next £8,000 • 25% on next £15,000 • 28% on next £65,000 • 25% on next £395,0000 • 18% on next £200,0000 • 5% on balance GIB allowances of £5,000 for approved expenditure on premises enhancement in Gibraltar and up to £1,500 of mortgage interest. Up to £1,500 allowance for employee pension contributions and up to £3,000 for medical insurance Up to £3,000 for installation of solar energy boilers Tax rate applicable to trusts: 10%	Non-residents are taxed under the Allowance Based System applicable to residents, but may not receive any personal allowances and do not enjoy the reduced rate tax band
		Residents	**Non-residents**
Capital Gains Tax (CGT)	General description	There is no capital gains tax, estate duty tax or wealth or other capital taxes	
		Domiciled	**Non-domiciled**
Inheritance Tax (IHT)	General description	There is no inheritance tax in Gibraltar	

IV   WITHHOLDING TAXES

Under domestic law	Payments to residents	Payments to non-residents
Dividends	Nil	
Interest	Nil	
Royalties	Nil	

V INDIRECT TAXES

		Residents	Non-residents
Value Added Tax (VAT)	General description	No VAT in Gibraltar	
Stamp Duty		• Capital transactions are payable at a fixed rate of £10 (applicable to both share and loan capital) • On real estate: First- and second-time buyers – 0% up to £260,000 Otherwise: Up to £200,000 – 0% Between £200,001 and £350,000 – 2% on first £250,000 and 5.5% on balance Over £350,000 – 3% on first £350,000 and 3.5% on balance • Mortgages are subject to stamp duty at 0.13% (on mortgages not exceeding £200,000) or 0.2% (on mortgages exceeding £200,000)	

Greece

*(Eleni Kaprani, Certified Auditors Nexia – Eurostatus SA,
ekaprani@eurostatus-nexia.gr)*

I   MAIN LEGAL FORMS

Legal form / Characteristics	Partnership and Limited Liability Partnership (OE or EE in Greek) – Private Company (IKE)	Limited Liability Partnership (LTD)	Société Anonyme Company or Limited by Shares Liability Company (AE)
Partners/shareholders • Number • Restrictions	• Two or more – One or more for IKE • None	• One or more • None	• One or more • None
Directors	Management by one or more partners or appointed administrator(s)	Management by one or more administrator(s) appointed by the partners	Management by directors[1]
Establishment	Private document	Notarial deed	Notarial deed
Registration	Registered with the General Commercial Registry (GEMI)	Registered with the General Commercial Registry (GEMI)	Registered with the General Commercial Registry (GEMI)
Minimum capital	None	None	€24,000 divided into shares
Liability	• For OE unlimited for all partners • For EE unlimited for at least one partner • For IKE limited to capital contributions	Limited to subscribed capital	Limited to share capital

---

1   Private company must have at least three directors. As of 2008, a corporate entity can be appointed as director, with a representative thereof.

Legal form / Characteristics	Partnership and Limited Liability Partnership (OE or EE in Greek) – Private Company (IKE)	Limited Liability Partnership (LTD)	Société Anonyme Company or Limited by Shares Liability Company (AE)
Governance	Civil law, administrator(s), partners' meetings	Company Law 3190/55, administrator, partners' meeting. Decisions in partners' meetings require both majority in capital and majority in number of shareholders	Company Law 2190/20, Managing Director, Board of Directors, shareholders' meeting – corporate governance
Audit requirements	None, unless two of the following criteria apply: • turnover more than €8m • assets more than €4m • more than 50 employees	No audit unless two of the following criteria apply: • turnover more than €8m • assets more than €4m • more than 50 employees	None if Private, unless two of the following criteria apply: • turnover more than €8m • assets more than €4m • more than 50 employees
Taxation	Corporate tax	Corporate tax	Corporate tax

II CORPORATION TAX

Legal Form / Description	Resident corporation	Permanent establishment (PE)
General description	Corporate tax	Corporate tax
Taxable entities	Legal persons or entities incorporated or established under Greek Law, or having their registered address in Greece or legal persons and legal entities that have the effective place of management or control in Greece (excluding shipping companies)	PE located in Greece, foreign companies holding real estate in Greece
Taxable income	Worldwide profits	Profits triggered by PE in Greece, or holding and selling real estate in Greece
Calculation of taxable profits	Accounting Profit +/– temporary or permanent tax adjustments[2,3]	
Interest payments	• Deductible, if tested with the average interest rate published by Bank of Greece for interest on credit limits to non-financial corporations restrictions to be observed[3] • Thin capitalization is determined in relation to the taxable profits before interest, tax and depreciations (EBITDA)	
Related party transactions	Strict requirements for Transfer Pricing Documentation and annual disclosure to the tax authorities of a Summary Information with details on transactions (amounts, transaction type and documentation method) per related party	
Tax year, return and payment	Tax period coincides with the accounting period which is normally the calendar year (1 January – 31 December). Legal persons or entities with double-entry books can have their year ended on 30 June, or at any other date to follow the year end of their shareholder, if a foreign company participates with more than 50%. A company/corporate tax return is filed within 6 months after accounting year end	
	Company/corporate tax is paid upon filing, together with additional 100% of the tax as prepayment for next year. Tax can be paid in monthly instalments up to 8 months	
	The above percentage of prepayment is reduced to 50% for the newly established business	
Capital gains	Capital gains are treated as ordinary business profits and are taxed accordingly	

2 Expenses or purchase of goods, assets and services from companies established in 'black list' countries or countries with 'favourable tax regimes' are not tax deductible unless the company presents evidence that these represent actual business transactions and do not have the aim of tax avoidance or tax evasion.

3 No interest deduction in the case of acquisition of 'Black List' shares or in favourable tax regimes. 'Black list' countries are non-EU countries mentioned in the OECD List and those that have not signed with Greece and at least 12 other countries an Administrative Mutual Assistance Agreement. 'Favourable tax regimes' include EU countries and any other country where the transaction is not subject to or actually taxed or if the corresponding tax is less than 50% of the tax that would be due in Greece. For transactions with 'favourable tax regimes', the Greek company can prove that the transactions reflect actual and usual transactions and do not result in the transfer of profits, or income, or capital, with the aim to avoid or evade taxes in Greece.

Legal Form / Description	Resident corporation	Permanent establishment (PE)
Losses	Losses from foreign country sources can only be offset against income from foreign country sources. Current year trading losses can be offset against other current year profits	
	Losses exceeding trading losses can be carried forward and set off against profits of the subsequent 5 years, with some restrictions in the use of losses in case of change of ownership	
Tax group	Not allowed	
Tax rate	• 29%	

III TAXES FOR INDIVIDUALS

		Residents	Non-residents
Income Tax	**General description**	Tax levied on the chargeable income of a chargeable person for a year of assessment	
	Taxable entities and taxable income	Residents are liable to tax on their worldwide income. An individual is classified as a tax resident of Greece provided that a) he/she maintains in Greece his primary residence or habitual abode or the centre of his/her vital interests or b) he/she is physically present in Greece for a period exceeding 183 days during any 12-month period consecutively or sporadically for the fiscal year, during which the 12-month period is completed	Non-residents are liable to tax on their Greek source income. Non-resident status must be evidenced
	Types of taxable income	• Property income (usually rent) • Income from capital investment (interest, sale of goodwill, dividends, royalties, income from real estate) • Income from business activities • Capital gains	
	Calculation of income	• The net taxable income is determined after the deduction of certain allowances and expenses from the taxpayer's total income • Employees are taxed on the Pay as You Earn (PAYE) system[4] • The tax is calculated based on a tax scale which is amended regularly	
	Tax year, tax assessment and tax payment	• Tax year – calendar year • Tax assessment – individual self-assessment returns for each taxpayer • Individuals are assessed on income earned on different dates, according to the type of income, starting from January to December following the year of the corresponding income earned	
	Losses	Trading losses are carried forward for 5 years to be offset against profits	

4 PAYE withholding tax is calculated based on the applicable tax scale prevailing for the year. PAYE tax is withheld from the employee and it is the employer's obligation to pay it to the Tax Office every 2 months. Any penalties for late payment or non-payment of PAYE tax are imposed on the company.

		Residents					Non-residents	

Income Tax – *contd*

	Tax rates	A. TAX SCALE FOR INCOME FROM SALARIES, PENSIONS AND PERSONAL BUSINESS ACTIVITIES

Income Bracket (€)	Tax Rate	Scale Tax (€)	Total Income (€)	Total Tax (€)
≤20,000	22%	4,400	20,000	4,400
>20,000 ≤30,000	29%	2,900	30,000	7,300
>30,000 ≤40,000	37%	3,700	40,000	11,000
>40,000	45%			

B. TAX SCALE FOR INCOME FROM REAL ESTATE PROPERTY

Income Bracket (€)	Tax Rate	Scale Tax (€)	Total Income (€)	Total Tax (€)
≤12,000	15%	1,800	12,000	1,800
>12,000 ≤35,000	35%	8,050	35,000	9,850
>35,000	45%			

Income from dividends: 15%
Income from interest: 15%
Income from royalties: 20%
Any increase in assets deriving from an illegal or unjustified or unknown source or cause is considered as income from business and taxed at 33%

		Residents	Non-residents

Capital Gains Tax (CGT)

General description	Tax on increase in the value of asset between acquisition and disposal, not chargeable to income or corporate tax	
Taxable entities and chargeable assets	• Any person resident in Greece • Applicable to real estate located in Greece and participations in companies worldwide	Any person owning real estate or participating in Greece domiciled companies[5]
Calculation of gain	Real estate (including participation in entities attracting more than 50% of their value from real estate property in Greece): Sales price less acquisition cost with reductions based on the years of retention. The gain resulting from contract values is tested against minimum values based on site location and other characteristics of the real estate applicable at the time of sale and acquisition and the tax is calculated at the highest gain resulting Securities (including transfer of business as a going concern and transfer of participation in partnerships): Net sales price less net acquisition cost. In the case of non-public entities, the gain is tested against the value of the entity as calculated based on a formula depending on profits, equity and real estate assets of an enterprise and the tax is imposed on the higher gain resulting	

5 Double Tax Treaty to be observed.

		Residents	Non-residents
Capital Gains Tax (CGT) – *contd*	Tax year, tax assessment and tax payment	Capital Gains tax resulting from the transfer of real estate property is payable before the signing of the sales contract	
		Capital gains from the sale of securities are declared in the Annual Income Tax Return regardless of whether proceeds have been collected or not	
	Losses	Losses from transfer of securities are not deducted against other types of income, but they can be carried forward for 5 years to be set off against future capital gains from the same source. Losses from the transfer of real estate property are not deductible and cannot be carried forward	
	Tax rates	Real estate: 15%	
		Securities: 15%	
		The above rates are applicable on the condition that, based on the number of transactions during certain periods, the individual is not considered to exercise business, ie trade of real estate property or trade of securities	

		Domiciled	Non-domiciled
Inheritance Tax (IHT)	General description	Tax charged on a chargeable transfer of value made by a lifetime gift or estate on death	
	Taxable entities and chargeable assets	• The *movable and immovable estate* of the deceased or the donor is subject to taxation in Greece *if the assets are situated in Greece*, regardless of the nationality or residence of the deceased or the donor and the heirs or the beneficiaries • The *movable estate* (ie tangible and intangible assets other than real estate property such as cash, bank deposits, stocks, bonds, etc) *of Greek tax residents* situated abroad is subject to taxation in Greece • *Real estate situated abroad* is not taxed in Greece • The *movable estate of a foreign tax resident*, individual or legal entity situated abroad, which is donated to a Greek tax resident, is subject to taxation in Greece • Any *annuity* received by an heir, *from the estate of a Greek tax resident* is not subject to income tax, but is subject to inheritance tax at the time of the inheritance • The tax is calculated based on a tax scale, which is different, almost every year depending on the total value of the assets and the kinship between the deceased or the donor and the heir or the beneficiary. From the tax due in Greece, any relevant tax paid abroad, for the taxable assets, is deducted subject to certain conditions • If assets are situated in Greece, they are subject to taxation regardless of nationality of the deceased or beneficiaries • The movable estate of Greek tax residents situated abroad is subject to taxation in Greece	
	Calculation of charge	Value of estate less allowances	
	Taxable events	Gifts (money or assets) during life, inheritance	
	Allowances	Various allowances for primary residence based on family kinship	
	Tax rates	Tax rates vary between 0% and 40% depending upon total value of assets and the kinship between the deceased and the beneficiary	

IV   WITHHOLDING TAXES

Under domestic law	Payments to residents	Payments to non-residents
Dividends	15%	15%[6]
Interest	15%	15%[6]
Royalties	20%	20%[6]
On payments to artists and sportsmen or technical assistance /management fees	0% to entities or 20% to self-employed professionals	20%[6]

Reduced or maximum rate available under the relevant Double Taxation Treaty			
Country	Dividends	Interest	Royalties
Albania	5%	5%	5%
Armenia	10%	5%	5%
Austria	5% or 15%	10%	7%
Azerbaijan	8%	8%	8%
Belgium	5% or 15%	15%	5%
Bosnia-Herzegovina	5% or 15%	10%	10%
Bulgaria	10%	10%	10%
Canada	5% or 15%	10%	10%
China	5% or 10%	10%	10%
Croatia	5% or 10%	10%	10%
Cyprus	25%	10%	10% or Nil
Czech Republic	local	10%	10%
Denmark	38%	8%	5%
Egypt	10%	15%	15%
Estonia	5% or 15%	10%	10%
Finland	47%	10%	10%
France	local	10%	5%
Georgia	8%	8%	5%
Germany	25%	10%	Nil
Hungary	45%	10%	10%
Iceland	5% or 15%	8%	10%
India	local	local	local
Ireland	5% or 15%	5%	5%
Israel	local	10%	10%
Italy	15%	10%	5%
Korea	5% or 15%	8%	10%
Kuwait	5%	5%	15%
Latvia	5% or 10%	10%	10%
Lithuania	5% or 15%	10%	5% or 10%
Luxembourg	38%	8%	5% or 7%
Malta	5% or 10%	8%	8%
Mexico	10%	10%	10%
Moldova	5% or 15%	10%	8%

6   Reduced rates of withholding tax may apply where there is an appropriate double tax treaty or if the EC Parent-Subsidiary Directive applies.

Reduced or maximum rate available under the relevant Double Taxation Treaty			
Country	Dividends	Interest	Royalties
Morocco	5% or 10%	10%	10%
Netherlands	35%	8% or 10%	5% or 7%
Norway	40%	10%	10%
Poland	local	10%	10%
Portugal	15%	15%	10%
Qatar	5%	5%	5%
Romania	25%	10%	5% or 7%
Russian Federation	5% or 10%	7%	7%
San Marino, Republic of	5% or 10%	10%	5%
Saudi Arabia	5%	10%	10%
Serbia	5% or 15%	10%	10%
Slovakia	local	10%	10%
Slovenia	10%	10%	10%
South Africa, Republic of	5% or 15%	8%	5% or 7%
Spain	5% or 10%	8%	6%
Sweden	local	10%	5%
Switzerland	35%	7%	5%
Tunisia	35%	15%	12%
Turkey	15%	12%	10%
Ukraine	5% or 10%	10%	10%
United Arab Emirates	5%	5%	5%
United Kingdom	local	Nil	Nil
United States	local	Nil or local	Nil
Uzbekistan	8%	10%	8%

Local: domestic rates apply.

Note: the above rates are only available provided the specific Treaty criteria are satisfied and special DTT forms are obtained. It is possible that lower rates than those shown above may be available provided that certain criteria are satisfied. As treaties will not be identical, guidance should be sought in all cases.

V   INDIRECT TAXES

		Residents	Non-residents
Value Added Tax (VAT)	General description	Tax on the supply of goods and services (VAT)	
	Entities obliged to levy VAT	Any individual, partnership, corporation or other entity, which carries out economic activities	
	Taxable activities	Supply of goods and services, import of goods, intra-Community acquisition of goods, etc	
	Taxable activities – zero-rated (examples)	Export of goods and supply of certain services with another EU Member State, or abroad	
	Exemptions (examples)	• Transactions related to the lease of any property located in Greece or related to the sale of property built prior to 1 January 2006, or property subject to property transfer tax • Banking and insurance services • Educational supplies of services • Certain welfare services including hospital and medical care services only if they are rendered from State Hospitals and individual medical professionals	
	Refund of VAT	• VAT paid on supplies and services is deductible as input tax, if incurred in the course or furtherance of the business and for the purpose of executing taxable supplies (including zero-rated supplies) • There is no credit for input tax incurred which relates to the provision of exempt supplies Where mixed supplies occur (taxable and exempt supplies), subject to de minimis provisions, input tax must be apportioned and recovered according to a partial exemption method	• EC 8th Directive refund system for non-resident businesses established within the EU, providing its business is not otherwise required to be registered in Greece • Strict time-limits apply to claims
	Tax liability	Normally the supplier of goods and services is responsible for charging VAT	
	Tax rates	• Standard rate = 24% • Reduced rate of 13% for basic consumer goods • Reduced rate of 6% for books, newspapers, magazines and theatre tickets • Special reduced rates for certain Greek islands 4%–9%–17%	

			Residents	**Non-residents**
Value Added Tax (VAT) – *contd*		Administrative obligations	• Formal requirements concerning business records and invoices • Quarterly or monthly self-assessment VAT return plus quarterly or monthly payment of any VAT liability to Greek Tax Authorities • VAT groups not allowed • Certain arrangements may need to be disclosed • VAT identification number must be shown on all invoices issued EU Invoicing Directive must be adhered to	• Registration for VAT purposes, if making supplies of goods and services in Greece • Appointment of fiscal tax representative obligatory for non-EU providers • As from May 2013, self-registration is allowed for VATable entities established in an EU Member state
Real Property Taxes	Annual Real Estate Property Tax	General description	Holding of rights on 1 January each year (full ownership, bare ownership, usufruct, right of occupancy or use) in real estate property situated in Greece is subject to real property tax (ENFIA), regardless of the permanent residence of the entity or of the individuals	
		Tax rate for legal entities	The basic tax is calculated at fixed amounts per square meter (ranging from €2 to €13 per square metre for buildings and €0.0037 to €11.25 for land, depending on the location) multiplied by + or – coefficients depending on the type of right, age of building, location of the site and other characteristics. A supplementary tax is imposed on all real estate owned by legal entities at the rate of 5.5% of the objective tax value with certain exceptions depending on use of the real estate for certain business activities Property used for self-producing or carrying any type of business is no longer exempt from additional ENFIA and now taxed at the rate of 1%	
		Tax rates for individuals	The basic tax is calculated as above A supplementary tax is imposed on individuals owning real estate exceeding €300,000 in total, calculated at rates ranging from 0.0% up to 1.15% depending on the total objective tax value owned	
	Special annual real property tax		This is an additional tax imposed on the taxable value of real estate property situated in Greece, owned by legal entities established in non-EU countries or in countries with which Greece has not signed an Administrative Mutual Assistance Agreement. It is also imposed on any other private legal entity which holds real estate property in Greece, having commercial income less than real or imputed income from property and does not disclose the physical persons who are the beneficial owners of the company The tax rate is 15%	
Stamp Duty			Levied on transactions, which are not subject to VAT, or special transfer taxes, such as loans, credit facilities, rents, shareholders' deposits other than for capital increase or shareholders' withdrawals other than dividends, transfer of liabilities, etc The rate varies from 1.2%–3.6% according to the type of transaction	

Nexia International does not accept liability for any loss arising from any action taken, or omission, on the basis of this publication. Professional advice should be obtained before acting or refraining from acting on the contents of this publication. Membership of Nexia International, or associated umbrella organizations, does not constitute any partnership between members, and members do not accept any responsibility for the commission of any act, or omission to act by, or the liabilities of, other members.

Nexia International is the trading name of Nexia International Limited, a company registered in the Isle of Man. Company registration number: 53513C. Registered office: 2nd floor, Sixty Circular Road, Douglas, Isle of Man, IM1 1SA

Guatemala

(Marco Monterroso, mmonterroso@wgarciayasociados.com)

I MAIN LEGAL FORMS

Legal form / Characteristics	Partnership and Limited Liability Partnership (LLP)	Private corporation (Ltd) and Public corporation (Plc)
Partners/shareholders • Number • Restrictions	Partnership: No limit LLP: No limit	Private corporation (Sociedad Anonima (SA)) and Public Corporation: Minimum of 2 All shares must be nominative
Directors	Three as minimum (Board)	
Establishment	Articles of Incorporation (Código de Comercio)	
Registration	Partnership, LLP and SA: Before a Public Notary and then registered at Registro Mercantil Public Corporation: Are created by Decrees issued by the Congress	
Minimum capital	Partnership: Q5,000.00 minimum LLP: Q5,000.00 minimum	Q5,000.00 minimum
Liability	Partnership: Social obligations are guaranteed by a given capital and partners are only required to respond to the amount of their stock LLP: For social obligations, only assets of the company respond Both are limited to capital	Paid-in capital
Governance	• Board or only one Administrator A legal representative needs to be appointed	• Shareholders • Board or only one Administrator
Audit requirements	Partnership financial statements are required by Código de Comercio	Full accounting, not all companies are required by Sat (responsible for the tax system in Guatemala) to be audited Some public corporation are audited by Contraloría General de Cuentas
Taxation	Corporation tax on income from a source in Guatemala	Corporation tax on income from a source in Guatemala

II   CORPORATION TAX

Legal form / Description	Resident corporation	Permanent establishment (PE)
General description	Corporation tax	
Taxable entities	Anyone deriving Guatemalan sourced income	
Taxable income	Income from goods and services provided in Guatemala	
Calculation of taxable profits	• Gross income minus deductions (traditional method) • 7% over invoiced monthly	
Interest payments	Normally deductible for entities under Central Bank system	
Related party transactions	Since 1 January 2015, it is mandatory to present a study of transfer prices with related parties transactions	
Tax year, return and payment	The general tax year is from 1 January to 31 December of each year. Return and payment must be submitted no later than 31 March of the following year	
Capital gains	Current laws, starting 1 January 2013, provide for an applicable tax rate on capital from furniture and real estate and gains at 10%	
Losses	Losses other than capital losses may not be carried back or forward. Capital losses may only be offset by two years with capital gains	
Tax group	No consolidation is possible	
Tax rate	Companies are subjected to income taxes, known as the income on lucrative activities regime, with the rate of 25% There is also an optional simplified regime on income from lucrative activities with rates between 5% to 7%	

III   TAXES FOR INDIVIDUALS

<table>
<tr><td rowspan="9">Income Tax</td><td></td><td>Residents</td><td>Non-residents</td></tr>
<tr>
<td>General Description</td>
<td>Individuals residing in Guatemala and receiving income from labor under a dependency relationship

An individual who remains in the country for more than 183 days during the calendar year, although not continuously</td>
<td>Non-resident taxpayers who act with or without a permanent establishment in the country. Also any transfer or credit note to their headquarters abroad, without consideration by permanent establishments of non-resident entities in the country</td>
</tr>
<tr>
<td>Taxable entities and taxable income</td>
<td>Individuals and legal entities are taxable</td>
<td>Individuals and legal entities are taxable</td>
</tr>
<tr>
<td>Types of taxable income</td>
<td colspan="2">Every kind of income derived from any source

A very extensive definition of income has been traditionally taken by the Tax Authorities</td>
</tr>
<tr>
<td>Calculation of income</td>
<td colspan="2">• Income on lucrative activities regime
• Optional simplified regime on income from lucrative activities
• Labor under a dependency relationship</td>
</tr>
<tr>
<td>Tax year, tax assessment and tax Payment</td>
<td colspan="2">Three months after taxation year-end is the deadline to file tax returns</td>
</tr>
<tr>
<td>Losses</td>
<td colspan="2">Losses, other than capital losses may not be carried back or forward. Capital losses may only be offset by two years with capital gains</td>
</tr>
<tr>
<td>Tax rates</td>
<td colspan="2">With permanent establishment:
• Income on lucrative activities regime, with the rate of 25%
• Optional simplified regime on income from lucrative activities with rates of 5% to 7%
• Personal tax: Dependency relationships (only residents)</td>
</tr>
<tr>
<td></td>
<td colspan="2">

Taxable base Fixed tax amount	Marginal rate on excess	(GTQ)
0.01 to 300,000	0	5%
Over 300,000	15,000	7%

*Fixed amount of 15,000 plus 7% on the surplus of 300,000</td>
</tr>
<tr>
<td></td>
<td></td>
<td>While not fulfilling the conditions to be classified as a Guatemalan resident, non-resident taxed at 15%, as specified in tax rates for non-residents without a permanent establishment. The taxable income is constituted by the amount that had been paid or credited into account</td>
</tr>
</table>

		Residents	**Non-residents**
Capital Gains Tax (CGT)	General description	Obtaining capital income and the realization of capital gains and losses, in cash or in kind arising from assets	
	Taxable entities and chargeable assets	• Revenue from capital • Revenue from real estate other than trading in such goods	
	Calculation of gain	• Income from capital: consists of the income generated in cash or in kind, unless specifically exempt income from capital • Income from real estate: the income is generated in cash or in kind less 30% of that income deducted as expenses, unless proven otherwise Otherwise the gain is calculated as the price of the sale of the property or rights less the cost of goods recorded in accounting books	
	Tax year, tax assessment and tax payment	Capital gains must be paid within 10 days of the end of the month immediately following	
	Losses	Can be offset against future capital gains, up to a maximum of two (2) years from the time the loss occurred	
	Tax rates	Current laws, starting 1 January 2013, provide for an applicable tax rate on capital from furniture and real estate and gains at 10%	Current laws, starting 1 January 2013, provide for an applicable tax rate on capital from furniture and real estate and gains at 10%, royalties at 15%, and payments to artists and sportsmen at 15%

		Domiciled	**Non-domiciled**
Inheritance Tax (IHT)	General description	There is inheritance tax for bequests and donations mortis causa, movable property, cash, registered shares or marketable securities, regardless of domiciled or non-domiciled	
	Taxable entities and chargeable assets	Individuals and legal entities are taxable when they receive any inheritance, bequests or donation	
	Calculation of charge	The calculation takes into account the relationship the recipient had with the deceased	
	Taxable events	The tax payment shall be based on the value of the property being transmitted by inheritance, bequest or donation, making deductions like debts, taxes and contributions and others	
	Allowances	None	

Tax rates

	Children, spouses or partners	Ancestors and descendants, except adopter and adopted children	Collateral consanguinity 2nd	3rd	4th	Relatives legal strange affinity
	%	%	%	%	%	% %
Up to Q50,000.00	1	2	3	5	7	9 12
Up to Q100,000.00	2	3	4	6	9	10 14
Up to Q200,000.00	3	4	5	7	10	11 16
Up to Q300,000.00	4	5	6	8	11	12 18
Up to Q500,000.00	5	6	7	9	12	13 20
Higher amounts	6	7	8	10	13	14 25

IV WITHHOLDING TAXES

Under domestic law	Payments to residents	Payments to non-residents
Dividends	10%	10%
Interest	10%	10%
Royalties	10%	15%
On payments to artists and sportsmen	10%	15%

Guatemala has not signed any tax treaties with foreign jurisdictions.

V   INDIRECT TAXES

		Residents	Non-residents
Value Added Tax	General description	VAT is collected on the exchange of goods or services at the local level as well as on the cross-border provision of services and the importation of goods	
	Entities obliged to levy VAT	Companies or individuals who sell goods or provide services locally and are legally registered	
	Taxable activities	All the activities except the export of goods and services	
	Taxable activities – zero-rated (examples)	Companies incorporated as a free zone and Maquilas which enjoy ten years of zero-rated	
	Exemptions (examples)	Exportation of goods and services are tax exempt These exemptions include: • Services provided by entities controlled by the Superintendence of Banks, stock exchange brokers, insurance and reinsurance operations • Issuance and transfer of some securities • Grants and donations to not-for-profit entities • Transactions among cooperative entities and their participants • Importation of furniture by cooperative entities, exclusively for their operations • Importations under the temporary importation system VAT tax returns shall be filed in a monthly basis within a month following that month reported in the tax return. The tax amount in debt shall be payable in the due date	
	Refund of VAT	Compensation of tax credits and debits	
	Tax liability	Any consumer must pay VAT on goods purchased	
	Tax rates	12% tax rate	
	Administrative obligations	Tax monthly accounting Payment – next month	
Real Property Taxes		VAT only for the first seller	
Stamp Duty		For Real Property: 3% stamp duty applies from the second sale	

Honduras

*(Ronald F Romero, Nexia Auditores & Consultores, rromero@nexiahonduras.com;
Julio Gomez, Nexia Auditores & Consultores, jgomez@nexiahonduras.com)*

I MAIN LEGAL FORMS

Legal form / Characteristics	Partnership and Limited Liability Partnership (LLP)	Private corporation (Ltd) and Public corporation (Plc)
Partners/shareholders • Number • Restrictions	• Minimum 2 partners • None	• Ltd – Minimum 2 shareholders; Plc – not applicable • None
Directors	• A general director	General Manager
Establishment	A social deed registered	A social deed registered (Ltd)
Registration	Public Register of Property, Tax Authorities, Social Security, INFOP, RAP, Commerce Chamber	Public Register of Property, Tax Authorities, Social Security, INFOP, RAP
Minimum capital	HNL5,000 (US$263)	HNL25,000 (US$1,314)
Liability	Just for the subscribed capital for each partner	Just for the subscribed capital for each shareholder
Governance	A general director	Board of directors
Audit requirements	Only if the National Commission of Banks and Insurances requires	Only if the National Commission of Banks and Insurances requires
Taxation	Income Tax Law, Municipal Taxes Law	Income Tax Law, Municipal Taxes Law

II   CORPORATION TAX

Description / Legal form	Resident corporations and Non-resident corporations with a Permanent establishment (PE)
General description	Corporation tax
Taxable entities	Corporations and branches incorporated in Honduras
Taxable income	Profits arising from operations (income before income tax)
Calculation on taxable profits	*Income tax:* Profits arising from operations (income before income tax) 25%; and a solidarity tax contribution of 10% for 2011, 6% for 2012, 5% for 2013 and 4% for 2014 on the excess of HNL1m income before income tax (this calculation is not deductible) *Net asset tax:* Alternative tax, used when there are no profits, or income tax is less than this calculation Calculated using the total assets less a deductible amount of HNL3m, with an applicable rate of 1% *Total revenues tax:* Currently a new alternative tax is in the process of approval in the National Congress, and proposes to apply a 1% charge on the total yearly revenues for all entities with revenues over HNL100m, only if income tax and net assets tax are less than this tax
Interest payments	Interests on borrowing are deductible, except if interests are paid to partners
Related party transactions	There is no restriction, only if the transactions cause benefits between companies
Tax year, return and payment	Tax year is the calendar year (January to December), except for companies with special tax year
Tax group	None
Tax rate	• Income tax 25% • Solidarity tax 5% (on the excess of HNL1m) • VAT 12% • Capital gains 10% • Net asset tax (when there are no profits) 1% over the excess of total assets less a deductible of HNL3m

III TAXES FOR INDIVIDUALS

<table>
<tr><th></th><th></th><th>Residents</th><th>Non-residents</th></tr>
<tr><td rowspan="7">Income Tax</td><td>General description</td><td>Applied to Honduran source coming from activities generating personal income</td><td>Not applied to non-residents. Except for individuals that generate occasional income within the Honduran territory</td></tr>
<tr><td>Taxable entities and taxable income</td><td>Individuals and legal entities are taxable</td><td>Individuals and legal entities are taxable</td></tr>
<tr><td>Calculation of income</td><td>Salary income is computed by applying a progressive table which starts from 0% to 25%</td><td>Subject to withholdings under a variable tax rate (5% to 35%) (depending on the type of income)</td></tr>
<tr><td>Tax year, tax assessment and tax payment</td><td>Tax year – Calendar year; annual return filled within 4 months; payments can be made on presentation of the return, or by quarterly payments in advance. Individuals with annual income lower than HNL150,000 (US$7,865) are exempt from income tax</td><td>Payments can be made once the income has been received</td></tr>
<tr><td>Losses</td><td>None</td><td>None</td></tr>
<tr><td>Tax rates</td><td>0% to 25%</td><td>5% to 35%</td></tr>
<tr><td rowspan="6">Capital gains tax (CGT)</td><td>General description</td><td>Tax on increase in the value of assets between acquisition and disposal</td><td>Tax on increase in the value of assets between acquisition and disposal</td></tr>
<tr><td>Taxable entities and chargeable assets</td><td>Individual; the net value of property transfer</td><td>Only assets located in Honduras</td></tr>
<tr><td>Calculation of gain</td><td>On the excess of the cost and sales price</td><td>On the excess of the cost and sales price</td></tr>
<tr><td>Tax year, tax assessment and tax payment</td><td>Calendar year; by a return filled within 4 months; payments are made on presentation of return</td><td>Calendar year; by a return filled within 4 months; payments are made on presentation of return</td></tr>
<tr><td>Losses</td><td>None</td><td>None</td></tr>
<tr><td>Tax rates</td><td>10%</td><td>10%</td></tr>
<tr><td rowspan="5">Inheritance tax (IHT)</td><td></td><td>**Domiciled**</td><td>**Non-domiciled**</td></tr>
<tr><td>General description</td><td>Tax for recipients on inheritances</td><td>Tax for recipients on inheritances</td></tr>
<tr><td>Taxable entities and chargeable assets</td><td>Individuals</td><td>Individuals</td></tr>
<tr><td>Taxable events</td><td>Inheritances received</td><td>Inheritances received</td></tr>
<tr><td>Tax rates</td><td>10%</td><td>10%</td></tr>
</table>

IV   WITHHOLDING TAXES

Under domestic law	Payments to residents	Payments to non-residents
Dividends	10%	10%
Interests	10%	10%
Royalties	10%	10%
On payments to artists and sportsmen	10%	10%

Honduras has not entered into any double tax treaties that might reduce the rates above.

V   INDIRECT TAXES

		Residents	Non-residents
Value Added Tax (VAT)	General description	Tax on the purchase and supply of goods and services	
	Entities being obliged to levy VAT	Individuals and all entities, except for entities previously authorised by tax authorities or special regime	
	Taxable activities – zero-rated (examples)	Purchase and supply of qualified goods and services	Purchase and supply of qualified goods and services
	Taxable activities – zero-rated	• Exports • entities under special regime (diplomatic and international officer)	None
	Exemptions (examples)	• Financial services • healthcare • social services • education • duty-free stores • certain goods and services exempt: medicines, computers and IT systems	None
	Refund of VAT	None	None
	Tax liability	Individuals and all entities	Individuals and all entities
	Tax rates	12% general 15% liquors and tobacco 16% hotels	12% general 15% liquors and tobacco 16% hotels
	Administrative obligations	To be registered as a Withholding Agent with Tax Authorities; file and paid (when applicable) monthly VAT returns	None
Real Property Taxes		Not applicable, but a tax of 1.5% on the transaction value must be declared and paid	Not applicable, but a tax of 1.5% on the transaction value must be declared and paid
Stamp Duty		None	

Hong Kong

(Brenda Chan, Nexia Charles Mar Fan & Co, brenda@charles-marfan.com)

I MAIN LEGAL FORMS

Characteristics / Legal form	Partnership and Limited Liability Partnership (LLP)	Private corporation (Ltd) and Public corporation (Plc)
Partners /shareholders • Number • Restrictions	Partnership: at least two and cannot be more than 20 partners Limited Partnership: at least two and shall not consist of more than 20 persons and must consist of at least one general partner and one limited partner Restrictions: none	Ltd: at least one and not more than 50 shareholders Plc: one or more
Directors	Management by partners	Ltd: at least one director Plc: at least two directors
Establishment	By partnership agreement	Set up under the Companies Ordinance
Registration	Partnership: not necessary to be registered with the Hong Kong Companies Registry Limited Partnership, Ltd, Plc: registered with the Hong Kong Companies Registry	
Minimum capital	None	• None (for practical purposes this is not usually less than HK$1,000 or the equivalent in a foreign currency) • A minimum of one share can be issued to each shareholder

Legal form / Characteristics	Partnership and Limited Liability Partnership (LLP)	Private corporation (Ltd) and Public corporation (Plc)
Liability	Partnership: • jointly and severally liable for all debts and obligations Limited Partnership: • general partners shall be liable for all debts and obligations • limited partners shall be liable for debts and obligations within the amount they have agreed to contribute	Limited to share capital subscribed
Governance	Governed by the partners	Governed by the Board of Directors • secretary • shareholders' meeting • annual general meeting
Audit requirements	None	Annually
Taxation	Subject to profits tax on their profits arising in and derived from Hong Kong. Partnerships are transparent for tax purposes	
Usage	Professional practices	All other businesses

II CORPORATION TAX

Description / Legal form	Resident corporation	Permanent establishment (PE)
General description	Profits tax	
Taxable entities	Companies and partnerships	PE located in Hong Kong
Taxable income	Profit arising in or derived from Hong Kong	Profits derived by PE in Hong Kong
Calculation of taxable profits	Accounting profit is adjusted for various tax add-backs and allowances to arrive at profits chargeable to profits corporation tax	
Interest payments	Interest expenses are tax deductible if related to the generation of taxable profits	
Related party transactions	All related party transactions must take place on an arm's length basis	
Tax year, return and payment	Tax returns are issued in April each year and are required to be filed within one month However, by special concession the following extensions for filing are usually granted: *Year-end* / *Filing date* 1 April to 30 November — 30 April of the following year 1 December to 31 December — 15 August of the following year 1 January to 31 March — 15 November of the same year	
Capital gains	Not taxable	
Losses	Net operating tax losses may be carried forward and set off against future taxable profits	
Tax group	None	
Tax rate	• 16.5% for limited companies • 15% for partnerships	

III TAXES FOR INDIVIDUALS

		Residents	Non-residents
Income Tax	General description	Tax levied on the chargeable income of a chargeable person for a year of assessment	
	Taxable entities and taxable income	Resident individuals are taxed on income arising in and derived from Hong Kong	Non-resident individuals are taxable on income derived in Hong Kong
	Types of taxable income	• Property income (usually rent) • Income from business activities • Employment income from personal services or pensions	
	Calculation of income	• Property income less 20% allowance for repairs and outgoings • Income from business activities is adjusted for various add-backs and allowances to arrive at profits chargeable to tax • Employment income or pensions on gross basis	
	Tax year, tax assessment and tax payment	Tax year – ends on 31 March each year Tax assessment – individual self-assessment returns for each taxpayer Return forms are issued on 1 April each year and must be submitted within one month	
	Losses	Losses may be carried forward and set off against future income on the election of personal assessment (combining all heads of income for assessment)	
	Tax rates	*Band* *(HK$)* First 40,000 Next 40,000 Next 40,000 On the remainder Standard rate	*Rate* *(%)* 2 7 12 17 15
Capital Gains Tax (CGT)	General description	Not taxable	
		Domiciled	**Non-domiciled**
Inheritance Tax (IHT)	General description	No inheritance tax	

IV WITHHOLDING TAXES

Under domestic law	Payments to residents	Payments to non-residents[1]
Dividends	Nil	Nil
Interest	Nil	Nil
Royalties	Nil	4.95%/16.5%
On payments to artists and sportsmen	Nil	10%/11%

Reduced rate available under the relevant Double Taxation Treaty			
Country	Dividends	Interest	Royalties
Austria	Nil	Nil	3%
Belgium	Nil	Nil	4.95%
Brunei	Nil	Nil	4.95%
Canada	Nil	Nil	4.95%
China	Nil	Nil	4.95%
Czech Republic	Nil	Nil	4.95%
France	Nil	Nil	4.95%
Guernsey	Nil	Nil	4%
Hungary	Nil	Nil	4.95%
Indonesia	Nil	Nil	4.95%
Ireland	Nil	Nil	3%
Italy	Nil	Nil	4.95%
Japan	Nil	Nil	4.95%
Jersey	Nil	Nil	4%
Korea	Nil	Nil	4.95%
Kuwait	Nil	Nil	4.95%
Liechtenstein	Nil	Nil	3%
Luxembourg	Nil	Nil	3%
Malaysia	Nil	Nil	4.95%
Malta	Nil	Nil	3%
Mexico	Nil	Nil	4.95%
Netherlands	Nil	Nil	3%
New Zealand	Nil	Nil	4.95%
Portugal	Nil	Nil	4.95%
Russia	Nil	Nil	3%
Qatar	Nil	Nil	4.95%
South Africa	Nil	Nil	4.95%
Spain	Nil	Nil	4.95%
Switzerland	Nil	Nil	3%
Thailand	Nil	Nil	4.95%
United Arab Emirates	Nil	Nil	4.95%
United Kingdom	Nil	Nil	3%
Vietnam	Nil	Nil	4.95%

Note: the above rates are only available provided the specific Treaty criteria are satisfied. It is possible that lower rates than those shown above may be available provided that certain criteria are satisfied. As treaties will not be identical, guidance should be sought in all cases.

1 Reduced rates of withholding tax may apply where there is an appropriate double tax treaty.

V   INDIRECT TAXES

		Residents	Non-residents
Value Added Tax (VAT)	General description	Tax on the supply of goods and services (VAT)	
	Entities being obliged to levy VAT	There is no VAT or sales tax, with the exception of a first registration tax on automobiles	
Real Property Taxes		Stamp duty on transfer of immovable property in Hong Kong ranges from 1.5%–8.5% based on the value of the properties	
		For properties resold within less than 36 months, special stamp duty ranges from 10%–20%	
		For buyer of residential properties, buyer stamp duty of 15% is due	
Stamp Duty		On transfer of Hong Kong stock: 0.1% of the amount of the consideration	

Nexia International is the trading name of Nexia International Limited, a company registered in the Isle of Man. Company registration number: 53513C. Registered office: 2nd floor, Sixty Circular Road, Douglas, Isle of Man, IM1 1SA

Hungary

(Jozsef Lang, ABT Hungaria Kft., jozsef.lang@abt.hu)

I MAIN LEGAL FORMS

Legal form / Characteristics	Partnership and Limited Liability Partnership (LLP)	Private corporation (Ltd) and Public corporation (Plc)
Partners/shareholders • Number • Restrictions	*Unlimited partnership (Kkt):* • No restrictions on number or type of partners • Each partner has unlimited liability *Limited partnership (Bt):* • General partner has unlimited liability, limited partners have limited liability • The number of partners is not restricted, but at least one limited partner and one general partner is required Restriction: an individual who has unlimited liability in one business cannot be an unlimited partner in another	*Limited liability company (Kft):* • No restrictions on number or type of partners *Public limited company (Rt):* • No restrictions on number or type of directors • There are two types of Rt *Closed Company Limited by Shares (ZRt):* its shares are not available for the public *Public Company Limited by Shares (NyRt):* its shares are listed on the stock exchange for the public
Directors	Kkt: each member is entitled to manage independently Bt: general partner(s)	Kft: managing director(s) ZRt and NyRt: Director or Board of Directors
Establishment	Kkt: by agreement and acceptance of the Memorandum of Association Bt: by agreement and acceptance of the Memorandum of Association	Kft: by agreement and acceptance of the Memorandum of Association ZRt and NyRt: by agreement and acceptance of the Articles of Association and by issuing shares
Registration	Registration at the Company Registrar (filing the Memorandum of Association and some other prescribed documents to the Court of Registry)	

Legal form / Characteristics	Partnership and Limited Liability Partnership (LLP)	Private corporation (Ltd) and Public corporation (Plc)
Minimum capital	Kkt: no minimum capital Bt: no minimum capital	Kft: minimum of HUF3m (€10,000) ZRt: minimum of HUF5m (€17,000) NyRt: minimum of HUF20m (€68,000)
Liability	Kkt: unlimited up to assets of the partnership; members – unlimited and jointly Bt: unlimited up to assets of the Bt; members – unlimited for the general partner(s), limited for the external (limited) partner(s)[1]	Kft: unlimited up to assets of the Ltd company; members – limited up to their capital contribution, plus up to the extra contribution, if there is any ZRt and NyRt: unlimited up to assets of the Plc; members – limited up to the face value or issue value of their shares
Audit requirements	Auditing of books is compulsory for all undertakings keeping double-entry books, if: • annual net sales exceed HUF300 million on average for the 2 financial years preceding the financial year under review, and/or • the average number of employees of the 2 financial years preceding the financial year under review exceeds 50 persons Irrespective of the above, auditing of the books is compulsory if having more than HUF10 million unpaid tax liability for more than 60 days	
Taxation	Corporation tax (or simplified taxation with special conditions for small sized companies having private shareholder)	Corporation tax
	Special taxation based on cash flow and personnel cost is applicable for small sized companies	
Usage	Kkt: limited use Bt: LP is the second most common business form	Most companies operate in the business form of Kft The companies with more significant economic role and businesses with higher need of capital investment generally operate in the form of ZRt

---

1   The limited partner might remain to be liable for the liability of the LP within 5 years following the termination of his former status of general partner.

II CORPORATION TAX

Description \ Legal form	Resident corporation	Permanent establishment (PE)
General description	Corporation tax on profits	
Taxable entities	Created under Hungarian law or with their place of management in Hungary	PE of foreign enterprises carrying out taxable activity in Hungary
Taxable income	Worldwide income	Hungarian source income
Calculation of taxable profits	Accounting profits adjusted for prescribed items 'Expected minimum profit' – if the profit before tax and the tax base for corporate income tax is less than the 'expected minimum profit', then the corporate income tax (9%) is to be paid on the latter, eg even a loss-making company may have to pay corporate income tax unless it files a declaration about its costs and expenses as main reason of the loss	
Interest payments	Deductible as a business cost, subject to thin capitalisation rules (1:3 – equity:debt)	
Related party transactions	Transactions must be conducted on an arm's length basis	
Tax year, return and payment	Usually the calendar year, unless the taxpayer decides otherwise Advance payments must be made on a monthly or quarterly basis (over HUF100m annual sales an extra advance payment is due by 20th of the last month of the business year) Returns must be filed by the last day of the 5th month following the tax year (which is 31 May where tax year equals calendar year)	
Capital gains	Capital gains are taxed as business profit	
Losses	Losses from 2015 may be carried forward for 5 years, but not carried back. Losses can be carried over from previous years only up to 50% of the actual tax base. Losses of years before 2015 (when an indefinite loss carry forward rule was in force) can be used by 31 December 2025 at the latest	
Tax group	Not available	
Tax rate	9% from 2017 Before 2017, the headline rate was: 19% and a beneficial rate of 10% was applicable to taxable profits of HUF500m (€1.7m) or lower	

III   TAXES FOR INDIVIDUALS

<table>
<tr><th colspan="2"></th><th>Residents</th><th>Non-residents</th></tr>
<tr><td rowspan="9">Income Tax</td><td>General description</td><td colspan="2">Federal tax on income of individuals</td></tr>
<tr><td>Taxable entities and taxable income</td><td>Those with a habitual residence in Hungary. Tax levied on the worldwide income of the individual</td><td>Domiciled neither in Hungary nor with a habitual residence in Hungary. Hungarian-source income subject to tax</td></tr>
<tr><td>Types of taxable income</td><td><ul><li>Income from employment</li><li>Income from self-employment</li><li>Capital gains on movable and immovable property</li><li>Benefits-in-kind</li><li>Income from capital assets, eg rent</li></ul></td><td>Same types of income, taxation treaties between the countries are applicable

Non-residents are taxable on Hungary-source income only</td></tr>
<tr><td>Calculation of income</td><td colspan="2"><ul><li>Employment income: full amount of income is taxable</li><li>Income from self-employment: by calculation of the entrepreneurial profit (revenue minus costs) or in a lump sum method</li><li>Capital gains on movable and immovable property: by calculation of the selling price minus the amount of purchase price and some costs that belonged to the acquisition</li><li>Benefits-in-kind: market value of the benefits including VAT</li><li>Income from capital assets: depending on the type of income derived (transfer of securities, interest, security lending, dividend, Stock Exchange transactions)</li></ul></td></tr>
<tr><td>Tax year, tax assessment and tax payment</td><td colspan="2">The tax year is the calendar year

Tax is collected by way of self-assessment

Income tax returns must be filed by 20 May of the following year, self-employed have until 25 February

Advance payments are required</td></tr>
<tr><td>Losses</td><td colspan="2">Losses from 2015 may be carried forward for 5 years, but not carried back. Losses can be carried over from previous years only up to 50% of the actual tax base. Losses of years before 2015 (when an indefinite loss carry forward rule was in force) can be used by 31 December 2025 at the latest</td></tr>
<tr><td>Tax rates</td><td colspan="2">15%</td></tr>
</table>

		Residents	Non-residents
Capital Gains Tax (CGT)	General description	Capital gains levied on immovable property and rights, interest and profit on shares	
	Taxable entities and chargeable assets	Individuals • The net value of property transfer or of establishing and transferring rights thereon • The interest of bank deposits and securities • Profit between the selling and purchase price or investment of shares	Individuals, if the property is situated in Hungary
	Calculation of gain	The gain is the income minus the amount of the purchase price and certain costs related to the acquisition of the immovable property or shares (eg stamp duty, certain allowable improvement expenditure, commission, administration cost, etc) In case of interest the gain is the amount calculated according to the contract or public conditions	
	Tax year, tax assessment and tax payment	Tax year – calendar year Period of assessment – The year of receipt of the income Tax payable on the deadline for submitting tax return (in case of interest and profit on shares the tax is withheld by the payer)	
	Losses	Not taxable under personal income tax, cannot be carried forward	
	Tax rates	Headline rate: 15% In case of housing properties the tax can be reduced • by 10% of the taxable gain in the 2nd year following the year of acquisition • by 40% of the taxable gain in the 3rd year following the year of acquisition • by 70% of the taxable gain in the 4th year following the year of acquisition This method will result in exemption on income from housing property selling after 5 years In case of other properties, 10–100% tax discount can be applied between the 6th and 15th years of ownership	

		Domiciled	**Non-domiciled**
Inheritance Tax (IHT)	General description	IHT is levied on property passing on the basis of an inheritance, a legacy or will, an acquisition of a legal share of an inheritance and a donation in the event of death	
	Taxable entities and chargeable assets	Individuals The net value of the inheritance constitutes the taxable base	There is no inheritance tax but there is an inheritance fee if the property is situated in Hungary
	Calculation of charge	Net value of inheritance subject to some allowances	
	Taxable events	Inheritance upon the death of the person leaving the property	
	Allowances (examples)	• Inheritance of savings deposits, movable inheritance up to a market value of HUF300,000 per heir • Inheritance of usufruct or use of residential property by the surviving spouse • Linear inheritance is exempt	
	Tax rates	18% except housing properties (9%)	

IV WITHHOLDING TAXES

Under domestic law	Payments to residents	Payments to non-residents[2]

Dividends	• No tax on dividend to corporates
	• For private persons
	  – 15% personal income tax, and
	  – 14% health contribution if the social security payment on the person's other revenues is not more than HUF450,000 (€1,500)
		• No tax on dividends to corporates
		• In case of dividends to individuals: 5–20% of withholding tax might be levied
		• In case of dividends from security listed on any regulated market of any EEA Member State: 10% of withholding tax is levied

Interest	• No tax on interest between companies • 15% on bank investments (deposit, securities, etc) of private persons	• No tax on interest between companies • Interest to private persons has to be reported (a certificate of residency is required) • Tax on bank investments of private persons (deposit, securities, etc) are withheld according to the treaty
Royalties	• No tax on royalties paid between companies • Private person's income from royalties are subject to personal income and social security taxes depending on the person's tax status	• No tax on royalties paid between companies • Tax of private person's income from royalties depends on the person's tax status

Reduced rate available under the relevant Double Taxation Treaty			
Country	**Dividends**	**Interest**	**Royalties**
Albania	10%	Nil	5%
Armenia	10%	10%	5%
Australia	15%	10%	10%
Austria	10%	Nil	Nil
Azerbaijan	8%	8%	8%
Bahrain	5%	Nil	Nil
Belarus	15%	5%	5%
Belgium	10%	15%	Nil
Bosnia and Herzegovina	10%	Nil	10%
Brazil	15%	15%	25%
Bulgaria	10%	10%	10%
Canada	15%	10%	10%
China	10%	10%	10%
Croatia	10%	Nil	Nil
Cyprus	15%	10%	Nil
Czech Republic	15%	Nil	10%
Denmark	15%	Nil	Nil
Egypt	20%	15%	15%
Estonia	15%	10%	10%
Finland	15%	Nil	5%

2 Reduced rates of withholding tax may apply where there is an appropriate double tax treaty.

Reduced rate available under the relevant Double Taxation Treaty			
Country	Dividends	Interest	Royalties
France	15%	Nil	Nil
Germany	15%	Nil	Nil
Georgia	5%	Nil	Nil
Greece	10%	10%	10%
Hong Kong	10%	5%	5%
Iceland	10%	Nil	10%
India	10%	10%	10%
Indonesia	15%	15%	15%
Iran (expected from 2017)	Nil	5%	5%
Ireland	15%	Nil	Nil
Israel	15%	Nil	Nil
Italy	10%	Nil	Nil
Japan	10%	10%	10%
Kazakhstan	15%	10%	10%
Kosovo	5%	Nil	Nil
Kuwait	Nil	Nil	10%
Latvia	10%	10%	10%
Liechtenstein	10%	Nil	Nil
Lithuania	15%	10%	10%
Luxembourg	10%	Nil	Nil
Macedonia	15%	Nil	Nil
Malaysia	10%	15%	15%
Malta	15%	10%	10%
Morocco	12%	10%	10%
Mexico	15%	10%	10%
Moldova	15%	10%	Nil
Mongolia	15%	10%	5%
Netherlands	15%	Nil	Nil
Norway	10%	Nil	Nil
Pakistan	20%	15%	15%
Philippines	20%	15%	15%
Poland	10%	10%	10%
Portugal	15%	10%	10%
Qatar	5%	Nil	5%
Republic of Korea	10%	Nil	Nil
Romania	15%	15%	10%
Russia	10%	Nil	Nil
San Marino	15%	Nil	Nil
Saudi Arabia	5%	Nil	8%
Serbia and Montenegro	15%	10%	10%
Singapore	10%	5%	5%
Slovakia	15%	Nil	10%
Slovenia	15%	5%	5%
South Africa	15%	Nil	Nil
Spain	15%	Nil	Nil

Reduced rate available under the relevant Double Taxation Treaty			
Country	Dividends	Interest	Royalties
Sweden	15%	Nil	Nil
Switzerland	10%	Nil	Nil
Taiwan	10%	10%	10%
Thailand	20%	25%	15%
Tunisia	12%	12%	12%
Turkey	15%	10%	10%
Turkmenistan (from 2017)	15%	10%	10%
United Arab Emirates	Nil	Nil	Nil
United Kingdom	15%	Nil	Nil
Ukraine	15%	10%	5%
Uruguay	15%	15%	15%
United States	15%	15%	Nil
Uzbekistan	10%	10%	10%
Vietnam	10%	10%	10%

Note: the above rates are only available provided the specific Treaty criteria are satisfied. It is possible that lower rates than those shown above may be available provided that certain criteria are satisfied. As treaties will not be identical, guidance should be sought in all cases.

V   INDIRECT TAXES

		Residents[3]	Non-residents
Value Added Tax (VAT)	General description	Tax on the supply of goods and services, imports and others	
	Entities obliged to levy VAT	All natural persons and legal entities that supply goods or services on a regular basis (taxable persons)	
		Non-taxable persons: in some cases, eg intra-Community acquisition of new means of transport	
	Taxable activities	Supply of goods and services within the territory of Hungary, intra-Community acquisitions, importation of goods, etc	
	Taxable activities – zero-rated (examples)	Export, transactions that are regarded in the same way as export and international transport	
	Exemptions (examples)	Financial services, healthcare, social services, education, leasing or letting immovable properties (option to tax is available), etc	
	Refund of VAT	Possession of invoice issued for the taxpayer, if certain legal requirements are met Some other pre-conditions must also be met for refunding	In line with the 8th and 13th VAT Directives Possession of invoice issued for the taxpayer and meeting the entire legal requirement are also necessary
	Tax liability	Tax assessment, tax payment, submitting tax return	
	Tax rates	Standard rate of 27%; reduced rates of 18% applied to foods and hotel services and (from 2017) internet service, and food and beverages prepared and sold in restaurants; 5% applied to books, medical supplies, live lambs, goats and half-carcases of lambs and goats, pork, certain new flats and housing properties among other items, and (from 2017) poultry, eggs and milk	
	Administrative obligations	Filing tax return on a monthly, quarterly or annual basis, depending on the VAT performance of the VAT subject to strict invoicing rules (new companies have to file monthly returns from 2015 in the 1st and 2nd years irrespective of their VAT performance) Monthly detailed reports have to be filed on invoices including more than HUF100,000 VAT; from 1 July 2017, online connection of invoicing software is planned	Filing the application, the invoices, bank account statements, contracts, etc until 30 June of the subsequent year
Real Property Taxes		Real estate: 4% up to HUF1 billion; 2% over HUF1 billion, maximum HUF200 million	
		Housing properties are subject to 2% tax up to HUF4m, and 4% over it	
		Calculation on the basis of market value	
Stamp Duty		Gift: 18% except housing properties (9%)	
		Transfer tax for movable property, certain rights: 4%	
		Procedural duty (court, public/central administration)	

---

3   In the context of this VAT schedule, 'residents' are domestic VAT taxpayers as well as foreigners registered in Hungary for VAT purposes.

India

*Maulik Doshi (maulik.doshi@skpgroup.com) and Pratik Shah
(pratik.shah@skpgroup.com)*

I MAIN LEGAL FORMS

Legal form / Characteristics	Partnership and Limited Liability Partnership (LLP)	Private corporation (Ltd) and Public corporation (Plc)
Partners/shareholders • Number • Restrictions	General Partnership: Minimum – 2 Partners Maximum – 20 Partners Limited Liability Partnership (LLP): Minimum – 2 Partners No maximum limit Foreign Direct Investment (FDI) not allowed in Indian General Partnership firm but allowed in LLP subject to specified conditions Foreign investment in LLP is permitted under the automatic route if the LLP is engaged in sector where 100% FDI is permitted and there are no attendant FDI-linked performance conditions to the sector	Private Company (Ltd): Minimum – 2 Shareholders Maximum – 200 Shareholders Public Company (Plc): Minimum – 7 Shareholders No maximum limit One Person Company – where the company to be formed is a private company, by subscribing their names or his name to a memorandum Cross-border mergers and amalgamations between companies registered in India and those incorporated outside India are permissible subject to certain conditions

Legal form / Characteristics	Partnership and Limited Liability Partnership (LLP)	Private corporation (Ltd) and Public corporation (Plc)
Directors	General Partnership: Managing Partner LLP: 2 Designated Individual Partners (1 Partner needs to be an Indian Resident) Or, in case of a LLP in which all the partners are bodies corporate or LLPs in which one or more partners are individuals and bodies corporate: at least 2 individuals who are partners of such a limited liability partnership or nominees of such body corporate shall act as designated partners	Ltd: Minimum – 2 Directors Concept of independent director is introduced At least one director should be resident in India for at least 182 days Plc: Minimum – 3 Directors Concept of independent director is introduced Every listed company to have at least one third of the total number of Directors as Independent Directors In above cases, at least one director should be resident in India for at least 182 days Also, in prescribed classes, there should be at least one woman director Concept of Key Managerial Personnel (KMP) has been introduced for specified companies
Establishment	Partnership: Partnership Deed LLP: LLP Agreement	Memorandum and Articles of Association
Registration	Registration of general partnership firm: Registrar of Firms Registration is optional. But rights restricted if not registered Not mandatory subject to conditions Mandatory registration of LLP: online with Ministry of Corporate Affairs Registration with Indian Income Tax and Indirect Tax Authorities	Registrar of Companies Registration with Indian Income Tax and Indirect Tax Authorities Other registrations as may be required under other Acts depending upon the activities and location of registered office of the Company
Minimum capital	No minimum capital	No Minimum Capital for Ltd & Plc
Liability	Partnership: unlimited liability LLP: typically, limited to contribution of partners	Shareholders' liability is limited to share capital

Legal form / Characteristics	Partnership and Limited Liability Partnership (LLP)	Private corporation (Ltd) and Public corporation (Plc)
Governance	General Partnership: Partners LLP: Designated Partners	Board of Directors Minimum of 4 meetings to be held in a year with a time gap between two meetings not less than 120 days Participation of Director through video conferencing and other audio-visual means allowed Directors remaining absent from all the meetings in a year would have to vacate the office even if the leave of absence is granted
Audit requirements	General Partnership: Optional LLP: mandatory if: • Turnover exceeds INR4m; or • Total contribution in LLP exceeds INR2.5m Mandatory tax audit if turnover exceeds INR10m for general partnership as well as LLP	Audit under Indian Companies Act: mandatory Mandatory tax audit if turnover exceeds INR10m In listed and such classes of companies, compulsory rotation of individual auditors in every five years' term and of audit firm in two terms of five years. An individual auditor/ audit firm who have completed the aforesaid term thereunder shall not be eligible for reappointment in the same company for a period of 5 years
Corporate social responsibility	Not mandatory	Corporate social responsibility is mandatory for all companies having a **turnover** of rupees one thousand crore or more or a **net profit** of rupees five crore or more in a financial year and companies having **net worth** of rupees five hundred crore or more A company falling under the above criteria is required to mandatorily contribute 2% of its average net profits made during the three immediately preceding years
Investments	General Partnership: There is no specific restriction in the Act LLP: LLP can invest overseas under automatic route or with approval as the case may be	A company cannot make investment through more than two layers of investment companies subject to certain exemptions
Year ending	General Partnership: No such specific requirement LLP: No such specific requirement	Year ending for all companies should be 31 March of the year, except companies which are either holding or subsidiary of foreign entity requiring consolidation of accounts outside India Existing companies need to align their financials within 2 years
Taxation	Partnership/LLP: taxed as a separate entity	Corporation tax

II CORPORATION TAX

Description / Legal Form	Resident corporation	Permanent establishment (PE)
General description	Indian Corporation Tax	
Taxable entities	• Companies incorporated in India • If Place of Effective Management[1] of the company is in India during the year	Foreign companies with PE situated in India
Taxable income	Taxable on worldwide income	Taxable on income attributable to PE/derived by PE in India
Calculation of taxable profits	• Accounting profit adjusted for add-backs and allowances Also, specific weighted deductions are granted on carrying out specified business activities	
Interest payments	Interest payments are generally deductible. No thin capitalisation rules[2]	
Dividend income	• Dividend income earned from a specified foreign company shall be chargeable to tax at 15.45%.[3] Dividends from other foreign companies taxable at maximum tax rate applicable for companies • Dividend income received from Indian company (ie a company incorporated in India) is exempt from tax in hands of any recipient	
Related party transactions	• Transaction need to be on arm's length basis • Conditions and mechanisms have been proposed to determine the arm's length price using multiple year data and 'range concept' for certain transactions • Transfer Pricing provisions widened to include specified domestic transactions with related parties • Advance Pricing Agreements (APA) regulations introduced to determine arm's length price in advance • Safe Harbour Rules for transfer pricing have been notified for specified industries • Transfer Pricing Documentation mandatory for transactions value exceeding INR10m In line with the OECD Report on Action 13 of BEPS Action Plan, Country by Country (CbC) Reporting is proposed to be introduced if the total turnover of group exceeds INR54 billion (EUR750m) • Filing of a CA certificate in a prescribed Form (No 3CEB) Certain compliance/filing required with Indian tax authorities	

1 The 'Place of Effective Management' means a place where key management and commercial decisions that are necessary for the conduct of the business of an entity as a whole are, in substance, made (with effect from 1 April 2016).
2 Thin capitalisation rules are proposed to be introduced by way of General Anti Avoidance Rule (GAAR) with effect from 1 April 2017.
3 Surcharge of 12% shall be applicable if the dividend exceeds INR10m.

Legal Form / Description	Resident corporation	Permanent establishment (PE)
Tax year, return and payment	Tax year runs from 1 April to 31 March irrespective of accounting period	

Tax Return

Due date	Assessees
30 November	Taxpayers to whom transfer pricing provisions are applicable
30 September	All other taxpayers

Tax payments need to be made in advance on quarterly basis

Due date	Amount of advance taxes
15 June	Up to 15% of total taxes
15 September	Up to 45% of total taxes less tax paid in first instalment
15 December	Up to 75% of total taxes less tax paid in first and second instalments
15 March	Entire taxes as reduced by tax already paid in first, second and third instalments

Capital gains[5]	Concept of short-term and long-term capital gains
	Short-term: less than or equal to 12 months for listed shares/ 24 months for unlisted shares/36 months for other assets
	Long-term: greater than 12 months for listed shares/24 months for unlisted shares/36 months for other assets

Taxation of Capital Gains	Taxation of Capital Gains
Short-term capital gains –	For PE situated in India,[5,6] short-term capital gains –
• listed shares – taxable at 15.45%[4]	• Listed shares – taxable at 15.45%[4]
• unlisted shares and other assets – taxable at 30.9%[4]	• Unlisted shares and other assets – Taxable at 41.2%[4]

4 Additional surcharge of 7% in case of resident companies and 2% in case of foreign companies/ PE would be applicable on the basic rate if the taxable income in India exceeds INR10m but does not exceed INR100m. However, if the taxable income of Indian companies and foreign companies/PE in India exceeds INR100m, the additional surcharge applicable shall be 12% and 5% on basic rate respectively.

5 Definitions of 'Capital Asset' and 'Transfer' clarified. Hence, transfer of shares of company registered outside India shall also be taxable in India if the shares of company incorporated outside India derive their substantial value from interests or rights in shares or any asset located in India.

The share of the foreign company shall be deemed to derive substantial value from Indian assets, if the fair value of the Indian assets:

• exceeds INR100m; and

• said value represents at least 50% of the value of all the assets owned by the foreign company. The amount to be taxed in India to be proportional to the value of the Indian assets to global assets of the foreign Company.

Exemption provided from indirect transfer to:

• small shareholders (ie shareholders who hold less than 5% voting power or share capital, and no right of management and control in the foreign entity); or

• foreign amalgamations and demergers, subject to certain conditions.

6 In case of non-residents, one needs to also examine the treaty provisions. For claiming treaty benefits, tax residency certificate (TRC) from government of home country is imperative. Further,

Legal Form / Description	Resident corporation	Permanent establishment (PE)
	Long-term capital gains – • listed shares – exempt if such transaction is chargeable to securities transaction tax • unlisted shares and other assets – taxable at 20.6%[4] Buy-back of unlisted shares: Capital gain exempt in hands of shareholders However, company is liable to pay buyback tax (discussed later)	For PE situated in India,[6] long-term capital gains – • listed shares – exempt if such transaction is chargeable to securities transaction tax • unlisted securities[7] – taxable at 10.3%[3] • Other assets – taxable at 20.6%[4] Buy-back of unlisted shares: Capital gain exempt in hands of shareholders However, company is liable to pay buyback tax (discussed later)
Losses	Business losses - Carry forward restricted to 8 years Capital losses – Carry forward restricted to 8 years subject to certain conditions[8]	
Tax group	None	
Tax rate[9]	30.9%[10, 11] (basic rate of 30% + education cess of 3%)[4] For patent box regime, separate rates have been provided[12]	41.2% (basic rate of 40% + education cess of 3%)[4]

it is also imperative to carry out an analysis of allied regulatory laws and Indian Exchange Control Regulations to determine the permissibility of permanent establishments of non-residents in India to trade in/acquire listed and unlisted securities in India.

7 Subject to fulfilment of condition that indexation benefit and currency fluctuation benefits not to be availed.

8 Long-term capital loss can be set off against long-term capital gains only. Short-term capital loss can be set off against short-term capital gains as well as long-term capital gains.

9 Minimum Alternate Tax (MAT) at 19.055% (plus applicable surcharge)[4] is levied where income tax on taxable profits of company is lower than 18.50% of the book profits. However, MAT will not be applicable to foreign companies on:
   (a) the capital gains arising on transactions in securities; or
   (b) the interest, royalty or fees for technical services chargeable to tax on gross basis (not attributable to PE).
   MAT shall not be applicable to foreign companies not having any permanent establishment in India or which are not required to be registered as per the companies law in India.

10 Tax rate of 29.87% (basic rate of 29% + education cess of 3%)[4] with effect from 1 April 2016 if the turnover or gross receipts of PY 2014-15 does not exceed INR50m

11 Tax rate of 25.75% (basic rate of 25% + education cess of 3%)[4] shall be applicable if the following conditions are satisfied:

   • The company is engaged in manufacturing and has been set up and registered on or after 1 March 2016.
   • The company has not claimed any tax incentives, as prescribed.

12 Concessional tax rate of 10.30%[4] on royalty for patent registered and developed in India. There is also an exemption from levy of MAT (book profits tax) on such income.

III TAXES FOR INDIVIDUALS

		Residents	Non-residents
Income Tax	General description	Concept of residents, not ordinarily resident and non-resident	
	Taxable entities and taxable income	Residents are taxed on their worldwide income	Not ordinarily residents and non-residents are taxed on the following streams of income: • Income received or deemed to be received in India by or on behalf of such person • Income accruing or arising or deemed to accrue or arise in India • Income from a business controlled from India or from a profession set up in India although the same may not accrue or arise in India
	Types of taxable income	• Employment income • Property income • Income from business or profession • Capital gains • Investment income – interest, dividend, etc	
	Calculation of Income	Calculation of taxable income is dependent upon nature of income, since certain specific deductions may be available	
	Tax year, tax assessment and tax payment	Tax year runs from 1 April to 31 March Tax Return *Due date* *Assesses* 30 November Taxpayers to whom transfer pricing provisions are applicable 30 September All taxpayers for whom tax audit is applicable 31 July All other taxpayers Advance tax payments need to be made in four instalments: *Due date* *Amount of advance taxes* 15 June Up to 15% of total taxes 15 September Up to 45% of total taxes less tax paid in first instalment 15 December Up to 75% of total taxes less tax paid in first and second instalments 15 March Entire taxes as reduced by tax already paid in first, second and third instalments	
	Losses	Business loss allowed to be carried forward up to 8 years	
	Tax rates	Graduated rates of taxation: The following bands and rates are provided by Finance Act 2016 *Taxable income (INR)* *Rate of income tax* 0–250,000 Nil 250,001–500,000 10%[12] of the income falling within this band[14] 500,001–1,000,000 20%[13] of the income falling within this band Above 1,000,000 30%[13] of the amount exceeding INR1m	

		Residents	Non-residents
Income Tax – *contd*		• The above rates undergo a change in case of resident individuals who are senior residents (ie of 60 years) or super senior (ie of 80 years) • Alternate Minimum Tax at 19.055% (plus applicable surcharge)[13] is levied where the regular income tax payable is lower than 18.50% of the adjusted total income and if such adjusted total income exceeds INR2m. Alternate minimum tax shall apply only if there is income from business or profession and tax holiday/deduction is claimed	
Capital Gains Tax (CGT)	General Description	Gains arising from transfer of capital asset liable to capital gains tax[5]	
	Taxable entities and chargeable assets	Chargeable capital assets refer to property of any kind held by the taxpayer whether or not connected with the business, except: • stock in trade • personal effects • agricultural land situated in rural areas of India	
	Calculation of gain	Concept of short-term and long-term capital gains Short-term: less than or equal to 12 months for listed shares/24 months for unlisted shares/36 months for other assets Long-term: greater than 12 months for listed shares/24 months for unlisted shares/36 months for other assets	
	Tax year, tax assessment and tax payment	Tax year/assessment year runs from 1 April to 31 March Advance tax payments need to be made in four instalments	
	Losses	Carry forward restricted to 8 years subject to certain conditions[8]	
	Tax rates	Short term capital gains – • Listed shares – taxable at 15.45%[13,15] • Unlisted shares and other assets – taxable at 30.9%[13,15] Long term capital gains – • Listed shares – exempt if such transaction is chargeable to securities transaction tax • Unlisted shares and other assets – taxable at 20.6%[13,15]	Short term capital gains[4] – • Listed shares – taxable at 15.45%[13] • Unlisted shares and other assets – taxable at 41.2%[13] Long term capital gains[5] – • Listed shares – exempt • Unlisted securities[7] – taxable at 10.3%[13] • Other assets – taxable at 20.6%[13]

13 From 1 April 2016, surcharge @ 15% shall be levied if the total income exceeds INR10m.
14 In the case of residents, with effect from 1 April 2016, rebate of INR5,000 shall be granted if taxable income is within the band.
15 Subject to benefit of bands.

		Residents	Non-residents
Inheritance Tax (IHT)	General description	No concept of inheritance tax in India. In India, wealth tax was levied prior to 1 April 2015, when the net worth of specified person exceeded a prescribed limit	
	Taxable Entities	Wealth tax has been abolished from 1 April 2015	
	Chargeable assets	Prior to 1 April 2015, chargeable/specified assets included guest houses, residential houses (including farm houses), commercial buildings, motor cars, jewellery, yachts, boats and aircraft, urban lands, cash-in-hand in excess of INR0.05m. It also included deemed assets such as assets transferred by one spouse to another, assets held by minor child, etc Residents – assets located in India and abroad Non-residents – assets located in India	
	Calculation of Charge	Prior to 1 April 2015, wealth tax was on net wealth of taxpayer. Net wealth defined as gross value of chargeable / specified assets less debts incurred / owed in respect of the said assets as on the valuation date (ie 31 March)	
	Taxable events	Prior to 1 April 2015, wealth tax levied on net wealth of taxpayer exceeding INR3m as on the valuation date	
	Allowances	Prior to 1 April 2015, certain allowances had been specified depending on the nature of assets	
	Tax rates	Prior to 1 April 2015, 1% of the net wealth in excess of INR3m	

IV   WITHHOLDING TAXES[16]

Under domestic law	Payments to residents	Payments to non-residents
Dividends	Nil[17] However, dividends are subject to dividend distribution tax at 20.36% (basic rate of 15% grossed up to 17.647% + surcharge of 12% + education cess of 3%) Further, any income distributed on the buy-back of shares is subject to distribution tax of 23.072% on distributed income[18] (basic rate of 20% + surcharge of 12% + education cess of 3%)	Nil However, dividends are subject to dividend distribution tax at 20.36% (basic rate of 15% grossed up to 17.647% + surcharge of 12% + education cess of 3%) Further, any income distributed on the buy-back of shares is subject to distribution tax of 23.072% on distributed income[18] (basic rate of 20% + surcharge of 12% + education cess of 3%)
Interest	10%[19]	In case of foreign currency loan – 5.15%/20.6%[20, 21] In case of Indian currency loan – 30.90%[20] / 41.20%[21]

16 Every recipient deriving income from India is required to obtain a Permanent Account Number (PAN) in India. In the absence of PAN, the withholding tax rate applicable in India would be at a higher rate and not as per the rate specified by treaty. With effect from 1 June 2016, a non-resident would be able to avail the beneficial rate as per treaty without obtaining PAN, subject to fulfilment of conditions as may be prescribed (furnishing of Tax Identification No, contact details and address of the country in which the payee is a non-resident).
   To avail tax treaty benefits, a non-resident is required to furnish a Tax Residency Certificate obtained from the Government of the home country.
17 Dividends received by resident individual, HUF or a firm from domestic companies in excess of INR1m will be charged to tax @ 10% on gross basis.
18 Distributed income would mean consideration paid by company on buy-back of shares as reduced by the amount which was received by company for issue of such shares. The amount which was received by the company for issue of shares shall be determined by the method as prescribed in the rules notified by the tax department.
19 For interest other than interest on securities the applicable rate of 10% would apply if the interest income exceeds the limit of INR5,000. In case of interest on securities (like interest on debentures) the applicable rate of 10% would apply if the interest income exceeds the limit of INR5,000.
20 Withholding taxes at the rate of 5% (plus applicable surcharge and cess) shall be applicable in case of foreign loans acquired during a specified period subject to specified conditions. Otherwise, taxes would be withheld at the rate of 20% (plus applicable surcharge and cess).
21 For companies, the rate of tax would further increase by a surcharge of 2% on the base rate where the income exceeds INR10m but not INR100m and 5% on the base rate where the income exceeds INR100m. For individuals, if the taxable income exceeds INR10m, a surcharge at the rate of 15% is applicable from PY 2016–17.

Royalties	10%[21, 22]	10.30%[21]
Fees for Technical Services	10%[21, 22]	10.30%[21]
On payments to artists and sportsmen	Sportsmen – 10% Artists (individual) – 10%	Sportsperson – 20.6%[21] Artists (individual) – 20.6%[21]

India's Double Taxation Avoidance Agreements in Force				
Country	Dividends (Note 2)	Interest	Royalties	Fees for Technical Services
Albania	10%	10%	10%	10%
Armenia	10%	10%	10%	10%
Australia	15%	15%	15%[7]	No Separate Provision
Austria	10%	10%	10%	10%
Bangladesh	10%/15%	10%	10%	No Separate Provision
Belarus	10%/15%	10%	15%	15%
Belgium	15%	15%[2]	10%	10%
Bhutan	10%	10%	10%	10%
Botswana	7.5%/10%	10%	10%	10%
Brazil	15%	15%	15%[1]	15%
Bulgaria	15%	15%	20%[6]	20%
Canada	15%/25%	15%[4]	15%[7]	15%[7]
China	10%	10%	10%	10%
Colombia	5%	10%	10%	10%
Croatia	5%/15%	10%	10%	10%
Cyprus (proposed to be effective from 1 April 2017)	10%	10%[5]	10%	10%
Czech Republic	10%	10%	10%	10%
Denmark	15%/25%	15%[2]	20%	20%
Estonia	10%	10%	10%	10%
Ethiopia	7.5%	10%	10%	10%
Finland	10%	10%[4]	10%	10%
Fiji	5%	10%	10%	10%
France	10%	10%	10%	10%
Georgia	10%	10%	10%	10%
Germany	10%	10%	10%	10%
Greece	Refer DTAA	Refer DTAA	Source Country tax – royalty	No Separate Provision

22 The applicable rate of 10% would apply if the income from royalty/ fees for technical services exceeds INR30,000.

Other

An equalisation levy of 6% shall be levied on gross amount of consideration for online advertisement or other specified e-commerce services received or receivable by non-resident not having permanent establishment in India. No such levy shall be made if the amount of consideration for specified services does not exceed INR0.1m. The consideration subject to equalisation levy will be exempt from income-tax in India.

India's Double Taxation Avoidance Agreements in Force				
Country	Dividends (Note 2)	Interest	Royalties	Fees for Technical Services
Hungary	10%	10%	10%	10%
Iceland	10%	10%	10%	10%
Indonesia	10%/15%	10%	15%	No Separate Provision
Ireland	10%	10%	10%	10%
Israel	10%	10%	10%	10%
Italy	15%/25%	15%	20%	20%
Japan	10%	10%	10%	10%
Jordan	10%	10%	20%	20%
Kazakhstan	10%	10%	10%	10%
Kenya	15%	15%	20%	17.5%
Korea (proposed to be effective from 1 April 2017)	15%	10%	10%	10%
Kuwait	10%	10%	10%	10%
Kyrgyzstan	10%	10%	15%	15%
Latvia	10%	10%	10%	10%
Libya	Refer DTAA	Refer DTAA	Source Country tax – royalty	No Separate Provision
Lithuania	5%/15%	10%	10%	10%
Luxembourg	10%	10%	10%	10%
Malaysia	5%	10%	10%	10%
Malta	10%	10%	10%	10%
Mauritius (from 1 April 2017)	5%/15%	7.5%	15%	10%
Macedonia	10%	10%	10%	10%
Mongolia	15%	15%	15%	15%
Montenegro	5%/15%	10%	10%	10%
Morocco	10%	10%	10%	10%
Mozambique	7.5%	10%	10%	No Separate Provision
Myanmar	5%	10%	10%	No Separate Provision
Namibia	10%	10%	10%	10%
Nepal	5%/10%	10%	15%	No Separate Provision
Netherlands	10%	10%	10%	10%
New Zealand	15%	10%	10%	10%
Norway	10%	10%	10%	10%
Oman	10%/12.5%	10%	15%	15%
Philippines	15%/20%	15%[2]	15%	No Separate Provision
Poland	10%	10%	15%	15%
Portugal	10%/15%	10%	10%	10%
Qatar	5%/10%	10%	10%	10%
Romania	10%	10%	10%	10%
Russian Federation	10%	10%	10%	10%
Saudi Arabia	5%	10%	10%	No Separate Provision
Serbia	5%/15%	10%	10%	10%
Singapore	10%/15%	15%[2]	10%	10%

India's Double Taxation Avoidance Agreements in Force				
Country	Dividends (Note 2)	Interest	Royalties	Fees for Technical Services
Slovenia	5%/15%	10%	10%	10%
South Africa	10%	10%	10%	10%
Spain	15%	15%	20%	20%
Sri Lanka	7.5%	10%	10%	10%
Sudan	10%	10%	10%	10%
Sweden	10%	10%	10%	10%
Switzerland	10%	10%[5]	10%	10%
Syria	5%/10%	10%	10%	No Separate Provision
Tajikistan	5%/10%	10%	10%	No Separate Provision
Tanzania	5%/10%	10%	10%	No Separate Provision
Thailand	15%/20%	25%[2]	15%	No Separate Provision
Trinidad and Tobago	10%	10%	10%	10%
Turkey	15%	15%[2]	15%	15%
Turkmenistan	10%	10%	10%	10%
Ukraine	10%/15%	10%[5]	10%	10%
Uganda	10%	10%	10%	10%
United Arab Emirates	10%	12.5%[3]	10%	No Separate Provision
United Arab Republic	Refer DTAA	Refer DTAA	Source Country tax – royalty	No Separate Provision
United Mexican States	10%	10%	10%	10%
United Kingdom	10%/15%	15%[2]	10%/15%	10%/15%
United States	15%/25%	15%[2]	10%/15%	10%/15%
Uruguay	5%	10%	10%	10%
Uzbekistan	10%	10%[5]	10%	10%
Vietnam	10%	10%[5]	10%	10%
Zambia	5%/15%	10%	10%	10%

Note 1: the above rates are only available provided the specific Treaty criteria are satisfied. It is possible that lower rates than those shown above may be available provided that certain criteria are satisfied. As treaties will not be identical, guidance should be sought in all cases.

Note 2: Dividends received from Domestic Company (company incorporated in India) on which Dividend Distribution tax (DDT) has been paid by such company are exempt in the hands of shareholders under section 10(34) of Income Tax Act. Accordingly, the rates mentioned in the above table do not have any practical application as such.

1 In case of royalties arising from use of trademarks, the applicable rate would be 25%.
2 In case of interest on bank loans, rates are 10%.
3 In case of interest on bank loans, rates are 5%.
4 Interest shall be taxed in the country in which it arises and according to domestic laws.
5 Interest received from transaction approved by source country's government will be exempt.
6 Where the payment received is for the use of or the right to use any copyright of a literary, artistic or scientific work, the applicable rate would be 15%.
7 In the case of royalties and fees for technical services relating to payments for the use of or the right to use industrial, commercial or scientific equipment, the rate is 10%.

V   INDIRECT TAXES AND VAT

		Overview
Indirect Taxes and Value Added Tax (VAT)	General description	*VAT:* Levied by State Government on intra-state sale of goods in India *CST:* Levied by Central Government on inter-state sale of goods in India *Service Tax:* Levied by Central Government on provision of services in India (except the states of Jammu and Kashmir). The service tax legislation is based on 'negative list' regime for applicability of service tax with effect from 1 July 2012. Further, certain specified services are taxable under reverse charge mechanism (RCM) when procured from specified person such as 'works contract', 'rent-a-cab' etc. The RCM is where the service receiver is liable to pay service tax *Excise Duty:* Levied by Central Government on manufacture of goods in India *Customs Duty:* Levied by Central Government on import of goods from outside India and on certain specified export of goods
	Entities obliged to levy	*VAT and CST:* All entities – individual, companies, firm, society, club and even Government selling goods beyond threshold limit as specified by respective State Governments *Service tax:* All entities – individual, companies, firm, society and even Government providing specified services beyond threshold limit of INR1m in a financial year. Specified entities receiving certain specified services are liable to levy under RCM without any threshold limit *Excise Duty:* All entities – individual, companies, firm, society, club and even Government manufacturing goods beyond a prescribed threshold limit *Customs Duty:* All entities – individual, companies, firm, society, club and even Government importing goods without any threshold limit
	Taxable activities	*VAT and CST:* Sale of goods in India, including certain transactions specified as deemed sale such as leasing, works contract, hire-purchase etc *Service Tax:* On provision of services including import and export of services in specified circumstances *Excise Duty:* Applicable on manufacturing but payable on removal of manufactured goods from the factory

		Overview
Indirect Taxes and Value Added Tax (VAT) – *contd*		*Customs Duty:* On import and clearance of goods from customs area for home consumption
	Taxable activities – zero-rated (examples)	*VAT and CST:* Export of goods subject to fulfillment of prescribed conditions *Service tax:* Export of services subject to fulfillment of prescribed conditions *Excise Duty:* Export of goods manufacture in India subject to fulfillment of prescribed conditions
	Exemptions (examples)	*VAT:* *Goods* of basic necessities and of local importance as specified by respective State Governments like grains, pulses, water, etc *Service tax:* Prescribed services in negative list such as services related to agriculture, transmission or distribution of electricity, education, etc. Prescribed services in exemption list such as services provided to United Nations, Health care services, etc *Excise Duty:* Prescribed exemptions such as animal products, grains, vegetables, certain pharmaceuticals, etc *Customs Duty:* Prescribed exemptions such as scientific and research equipment, certain raw materials for manufacture in India, etc
	Refund	*VAT:* Unutilised VAT credit at the end of reporting period can be claimed as cash refund depending on state-specific provisions *Service tax:* Exporter of services can claim cash refund of unutilised CENVAT credit subject to prescribed conditions and timeline *Excise Duty:* Exporter of goods can claim cash refund of unutilised CENVAT credit subject to prescribed conditions and timeline
	Tax liability	*VAT and CST:* Person selling the goods is liable to charge the tax to the purchaser and pay the tax to the Government *Service Tax:* Person providing services is liable to charge the tax to the receiver and pay the tax to the Government. In case of RCM, receiver of services is responsible to pay tax *Excise Duty:* Person manufacturing and removing goods from the factory of production is liable to charge the duty to the purchaser of goods and pay the duty to the Government *Customs Duty:* Person responsible for import of goods in India is liable to pay the duty to the Government

		Overview
Indirect Taxes and Value Added Tax (VAT) – contd	Tax rates	*VAT:* VAT Rate differs from product to product and state to state: – For basic necessities – 0% – For goods of general importance – 4 to 6.5% – Others – 12.5% and above *CST:* Concessional rate of 2% if prescribed statutory Form (ie Form C) is obtained from purchaser *Service tax:* Service Tax – 15% (including Swachh Bharat Cess of 0.5% and Krishi Kalyan Cess of 0.5%) *Excise Duty:* Excise Duty Rate differs depending on product classification under Excise Tariff: – Excise Duty (generic rate) – 12.5% *Customs Duty:* Custom Duty Rate differs depending on product classification under Customs Tariff which is based on HS Codes: – Basic Customs Duty (generic rate) - 10% *(peak rate of duty shall be 29.45%)*
	Administrative obligations	*VAT and CST:* Registration with State VAT authorities beyond the threshold limit prescribed by State VAT laws Payment of VAT on monthly/quarterly/six-monthly basis depending on the turnover Filing of returns on monthly/quarterly/six-monthly basis depending on the turnover *Service tax:* Registration requirements for the provider beyond the threshold of INR0.9m and recipients of service (if RCM is applicable) without threshold Payment of service tax on monthly basis Filing of returns on six-monthly/annual basis *Excise Duty:* Registration requirements for the manufacturer of goods beyond a threshold limit of INR15m Payment of excise duty on monthly basis Filing of returns on monthly/quarterly/annual basis *Customs Duty:* Registration requirements for the importer of goods Payment of customs duty as and when goods are imported
	Local taxes	Apart from the taxes and duties mentioned above, there are local taxes that are levied and administered by state government, local municipal authority, etc. Such taxes typically cover Entry Tax, Local Body Tax, Octroi, Cess, etc

		Overview
Indirect Taxes and Value Added Tax (VAT) – *contd*	Upcoming Goods and Services Tax (GST)	GST is proposed to subsume most of present Federal and State indirect taxes such as Central Excise, Service tax, VAT, Central Sales Tax, Entry Tax, Countervailing Duties, etc
		'Dual GST' structure is proposed (Central GST and State GST)
		GST is expected to bring about uniformity in tax regime with wider tax base, reduction in cascading effect leading to lower transaction costs
		GST Bill for Constitutional Amendment was passed by both the houses of the Indian Parliament and enacted as Act in September 2016. The draft legislation known as 'Model GST Law' was released in public for discussion purposes on 14 June 2016. Further documents such as draft GST Rules and Formats on invoices, registration, payment, returns and refunds have also been released by the Government of India, and the revised version of 'Model GST Law' was released on 26 November 2016 by the Government of India
		It is proposed that GST would be implemented in India by 1 April 2017

Indonesia

(Rochmat, KAP Kanaka Puradiredja Suhartono, rochmat@kanaka.co.id)

I MAIN LEGAL FORMS

Characteristics / Legal form	Partnership	Private corporation and Public corporation
Partners/shareholders	Two or more	Two or more
• Number	None	None
• Restrictions		
Directors	Management by Partners	Management by Directors[1]
Establishment	Established by notary deed	Established by Notary deed
Registration	Registration with Public Court and then registered at State Gazette	Registration with Ministry of Law and Human Rights and then registered at State Gazette
Minimum capital	None	IDR50,000,000[2]
Liability	Unlimited	Limited to shareholders' contributions
Governance	Partners, General Meeting	Board of Directors, Shareholders' Meeting
Audit requirements	None	Audit is required if: The company operation is to collect or manage public funds The company issues bonds to the public The company is a public company The company has assets and/or business turnover minimum IDR50 million
Taxation	Transparent	Indonesia resident companies are subject to corporation tax

---

1 Management of corporations is performed by directors and supervised by commissioners. Both private and public companies must have at least one director and one commissioner, who are natural persons, ie not corporate bodies. The expatriates can act as a director or a commissioner in the Indonesian companies, except human resources and government relation.
2 For foreign investment company a start-up minimum investment value of at least IDR10,000,000,000 (ten billion Rupiah) (excluding value of land and building) with a minimum issued and paid-up capital of IDR2,500,000,000 (two billion and five hundred million Rupiah) or the equivalent in US Dollars.

II   CORPORATION TAX

Description / Legal Form	Resident corporation	Permanent establishment (PE)
General description	Indonesia Corporation Tax	
Taxable entities	Companies incorporated and domiciled in Indonesia	PE located in Indonesia
Taxable income	Worldwide profits	Profits derived by PE in Indonesia
Calculation of taxable profits	Accounting profit is adjusted for various tax add-backs and allowances to profits chargeable to corporation tax, with the exception of businesses subject to a tax on gross turnover	
Interest payments	Interest expenses are tax deductible except interest for loan to buy stock which cannot be deductible as interest expense if dividend received by the company is not subject to income tax	
Related party transactions	All related party transactions must take place on arm's-length basis	
Tax year, return and payment	Tax period normally coincides with accounting period	
	Tax return must be submitted to the tax office within 4 months from the end of the accounting period	
	Tax payment should be made before the tax return is submitted but most companies pay tax in monthly instalments	
Capital gains	Capital gains are subject to corporation tax at normal rates	
Losses	Tax losses can be carried forward and set off against income derived in the following 5 years	
Tax group	Group relief applicable only for dividend income if a company holds participating minimum 25% ownership of another taxpayer	
Tax rate	Generally: 25%	
	Specific:	
	a. 20% for public companies that satisfy a minimum listing requirement of 40%	
	b. 1% and should be final for small enterprises with turnover of IDR4.8 billion per annum and below	
	For businesses that are subject to deemed profit calculations:	
	a. 1.2% and should be final for domestic shipping company	
	b. 1.8% and should be final for domestic airline company	
	c. 2.64% and should be final for foreign shipping and airline company	
	d. 2% up to 6% (depend on services) and should be final for construction company	
	e. 3.75% and should be final for foreign drilling of oil and gas company	

III TAXES FOR INDIVIDUALS

		Residents	Non-residents
Income Tax	General description	Tax levied on the chargeable income of a chargeable person for a year of assessment	
	Taxable entities and taxable income	Residents are taxed on their worldwide income Professionals and businessmen have an option of maintaining full bookkeeping records or only a record of income derived	Non-residents are liable to tax on income arising in Indonesia, subject to provisions in double taxation agreements
	Types of taxable income	Property income Income from business activity Employment income Miscellaneous income – annual profits, capital gain, etc	
	Calculation of income	Actual income received reduced by deductible expenses and non-taxable income	
	Tax year, tax assessment and tax payment	Tax year – fiscal year – 1 January to 31 December Tax assessment – individual self-assessment return for each taxpayer to be filed by 31 March Tax payment due – 31 March following the tax year	Tax year – fiscal year – 1 January to 31 December Tax assessment – with credits for any withholding tax payments Tax payment due – anytime via withholding tax
	Losses	Losses are treated the same as treatment of losses for corporate taxes but only for professionals and businessmen who choose to maintain full bookkeeping	No loss carried forward allowed
	Tax rates	Scale rate as follows: *Chargeable income* *Tax rate (%)* 0 to IDR50,000,000 5% IDR50,000,000–IDR250,000,000 15% IDR250,000,000–IDR500,000,000 25% Above IDR500,000,000 30%	20% from taxable income, or subject to provisions in double taxation agreements
		Residents	**Non-residents**
Capital Gains Tax (CGT)	General description	No specific capital gains tax applicable; capital gains are subject to individual income tax at normal rates	
	Taxable entities and chargeable assets		
	Calculation of gain		
	Tax year, tax assessment and tax payment		
	Losses		
	Tax rates		

		Domiciled	Non-domiciled
Inheritance Tax (IHT)	General description	Inheritance is not subject to tax	
	Taxable entities and chargeable assets		
	Calculation of charge		
	Taxable events		
	Allowances		
	Tax rates		

IV WITHHOLDING TAXES

Under domestic law	Payments to residents	Payments to non-residents
Dividends	15% from gross amount for corporations	20%
	10% final from gross amount for individuals	
	Not subject to tax for a company which holds participating ownership in another taxpayer of a minimum 25%	
Interest	15% from gross amount	20%
	20% from gross amount for interest from time deposit	
Royalties	15% from gross amount	20%
On payments to artists and sportsmen	Progressive from 5%–30%	20%

Reduced rate available under the relevant Double Taxation Treaty			
Country	Dividends	Interest	Royalties
Algeria	15%	15%	15%
Australia	15%	10%	15%
Austria	15%	10%	10%
Bangladesh	15%	10%	10%
Belgium	15%	10%	10%
Brunei	15%	15%	15%
Bulgaria	15%	10%	10%
Canada	15%	10%	10%
China	10%	10%	10%
Croatia	10%	10%	10%
Czech Republic	15%	12.5%	12.5%
Denmark	20%	10%	15%
Egypt	15%	15%	15%
Finland	15%	10%	15%
France	15%	15%	10%
Germany	15%	10%	15%
Hong Kong	5%	10%	5%
Hungary	15%	15%	15%
India	15%	10%	15%
Iran	7%	10%	12%
Italy	15%	10%	15%
Japan	15%	10%	10%
Jordan	10%	10%	10%
Kuwait	10%	5%	20%
Luxembourg	15%	10%	12.5%
Malaysia	10%	10%	10%
Mexico	10%	10%	10%
Mongolia	10%	10%	10%
Morocco	10%	10%	10%
Netherlands	10%	10%	10%
New Zealand	15%	10%	15%

Reduced rate available under the relevant Double Taxation Treaty			
Country	Dividends	Interest	Royalties
North Korea	10%	10%	10%
Norway	15%	10%	15%
Pakistan	15%	15%	15%
Papua New Guinea	15%	10%	10%
Philippines	20%	15%	15%
Poland	15%	10%	15%
Portugal	10%	10%	10%
Qatar	10%	10%	5%
Romania	15%	12.5%	15%
Russia	15%	15%	15%
Seychelles	10%	10%	10%
Singapore	15%	10%	15%
Slovakia	10%	10%	15%
South Africa	15%	10%	10%
South Korea	15%	10%	15%
Spain	15%	10%	10%
Sri Lanka	15%	15%	15%
Sudan	10%	15%	10%
Suriname	15%	15%	15%
Sweden	15%	10%	15%
Switzerland	15%	10%	10%
Syria	10%	10%	20%
Taiwan	10%	10%	10%
Thailand	20%	15%	15%
Tunisia	12%	12%	15%
Turkey	15%	10%	10%
Ukraine	15%	10%	10%
United Arab Emirates	10%	5%	5%
United Kingdom	15%	10%	15%
United States of America	15%	10%	10%
Uzbekistan	10%	10%	10%
Venezuela	15%	10%	20%
Vietnam	15%	15%	15%
Zimbabwe	20%	10%	15%

Note: the above rates are only available provided the specific Treaty criteria are satisfied. It is possible that lower rates than those shown above may be available provided that certain criteria are satisfied. As treaties will not be identical, guidance should be sought in all cases.

V INDIRECT TAXES

		Residents	Non-residents
Value Added Tax (VAT)	General description	Tax on the supply of goods and services	
	Entities obliged to levy VAT	Any individual, partnership, corporation or other body, which carries out taxable activities	
	Taxable activities	Supply of goods and services, import of goods, intra-community acquisition of goods, etc	
	Taxable activities – zero-rated (examples)	Export of goods and certain services	
	Exemptions (examples)	Products of mining or drilling taken directly from the source	
		Taxable goods delivery to the broker or through an auctioneer	
		Daily necessities needed by public	
		Financial, insurance, social, medical, and religious services	
	Refund of VAT	VAT is computed by deducting the input tax amount from the output tax amount chargeable on the goods or services supplied by the taxpayer. The input tax which exceeds the output tax is refundable	
	Tax liability	The supplier of goods and services is responsible for charging VAT	
	Tax rates	Standard rate: 10%	
		Export rate: 0%	
	Administrative obligations	Monthly self-assessment VAT in minus VAT out to tax office	
Real Property Taxes		There is both an annual tax and a transfer tax on land and buildings	
Stamp Duty		IDR3,000 for transactions IDR250,000 up to IDR1,000,000	
		IDR6,000 for transactions IDR1,000,000 and above	

Iraq

(Ahmed Al-Juboori, Ahmed Al-Juboori & Co. LLP, acc.firm@aljuboori.net)

I MAIN LEGAL FORMS

Legal form / Characteristics	Sole Owner Enterprise, Simple Company, Partnership	Joint Stock Company, Joint Liability Company, Limited Liability Company (LLC)
Partners/shareholders • Number • Restrictions	One person or more than one persons	Private: one person or more than one person PLC: no less than 3 and no more than 100
Directors	Management by the partners or by director	Board directors
Establishment	Register in Ministry of Trade – Register of companies	Register in Ministry of Trade – Register of companies
Registration	A notarized establishment contract signed by all the partners will suffice and a copy of the establishment contract should be placed with the registrar of companies	The registration process of the companies takes between eight to 12 weeks to be completed from the date of submission of the application to the registrar of companies
Minimum capital	IQD 500,000 (approx US$400)	Private: IQD 1,000,000 (US$800) PLC: IQD 2,000,000 (US$1,600)
Liability	Partnership: unlimited LLP: unlimited	Private and PLC: Limited according to the capital
Governance	Partners and General Manager	Private: Directors PLC: audit committee + Directors
Audit requirements	Should be audited	Should be audited
Taxation	Tax on worldwide profits since the capital is from Iraq	Tax on worldwide profits since the capital is from Iraq
Usage	Financial organizations and Government	Financial organizations and Government However, Iraqi companies should have an Arabic name and therefore most of the foreign companies cannot keep their names as they do not have an Arabic meaning

II CORPORATION TAX

Legal form / Description	Resident corporation	Permanent establishment (PE)
General description	General committee of Tax – Iraq	
Taxable entities	Corporations registered in Iraq	PE located in Iraq
Taxable income	All turnover from Iraqi source and Iraqi Fund	All turnover from Iraqi source and Iraqi Fund to the PE located in Iraq
Calculation of taxable profits	Accounting profit as adjusted for various expenses which are added back to profit to reach taxable income	Accounting profit as adjusted for various expenses which are added back to profit to reach taxable income
Interest payments	No restriction on allowable interest payments	No restriction on allowable interest payments
Related party transactions	All related party transactions will be included in calculations	All related party transactions will be included in calculations
Tax year, return and payment	Tax year ends on 31 December Tax summated should be done before 1 June every year. Corporate tax payment should been done annually and payroll tax should be done monthly	Tax year ends on 31 December Tax summated should be done before 1 June every year. Corporate tax payment should been done annually and payroll tax should been done monthly
Capital gains	Capital gains are taxable at the normal corporate income tax rate All gains can be transferred to any place out of Iraq or in Iraq	Capital gains are taxable at the normal corporate income tax rate All gains can be transferred to any place out of Iraq or in Iraq
Losses	Can be carried forward for next five years	Can be carried forward for next five years
Tax group	There is no tax group	There is no tax group
Tax rate	15% profit on all activity and 35% for oil and gas businesses	15% profit on all activity and 35% for oil and gas businesses

III TAXES FOR INDIVIDUALS

		Residents	Non-residents
Income Tax	General description	Tax depending on personal income during the year	
	Taxable entities and taxable income	Individuals, trusts	Liable to tax on income earned in Iraq regardless of the place of receipt
	Types of taxable income	– Rent from property – Trading activity – Employment income	– Rent from property – Trading activity – Employment income
	Calculation of income	Property rent: 10% Trading activity: 15% Employment income: 15%	Property rent: 10% Trading activity: 15% Employment income: 15%
	Tax year, tax assessment and tax payment	5 months after the end of year and the payment is the same	5 months after the end of year and the payment is the same
	Losses	Any losses can be carried forward for the next 5 years	Any losses can be carried forward for the next 5 years
	Tax rates	up to IQD 500,000 3% IQD 500,000–1000,000 5% IQD 1,000,000–2,000,000 10% More than IQD 2,000,000 15%	up to IQD 500,000 3% IQD 500,000–1000,000 5% IQD 1,000,000–2,000,000 10% More than IQD 2,000,000 15%
Capital Gains Tax (CGT)	General description	All gains and losses on disposals of capital assets	
	Taxable entities and chargeable assets	All individuals resident in Iraq	Assets located in Iraq and owned by non-residents are subject to CGT
	Calculation of gain	Proceeds less attributable costs	Proceeds less attributable costs
	Tax year, tax assessment and tax payment	Before 31 May every year	Before 31 May every year
	Losses	Can be carried forward for 5 years	
	Tax rates	Taxed as a part of income	Taxed as a part of income
		Domiciled	**Non-domiciled**
Inheritance Tax (IHT)	General description	Tax on all property and lottery winnings over IQD 10,000 under Tax law No 7 of year 1966	
	Taxable entities and chargeable assets	A person who lives in Iraq is taxable	A person who has property in Iraq and does not live in Iraq is taxable
	Calculation of charge	Proceeds from gift less expenses	Proceeds from gift less expenses
	Taxable events	Gifts in life and death Prizes of all kinds	Gifts in life and death Prizes of all kinds
	Allowances	N/A	N/A
	Tax rates	5%–35%	5%–35%

IV   WITHHOLDING TAXES

Under domestic law	Payments to residents	Payments to non-residents
Dividends	Nil	Nil
Interest	Nil	A tax of 15% applies to payments of interest from an Iraqi LLC or branch to a non-Iraq resident (eg the foreign parent company or non-resident bank)
Royalties	Nil	Nil

There are also payroll and social security taxes to be withheld from earnings in Iraq.

Iraq has a number of Double Taxation Treaties, including with the Council of Arab Economic Unity (CAEU). However, these are mainly ignored.

V INDIRECT TAXES

		Residents	Non-residents
Value Added Tax	General description	In Iraq, there is no general indirect taxation or any general sales tax	
	Entities obliged to levy VAT		
	Taxable activities		
	Taxable activities – zero-rated (examples)		
	Exemptions (examples)		
	Refund of VAT		
	Tax liability		
	Tax rates		
	Administrative obligations		
Real Property Taxes			
Stamp Duty			

Ireland

(John Fisher, Gordon Hayden, Smith & Williamson, john.fisher@
smithandwilliamson.com, gordon.hayden@smithandwilliamson.com)

I MAIN LEGAL FORMS

Legal form / Characteristics	Partnership and Limited Liability Partnership (LLP)	Private corporation (Ltd)/(DAC) and Public corporation (Plc)
Partners/shareholders • Number • Restrictions	Two or more but a maximum of 20 persons (exception in the case of professional partnerships) No concept of an LLP exists under Irish law	Company limited by shares (Ltd) Designated Activity Company (DAC) – Ltd by shares, differs in some aspects to a company limited by shares. Applies to companies which require an objects clause or those that are prohibited from being a company limited by shares; for example, an insurance undertaking, or those companies that wish to list debt securities but are not Plcs, will need to register as a DAC
Directors		Ltd – one director DAC – at least two directors
Establishment	Partnership deed	Constitution (including a memorandum and articles of association)
Registration		Filed with Registrar of Companies
Minimum capital	N/A	Plc: €25,000 of share capital must be issued, of which 25% must be paid up Ltd: One share per shareholder
Liability	Joint and several liability with no limitations	Limited to unpaid capital subscribed
Audit requirements		Mandatory except for smaller private companies/groups under certain circumstances
Taxation	Transparent assessed on partners	Taxable on worldwide profits if resident in Ireland

II   CORPORATION TAX

Legal form / Description	Resident corporation	Permanent establishment (PE)
General description	Corporation tax	
Taxable entities	From 1 January 2015, all Irish incorporated companies will be considered tax resident in Ireland unless they are considered tax resident in another location by virtue of a tax treaty which Ireland has with that other territory. In addition, any company which is considered to be managed and controlled in Ireland will be considered Irish	Companies operating a branch or agency in Ireland
Taxable profits	Total worldwide profits (income and gains)	• Trading income arising directly or indirectly through a branch or agency in the state; and • any income or chargeable gains from property owned or used by, or held by or for, a branch or agency
Calculation of taxable profits	• Income is calculated under various schedules and cases and taxed thereon • Corporation tax is imposed on the company's profits, which includes business/trading profits, passive income and capital gains • Company chargeable gains on development land and shares deriving their value from development land are subject to capital gains tax	
Interest payments	• Interest on borrowings used for trade or rental purposes is generally tax deductible on an accruals basis • Interest on borrowings used for non-trade purposes, such as acquisition of shares in another company, is deductible on a paid basis, subject to certain conditions • There are restrictions where intra-group transactions are financed by intra group debt • No thin capitalisation restrictions other than payments to a non-Irish resident 75% affiliate outside the EU that may be reclassified as dividends/distributions in certain limited cases	
Related party transactions	Transfer pricing legislation applies to trading transactions between connected parties in certain circumstances	
Tax year, return and payment	The tax year is the accounting year Corporation tax returns (together, in certain cases, with iXBRL financial statements) are due for submission to the Irish Revenue on the 23rd day of the ninth month (where they elect to pay and file electronically via the Revenue's Online System (ROS), otherwise it is the 21st) following the end of the accounting period to which it relates Companies generally must pay 90% of their corporation tax liability on the 23rd day (if paying via ROS online, otherwise it is 21st) of the 11th month of the accounting period. In addition to the above, 'large companies', defined as companies with a previous year tax liability in excess of €200,000, must pay 45% of their corporation tax liability approximately 6 months before their year end. 'Large companies' must then account for 90% of their total tax liability for the year by the payment due date in the 11th month	
Taxation of capital gains	Chargeable gains are subject to corporation tax/capital gains tax at an effective rate of 33%	

Legal form / Description	Resident corporation	Permanent establishment (PE)
Taxation of income	Trading income is subject to the standard rate of corporation tax at 12.5%	
	Income from a foreign trade is taxed at 25%	
	Passive income, including rental income and interest income, is generally taxed at 25%	
Losses	• Trading losses may be set off against trading profits of the company in the same accounting period or preceding accounting period (of equal length) or alternatively can be carried forward indefinitely for use in the same trade • Trading losses can also be set against other income and gains of the current and preceding year on a 'value basis'. This means that the amount of the loss which is needed to shelter other income will depend on the tax rate which would have been applicable to that other income in the absence of loss relief	
Tax group	Each company in a group is taxed separately. Group relief may be claimed on a current period basis. A group consists of a parent company and all of its 75% subsidiaries. All group members must be resident in an EU Member State, an EEA Member State or a state with which Ireland has a Double Taxation Agreement, or be listed on a recognised stock exchange	

III TAXES FOR INDIVIDUALS

	Residents	Non-residents
General description	Income tax and capital gains tax	
Important definitions relevant to the scope of Irish taxation for individuals	• An individual is tax resident if he is present in Ireland at any time or several times in the tax year for a period in the whole amounting to 183 days or more; or • At any time or several times in the tax year and the preceding tax year for a period in the whole amounting to 280 days or more (no account is taken for a period in the whole amounting to 30 days or less in one of these years) • An individual will be considered to have spent a day in Ireland if they have been present in the country at any time during that day • An individual is ordinarily resident tax in Ireland for a tax year if he has been resident for each of the 3 consecutive tax years preceding that year • Domicile is a legal concept and generally a person is domiciled in the country of which he is a national. A person's domicile can change and the circumstances of each situation have to be considered • There are specific provisions for non-domiciled individuals	

Income Tax		Individual resident, ordinarily resident and domiciled	Individual not resident but ordinarily resident and domiciled
	Taxation of income	Liable to Irish income tax on his worldwide income	Liable to Irish income tax on worldwide income with the exception of income from: • a trade or profession no part of which is carried on in Ireland • an office or employment all of the duties of which are performed outside Ireland • other sources of foreign income not exceeding €3,810
	Types of taxable income	• Rental and investment income • Trading profits • Employment and pension income	• Rental and investment income excluding foreign income not exceeding €3,810 • Trading profits excluding profits where the trade is wholly exercised outside of Ireland • Employment income excluding income where the employment is wholly exercised outside of Ireland and • Pension income
	Calculation of income	Income is calculated under various schedules and cases and taxed thereon	

		Residents	Non-residents
Income Tax – *contd*	Tax year, tax assessment and tax payment	• The tax year is the calendar year • Income tax on employment income is taxed at source and collected through the operation of PAYE • Generally, where an individual has income other than employment income subject to PAYE, he will be taxed under the self-assessment system, under which the taxpayer is obliged to submit a tax return to the Irish Revenue by 31 October in the year that follows the tax year of assessment • Under self assessment, preliminary income tax is paid on 31 October in the current year of assessment and the balance is payable on 31 October following the year of assessment (ie the date on which the return is filed) • Taxpayers can opt to file tax returns electronically and may avail of an extended deadline for the submission of their tax return where they elect to pay and file electronically via the Revenue's Online System	
	Losses	Generally, losses may be carried forward indefinitely for offset against profits arising from the same source Trading losses may shelter current year income from other sources, subject to the trader being a sole trader or active partner Carry back of trade losses for 3 years is provided where there is a permanent discontinuance of the trade to which the loss relates	
	Tax rates	• The standard rate of income tax is 20% • The marginal rate of income tax is 40% • PRSI (Social Insurance contributions) applies at a rate of 4% to gross income. Employers PRSI is in general charged at a rate of 10.75% • A Universal Social Charge applies at various rates ranging from 0.5% to 10.5% for 2017	
		Irish resident/ordinarily resident and domiciled	**Non-resident**
Capital Gains Tax (CGT)		Liable to CGT on gains accruing on the disposal of worldwide assets	Liable to CGT on the disposal of 'specified assets' (eg land, buildings, minerals, exploration rights) in the state and on shares deriving their value or the greater part of their value from certain 'specified assets'
	Taxation of chargeable capital	• Computed in accordance with the CGT rules • The tax year for payment purposes is split into an 'initial period' running from 1 January to 30 November and a 'later period' running for one month to 31 December • CGT for the initial period ending 30 November is due for payment on 15 December in that year • CGT for the later period ended 31 December is due for payment on 31 January following the year of assessment • Details of chargeable gains for a tax year are due for submission to the Irish Revenue on 31 October following the year of assessment	
	Losses	Generally losses can be set off against gains realised in the same year or carried forward for utilisation in subsequent years	
	Tax rates	The rate of CGT is 33% Capital gains arising on the disposal of certain offshore funds are taxed at other rates	

		Irish resident/ordinarily resident and domiciled	Non-resident
Inheritance Tax and Gidt Tax (CAT)	The territorial scope of Irish capital acquisitions tax	Levied on the recipients of gifts or inheritances Generally, Irish capital acquisitions tax (CAT) will arise on gifts or inheritances taken where: • the disponer is resident or ordinarily resident in the state; • the donee is resident or ordinarily resident in the state; • property is situated in the state	
	Calculation of charge	Computed in accordance with the Capital Acquisition Tax Rules	
	Tax-free group thresholds	• Threshold (A) €310,000 – where the donee is a child or in some cases a parent of the disponer • Threshold (B) €32,500 – where the donee is a lineal ancestor or descendant (eg brother, sister, or a child of a brother or sister) • Threshold (C) €16,250 – other	
	Tax rates	The rate of CAT is 33%	

IV   WITHHOLDING TAXES

Under Domestic Law	Payments to residents	Payments to non-residents[5]
Dividends	Resident companies: Exempt	20%
	Resident individuals: 20%	
Interest	20%[1]	20%[2]
Royalties	Patent royalties: 20%[3]	20%[4]
	Other royalties: Nil	

Reduced rate available under the relevant Double Taxation Treaty		
Country	Dividends paid to other 'qualifying' companies	Interest	Royalties[6]
---	---	---	---
Albania	Nil	7%	7%
Armenia	Nil	10%	5%
Australia	Nil	10%	10%
Austria	Nil	Nil	10%
Bahrain	Nil	Nil	Nil
Belarus	Nil	5%	5%
Belgium	Nil	15%	Nil
Bosnia	Nil	Nil	Nil
Botswana	Nil	7.5%	7.5%
Bulgaria	Nil	5%	10%
Canada	Nil	10%	10%
Chile	Nil	15%	10%
China	Nil	10%	10%
Croatia	Nil	Nil	10%
Cyprus	Nil	Nil	5%
Czech Republic	Nil	Nil	10%
Denmark	Nil	Nil	Nil
Egypt	Nil	10%	10%
Estonia	Nil	10%	10%
Ethiopia	Nil	5%	5%
Finland	Nil	Nil	Nil
France	Nil	Nil	Nil
Georgia	Nil	Nil	Nil

1   There is an exemption where there is a 51% relationship between the payer and payee.
2   No withholding tax should apply where the conditions set out in the Irish legislation implementing the EU Interest and Royalty Directive 2003/49/EC apply and also in other specific circumstances.
3   There is an exemption where there is a 51% relationship between the payer and payee.
4   Exemptions can apply under the domestic legislation, eg EU Interest and Royalty Directive 2003/49/EC, where the recipient is tax resident in a country with which there is a double taxation agreement.
5   This is the maximum rate that may be imposed. Lower rates may apply depending on the circumstances.
6   Under the domestic legislation most payments should qualify for the 0% rate. The rate shown is the maximum rate that may be imposed. Payments related to copyrights, literary, dramatic, musical rights, etc may be taxed at different lower rates.

Reduced rate available under the relevant Double Taxation Treaty		
Country	**Dividends paid to other 'qualifying' companies**	**Interest**	**Royalties**[6]
Germany	Nil	Nil	Nil
Greece	Nil	5%	5%
Hong Kong	Nil	10%	3%
Hungary	Nil	Nil	Nil
Iceland	Nil	Nil	10%
India	Nil	10%	10%
Israel	Nil	10%	10%
Italy	Nil	10%	Nil
Japan	Nil	10%	10%
Kuwait	Nil	Nil	5%
Latvia	Nil	10%	10%
Lithuania	Nil	10%	10%
Luxembourg	Nil	Nil	Nil
Macedonia	Nil	Nil	Nil
Malaysia	Nil	10%	8%
Malta	Nil	Nil	5%
Mexico	Nil	10%	10%
Moldova	Nil	5%	5%
Montenegro	Nil	10%	10%
Morocco	Nil	10%	10%
Netherlands	Nil	Nil	Nil
New Zealand	Nil	10%	10%
Norway	Nil	Nil	Nil
Pakistan	Nil	10%	10%
Panama	Nil	5%	5%
Poland	Nil	10%	10%
Portugal	Nil	15%	10%
Qatar	Nil	Nil	5%
Republic of Korea	Nil	Nil	Nil
Romania	Nil	3%	3%
Russia	Nil	Nil	Nil
Saudi Arabia	Nil	Nil	8%
Serbia	Nil	10%	10%
Singapore	Nil	5%	5%
Slovakia	Nil	Nil	10%
Slovenia	Nil	5%	5%
South Africa	Nil	Nil	Nil
Spain	Nil	Nil	10%
Sweden	Nil	Nil	Nil
Switzerland	Nil	Nil	Nil
Thailand	Nil	15%	15%
Turkey	Nil	15%	10%
Ukraine	Nil	10%	5%
United Kingdom	Nil	Nil	Nil

Reduced rate available under the relevant Double Taxation Treaty			
Country	Dividends paid to other 'qualifying' companies	Interest	Royalties[6]
United Arab Emirates	Nil	Nil	Nil
United States	Nil	Nil	Nil
Uzbekistan	Nil	5%	5%
Vietnam	Nil	10%	15%
Zambia	Nil	10%	10%

Note: the above rates are only available provided the specific Treaty criteria are satisfied. It is possible that lower rates than those shown above may be available provided that certain criteria are satisfied. As treaties will not be identical, guidance should be sought in all cases. There are different dates under the treaties where certain taxes become effective. Specific advice should always be sought as some of the provisions will have effect later than others. Also there are provisions under the domestic legislation where certain reliefs have effect before the entry into force of the treaty.

V   INDIRECT TAXES

<table>
<tr><td rowspan="7">Value Added Tax (VAT)</td><td></td><td>**Residents**</td><td>**Non-residents**</td></tr>
<tr><td>Entities obliged to levy VAT</td><td colspan="2">Any person who makes taxable supplies of goods and services within the state in the course or furtherance of business in excess of the thresholds in any continuous period of 12 months (registration threshold of €37,500 for services and €75,000 for goods)

• On intra-Community acquisitions of goods
• Goods imported into the state from outside the EU
• A person who is not established in the state who supplies goods or services in the state
• Distance sales to customers who are not registered for VAT (registration threshold of €35,000)</td></tr>
<tr><td>Taxable activities and tax rates</td><td colspan="2">• Zero rate – includes most food and drink of a kind for human consumption, most clothing for children under 11 years of age, certain medical equipment and appliances
• 5.4% rate – certain farmers
• 9% rate - new reduced rate of VAT for tourism-related activities including restaurants, hotels and holiday accommodation, cinemas, hairdressing and newspapers
• 13.5% rate – reduced rate for items including immovable goods, services consisting of the development of immovable goods
• 23% rate – all other goods and services not specifically legislated to be taxed under any other rate</td></tr>
<tr><td>Exemptions (examples)</td><td colspan="2">• Exempt – certain lettings of immovable property, medical, dental and optical services, insurance services, banking and stock exchange activities</td></tr>
<tr><td>Refund of VAT</td><td>If incurred in course of furtherance of a business, VAT paid on supplies and services will be deductible as an input credit against VAT payable

A business will not be entitled to an input credit where the supplies and services are related to the provision of a VAT exempt supply

Input credit may be apportioned on a pro-rata basis between exempt and non-exempt supply where mixed usage occurs</td><td>The general position is that, under EU VAT legislation, a VAT registered person who is engaged in business outside the State, and who is not engaged in business in the State, may claim repayment of Irish VAT on most business purchases in the State</td></tr>
<tr><td>Tax liability</td><td colspan="2">See above</td></tr>
<tr><td>Administrative obligations</td><td colspan="2">Registration for VAT

Bi-monthly VAT returns or less frequently based on prior agreement with Revenue</td></tr>
</table>

	Residents	Non-residents
Real Property Taxes	Local municipal authorities levy 'rates' on the occupation of commercial property	
	An annual local property tax was introduced in 2013 in respect of residential property and is calculated based on the market value of the property	
Stamp Duty	Residential property: • Property valued up to €1,000,000 – 1% • Balance – 2%	
	Commercial property: • A single lower rate of 2% has applied since 7 December 2011	
	Shares: • 1% of all transactions above €1,000	
	No capital duty arises on the issue of shares	

Isle of Man

*(Stewart Fleming, Abacus Trust Company Limited,
stewart.fleming@abacusiom.com)*

I   MAIN LEGAL FORMS

Legal form / Characteristics	Partnership and Limited Partnership (LP) (No LLPs exist in the Isle of Man (IOM))	Private corporation (Ltd) and Public corporation (Plc)
Partners/shareholders • Number • Restrictions	• Two or more • None	• One or more • None
Directors	Management by partners or general partner within an LP	Management by directors
Establishment	Partnership deed	Articles of Association
Registration	IOM registry	
Minimum capital	None	1931 company – £1 for Ltd and £2 for Plc 2006 company – no minimum
Liability	Unlimited but limited partners of LP may be limited to capital	Limited to capital
Governance	Partners, general meeting	Managing director/Board of Directors, secretary, registered agent, shareholders' meeting
Audit requirements	None	*1931 company:* No audit requirement for Ltd providing it meets two of the following conditions: • turnover does not exceed £5.6m • total assets do not exceed £2.8m • no more than 50 employees Audit is required for Plc *2006 company:* No audit requirement

Characteristics \ Legal form	Partnership and Limited Partnership (LP) (No LLPs exist in the Isle of Man (IOM))	Private corporation (Ltd) and Public corporation (Plc)
Taxation	Partnerships are tax transparent. Partners are subject to IOM income tax on their share of the profits. Non-IOM resident partners are only taxed on certain IOM source income such as IOM rents and trading income	Resident companies are subject to income tax on their profits derived anywhere in the world
Usage	Varied, including professional and financial organisations	Small and medium-sized enterprises Plc used for larger companies seeking listing on AIM, etc

II CORPORATION TAX

Description / Legal form	Resident corporation	Permanent establishment (PE)
General description	Corporation tax	
Taxable entities	Companies resident in the IOM are subject to Manx income tax on their worldwide income	Companies incorporated and controlled outside of IOM, engaged in business within the IOM through a branch are liable to Manx non-resident income tax on the profit arising from the business of the branch
Taxable income	Worldwide profits	Profits derived by the branch in IOM
Calculation of taxable profits	Accounting profit is adjusted for various tax add-backs and allowances to arrive at profits chargeable to income tax	
Interest payments	Interest expenses for trading companies are fully tax deductible. However, the company must take into account the arm's length principle	
Related party transactions	All related party transactions must take place on arm's length basis	
Tax year, return and payment	Tax returns are due in respect of an accounting period and submission of the return is required within 12 months and 1 day of the end of the accounting period	
Capital gains	There is no capital gains tax	
Losses	Trading losses of a company may be offset against any other income in the same accounting period, carried back 1 year or carried forward and offset against future income of the same trade	
Tax group	A group comprises a parent company and its 75% subsidiaries	Not applicable for non-resident companies
Tax rate	The standard rate of corporate income tax in IOM is 0%. A 10% rate applies to income received from certain banking activities, and (up to 5 April 2015) on income derived from IOM land and property. With effect from 6 April 2015; a 20% income tax rate applies to income derived from IOM land and property. There is a land development tax holiday which provides an exemption from income tax for up to five years where certain conditions are met. With effect from 6 April 2013, corporate taxpayers which carry on retail business in the IOM and have taxable income of more than £500,000 are subject to the 10% rate	

III   TAXES FOR INDIVIDUALS

		Residents	Non-residents
Income Tax	General description	Tax levied on the chargeable income of a chargeable person for a year of assessment	
	Taxable entities and taxable income	Residents are taxed on their worldwide income with relief for double taxation	Non-residents are taxed on income arising in IOM
	Types of taxable income	• Property income • Savings and investment income but not bank interest and IOM company dividends for non-residents • Income from business activities • Employment from personal services or pensions • Income from trusts and estates but not non-IOM source for non-residents	
	Calculation of income	Generally that received in the year	
	Tax year, tax assessment and tax payment	• Tax year – runs from 6 April to the following 5 April • Tax assessment – individual returns and assessments for each taxpayer • Returns must be filed by 6 October following the year of assessment • Wages and salaries paid to employees are subject to tax deduction at source	
	Losses	Losses created by trading activities can be offset against other income or carried forward against future profits	
	Tax rates	Income is subject to Manx income tax at the standard rate of 10% on the first £8,500 of taxable income and thereafter at the higher rate of 20%. Personal allowance – £10,500	Non-residents are subject to income tax at a rate of 20%. Personal allowance – £Nil
Capital Gains Tax (CGT)	General description	Tax on increase in the value of asset between acquisition and disposal, not chargeable to income or corporate tax	
	Taxable entities and chargeable assets	There is no CGT in the IOM	
		IOM domiciled	**Non-IOM domiciled**
Inheritance Tax (IHT)	Taxable entities and chargeable assets	There is no estate or inheritance tax in the IOM	

IV WITHHOLDING TAXES

Under domestic law	Payments to residents	Payments to non-residents
Dividends	Nil	Nil
Interest	Nil	Nil, although in limited cases involving Isle of Man land, a 20% withholding may apply
Royalties	Nil	Nil
On payments to artists and sportsmen	Nil	Nil

Although the Isle of Man has an increasing number of double tax treaties in place, these will have little impact, given the general lack of withholding taxes. Where interest relates to land, treaty relief may be available should the necessary criteria be satisfied. However, professional advice should be sought.

V   INDIRECT TAXES

<table>
<tr><th></th><th></th><th>Residents</th><th>Non-residents</th></tr>
<tr><td rowspan="9">Value Added Tax (VAT)</td><td>General description</td><td colspan="2">Tax on the supply of goods and services</td></tr>
<tr><td>Entities obliged to levy VAT</td><td colspan="2">Generally any individual, partnership, corporation or other body which carries out taxable activities in the IOM or UK, subject to a turnover limit of £83,000, although other criteria also exist</td></tr>
<tr><td>Taxable activities</td><td colspan="2">VAT is charged on the purchase and sale of goods and services

VAT sales are either exempt, zero-rated or standard-rated</td></tr>
<tr><td>Taxable activities – zero-rated (examples)</td><td colspan="2">Export of goods and supply of services with another EU Member State</td></tr>
<tr><td>Exemptions (examples)</td><td colspan="2">Banking and insurance services</td></tr>
<tr><td>Refund of VAT</td><td colspan="2">If appropriate it may be obtained on submission of the VAT return</td></tr>
<tr><td>Tax liability</td><td colspan="2">Normally the supplier of goods and services is responsible for charging VAT</td></tr>
<tr><td>Tax rates</td><td colspan="2">• Standard rate = 20%
• Reduced rate = 5% (certain residential work)
• Zero rate = 0%</td></tr>
<tr><td colspan="2">Real Property Taxes</td><td colspan="2">There is no property tax</td></tr>
<tr><td colspan="2">Stamp Duty</td><td colspan="2">There is no stamp duty</td></tr>
</table>

Israel

(Guy Faigenboim, guy@slcpa.co.il)

I   MAIN LEGAL FORMS

Legal form / Characteristics	Partnership and Limited Partnership	Private corporation (Ltd) and Public corporation (Plc)
Partners/shareholders • Number • Restrictions	Limited Partnerships Minimum two partners in partnerships None	Ltd: No minimum Plc: Two partners minimum
Directors	N/A	No minimum except for listed companies
Establishment	Partnership agreement	Articles of Incorporation
Registration	Registrar of Companies	
Minimum capital	None	None
Liability	Joint and several liability	Limited to share capital
Governance	Partners	Management Board
Audit requirements	None	Mandatory
Taxation	Transparent. Partners assessed on share of worldwide profits	Corporation tax on worldwide profits/gains

II   CORPORATION TAX

Legal form / Description	Resident corporation	Permanent establishment (PE)
General description	Corporation tax	
Taxable entities	Incorporated in Israel/control and management in Israel	PE in Israel
Taxable income	Worldwide profits	Income derived in Israel
Calculation of taxable profits	Levied on gross income less certain allowable deductions	
Interest payments	Deductible subject to regular expenses deductions rules	
Related party transactions	Related party transactions should take place on arm's length basis	
Tax year, return and payment	Tax year – calendar year Tax returns are due within 5–12 months after the year-end Estimated tax liability must be paid in either 10 or 12 instalments based on a percentage of the company's turnover	
Capital gains	Taxed regarding the tax rate, as part of business profits	
Losses	Can be carried forward indefinitely subject to anti-avoidance rules	
Tax group	None	
Tax rate	2012: 25% 2013: 25% From 2014: 26.5%	2012: 25% 2013: 25% From 2014: 26.5%

III TAXES FOR INDIVIDUALS

		Residents	Non-residents
Income Tax	General description	Income tax	
	Types of taxable income	• Regular income • Interest • Royalties • Rent • Capital gains	Only taxed on Israeli source income
	Calculation of income	Levied on gross income less certain allowable deductions	
	Tax year, tax assessment and tax payment	Tax year – calendar year Tax returns are due within 5–12 months after the year-end Estimated tax liability must be paid in either 10 or 12 instalments based on a percentage of the individual's turnover	
	Losses	May be offset against other profits (in general against the same kind of profit) and/or carried forward indefinitely	
	Tax rates	• Regular income: From 2012: 10%–48% • Capital gain: 25%/30% • Interest: 15%/25%/the same as the rates for regular income • Royalties: the same as the rates for regular income • Rent: the same as the rates for regular income (except from flats / real estate abroad – lower rates)	
Capital Gains Tax (CGT)	General description	Capital gains/real estate tax	
	Calculation of gain	Levied on gross income less certain allowable deductions	
	Tax year, tax assessment and tax payment	The tax year is the calendar year Estimated tax liability must be paid within 30 days after the sale	
	Losses	May be offset against other gain and/or carried forward indefinitely	
	Tax rates	15%, 20% and 25%	
		Domiciled	**Non-domiciled**
Inheritance Tax (IHT)	General description	Neither estate nor gift tax are imposed in Israel	

IV   WITHHOLDING TAXES

Under domestic law	Payments to Residents	Payments to non-residents[1]
Dividends	25%	25%
Interest	25%	25%
Royalties	25%	25%
On payments to artists and sportsmen	25%	25%

Reduced rate available under the relevant Double Taxation Treaty			
Country	Dividends	Interest	Royalties
Austria	25%	15%	10%
Belarus	10%	10%	10%
Belgium	15%	15%	10%
Brazil	15%	15%	15%
Bulgaria	12.5%	10%	12.5%
Canada	15%	15%	15%
China	10%	10%	10%
Croatia	15%	10%	5%
Czech Republic	15%	10%	5%
Denmark	25%	25%	10%
Estonia	5%	5%	Nil
Ethiopia	15%	10%	5%
Finland	15%	10%	10%
France	15%	10%	10%
Germany	25%	15%	5%
Greece	25%	10%	10%
Hungary	15%	Nil	Nil
India	10%	10%	10%
Ireland	10%	10%	10%
Italy	15%	10%	10%
Jamaica	22.5%	15%	10%
Japan	15%	10%	10%
Korea, Republic of	15%	10%	5%
Latvia	15%	10%	5%
Lithuania	15%	10%	10%
Luxembourg	15%	10%	5%
Mexico	10%	10%	10%
Moldova	10%	5%	5%
Netherlands	15%	15%	10%
Norway	25%	25%	10%
Philippines	15%	10%	15%
Poland	10%	5%	10%
Portugal	15%	10%	10%
Romania	15%	10%	10%
Russia	10%	10%	10%

1   Reduced rates of withholding tax may apply where there is an appropriate double tax treaty.

Reduced rate available under the relevant Double Taxation Treaty			
Country	Dividends	Interest	Royalties
Singapore	10%	7%	5%
Slovakia	10%	10%	5%
Slovenia	15%	5%	5%
South Africa	25%	25%	Nil
Spain	10%	10%	7%
Sweden	Nil	25%	Nil
Switzerland	15%	10%	5%
Taiwan	10%	10%	10%
Thailand	15%	15%	15%
Turkey	10%	10%	10%
Ukraine	15%	10%	10%
United Kingdom	15%	15%	Nil
United States	25%	17.5%	15%
Uzbekistan	10%	10%	10%
Vietnam	10%	10%	15%

Note: the above rates are only available provided the specific Treaty criteria are satisfied. As treaties will not be identical, guidance should be sought in all cases. It is possible that lower rates than those shown above may be available provided that certain criteria are satisfied.

V   INDIRECT TAXES

<table>
<tr><th></th><th></th><th>Residents</th><th>Non-residents</th></tr>
<tr><td rowspan="10">Value Added Tax (VAT)</td><td>General description</td><td colspan="2">Tax on the supply of goods and services</td></tr>
<tr><td>Entities obliged to levy VAT</td><td colspan="2">• Corporation
• Licensed dealer</td></tr>
<tr><td>Taxable activities</td><td colspan="2">• Sale of goods
• Services</td></tr>
<tr><td>Taxable activities – zero-rated (examples)</td><td colspan="2">Unprocessed fruit and vegetables, exports provided to tourists and certain other income from foreign sources</td></tr>
<tr><td>Exemptions (examples)</td><td colspan="2">Certain structural alterations</td></tr>
<tr><td>Refund of VAT</td><td colspan="2">Monthly basis</td></tr>
<tr><td>Tax liability</td><td colspan="2">Businesses selling goods and services</td></tr>
<tr><td>Tax rates</td><td colspan="2">Uniform rate of 18%</td></tr>
<tr><td>Administrative obligations</td><td colspan="2">• Monthly report
• Monthly payment</td></tr>
<tr><td colspan="2">Real Property Taxes</td><td colspan="2">No real property tax</td></tr>
<tr><td colspan="2">Stamp Duty</td><td colspan="2">No stamp taxes</td></tr>
</table>

Nexia International is the trading name of Nexia International Limited, a company registered in the Isle of Man. Company registration number: 53513C. Registered office: 2nd floor, Sixty Circular Road, Douglas, Isle of Man, IM1 1SA

Italy

(Salvatore Tarsia, TCFCT – Studio Associato Consulenza Societaria e Tributaria, s.tarsia@tcfct.it)

I MAIN LEGAL FORMS

Legal form / Characteristics	Partnership and Limited Liability Partnership (LLP)	Private corporation (Ltd) and Public corporation (Plc)
Partners/shareholders • Number • Restrictions	No limitations No concept of LLPs	
Directors	One or more (joint or severally)	One or more (sole director or Board of Directors)
Establishment	Public deed	
Registration	Commercial Register	
Minimum capital		Ltd: €10,000 (possibility to set up a 'Simplify Ltd' company with minimum capital of €1 – bylaw imposed) Plc: (limited by shares) €50,000
Liability	Joint and several liability for partners	Limited to capital
Governance	By partners	Sole director or Board of Directors
Audit requirements	No	Public companies only Ltd: only for certain requirements
Taxation	Tax transparent	Resident companies are subject to corporation tax on their profits derived anywhere in the world Tax transparent taxation rule is applicable only per option

II   CORPORATION TAX

Description \ Legal form	Resident corporation	Permanent establishment (PE)
General description	Joint Stock Companies are subject to IRES (Corporate Income Tax)	PE of Foreign Companies are subject to IRES (Corporate Income Tax)
Taxable entities	Taxable entities are both resident and non-resident. Italian resident companies are taxed on their worldwide income	PEs located in Italy are taxed on their worldwide incomes if realised through the PE
Taxable income	Worldwide profits	Worldwide profits realised through the PE
Calculation of taxable profits	Accounting profit is adjusted for various tax add-backs and allowances to obtain the taxable profit	
Interest payments	Interest expenses are deductible according to the following tests: • Test 1: There is no restriction if the positive interest exceeds the negative interest • Test 2: The excess interest expenses not deducted according to test 1 can be deducted up to an amount equal to 30% of EBITDA (earnings before interest, taxes, depreciation and amortisation); the excess will be available for carry forward to future years	
Related party transactions	All related party transactions must take place on arm's length basis	
Tax year, return and payment	The tax year corresponds to the company's financial year The tax return must be filed within 9 months after the year-end Businesses are always required to file the tax return	
Capital gains	Capital gains on the disposal of shares are tax exempt for 95% subject to four conditions (participation exemption). If the conditions are not met, capital gains are fully taxable as corporate income	
Losses	Tax losses can be carried forward indefinitely Only 80% of future profits can be offset against tax losses carried forward	
Tax group	Domestic tax group Worldwide tax group	
Tax rate	27.5% to 24%[1,2,3,4]	

---

1   Resident companies are also subject to IRAP, a regional tax (3.9%) whose taxable basis is usually higher than the corporate income taxable basis, because financial costs and financial revenues are not relevant. Employees' costs are relevant only to open-ended contract.
2   Companies that close for five years with a tax loss, on the sixth year will have to pay an additional 10.5% CIT.
3   From 2017 the CIT rate will be 24%.
4   Companies operating in the credit and financial sector are liable to an additional 3.5% tax rate.

III TAXES FOR INDIVIDUALS

<table>
<tr><td colspan="2"></td><th>Residents</th><th>Non-residents</th></tr>
<tr><td rowspan="8">Income Tax</td><td>General description</td><td colspan="2">Tax levied on the chargeable income of a chargeable person for a year of assessment</td></tr>
<tr><td>Taxable entities and taxable income</td><td>Residents are taxed on their worldwide income with some relief for double taxation</td><td>Non-residents are taxed on income arising in Italy</td></tr>
<tr><td>Types of taxable income</td><td colspan="2">• Property income (usually rent)
• Income from capital investment (interest, sale of goodwill, dividends, royalties, annuities)
• Employment income
• Self-employment income
• Business activities income
• Other income</td></tr>
<tr><td>Calculation of income</td><td colspan="2">The taxable basis is the sum of all kinds of income. The tax rate on individual income (IRE) is progressive</td></tr>
<tr><td>Tax year, tax assessment and tax payment</td><td colspan="2">Tax year – is always calendar year

Tax assessment – individuals are not required to file a tax return where they:

• do not receive any income
• receive only exempt income
• receive income solely from employment or pensions

Business entities are always required to file the annual tax return

The annual tax return must be filed by 30 September of the following year

The taxes are paid on 16 June and 30 November</td></tr>
<tr><td>Losses</td><td colspan="2">Tax losses deriving from a business activity (enterprise owned by an individual) or self-employed activity, or partnership, can be offset with other incomes, and cannot be carried forward</td></tr>
<tr><td>Tax rates</td><td colspan="2">

Band (€)	%
0–15,000	23
15,001–28,000	27
28,001–55,000	38
55,001–75,000	41
75,001+	43

An additional local tax can apply depending on the city and the region of residence, with rates from 1.23% to 4.13%</td></tr>
</table>

		Residents	Non-residents
Capital Gains Tax (CGT)	General description	Capital gain obtained as difference between sale and purchase price is a taxable income	
	Taxable entities and chargeable assets	Capital gains are included in the income of a taxpayer in the year in which they are cashed. Capital gains on disposals of real estate owned for more than 5 years are tax exempt. If sold within 5 years a 20% final withholding tax is applied	
	Calculation of gain	Selling price less purchase price	
	Tax year, tax assessment and tax payment	Income tax rules apply	
	Losses	The losses on disposal of participation can be carried forward for 4 years and utilised to offset with increases of the same nature	
	Tax rates	• 20% on capital gain on real estate disposal if sold within 5 years • 26% on capital gain on participation disposal, but not for a qualifying participation • The capital gain on qualifying participation disposals is exempt for 50.28% of the gain and the balance is taxed at progressive rate as indicated above	

		Residents	Non-residents
Inheritance Tax (IHT)	General description	Inheritance and donation tax reintroduced from 3 October 2006 (depending on circumstances) Donation tax reintroduced from 29 November 2006 (depending on circumstances)	
	Taxable entities and chargeable assets	• Inheritance tax: the deceased is resident in Italy • Donation tax: the donor is resident in Italy • Inheritance tax: the deceased's estate • Donation tax: all assets donated	Only assets existent in Italy
	Calculation of charge	See below under tax rates	
	Taxable events	Death Donation	
	Allowances	Nil	
	Tax rates	Inheritance – gift to: • spouse/lineal relatives: 4%. Tax-free franchise €1m per each beneficiary • brothers and sisters: 6%. Tax-free franchise €100,000 per each beneficiary • other relatives until fourth degree: 6% • lineal relatives by marriage: 6% • collateral relatives by marriage until third degree: 6% • other: 8% Further tax on real estate: • *Inheritance*: 3% on the value of the real estate inherited, or €400 if it is the first house for the beneficiary • *gift*: 3% on the value of the real estate donated, or €400 if it is the first house for the beneficiary	

IV WITHHOLDING TAXES

Under Domestic Law	Payments to residents	Payments to non-residents[5]
Dividends	*Dividends paid to an Italian individual:* • 26% for non-qualified participation • 0% for qualified participation *Dividends paid to an Italian company:* • 0% in any case	*Dividends paid by an Italian company:* • to non-resident individual: 26% *final* withholding tax subject to double tax treaty relief • *no* withholding tax under the EU Parent-Subsidiary Directive
Interest	Nil	• No withholding tax on interest paid to EU resident companies if EU Directive 2003/49/EEC is applicable • Interest on loan paid to foreign companies is subject to a 20% withholding tax subject to double tax treaty relief
Royalties	20%	30%
On payments to artists and sportsmen	20%	30%

Reduced rate available under the relevant Double Taxation Treaty			
Country	Dividends	Interests	Royalties
Albania	10%	5%	5%
Algeria	15%	15%	15%
Argentina	15%	20%	18%
Armenia	10%	10%	7%
Australia	15%	10%	10%
Austria	15%	10%	10%
Azerbaijan	10%	10%	10%
Bangladesh	15%	15%	10%
Belarus	15%	8%	6%
Belgium	15%	15%	5%
Brazil	15%	5%	15%
Bulgaria	10%	Nil	5%
Canada	15%	15%	10%
China	10%	10%	10%
Congo	15%	Nil	10%
Croatia	15%	10%	5%
Cyprus	15%	10%	Nil
Czech Republic	15%	Nil	5%
Denmark	15%	10%	5%
Ecuador	15%	10%	5%

---

5   Reduced rates of withholding tax may apply where there is an appropriate double tax treaty.

Reduced rate available under the relevant Double Taxation Treaty			
Country	Dividends	Interests	Royalties
Egypt	20%	25%	15%
Estonia	15%	10%	10%
Ethiopia	10%	10%	20%
Finland	15%	15%	5%
Former Yugoslavia (still working for Bosnia, Serbia and Montenegro)	10%	10%	10%
Former Soviet Union (still working for Moldova, Kyrgyzstan and Tajikistan)	15%	Nil	Nil
France	15%	10%	5%
Georgia	10%	Nil	Nil
Germany	15%	10%	5%
Ghana	15%	10%	10%
Greece	35%	10%	5%
Hong Kong	10%	12.5%	15%
Hungary	10%	Nil	Nil
Iceland	15%	Nil	5%
India	25%	15%	20%
Indonesia	15%	10%	15%
Ireland	15%	10%	Nil
Israel	15%	10%	10%
Ivory Coast	18%	15%	10%
Japan	15%	10%	10%
Jordan	10%	10%	10%
Kazakhstan	15%	10%	10%
Kuwait	5%	Nil	10%
Latvia	15%	10%	10%
Lebanon	15%	Nil	Nil
Lithuania	15%	10%	10%
Luxembourg	15%	10%	10%
Macedonia	10%	10%	12%
Malaysia	10%	15%	15%
Malta	15%	10%	10%
Mauritius	40%	Nil	15%
Mexico	15%	15%	15%
Moldova	15%	5%	5%
Morocco	15%	10%	10%
Mozambique	15%	10%	10%
Netherlands	15%	10%	5%
New Zealand	15%	10%	10%
Norway	15%	15%	5%
Oman	10%	5%	10%
Pakistan	25%	30%	30%

Reduced rate available under the relevant Double Taxation Treaty			
Country	Dividends	Interests	Royalties
Philippines	15%	15%	25%
Poland	10%	10%	10%
Portugal	15%	15%	12%
Qatar	15%	5%	5%
Romania	10%	10%	10%
Russia	10%	10%	Nil
San Marino	15%	13%	10%
Saudi Arabia	10%	5%	10%
Senegal	15%	15%	15%
Singapore	10%	12.5%	20%
Slovakia	15%	Nil	5%
Slovenia	15%	10%	5%
South Africa	15%	10%	6%
South Korea	15%	10%	10%
Spain	15%	12%	8%
Sri Lanka	15%	10%	15%
Sweden	15%	15%	5%
Switzerland	15%	12.5%	5%
Syria	10%	10%	18%
Tanzania	10%	15%	15%
Thailand	20%	10%	15%
Trinidad & Tobago	20%	10%	5%
Tunisia	15%	12%	16%
Turkey	15%	15%	10%
Uganda	15%	15%	10%
Ukraine	15%	10%	7%
United Arab Emirates	15%	Nil	10%
United Kingdom	15%	10%	8%
United States	15%	10%	8%
Uzbekistan	10%	5%	5%
Venezuela	10%	10%	10%
Vietnam	15%	10%	10%
Zambia	15%	10%	10%

Note: the above rates are only available provided the specific Treaty criteria are satisfied. It is possible that lower rates than those shown above may be available provided that certain criteria are satisfied. As treaties will not be identical, guidance should be sought in all cases.

V   INDIRECT TAXES

<table>
<tr><td colspan="2"></td><th>Residents</th><th>Non-residents</th></tr>
<tr><td rowspan="10">Value Added Tax (VAT)</td><td>General description</td><td colspan="2">Tax on the supply of goods and services (VAT)</td></tr>
<tr><td>Entities obliged to levy VAT</td><td colspan="2">All subjects (individual or companies) that perform a business activity or self-employed activity in Italy</td></tr>
<tr><td>Taxable activities</td><td colspan="2">Supply of goods and services, import of goods and services, intra-Community acquisition of goods</td></tr>
<tr><td>Taxable activities/ zero-rated (examples)</td><td colspan="2">• Export of goods
• Export of services</td></tr>
<tr><td>Exemptions (examples)</td><td colspan="2">• The most important are the following activities: financial; banking; insurance; medical; rent/sale of buildings (if the lessee/buyer is a VAT subject)</td></tr>
<tr><td>Refund of VAT</td><td colspan="2">Permitted if some conditions are met</td></tr>
<tr><td>Tax liability</td><td colspan="2">Normally the supplier of goods and services is responsible for charging VAT

Reverse charge for certain supplies of goods and services</td></tr>
<tr><td>Tax rates</td><td colspan="2">Ordinary rate is 22%; there are also reduced rates of 10% and 4% in particular cases</td></tr>
<tr><td>Administrative obligations</td><td>Record of all VAT books, registration of invoices issued, payment of VAT, filing of annual VAT returns, filing of Intrastat (only for intra-EU transactions)</td><td>If the non-resident has no VAT direct registration (applicable only for EU companies) or VAT representative, NO administrative obligations are required</td></tr>
<tr><td colspan="2">Property Tax</td><td colspan="2">Properties (real estate and land only) are subject to municipal taxes: IMU, TASI and TARI calculated on the cadastral value of the property. The value is not the market value</td></tr>
<tr><td colspan="2">Stamp Duty Registration Tax</td><td colspan="2">Stamp duty and registration tax is levied on deeds, documents, contracts and registers and it could be fixed rate (€200) or progressive up to 15%</td></tr>
</table>

Japan

(Masanobu Muramatsu, Gyosei & Co, m-muramatsu@gyosei-grp.or.jp)

I MAIN LEGAL FORMS

Legal form / Characteristics	Partnership and Limited Liability Partnership (LLP)	Private corporation (Ltd) and Public corporation (Plc)
Partners/shareholders • Number • Restrictions	General partnership: at least two Limited partnership: one general partner and at least one limited partner None	Ltd: at least one Plc: at least 400 to keep listing on the Tokyo Stock Exchange (Minimum required number is determined by each stock exchange market) None
Directors	N/A	Ltd: at least one Plc: at least two
Establishment	General partnership (Nini-Kumiai or 'NK'): Civil law Limited partnership (Tokumei Kumiai or 'TK'): Commercial Code	Corporation law
Registration	Not required	At the local legal bureau
Minimum capital	None	JPY 1
Liability	NK: unlimited liability GP in TK: unlimited liability LP in TK: limited to capital contribution	Limited to capital contribution
Governance	Partnership agreement	Prescribed in corporation law
Audit requirements	None	Paid-in capital of JPY 500 million or more, or liabilities of JPY 20 billion or more
Taxation	At a partner level	At an entity level

II CORPORATION TAX

Legal form / Description	Resident corporation	Permanent establishment (PE)
General description	Corporation tax (National tax),Corporate Inhabitant tax (Local tax) and Enterprise tax (Local tax)	
Taxable entities	A domestic corporation with its head office or a main office in Japan	A foreign corporate entity with a PE in Japan
Taxable income	Any income wherever the income source is	Any income, wherever the income source is, attributable to the PE in Japan
Calculation of taxable profits	Book/tax differences are added to or deducted from book income	
Interest payments	Interest is deductible on accruals basis, but interest on an inter-company loan is subject to a thin capitalisation rule or an earnings stripping rule, whichever disallowed interest is larger	Interest, including that on inter-office (PE) loan, is deductible on accrual basis, but the deduction of interest on PE's excess liability shall be disallowed. Also, interest on an inter-company loan shall be subject to an earnings stripping rule if the disallowed interest is larger than interest on PE's excess liability
Related party transactions	Foreign related party transactions are subject to a transfer pricing rule	Foreign related party transactions, as well as inter-office transactions, are subject to a transfer pricing rule
Tax year, return and payment	A tax period is the accounting period stipulated in the article of incorporation, but its duration shall not exceed 1 year. A filling due date and tax payment due date are the corresponding date of the second month subsequent to the end of the tax period, but one month (two months for a consolidated return) extension to file a tax return, but not payment, shall be permitted if an application is filed. Payment of estimated tax, of which amount is a half of prior year's tax due, is required once a year, of which due date is usually the corresponding date of the second month subsequent to the end of the first six months period	Same as those for a domestic corporation, except that a tax period is the accounting period for its head office
Capital gains	Not separately taxed from income gain and standard tax rate is applied	

Legal form / Description	Resident corporation	Permanent establishment (PE)
Losses	Net operating losses (NOL) for a 'blue return filer' may be carried forward for 10 years (7 years for NOL incurred in a tax period ended before 1 April 2008, and 9 years for NOL incurred in a tax period ended before 1 April 2018), but NOL deduction for a large corporation, of which capital is more than JPY 100 million, is limited to 60% (55% and 50% from the tax period beginning on and after 1 April 2017 and 1 April 2018, respectively) of current year's taxable income	
	There are no restrictions on offset of capital losses with operating income	
	One year carry-back of NOL is currently suspended for a large corporation	
Tax group	The consolidated tax return system is available for a domestic parent and its wholly-owned domestic subsidiaries	Not available
Tax rate	• Corporation tax (national tax): 23.4% (23.2% from the tax period beginning on and after 1 April 2018) in general, 19% (15% for each tax period beginning from 1 April 2012 to 31 March 2017) for a medium or small corporation, of which capital is not more than JPY 100 million, with taxable income of not more than JPY 8 million • Earnings profit tax for a closely held corporation (national tax): progressive tax rate of 10%/15%/20% on undistributed earnings. The closely held corporation is a corporation with capital of more than JPY 100 million, in which more than 50% interest is directly or indirectly owned by one individual shareholder • Inhabitant tax (local tax): 12.9% (7.0% from the tax period beginning on and after 1 October 2019) of corporation tax due (or 3.02% (1.62 % for 1 October 2019 onwards) of taxable income). A local government may raise the tax rate up to 16.3% (10.4% from the tax period beginning on and after 1 October 2019) (or 3.81% (2.41% for 1 October 2019 onwards) of taxable income). The tax rate for a corporation located in Tokyo Metropolitan area is 16.3% (or 3.81%) • Enterprise tax (local tax): progressive standard tax rate is 0.3%/0.5%/0.7% (1.9%/2.7%/3.6% for the tax period beginning on and after 1 October 2019) for a large corporation and 3.4%/5.1%/6.7% (5.0%/7.3%/9.6% for the tax period beginning on and after 1 October 2019) for a medium and small corporation. In addition to income-base taxation, a large corporation is also subject to business-scale-base taxation where the tax rate is 1.2% on added value and 0.5% on paid-in capital. A local government may raise the tax rate by a maximum of 200%. The income-base tax rate for a large corporation located in Tokyo Metropolitan area is 0.395%/0.635%/0.88% on taxable income • Surtax (national tax) on taxable income shall be also levied at the tax rate of 1.24%/2.07%/2.90% (414.2% of standard tax rate for enterprise tax) for a large corporation and 1.47%/2.20%/2.89% (43.2% of standard tax rate for enterprise tax) for a medium and small corporation. It shall be abolished from the tax period beginning on and after 1 October 2019 • Surtax (national tax) on corporation tax due shall be levied at the tax rate of 4.4% (10.3% from the tax period beginning on and after 1 October 2019) • Taking all of the above taxes into account, combined marginal tax rate or theoretical effective tax rate on income for a large corporation is 30.86% (30.62% for the tax period beginning on and after 1 April 2018)	

III TAXES FOR INDIVIDUALS

<table>
<tr><td colspan="2"></td><th>Residents</th><th>Non-residents</th></tr>
<tr><td rowspan="8">Income Tax</td><td>Taxable entities and taxable income</td><td>Individuals are resident if they have a Japanese domicile or have resided continuously in Japan for a year or more. Resident is classified as permanent resident (residing over 5 years) or non-permanent resident. A permanent resident is taxed on worldwide income. A non-permanent resident is subject to tax on Japanese source income and foreign source income paid in or remitted into Japan</td><td>Japanese source income</td></tr>
<tr><td>Types of taxable income</td><td colspan="2">• Business income
• Employment (salary) income
• Severance benefits or pension income
• Real estate income
• Capital gain (see below)
• Dividend income
• Interest income
• Royalty income
• Other income</td></tr>
<tr><td>Calculation of income</td><td>Generally, subject to 'net taxation system' where taxable income is calculated as gross revenue minus relevant expenses and itemised deduction/personal exemption</td><td>Generally, subject to 'gross taxation system' where taxable income is equal to gross revenue, but for a non-resident with PE, subject to 'net taxation system'</td></tr>
<tr><td>Tax year, tax assessment and tax payment</td><td colspan="2">Tax period is the calendar year

Income tax returns should be filed for the period between 16 February and 15 March in the following year. For employees with a salary of less than JPY 20 million, annual adjustment should be made by the employer and there is no need to file the tax returns

Generally, tax payments are made by a withholding agent (a payer of income). If the net tax due for the prior tax period is not less than JPY 150,000, a payment of an estimated tax as one-third of the net tax due is required in July and November, respectively</td></tr>
<tr><td>Losses</td><td colspan="2">Losses, other than capital losses, for a 'blue return filer' may be carried forward for 3 years. One year carry-back of the losses is permitted. As to capital losses, see below</td></tr>
<tr><td>Tax rates</td><td>Progressive rate for national taxes under net taxation: 5%/10%/20%/23%/33%/40% on taxable income and 10% on taxable income for local inhabitant tax for residents and non-residents with PE who are subject to net taxation

0.105%/0.21%/0.42%/0.483%/0.693%/0.84% of surtax (2.1% of National Tax due) shall be levied for 25 years from 2013 tax year to 2037 tax year</td><td>Under gross taxation, 15.315% or 20.42% (including surtax) depending on the character of income</td></tr>
</table>

		Residents	Non-residents
Capital Gains Tax (CGT)	Taxable entities and chargeable assets	Capital gain on real estate properties and equity securities is taxed separately from other capital gain and income gain	
		A non-resident without PE is exempted from tax on capital gain on disposal of a listed company's equity security	
		A resident who holds securities with the value of not less than JPY 100 million and moves to a foreign country is subject to an exit tax where net built-in gain on the securities shall be taxed	
	Calculation of gain	Generally, capital gain is calculated as gross revenue minus adjusted basis of a property minus relevant expenses	
	Tax year, tax assessment and tax payment	Calendar year	
	Losses	Generally, capital losses may be offset against income gains. However, offset of capital loss on disposal of equity and debt securities shall be limited to capital gains on equity and debt securities, dividend income, and interest income on debt securities	
		No carry-forward or carry-back of capital losses shall be permitted, except for loss on disposal of a listed company's equity security and/or a public offering debt security, and loss on disposal of certain residential real estate property, which can be carried forward for 3 years. Offset of the carry-forward loss on a listed company's equity security and/or a public offering debt security is subject to the limitation as above	
	Tax rates	Capital gain on real estate: 20.315% (including surtax and inhabitant tax) for a real estate property held for long-term (more than 5 years), and 39.63% for one held for short-term	
		Capital gain on any equity and debt securities: 20.315%	
		Tax rates shown as above include surtax and inhabitant tax and therefore they are for residents and non-residents with PE	

		Domiciled	Non-domiciled
Inheritance Tax (IHT)	Taxable entities and chargeable assets	A domiciled heir is subject to IHT on any inheritance succeeded regardless of its location	A non-domiciled heir who has Japanese nationality and had been domiciled anytime within 5 years prior to inheritance or bequest is subject to IHT on any inheritance succeeded regardless of its location. Other non-domiciled heirs are subject to IHT only on inheritance located in Japan
	Calculation of charge	Taxable estate is calculated as taxable value of assets minus liabilities/funeral expenses plus any gifts to heirs within 3 years prior to the death minus basic exemption	
	Taxable events	Inheritance or bequest	
	Allowances	Basic exemption of JPY 30 million plus JPY 6 million for each statutory heir	
	Tax rates	Progressive rate of 10%/15%/20%/30%/40%/45%/50%/55%	
		10% is applied to the taxable estate of the first JPY 10 million and 55% on any in excess of JPY 600 million	

IV   WITHHOLDING TAXES

Under Domestic Law	Payments to residents	Payments to non-residents[1]
Dividends	20.315% for a listed company's dividends; 20.42% for other dividends	15.315% for a listed company's dividends; 20.42% for other dividends
Interest	20.315% for interest on debt securities and bank deposits; Nil for interest on loans	15.315% for interest on debt securities and bank deposits; 20.42% for interest on loans
Royalties	10.21%/20.42%; 20.42% shall be applied to the amount in excess of JPY 1 million	20.42%
On payments to professionals, artists and sportsmen, etc	10.21%/20.42%; 20.42% shall be applied to the amount in excess of JPY 1 million	20.42%

Reduced rate available under the relevant Double Taxation Treaty			
Country	Dividends[2]	Interest	Royalties
Armenia	15%	10%	10%
Australia	10%	10%	5%
Austria	20%	10%	10%
Azerbaijan	15%	10%	10%
Bangladesh	15%	10%	10%
Belarus	15%	10%	10%
Belgium	15%[8]	10%	10%[8]
Brazil	12.5%	12.5%	12.5%[4]
Brunei Darussalam	10%	10%	10%
Bulgaria	15%	10%	10%
Canada	15%	10%	10%
Chile[6]	15%	10%[7]	10%
China	10%	10%	10%
Czech Republic	15%	10%	10%
Denmark	15%	10%	10%
Egypt	15%	N/A	15%
Fiji Islands	10%	10%	Nil
Finland	15%	10%	10%
France	10%	10%	Nil
Georgia	15%	10%	10%
Germany	15%	Nil	Nil
Hong Kong	10%	10%	5%
Hungary	10%	10%	10%
India	10%	10%	10%

---

1   Including foreign corporations. Reduced rates of withholding tax may apply where there is an appropriate double tax treaty.

Reduced rate available under the relevant Double Taxation Treaty			
Country	Dividends[2]	Interest	Royalties
Indonesia	15%	10%	10%
Ireland	15%	10%	10%
Israel	15%	10%	10%
Italy	15%	10%	10%
Kazakhstan	15%	10%	10%[3]
Kuwait	10%	10%	10%
Kyrgyzstan	15%	10%	10%
Luxembourg	15%	10%	10%
Malaysia	15%	10%	10%
Mexico	15%	15%	10%
Moldova	15%	10%	10%
Netherlands	10%	10%	Nil
New Zealand	15%	10%	5%
Norway	15%	10%	10%
Oman	10%	10%	10%
Pakistan	10%	10%	10%
Philippines	15%	10%	10%
Poland	10%	10%	10%
Portugal	10%	10%	5%
Qatar	10%	10%	5%
Republic of Korea	15%	10%	10%
Romania	10%	10%	10%
Russia	15%	10%	10%
Saudi Arabia	10%	10%	10%
Singapore	15%	10%	10%
Slovakia	15%	10%	10%
Slovenia[6]	5%	5%	5%
South Africa	15%	10%	10%
Spain	15%	10%	10%
Sri Lanka	20%	N/A	10.21%
Sweden	10%	Nil	Nil
Switzerland	10%	10%	Nil
Taiwan	10%	10%	10%
Tajikistan	15%	10%	10%
Thailand	20%	25%	15%
Turkey	15%	15%	10%
Turkmenistan	15%	10%	10%
Ukraine	15%	10%	10%
United Arab Emirates	10%	10%	10%
United Kingdom	10%	Nil	Nil
United States	10%	10%[5]	Nil

Reduced rate available under the relevant Double Taxation Treaty			
Country	Dividends[2]	Interest	Royalties
Uzbekistan	15%	10%	10%
Vietnam	10%	10%	10%
Zambia	Nil	10%	10%

Note: The above rate is only available provided the specific treaty criteria are satisfied. It is possible that lower rates than those shown above may be available provided that certain criteria are satisfied. As treaties will not be identical, guidance should be sought in all cases.

2   An applicable rate changes depending on the percentage of shares held by the recipients and other factors.
3   By the protocol, treaty rate shall be substantially reduced to 5%.
4   Treaty rate of royalty for trademarks and for copyright of cinematograph films shall be 20.42% and 15%, respectively.
5   Treaty rate reduction to nil has been ratified by Japanese Diet, but instrument of ratification not yet exchanged.
6   The tax treaty has been newly signed, but not yet been ratified by Japanese Diet.
7   For 2 years from the date on which the convention enters into force, the rate of 15% shall apply in place of 10%.
8   The overall revised tax treaty, where the treaty rate for dividends and for royalties is reduced to 10% and nil respectively, has been signed, but not yet been ratified by Japanese Diet.

V   INDIRECT TAXES

		Residents	Non-residents
Value Added Tax (VAT)	General description	Consumption tax	
	Entities obliged to levy VAT	A corporation and a proprietor of which taxable sales for the 'base period (the year 2 years prior to the current tax year)' is more than JPY 10 million, and any business entities withdrawing the foreign goods from the bonded area and bringing them into Japan. A newly incorporated corporation would be obliged to levy the consumption tax from the year of incorporation if either criteria of (a) its registered paid-in capital is not less than JPY 10 million or (b) more than 50% of its interest is owned by a corporation, of which taxable revenue is more than JPY 500 million, is met	
	Taxable activities	• Sales of goods and rendering services in Japan • The importation of foreign goods into Japan • The 'B2B' Internet Service transaction and the transaction in respect of personal activities exercised by a foreign entertainer/sportsperson shall be subject to a reverse charge mechanism	
	Taxable activities – zero-rated (examples)	Export of goods and rendering services to non-residents (individuals and foreign corporations)	
	Exemptions (examples)	• Transfer of land • Education services • Transfer of monetary assets/currency • Loan interest and insurance premium	
	Refund of VAT	Input tax in excess of output tax	
	Tax liability	Output tax minus input tax	
	Tax rates	8% (10% from 1 October 2019) of sales value or CIF price plus custom duty (Lower rate of 8% for foods shall be introduced from 1 October 2019)	
	Administrative obligations	• Filing a monthly/quarterly/semi-annual/annual tax return and accompanying payments of tax due are required, depending on the amount of prior year's tax due. The filing and payment due date is the end of the second month subsequent to the end of the tax return period • In order to take a tax credit of input tax against output tax, purchase records and relevant invoices shall be kept • In order to be able to issue a CT (consumption tax) invoice, a registration for a taxable business entity shall be required from 1 October 2021	
Real Property Taxes		An owner of real estate property and personal property placed in business as of 1 January each year is levied RPT on the taxable value of those properties at the tax rate of 1.4%	
Stamp Duty		Stamp Duty is levied on taxable documents such as buy/sell agreement, promissory notes, consignment agreement, certificate of equity security etc. Tax due varies depending on a type of taxable documents and a contract amount	

Nexia International does not accept liability for any loss arising from any action taken, or omission, on the basis of this publication. Professional advice should be obtained before acting or refraining from acting on the contents of this publication. Membership of Nexia International, or associated umbrella organizations, does not constitute any partnership between members, and members do not accept any responsibility for the commission of any act, or omission to act by, or the liabilities of, other members.

Nexia International is the trading name of Nexia International Limited, a company registered in the Isle of Man. Company registration number: 53513C. Registered office: 2nd floor, Sixty Circular Road, Douglas, Isle of Man, IM1 1SA

Jordan

(Sinan S Ghosheh, Gosheh & Co, sinan@ghosheh.com)

I MAIN LEGAL FORMS

Legal form / Characteristics	Partnership and Limited Liability Partnership (LLP)	Private corporation (Ltd) and Public corporation (Plc)
Partners/shareholders • Number • Restrictions	One and more	Private: 1 or more PLC: 3 or more
Directors	Management by partners or directors	Board of Directors
Establishment	Register at Ministry of Trade – controller	Register at Ministry of Trade – controller
Minimum capital	JD1,000	PLC: JD500,000 Private: JD50,000
Liability	Partnerships: unlimited LLPs: limited to capital	Limited to capital
Governance	Partners, managers and general meeting	Audit committee General assembly
Audit requirements	No audit to partner Audit for LLP	Audit
Taxation	Partners and LLP taxed on worldwide profits since the capital is from Jordan	Corporation tax on worldwide profits since the capital is from Jordan
Usage	Financial organisations and governments	Financial organisations and governments

II   CORPORATION TAX

Legal form / Description	Resident corporation	Permanent establishment (PE)
General description	Jordan corporation tax	
Taxable entities	Companies incorporated in Jordan and their subsidiaries, and 10% of profit of all branches outside Jordan	PE located in Jordan
Taxable income	Income and gains derived from sources within Jordan	Profit, income and gains attributable to the PE located in Jordan
Calculation of taxable profits	Accounting profit is adjusted for various expenses which are added back to profit to reach taxable income, such as allowances to and losses from portfolio investments	
Interest payments	Interest on debt capital is allowed	
Related party transactions	All related party transactions will be included in calculations	
Tax year, return and payment	Tax period normally coincides with accounting period, normally 12 months	
	Tax return must be submitted within 4 months from the end of the accounting period	
	Tax payment should be made every 6 months	
Capital gains	Capital gains is exempted where amount does not exceed depreciation	
Losses	Excess trading losses can be carried forward without period limit	
Tax group	Industry, financial, trading and service, and others	
Tax rate	Industry 14%	
	Financial 35%	
	Trading and service 20%	
	Others 24%	

III TAXES FOR INDIVIDUALS

		Residents	Non-residents
Income Tax	General description	Tax depending on personal income during year	
	Taxable entities and taxable income	Individuals, trustees	Non-residents are liable to tax on income earned in Jordan
	Types of taxable income	• Rent from property • Trading • Savings at bank • Employment income	

	Calculation of income	• Property – 10% accrual basis
		• Trading – current year basis
		• Savings – 5% of interest received
		• Employment – income/benefit received:
		  – married person – over JD24,0000
		  – single person – over JD12,0000	

	Tax year, tax assessment and tax payment	4 months after the end of the fiscal year and the payment is the same	
	Losses	Any losses are carried forward for an unlimited period	
	Tax rates	• First JD10,000 – 7% • Second JD10,000 – 14% • Over JD20,000 – 20%	

		Residents	Non-residents
Capital Gains Tax (CGT)	General description	Tax on increase in the value of used asset over book value is not taxable	
	Taxable entities and chargeable assets	All companies, LLPs and Public Companies	
	Calculation of gain	• Disposal proceeds less allowable expenditure • Additional reliefs available, depending on type of asset	
	Tax year, tax assessment and tax payment	Same as fiscal year of companies (4 months after fiscal year)	
	Losses	Utilised against gains in year, and not accepted as loss on calculation as taxable income	
	Tax rates	The exemption must not exceed the depreciation allowance and the rate is 14%	

		Domiciled	Non-domiciled
Inheritance Tax (IHT)	General description	No tax on transfer of the estate on death, but income from prizes and lotteries over JD1,000 is taxable	
	Taxable entities and chargeable assets	The person who is resident in Jordan is taxable	
	Calculation of charge	Proceeds from gift less expense	
	Taxable events	Prizes and lotteries	
	Allowances	–	
	Tax rates	15%	

IV   WITHHOLDING TAXES

Under domestic law	Payments to residents	Payments to non-residents[1]
Dividends	Nil	Nil
Interest	5%	5%
Royalties	10%	10%
On payments to artists and sportsmen	Normal income tax	

---

1   Although Jordan has tax treaties with a number of countries, these do not reduce the rates of withholding tax shown above.

V INDIRECT TAXES

		Residents	Non-residents
Value Added Tax	General description	Tax on the supply of goods and services	
	Entities obliged to levy VAT	Any individual, partnership, corporation or other body, which carries out taxable activities in Jordan	
		Subject to turnover threshold according to types of activities as follows: • services and industry turnover – over JD30,000 per year • trade turnover – over JD75,000 per year	
	Taxable activities	Supply of goods and services, import of goods, intra-Community acquisition of goods	
		Place of supply of goods and services must be in Jordan	
	Taxable activities – zero-rated (examples)	• Goods related to children, food and special sick people • Sale of books and printing of leaflets	
	Taxable activities – exemptions (examples)	• Education commission and banking interest • Olive oil • Gold	
	Refund of VAT	VAT paid on supplies and services is deductible as input tax, if incurred in the course or furtherance of the business and for the purpose of making taxable supplies (including zero-rated supplies)	
		There is no credit for input tax incurred which relates to the provision of exempt supplies	
		Where mixed supplies occur (taxable and exempt supplies), subject to de minimis provisions, input tax must be apportioned and recovered according to a partial exemption method. Agreement with tax authorities is required for non-standard partial exemption methods	
	Tax rates	Standard rate – 16%	
		Zero rate – 0%	
	Administrative obligations	Formal requirements concerning business records and invoices	
		Self-assessment every two months plus quarterly payment	
	Special VAT rates	Some goods and service have special VAT rates, eg: • Alcoholic goods • Cigarettes • Steel for construction	
		The rates can reach 100%	
Real Property Taxes		10% of the value of property at point of sale	
Stamp Duty		0.3% of transactions related to purchase and sale of securities over JD1,000	

Kazakhstan

(Vitaly Sipakov, NEXIA KZ, LLP, Almaty, sipakov@nexia.kz)

I MAIN LEGAL FORMS

Characteristics / Legal form	Partnership and Limited Liability Partnership (LLP)	Private corporation (Ltd) and Public corporation (Plc)
Partners/shareholders • Number • Restrictions	There are no restrictions	There are no restrictions
Directors	Management by Director of Boards (specified by largest investment into authorized fund)	Board of Directors (Shareholders, within the number of shares)
Establishment	State registration is implemented by Ministry of Justice with foundation agreement to be presented	Partnership is established by one or several founders; shareholders' agreement should be notarially certified and presented to the Ministry of Justice
Registration	Ministry of Justice	Ministry of Justice
Minimum capital	$638 (100 monthly calculation index)	$318,708 (50,000 monthly calculation index)
Liability	Members of LLP are liable to contribute to the authorized fund that amount which is specified in agreement on time	Shareholder should: pay off for shares; inform registrar and nominal shareholder about changes of data related to the number of shareholders within 10 days
Governance	General meeting is supreme body of governance. All members are permitted to take part in discussion and vote	Shareholders' general meeting; Board of Directors; Executive board – collegiate body; Other bodies suggested by law and regulations
Audit requirements	No formal requirements except some urgent cases: in case of argument requested by court to audit obligatory	Annual audit is obligatory by law

Characteristics / Legal form	Partnership and Limited Liability Partnership (LLP)	Private corporation (Ltd) and Public corporation (Plc)
Taxable items	Part of the net profit:	Part of the net profit:
	Residents of the Republic of Kazakhstan (RoK):	Non-residents of the Republic of Kazakhstan (RoK):
	Individuals are not obligated after 3rd year of possession;	Individuals and legal entities are not obligated after 3rd year of possession;
	Legal bodies are not obligated	5% – up to three years

II CORPORATION TAX

Description \ Legal Form	Resident corporation	Permanent establishment (PE)
General description	Tax levied on the taxable profit of a chargeable company for a year of assessment	
Taxable entities	Companies incorporated in Kazakhstan and/or foreign companies with central management and control located in Kazakhstan	PE located in Kazakhstan
Taxable income	Worldwide profits	Profits derived by PE in Kazakhstan
Calculation of taxable profits	Taxable income is defined as the difference between the cumulative revenue minus adjustments and deductions	
Interest payments	Deductions of interest shall be within the limits of the amount calculated by the special formula	Deductions of interest shall be within the limits of the amount calculated by the special formula
Related party transactions	All related party transactions must take place on arm's length basis	
Tax year, return and payment	Tax period coincides with calendar year. Tax return must be submitted to tax authorities by 31 March. Tax payment should be made within 10 days after date of submission	
Capital gains	Capital gains are subject to corporation tax at normal rates	
Losses	Within a year losses can be offset against other current year profits	
	A current year loss can be carried back one year and carried forward 10 years	
Tax group	Each tax agent is the independent tax bearer. The tax group is not considered	
Tax rate	Tax rate for each category of business except agricultural producers – 10%	Tax rate for each category of business except agricultural producers – 10%
	For agricultural producers – 10%	For agricultural producers – 10%
	Income is taxed at the payment source of residents by 15%	Net profit is taxed by 15%; 5% – on international transportation, reinsurance of risks
		Income of the person registered in a state with the preferential taxation – 20%
		Income from capital gain, dividends, interest, royalty – 15%

III   TAXES FOR INDIVIDUALS

		Residents	Non-residents
Personal Income Tax	General description	Taxable items are defined as the difference between the taxable income, in view of adjustments, and the tax deductions in cases, in accordance with the procedure and in amounts specified by the Tax Code of RK	
	Taxable entities and taxable income	Individuals who are resident in Kazakhstan are liable to tax on their worldwide income	Individuals who are not resident in Kazakhstan are liable to tax on income arising in Kazakhstan
	Types of taxable income	Individual income of the worker Pension payments from pension funds Dividends, compensation, prizes Grants Income from insurance contracts Income gained from tax agent	Goods, services sale income Dividends Compensation Property leasing Other
	Calculation of income	Individual income multiplied by tax rate	
	Tax year, tax assessment and tax payment	1. Withholding personal income tax: Tax period coincides with 1 quarter. Tax return should be submitted to the tax authorities not later than 15th of second month after tax period. Tax payment should be made within 25 calendar days after the end of the month in which the payment of the income was made 2. Non-withholding personal income tax: Tax period coincides with calendar year. Tax return must be submitted to tax authorities by 31 March. Tax payment should be made within 10 days after date of submission	
	Losses	Not applied	
	Tax rates	10% 5% – as income from dividends	10% 5% – as income from dividends
		Residents	**Non-residents**
Capital Gains Tax (CGT)	General description	Subject to income tax	
	Taxable entities and chargeable assets		
	Calculation of gain		
	Tax year, tax assessment and Tax payment		
	Losses		
	Tax rates		

		Domiciled	Non-domiciled
Inheritance Tax (IHT)	General description	There are no inheritance taxes or gift taxes	
	Taxable entities and chargeable assets		
	Calculation of charge		
	Taxable events		
	Allowances		
	Tax rates		

IV   WITHHOLDING TAXES

Under domestic law	Payments to residents	Payments to non-residents
Dividends	15%	15%
Interest	15%	15%
Royalties	20%	20%
On payments to artists and sportsmen	10%	10%

Reduced rate available under the relevant Double Taxation Treaty			
Country	Dividends	Interest	Royalties
Armenia	10%	10%	10%
Austria	15%	10%	10%
Azerbaijan	10%	10%	10%
Belarus	15%	10%	15%
Belgium	15%	10%	10%
Bulgaria	10%	10%	10%
Canada	15%	10%	10%
China	10%	10%	10%
Czech Republic	10%	10%	10%
Estonia	15%	10%	15%
Finland	15%	10%	10%
France	15%	10%	10%
Georgia	15%	10%	10%
Germany	15%	10%	10%
Hungary	15%	10%	10%
India	10%	10%	10%
Iran	15%	10%	10%
Italy	15%	10%	10%
Japan	15%	10%	10%
Kyrgyzstan	10%	10%	10%
Latvia	15%	10%	10%
Lithuania	15%	10%	10%
Malaysia	10%	10%	10%
Moldova	15%	10%	10%
Mongolia	10%	10%	10%
Netherlands	15%	10%	10%
Norway	15%	10%	10%
Pakistan	15%	12.5%	15%
Poland	15%	10%	10%
Republic of Korea	15%	10%	10%
Romania	10%	10%	10%
Russia	10%	10%	10%
Singapore	10%	10%	10%
Slovakia	15%	10%	10%
Spain	15%	10%	10%
Sweden	15%	10%	10%
Switzerland	15%	10%	10%

Reduced rate available under the relevant Double Taxation Treaty			
Country	Dividends	Interest	Royalties
Tajikistan	15%	10%	10%
Turkey	10%	10%	10%
Turkmenistan	10%	10%	10%
Ukraine	15%	10%	10%
United Kingdom	15%	10%	10%
United States	15%	10%	10%
Uzbekistan	10%	10%	10%

Note: the above rates are only available provided the specific Treaty criteria are satisfied. It is possible that lower rates than those shown above may be available provided that certain criteria are satisfied. As treaties will not be identical, guidance should be sought in all cases.

V   INDIRECT TAXES

		Residents	Non-residents
Value Added Tax (VAT)	General description	Tax on the amount by which the value of an article has been increased at each stage of its production or distribution	
	Entities obliged to levy VAT	Individual entrepreneur; juridical persons-residents (except state authorities); non-residents acting through permanent establishment; reliable persons who realize goods, service based on agreement of reliance	
	Taxable activities	Taxable turnover, except some exemptions Taxable import	
	Taxable activities – zero-rated (examples)	Export of goods, except ferrous and non-ferrous goods; international transportation	
	Exemptions (examples)	Turnover of goods and services related to contribution to the authorized fund, financial services, transfer of property to financial leasing, exploration work, import of some goods including those which were imported by zero tax rate Import of foreign currency; medicine; sell or rent of immovable property	
	Refund of VAT	1) If extra VAT is paid to the fund (excess) 2) VAT is paid to Supplier of goods and services at the expense of Grant 3) If overall Sales Tax exceeds VAT chargeable as per declaration at the end of tax period 4) VAT paid by diplomatic representatives of foreign states and equal representatives of consulate general, or members of family related to such persons	
	Tax liability	Supplier of goods and services is liable to pay VAT where he is registered	For the non-resident who has not been registered as a payer of VAT, the obligation to pay VAT lies with the buyer
	Tax rates	12% – on taxable turnover and import 0% – on export of goods, except ferrous and non-ferrous metals and international transportation	
	Administrative obligations	Compulsory registration in tax authorities. Declaration to be presented within tax period but not later than 15th of second month after tax period	Non-residents are not obliged to register, except those non-residents with permanent establishment
Excise		Rates on excise are fixed in absolute value per unit of measure in a full scale Rates on excise of alcohol are fixed in accordance with above-mentioned condition or depending on capacity of spirits level in it Rates on wine production and alcohol are fixed depending on further use of alcohol	

Nexia International does not accept liability for any loss arising from any action taken, or omission, on the basis of this publication. Professional advice should be obtained before acting or refraining from acting on the contents of this publication. Membership of Nexia International, or associated umbrella organizations, does not constitute any partnership between members, and members do not accept any responsibility for the commission of any act, or omission to act by, or the liabilities of, other members.

Nexia International is the trading name of Nexia International Limited, a company registered in the Isle of Man. Company registration number: 53513C. Registered office: 2nd floor, Sixty Circular Road, Douglas, Isle of Man, IM1 1SA

Kenya

(Charles Gitau, Carr Stanyer Gitau & Co. Certified Public Accountants, csg@carrstanyergitau.com)

I   MAIN LEGAL FORMS

Legal form / Characteristics	Partnership and Limited Liability Partnership (LLP)	Private corporation (Ltd) and Public corporation (Plc)
Partners/shareholders • Number • Restrictions	• Maximum of 20 • No restrictions No concept of LLPs	Ltd: minimum of two Plc: minimum of seven
Directors	Partners	Ltd: one Plc: three Have full control in management of the company
Establishment	Partnership deed	Memorandum and Articles of Association
Registration	Registrar of Business Names under The Registration of Business Names Act (Cap 499)	Registrar of Companies under The Companies Act (Cap 486)
Minimum capital	None	Kshs 2,000 for corporations having a share capital and none for corporations without a share capital (corporations limited by guarantee)
Liability	Unlimited	• Limited to share capital for corporations having share capital • Limited up to the guaranteed amount by the directors for corporations limited by guarantee
Governance	Partnership deed	Board of Directors, Articles of Association
Audit requirements	None	Statutory audits
Taxation	Transparent	Corporation tax on taxable profits
Usage	Professional services and small and medium-sized enterprises (SMEs)	Most forms of business except professional partnerships

II   CORPORATION TAX

Legal form / Description	Resident corporation	Permanent establishment (PE)
General description	Tax levied on chargeable profits	
Taxable entities	Incorporated under Kenyan law, or, for an overseas company, management and control exercised in Kenya	PEs located in Kenya
Taxable income	Worldwide profits	Profits derived in Kenya only
Calculation of taxable profits	Business profit adjusted to allow for capital deductions, disallowable non-business expenses and to exclude non-chargeable income	
Interest payments	Deductible/allowable, subject to thin capitalisation rules	
Related party transactions	Related party transactions should take place at arms' length prices	
Tax year, return and payment	Tax year may be either a calendar year or the financial year of the company	
	Self-assessment tax returns should be filed within 6 months following the end of the year of assessment	
	Tax is payable in instalments if certain thresholds are exceeded	
Capital gains	• Individuals (including unincorporated institutions) – on transfer of land and shares excluding those listed on the NSE • Company – on transfer of assets, excluding shares listed on the NSE, that are not subject to corporation tax • Rate – 5% of the gain • On transfer of property – payable on or before the date the application for the transfer of property is made at the Lands Office	
Losses	Tax losses are carried forward for a maximum number of 9 years for offset against future profits from the same source of income; extension of the said period can be granted through application to the commissioner giving evidence of inability to extinguish the loss within that period	
Tax group	None	

Legal form / Description	Resident corporation	Permanent establishment (PE)
Tax rate	• 30% • Unincorporated entities with turnover of up to Kshs 5 million: 3% (excluding rental, management, professional and training income) • On gross residential rental income up to Kshs 10 million p.a. – 10% (payable monthly by 20th of the subsequent month) Export Processing Zone enterprises: • First ten years – Nil • Next ten years – 25% Special Economic Zone enterprise, developer or operator: • First ten years – 10% • Next ten years – 15% Newly listed companies (NLC) following the year of listing: • Lists at least 20% of its shares: 27% for 3 years • Lists at least 30% of its shares: 25% for 5 years • Lists at least 40% of its shares: 20% for 5 years • Introduction of shares without listing: 25% for 5 years Income of a registered Unit Trust, Collective Investment – Exempt Exemption from income tax accorded, on application to the Commissioner, to organisations established solely for the purposes of relief of poverty or distress of the public or for the advancement of religion or education. Tax exemption status is renewable once every 5 years	• 37.5% for non-resident corporations • 37.5% for permanent establishment of a non-resident company

III TAXES FOR INDIVIDUALS

		Residents	Non-residents
Income Tax	Taxable entities and taxable income	• Individuals with a permanent home in Kenya who have been present in Kenya for more than 183 days in the tax year or averaged at least 122 days in the previous 2 tax years	Income derived in Kenya only
	Types of taxable income	• Employment income • Business income • Rental income • Interest income • Farming income • Insurance commission income • Other income	
	Calculation of income	Based on all sources of income adjusted to allow for personal relief and other qualifying reliefs	
	Tax year, tax assessment and tax payment	Tax year – calendar year Returns should be filed within 6 months of the end of the year of assessment Tax computed on PAYE basis; can be remitted monthly	
	Tax rates	Progressive tax rates from 10%–30%	
Capital Gains Tax (CGT)	General description	Individuals (including unincorporated institutions) – on transfer of land and shares excluding those listed on the NSE • Company – on transfer of assets, excluding shares listed on the NSE, that are not subject to corporation tax • Rate – 5% of the gain • On transfer of property – payable on or before the date the application for the transfer of property is made at the Lands Office • Transfer of property between spouses, or to a company 100% owned by either or both of the spouses or immediate family members, is exempt	
Inheritance Tax (IHT)	General description		No estate taxes

IV WITHHOLDING TAXES

Under domestic law	Payments to residents	Payments to non-residents[1]
Dividends	5%	• 5% to citizens of the East African Community Partner States • 10% to other non-residents
Interest	15%	15%
Royalties	5%	20%
On payments to artists and sportsmen	Nil	20%

There are a wide range of withholding taxes on other sources of income, for example:

	Resident	Non Resident
Telecommunication services	–	5%
Dividends paid to companies having 12.5% or more voting power	Exempt	10%
Renting property other than immovable	–	15%
Rent – land and buildings	10%	30%
Interest on bearer bonds with maturity of 10 years and above	10%	15%
Housing bond interest	10%	15%
Deemed interest on interest-free loans in respect of thin capitalisation	–	15%
Pension and taxable withdrawals from pension /provident funds	10–30%	5%
Insurance commissions	10%	Not specified
Contractual fees	3%	20%
Management, professional or training fees	5%	20%
Surplus pension fund withdrawals	30%	30%
Shipping business or aircraft	–	2.50%
Winnings from betting & gaming paid by bookmakers	7.50%	7.50%

Reduced rate available under the relevant Double Taxation Treaty			
Country	Dividends	Interest	Royalties
Canada	10%	15%	15%
Denmark	10%	15%	20%
France	10%	12%	10%
Germany	10%	15%	15%
India	10%	15%	20%
Norway	10%	15%	20%
Sweden	10%	15%	20%
United Kingdom	10%	15%	15%
Zambia	10%	15%	20%

Note: the above rates are only available provided the specific Treaty criteria are satisfied. It is possible that lower rates than those shown above may be available provided that certain criteria are satisfied. As treaties will not be identical, guidance should be sought in all cases.

---

1 Reduced rates of withholding tax may apply where there is an appropriate double tax treaty.

V   INDIRECT TAXES

		Residents	Non-residents
Value Added Tax	Entities obliged to levy VAT	Registration threshold is turnover of Kshs 5 million with effect from 15 June 2007 Registration can also be done voluntarily even if the turnover is below the threshold required	
	Taxable activities	VAT is levied on the supply of goods and services in the course of furtherance to business	
	Taxable activities – zero-rated (examples)	• Export of goods or services outside Kenya • Supply of goods or services to an export processing zone enterprise • Supply of coffee and tea for export to coffee and tea auction centres in Kenya	
	Exemptions (examples)	• Financial services subject to certain exclusions • Insurance and reinsurance services • Agricultural, animal husbandry and horticultural services	
	Refund of VAT	To submit a claim, must be registered for VAT and be compliant to VAT Act rules and regulations	Applies to companies whose management and control is exercised from outside Kenya. To submit a claim, must be registered for VAT and be compliant with VAT Act rules and regulations
	Tax liability	Based on monthly VAT returns	
	Tax rates	• Standard rate of 16% • 0% for zero-rated supplies	
	Administrative obligations	VAT returns and payments remitted on or before 20th day of the month following that in which the sales were made	
Turnover Tax		For taxable resident persons with business income whose annual turnover exceeds Kshs 500,000 and does not exceed Kshs 5 million with effect from 1 January 2007	
Real Property Taxes		Stamp Duty Land Tax – 4%	
Stamp Duty		1%	

Korea, Republic of

(Nexia Samduk, Hyunsoo KWON, hskwon@nexiasamduk.kr; Young Chang KWON, vitalset@nexiasamduk.kr)

I MAIN LEGAL FORMS

Legal form Characteristics	Limited Partnership (LP), Unlimited Partnership Company (UP) and Limited Liability Partnership Company (LLP)	Limited Liability Company-1 (LLC-1), Limited Liability Company-2 (LLC-2), Stock Company
Partners /shareholders • Number • Restrictions	LP: • two or more • no managing partner can transfer shares without the consent of all the partners • a partner with limited liability may transfer his/her shares in accordance with the partnership agreement UP: • two or more • no partner shall, without the consent of all other partners, transfer all or part of his/her shares in the company to another person LLP: • two or more • no partner with unlimited liability can transfer shares without the consent of all the partners. A partner with limited liability may transfer to another person the whole or part of his/her shares with the consent of all the partners with unlimited liability	LLC-1: • one or more • a member may transfer the whole or part of his/her shares to any other person only if a resolution of a general members' meeting is adopted by the affirmative votes of a majority of all the members and of the three-quarters of the total votes LLC-2:[1] • one or more • no member can transfer shares without the consent of other member • non-managing member can transfer shares with the consent of managing members. If there is no managing member, a member can transfer shares with the consent of all members Stock Company: • one or more • shares shall be transferable to other persons. Provided That the Articles of Incorporation may subject the transfer of shares to the requirement of approval of the Board of Directors

---

1   First introduced in 2012 in Korea. Internally LLC-2 operates like a partnership, but externally members have limited liability.

Legal form / Characteristics	Limited Partnership (LP), Unlimited Partnership Company (UP) and Limited Liability Partnership Company (LLP)	Limited Liability Company-1 (LLC-1), Limited Liability Company-2 (LLC-2), Stock Company
Directors	UP: each of partners shall represent the company LLP: one or more of the partners with unlimited liability shall represent the company	LLC-1: directors shall be elected at a general members' meeting Stock Company: – minimum requirement of three directors and one statutory auditor for capital of KRW1bn or over – minimum requirement of one director for capital of less than KRW1bn
Establishment	The company's Articles of Incorporation should be made	Stock Company: at least one promoter shall be required for the incorporation
Registration	A company's incorporation is registered with the appropriate district court controlling the area of head office	
Minimum capital	LP: no minimum capital UP: no minimum capital LLP: no minimum capital	LLC-1: no minimum capital LLC-2: no minimum capital Stock Company: no minimum capital
Liability	LP: general partner with unlimited liability and limited partners with limited liability UP: joint, several and unlimited liability LLP: general partner with unlimited liability and limited partners with limited liability	LLC-1 and LLC-2: limited to the amount of shareholder contributions to the company Stock company: limited to the subscription amount of shares
Governance	LP: each of general partners has the right and duty to manage partnership unless otherwise prescribed by the partnership agreement UP: each partner has the right and duty to manage the affairs of the company LLP: every partner with unlimited liability shall have the right and duty to manage the affairs of the company	LLC-1: management of the company's business shall be determined by a majority vote of the directors LLC-2: managing member has the right and duty to manage the affairs of the company Stock Company: a Board of Directors, by resolution, shall make decisions on management of affairs, appointment or dismissal of managers and establishment, transfer or abolition of branch offices
Audit requirements	N/A	LLC-1 and LLC-2: N/A Stock Companies with one of the following conditions: • total assets exceeding KRW12bn • total liabilities exceeding KRW7bn and total assets exceeding KRW7bn • total employees exceeding 300 and total assets exceeding KRW7bn

Legal form / Characteristics	Limited Partnership (LP), Unlimited Partnership Company (UP) and Limited Liability Partnership Company (LLP)	Limited Liability Company-1 (LLC-1), Limited Liability Company-2 (LLC-2), Stock Company
Taxation	• Resident companies are subject to corporation tax on their worldwide income • Partnerships and Partnership Companies can choose to be transparent for tax purposes	
Usage	LP (Hapja Johap): no juristic personality UP (Hapmyung Hoesa) LLP (Hapja Hoesa)	LLC-1 (Yuhan Hoesa) LLC-2 (Yuhan Chegim Hoesa) Stock Company (Chusik Hoesa) Corporations predominantly conduct business as Chusik Hoesa

II   CORPORATION TAX

Legal form / Description	Resident corporation	Permanent establishment (PE)
General description	Corporation tax	
Taxable entities	Companies are liable to corporation tax on their worldwide income	PE located in Korea on all Korean source income
Taxable income	Worldwide profits	Profits derived by PE in Korea
		No corporation tax is levied on the liquidation income of PE
Calculation of taxable profits	Accounting profit is adjusted for various tax add-backs and allowances to arrive at profits chargeable to corporation tax (PCTCT)	
Interest payments	• In principle, all interest payments on loans and other debts of a company are considered to be business expenses and therefore deductible • A thin capitalisation rule for the borrowing from overseas controlling shareholders exceeding 2 times the equity held by them (6 times for financial institutions) is applied and therefore the corresponding interest expenses are non-deductible	
Related party transactions	All related party transactions must take place on an arm's length basis	
Tax year, return and payment	• A corporation may determine its fiscal year, and where a corporation fails to determine its fiscal year, the fiscal year shall be 1 January to 31 December each year • A corporation tax return must be filed and corporation tax must be paid within 3 months from the last day of its fiscal year • Where the corporation tax amount to be paid is greater than KRW10m and less than KRW20m, the amount in excess of KRW10m may be paid in instalments within one month of the expiration date of the payment period (two months for SMEs) • Where the tax amount to be paid exceeds KRW20m, 50% or less of the tax amount may be paid in instalments	
Capital gains	Normal corporation tax is charged on capital gains from the disposal of land and buildings	
Losses	• Tax losses can be carried forward for 10 years (5 years for losses incurred before the fiscal year commencing 1 January 2009) • Carry back of tax losses is generally not allowed except for one year carry back of losses which is available to small and medium sized companies	
Tax group	Optional: fiscal unity with 100% owned companies only	
Tax rate	In fiscal year 2012 and thereafter • Taxable income not exceeding KRW200m – 10% of taxable income • Taxable income between KRW200m and 20bn – KRW20m plus 20% of the amount in excess of KRW200m • Taxable income exceeding KRW20bn – KRW3.98bn plus 22% of the amount in excess of KRW20bn • A local income surtax of 10% on corporation tax liability is assessed each year	

III TAXES FOR INDIVIDUALS

		Residents	Non-residents
Income Tax	General description	Tax levied on the chargeable income of a chargeable person for a year of assessment	
	Taxable entities and taxable income	Residents are taxed on their worldwide income	Non-residents are taxed on income arising in Korea
	Types of taxable income	• Global income – interest, dividends, business income, wage and salary income, pension income and other income • Schedular income – retirement income and capital gains	• Korean source income • Schedular income (both with or without PE) – retirement income and capital gains
	Calculation of income	• Global income is aggregated and taxed progressively • A combined income of dividend and interest exceeding KRW20m is subject to aggregate taxation on financing income • Schedular income is taxed separately at varying tax rates	
	Tax year, tax assessment and tax payment	• Tax year – taxes are assessed for the calendar year • Tax assessment – a resident who receives global income, retirement income and capital gains in a tax year is required to file a return for each category of income by the end of May of the following year • Tax payment: – where the income tax amount to be paid is greater than KRW10m and less than KRW20m, the excess over KRW10m may be paid in instalments within two months of the expiration date of the payment period – where the income tax amount to be paid exceeds KRW20m, 50% or less of the income tax amount may be paid in instalments	
	Losses	• Net Operating Losses (NOL) carryover is allowed for 10 years for the fiscal years starting after 31 December 2008 (5 years for the prior years) • Carry back of losses for 1 year is available	
	Tax rates		

Income band (KRW)	Tax rate (%): For the income arising after 1 January 2014
12m or less	6
12m to 46m	15
46m to 88m	24
88m to 150m	35
Over 150m	38

• A local income surtax is assessed at a rate of 10% of the income tax liability

		Residents	Non-residents
Capital Gains Tax (CGT)	General description	Gains arising from the disposal of capital assets are included in an individual's taxable income, but are taxed separately from global income	
	Taxable entities and chargeable assets	• Gains arising from the transfer of land or buildings • Gains arising from the transfer of rights related to real estate • Gains arising from transfer of shares in a non-listed company • Gains arising from transfer of specific listed shares (major shareholders' shares who own more than 1% (2% for KOSDAQ) or total market value held by a shareholder is KRW2.5bn (KRW2bn for KOSDAQ) or more)	• Gains derived from the transfer of land and buildings located in Korea • Gains arising from the transfer of investments in a domestic corporation or other securities issued by a domestic corporation or the domestic business place of a foreign corporation. However, gains arising from the transfer by a non-resident of domestically listed shares or corporate shares registered with the KOSDAQ (Korean Securities Dealers Automated Quotations) shall not be taxed, subject to the reciprocity principal
	Calculation of gain	• Gain on transfer = selling price − necessary expenses • Amount of capital gain = gain on transfer − special deduction for long-term possession of land and buildings − capital gains deduction • Necessary expenses include acquisition costs, costs of instalments or improvements, and other capital expenditure	
	Tax year, tax assessment and tax payment	A resident who transfers assets subject to capital gains is required to file a return and pay the tax due on the capital gains within 2 months from the end of the month to which the date of transfer belongs (In the case of shares, 2 months from the end of the quarter to which the date of transfer belongs)	
	Losses	• Capital losses are deductible only against capital gains • Unused losses may not be carried forward	
	Tax rates	• Capital gains from transfers of land, buildings, and rights to real estate are taxed at a rate of 6% to 70% • Capital gains arising from transfers of shares are taxed at a rate of 10% to 30%	

		Domiciled	Non-domiciled
Inheritance Tax (IHT)	General description	• A person or a company that acquires property through inheritance or bequest is liable to IHT • An inheritee that is a for-profit company is exempt from IHT	
	Taxable entities and chargeable assets	Levied after deducting certain amounts from the total value of the assets acquired on death of an inheritor and assets gifted to an inheritor within the preceding 10 years	
	Calculation of charge	• In principle, inherited properties are evaluated by the market price prevailing at the time of inheritance • A 10% credit is granted to those taxpayers who submit their tax returns on time	
	Taxable events	• IHT covers all property bequeathed by a resident and all property in Korea bequeathed by a non-resident	
	Allowances	• Public imposts, funeral expenses between KRW5m and KRW10m, debts left by the bequeathed • Basic deduction: KRW200m • Deduction for spouse: from KRW500m to KRW3bn • Other deductions	
	Tax rates	Rates of inheritance tax increase in bands from 10% on the first KRW100m of the statutory inheritance to 50% on the excess of KRW3bn	

IV   WITHHOLDING TAXES

Under domestic law	Payments to residents	Payments to non-residents[2]
Dividends	14%	20%
Interest	14%	20% (14% for bonds)
Royalties	Nil	20%
On payments to artists and sportsmen	20%	20%

Reduced rate available under the relevant Double Taxation Treaty[3]			
Country	Dividends	Interest	Royalties
Albania	10%	10%	10%
Algeria	15%	10%	10%
Australia	15%	15%	15%
Austria	15%	10%	10%
Azerbaijan	7%	10%	10%
Bahrain	10%	5%	10%
Bangladesh	15%	10%	10%
Belarus	15%	10%	5%
Belgium	15%	10%	10%
Brazil	10%	15%	25%
Bulgaria	10%	10%	5%
Canada	15%	10%	10%
Chile	10%	15%	10%
China	10%	10%	10%
Croatia	10%	5%	Nil
Colombia	10%	10%	10%
Czech Republic	10%	10%	10%
Denmark	15%	15%	15%
Ecuador	10%	12%	12%
Egypt	15%	15%	15%
Estonia	10%	10%	10%
Fiji	15%	10%	10%
Finland	15%	10%	10%
France	15%	10%	10%
Gabon	15%	10%	10%
Germany	15%	10%	10%
Greece	15%	8%	10%
Hungary	10%	Nil	Nil
Iceland	15%	10%	10%
India	20%	15%	15%
Indonesia	15%	10%	15%
Iran	10%	10%	10%
Ireland	15%	Nil	Nil

2   Reduced rates of withholding tax may apply where there is an appropriate double tax treaty.
3   As of 1 January 2016.

Reduced rate available under the relevant Double Taxation Treaty[3]			
Country	Dividends	Interest	Royalties
Israel	15%	10%	5%
Italy	15%	10%	10%
Japan	15%	10%	10%
Jordan	10%	10%	10%
Kazakhstan	15%	10%	10%
Kuwait	5%	5%	15%
Kyrgyzstan	10%	10%	10%
Laos	10%	10%	5%
Latvia	10%	10%	10%
Lithuania	10%	10%	10%
Luxembourg	15%	10%	15%
Malaysia	15%	15%	15%
Malta	15%	10%	Nil
Mexico	15%	15%	10%
Mongolia	5%	5%	10%
Morocco	10%	10%	10%
Myanmar	10%	10%	15%
Nepal	10%	10%	15%
Netherlands	15%	15%	15%
New Zealand	15%	10%	10%
Nigeria	7.5%	7.5%	7.5%
Norway	15%	15%	15%
Oman	10%	5%	8%
Pakistan	12.5%	12.5%	10%
Panama	15%	5%	10%
Papua New Guinea	15%	10%	10%
Peru	10%	15%	15%
Philippines	25%	15%	15%
Poland	10%	10%	10%
Portugal	15%	15%	10%
Qatar	10%	10%	5%
Romania	10%	10%	10%
Russia	10%	Nil	5%
Saudi Arabia	10%	5%	10%
Singapore	15%	10%	15%
Slovakia	10%	10%	10%
Slovenia	15%	5%	5%
South Africa	15%	10%	10%
Spain	15%	10%	10%
Sri Lanka	15%	10%	10%
Sweden	15%	15%	15%
Switzerland	15%	10%	10%
Thailand	10%	15%	15%
Tunisia	15%	12%	15%
Turkey	20%	15%	10%

Reduced rate available under the relevant Double Taxation Treaty[3]			
Country	Dividends	Interest	Royalties
Ukraine	15%	5%	5%
United Arab Emirates	10%	10%	Nil
United Kingdom	15%	10%	10%
United States	15%	12%	15%
Uruguay	15%	10%	10%
Uzbekistan	10%	5%	5%
Venezuela	15%	10%	10%
Vietnam	10%	10%	15%

Note: the above rates are only available provided the specific treaty criteria are satisfied. It is possible that lower rates than those shown above may be available provided that certain criteria are satisfied. As treaties will not be identical, guidance should be sought in all cases.

V INDIRECT TAXES

		Residents	Non-residents
Value Added Tax (VAT)	General description	Tax on the supply of goods and services (VAT)	
	Entities subject to VAT	Taxpayers include individuals, corporations, national and local governments, association of local authorities, any bodies of persons, and unincorporated foundations of any other organisations are generally subject to VAT	
	Taxable activities	• The supply of goods and services • The importation of goods	
	Taxable activities – zero-rated (examples)	A zero rate applies to the supply of goods for export, services furnished from outside the Republic of Korea, international transportation services by ships or aircraft and foreign currency earnings derived from goods or services supplied to a non-resident or foreign corporation with no permanent establishment in Korea	
	Exemptions (examples)	The supply of the following goods or services is subject to exemption and input tax incurred thereon is not refundable: basic life necessities and services, social welfare services, goods or services related to culture, human services, goods or services supplied by the government, local authorities and duty exempt goods	
	Refund of VAT	VAT is computed by deducting the input tax amount from the output tax amount chargeable on the goods or services supplied by the taxpayer. The input tax which exceeds the output tax is refundable	
	Tax liability	A trader is required to file a return on the tax base and tax amount payable or refundable within 25 days (50 days in the case of foreign corporations) from the date of termination of each preliminary return period and from each taxable period	
	Tax rates	Standard rate = 10%	
Property Taxes		An annual tax ranging from 0.07% to 4% is charged on the statutory value of land, buildings, houses, vessels, and aircraft. Five times the property tax rate is applied to property that is newly constructed or expanded in the Seoul metropolitan area for five years from its relevant registration date	
Stamp Duty		Stamp tax is levied on a person who prepares a document certifying establishment, transfer, or change of rights to property in Korea. The stamp tax ranges from KRW100 to KRW350,000, depending on the type of taxable document	

Kuwait

(Nayer Nazar, Nazar & Partners, nazarnexia@hotmail.com)

I MAIN LEGAL FORMS

Characteristics \ Legal form	Partnership and Limited Liability Partnership (LLP)	Private corporation (Ltd) and Public corporation (Plc)
Partners/shareholders • Number • Restrictions	SPC – owned by one person – unlimited liability (Kuwaiti or GCC) Partnership – minimum of 2 persons – Kuwaiti Unlimited liability WLL companies – minimum 2 persons – 51% of capital Kuwaiti – limited to the capital	KSC (closed) – not less than 5 persons. Limited to capital KSC – Public shareholding Limited to capital
Directors	Management by Partners	Board of Directors
Establishment	Ministry of Commerce and other authorities according to activity	Ministry of Commerce and other authorities according to activity
Registration	Registration through Ministry of Commerce	Registration through Ministry of Commerce and financial institutes
Minimum capital	KWD1,000. This is the minimum capital and depends on the activity	KSC (public) – KWD250,000 KSC (closed) – KWD10,000 Minimum capital and depends on the activity
Liability	Unlimited (SPC) Limited to capital	Limited to capital (shares)
Governance	Manager or as per Article of Association	Managing Director – Board of Directors – Shareholders' general meeting
Audit requirements	SPC and partnership – not required WLL – Independent audit required by law	Independent audit required by law KSC – public shareholding (listed) – two auditors required
Taxation	No tax	No tax

Notes: According to Ministerial Order No 237 of 2011, GCC (Gulf Cooperation Council) Companies are allowed to operate in Kuwait and are treated as Kuwaiti Companies, and could be owned 100% by GCC nationals.

• The Companies Law No 25 was issued and published in November 2012 and cancelled by the 'Companies Law No 1' which was issued on 24 January 2016 and published on 1 February 2016.

The main legal forms are the same. New legal forms included in the Law such as 'Sole person limited company' and professional companies such as Accounting, Lawyers, Medical companies.

II CORPORATION TAX

Legal Form / Description	Resident corporation	Permanent establishment (PE)
General description	Tax levied on taxable profit (net profit), only from foreign companies (companies formed and registered under the law of any country but carrying on business in Kuwait) and foreign partners (companies not individuals) in a resident company	
	Zakat tax 1% of net profit after accounting adjustments imposed on Kuwaiti shareholding companies (closed and public)	
Taxable entities	Only non-resident companies and the foreign partner company	
Taxable income	Net profit of the non-resident companies from its operations, plus any amount receivable for any other income in Kuwait (interest, royalties, technical services, management fees)	
Calculation of taxable profits	Accounting profit is adjusted for various tax add-backs and allowances to arrive at taxable profit	
Interest payments	Interest paid to local banks related to company's Kuwait operations is accepted as expenses. Interest income is taxable	
Related party transactions	10%–15% has to be deducted from the invoice value of materials imported to the Kuwaiti branch from head office or related parties abroad (transfer pricing)	
Tax year, return and payment	Tax period is 12 months (not more than 18 months for first return)	
	Tax return must be submitted to authorities not later than 3.5 months from end of the financial year	
	Tax paid within 30 days of submission 1% of the tax due for each 30 days as delay penalty	
Capital gains	Capital gains on the sale of assets and shares by foreign shareholders are subject to tax at 15%	
Losses	The losses of a year can be carried forward to the next two years only	
Tax group	Non-resident group is taxed and treated as one company	
Tax rate	Tax is imposed on non-resident companies (a branch of a foreign company) at rate of 15% of net profit for its operations in Kuwait for the financial period	
	1% is Zakat tax of net profit of Kuwaiti shareholding companies (public and closed)	

III TAXES FOR INDIVIDUALS

		Residents	Non-residents
Income Tax	General description	No tax imposed on individuals (residents and non-residents)	
	Taxable entities and taxable income		
	Types of taxable income		
	Calculation of income		
	Tax year, tax assessment and tax payment		
	Losses		
	Tax rates		
		Residents	Non-residents
Capital Gains Tax (CGT)	General description	No capital gains tax	
	Taxable entities and chargeable assets		
	Calculation of gain		
	Tax year, tax assessment and tax payment		
	Losses		
	Tax rates		
		Domiciled	Non-domiciled
Inheritance Tax (IHT)	General description	No inheritance tax	
	Taxable entities and chargeable assets		
	Calculation of charge		
	Taxable events		
	Allowances		
	Tax rates		

IV   WITHHOLDING TAXES

Under domestic law	Payments to residents	Payments to non-residents
Dividends	Nil	15%
Interest	Nil	15%
Royalties	Nil	15%
On payments to artists and sportsmen	Nil	15%

Gains from the above items of non-resident Companies are taxable at 15% of the profit.

Whilst Kuwait has tax treaties with the countries listed below, and others which are being ratified, there is uncertainty as to how these will be interpreted by the State and advice should be taken in each case.

Reduced rate available under the relevant Double Taxation Treaty			
Country	Dividends	Interest	Royalties
Austria	Nil	Nil	10%
Belarus	5%	5%	10%
Belgium	10%	Nil	10%
Bulgaria	5%	5%	10%
Canada	15%	10%	10%
China	5%	5%	10%
Croatia	10%	10%	10%
Cyprus	10%	10%	5%
Czech Republic	5%	Nil	10%
Ethiopia	5%	5%	30%
France	Nil	Nil	Nil
Germany	15%	Nil	10%
Hungary	Nil	Nil	10%
India	10%	10%	10%
Indonesia	10%	5%	20%
Italy	5%	Nil	10%
Jordan	5%	5%	30%
Korea, Republic of	10%	10%	15%
Lebanon	Nil	Nil	30%
Malta	15%	Nil	10%
Mauritius	Nil	5%	10%
Mongolia	5%	5%	10%
Netherlands	10%	Nil	5%
Pakistan	10%	10%	10%
Poland	5%	5%	15%
Romania	1%	1%	20%
Russian Federation	5%	Nil	10%
Singapore	Nil	7%	10%
South Africa	Nil	Nil	Nil
Sri Lanka	10%	10%	20%
Sudan	5%	5%	10%

Reduced rate available under the relevant Double Taxation Treaty			
Country	Dividends	Interest	Royalties
Switzerland	15%	10%	10%
Syria	Nil	10%	20%
Tunisia	10%	2.5%	5%
Turkey	10%	10%	10%
Ukraine	5%	Nil	10%
United Kingdom	15%	Nil	10%

Note: the above rates are only available provided the specific Treaty criteria are satisfied. It is possible that lower rates than those shown above may be available provided that certain criteria are satisfied. As treaties will not be identical, guidance should be sought in all cases.

V   INDIRECT TAXES

		Residents	Non-residents
Value Added Tax (VAT)	General description	There is no VAT	
	Entities obliged to levy VAT		
	Taxable activities		
	Taxable activities – zero-rated (examples)		
	Exemptions (examples)		
	Refund of VAT		
	Tax liability		
	Tax rates		
	Administrative obligations		
Real Property Taxes		0.5% of property value – transfer and/or registration	
Stamp Duty		Custom duty for goods and materials import is 4% of the invoice amount	
		Health insurance for non-Kuwaitis is KWD50 per year	
		Residential visa and other official stamp duties not more than KWD10	

Lebanon

(Mosbah Majzoub, Majzoub & Partners CPAs, info@majzoubcpas.com)

I MAIN LEGAL FORMS

Legal form / Characteristics	Partnership and Limited Liability Partnership (LLP) (Personal Companies)	Private corporation (Ltd) and Public Corporation (Plc) (Capital Companies)
Partners/shareholders • Number • Restrictions	There are 3 categories of partnerships: *General partnership (Sociétéen Nom Collectif – SNC):* Partnerships are associations of 2 or more people *Partnership in commendam (Sociétéen Commandite Simple – SCS):* This is a limited partnership with 2 types of partners. General partners own and manage the business and are liable for all its obligations. The liability of limited partners is limited to their investment *Co-Partnership (Joint Ventures):* Each party is responsible for their own liabilities	There are 5 categories of corporations: *Joint Stock Company (Société Anonyme Libanaise – SAL):* A SAL has a minimum of 3 shareholders *Limited Liability Company (Société à Responsabilité Limitée – SARL):* This type of hybrid company consists of between 3 and 20 partners *Corporation in Commendam:* A company in commendam is a limited partnership company with no specific capital requirements *Holding Company:* It is incorporated under the form of a joint-stock company and is subject to the same legal system governing joint-stock companies as provided by the Commercial Law *Offshore Company:* It is incorporated under the form of a joint-stock company and is subject to the same legal system governing joint-stock companies as provided by the Commercial Law The taxation is limited to US$667 The object of the company is limited by law (refer to next pages)
Directors	Appointment of manager based on formation documents	*Joint Stock Company:* minimum 3, maximum 12 *Holding Company:* at least 2 Lebanese citizens must be on the Board of Directors

Legal form / Characteristics	Partnership and Limited Liability Partnership (LLP) (Personal Companies)	Private corporation (Ltd) and Public Corporation (Plc) (Capital Companies)
Registration	*General Partnership:* must be registered with the Commercial Register *Joint Stock Company:* same as LLCs *Limited Liability Company (LLC):* the Articles of Incorporation must be notarised and filed in the Commercial Register	
Minimum capital	Partnerships: none	*Joint Stock Company (Société Anonyme Libanaise – SAL):* minimum capital LBP30m (US$20,000), with one-fourth paid-up at the time of registration *Limited Liability Company (Société à Responsabilité Limitée – SARL):* minimum capital of at least LBP5m (US$3,300), wholly paid-up at the time of registration
Liability	Unlimited liability	Limited to the extent of the share capital
Governance	General partners per Articles of Partnership and/or Memorandum of Association	Board of Directors and ultimately the equity shareholders in a General Assembly Meeting
Audit requirements	If turnover more than US$500,000 Or if required under the Articles of Partnership/ Memorandum of Association	*Joint Stock Company:* two auditors should be appointed LLC should appoint one auditor
Taxation	Each partner is subject to personal income tax in proportion of their share in the company	Corporate Tax applied

II CORPORATION TAX

Legal Form / Description	Partnership and Limited Liability Partnership (LLP) (Personal Companies)	Private corporation (Ltd) and Public corporation (Plc) (Capital Companies)
General description	Corporation tax	
Taxable entities	Companies resident in Lebanon are taxed on their worldwide income	
Taxable income	Income realised in Lebanon	
Calculation of taxable profits	Accounting profit is adjusted for various tax add-backs and allowances to arrive at the profits assessable to corporation tax	
Interest payments	Interest charges are fully deductible under the condition that taxes on interest are already deductible at the source (5%–10%)	
Related party transactions	All related party transactions must take place on arm's length basis	
Tax year, return and payment	Filed annually with accounts after year end	
Capital gains	Capital Gains on assets are taxed at 10%	
	Holding companies' Capital Gains on assets held for less than 2 years are taxed at 10%	
Losses	Losses can be carried forward for a maximum period of 3 years	
Tax group	None	
Tax rate	15%	

III TAXES FOR INDIVIDUALS

<table>
<tr><th></th><th></th><th>Residents</th><th>Non-residents</th></tr>
<tr><td rowspan="8">Income Tax</td><td>General description</td><td colspan="2">Income Tax is levied on any earning generated in Lebanon of a chargeable person for a year of assessment</td></tr>
<tr><td>Taxable entities and taxable income</td><td>All individuals are taxed, based on profits from industrial, commercial and non-commercial trade. No income is exempt from tax except by explicit provision in legislation</td><td>On all sources of income arising within Lebanon</td></tr>
<tr><td>Types of taxable income</td><td colspan="2">• Personal earnings: salaries, overtimes, bonuses
• Earnings generated from partnerships
• Profits from Joint Stock Company and limited liability company
• Income generated from stocks, bonds, shares</td></tr>
<tr><td>Calculation of Income</td><td colspan="2">Gross salary less allowances and pension contributions</td></tr>
<tr><td>Tax year, tax assessment and tax payment</td><td colspan="2">Partnerships and individuals 31 March following the 31 December year-end</td></tr>
<tr><td>Losses</td><td colspan="2">Set off against taxable income</td></tr>
<tr><td>Tax rates</td><td colspan="2">

Band (LBP)	Rate (%)
0–6,000,000	2
6,000,001–15,000,000	4
15,000,001–30,000,000	7
30,000,001–60,000,000	11
60,000,001–120,000,000	15
120,000,001 +	20

</td></tr>
<tr><td rowspan="4">Capital Gains Tax (CGT)</td><td>Taxable entities, chargeable assets and calculation of the gain</td><td colspan="2">Any resident persons</td></tr>
<tr><td>Tax year, tax assessment and tax payment</td><td colspan="2">Tax declarations are due on:
31 January sole proprietorship using lump sum method
31 March partnerships and sole proprietorships using real profit method
31 May for corporate entities</td></tr>
<tr><td>Losses</td><td colspan="2">Capital losses can be offset against taxable income of the same year</td></tr>
<tr><td>Tax rates</td><td colspan="2">10%</td></tr>
</table>

		Domiciled	**Non-domiciled**
Inheritance Tax (IHT)	General description	Inheritance taxes are levied at progressive rates depending on the degree of kinship between the deceased and the heir	
	Taxable entities and chargeable assets	The estate through the executor of the will. Value of inheritance less permitted exemption amounts and allowances	
	Calculation of charge	Gross estate less expired or irrecoverable debts and burial expenses	
	Taxable events	Transfer/transmission of ownership to beneficiary	
	Allowances	Each heir may be entitled to a tax-exempt amount, depending on the heir's relationship to the deceased	
		Relationship *Exemption amount*	
		Child, spouse or parent LBP40m (US$25,988)	
		Other descendants LBP16m (US$10,395)	
		Other persons LBP8m (US$5,198)	
	Tax rates	*Tax rate*	
		Up to LBP30m (US$19,491) 3%–16%	
		LBP30m–LBP60m (US$38,982) 5%–21%	
		LBP60m–LBP100m (US$64,970) 7%–27%	
		LBP100m+ (US$64,970+) 10%–33%	

IV   WITHHOLDING TAXES

Under domestic law	Payments to residents	Payments to non-residents[1]
Dividends	10%	10%
Interest	10%	5%
Royalties	Nil	7.5%
On payments to artists and sportsmen	Nil	15% of 50% of income

Reduced rate available under the relevant Double Taxation Treaty			
Country	Dividends	Interests	Royalties
Algeria	15%	15%	10%
Armenia	10%	8%	5%
Bahrain	Nil	Nil	Nil
Belarus	7.5%	5%	5%
Bulgaria	5%	7%	5%
Cyprus	5%	5%	Nil
Czech Republic	5%	Nil	10%
Egypt	10%	10%	5%
France	Nil	Nil	Nil
Iran	5%	5%	5%
Italy	15%	Nil	Nil
Jordan	10%	10%	10%
Kuwait	Nil	Nil	5%
Malaysia	5%	10%	8%
Malta	5%	Nil	5%
Morocco	10%	10%	10%
Pakistan	10%	10%	7.5%
Poland	5%	5%	5%
Qatar	Nil	Nil	Nil
Romania	5%	5%	5%
Russia	10%	5%	5%
Senegal	10%	10%	10%
Sultanate of Oman	10%	10%	10%
Syria	5%	10%	18%
Tunisia	5%	5%	5%
Turkey	15%	10%	10%
United Arab Emirates	Nil	Nil	5%
Ukraine	15%	10%	10%
Yemen	10%	5%	7.5%

Note: the above rates are only available provided the specific Treaty criteria are satisfied. It is possible that lower rates than those shown above may be available provided that certain criteria are satisfied. As treaties will not be identical, guidance should be sought in all cases.

---

1 Reduced rates of withholding tax may apply where there is an appropriate double tax treaty.

V INDIRECT TAXES

		Residents	Non-residents
Value Added Tax (VAT)	General description	The supply of goods and services carried out by a taxable person, for consideration, within the Lebanese territory	
		Import transactions undertaken by any person, whether that person is taxable or not	
	Entities obliged to levy VAT	Registration for VAT purposes is compulsory for businesses with turnover of LBP150m or more, per year	
		Registration for VAT purposes is voluntary where the turnover is less than that specified for compulsory registration	
	Taxable activities	The supply of goods and services carried out by a taxable person, for consideration, within the Lebanese territory	
		Import transactions undertaken by any person, whether that person is taxable or not	
	Taxable activities – zero-rated (examples)	Exempted activities: tax shall not be charges in respect of the transactions carried out within the Lebanese territory and related to any of the following activities: • Medical services • Education • Insurance and reinsurance • Banking and financial services • Non-profit organisations • Collective transport • Betting, lotteries and other forms of gambling • Sale of properties • Residential letting of properties • Farming Exempted goods: tax shall not be charged in respect of the following goods: • Livestock, poultries, live fish and agricultural alimentary products sold in their raw state • Food and cooking essentials • Publications • Gas for household consumption (butane) • Seeds, fertilizers, feeds and agricultural pesticides • Agricultural machinery • Medicines, drugs and pharmaceutical products • Medical equipment • Precious and semi-precious stones and metal • Yachts and other excursion or sports sailboats with a length exceeding 15 metres that are only owned by non-Lebanese	
	Exemptions (examples)	Schools, hospitals, medicines, and other exempt essential items, such as certain foods	
	Refund of VAT	The tax is calculated at the end of each quarter of the calendar year	
		If, at the end of a tax period, the amount of the deductible tax exceeds the amount of the tax due, then the excess shall be carried forward to the following period	
	Tax liability	Normally the supplier of goods and services is responsible for charging VAT	
	Tax rates	Taxable rate of 10%	
	Administrative obligations	Registered entity for VAT	

	Residents	**Non-residents**
Real Property Taxes	LBP74,000 (flat taxes)	
	+ 5% of property value (transfer tax)	
	+ 5% of the sum of transfer tax and flat taxes (municipal tax)	
	+ LBP5,000 (stamp duty on new deed)	
	+ 0.3% of property value (stamp duty)	
	+ 0.1% of property value (bar association tax)	
Stamp Duty	A stamp duty of 0.3% is levied on various documents	

VI NATIONAL SOCIAL SECURITY FUND (NSSF)

The National Social Security Fund (NSSF) provides employees with insurance coverage for sickness and maternity care. It also covers family allowances, end-of-service pension, and work related accidents and diseases. Any employee or labourer in any sector is eligible to enrol in the program. Employers are required to register in NSSF all Lebanese employees working for local and international firms. Foreign employees with a valid work permit and residence permit are entitled to join NSSF, provided their home country offers equivalent or better programs to Lebanese residents employed there. Foreign Nationals are not entitled for end-of-service benefits. Employer contribution is 6% of salary toward family allowances (with a ceiling of 1,500,000 L.L from the salary for the family), and 7% for health (with a ceiling of 2,500,000 L.L from the salary for the health), and a flat 8.5% for end of service. The employee pays a 2% for health coverage with a monthly ceiling of LBP50,000.

END OF SERVICE

At the age of 60, an employee can ask for early retirement and end-of-service compensation (paid only once) provided 20 years of service have been completed. Noting that the retirement age is 64, an employee no longer benefits from the NSSF. An employee can continue working after 64 if the company's by-law allows him, but he will no longer benefit from the end of service. The end of service indemnity will allow the employee to receive a month's wage equivalent to the last salary for every year worked.

FAMILY, TRANSPORTATION AND EDUCATION ALLOWANCE

Employees are entitled to family, transportation, and education allowances, attached to the husband's rather than wife's salary, except if the female employee is a widow or sole provider.

A married employee registered with NSSF receives a spouse allowance of LBP60,000 and an additional LBP33,000 for every child (maximum 5 children); this amount is paid by the NSSF through the employers.

Employees are given LBP8,000 transport allowance for every day they go to work; this amount is free of tax.

Education allowance is a lump sum for children up to the age of 25, attending school or university. A LBP300,000 (US$200) is allowed per child attending a public school or the Lebanese University, with a ceiling of LBP1.5 million. If the child is in a private school or university, the allowance increases to LBP750,000 (US$500) per child, but the same ceiling applies. This allowance does not form part of the NSSF employer contributions but is accounted for as operational expenses, and it is free of tax.

NSSF HEALTH BENEFITS

Once an employee is registered, the NSSF covers the employee and dependants in maternity, sickness, and work-related accidents. The employee is liable for 10% of all hospitalization costs and 20% of medication and examination expenses. Exceptions are made for pre-maternity and post-maternity examinations, which the NSSF pays in full.

COMPLIANCE

The law requires all companies to contribute to the NSSF Fund. Firm with less than 10 employees have to submit reports and pay contributions every three months. Larger enterprises that contain more than 10 employees must submit their reports and settle their contribution on a monthly basis. Evading the payments will impose fines on the employer. Fines are calculated by 0.5% or 0.05% for each day late for non-payment of the contribution amount.

Liechtenstein

(Urs Schnider, Axalo Steuerberatung AG, urs.schnider@axalo.com)

I MAIN LEGAL FORMS

Legal form / Characteristics	Company limited by Shares (Aktiengesellschaft, AG)	Foundation (Stiftung)	Establishment (Anstalt)
Structure	Corporation At least two founders are necessary for the formation act. Afterwards a one-man company is possible	Independent assets devoted to a particular use	Unique legal form, intermediate between corporation and foundation
Legal entity	Yes	Yes	Yes
Mandatory persons	• General Assembly • Board of Directors • Audit Company	• Board of Foundation • Audit Company (if purpose is charitable)	• Founder (bearer of the founder's rights) • Board of Directors • Audit Company (if purpose is commercial)
Minimum capital	CHF50,000	CHF30,000	CHF30,000
Usage	All commercial purposes, eg trading, production and financial business, but also non-commercial purposes	• Asset management • Organisation of family assets • Allocation to beneficiaries of a defined group • Holding function • Including non-commercial activities and purposes (unsuitable for commercial purposes)	• Universal use • All commercial purposes • Also suitable assets management tool

Characteristics \ Legal form	Company limited by Shares (Aktiengesellschaft, AG)	Foundation (Stiftung)	Establishment (Anstalt)
Registration	Public Register, compulsory and constitutive	• In practice, foundations are 'deposited' with the Public Register, with no right of inspection for third parties (family foundations and foundations with designated or definable beneficiaries) • In other cases (eg charitable purpose): compulsory and constitutive • Registration is also permitted for foundations which may be deposited	Public Register, compulsory and constitutive
Beneficiaries	Shareholders (as dividends and liquidation proceeds)	Beneficiaries in accordance with the provisions of the by-laws	Beneficiaries in accordance with the provisions of the by-laws It is presumed by law that the founder and/or his legal successors are the beneficiaries, unless other provision is made
Legal basis	Art 261 et seq Company Act (PGR), large number of mandatory legal provisions	Art 552 et seq PGR, hardly any mandatory legal provisions	Art 534 et seq PGR, hardly any mandatory legal provisions
Tax on distributions	No coupon taxes on distributions which are generated from 1 January 2011 Retained earnings which are generated until 31 December 2010 have to be taxed with coupon tax of 4% before or on the date of distribution (FIFO principle) No income tax on dividends since 2011	No coupon tax at all No income tax	No coupon tax at all No income tax

Legal form / Characteristics	Company limited by Shares (Aktiengesellschaft, AG)	Foundation (Stiftung)	Establishment (Anstalt)
Capital tax	No capital tax for companies subject to new Tax Act 44	No capital tax for companies subject to new Tax Act 44	See AG
	Capital tax of 1% of paid-in capital plus reserves, at least CHF1,200, for companies subject to old Tax Act 83 and 84 during the transitional period until 31 December 2013	Capital tax of CHF1,200 for foundations subject to old Tax Act 83 and 84 during the transitional period until 31 December 2013	
Taxes for companies operating in Liechtenstein	See below		
Usage	Suitable for all commercial transactions, with a well-understood legal form	A suitable instrument for asset investment and holding functions with few formalities as well for charitable purposes	Flexible but in other jurisdictions unknown legal form, suitable for all purposes

II   CORPORATION TAX

Legal form / Description	Resident corporation	Permanent establishment (PE)
General description	Tax on profits	
Taxable income	Resident companies	Property or branches located in Liechtenstein
Taxable income	Worldwide profits	Profits derived by the PE in Liechtenstein
Calculation of taxable profits	**General position** • 12.5%, with a minimum CHF1,200 (from 1 January 2017: CHF1,800) • the taxable profit can be reduced by an interest equity deduction of (currently) 4% • 30% of net profit is taxable at least while loss-offsetting • dividend income and capital gains on shares are not taxable income **Private asset structures** Description: A private asset structure will only be taxed with the minimum profit tax of CHF1,200 (from 1 January 2017: CHF1,800), if the following requirements are fulfilled: • No economic activities • The only purpose is the purchase, the holding, administration and the sale of 'bankable assets' as defined in the EU Markets in Financial Instrument Directive (MiFID), Vermögensverwaltungsgesetz Art 4 Abs1 Bst (g) • The shares (if any) are not publicly offered or traded • No promotion for share/stockholders and/or investors • No receipt of compensation or reimbursements by share/stockholders, investors or third parties • No legal entities as shareholders • Participation in other legal entities (>20%) is permitted, if neither the PVS nor owners nor beneficiaries influence the administration of such legal entities • Articles must provide for its treatment as a PVS No income tax for companies subject to old Tax Law 83 and 84 during the transitional period until 31 December 2013 (but therefore capital tax) – see above	

III TAXES FOR INDIVIDUALS

<table>
<tr><td rowspan="5">Income Tax</td><td>General description</td><td>Tax levied on the chargeable person for a year of assessment</td></tr>
<tr><td>Taxable entities and taxable income</td><td>Residents: worldwide income

Non-residents: Income arising in Liechtenstein – The income of general partnerships and limited partnerships is not subject to income taxes in Liechtenstein if the domicile of the individual is abroad and there is no permanent establishment in Liechtenstein

Liechtenstein income tax law is governed by the principle of family taxation, ie married persons are treated as a unit for purposes of income taxes and their tax liability is calculated jointly. Family taxation also includes minor children who live in a joint household with their parents</td></tr>
<tr><td>Types of taxable income</td><td>Income includes all periodic and non-recurrent income such as earnings from employment and self-employment, annuities, pensions, daily allowances from unemployment, health, and accident insurance, as well as lump-sum compensation. The Tax Act provides for different types of deductions (production costs, social insurance) as well as certain tax-exempt amounts. Capital income and capital gains are exempted</td></tr>
<tr><td>Tax rates</td><td>The national tax shall be calculated according to the taxable income including the wealth tax converted into income with 4% of the net wealth. The tax rates are between 1–8%, which also includes deductions. Municipalities add additional surcharges of at most 200% to the overall national tax liability. Assuming a municipal tax surcharge of 200%, the maximum tax rate is 24%</td></tr>
<tr><td>General description</td><td>Tax levied on the chargeable person for a year of assessment</td></tr>
<tr><td>Asset Tax</td><td>Taxable entities and taxable assets</td><td>Residents: worldwide assets (foreign real estate property is treated separately under the exemption of progression)

Non-residents: all domestic assets

The assets of the general partnerships and limited partnerships are not subject to asset tax in Liechtenstein, if the domicile of the individual is abroad and there is no permanent establishment in Liechtenstein

Liechtenstein asset tax law is governed by the principle of family taxation, ie married persons are treated as a unit for purposes of asset taxes and their tax liability is calculated jointly. Family taxation also includes minor children who live in a joint household with their parents</td></tr>
</table>

Asset Tax – *contd*	Types of taxable assets	The entirety of moveable and immoveable assets and earnings on these assets is subject to asset tax. No taxes are due on earnings (eg rental income) from real property
	Tax rates	The national tax shall be calculated according to the taxable income including the wealth tax converted into income with 4% of the net wealth. The tax rates are between 1–8%, which also includes deductions. Municipalities add additional surcharges of at most 200% to the overall national tax liability. Assuming a municipal tax surcharge of 200%, the maximum tax rate is 24%
Estate Tax and Inheritance Tax	General description	No estate tax and inheritance tax as from 1 January 2011

IV WITHHOLDING TAXES

Under Domestic Law	Payments to residents	Payments to non-residents
Dividends	Nil	No taxes on dividends as earnings from 1 January 2011 thenceforth 4% coupon tax on retained earnings generated until 31 December 2010. By applying for taxation of retained earnings, the latter will be taxed with 4%
Interest	Nil	EU interest taxation on bank interest income
Royalties	Nil	Nil
On payments to artists and sportsmen	Nil	Wage withholding tax/tax at source from 4% to 14%

Reduced rate available under the relevant Double Taxation Treaty			
Country	Dividends	Interest	Royalties
Austria	15%	Nil	10%
Germany	15%	Nil	Nil
Hong Kong	Nil	Nil	3%
Luxembourg	15%	Nil	Nil
San Marino	5%	Nil	Nil
Switzerland	0–15%	Nil	Nil
United Kingdom	15%	Nil	Nil
Uruguay	10%	10%	10%

The lower of the domestic and treaty rate will apply.

Note: the above rates are only available provided the specific Treaty criteria are satisfied. It is possible that lower rates than those shown above may be available provided that certain criteria are satisfied. As treaties will not be identical, guidance should be sought in all cases.

V   INDIRECT TAXES

		Residents	Non-residents
Value Added Tax (VAT)	General description	Liechtenstein is part of the Swiss VAT system and has virtually the same VAT law (see VAT Switzerland)	
	Entities obliged to levy VAT		
	Taxable activities		
	Taxable activities – zero-rated (examples)		
	Exemptions (examples)		
	Refund of VAT		
	Tax liability		
	Tax rates		
	Administrative obligations		
Real Property Taxes		Official fees are charged on the transfer of ownership of real estate (land or land and building)	
General description		Profits attained through the sale of real property located in Liechtenstein are subject to real estate capital gains tax. If a profit is attained through the sale of real property located in Liechtenstein, the seller must pay real estate profit tax. Sales include transfers through foreclosure sales or expropriation	
Taxable entities and chargeable assets		Real estate profits are the amount by which the proceeds of the sale exceed the investment costs (purchase price and expenditures increasing value)	
		In the case of sales pursuant to a contract, the sales profit equals the purchase price including all further services of the buyer	
Calculation and tax rates		The real estate capital gains tax has the same tax scale as the tax rate of individuals (24%)	
Stamp Duty		Swiss legislation on Stamp Tax is applicable in Liechtenstein (see Stamp Tax Switzerland). Swiss Tax Authorities are responsible for levying Stamp Tax in Liechtenstein	

Luxembourg

(Lut Laget, tax, audit & accountancy Sàrl, vgd.luxembourg@vgd.eu)

I MAIN LEGAL FORMS

Characteristics \ Legal form	SENC; SC (Partnership) and SECS; SECA (Limited Partnership)	Private corporation (Sàrl) and Public corporation (SA)
Partners/shareholders • Number • Restrictions	*General partnership – Société en nom collectif (SENC)*: two or more	*Public limited liability company – Société Anonyme (SA)*: one or more
	Limited partnership – Société en commandite simple (SECS): two or more: • one or more managing partners (associé(s) commandité(s)); and • one or more capital partners (associé(s) commanditaire(s))	*Private limited liability company – Société à responsabilité limitée (Sàrl)*: one or more (max: 100)
	Partnership limited by shares – Société en commandite par actions (SECA): at least one or more	
	Cooperative Society – Société Coopérative (SC): at least seven or more	
Directors	*SENC*: Management by partners (gérant(s))	*SA*: the board of directors – management by directors[1]
	SECS: the managing director (gérant) is (one of) the founding managing partner(s), appointed in the Articles of Incorporation	*Sàrl*: one managing director at least
	SECA: the managing director (gérant) is (one of) the founding managing partner(s), appointed in the Articles of Incorporation	
	SC: one or more managers	

---

1 At least three, or one where only one shareholder.

Legal form / Characteristics	SENC; SC (Partnership) and SECS; SECA (Limited Partnership)	Private corporation (Sàrl) and Public corporation (SA)
Establishment	*SENC*: private agreement, except *SECA* (notarial deed)	Notarial deed
	SECS: private agreement, except *SECA* (notarial deed)	
	SECA: notarial deed	
	SC: Private agreement, except *SECA* (notarial deed)	
Registration	Registration and deposit in the 'Registre de Commerce et des Sociétés' (RCS)	Registration and deposit in the 'Registre de Commerce et des Sociétés' (RCS)
Minimum capital	*SENC & SECA*: no minimal capital required	*SA*: €30,000
	SECA: €30,000	*Sàrl*: €12,000
	SC: variable capital, freely determined	
Liability	*SENC*: unlimited	Limited liability; limited for all shareholders
	SECS: managing partners have a joint and unlimited liability; capital partners only liable for their contribution	
	SECA: managing partners have a joint liability; capital partners are only liable for their contribution (shareholders)	
	SC: freely determined by the Articles of Incorporation	
Governance	*SENC*: each director solely	*SA*: Board of Directors (Conseil d'Administration) – day-to-day management to the managing director (Administrateur Délégué) – Executive Committee (Directoire) – Audit Committee (Conseil de Surveillance) – shareholders' meeting (Assemblée Générale)
	SECS: joint governance by director and managing partners – right of veto of the managing director – shareholders' meeting (Assemblée Générale)	
	SECA: joint governance by director and managing partners – right of veto of the managing director – shareholders' meeting (Assemblée Générale)	*Sàrl*: each director solely – shareholders' meeting (Assemblée Générale)
	SC: determined by the Articles of Incorporation – shareholders' meeting (Assemblée Générale)	

Legal form / Characteristics	SENC; SC (Partnership) and SECS; SECA (Limited Partnership)	Private corporation (Sàrl) and Public corporation (SA)
Audit requirements	*SENC*: N/A *SECS*: N/A *SECA*: at least three auditors *SC*: one or more auditor	*SA*: internal audit by one or more auditors (commissaire) – or external audit by auditor (réviseur d'entreprises) if: • turnover: €4.4m • balance sheet total: €8.8m • employed staff: 50 *Sàrl*: internal audit by one or more auditors if more than 60 shareholders – external audit as SA above
Taxation	*SENC*: transparent *SECS*: transparent *SECA*: corporate income tax *SC*: corporate income tax	• Corporate income tax on profits and fortune tax on net fortune[2,3,4]

2   Favourable tax regime for SOPARFI (Sociétés de Participations Financières).
3   Revenue of intellectual properties, 80% of income is tax-free (until 30 June 2021).
4   SPF tax of 0.25% on net fortune with specific exemptions.

II   CORPORATION TAX

Legal form / Description	Resident corporation	Permanent establishment (PE)
General description	Corporate tax	
Taxable entities	Resident companies are subject to corporate tax on their worldwide income	Non-resident companies having a PE in Luxembourg
Taxable income	Worldwide profits	All PE-income
Calculation of taxable profits	Profit of commercial balance sheet, but some types of income and expenses are treated differently for fiscal purposes	Income taxes are calculated on: • income attributable to the PE • dividends, interests, royalties and capital gains • income from immovable property in Luxembourg • interest on loans secured by immovable property in Luxembourg
Losses during the year	Losses can be carried forward against future income; from 2017, limited to 17 years	
Interest payments	Deductible, but thin capitalisation restrictions to be observed	
Related party transactions	New requirements in terms of transfer pricing and substance from 1 January 2017	
Tax year, return and payment	Tax year corresponds to calendar year. Companies with different accounting periods: tax year is the year ending in the calendar in question	Tax year corresponds to calendar year. PE with different accounting periods: tax year is the year ending in the calendar in question
Capital gains	No special capital gains tax[5]	
Losses	Losses arising during the year can be deducted from operating profits. Any unused balance of losses can be carried forward for 17 years	

[5]

Total of Balance Sheet (€)	Minimum wealth tax (€)
≤350,000	535
>350,000 and ≤2,000,000	1,605
>2,000,000 and ≤10,000,000	5,350
>10,000,000 and ≤15,000,000	10,700
>15,000,000 and ≤20,000,000	16,050
>20,000,000 and ≤30,000,000	21,400
>30,000,000	32,100

For SOPARFI companies, the minimum wealth tax payable is €4,815.

Legal form / Description	Resident corporation	Permanent establishment (PE)
Tax group	Available under strict conditions	
Tax rate	• Corporate income tax: between 15% and 21%[6] • Municipal business tax: around 6.75% to 7.5%[7] • Net worth tax: Annual tax at 0.5% of the unitary value of the company as at 1 January each year. Tax minimum following the total of the balance sheet[8]	

6 Capital gains deriving from the sale of shareholdings in other companies are excluded from taxation if the company gives the Luxembourg tax authorities an undertaking that it intends to hold the shares for at least 12 months and if they represent at least a 10% shareholding (or if less, that acquisition cost was at least €6m).

7 – 15% for income less than €25,000
   – 18% for income above €25,000 from 2018 (19% in 2017)
   There is a 7% employment fund surcharge calculated on income tax.

8 A charge of about 7.5% in respect of municipal services is calculated on the income after a reduction of €17,500. This latter component can vary according to location: in Luxembourg City it fell to 6.75%.

III   TAXES FOR INDIVIDUALS

<table>
<tr><td></td><td></td><td>Residents</td><td>Non-residents</td></tr>
<tr><td rowspan="8">Income Tax</td><td>General description</td><td colspan="2">Tax levied on the chargeable income of individuals</td></tr>
<tr><td>Taxable entities and taxable income</td><td>Residents are taxed on their worldwide income[9]</td><td>Non-residents are taxed on income arising in Luxembourg</td></tr>
<tr><td>Types of taxable income</td><td>
• Employment income
• Business income
• Income from professions
• Capital gains
• Others</td><td></td></tr>
<tr><td>Calculation of income</td><td>Taxable income is calculated by reference to specified categories, according to different rules, though losses made in one category may be offset against the income from another</td><td></td></tr>
<tr><td>Tax year, tax assessment and tax payment</td><td>The tax year is the calendar year

Returns should be filed within 3 months of the end of the year

Quarterly prepayments, final payment or refund after tax assessment</td><td></td></tr>
<tr><td>Losses</td><td colspan="2">Losses from a business or profession can be carried forward without limit. The offset of other losses is restricted</td></tr>
<tr><td>Tax rates</td><td colspan="2">Income tax rates are progressive: from 0% to 42%

Luxembourg income tax liability is based on the individual's personal situation (eg family status). Three tax classes have been defined:

• Class 1
• Class 1a
• Class 2</td></tr>
</table>

9   Double tax treaty to be observed.

		Residents	Non-residents
Capital Gains Tax (CGT)	General description	Profits realised on the disposal of movable and immovable property[10]	
	Taxable entities and chargeable assets	All assets acquired on a speculative basis	
	Calculation of gain	Difference between the sales price and acquisition costs (these are adjusted to take account of inflation)	
	Tax year, Tax assessment and Tax payment	The tax year is the calendar year Included in the normal tax declaration	
	Losses	Offset against taxable income	

	Tax rates	• Capital gains on real estate:
		  – is subject to progressive income tax rates if disposal takes place within 2 years of acquisition
		  – is subject to a reduced tax rate if disposal takes place more than 2 years after acquisition: the reduced tax rate will not exceed 19.5%
		• Capital gains on shares:
		  – the capital gain realised by an individual on the sale of a shareholding of more than 10% held for more than 6 months will be taxed under the same regime as capital gains arising from the sale of real estate more than 2 years after purchase
		• Others: taxed at normal tax rate	

		Residents	Non-residents
Inheritance Tax (IHT)	General description	Death and succession duties	
	Taxable entities and chargeable assets	The worldwide property of an individual domiciled in Luxembourg at the time of his death is subject to estate duty except on property located abroad	Property located in Luxembourg
	Calculation of charge	Various rates depending on relationship to deceased	
	Taxable events	Inheritances	

	Tax rates	Rates vary according to the nature of the relationship with the beneficiary and the value of the estate:
		• Individual heirs:
		  – direct descendants: nil
		  – spouse with children: nil
		  – spouse without children: 5%
		  – brothers and sisters: 6%–15%
		  – others: 10%–15%
		No difference for resident and non-resident heirs	

10 The capital gain on the sale of taxpayers' main residence is tax exempt.

IV WITHHOLDING TAXES

Under domestic law	Payments to residents	Payments to non-residents
Dividends	15%	15%[11,12]
Interest	20%	Nil
Royalties	Nil	Nil
On payments to artists and sportsmen	10%	Nil

Reduced rate available under the relevant Double Taxation Treaty			
Country	Dividends[13]	Interest[13]	Royalties[13]
Andorra	5/15%	Nil	Nil
Armenia	0/15%	10%	5%
Austria	0/5/15%	Nil	Nil
Azerbaijan	0/5/10%	10%	10%
Bahrain	0/10%	Nil	Nil
Barbados	0/15%	Nil	Nil
Belgium	0/10/15%	15%	Nil
Brazil	0/15/25%	15%	15%
Bulgaria	0/5/15%	10%	5%
Canada	0/5/15%	10%	10%
China	0/5/10%	10%	10%
Croatia	5/15%	10%	5%
Czech Republic	0/5/10%	Nil	10%
Denmark	0/5/15%	Nil	Nil
Estonia	0/10%	10%	10%
Finland	0/5/15%	Nil	5%
France	0/5/15%	10%	Nil
Georgia	0/5/10%	Nil	Nil
Germany	0/5/15%	Nil	5%
Guernsey	0/5/15%	Nil	Nil
Greece	0/7.5%	8%	7%
Hong Kong	0/10%	Nil	3%
Hungary	0/5/15%	Nil	Nil
Iceland	0/5/15%	Nil	Nil

11 Reduced rates of withholding tax may apply where there is an appropriate double tax treaty.

12 No withholding tax on dividends paid to companies resident in other EU countries under some conditions according to the EU Parent-Subsidiary Directive. The withholding tax exemption under the domestic participation exemption regime will not apply if the transaction is characterised as 'not genuine' within the meaning of the General Anti Abuse Rule. However, the GAAR does not apply to transactions where dividends are distributed to a non-resident (including EU) corporate entity that is resident in a tax treaty partner country and fully subject to an income tax comparable to the Luxembourg corporate income tax.

13 Where the domestic rate of withholding tax is lower than the treaty rate, the domestic rate will usually apply.

Reduced rate available under the relevant Double Taxation Treaty			
Country	Dividends[13]	Interest[13]	Royalties[13]
India	0/10%	10%	10%
Indonesia	0/10/15%	10%	10%
Ireland	0/5/15%	Nil	Nil
Isle of Man	0/5/15%	Nil	Nil
Israel	0/5/15%	10%	5%
Italy	0/5/15%	10%	10%
Japan	0/5/15%	10%	10%
Jersey	0/5/15%	Nil	Nil
Kazakhstan	0/5/15%	10%	10%
Latvia	0/5/10%	10%	10%
Laos	0/5/15%	10%	5%
Liechtenstein	0/5/15%	Nil	Nil
Lithuania	0/5/15%	10%	10%
Macedonia	0/5/15%	Nil	Nil
Malaysia	0/5/10%	10%	8%
Malta	0/5/15%	Nil	10%
Mauritius	0/5/10%	Nil	Nil
Mexico	0/5/15%	10%	10%
Moldova	0/5/10%	5%	5%
Monaco	0/5/15%	Nil	Nil
Mongolia	15%	10%	5%
Morocco	0/10/15%	10%	10%
Netherlands	0/2.5/15%	Nil	Nil
Norway	0/5/15%	Nil	Nil
Panama	0/5/15%	5%	5%
Poland	0/15%	10%	10%
Portugal	0/15%	15%	10%
Qatar	0/5/10%	Nil	5%
Romania	0/5/15%	10%	10%
Russia	0/5/15%	Nil	Nil
San Marino	0/15%	Nil	Nil
Saudi Arabia	0/5%	Nil	5%–7%
Seychelles	0/10%	5%	5%
Singapore	0/5/10%	10%	10%
Slovakia	0/5/15%	Nil	10%
Slovenia	0/5/15%	5%	5%
South Africa	0/5/15%	Nil	Nil
South Korea	0/5/15%	10%	15%
Spain	0/5/15%	10%	10%
Sri Lanka	0/7.5/10%	10%	10%
Sweden	0/15%	Nil	Nil
Switzerland	0/5/15%	10%	Nil
Taiwan	0/10/15%	15%	10%
Tajikistan	0/15%	12%	10%
Thailand	0/5/15%	15%	15%

Reduced rate available under the relevant Double Taxation Treaty			
Country	Dividends[13]	Interest[13]	Royalties[13]
Trinidad & Tobago	0/5/10%	10%	10%
Tunisia	0/10%	10%	12%
Turkey	0/5/20%	15%	10%
United Arab Emirates	0/5/10%	Nil	Nil
United Kingdom	0/5/15%	Nil	5%
United States	0/5/15%	Nil	Nil
Uzbekistan	0/5/15%	10%	5%
Vietnam	0/5/10/15%	10%	10%

Note: the above rates are only available provided the specific Treaty criteria are satisfied. It is possible that lower rates than those shown above may be available provided that certain criteria are satisfied. As treaties will not be identical, guidance should be sought in all cases.

V   INDIRECT TAXES

<table>
<tr><th></th><th></th><th>Residents</th><th>Non-residents</th></tr>
<tr><td rowspan="10">Value Added Tax (VAT)</td><td>General description</td><td colspan="2">Tax on the supply of goods and services (VAT)</td></tr>
<tr><td>Entities obliged to levy VAT</td><td colspan="2">Nature of entity is of no relevance. The kind of transaction triggers the VAT status</td></tr>
<tr><td>Taxable activities</td><td colspan="2">All goods and services excluding in particular cases the supply and leasing of immovable property (option for VAT is possible upon request)</td></tr>
<tr><td>Taxable activities – zero-rated (examples)</td><td colspan="2">• Gold
• Export</td></tr>
<tr><td>Exemptions (examples)</td><td colspan="2">Insurances

Hospitals

Education

Cultural activities (associations)</td></tr>
<tr><td>Refund of VAT</td><td>Company can demand a refund on the tax declaration but tax authorities reimburse only after control</td><td>Foreign companies may receive a reimbursement of VAT on exports of goods and services on a quarterly or an annual basis by internet on www.vatrefund.lu after control of administration</td></tr>
<tr><td>Tax liability</td><td colspan="2">The supplier of goods and services is generally liable</td></tr>
<tr><td>Tax rates</td><td colspan="2">• Standard rate: 17%

• Intermediate rate: 14%

• Reduced rate: 8%

• Super reduced rate: 3%</td></tr>
<tr><td>Administrative obligations</td><td>Monthly, quarterly or annual declaration to the tax authorities</td><td>Any business making taxable supplies or services has to register for VAT</td></tr>
<tr><td colspan="4"></td></tr>
<tr><td colspan="2">Real Property Taxes</td><td colspan="2">Levied by each town at varying rates</td></tr>
<tr><td colspan="2">Stamp Duty</td><td colspan="2">On certain legal contracts</td></tr>
</table>

Malaysia

(Jason Sia, Nexia SSY, jasonsia@nexiassy.com)

I MAIN LEGAL FORMS

Legal form / Characteristics	Partnership (P) / Limited Liability Partnership (LLP)	Private limited company (Sdn Bhd) and Public limited company (Berhad)
Partners/shareholders • Number • Restrictions	Minimum: two P Maximum: not more than 20 (except lawyers, doctors and accountants) LLP Maximum: no limit	Minimum: two Maximum: public – no limit private – 50
Partners/Directors	Every P shall have at least two partners, each of whom has his principal or only place of residence within Malaysia Every LLP shall have at least two partners. The partner who also acts as the compliance officer shall be a citizen or permanent resident in Malaysia and ordinarily resides in Malaysia	Every company shall have at least two directors, each of whom has his principal or only place of residence within Malaysia
Establishment	P: Partnership deed LLP: Limited Liability Partnership Agreement	Memorandum and Articles of Association
Registration	Registered under Companies Commission of Malaysia	
Minimum capital	P & LLP: Not applicable	Minimum two ordinary shares of MYR1 each
Liability	P: Collectively responsible for all debts of firm Partners' liability to pay the firm's debt is unlimited LLP: Limited to assets of the LLP	Limited to the share capital invested by the shareholders in the company
Governance	P: Partnership Act 1961 LLP: Limited Liability Partnerships Act 2012	Companies Act 1965 (Act 125)

Legal form / Characteristics	Partnership (P) / Limited Liability Partnership (LLP)	Private limited company (Sdn Bhd) and Public limited company (Berhad)
Audit requirements	P & LLP: No audited accounts required	Every auditor of a company shall report to the members on the accounts required to be laid before the company in general meeting and on the company's accounting and other records relating to those accounts. If it is a holding company for which consolidated accounts are prepared, he shall also report to the members on the consolidated accounts
Taxation	P: Share of income of partners is assessed at individual levels LLP: Resident partnerships are subject to income tax on the partnerships' profits derived on a territorial basis	Resident companies are subject to corporation tax on their profits derived on a territorial basis

II CORPORATION TAX

Legal form / Description	Resident corporation[1]	Permanent establishment (PE)
General description	Income tax	
Taxable entities	Resident companies are liable to income tax on income accruing in or derived from Malaysia	PE located in Malaysia is liable to income tax on income accruing in or derived from Malaysia
Taxable income	Profits or gains derived in Malaysia	
Calculation of taxable profits	Accounting profit before tax is adjusted for various tax add-backs and allowances to arrive at profit chargeable to corporation tax (PCTCT)	
Interest payments	Interest incurred *wholly* in the production of gross income is allowable as a deduction for tax purposes	
Related party transactions	All related party transactions must take place on an arm's length basis	
Tax year of assessment, return and payment	The tax basis year of assessment (Y/A) corresponds to the calendar year but a company may adopt any accounting period as its basis period which ends in the basis year of assessment for a year of assessment. All companies must complete and submit their tax returns within 7 months from the end of their accounting year	
Capital gains	Any gain on the disposal of real property or shares in a real property company (RPC[2]) is exempt from real property gains tax (RPGT) as from 1 April 2007. With effect from 1 January 2010, any gain on the disposal of real property or shares in a RPC within 5 years of purchase is subject to tax of between 5% to 10%. With effect from 1 January 2013, the tax rates have been increased to between 10% to 15%. With effect from 1 January 2014, the tax rates have been revised to between 0% to 30%	
Losses	Current year business losses are allowed to be deducted against other sources of income during the same year of assessment Unabsorbed losses are allowed to be carried forward to be set off against future business income	

---

1 A company (or a body of persons) carrying on a business is resident in Malaysia if, at any time in the basis year of assessment, the management and control of its business is exercised in Malaysia.
2 A RPC is a company holding real property or shares in another RPC of which the defined value of the company is not less than 75% of the value of the company's total tangible assets.

Legal form / Description	Resident corporation[1]	Permanent establishment (PE)
Tax rate	Year of assessment 2009 to 2015 – 25% Year of assessment 2016 and onwards – 24% Preferential SME tax rate for companies incorporated in Malaysia with a paid-up ordinary share capital of MYR2.5 million or less at the beginning of the basis period is as follows:	

Chargeable income	Year of Assessment		
	2009 to 2015	2016	2017 and onwards
First MYR500,000	20%[3]	19%[3]	18%[3]
On subsequent chargeable income	25%	24%	24%[4]

3 Preferential tax rates not applicable if more than:
   (a) 50% of the paid-up capital in respect of ordinary shares of the company is directly or indirectly owned by a related company;
   (b) 50% of the paid-up capital in respect of ordinary shares of the related company is directly or indirectly owned by the first mentioned company; or
   (c) 50% of the paid-up capital in respect of ordinary shares of the first mentioned company and the related company is directly or indirectly owned by another company.
   'Related company' is defined as a company which has a paid up capital exceeding MYR2.5 million in respect of ordinary shares at the beginning of the basis period for a year of assessment.
4 A reduction in the income tax rate, based on the percentage of increase in chargeable income as compared to the immediate preceding year of assessment, will be given to entities if they fulfil the criteria. The reduction in the income tax rate for Y/A 2017 and Y/A 2018 is as follows:

Percentage of increase in chargeable income as compared to the immediate preceding year of assessment	Percentage point reduction on income tax rate	Reduced income tax rate on increase in chargeable income (%)
Less than 5%	NIL	24
5%–9.99%	1	23
10%–14.99%	2	22
15%–19.99%	3	21
20% and above	4	20

III TAXES FOR INDIVIDUALS

<table>
<tr><th></th><th></th><th>Residents</th><th>Non-residents</th></tr>
<tr><td rowspan="9">Income Tax</td><td>General description</td><td colspan="2">Tax levied on the chargeable income of a chargeable person for a year of assessment</td></tr>
<tr><td>Taxable entities and taxable income</td><td>Residents are taxed on their territorial income with some relief for double taxation</td><td>Non-residents are taxed on income arising in Malaysia. No entitlement to reliefs</td></tr>
<tr><td>Types of taxable income</td><td colspan="2">• Property income (usually rent)
• Income from capital investment (interest, dividends, royalties, annuities)
• Income from business activities
• Employment from personal services or pensions</td></tr>
<tr><td>Calculation of income</td><td colspan="2">Accounting profit is adjusted for various tax add-backs and allowances to arrive at profits chargeable to tax</td></tr>
<tr><td>Tax year, tax assessment and tax payment</td><td colspan="2">Tax year – calendar year

Tax assessment – Taxpayers must complete and submit tax returns by 30 April (for a person not carrying on a business) or 30 June (for a person carrying on a business, ie sole proprietor, club, association and Hindu Joint family)</td></tr>
<tr><td>Losses</td><td colspan="2">Business losses can be utilised against other sources of income in the basis year and any unutilised business losses can be offset against income from business sources in subsequent years. Losses can be carried forward indefinitely until permanent cessation of the business</td></tr>
<tr><td>Tax rates</td><td>Scale rate for Y/A 2013 to Y/A 2014</td><td>26% flat rate</td></tr>
</table>

Chargeable income (MYR)	Tax rate (%)	Tax payable (MYR)
First 5,000	0	0
Next 15,000	2	300
On 20,000		300
Next 15,000	6	900
On 35,000		1,200
Next 15,000	11	1,650
On 50,000		2,850
Next 20,000	19	3,800
On 70,000		6,650
Next 30,000	24	7,200
On 100,000		13,850
Next 150,000	26	39,000
On 250,000		52,850
Exceeding 250,000	26	

		Residents			Non-residents
Income Tax – contd		With effect from Y/A 2015, the scale rate have been revised as follows:			25% flat rate
		Chargeable income (MYR)	*Tax rate (%)*	*Tax payable (MYR)*	
		First 5,000	0	0	
		Next 15,000	1	150	
		On 20,000		150	
		Next 15,000	5	750	
		On 35,000		900	
		Next 15,000	10	1,500	
		On 50,000		2,400	
		Next 20,000	16	3,200	
		On 70,000		5,600	
		Next 30,000	21	6,300	
		On 100,000		11,900	
		Next 150,000	24	36,000	
		On 250,000		47,900	
		Next 150,000	24.5	36,750	
		On 400,000		84,650	
		Exceeding 400,000	25		
		With effect from Y/A 2016, the scale rate have been revised as follows:			28% flat rate
		Chargeable income (MYR)	*Tax rate (%)*	*Tax payable (MYR)*	
		First 5,000	0	0	
		Next 5,000	1	50	
		On 10,000		50	
		Next 10,000	1	100	
		On 20,000		150	
		Next 15,000	5	750	
		On 35,000		900	
		Next 15,000	10	1,500	
		On 50,000		2,400	
		Next 20,000	16	3,200	
		On 70,000		5,600	
		Next 30,000	21	6,300	
		On 100,000		11,900	
		Next 50,000	24	12,000	
		On 150,000		23,900	
		Next 100,000	24	24,000	
		On 250,000		47,900	
		Next 150,000	24.5	36,750	
		On 400,000		84,650	
		Next 200,000	25	50,000	
		On 600,000		134,650	
		Next 400,000	26	104,000	
		On 1,000,000		238,650	
		Exceeding 1,000,000	28		

		Residents	Non-residents
Capital Gains Tax (CGT)	General description	Malaysia does not generally tax capital gains. Gains from the disposal of real property or shares in real property companies are subject to real property gains tax	
Inheritance Tax (IHT)	General description	No inheritance taxes	

IV   WITHHOLDING TAXES

Under domestic law	Payments to residents	Payments to non-residents[5]
Dividends	Nil	Nil
Interest	Nil	15%
Royalties	Nil	10%
Contract payments	Nil	10% of the service portion of the contract 3% of the service portion of the contract in respect of the employee's tax
Special classes of income	Nil	10%
On payments to public entertainers (eg artists and sportsmen)	Nil	15%
Other income under Section 4(f) of Income Tax Act 1967[8]	Nil	10%

Reduced rate available under the relevant Double Taxation Treaty					
Country	Dividends	Interest	Royalties	Technical fees	Section 4(f) income[8]
Albania	Nil	10%	10%	10%	10%
Argentina[6]	Nil	15%	10%	10%	10%
Australia	Nil	15%	10%	Nil	10%
Austria	Nil	15%	10%	10%	10%
Bahrain	Nil	5%	8%	10%	10%
Bangladesh	Nil	15%	10%	10%	10%
Belgium	Nil	10%	10%	10%	10%
Bosnia-Herzegovina	Nil	10%	8%	10%	10%
Brunei	Nil	10%	10%	10%	10%
Canada	Nil	15%	10%	10%	10%
Chile	Nil	15%	10%	5%	10%
China	Nil	10%	10%	10%	10%
Croatia	Nil	10%	10%	10%	10%
Czech Republic	Nil	12%	10%	10%	10%
Denmark	Nil	15%	10%	10%	10%
Egypt	Nil	15%	10%	10%	10%
Fiji	Nil	15%	10%	10%	10%
Finland	Nil	15%	10%	10%	10%
France	Nil	15%	10%	10%	10%
Germany	Nil	10%	7%	7%	Nil
Hong Kong	Nil	10%	8%	5%	10%
Hungary	Nil	15%	10%	10%	10%

5   Reduced rates of withholding tax may apply where there is an appropriate double tax agreement.
6   Limited agreements.
7   Income Tax Exemption Order.
8   Section 4(f) income refers to gains and profits not specifically provided for under Section 4 of the Income Tax Act 1967. Such income includes commissions and guarantee fees.

Reduced rate available under the relevant Double Taxation Treaty					
Country	Dividends	Interest	Royalties	Technical fees	Section 4(f) income[8]
India	Nil	10%	10%	10%	10%
Indonesia	Nil	10%	10%	10%	10%
Iran	Nil	15%	10%	10%	10%
Ireland	Nil	10%	8%	10%	10%
Italy	Nil	15%	10%	10%	10%
Japan	Nil	10%	10%	10%	10%
Jordan	Nil	15%	10%	10%	Nil
Kazakhstan	Nil	10%	10%	10%	10%
Kuwait	Nil	10%	10%	10%	10%
Kyrgyzstan	Nil	10%	10%	10%	10%
Laos	Nil	10%	10%	10%	10%
Lebanon	Nil	10%	8%	10%	10%
Luxembourg	Nil	10%	8%	8%	10%
Malta	Nil	15%	10%	10%	10%
Mauritius	Nil	15%	10%	10%	10%
Mongolia	Nil	10%	10%	10%	10%
Morocco	Nil	10%	10%	10%	10%
Myanmar	Nil	10%	10%	10%	10%
Namibia	Nil	10%	5%	5%	10%
Netherlands	Nil	10%	8%	8%	10%
New Zealand	Nil	15%	10%	10%	10%
Norway	Nil	15%	10%	10%	10%
Pakistan	Nil	15%	10%	10%	10%
Papua New Guinea	Nil	15%	10%	10%	10%
Philippines	Nil	15%	10%	10%	10%
Poland	Nil	15%	10%	10%	10%
Qatar	Nil	5%	8%	8%	10%
Republic of Korea	Nil	15%	10%	10%	10%
Romania	Nil	15%	10%	10%	10%
Russia	Nil	15%	10%	10%	10%
San Marino	Nil	10%	10%	10%	10%
Saudi Arabia	Nil	5%	8%	8%	10%
Senegal	Nil	10%	10%	10%	10%
Seychelles	Nil	10%	10%	10%	10%
Singapore	Nil	10%	8%	5%	10%
South Africa	Nil	10%	5%	5%	10%
Spain	Nil	10%	7%	5%	10%
Sri Lanka	Nil	10%	10%	10%	10%
Sudan	Nil	10%	10%	10%	10%
Sweden	Nil	10%	8%	8%	10%
Switzerland	Nil	10%	10%	10%	10%
Syria	Nil	10%	10%	10%	10%
Taiwan[7]	Nil	10%	10%	7.5%	10%

Reduced rate available under the relevant Double Taxation Treaty					
Country	**Dividends**	**Interest**	**Royalties**	**Technical fees**	**Section 4(f) income[8]**
Thailand	Nil	15%	10%	10%	10%
Turkey	Nil	15%	10%	10%	10%
Turkmenistan	Nil	10%	10%	10%	Nil
United Arab Emirates	Nil	5%	10%	10%	10%
United Kingdom	Nil	10%	8%	8%	10%
United States[6]	Nil	15%	10%	10%	10%
Uzbekistan	Nil	10%	10%	10%	10%
Venezuela	Nil	15%	10%	10%	10%
Vietnam	Nil	10%	10%	10%	10%
Zimbabwe	Nil	10%	10%	10%	10%

Note: the above rates are only available provided the specific Treaty criteria are satisfied. It is possible that lower rates than those shown above may be available provided that certain criteria are satisfied. As treaties will not be identical, guidance should be sought in all cases.

V INDIRECT TAXES

	Residents	Non-residents
General description	Types of indirect taxes in the country are: • Customs duties • Excise duties • Service tax *(replaced by Goods and Services Tax ('GST') with effect from 1 April 2015)* • Sales tax *(replaced by GST with effect from 1 April 2015)*	
Customs duties • Import duties • Export duties	Levied on goods imported into or exported from Malaysia	
	Certain types of goods are exempted from customs duties under specific exemption orders	
	• Import duties rates are either specific or ad valorem from 2%–300% • Export duties rates are either specific or on cost plus concept	
Excise duties	Imposed on certain locally manufactured goods (eg beer, stout, other intoxicating liquors, cigarettes, motor vehicles and playing cards)	
	Rates are either specific or ad valorem	
Service tax *(replaced by GST with effect from 1 April 2015)*	Consumption tax levied and charged on any taxable services provided by any taxable person	
	Rate is 6% of the price, charge or premium of the taxable service	
Sales tax *(replaced by GST with effect from 1 April 2015)*	Single stage tax imposed on all goods manufactured in or imported into Malaysia unless specifically exempted	
	Rates are ad valorem from 5%–10%	
Goods and Services Tax (GST) General description	Tax on the supply of goods and services (GST). Business with taxable turnover of MYR500,000 or more for a period of 12 months or less is required to be registered	
Entities obliged to levy GST	GST has been implemented on 1 April 2015, replacing the Sale and Service taxes, at standard rate of 6% except for goods and services listed under Exempt Order, Zero-rated Order or Relief Order	

Real Property Taxes	With effect from 1 January 2014, the RPGT rates have been revised as follows:

Date of disposal	Real Property Gains Tax Rates		
	Companies	Individual (Citizen & permanent resident)	Individual (Non-Citizen)
Within 3 years from date of acquisition	30%	30%	30%
In the 4th year	20%	20%	30%
In the 5th year	15%	15%	30%
In the 6th year and subsequent years	5%	0%	5%

Stamp Duty	Chargeable on certain instruments and documents
	Rate of duty varies (fixed or ad valorem) according to the nature of the instrument/documents and transacted values according to the First Schedule to the Stamp Act 1949

Nexia International does not accept liability for any loss arising from any action taken, or omission, on the basis of this publication. Professional advice should be obtained before acting or refraining from acting on the contents of this publication. Membership of Nexia International, or associated umbrella organizations, does not constitute any partnership between members, and members do not accept any responsibility for the commission of any act, or omission to act by, or the liabilities of, other members.

Nexia International is the trading name of Nexia International Limited, a company registered in the Isle of Man. Company registration number: 53513C. Registered office: 2nd floor, Sixty Circular Road, Douglas, Isle of Man, IM1 1SA

Malta

(Karl Cini, Nexia BT, karl.cini@nexiabt.com)

I MAIN LEGAL FORMS

Legal form / Characteristics	Partnership and Limited Liability Partnership (LLP)	Private corporation (Ltd) and Public corporation (Plc)
Partners/shareholders • Number • Restrictions	Two types of partnerships are possible, namely: • *En nom collectif:* unlimited partnership, where all partners' liability is unlimited, joint and several • *En commandite:* limited partnership, where at least one partner's liability has to be unlimited	*Ltd:* • minimum: one shareholder (as long as the sole shareholder and sole director are not themselves corporate entities, and the objects clause is restricted to one main activity) • maximum: 50 shareholders *Plc:* • minimum: two shareholders • maximum: no limit
Directors	Management by partners	Minimum: one director Maximum: no limit
Establishment	Deed of partnership	Memorandum and Articles of Association
Registration	Filing of deed of partnership at the Registry of Companies	Filing of Memorandum and Articles at the Registry of Companies
Minimum capital	*En nom collectif:* none *En commandite:* its capital may or may not be divided into shares. No minimum	Ltd: €1,164.69 with at least 20% thereof paid upon subscription Plc: €46,587.47 with at least 25% thereof paid upon subscription
Liability	*En nom collectif:* unlimited *En commandite:* unlimited and joint and several liability of one or more general partners and liability limited to the amount, if any, unpaid on the contribution of one or more limited partners	Limited to the portion, if any, of unpaid, but subscribed for, share capital
Governance	Partners	Board of Directors
Audit requirements	None	Audit required
Taxation	Transparent	Worldwide basis

II CORPORATION TAX

Legal form / Description	Resident corporation	Permanent establishment (PE)
General description	Income tax	
Taxable entities	Resident companies	PE located in Malta
Taxable income	• Worldwide profits for resident companies incorporated and managed and controlled in Malta • Source basis for resident companies not incorporated and managed and controlled in Malta • Source and remittance (except foreign capital gains) basis for resident companies not incorporated but managed and controlled in Malta	Profits allocated to the PE in Malta
Calculation of taxable profits	Accounting profits as adjusted for various disallowable expenses and tax allowances Dividends from qualifying participations are exempt	
Interest payments	Interest on any borrowed money is an allowable deduction if it is paid on capital employed in acquiring income	
Related party transactions	Arm's length basis	
Tax year, return and payment	Fiscal year is the calendar year Malta operates a self-assessment system. Tax is payable at the time the self-assessment is filed. For companies the tax return date is 9 months after the financial year end, but not earlier than 31 March of each year Companies and self-employed persons pay tax under the provisional tax system (PT). PT payments are due every 4 months. Where the tax liability is not fully covered by the PT the balance must be paid at the time the relative tax return is due Special rules apply to tax due by companies deriving foreign income	
Capital gains	Capital gains are added to the income of the recipient and chargeable to tax accordingly in Malta. The only capital gains subject to tax are those made on transfer of: • immovable property • securities and shares (but excluding those quoted on the Malta Stock Exchange) • beneficial interest in a trust • business, goodwill, trademarks, trade names, patents and copyrights Capital gains from qualifying participations are exempt Capital gains realised on the transfer of shares by non-residents are exempt from Malta income tax (with the exception of shares in companies, the assets of which consist wholly or principally of immovable property situated in Malta)	
Losses	Trading losses can be carried forward without time limit and offset against future profits arising from the same trade including capital gains Capital losses can be carried forward without time limit but may only be set off against capital gains	

Description / Legal form	Resident corporation	Permanent establishment (PE)
Tax group	A company may surrender its losses in favour of any group company subject to certain conditions. For this purpose two companies are considered to form part of a group if the shares of one company are owned to the extent of more than 50% by the other, or both of them are to the extent of more than 50% subsidiaries of a third company	Not available
Tax rate	35%[1]	

---

1 Various credits are available for participating holdings, trading income and income derived from passive assets in addition to credits for foreign losses suffered on the income.

III   TAXES FOR INDIVIDUALS

		Residents	Non-residents
Income Tax	General description	Tax levied on the chargeable income of a chargeable person for a year of assessment. A person's liability to tax in Malta hinges on the twin concepts of residence and domicile **Special tax status holders (under the Global Resident Programme rules)** A flat rate of 15% is applicable on all foreign source income received in Malta by third country nationals provided certain conditions are satisfied, such as the purchase or rental of immovable property in Malta meeting certain thresholds. This is subject to a minimum tax payment of €15,000 This programme does not grant tax residence in Malta to the applicant and his dependants. To become tax resident, the applicant must establish ties with Malta **Special tax status holders (under the Residence Programme rules)** A flat rate of 15% is applicable on all foreign source income received in Malta by EU/EEA nationals provided certain conditions are satisfied, such as the purchase or rental of immovable property in Malta meeting certain thresholds. This is subject to a minimum tax payment of €15,000 **Special tax status holders (under the Highly Qualified Persons rules)** A flat rate of 15% is applicable on chargeable employment income in a senior position derived from a Maltese employer in the financial sector, remote gaming or aviation sector licensed under the Malta Financial Services Authority (MFSA), the Lotteries and Gaming Authority (LGA) or Authority for Transport in Malta (TM) respectively. This is subject to a minimum employment income of €81,205 adjusted annually for inflation. The benefits under this rule are available for 5 consecutive years for EEA and Swiss nationals and 4 years for non-EU citizens **Special Scheme for Expatriates** Subject to certain conditions, employment income arising to an expatriate working in Malta in respect of work or duties carried out in Malta is subject to tax in Malta at 15% **Special tax status holders for EU/EEA and Swiss Nationals (under the Malta Retirement Programme Rules)** A flat rate of 15% on income received in or remitted to Malta, provided that 75% of such person's income consists of pension income. This is subject to a minimum tax payment of €7,500 per annum plus an amount of €500 per dependant	
	Taxable entities and taxable income	Persons that are both ordinarily resident and domiciled in Malta are subject to income tax on their worldwide income and certain capital gains Persons that are resident but not domiciled in Malta are taxable on income arising outside Malta that is remitted to Malta, unless the individual has or has applied for a long-term residence or a permanent residence status, in which case, such individual would be taxable on a worldwide basis	Taxable on any income and certain capital gains arising in Malta

		Residents		Non-residents
Income Tax – *contd*	Types of taxable income	• Gains or profits from trade, profession or vocation • Employment income including certain fringe benefits • Investment income • Rent, royalties, premiums and any other profit arising from property • Other gains or profits not taxed elsewhere		
	Calculation of income	Income is generally taken to be the gross amount received less any allowances and generally on an accruals basis. Fringe benefits are calculated according to the value of the benefit based on calculations as prescribed by the Inland Revenue Department		
	Tax year, tax assessment and tax payment	Tax year – calendar year Tax assessment – individual self-assessment Tax payment – by 30 June of the following year (also filing date)		
	Losses	Trading losses can be carried forward and set off against any type of income Capital losses can be carried forward but may only be set off against capital gains		
	Tax rates	**Single rates**		**Single and married**

Chargeable income (€)	Rate (%)
0–9,101	0
9,101–14,500	15
14,501–19,500	25
19,500 – 60,000	25
60,001 and over	35

Married rates

Chargeable income (€)	Rate (%)
0–12,700	0
12,701–21,200	15
21,201–28,700	25
28,701–60,000	25
60,001 and over	35

Chargeable income (€)	Rate (%)
0–700	0
701–3,100	0.2
3,101–7,800	0.3
7,801 and over	0.35

Non-resident individuals who can prove that more than 90% of their worldwide income is arising from Malta can have their income taxed in Malta under the residents' rates of taxation. Certain conditions apply

		Residents	Non-residents
Income Tax – *contd*		**Parent rates**	
		Chargeable income (€) *Rate (%)*	
		0–10,500 0	
		10,501–15,800 15	
		15,801–21,200 25	
		21,201–60,000 25	
		60,001 and over 35	
		There are certain conditions to be met in order for individuals to opt for the parent rates	
Capital Gains Tax (CGT) / Property Tax	General description	Taken to be gains made on the disposal of certain assets	
	Taxable entities and chargeable assets	Any person resident in Malta in the year during which the gain arises is taxable Chargeable assets being: • immovable property (subject to final tax) • securities and shares (but excluding those quoted on the Malta Stock Exchange) • beneficial interest in a Trust • business, goodwill, trademarks, trade names, patents and copyrights	
	Calculation of gain / Property Transfer Tax	Gain is based on the disposal proceeds less cost of acquisition and other allowable expenditure. Transfers of immovable property situated in Malta are subject to a final Property Transfer Tax system at the rate of 8% on the transfer value, subject to the following exceptions: a. 5% on the transfer value in the case of individuals who are not property traders where the property is transferred within 5 years of acquisition; b. 10% on the transfer value in the case of property sold by companies or individuals where the property disposed has been acquired before 1 January 2004	

		Residents	Non-residents
Capital Gains Tax (CGT) / Property Tax – *contd*	Tax year, tax assessment and tax payment	Capital gains are recorded in the tax return of the individual. The tax year is hence a calendar year For the majority of transfers, a provisional tax payment of 7% of the transfer value is payable upon transfer, with the resultant tax due, if any, to be paid by 30 June of the following year	
	Losses	Capital losses are set off against any capital gains made during that year Unutilised capital losses can be carried forward indefinitely, to be set off against future capital gains	
	Tax rates	Capital gains, with the exception of transfers of immovable property which are subject to a Final Property Transfer Tax system, are recorded in the individual's tax return for that year and added to the other income. The applicable tax rate will then apply on the total income	

		Domiciled	Non-domiciled
Inheritance Tax (IHT)	General description	There is no inheritance or gift tax in Malta. The transmission of property and company shares is, however, subject to tax under the Duty on Documents and Transfers Act. Duty will be due at the rate of: €5 per €100 or part thereof in the case of real estate; €2 per €100 or part thereof in the case of shares in companies that do not have immovable property situated in Malta; and €5 per €100 in other cases	

IV   WITHHOLDING TAXES

Under domestic law	Payments to residents	Payments to non-residents
Dividends	None (a 15% tax would apply when dividends are paid from a company's untaxed account to a Maltese resident individual)	Nil
Interest	Nil	Nil
Royalties	Nil	Nil
On payments to artists and sportsmen	Nil	10% (applicable to foreign entertainers performing in Malta)

Income arising in Malta and paid to non-residents may attract withholding tax. The rate at which tax is withheld depends on the nature of the recipient.

Reduced rate available under the relevant Double Taxation Treaty		
Country	Dividends Rates for minor shareholding	Interest	Royalties
Albania	15%	5%	5%
Australia	15%	15%	10%
Austria	15%	5%	10%
Azerbaijan[3]	Nil	8%	8%
Bahrain	Nil	Nil	Nil
Barbados	15%	5%	5%
Belgium	15%	10%	10%
Bulgaria	Nil	Nil	10%
Canada	15%	15%	10%
China	5%	10%	7%
Croatia	5%	Nil	Nil
Curacao[3]	5%	Nil	Nil
Cyprus	15%	10%	10%
Czech Republic	5%	Nil	5%
Denmark	15%	Nil	Nil
Egypt	10%	10%	12%
Estonia	15%	10%	10%
Finland	15%	10%	10%
France	0%	5%	10%
Georgia	Nil	Nil	Nil
Germany	15%	Nil	Nil
Greece	10%	8%	8%
Guernsey	Nil	Nil	Nil
Hong Kong	Nil	Nil	3%
Hungary	15%	10%	10%
Iceland	15%	Nil	5%

2   Denotes that treaty is signed but not yet in force.
3   A new treaty/Protocol has been signed but is not yet in force.

Reduced rate available under the relevant Double Taxation Treaty			
Country	Dividends Rates for minor shareholding	Interest	Royalties
India	10%	10%	10%
Ireland	5%	Nil	5%
Isle of Man	Nil	Nil	Nil
Israel	15%	5%	Nil
Italy	15%	10%	10%
Jersey	Nil	Nil	Nil
Jordan	10%	10%	10%
Korea	15%	10%	Nil
Kuwait	Nil	Nil	10%
Latvia	10%	10%	10%
Lebanon	5%	Nil	5%
Libya	15%	5%	5%
Liechtenstein	Nil	Nil	Nil
Lithuania	5%	10%	10%
Luxembourg	15%	Nil	10%
Malaysia	Nil	15%	15%
Mauritius	Nil	Nil	Nil
Mexico	Nil	5%/10%	10%
Moldova	Nil	5%	5%
Montenegro	5%	10%	5%
Morocco	10%	10%	10%
Netherlands	15%	10%	10%
Norway	15%	10%	10%
Pakistan	Nil	10%	10%
Poland	15%	10%	10%
Portugal	15%	10%	10%
Qatar	Nil	Nil	Nil
Romania	5%	5%	5%
Russia	10%	5%	5%
San Marino	10%	Nil	Nil
Saudi Arabia	5%	Nil	5%/7%
Serbia	5%	10%	5%/10%
Singapore	Nil	7%/10%	10%
Slovakia	5%	Nil	5%
Slovenia	15%	5%	5%
South Africa	10%	10%	10%
Spain	5%	Nil	Nil
Sweden	15%	Nil	Nil
Switzerland	15%	10%	Nil
Syria	Nil	10%	18%
Tunisia	10%	12%	12%
Turkey	15%	10%	10%
Ukraine[2]	15%	Nil	Nil

Reduced rate available under the relevant Double Taxation Treaty			
Country	Dividends Rates for minor shareholding	Interest	Royalties
United Kingdom	Nil	10%	10%
United Arab Emirates	Nil	Nil	Nil
Uruguay	15%	10%	5%/10%
United States	15%	10%/15%	10%
Vietnam[3]	15%	10%	5%/10%/15%

Where the treaty rate is higher than the domestic rate, the domestic rate will usually apply.
Note: the above rates are only available provided the specific Treaty criteria are satisfied. It is possible that lower rates than those shown above may be available provided that certain criteria are satisfied. As treaties will not be identical, guidance should be sought in all cases.

V INDIRECT TAXES

		Residents	Non-residents
Value Added Tax (VAT)	General description	Tax on the supply of goods and services (VAT)	
	Entities obliged to levy VAT	Registration is compulsory for suppliers of goods with annual turnover over €28,000 and suppliers of services over €19,000. However, those with a turnover below these thresholds need to be registered with an exempt status. Entities include individuals, partnerships, corporations or other bodies. Following distance selling rules, foreign EU-based suppliers exceeding the current threshold of €35,000 sales made in Malta over a period of a year need to register in Malta	
	Taxable activities	All supplies of goods and services that take place in Malta, intra-Community acquisitions and imports	
	Taxable activities – zero-rated (examples)	Zero rating applies to exports and intra-Community supplies, international transport, domestic passenger transport, food, pharmaceuticals and the supply and repair of ships and aircraft	
	Exemptions (examples)	Exemptions include the sale and leasing of immovable property, banking and insurance services, health, education and broadcasting	
	Refund of VAT	VAT paid on supplies and services is deductible as input tax, if incurred in the course or furtherance of the business and for the purpose of making taxable supplies (including zero-rated supplies) There is no credit for input tax incurred which relates to the provision of exempt supplies Where mixed supplies occur (taxable and exempt), input tax must be apportioned and recovered according to a partial attribution method stipulated in the law	EC 8th Directive refund system applies for non-resident businesses established within the EU, as long as its businesses do not require a registration in Malta EC 13th Directive refund system for non-resident businesses established outside the EU, as long as its businesses do not require a registration in Malta Such claims are required to be made to the Maltese VAT department within strict time limits
	Tax liability	Normally the supplier of goods and services is responsible for charging VAT Reverse charge system applies for certain types of goods and services (eg accountancy and consultancy services received from businesses established in EU but outside Malta)	
	Tax rates	Standard rate = 18% A reduced 7% rate applies to the supply of holiday accommodation, and a 5% rate applies on electricity, printed matter and confectionery Zero rate = 0%	
	Administrative obligations	Formal requirements concerning business records and invoices Quarterly self-assessment VAT return. Returns are to be submitted one and a half months following the end of the quarter together with the payment of any VAT liability to the Commissioner of VAT (special arrangements allow for monthly returns to be filed) VAT invoices required to contain some basic data including the respective VAT identification number	Registration for VAT purposes if making supplies of goods and services in Malta

	Residents	Non-residents
Property Stamp Duty	Chargeable on the transfer, whether inter vivos or by way of inheritance, of immovable property	
	The rate is €5 per €100 or part thereof payable by the buyer	
	Exemptions include transfers of property between group companies, partitioning of property by joint owners and transfers between spouses (amongst others)	
Stamp Duty on transfers of shares	Stamp duty is also chargeable on the transfer, whether inter vivos or by way of inheritance, of securities. The tax in this case is €2 per €100 or part thereof but is increased to €5 per €100 or part thereof in the case of shares in property companies	
	Duty at various rates is also chargeable on emphyteutic grants, auction sales, credit cards and insurance policies (with the exemption of policies relating to health, marine, aviation, export finance and re-insurance)	

Mauritius

(Ouma Shankar (Swaraj) Ochit, Nexia Baker & Arenson, nexiamtius@intnet.mu)

I MAIN LEGAL FORMS

Legal form / Characteristics	Partnership and Limited Liability Partnership (LLP)	Private corporation (Ltd) and Public corporation (Plc)
Partners/shareholders • Number • Restrictions	*Société and LLP* • Two or more associates/partners	• Minimum: one • Private company: maximum 25 shareholders
Directors	All partners unless stated otherwise in the partnership deed	Minimum one director
Establishment	Partnership deed	Constitution of the Company
Registration	Must be registered with the Registrar of Companies	
Minimum capital	No minimum capital	
Liability	Société: liability of associates is unlimited LLP: at least one partner's liability is unlimited	Limited by shares or by guarantee or both shares and guarantee
Governance	The Code de Commerce (Amendment) Act, Act 21 of 1985	Companies Act 2001
Audit requirements	No audit required	Financial statements must be audited unless it is a small private company whose annual turnover of its last preceding accounting period is less than MUR50m
Taxation	Transparent, but the individual partners are directly liable for their respective share of income, except for a non-resident société which is treated as a company	Corporate tax, as an opaque entity

II   CORPORATION TAX

Legal form / Description	Resident corporation	Permanent establishment (PE)
General description	Tax on income from chargeable sources for a chargeable year of assessment	
Taxable entities	Companies, trusts and trustees of unit trust schemes	PE located in Mauritius
Taxable income	Worldwide income	Income arising or deemed to arise in Mauritius
Calculation of taxable profits	Profit as adjusted for tax purposes	
Interest payments	Deductible, provided incurred in the production of income, no thin capitalisation rules	
Related party transactions	Transactions not carried out at arm's length may be subject to tax adjustments	
Tax year, return and payment	Annual return to be filed not later than 6 months from the end of the month in which its accounting period ends	
	Besides the annual return, companies are required to file quarterly Advance Payment System (APS) Statements and at the same time pay the tax based on either the chargeable income of the preceding year or the actual chargeable income of the quarter, unless in the preceding year:	
	(a) the company's gross income did not exceed MUR10m; or	
	(b) it had no chargeable income	
Capital gains	No CGT in Mauritius	
Losses	May be carried forward and set off against its income derived in the following 5 income years. The time limit of 5 years is not applicable for the carry forward of the loss attributable to annual allowances in respect of capital expenditure incurred on or after 1 July 2006	
Tax group	None	
Tax rate	15% (Global Business Companies, Category 1 are taxed at a maximum effective rate of 3%)	
Corporate Social Responsibility (CSR)	Every company shall set up a CSR Fund equivalent to 2% of its chargeable income of the preceding year	
	A Global Business Company, Category 1 and a bank for its segment B business have no CSR Fund obligations	

III TAXES FOR INDIVIDUALS

		Residents	Non-residents
Income Tax	General description	Income tax	
	Taxable entities and taxable income	Any individual present in Mauritius for a period of 183 days or more in an income year or for an aggregated period of 270 days or more in the current income year and the 2 preceding income years	Income derived from sources in Mauritius
	Types of taxable income	Income related to employment and income derived from trade, business, profession and rent	
	Calculation of income	Chargeable income is the amount remaining after deducting from the net income, the income exemption threshold to which the individual is entitled	
	Tax year, tax assessment and tax payment	Tax year ends on 30 June and tax returns should be filed within 3 months from the end of the tax year	
		PAYE system is in operation, and is based on a cumulative basis	
		Current Payment System (CPS) concerns self-employed persons with income derived from trade, business, professional and rent. The individual must submit the CPS return on a quarterly basis and at the same time pay the tax based on either the income of the preceding year or the actual chargeable income, unless: in respect of the preceding year (a) his gross income did not exceed MUR4m; or (b) the actual tax payable does not exceed MUR500	
	Losses	May be carried forward to offset against business income derived in the 5 succeeding income years	
	Tax rate	15%	
Capital Gains Tax (CGT)	General description	No capital gains tax in Mauritius	
		Mauritius domiciled	**Non-Mauritius domiciled**
Inheritance Tax (IHT)	General description	No gift or inheritance taxes in Mauritius	

IV   WITHHOLDING TAXES

Under Domestic Law	Payments to residents	Payments to non-residents[1]
Dividends	Nil	Nil
Interest	Nil	15% (exempt for a GBC 1 company from its foreign source income)
Royalties	10%	15% (exempt for a GBC 1 company from its foreign source income)
On payments to artists and sportsmen	Nil	10%
On management fees	5%	10%
Payments made by any person, other than an individual, to a non-resident for any services rendered in Mauritius	Nil	10%

Reduced rate available under the relevant Double Taxation Treaty (Maximum tax rates applicable in the State of Source)			
Country	Dividends	Interest[2]	Royalties
Bangladesh, People's Republic of	10%	Normal rate	Normal rate
Barbados	5%	5%	5%
Belgium	5%/10%	10%	Exempt
Botswana	5%/10%	12%	12.5%
China, People's Republic of	5%	10%	10%
Congo	0%/5%	5%	Exempt
Croatia	Exempt	Exempt	Exempt
Cyprus	Exempt	Exempt	Exempt
Egypt	5%/10%	10%	12%
France	5%/15%	Same rate as under domestic law	15%
Germany	5%/15%	Exempt	10%
Guernsey	Exempt	Exempt	Exempt
India	5%/15%	Same rate as under domestic law	15%
Italy	5%/15%	Same rate as under domestic law	15%
Kuwait	Exempt	Exempt	10%
Lesotho	10%	10%	10%
Luxembourg	5%/10%	Exempt	Exempt
Madagascar	5%/10%	10%	5%
Malaysia	5%/15%	15%	15%
Malta	Exempt	Exempt	Exempt
Monaco	Exempt	Exempt	Exempt
Mozambique	8%/10%/15%	8%	5%

1   Reduced rates of withholding tax may apply where there is an appropriate double tax treaty.

Reduced rate available under the relevant Double Taxation Treaty (Maximum tax rates applicable in the State of Source)			
Country	Dividends	Interest[2]	Royalties
Namibia	5%/10%	10%	5%
Nepal	5%/10%/15%	10%/15%	15%
Oman	Exempt	Exempt	Exempt
Pakistan	10%	10%	12.5%
Qatar, State of	Exempt	Exempt	5%
Rwanda	10%	10%	10%
Senegal	Exempt	Exempt	Exempt
Seychelles	Exempt	Exempt	Exempt
Singapore	Exempt	Exempt	Exempt
South Africa	5%/10%	10%	5%
Sri Lanka	10%/15%	10%	10%
Swaziland	7.5%	5%	7.5%
Sweden	0%/15%	Exempt	Exempt
Thailand	10%	10%/15%	5%/15%
Tunisia	Exempt	2.5%	2.5%
Uganda	10%	10%	10%
United Arab Emirates	Exempt	Exempt	Exempt
United Kingdom	10%/15%	Same rate as under domestic law	15%
Zambia	5%/15%	10%	5%
Zimbabwe	10%/20%	10%	15%

Where the treaty rate is higher than the domestic rate, the domestic rate will usually apply.

Note: the above rates are only available provided the specific Treaty criteria are satisfied. It is possible that lower rates than those shown above may be available provided that certain criteria are satisfied. As treaties will not be identical, guidance should be sought in all cases.

---

2   Where interest is taxable at rate provided in the domestic law of the State of source or at a reduced treaty rate, provision is usually made in the treaty to exempt interest receivable by a Contracting State itself. Its local authorities, its Central Bank/all banks carrying on bona fide banking business and any other financial institutions as may be agreed upon by both Contracting States.

V   INDIRECT TAXES

		Residents	Non-residents
Value Added Tax (VAT)	Entities obliged to levy VAT	• Any business person with a turnover of taxable supplies of more than MUR6m must register with VAT Department, Mauritius Revenue Authority • Persons engaged in certain businesses or professions may also be required to register, irrespective of their turnover	
	Taxable activities	Goods and services produced or improved locally	
	Taxable activities – zero-rated (examples)	Exports and other items as specified in the VAT Act	
	Exemptions (examples)	Certain essential goods and services	
	Refund of VAT	On capital goods in excess of MUR100,000 and input tax relating to zero-rated supplies	
	Tax liability	Liable to pay tax for a period prior to registration if the person should have been registered	
	Tax rate	Standard rate of 15%	
	Administrative obligations	A return together with payment of tax to be submitted monthly, unless the annual turnover is less than MUR10m, in which case the return is submitted quarterly	
Registration duties on immovable properties		5% on value of immovable property transferred payable by purchaser	
Registration duty on loans		Duties of fixed amounts are levied upon registration of a loan agreement	
Real Property Taxes		Land Transfer Tax payable by the seller at the rate of 5% if the property transferred has been acquired more than 5 years from date of transfer. If transfer made within 5 years the rate is 10%	

Nexia International does not accept liability for any loss arising from any action taken, or omission, on the basis of this publication. Professional advice should be obtained before acting or refraining from acting on the contents of this publication. Membership of Nexia International, or associated umbrella organizations, does not constitute any partnership between members, and members do not accept any responsibility for the commission of any act, or omission to act by, or the liabilities of, other members.

Nexia International is the trading name of Nexia International Limited, a company registered in the Isle of Man. Company registration number: 53513C. Registered office: 2nd floor, Sixty Circular Road, Douglas, Isle of Man, IM1 1SA

© Nexia International 2017

Mexico

(Alfredo Solloa, SOLLOA-NEXIA S.C., alfredo.solloa@solloacp.com.mx)

I MAIN LEGAL FORMS

Legal form / Characteristics	Partnership and Limited Liability Partnership (LLP)	Private corporation (Ltd) and Public corporation (Plc)
Official name	Sociedad Civil (SC) Sociedad de Responsabilidad Limitada (S de RL)	Sociedad Anónima (SA) which might be of fixed or variable equity (SA de CV) If publicly held: Sociedad Anónima Bursátil (SAB). Might also be of fixed or variable equity
Partners/shareholders • Number • Restrictions	• LLP: 50 maximum • Partnership: 2 minimum, no limit	• 2 minimum • No limit
Directors	Might be sole director or a board	
Establishment	A notary public issues the incorporation deed and it has to be registered in the public registry of property and commerce	
Registration	Registration before tax authorities, social security authorities and state payroll tax. Also, if foreign shareholders are involved, before the Foreign Investment Registry	
Minimum capital	• LLP: no minimum • Partnership: no minimum	• No minimum
Liability	The legal representative (with power of attorney) and in some cases the partners up to the amount of their contribution	
Governance	• LLP: Board of managers or sole • Partnership: One or more partners	Board of Administration (Board of Directors) or sole Administrator
Audit requirements	Option/right to audit if turnover exceeds 100 m pesos on prior year, fixed assets over 79 m pesos or above 300 employees	
Taxation	Mexican residents are subject to tax on all income, regardless of source (ie worldwide income)	
Usage	The Mexican LLC (Limited Liability Company) can be used in some countries as a pass-through vehicle Publicly held companies cannot use this type of entity	Mandatory for publicly held companies

II   CORPORATION TAX

Legal form / Description	Resident corporation	Permanent establishment (PE)
General description	Corporate income tax	Branch income tax
Taxable entities	Corporations incorporated in Mexico and/or overseas companies with central management and control located in Mexico	PE located in Mexico
Taxable income	Worldwide profits	Profits derived by PE in Mexico
Calculation of taxable profits	Accounting profit is adjusted for various tax add-backs and allowances to arrive to profits chargeable to corporation tax (PCTCT)	
Interest payments	Interest payments are tax deductible, and the comparisons with inflation rates generate gains or losses, which are taxable or tax deductible Thin capitalisation rule is 3:1 and where the liability exceeds the 3:1 ratio the interests paid in excess are non-deductible Thin capitalisation rule applies only to interest paid to related parties residing abroad	
Related party transactions	All related party transactions must take place on an arm's length basis and companies are obliged to substantiate such basis by preparing a formal annual transfer pricing study	
Tax year, return and payment	The tax year is the calendar year and tax is paid monthly or quarterly in advance depending on the level of revenue The annual tax return must be filed within 3 months after the end of the tax year	
Capital gains	Capital gains are subject to income tax at the same rate of corporations (30%). In some cases, capital gains are subject to withholding tax on gross proceeds	
Losses	Net operating tax losses may be carried forward for 10 years and set off against taxable profits	
Tax rate	30%	

III TAXES FOR INDIVIDUALS

		Residents	Non-residents
Income Tax	General description	Tax levied on income	
	Taxable entities and taxable income	Residents are taxed on their worldwide income	Non-residents are taxed on income from Mexican sources
	Types of taxable income	• Property income (usually rent) • Income from capital investment (interest, sale of goodwill, dividends, royalties, annuities) • Income from business activities and/or professional activities • Employment, personal services and pensions	
	Calculation of income	• Taxable income is generally computed by reducing the related costs of goods or the cost of acquisition • Rental income is entitled to a 35% blind deduction (optional) • Salary income is computed by applying a progressive table which starts from 0% and goes up to 35% income tax	
	Tax year, tax assessment and tax payment	The tax year is a calendar year Tax is usually withheld by the payer and is due the following month Annual tax for individuals is due before the end of April the following year	
	Losses	Can be credited in some very specific cases such as sale of assets and business activities	
	Tax rates	0–35%	
		Residents	**Non-residents**
CAPITAL GAINS TAX (CGT)	General description	No CGT exist as such in Mexico. However, the profit resulting from the sale of assets is included in the taxable income for income tax purposes	
	Taxable entities and chargeable assets	Capital gains are computed and added to the corporate/individual taxable income	Only assets located in the Mexican territory
	Calculation of gain	Liability is calculated by deducting historical cost adjusted to current value, accounting for inflation between the date of acquisition and the date of disposal	
	Tax year, tax assessment and tax payment	The tax year is the calendar year and tax is paid monthly or quarterly in advance The tax return must be filed within 4 months after the end of the tax year	
	Losses	Tax losses resulting from business income may be carried forward for 10 years and set off against future taxable profits except on the sale of stocks Individuals may carry forward losses in some other specific cases	
	Tax rates	0–35%	
		Domiciled	**Non-domiciled**
Inheritance Tax (IHT)	General description	There is no IHT in Mexico	

IV   WITHHOLDING TAXES

Under Domestic Law	Payments to residents	Payments to non-residents[1]
Dividends	10%	10%
Interest	Nil	From 4.9%–35%
Royalties	Nil	From 5%–35%
On payments to artists and sportsmen	Nil	From 25%–35%
On technical assistance to a non-treaty country	Nil	From 5%–35%

Reduced rate available under the relevant Double Taxation Treaty			
Country	Dividends	Interest	Royalties
Austria	10%	10%	10%
Australia	15%	15%	10%
Barbados	10%	10%	10%
Bahrain	Nil	10%	10%
Belgium	15%	15%	10%
Brazil	15%	15%	15%
Canada	15%	10%	10%
Chile	10%	15%	15%
China	5%	10%	10%
Colombia	Nil	10%	10%
Czech Republic	10%	10%	10%
Denmark	15%	15%	10%
Ecuador	5%	15%	10%
Estonia	Nil	10%	10%
Finland	Nil	15%	10%
France	5%	15%	15%
Germany	15%	10%	10%
Greece	10%	10%	10%
Hong Kong	0%	10%	10%
Hungary	15%	10%	10%
Iceland	15%	10%	10%
India	10%	10%	10%
Indonesia	10%	10%	10%
Ireland	10%	10%	10%
Israel	10%	10%	10%
Italy	15%	15%	15%
Japan	15%	15%	10%
Korea	15%	15%	10%
Kuwait	Nil	10%	10%
Lithuania	15%	10%	10%
Latvia	10%	10%	10%

---

1   Reduced rates of withholding tax may apply where there is an appropriate double tax treaty in force.

Reduced rate available under the relevant Double Taxation Treaty			
Country	Dividends	Interest	Royalties
Luxembourg	15%	10%	10%
Malta	Nil	10%	10%
Netherlands	15%	10%	10%
New Zealand	15%	10%	10%
Norway	15%	15%	10%
Panama	7.5%	10%	10%
Peru	15%	15%	15%
Poland	15%	15%	10%
Portugal	10%	10%	10%
Qatar	Nil	10%	10%
Romania	10%	15%	15%
Russia	10%	10%	10%
Singapore	Nil	15%	10%
Slovakia	Nil	10%	10%
South Africa	10%	10%	10%
Spain	15%	15%	10%
Sweden	15%	15%	10%
Switzerland	15%	10%	10%
Turkey	15%	15%	10%
Ukraine	15%	10%	10%
United Arab Emirates	Nil	10%	10%
United Kingdom	15%	15%	10%
United States	10%	15%	10%
Uruguay	5%	10%	10%

Where the domestic rate is lower than the treaty rate, the domestic rate will usually apply.

Note: the above rates are only available provided the specific Treaty criteria are satisfied. It is possible that lower rates than those shown above may be available provided that certain criteria are satisfied. As treaties will not be identical, guidance should be sought in all cases.

V INDIRECT TAXES

		Residents	Non-residents
Value Added Tax (VAT)	General description	Impuesto al Valor Agregado (VAT) Value Added Tax	
	Entities obliged to levy VAT	All entities or individuals (either residents or non-residents) performing activities in the Mexican territory are subject to VAT	
	Taxable activities	• Transfer of goods • Rendering services • Property income (rentals) • Importation	
	Taxable activities – zero-rated (examples)	• Food • Medicines • Primary activities (agriculture, fishing, catering) • Exports	
	Exemptions (examples)	• Books • Interest from financial institutions • Services rendered or goods transferred by not-for-profit organisations	
	Refund of VAT	Refunds paid within a period of 40 working days	Not allowed under general rules
	Tax liability	The supplier of the goods and services is responsible for charging VAT	
	Tax rates	• Standard rate = 16% • Rate on exports and food = 0% • The tax is computed on a cash-flow basis	
	Administrative obligations	• Apply for registration • File monthly returns • Withhold VAT in case of payments made to individuals • File monthly and annual information returns • Issue electronic invoices complying with special requirements	
Real Property Taxes		Owners of land and buildings pay tax to local councils, who apply rules to each city	
Stamp Duty		There are no stamp taxes	

Morocco

(Mohamed Ouedghiri, Nexia Fiducia, m.ouedghiri@nexiafiducia.ma)

I MAIN LEGAL FORMS

Legal form / Characteristics	Partnership and Limited Liability Partnership (LLP)	Ltd (private corporation) and Plc (public corporation)

Partners/shareholders
• Number
• Restrictions
	• **General partnership** – Société en nom collectif (SNC):
	  – at least two partners
	  – all partners have to be traders
	• **Limited partnership** – *Société en commandite simple* (SCS) and **Partnership limited by shares** – *Société en commandite par actions* (SCA):
	  – at least two partners
	  – two kinds of associates: one or more managing partners and one or more capital partners
		• **Private limited liability company** – *Société à responsabilité limitée* (SARL):
		one shareholder or more (maximum: 50)
		• **Public limited liability company** – *Société Anonyme* (SA):
		Minimum of five shareholders

Directors	• **General partnership:** Unless otherwise stipulated in the company's articles, all the partners are managers; it is also possible to appoint one or more managers, who may or may not be a partner	• **Public limited liability company:**
		• Classic system: Conseil d'administration (CA):
		  – between 3 and 12 members
		  – management of the company by the President of the CA or a general manager

Legal form / Characteristics	Partnership and Limited Liability Partnership (LLP)	Ltd (private corporation) and Plc (public corporation)
	• **Limited partnership:** one or more partners are jointly and severally liable. One or more managing directors can be appointed by the partners • **Partnership limited by shares:** managing directors cannot be appointed from among capital partners	• Dualistic system: – Directoire (Executive committee) and Conseil de surveillance (Audit committee): – directoire: maximum four members – The 'directoire' manages the company – The 'conseil de surveillance' • **Private limited liability company:** One or more managing director or managing partner
Establishment	Can be established by private agreement, a notarial deed is not required	
Registration	All entities to be registered at the Commercial Court and publication of by-laws	
Minimum capital	**General partnership:** no minimum capital required **Limited partnership:** no minimum capital required	• **Public limited liability company:** MAD300,000 • **Listed company:** MAD3,000,000 • **Private limited liability company:** no minimum capital required
Liability	**General partnership:** joint and unlimited liability for all debts **Limited partnership:** – managing partners: joint and unlimited liability for all debts – capital partners: liability limited to their contribution	**Public limited liability company** **Private limited liability company** Liability limited to contribution
Governance	**General partnership:** Partners **Limited partnership:** managing partners	**Public limited liability company:** – Classic system: Board of Directors and shareholders' meeting – Dualistic system: Board of Directors, audit committee and shareholders meeting **Private limited liability company** – Managing Directors or Managing Partners – Shareholders' meeting

Characteristics Legal form	Partnership and Limited Liability Partnership (LLP)	Ltd (private corporation) and Plc (public corporation)
Audit requirements	No obligation for audit, except if sales are higher than MAD50m	**Public limited liability company:** Statutory audit is always required. At least two external auditors are required concerning special business – bank, insurance, public corporation, etc **Private limited liability company** No obligation for audit except if sales are higher than MAD50m
Taxation	Subject to personal income tax on behalf of the major partner unless option for corporation tax	Resident companies are subject to corporate tax on the profits derived from activities in Morocco (including income and capital gains) and overseas profits attributed under the double tax treaty provisions

II CORPORATION TAX

General description	Corporation tax	
Taxable entities	Companies incorporated in Morocco	PE located in Morocco
Taxable income	Profits on business activities carried out in Morocco and overseas income attributed under the double tax treaty provisions	Profits derived by PE in Morocco
Calculation of taxable profits	• net taxable benefits less tax losses • accruals method of accounting	
Interest payments	Interest payments are deductible, unless paid to shareholders, in which case: • not deductible if the capital is not fully paid up; • deductible only on the amount of the loan not exceeding the company's nominal capital; and • the rate of interest is limited to the yearly average rate on treasury bonds	
Related party transactions	All related party transactions must take place on arm's length basis	
Tax year, return and payment	Company may choose its accounting year-end date: • Tax return must be filed within 3 months after the end of the accounting year • Tax is payable in quarterly instalments based on prior year profits • Balance of tax is payable on the tax return filing date	
Capital gains	• Capital gains are subject to corporation tax at standard rates • Capital gains on quoted transferable securities realised by non-resident companies are tax-free	
Losses	• Net operating tax losses may be carried forward for 4 years and set off against future taxable profits • The loss arising from depreciation can be carried forward indefinitely. This concerns intangible and tangible assets	
Tax group	None	

Tax rate	• Standard rates:
	  – 10% if profit is less or equal to MAD300 000
	  – 20% if profit is between MAD300 001 and MAD1,000,000
	  – 30% if profit is between MAD1,000,001 and MAD5,000,000
	  – 31% if profit is higher than MAD5,000,000
	
	• Special rates:
	  – 37% for Insurance, banking and leasing companies
	  – exemption for the first 5 years followed by imposition at permanent rate of 17.50% for exporting companies and hotels
	  – exemption for the first 5 years followed by imposition at permanent rate of 8.75% for services firms installed at 'Casablanca Finance City' (CFC) for their sales to export
	  – exemption for the first 5 years followed by imposition at temporary rate of 8.75% during 20 years for firms located in export processing zones
	  – 17.50% for mining, craft, private education, real estate, farms, during the first 5 years of their activity
	  – 8% of the amount of the project, excluding VAT, for non-resident companies as tenderer for work, construction or assembly projects, having opted for flat tax
	  – 10% for (i) offshore banks during the first 15 years, or (ii) regional or international headquarters based in CFC

III   TAXES FOR INDIVIDUALS

		Residents	Non-residents
Income Tax	General description	Tax levied on the chargeable income of an individual for the year of assessment	
	Taxable entities and taxable income	Residents are taxed on their worldwide income (including overseas income attributed under double tax treaty provisions)	Non-residents are taxable on all income arising in Morocco unless excluded under a double tax treaty
	Types of taxable income	• Professional income (from business activities) • Farming income • Wages and similar income • Real estate income and capital gains • Income and profits derived from securities	
	Calculation of income	Total taxable income is the aggregate of various descriptive categories. The net income of each of these categories is separately assessed according to its own rules	
	Tax year, tax assessment and tax payment	Fiscal year is the calendar year • Recovery by means of spontaneous payment after filing the return • Instalments are assessed annually on prior year income tax	
	Losses	Losses can only be offset against income arising from the same source	
	Tax rates	Rates between 0–38% are applied to total taxable income on a progressive tax brackets basis	
		Residents	Non-residents
Capital Gains Tax (CGT)	General description	Increase in the value of assets between acquisition and disposal, not chargeable to income tax	
	Taxable entities and chargeable assets	• Capital gains are normally assessed as income • Movable property sold by individuals is subject to a final tax fixed in special rules • Fixed assets sold by individuals are subject to a final tax of 20% of the gain subject to a minimum liability of 3% of gross proceeds • Special rates are provided for vacant land	• Capital gains on quoted transferable securities realised by non-residents are subject to income tax • Fixed assets sold by non-residents are subject to a final tax of 20% of the gain subject to a minimum liability of 3% of gross proceeds • Special rates are provided for vacant land
	Calculation of gain	See above	

	Residents	Non-residents
Capital Gains Tax (CGT) – *contd*	Tax year, tax assessment and tax payment	Regarding real estate assets, a statement has to be made within 30 days of the transfer, together with payment of the tax As to movable capital, the taxpayer has to make an annual statement of the profits and losses registered during the previous year at the latest on 31 March of the current year. Notice to pay the tax will be sent to him by the Tax Administration which is responsible for calculating the due tax	
	Losses	In the case of real estate assets no loss is allowed. A minimum tax of 3% is due to be paid on the basis of the selling price Regarding movable capital, there is a possibility of compensating losses and profits by carrying forward the net loss of one year over the 4 following years	
	Tax rates	See above	
There is no Inheritance Tax			

IV   WITHHOLDING TAXES

Under domestic law	Payments to residents	Payments to non-residents[1]
Dividends	15%	10%
Interest	30% to corporate entities	10%
	20% to non-corporates	
Royalties	Comprised in the total income and taxed on increasing progressive tax brackets basis (rates between 0–38%)	10%

Reduced rate available under the relevant Double Taxation Treaty			
Country	Dividends	Interest	Royalties
Austria[2]			
Bahrain	10%[3]	10	10
Belgium	10%[3]	10%	10%
Bulgaria	10%[3]	10%	10%
Canada	15%	15%	10%[4]
China[2]			
Czech Republic[2]			
Denmark	25%[3]	10%	10%
Egypt	12.5%[3]	20%	10%
Finland	15%	10%	10%
France	15%	10%	10%
Germany	15%	10%	10%
Hungary[2]			
India[2]			
Italy	15%[3]	10%	10%
Kuwait	10%[3]		
Lebanon	10%[3]	10%	10%[4]
Libya[2]			
Luxembourg	15%[3]	10%	10%
Malaysia[2]			
Malta[2]			
Netherlands	25%[3]	10%	10%
Norway	15%	10%	10%
Poland[2]			
Portugal	15%[3]	12%	10%
Romania[2]			

1   Reduced rates of withholding tax may be applied where there is an appropriate double tax treaty.
2   Treaties not provided by the Tax Authorities, in particular because they are not approved or are approved but have not been published.
3   If the recipient of the dividends is a company holding a minimum percentage of share capital and/or voting rights, varying from 5% to 25%, a lower rate may be available.
4   Royalties for the use or right to use copyright of literary, artistic or scientific works, excluding cinematograph films and television 5%; other royalties 10%.

Reduced rate available under the relevant Double Taxation Treaty			
Country	Dividends	Interest	Royalties
Russian Federation	10%	10%	10%
Senegal[2]			
South Korea[2]			
Spain	15%[3]	10%	10%[4]
Sweden[2]			
Switzerland	15%[3]	10%	10%
Tunisia[2]			
Turkey[2]			
The Arab Maghreb Union (AMU)[5]	10%	30%	30%
United Arab Emirates	10%[3]	10%	10%
United Kingdom	25%[3]	10%	10%
United States	15%[3]	15%	10%

Where the treaty rate is higher than the domestic rate, the domestic rate will usually apply.

Note: the above rates are only available provided the specific Treaty criteria are satisfied. It is possible that lower rates than those shown above may be available provided that certain criteria are satisfied. As treaties will not be identical, guidance should be sought in all cases.

5   Algeria, Libya, Mauritania, Morocco and Tunisia. Domestic legislation applies (dividends: 15%; interests: 30%; royalties: 30%).

V   INDIRECT TAXES

		Residents	Non-residents	
Value Added Tax (VAT)	General description	Tax on the supply of goods and services (VAT)		
	Entities obliged to levy VAT	Taxable businesses		
	Taxable activities	Supply of goods and services		
	Taxable activities – zero-rated (examples)	• Exports • Equipment acquired by new companies during the first 36 months since their business started • Equipment for special activities		
	Exemptions (examples)	Goods and services exported; agricultural activities		
	Refund of VAT	For export activities	For passengers	VAT on investment goods
	Tax liability	It is up to the firm providing the goods or services to recover the VAT amount charged to the client and transfer it to the Treasury	Regime of reverse charge system: payment of the VAT by the Moroccan client for a supplier or a provider of service not established in Morocco	
	Tax rates	Standard rate of 20% and lower rates of 14%, 10% and 7%		
	Administrative obligations	Filing return	Filing return	
Stamp Duty Land Tax		None		
Stamp Duty		At the rate of 0.25% on the cash receipts for companies with annual turnover higher than MAD2,000,000		

Mozambique

(Jeremias Cardoso da Costa; Nexia BKSC, Lda; jcdacosta@bksc.co.mz)

I MAIN LEGAL FORMS

Legal form / Characteristics	Partnership and Limited Liability Partnership (LLP)	Private corporation ((Pty) Ltd) and Public company (Ltd)
Partners/shareholders • Number • Restrictions	One or more Both individuals or companies can be partners	Private company ((Pty) Ltd): minimum one partner Public company (Ltd): minimum three partners if are individuals, and minimum one if partner is an entity
Restrictions	None	None
Directors	One (partners) or more	Private: one or more Public: three or more + fiscal council
Establishment	Partnership deed	Constitution
Registration	N/A	Registration with Commercial Conservatory
Minimum capital	MZN 20,000	1) MZN 20,000, except construction sector which have 7 categories where minimum capital vary from MZN 20,000 (class 1) to MZN 10m (class 7) 2) Foreign Direct Investment (FDI) to be eligible for Tax benefits with CPI (Investment Promotion Centre), minimum share capital is US$100k
Liability	No limited liability to all partners	Both have limited liability to capital for all shareholders
Governance	Partnership agreement	Commercial code, approved by law Directors' meetings Shareholders' meetings
Audit requirements	• No audit required • Turnover above MZN 2.5m require financial statements signed off by a Certified Accountant	• Private company ((Pty) Ltd): are not required to comply with audit, except when have CPI agreement in place • Public company (Ltd): are required to be audited

Legal form / Characteristics	Partnership and Limited Liability Partnership (LLP)	Private corporation ((Pty) Ltd) and Public company (Ltd)
Taxation	Members are taxed individually	Corporation tax on worldwide profits
Usage	Used by professionals and small unregistered businesses	(Pty) Ltd: small businesses, investment holding Ltd: all types of businesses including listed entities

II CORPORATION TAX

Description \ Legal form	Resident corporation	Permanent establishment (PE)
General description	• Levied on taxable income	
Taxable entities	• Entities incorporated in Mozambique	• Branches or agencies of foreign entities
Taxable income	• Worldwide income subject to certain exemptions for activities undertaken outside Mozambique	• Mozambican source income and sales of Mozambican Assets
Calculation of taxable profits	• Adjusted profits less allowable deductions	• Adjusted profits less allowable deductions, when have CPI agreement
Interest payments	• Deductible up to MAIBOR (12 months) + 2% spread and subject to thin capitalisation rules[1] • 20% Withholding tax at the source of income	• Deductible up to MAIBOR (12 months) + 2% spread and subject to thin capitalisation rules[1] • 20% Withholding tax at the source of income
Related party transactions	• Strict adherence to the arm's length principle and fiscal transparency	• Strict adherence to the arm's length principle and fiscal transparency
Tax year, return and payment	• Year End: 1 January to 31 December • Tax Return submission: End of May • Prepayment: 80% of prior year tax in 3 instalments	• Year End: 1 January to 31 December. However, international groups can request different year end • Tax Return submission: 31 May or 5th month of the year end • Prepayment: 80% of prior year tax in 3 instalments
Capital gains	• Worldwide gains taxed at corporate tax rate (32%)	• Worldwide gains taxed at corporate tax rate (32%), with the following scales: ○ 100% taxable if the asset is held less than 12 months ○ 85% taxable if the asset is held from 12 to 24 months ○ 65% taxable if the asset is held from 24 to 60 months ○ 55% taxable if the asset is held for more than 60 months • Double taxation treaties also applied
Losses	• Losses may be carried forward for 5 years provided that entity is trading	• Losses may be carried forward for 5 years provided entity is trading. However, if the entity benefits from corporate tax exemption (CPI), the loss is not deductible in the next profitable year

Description ╲ Legal form	Resident corporation	Permanent establishment (PE)
Tax group	• Asset transfers only. No tax consolidation of profits	• Asset transfers only. No tax consolidation of profits
Tax rate	• Standard rate: 32% • Agriculture: 10% • Undocumented expenses not allowed and taxed at 35%	• Standard rate: 32% • Agriculture: 10% • Undocumented expenses not allowed and taxed at 35%

1 The Mozambican Corporate Income Tax Code (CITC) includes some rules for thin capitalization (art 52).

The CITC states that, where loans from related foreign corporations exceed twice the corresponding equity in the borrowing Mozambican corporation, the interest on the excess borrowing is not tax deductible.

The Mozambican thin capitalization rules state that subsidiaries are considered and treated as thinly capitalized companies if and to the extent that, as at any date of the tax period, any of their relevant debt-to-equity ratios exceeds a factor of two.

For the application of the thin capitalization rules, a 'specially related non-resident' is an entity with special links with another, which includes any entity that:

• holds, either directly or indirectly, at least 25% of the share capital of the Mozambican company;
• though holding less than 25%, has a significant influence on its management; or
• both taxpayer and non-resident entity are under control of the same entity, which has participation in their share capital, either directly or indirectly.

Under any of above circumstances, interest made available (debit of income statement or paid) to such specially related non-residents is not allowed as a tax-deductible cost for the Mozambican company in the portion that corresponds to the excessive indebtedness, unless the company can prove that it could have obtained the same level of indebtedness at comparable conditions from unrelated parties, taking into account the nature of its business, its sector of activity, dimension, and other relevant criteria.

III TAXES FOR INDIVIDUALS

		Residents	Non-residents
Income Tax	General description	Residents are taxed on worldwide income and non-residents are taxed on income from Mozambican sources or deemed Mozambican sources	
	Taxable entities and taxable income	• A citizen ordinarily resident in Mozambique or anyone who spends in the country more than 180 days per tax year in the current year	Individual not resident in Mozambique
	Types of taxable income	• Wages and remunerations and allowances; commissions, business income; Dividends; Interest; Rentals; Royalties and Pensions	Commissions, Wages and allowances; Business income; Dividends; Interest; Rentals; Royalties and Pensions
	Calculation of income	Aggregate of gross income less exempt income less deductions	Aggregate of gross income less exempt income less deductions
	Tax year, tax assessment and tax payment	• Year End: 1 January to 31 December • Tax Return submission: End of March • No return is required to individuals whose sole income is derived from remuneration and does not exceed MZN 225,000 per year • Prepayment applicable only for business income	Year End: N/A Tax Return submission: N/A Prepayment: 20% withholding tax for an income received in Mozambique
	Losses	• No carry back	• No carry back
	Tax rates As at 1 January 2014	*Monthly Income (MZN)* *Tax (%)* 0–20,250 Nil 20,251–22,250 10 22,251–32,750 15 32,755–60,750 20 60,751–144,750 25 144,751+ 32	• 20% withholding tax for an income received in Mozambique • Double taxation treaties also applied

		Residents	**Non-residents**
Capital Gains Tax (CGT)	General description	Receipts and accruals of a capital nature subject to CGT with effect from 1 January 2014	
	Taxable entities and chargeable assets	Capital gains made on disposal of assets owned worldwide	Capital gains made on disposal of fixed property situated in Mozambique, including any interest in fixed property
	Calculation of gain	Worldwide gains taxed at corporate tax rate (32%), with the following scales: a) 100% taxable if the asset is held less than 12 months b) 85% taxable if the asset is held from 12 to 24 months c) 65% taxable if the asset is held from 24 to 60 months d) 55% taxable if the asset is held for more than 60 months	Worldwide gains taxed at corporate tax rate (32%), with the following scales: a) 100% taxable if the asset is held less or for 12 months b) 85% taxable if the asset is held from 12 to 24 months c) 65% taxable if the asset is held from 24 to 60 months d) 55% taxable if the asset is held for more than 60 months
	Tax year, tax assessment and tax payment	• Year End: 1 January to 31 December • Tax Return submission: End of March	• Year End: 1 January to 31 December • Tax Return submission: End of March
	Losses	• No carry back	• No carry back
	Tax rates	• Standard rate: 32% • Agriculture: 10%	• Standard rate: 32% • Agriculture: 10%

IV WITHHOLDING TAXES

Under domestic law	Payments to residents	Payments to non-residents (reduced rates may apply under double tax treaty)
Dividends	20%	20%
Interest	1) Fixed Deposits: 10% 2) Listed assets: 10%	20%
Royalties and management services	1) 20% 2) Telecommunication sector and Listed assets: 10%	20%
On payments to artists, sportsmen and gambling	1) 10% 2) Gambling and betting: 10%	20%

Reduced rate available under the relevant Double Taxation Treaty			
Country	Dividends	Interest	Royalties + Management fee
Botswana	0 / 12%[2]	10%	10%
India	7.5%	10%	10%
Italy	15%	0 /10%[3]	10%
Macau	10%	10%	10%
Mauritius	15 / 10 / 8%[4]	8%	5%
Portugal	15%	0 / 10%[5]	10%
South Africa	15 / 8%	0 / 8%[6]	5%
United Arab Emirates	0%[7]	0%[8]	5%
Vietnam	10%	10%	10%

Note: the above rates are only available provided the specific Treaty criteria are satisfied. It is possible that lower rates than those shown above may be available provided certain criteria are satisfied. As treaties will not be identical, guidance should be sought in all cases.

2 12% for dividend payments by a less than 25% owned subsidiary in Mozambique to its Botswana parent company. 0% for a dividend payments by a 25% or more owned subsidiary in in Mozambique to its Botswana parent company.
3 The 0% rate applies, inter alia, to interest paid or derived, by public bodies.
4 10% for dividend payments by a less than 25% owned subsidiary in Mozambique to its Mauritius parent company. 8% for a dividend payments by a 25% or more owned subsidiary in in Mozambique to its Mauritius parent company.
5 The 0% rate applies, inter alia, to interest paid or derived, by public bodies.
6 The 0% rate applies only for interest paid to a bank or to a public body.
7 Income is taxable only in the state of residence.
8 Income is taxable only in the state of residence.

V   INDIRECT TAXES

		Residents	Non-residents
Value Added Tax	General description	• Goods and services tax (GST) on the supply of goods and services • Any vendor whose taxable supplies exceed MZN 750,000.00 per annum	
	Entities obliged to levy VAT	• Any activity carried on in Mozambique other than government bodies	
	Taxable activities	• All types of services and goods, except exempted	
	Taxable activities – zero-rated (examples)	• A zero rate applies to the export of goods and services	
	Exemptions (examples)	• Government services, education, insurance and finance services; charitable; culture and sport and health and pharmacy	
	Refund of VAT	• By Tax credit or submission of VAT refund application	
	Tax liability	• Strict liability with entity rendering service or effecting sale	
	Tax rates	• 17%	
	Administrative obligations	• Submission of monthly returns. Precise accounting and legal tax invoices are required • VAT claim within 90 days of date of the tax invoice • Keep tax invoice archives for 5 years	
Real Property Taxes		• Local rates	
Stamp Duty		• Imposed at State level on various transactions and conveyances at either a fixed rate or at ad valorem rates	

Myanmar

(Henry Tan, Nexia TS, henrytan@nexiats.com.sg)

I MAIN LEGAL FORMS

Legal form / Characteristics	Partnership and Limited Liability Partnership (LLP)	Private corporation (Private Limited) and Public corporation (Public Limited)
Partners/shareholders • Number • Restrictions	**Partnership:** • Between two and 20 partners • Restriction on transferability of ownership LLP is not recognized as a form of business	**Private Corporation:** • Minimum two shareholders and not more than 50 shareholders • Restriction on right to transfer shares **Public Corporation:** • Minimum seven shareholders **FDI restrictions in case of Private and Public Corporations:** • Foreigners cannot directly invest in local companies • Under the Myanmar Foreign Investment Law (MFIL), an investment may be carried out in any of the following options: i. a wholly foreign-owned company in the business permitted by the Myanmar Investment Commission (MIC) ii. a joint venture between a foreign investor and a local partner (a Myanmar citizen, or a government department and organization) iii. investment made in line with systems specified in contract set by both foreign investor and local parties • Foreign investors are eligible for tax incentives only if they obtain investment permit from MIC and register under the MFIL
Directors	**Partnership:** • Management by partners	**Public Corporation:** • At least two directors

Legend form / Characteristics	Partnership and Limited Liability Partnership (LLP)	Private corporation (Private Limited) and Public corporation (Public Limited)
Establishment	**Partnership:** • Partnership Deed/Agreement	**Private and Public Corporations:** • Memorandum and Articles of Association
Registration	**Partnership:** • Registration is optional	**Private and Public Corporations:** • Registrar of Companies

Minimum capital	**Partnership:**
	• No minimum capital
		Private and Public Corporations:
		• No minimum share capital requirements except in case of insurance companies, foreign companies and branches of all foreign business
		• For foreign companies and branches, the minimum capital required in Myanmar is as follows:
		  i. Industrial, hotels and construction: US$150,000
		  ii. Services, travels and tours, bank representative offices and insurance representative offices: US$50,000

Liability	**Partnership:** • Unlimited • Partners are jointly and severally liable for all debts and obligations	**Private and Public Corporations:** • Limited
Governance	**Partnership:** • Partners' meetings	**Private and Public Corporations:** • Directors' meetings • Shareholders' meetings – A general meeting shall be held within 18 months from the date of incorporation and thereafter at least once in every calendar year and not more than 15 months after the holding of the last preceding general meeting
Audit requirements	**Partnership:** None	**Private and Public Corporations:** • Mandatory
Taxation	**Partnership:** • Taxed as a separate entity and not on the individual profit share of the partners • Partnership income is not taxed in the hands of the partners	**Private and Public Corporations:** • Profits taxed at corporate tax rates
Fiscal Year ending	The fiscal year begins on 1 April and ends on 31 March	

II CORPORATION TAX

Description \ Legal form	Resident corporation[1]
General description	Myanmar corporate income tax
Taxable entities	• A resident company is a company formed under the Myanmar Companies Act or any existing law such as MFIL
Taxable income	• Resident companies are taxed on a worldwide basis • MFIL companies are treated as resident companies but are not taxed on their foreign-sourced income
Calculation of taxable profits	• Income is categorized as income from profession, business, property, capital gains, other sources and undisclosed sources of income • Business includes securities, and interest income from bonds and debentures is treated as business income • Tax is levied on total income, after deduction of allowable expenditure and depreciation • Income from capital gains is assessed separately
Interest payments	• Interest payments are generally tax deductible • Interest expense relating to assets that produce non-income or exempt income is not tax deductible • There are no specific thin capitalisation rules
Related party transactions	• There are no transfer pricing rules applicable for related party transactions

Tax year, return and payment	• The taxable period of a company is the same as its financial year (income year), which is from 1 April to 31 March
	• Income earned during the financial year (from 1 April to 31 March) is assessed to tax in the assessment year, which is the year following the financial year
	• Due dates for filing returns:
	  • Every person who has assessable income during the tax year must file a return of income with the Internal Revenue Department within three months from the end of that year, ie by 30 June of the assessment year
	  • If a business is dissolved, an income tax return must be filed within one month from the time the business was discontinued
	  • Tax returns for capital gains under the income tax law are to be submitted within one month after the capital asset was disposed of
	• Advance income tax payments are made in quarterly instalments within the financial year based on estimated total income for the year, and are creditable against the final tax liability

Capital gains	• Income tax is levied on gains from the sale, exchange or transfer of capital assets • Capital asset means any land, building, vehicle and any capital assets of an enterprise, which include shares, bonds and similar instruments • Capital gains are calculated based on the difference between sale proceeds and the cost of assets and any additions, less tax depreciation allowed, less expenses incurred at the time of purchase or sale of capital asset • Capital gains are not taxable if the total value of the capital assets sold, exchanged or transferred within a year does not exceed MMK 10 million • The tax rate for taxpayers in the oil and gas industry is between 40% and 50% • From 1 April 2015, the tax rate is 10% for resident companies and non-resident companies

Legal form / Description	Resident corporation[1]
Losses	• Losses from any source may be set off against income accruing from any other sources in that year, except where the loss is from capital assets or a share of a loss from an association of persons • Losses that are not fully deducted in a year can be carried forward and set off against profits in the next three consecutive years, except where the loss is from capital assets or a share of a loss from an association of persons • Losses cannot be carried back
Tax group	There are no provisions that allow for group taxation
Tax rate	Tax rate from 1 April 2015 – 25%
Wealth tax	No wealth tax in Myanmar

1 Permanent Establishment (PE) – There is no definition of PE in the Myanmar Income Tax Act. The Myanmar tax authorities seek to collect taxes from a non-resident company on its income received from Myanmar by way of a withholding tax mechanism, regardless of whether the non-resident company has a PE in Myanmar or not. However, the term PE may be defined in the Double Tax Agreements (DTAs) that Myanmar has entered into with other countries. Subject to the DTA, a non-resident company which is a resident of the treaty country may not be subject to Myanmar income tax if it does not have a PE in Myanmar.

III TAXES FOR INDIVIDUALS

<table>
<tr><th></th><th></th><th>Residents</th><th>Non-residents</th></tr>
<tr>
<td rowspan="6">Income Tax</td>
<td>General description</td>
<td colspan="2">The taxation of income depends on the individual's residential status in Myanmar</td>
</tr>
<tr>
<td>Taxable entities and taxable income</td>
<td>
<ul>
<li>Myanmar nationals are treated as tax residents</li>
<li>Resident foreigners are foreigners who reside in Myanmar for not less than 183 days during the income year. Foreigners working for companies set up under the MFIL are treated as resident foreigners regardless of their period of stay in Myanmar</li>
<li>Resident nationals and resident foreigners are taxed on their worldwide income. However, the salary income of Myanmar citizens working outside Myanmar is exempt from tax</li>
</ul>
</td>
<td>
<ul>
<li>Non-resident foreigners are taxed only on income derived from sources within Myanmar</li>
</ul>
</td>
</tr>
<tr>
<td>Types of taxable income</td>
<td colspan="2">
<ul>
<li>Employment income is defined broadly and includes salary, wages, annuity and any fees, commissions or perquisites received in lieu of or in addition to any salary and wages</li>
<li>Non-employment income includes:
<ul>
<li>business income such as income from moveable properties, royalties and interest, profession or vocation</li>
<li>income from a profession</li>
<li>capital gains from the sale of capital assets</li>
<li>other income from investments except dividends received from an association of persons which are exempt from income tax</li>
<li>undisclosed sources of income and other sources of income</li>
</ul>
</li>
</ul>
</td>
</tr>
<tr>
<td rowspan="2">Calculation of income</td>
<td colspan="2">Taxable income after deducting any allowable expenses and/or allowances is assessed to tax</td>
</tr>
<tr>
<td>
<ul>
<li>Various deductions from total income available</li>
</ul>
</td>
<td>
<ul>
<li>No deductions from total income are available</li>
</ul>
</td>
</tr>
<tr>
<td>Tax year, tax assessment and tax payment</td>
<td colspan="2">
<ul>
<li>The income year runs from 1 April to 31 March</li>
<li>Income earned during the tax year is assessed to tax in the assessment year, which is the year following the tax year</li>
<li>Due dates for filing returns:
<ul>
<li>An employer is required to deduct income tax due from salaries at the time of payment to employees, and must pay the amount within seven days from the date of deduction</li>
<li>Except for individuals with only Myanmar employment income fully subject to withholding by the employer, every individual who has assessable income during the tax year must file a return of income with the Internal Revenue Department within three months from the end of that year, ie by 30 June of the assessment year</li>
<li>If a business is dissolved, an income tax return must be filed within one month from the time the business was discontinued</li>
<li>Tax returns for capital gains under the income tax law are to be submitted within one month after the capital asset was disposed of</li>
</ul>
</li>
<li>Advance income tax payments are made in quarterly instalments within the income tax year based on estimated total income for the year</li>
</ul>
</td>
</tr>
</table>

		Residents	**Non-residents**
Income Tax - *contd*	Losses	• Losses from any source may be set off against income accruing from any other sources in that year, except where the loss is from capital assets or a share of a loss from an association of persons • Losses that are not fully deducted in a year can be carried forward and set off against profits in the next three consecutive years, except where the loss is from capital assets or a share of a loss from an association of persons • Losses cannot be carried back	
	Tax rates	• Myanmar nationals and resident foreigners are taxed at progressive tax rates ranging from 0% to 25%	• Non-resident foreigners are taxed at progressive tax rates ranging from 0% to 25%
		• Income that escaped assessment is taxed at progressive rates ranging from 3% to 30% • Salaries of foreigners engaged under special permission in state-sponsored projects and enterprises and received in Kyats are taxed at a flat rate of 20% on their income from salary • No tax is payable if total income under salaries does not exceed MMK 2,000,000 in a year	
Capital Gains Tax (CGT)	General description	• Income tax is levied on gains from the sale, exchange or transfer of capital assets • Capital asset means any land, building, vehicle and any capital assets of an enterprise, which include shares, bonds and similar instruments • Capital gains are calculated based on the difference between sale proceeds and the cost of assets and any additions, less tax depreciation allowed, less expenses incurred at the time of purchase or sale of capital asset • From 1 April 2015, the tax rate is 10% for both resident individuals and non-resident individuals	

Other		• No wealth tax or inheritance tax in Myanmar
		• Social security contributions:
		  • An employer with more than five workers is required to provide Social Security Scheme benefits to his workers, such as general benefit insurance and insurance against employment-related injuries
		  • The rates of contribution by employees and employers are 2% and 3% of the total salary and wages respectively. However, at present, the maximum monthly contribution is limited to MMK 9,000 by the employer and MMK 6,000 by the employee
		  • The employer is obligated to withhold the employees' contributions from their pay
		  • The employee's contributions to the Social Security Scheme are deductible by the employee for his personal income tax purposes	

IV   WITHHOLDING TAXES

Under domestic law	Payments to residents[2]	Payments to non-residents[3]
Dividends	Nil	Nil
Interest	Nil	15%
Royalties	15%	20%
Payment made for procurement of goods within the country and services rendered	2%	3.5%

Reduced rate available under the relevant Double Taxation Treaty[4,5]			
Country	Dividends[6]	Interest[7]	Royalties
India	Nil	10%	10%
Korea (Republic of)	Nil	10%	15%[9]
Laos	Nil	10%	10%
Malaysia	Nil	10%	10%
Singapore	Nil	10%[8]	10%[9]
Thailand	Nil	10%	15%[10]
United Kingdom	Nil	Not covered	Nil
Vietnam	Nil	10%	10%

2   For residents, deductions as above shall be offset against tax due on final assessment.
3   For non-residents, the above withholding tax from payments to non-resident companies is a final tax.
4   Myanmar has concluded tax treaties with Bangladesh and Indonesia, but these treaties are pending ratification.
5   The above rates can be applied provided the specific treaty criteria are satisfied. It is possible that lower rates than those shown above may be available provided that certain criteria are satisfied. As treaties are not identical, guidance is recommended to be sought in all cases.
6   No withholding taxes on outbound dividends under the domestic legislation.
7   Interest is exempt from tax if it is paid to the Government of the other Contracting State, except for the Double Taxation treaty with the United Kingdom which does not cover interest.
8   The rate is 8% if the interest is paid to a bank or financial institution.
9   The rate is 10% in respect of payments for the use of, or the right to use, any patent, design or model, plan, secret formula or process, or the use of, or the right to use industrial, commercial or scientific equipment, or for information concerning industrial, commercial or scientific experience.
10   The rate is 5% in respect of payments for the use of, or the right to use, any copyrights of literary, artistic or scientific work, and 10% for consideration for any services of a managerial or consultancy nature, or for information concerning industrial, commercial or scientific equipment.

V   INDIRECT TAXES

		Overview
Commercial Tax (CT)	General description	• Commercial Tax (CT) is levied as a turnover tax on goods and services. CT is also levied on imported goods
	Entities obliged to levy CT	• Myanmar-resident entities are required to register for CT when the amount of income from sales and services for an income year is at least MMK 20 million (from 1 April 2015)
	Taxable activities	• CT applies to all goods and services produced or rendered in Myanmar, unless specifically exempted • CT is also levied on imported goods
	Exemptions (examples)	• Specific services are exempted from CT, eg banking services, home rental, life insurance etc • CT is exempt on all exports of goods except for five natural resource items (ie natural gas, crude oil, jade, gemstones and wood) and electricity • Certain essentials and basic commodities produced in the country are not subject to CT, eg milk powder, wheat grain, pulses, medicinal plants or herbs, raw cotton etc
	Refund of CT	• CT-registered entities can claim CT incurred on business purchases of goods, but not on services, subject to conditions
	Tax liability	• Entities that are registered for CT and importers
	Tax rate	• CT ranges from 0% to 120% with effect from 1 April 2015. The CT rate is generally 5%
	Administrative obligations	• Monthly payment of tax before 10th day of the month following the month of sale or receipt from service • Filing of quarterly return within one month from the end of the quarter • Filing of annual return within three months from the end of the year

Property Taxes		• Immovable property situated within the Yangon development is subject to property taxes as follows:
		  • general tax not exceeding 8% of the annual value
		  • lighting tax not exceeding 5% of the annual value
		  • water tax and not exceeding 6.5% of the annual value
		  • conservancy tax not exceeding 3.25% of the annual value
		• Foreign companies are prohibited from owning immovable property in Myanmar, hence property tax would not be relevant to foreign investors

Stamp Duty		• Stamp duty is levied on various types of instrument. Some of the stamp duty rates are as follows:
		  • 3% of the amount or value of the consideration for conveyances of properties, for the sale or transfer of immovable property, plus an additional 2%
		  • 0.3% of share value for the transfer of shares
		  • 2% of the amount or value secured for bonds
		  • 1.5% of the annual value of rent for lease agreements between one and three years, and 3% of the average annual value of rent and premium where the term of the lease agreement is more than 3 years

	Overview
Customs Duty	• Most imported goods, with a few exceptions, are subject to customs duty on importation and are required to be declared to the Myanmar Customs Department accordingly
	• Currently, the customs duty levied on the import of machinery, spare parts, and inputs generally ranges from 0% to 40% of the value of the goods imported
	• For exports of goods, export duty is levied on commodities
	• Companies registered under the MFIL and which have obtained permits from the MIC may, at the discretion of the MIC, be given relief from customs duty on machinery, equipment, instruments, machinery components, spare parts and materials used during the period of construction or expansion, and on raw materials for the first three years of commercial production
Excise duty	• Excise duty in the form of an excise licence fee is levied on alcoholic drinks

The Netherlands

(Chris Leenders, Koenen en Co Maastricht, c.leenders@koenenenco.nl)

I MAIN LEGAL FORMS

Legal form / Characteristics	Partnership (VOF) and Limited Liability Partnership (CV)	Private corporation (BV) and Public corporation (NV)
Partners/shareholders • Number • Restrictions	• Two or more • None[1]	• One or more • None
Directors	Management by partners	Management by director(s)[2]
Establishment	No formal requirements[3]	Notarial deed of incorporation
Registration	Chamber of Commerce and tax authorities	
Minimum capital	None	€0.01 for BV and €45,000 for NV
Liability	Unlimited[4]	Limited to capital[5]
Governance	Partners, general meeting, works council[6]	Managing Director/Board of Directors, supervisory board, shareholders' meeting, works council[7]
Audit requirements	No audit requirements for partnerships	No audit requirements if for two consecutive years at least two of the three conditions below were not exceeded: • Turnover does not exceed €12m • Total assets do not exceed €6m • Number of employees does not exceed 50

---

1 The limited partner should not legally represent the CV in external relations.
2 A private and a public company must have at least one director.
3 Partnership agreement in writing is advisable.
4 For CV unlimited liability will apply to at least one partner. Other partners' liability may be limited to their capital.
5 Management can be liable in case of misconduct.
6 Works council is required if 50 employees or more.
7 Capital gains are not taxed separately but included in the profit share/taxable income.

Legal form / Characteristics	Partnership (VOF) and Limited Liability Partnership (CV)	Private corporation (BV) and Public corporation (NV)
Taxation	Partners are subject to Dutch (corporate) income tax on their share of profits[7]	Dutch resident companies are subject to corporation tax on their profits derived anywhere in the world
Usage	Professional and financial organisations, joint ventures of small, medium-sized and large companies	BV used for small and medium-sized enterprises. NV used for larger companies and companies seeking listing on any market

II CORPORATION TAX

Legal form / Description	Dutch-resident corporation	Permanent establishment (PE)
General description	Tax levied on the taxable profit of a chargeable company for a year of assessment[8]	
Taxable entities	Companies incorporated in the Netherlands and/or foreign companies with central management and control located in the Netherlands	PE located in the Netherlands
Taxable income	Worldwide profits	Profits derived by PE in the Netherlands
Calculation of taxable profits	Accounting profit is adjusted for various tax add-backs, allowances and exemptions to arrive at the taxable profit Dividends from qualifying participations are exempted	
Interest payments	• Transfer pricing rules are in place that require funding arrangements to be at arm's length for interest payment to remain tax deductible • Anti-abuse provisions can deny interest deduction in certain cases • Anti-abuse provisions and case law can recategorise loans as capital	
Related party transactions	All related party transactions must take place on arm's length basis	
Tax year, return and payment	Tax period normally coincides with accounting period Tax return must be submitted to tax authorities within five months from the end of the accounting period[9] Tax payment should be made monthly during the accounting period[10]	
Capital gains	Capital gains are subject to corporation tax at normal rates Capital gains on qualifying participations are exempt	
Losses	Within a year losses can be offset against other current year profits A current year loss can be carried back one year and carried forward 9 years	
Tax group	A fiscal unity can be formed by a parent company and its 95% subsidiaries[11,12]	Foreign entities with Dutch PEs can unite the Dutch PEs in a fiscal unity[13]
Tax rate	Between 20% and 25% Profits (€) Rate Up to 200,000 20% 200,000+ 25%	

8 Capital gains are not taxed separately but treated/taxed as taxable profit.
9 The tax authorities grant tax advice firms an extension for their clients which enable them to file the returns proportionally over a period of 16 months after the end of the accounting period.
10 Interest is due for any over- or underpayment of tax.
11 Fiscal unity means that the group is treated as one company for corporation tax purposes and taxed on a consolidated basis.
12 A parent company could only form a fiscal unity with its subsidiary if it holds at least 95% of the shares and the voting rights of its subsidiary.
13 As long as the 95% ownership condition is met.

III   TAXES FOR INDIVIDUALS

<table>
<tr><td colspan="2"></td><th>Residents[14]</th><th>Non-residents</th></tr>
<tr><td rowspan="7">Income Tax</td><td>General description</td><td colspan="2">Tax levied on the taxable income of a chargeable person for a year of assessment[15]</td></tr>
<tr><td>Taxable entities and taxable income</td><td>Individuals who are resident in the Netherlands are liable to tax on their worldwide income</td><td>Individuals who are not resident in the Netherlands are liable to tax on income arising in the Netherlands, subject to provisions in double taxation agreements</td></tr>
<tr><td>Types of taxable income</td><td>• Worldwide income of a trade, profession or vocation (box 1)
• Worldwide employment income (box 1)
• Worldwide income from substantial shareholding (box 2)
• Worldwide property income (box 1 or 3)
• Worldwide savings and investment income (box 3)
• Worldwide income from trusts or estates (box 3)</td><td>• Dutch-sourced trading income of a trade, profession or vocation (box 1)
• Dutch employment income (box 1)
• Dutch-sourced income from substantial shareholding (box 2)
• Dutch property income (box 1 or 3)</td></tr>
<tr><td>Calculation of income</td><td colspan="2">• Box 1 – accrual basis, income/benefit received
• Box 2 – actual income received and in certain cases a deemed income
• Box 3 –

	Nominal rate	Effective rate
up to €25,000	Nil	Nil
€25,000 – 100,000	2.87% (2016: 4%)	0.86% (2016:1.2%)
€100,000 – 1,000,000	4.6% (2016: 4%)	1.38% (2016: 1.2%)
> €1,000,000	5.39% (2016: 4%)	1.62% (2016: 1.2%)[16]
</td></tr>
<tr><td>Tax year, tax assessment and tax payment</td><td colspan="2">Tax year – calendar year
Tax assessment – after submitting individual tax return
Tax payment due – during the tax year[17]</td></tr>
<tr><td>Losses</td><td colspan="2">• Box 1 – 3 years carry back, 9 years carry forward
• Box 2 – 1 year carry back, 9 years carry forward
• There are restrictions for loss compensation between the boxes</td></tr>
<tr><td>Tax rates</td><td colspan="2">• Box 1 – progressive (from 37% up to 52%)
• Box 2 – 25%
• Box 3 – 30%</td></tr>
</table>

14 Double taxation will be prevented by double tax treaty or the Dutch Unilateral Decree to prevent double taxation.
15 Capital gains are not taxed separately but treated/taxed as chargeable income.
16 Capital gains are 'included' and thus not taxed separately.
17 Interest is due for any over- or underpayment of tax.

		Residents[14]	Non-residents
Capital Gains Tax (CGT)	General description	Capital gains are not taxed separately but treated/taxed as chargeable income (if any)	
		Dutch residents	**Non-residents**
Inheritance Tax (IHT)	General description	Tax charged on a taxable transfer of value made by a lifetime gift or estate on death[18]	
	Taxable entities and chargeable assets	Estate or lifetime gifts received from a Dutch[19] deceased or donor	
	Calculation of charge	Value of the estate or lifetime gift	
	Taxable events	• Lifetime gifts • Estates on death and gifts made 180 days prior to death of donor	
	Allowances	There are various exemptions for estate and lifetime gifts under various conditions Charities are exempted from paying tax on estate and lifetime gifts	
	Tax rates	• 10%–20% for children and spouses • 18%–36% for grandchildren • 30%–40%for others	

18 Inheritance tax treaties can override the right of the Netherlands to tax a taxable estate or lifetime gift.
19 Dutch refers to Dutch residents, which includes foreign citizens residing in the Netherlands. Dutch citizens who were Dutch residents 10 years prior to the taxable event are treated as Dutch residents for inheritance tax purposes.

IV   WITHHOLDING TAXES

Under Domestic Law	Payments to residents	Payments to non-residents[20]
Dividends	15%	15%
Interest	Nil	Nil
Royalties	Nil	Nil
On payments to artists and sportsmen	Wage tax withholding	0%[21]

Reduced rate available under the relevant Double Taxation Treaty			
Country	Dividends	Interest	Royalties
Albania	15%	Nil	Nil
Argentina	15%	Nil	Nil
Armenia	15%	Nil	Nil
Aruba	15%	Nil	Nil
Australia	15%	Nil	Nil
Austria	15%	Nil	Nil
Azerbaijan	10%	Nil	Nil
Bahrain	10%	Nil	Nil
Bangladesh	15%	Nil	Nil
Barbados	15%	Nil	Nil
Belgium	15%	Nil	Nil
BES Islands (Bonaire, St Eustatius and Saba)	15%	Nil	Nil
Bosnia and Herzegovina	15%	Nil	Nil
Brazil	15%	Nil	Nil
Bulgaria	15%	Nil	Nil
Canada	15%	Nil	Nil
China	10%	Nil	Nil
Croatia	15%	Nil	Nil
Curaçao	15%	Nil	Nil
Czech Republic	10%	Nil	Nil
Denmark	15%	Nil	Nil
Germany	15%	Nil	Nil
Egypt	15%	Nil	Nil
Estonia	15%	Nil	Nil
Finland	15%	Nil	Nil
France	15%	Nil	Nil
Georgia	15%	Nil	Nil

20 Reduced rates of withholding tax may apply in the case of double tax treaty and under the EU Parent-Subsidiary Directive.

21 The 0% is applicable if the artist or sportsman is from a country which has a tax treaty with the Netherlands. Without a tax treaty thewithholding rate amounts to 20%.

Reduced rate available under the relevant Double Taxation Treaty			
Country	Dividends	Interest	Royalties
Ghana	10%	Nil	Nil
Greece	15%	Nil	Nil
Hungary	15%	Nil	Nil
Hong Kong	10%	Nil	Nil
Iceland	15%	Nil	Nil
India	15%	Nil	Nil
Indonesia	10%	Nil	Nil
Ireland	15%	Nil	Nil
Israel	15%	Nil	Nil
Italy	15%	Nil	Nil
Japan	10%	Nil	Nil
Jordan	15%	Nil	Nil
Kazakhstan	15%	Nil	Nil
Kuwait	10%	Nil	Nil
Latvia	15%	Nil	Nil
Lithuania	15%	Nil	Nil
Luxembourg	15%	Nil	Nil
Macedonia	15%	Nil	Nil
Malawi	15%	Nil	Nil
Malaysia	15%	Nil	Nil
Malta	15%	Nil	Nil
Morocco	15%	Nil	Nil
Mexico	15%	Nil	Nil
Moldova	15%	Nil	Nil
Mongolia	15%	Nil	Nil
Montenegro	15%	Nil	Nil
New Zealand	15%	Nil	Nil
Nigeria	15%	Nil	Nil
Norway	15%	Nil	Nil
Oman	10%	Nil	Nil
Panama	15%	Nil	Nil
Pakistan	15%	Nil	Nil
Philippines	15%	Nil	Nil
Poland	15%	Nil	Nil
Portugal	10%	Nil	Nil
Qatar	10%	Nil	Nil
Republic of Korea	15%	Nil	Nil
Romania	15%	Nil	Nil
Russia	15%	Nil	Nil
St Maarten	15%	Nil	Nil
Saudi Arabia	10%	Nil	Nil
Serbia	15%	Nil	Nil
Singapore	15%	Nil	Nil
Slovakia	10%	Nil	Nil
Slovenia	15%	Nil	Nil

Reduced rate available under the relevant Double Taxation Treaty			
Country	Dividends	Interest	Royalties
Soviet Union (former)	15%	Nil	Nil
Spain	15%	Nil	Nil
Sri Lanka	15%	Nil	Nil
Suriname	15%	Nil	Nil
Taiwan	10%	Nil	Nil
Thailand	15%	Nil	Nil
Tunisia	20%	Nil	Nil
Turkey	20%	Nil	Nil
Uganda	15%	Nil	Nil
Ukraine	15%	Nil	Nil
United Arab Emirates	10%	Nil	Nil
United Kingdom	10%	Nil	Nil
United States	15%	Nil	Nil
Uzbekistan	15%	Nil	Nil
Venezuela	10%	Nil	Nil

Where the treaty rate is above the domestic rate, the domestic rate usually applies.

Note: the above rates are only available provided the specific Treaty criteria are satisfied. It is possible that lower rates than those shown above may be available provided that certain criteria are satisfied. As treaties will not be identical, guidance should be sought in all cases.

V INDIRECT TAXES

<table>
<tr><td rowspan="8">Value Added Tax (VAT)</td><td></td><td>**Residents**</td><td>**Non-residents**</td></tr>
<tr><td>General description</td><td colspan="2">Tax on the supply of goods and services</td></tr>
<tr><td>Entities obliged to levy VAT</td><td colspan="2">• Any individual, partnership, corporation or other body, which carries out taxable activities in the Netherlands
• Other situations may also arise, eg distance selling, sale of assets, acquisitions from other EC member states</td></tr>
<tr><td>Taxable activities</td><td colspan="2">• Supply of goods and services, import of goods, intra-Community acquisition of goods, etc
• Regarding the payment of Dutch VAT, the place of the supply of goods and/or services must be in the Netherlands (following the third chapter of title IV and the first chapter of title V from the EU VAT Directive)</td></tr>
<tr><td>Taxable activities – zero-rated (examples)</td><td colspan="2">• Supply of goods from a VAT entrepreneur resident in the Netherlands to a VAT entrepreneur resident in another EU-country (intra-community delivery)
• Export of goods and certain services to anyone outside the EU</td></tr>
<tr><td>Exemptions (examples)

Reverse charge mechanism</td><td colspan="2">• Transactions related to the sale of any Dutch property used for more than 2 years and the lease of any Dutch property(option to tax for VAT available for commercial property)
• Banking and insurance services
• Educational supplies
• Certain welfare services including hospital and medical care services
• Where a service is provided by a VAT entrepreneur resident in the Netherlands to a VAT entrepreneur resident in another EU country, the payable VAT that corresponds to this service is 'reverse charged' to the recipient of the service (business-to-business activity)
• Where a VAT entrepreneur provides the delivery and/or the service is not resident in the Netherlands and does not have a permanent establishment in the Netherlands and the recipient of the service and/or the delivery is a VAT entrepreneur resident in the Netherlands or does have a permanent establishment in the Netherlands, the payable VAT is reverse charged to the recipient if the place of the service or the delivery is the Netherlands</td></tr>
<tr><td>Refund of VAT</td><td>• VAT paid on supplies and services is deductible as input tax, if incurred in the course or furtherance of the business and for the purpose of making taxable supplies (including zero-rated supplies)
• There is no credit for input tax incurred which relates to the provision of exempt supplies
• Where mixed supplies occur(taxable and exempt supplies), subject to anti-abuse provisions, input tax must be apportioned and recovered according to a partial exemption method</td><td>• EC 8th Directive refund system for non-resident businesses established within the EU, providing its business is not other wise required to be registered in the Netherlands
• EC 13th Directive refund system for non-resident businesses established outside the EU, providing its business is not otherwise required to be registered in the Netherlands
• Strict time limits apply to claims[22]</td></tr>
</table>

---

22 Filing the claim after the deadline will be rewarded normally, but any denial cannot be disputed in court.

		Residents	Non-residents
Value Added Tax (VAT)	Tax liability	• Normally the supplier of goods and services is responsible for charging VAT • With a licence, Dutch residents can defer the VAT payable upon import of goods into the EU to their Dutch VAT return[23]	
	Tax rates	• Standard rate = 21% • Reduced rate = 6% (eg food) • Zero rate = 0%	
	Administrative obligations	• Formal requirements concerning business records and invoices • Monthly or quarterly self-assessment VAT returns plus payment of any VAT liability to tax authorities • VAT groups are allowed subject to certain requirements • VAT identification number must be shown on all invoices issued • EU invoicing directive must be adhered to • Listings for the intra-community services and/or deliveries that were provided from the Netherlands should be filed on a monthly or quarterly basis	• Registration for VAT purposes, if making supplies of goods and services in the Netherlands • Appointment of fiscal tax representative possible but not obligatory
Real Property Taxes		• Transfer of Dutch property is taxed at 6% on value of transaction payable by the buyer and in some cases exemptions are applicable • Transfer of Dutch private dwellings is taxed at 2% of value on transaction payable by the buyer • The value of property is taxed by local governments	
Stamp Duty		Transaction-related insurances are taxed at 21% of the insurance premiums with a range of exemptions	

---

23 No cash flow because the reported import VAT is recovered as input VAT on the same return.

Nevis

(Graham Sutcliffe, Dixcart Management Nevis Limited,
graham.sutcliffe@dixcart.com)

I MAIN LEGAL FORMS

Characteristics / Legal form	Nevis IBC	Nevis LLC
Partners/shareholders • Number • Restrictions	Minimum: 1 None	Minimum: 1 member None
Directors	Minimum: 3 (unless less than 3 shareholders in which case number of directors can equal number of shareholders)	Minimum: 1
Establishment	Not required	Not required
Registration	At Offshore Registry	At Offshore Registry
Minimum capital	None	None
Liability	Limited liability	Limited liability
Governance	Regulated by Offshore Regulator	Regulated by Offshore Regulator
Audit requirements	None	None
Taxation	None	None

II   CORPORATION TAX

Legal Form / Description	Resident corporation	Permanent establishment (PE)
General description	Offshore companies are exempt	Offshore companies are exempt
Taxable entities		
Taxable income		
Calculation of taxable profits		
Interest payments		
Related party transactions		
Tax year, return and payment		
Capital gains		
Losses		
Tax group		
Tax rate		

III TAXES FOR INDIVIDUALS

		Residents	Non-residents
Income Tax	General description	No income tax	
	Taxable entities and taxable income		
	Types of taxable income		
	Calculation of income		
	Tax year, tax assessment and tax payment		
	Losses		
	Tax rates		
Capital Gains Tax (CGT)	General description	No capital gains tax	
	Taxable entities and chargeable assets		
	Calculation of gain		
	Tax year, tax assessment and tax payment		
	Losses		
	Tax rates		
		Domiciled	**Non-domiciled**
Inheritance Tax (IHT)	General description	No inheritance tax	
	Taxable entities and chargeable assets		
	Calculation of charge		
	Taxable events		
	Allowances		
	Tax rates		

IV WITHHOLDING TAXES

	Offshore companies	Local companies
Dividends	Nil	10%
Interest	Nil	10%
Royalties	Nil	10%
On payments to artists and sportsmen	Nil	10%

V   INDIRECT TAXES

		Residents	Non-residents
Value Added Tax (VAT)	General description	VAT at 17% on most goods. Some exemptions/ lower rates are available for certain goods and services. There are also import taxes on all goods coming in	
	Entities obliged to levy VAT	Any unless exempted such as offshore services	
	Taxable activities	Trading goods and services in St Kitts and Nevis unless exempt	
	Taxable activities – zero-rated (examples)	Electricity, water, some medicinal products	
	Exemptions (examples)	Offshore companies and those performing offshore registered agent services	
	Refund of VAT	Within two months	
	Tax liability	Net due or reclaimable after usual calculation (Output VAT – Input VAT)	
	Tax rates	17% or 7%	
	Administrative obligations	Monthly return if VATable	
Real Property Taxes		Purchase: 12% stamp duty payable by the seller. Aliens have to pay 10% alien land holding tax. Annual land taxes are based on value of land and building	
Stamp Duty		12% on sale or transfer of title of land/buildings. 1% on shares in local company	

Nexia International does not accept liability for any loss arising from any action taken, or omission, on the basis of this publication. Professional advice should be obtained before acting or refraining from acting on the contents of this publication. Membership of Nexia International, or associated umbrella organizations, does not constitute any partnership between members, and members do not accept any responsibility for the commission of any act, or omission to act by, or the liabilities of, other members.

Nexia International is the trading name of Nexia International Limited, a company registered in the Isle of Man. Company registration number: 53513C. Registered office: 2nd floor, Sixty Circular Road, Douglas, Isle of Man, IM1 1SA

New Zealand

(Doug Allcock, Nexia New Zealand,dallcock@nexiachch.co.nz)

I MAIN LEGAL FORMS

Legal form / Characteristics	Partnership	Limited Liability Partnership (LLP)	Limited liability company[1]
Partners/shareholders • Number • Restrictions	Two or more	Two or more (minimum one general, one limited – the limited cannot be a general partner)	One or more No restriction
Directors	Management by partners	Management by general partner only; limited partners should not manage the LLP as they will lose their limited liability to the extent they do so	Management by directors Must have at least one NZ resident director
Establishment	Deed	Deed	Constitution
Registration	General partnerships: none	Limited partnerships: companies office register	Companies: register with companies office (Ministry of Economic Development) Companies that elect to become look through companies ('LTC') must file an additional election with the Inland Revenue Department
Minimum capital	$0	$0	$1
Liability	Unlimited	Ltd partner: limited to capital, provided does not undertake general partner duties General partner: joint and several	Limited to capital LTC owners/shareholders personally liable for tax obligations of the company

---

1 It is possible for certain companies to elect to become 'look-through companies' ('LTCs') for tax purposes. These companies retain their status as a company for commercial purposes, but are treated as flow-through entities for tax purposes and taxed in a similar way to partnerships. LTCs can have a maximum of five 'counted owners' – certain persons such as family members are grouped as one person for this test.

Legal form / Characteristics	Partnership	Limited Liability Partnership (LLP)	Limited liability company[1]
Governance	Partners	Partners	Management/Directors
Audit requirements	None	None	Required for: • FMC Reporting entities and other publicly accountable entities • Large overseas companies that carry on business in New Zealand and large companies with 25% or more overseas ownership, unless the company is a subsidiary of a New Zealand company that has filed audited group financial statements Some opt-out options are available • The company is a wholly owned subsidiary of a company that has filed audited group financial statements with the Registrar of Companies • Companies with fewer than 10 shareholders, except if shareholders of the company who hold at least 5% of the voting shares require the company to have an audit
Taxation	Taxed in partners' hands per their share at their marginal rates	Flow-through of aggregated result at marginal rates	NZ resident company taxed on worldwide income LTC income flows through to owners and taxed at marginal rates
Usage	No restriction	No restriction	No restriction LTCs must have 5 maximum counted owners and must be NZ tax resident

II CORPORATION TAX

Description / Legal form	New Zealand resident corporation	Permanent establishment (PE)
General description	Company tax	Profits attributable to PE in New Zealand
Taxable entities	Incorporated in New Zealand, head office in New Zealand, director control or central management and control is exercised from New Zealand	Taxed as a branch in New Zealand
Taxable income	Worldwide income from all sources is taxable Comprehensive Controlled Foreign Company (CFC) and Foreign Investment Fund (FIF) regimes taxing passive income of foreign subsidiaries and other investments Comprehensive financial arrangements regime, taxing income (including unrealised foreign exchange movements) on an unrealised basis under spreading methods established by tax laws	Income derived from New Zealand Transfer pricing guidelines to be taken into account when calculating branch income
Calculation of taxable profits	Accounting profit adjusted by various add-backs/deductions – including timing adjustments, as calculated under tax rules	Profits attributable to New Zealand activities, calculated under New Zealand tax rules
Interest payments	Interest is deductible (for companies and for other entity types where there is a nexus to income) but subject to thin capitalisation rules – 60% safe harbour limit on interest bearing debt/total asset ratio of New Zealand group, or limitation on interest deductions if New Zealand group debt percentage exceeds 110% of the worldwide group debt percentage Thin capitalisation rules also apply to New Zealand tax resident companies who obtain interest bearing debt in New Zealand and then on-lend to foreign subsidiaries or associated companies – the safe harbour in this case is 75%	
Related party transactions	Cross-border related party transactions must comply with transfer pricing guidelines – an ability to demonstrate compliance with the arm's length principle using one of the OECD transfer pricing methods. There is also a potential for related party transactions to give rise to deemed dividends, fringe benefit tax (FBT) and non-resident withholding tax, particularly where consideration is not at market value	
Tax year, return and payment	Balance date is generally 31 March although companies may have alternative balance dates with approval in advance from the Inland Revenue Department Tax returns must be filed by 7 July but extended to the 31 March following balance date if filed by a tax agent Companies must pay provisional tax in 3 instalments – commencing 4 months after balance date. Underpayments of provisional tax attract use of money interest and, in some cases, late payment penalties Terminal tax payable 7 February or 7 April if returns are filed by a tax agent	

Legal form / Description	New Zealand resident corporation	Permanent establishment (PE)
Capital gains	No CGT in New Zealand. However, certain gains from land, financial arrangements and foreign investment transactions may be taxable[2] – subject to specific Controlled Foreign Company/Foreign Investment Fund/ financial arrangement regimes Related party capital gains may also be taxable in some circumstances	No CGT in New Zealand. However, certain gains from land, financial arrangements and foreign investment transactions may be taxable Related party capital gains may also be taxable in some circumstances Residential land sold within 2 years of acquisition (if purchased on or after 1 October 2015) subject to tax. Non-residents to provide IRD numbers and evidence of NZ bank details
Losses	Most losses are allowable and may be carried forward where 49% shareholder continuity maintained from the time the losses are incurred, or offset amongst group companies where 66% continuity maintained from the time the losses are incurred. Shareholder continuity is measured at the ultimate natural person or trust level; corporate shareholders are ignored	
Tax group	A consolidated group may file a tax return as one taxpayer where the members are 100% commonly owned and where an election is made with the Inland Revenue Department within 63 days of the start of the income year (in which the election is to apply) to be treated as a consolidated tax group	
Tax rate	Flat rate of 28%	28%, unless limited under specific DTA article (generally passive income only such as interest, dividends or royalties)

---

2 Legislation was enacted with effect from the 2008 income year which changed the way income from financial investments is taxed where shares are held in countries outside New Zealand and Australia (generally applies to direct shareholdings of less than 10%) – introduction of Fair Dividend Rate, de minimis exemptions apply to individuals. Different rules apply to indirect investments through Portfolio Investment Entities (PIEs) – investors will pay tax at rates between 0% and 28%.

III TAXES FOR INDIVIDUALS

<table>
<tr><th></th><th></th><th>Residents</th><th>Non-residents</th></tr>
<tr>
<td rowspan="8">Income Tax</td>
<td>General description</td>
<td colspan="2">Tax levied on a person's income for the year (worldwide for residents)

Non-residents are liable to tax on New Zealand sourced income</td>
</tr>
<tr>
<td>Taxable entities and taxable income</td>
<td>Overriding test is that persons with a permanent place of abode in New Zealand are resident

Note the Inland Revenue Department released guidance in March 2014 which widened the meaning of permanent place of abode – this change is likely to mean more individuals are considered New Zealand tax resident than in previous years

Second test is where a person is personally present in New Zealand for longer than a total of 183 days in any 12-month period

A new tax resident (not resident for 10 years prior) may be eligible for transitional residents exemption for first 48 months of tax residency on certain sources of income</td>
<td>Absent from New Zealand for more than 325 days in any 12-month period and does not maintain a permanent place of abode

Note the Inland Revenue Department released guidance in March 2014 which widened the meaning of permanent place of abode – this change is likely to mean more individuals are considered New Zealand tax resident than in previous years, even where a person has been absent for 325 days in a 12-month period</td>
</tr>
<tr>
<td>Types of taxable income</td>
<td colspan="2">
• Employment income (including free accommodation in some circumstances). New Zealand also taxes fringe benefits provided to employees (at the employer level)
• Business income
• Interest
• Rentals
• Dividends
• Royalties
• Certain land transactions (taxable developments, subdivisions, etc)
• Foreign investment – subject to CFC/FIF rules
• Foreign interests such as overseas bank accounts, loans, foreign pensions, may be subject to the financial arrangements, CFC or FIF rules
</td>
</tr>
</table>

		Residents	Non-residents
Income Tax – *contd*	Calculation of income	• Employment income – income when received, this is normally subject to tax at source (Pay As You Earn tax) • Business income – derived on accrual basis • Interest – individuals: income cash or accrual, expenditure on accrual basis • Rentals – generally income derived on cash basis, expenditure on accrual basis • Dividends – income derived on a cash basis, may be excluded if shares are subject to FIF or CFC regime • Royalties – income derived on a cash basis • Taxable land transactions – income derived on a cash basis • Foreign investment – see note under companies CGT • Foreign interests – income on an accrual basis, calculated under applicable regime, eg: CFC, FIF or financial arrangement rules	
	Tax year, tax assessment and tax payment	The tax year runs to 31 March. Residents are generally required to file a tax return where income has been received from sources with no tax deducted (ie other than New Zealand employment income/ interest and dividends) Returns must be filed by 7 July if no agent or 31 March if taxpayer has an agent	Non-resident returns required if New Zealand sourced income or profits attributable to New Zealand – same dates as residents
		Provisional tax is payable in three equal instalments Due 28th day of 5th, 9th and 13th months except for GST registered persons using ratio method or who are 6-monthly filers – payments due in December or April will be due 15 January and 7 May respectively Terminal tax due 7 February if no agent or 7 April if agent Temporary resident's tax exemption on foreign passive income for new migrants and returning New Zealanders (where non-resident for at least 10 years) applies from 1 April 2006 to exempt most sources of passive foreign income from tax in New Zealand for first 4 years of residency	
	Losses	May be utilised and carried forward indefinitely	
	Tax rates	Tax is levied on a graduated scale depending on the level of taxable income 10.5%–33%	10.5%–33% (see also note for residents)

		Residents	Non-residents
Capital Gains Tax (CGT)	General description	No CGT in New Zealand. However certain gains from land and foreign investment transactions may be taxable	
		Related party capital gains may be taxable in some situations	
		Residential land sold within 2 years of acquisition (if purchased on or after 1 October 2015) subject to tax. Non-residents to provide IRD numbers and evidence of NZ bank details	
	Taxable entities and chargeable assets		
	Calculation of gain		
	Tax year, tax assessment and tax payment		
	Losses	Capital losses are not deductible	
	Tax rates	Marginal or company tax rates may apply	
		Domiciled	**Non-domiciled**
Inheritance Tax (IHT)		Estate duty was abolished in 1993	
		Gift duty legislation was repealed with effect from 1 October 2011	

IV   WITHHOLDING TAXES

Under domestic law	Payments to residents	Payments to non-residents
Dividends	33% Withholding tax liability reduced to the extent imputation credits are attached to the dividends (in most cases 28% imputation credits and 5% withholding tax)	0% if dividends are fully imputed and paid to a non-resident who holds at least 10% of the voting interests 0% if dividends are fully imputed and paid to a non-resident who holds less than 10% of the voting interests where a double tax treaty would reduce the rate to below 15% 15% to the extent that dividends are fully imputed 30% to the extent that dividends are not imputed
Interest	10.5% to 33%	15% Approved Issuer Levy 2% on interest not paid to associated person where recipient has applied to the Inland Revenue Department for AIL treatment
Royalties	Tax payable at marginal rates 10.5% to 33%	15%
On payments to artists and sportsmen	Tax payable at marginal rates 10.5% to 33%	• 20% non-resident entertainers • 15% non-resident contractors

Notes:

• Rates may be reduced by Double Tax Agreements.
• It may be possible to reduce non-resident contractors' withholding tax rates in certain circumstances, where a certificate of exemption is obtained from the Inland Revenue Department.

Reduced rate available under the relevant Double Taxation Treaty			
Country	Dividends	Interest	Royalties
Australia	0% to 15%	10%	5%
Austria	15%	10%	10%
Belgium	15%	10%	10%
Canada	5% to 15%	10%	5%
Chile	15%	15%	5%
China	15%	10%	10%
Czech Republic	15%	10%	10%
Denmark	15%	10%	10%
Fiji	15%	10%	15%
Finland	15%	10%	10%
France	15%	10%	10%
Germany	15%	10%	10%
Hong Kong	0% to 15%	10%	5%
India	15%	10%	10%
Indonesia	15%	10%	15%

Reduced rate available under the relevant Double Taxation Treaty			
Country	Dividends	Interest	Royalties
Ireland	15%	10%	10%
Italy	15%	10%	10%
Japan	0% to 15%	10%	5%
Korea	15%	10%	10%
Malaysia	15%	15%	15%
Mexico	15%	10%	10%
Netherlands	15%	10%	10%
Norway	15%	10%	10%
Papua New Guinea	15%	10%	10%
Philippines	15%	10%	15%
Poland	15%	10%	10%
Russian Federation	15%	10%	10%
Singapore	5% to 15%	10%	10%
South Africa	15%	10%	10%
Spain	15%	10%	10%
Sweden	15%	10%	10%
Switzerland	15%	10%	10%
Taiwan	15%	10%	10%
Thailand	15%	10% to 15%	10% to 15%
Turkey	5% to 15%	10% to 15%	10%
United Arab Emirates	15%	10%	10%
United Kingdom	15%	10%	10%
United States of America	0% to 15%	10%	5%

Notes: the above rates are only available provided the specific Treaty criteria are satisfied. It is possible that lower rates than those shown above may be available provided that certain criteria are satisfied. As treaties will not be identical, guidance should be sought in all cases.

The tax Treaties may alter the domestic law definition of royalties in some cases, meaning items such as management fees may be subject to royalty withholding taxes in certain cases.

V   INDIRECT TAXES

<table>
<tr><th></th><th></th><th>Residents</th><th>Non-residents</th></tr>
<tr><td rowspan="13">Value Added Tax (GST)</td><td>General description</td><td colspan="2">Goods and Services Tax (GST)</td></tr>
<tr><td>Entities obliged to levy GST</td><td colspan="2">Where operating a taxable activity in New Zealand and turnover exceeds $60,000 per annum</td></tr>
<tr><td>Non-residents entitled to register</td><td colspan="2">From 1 April 2014, certain non-residents can register for GST under a special 'non-resident registration' category. Certain criteria must be satisfied to register. This registration type allows non-residents to recover any GST paid on purchases made in New Zealand where they are not carrying on a taxable activity in New Zealand</td></tr>
<tr><td>Taxable activities</td><td colspan="2">Any activity which is carried on continuously or regularly by any person, whether or not for a pecuniary profit, and involves or is intended to involve, in whole or in part, the supply of goods and services to any other person for a consideration; and includes any such activity carried on in the form of a business, trade, manufacture, profession, vocation, association, or club</td></tr>
<tr><td>Taxable activities – zero-rated (examples)</td><td colspan="2">Exports, sales of businesses, and commercial land sales where land is sold between two GST-registered persons</td></tr>
<tr><td>Exemptions (examples)</td><td colspan="2">Financial services

Residential rents

Donated goods and services</td></tr>
<tr><td>Refund of GST</td><td>Input tax claimable upon purchase of goods and services to the extent those goods and services are acquired for making taxable supplies

No input claim available for certain financial services

If intended taxable use % changes after purchase, then apportionment rules apply which will require an annual adjustment calculation</td><td>Non-residents can be registered and make input claims where carrying on a taxable activity in NZ

Non-residents are also able to register under a special 'non-resident registration category' which will allow them to claim GST inputs on expenses incurred in NZ if they are not making taxable supplies and satisfy other criteria</td></tr>
<tr><td>Tax liability</td><td colspan="2">Obligation is on supplier to charge GST where appropriate

Reverse charge (self-assessed) applies to some imported services where a non-resident supplies a resident recipient who makes more than 5% of non-taxable supplies</td></tr>
<tr><td>Tax rates</td><td colspan="2">• Standard rate = 15%
• Zero rate = 0%</td></tr>
<tr><td>Administrative obligations</td><td>Prescribed record keeping and tax invoice requirements

Returns filed monthly, 2-monthly or 6-monthly depending on turnover and choice

Grouping allowed where requirements met</td><td>Non-residents can be registered and make input claims where carrying on a taxable activity in New Zealand</td></tr>
<tr><td colspan="2">Real Property Taxes</td><td colspan="2">Local rates apply</td></tr>
<tr><td colspan="2">Stamp Duty</td><td colspan="2">There is no stamp duty</td></tr>
</table>

Nigeria

(Aliu Yesufu, Nexia Agbo Abel & Co., aliu@nexianigeria.com)

I MAIN LEGAL FORMS

Legal form / Characteristics	Partnership and Limited Liability Partnership (LLP)	Private corporation (Ltd) and Public corporation (Plc)
Partners/shareholders • Number • Restrictions	A minimum of two and maximum of 20 partners	• A minimum of one shareholder for Ltd and Plc • Maximum of 50 shareholders for Ltd • No restriction for Plc
Directors	N/A	A minimum of two directors for Ltd and Plc
Establishment	Partnership agreement or deed	Company Regulations (ie Memorandum or Articles of Association)
Registration	The Registrar (Corporate Affairs Commission) is responsible for the registration of all partnerships and companies	
Minimum capital	None required by law	25% of authorized share capital
Liability	Unlimited liability and every partner is jointly and severally responsible for them	Liability limited to the value of any unpaid liability on issued shares
Governance	The Board of Partners	The Board of Directors
Audit requirements	Audit not required by law	Audited accounts due by law not later than 6 months after every accounting year
Taxation	Corporate income tax for the firm PAYE for individual partners	Corporate income tax on worldwide profits for Nigerian companies and for non-resident companies income derived from Nigeria

II CORPORATION TAX

Description \ Legal form	Resident corporation	Permanent establishment (PE)
General description	Company income tax (CIT) is payable for each year of assessment on the profits of any company at a rate of 30%. These include profit accruing in, derived from, brought into or received from a trade, business or investment. The basis of assessment for both resident and non-resident companies is preceding year basis	
Taxable entities	Incorporated in the Federal Republic of Nigeria or having its management and control exercised from within Nigeria at any time during the year of assessment	The permanent establishment is the condition for liability to Nigerian tax of business profit made in Nigeria. If a company has a permanent establishment in Nigeria, it is liable to Nigerian tax on the profit from trade or business derived from Nigeria
Taxable income	Taxable profits	Profits derived by a PE in Nigeria
Calculation of taxable profits	All incomes/revenues accruing to the business less deductions allowable by law	
Interest payments	Payment of interest to both residents and non-residents attracts 10% withholding tax on the gross amount	
Related party transactions	Related party transactions should be at arm's length, and the tax authorities are empowered to adjust transactions considered not to be at arm's length. Transfer pricing regulations are applicable in Nigeria, and the rules are in line with the OECD and the UN models	
Tax year, return and payment	The fiscal year is 1 January to 31 December. Companies are expected to file their tax returns by the end of the sixth month after the end of their financial year, or by 30 June each year, whichever is earlier. However, a new company must file its returns within 18 months from the date of incorporation, or 6 months after its first accounting period, whichever is earlier	
	The filing requirements include a full set of audited financial statements, capital allowances and tax computations, together with the necessary forms disclosing relevant details about the earnings of the company for the tax year. The due date of payment of income tax is 2 months from the filing due date in the case of a lump sum payment or in such instalments as the tax authority may approve. In the case of instalments, evidence of payment of the first instalment must be submitted with the return	
Capital gains	Capital gains tax accrues on an actual year basis and it pertains to all gains accruing to a taxpayer from the disposal of chargeable assets. Where, however, the taxpayer is a non-resident company or individual, the tax will only be levied on the amount received or brought into Nigeria. The rate is 10% of net capital gain	
	Computation of capital gains tax is done by deducting, from the sum received or recoverable, the cost of acquisition to the person realizing the chargeable gain, plus expenditure incurred on the improvement expenses incidental to the realization of the asset; certain assets are, however, exempt from CGT	
	Capital gains arising from the disposal of fixed assets may be deferred by the application of roll over relief. Roll over relief can be claimed if the proceeds of the disposal are used to purchase a new asset of the same class as the disposed asset. This relief is applicable to certain classes of qualifying assets	

Description \ Legal form	Resident corporation	Permanent establishment (PE)
Losses	A loss incurred by a company in any trade or business during a preceding year of assessment is deductible in computing the total income of the company for income tax purposes. The amount deductible for any year of assessment is limited to the amount of assessable profits included in the total profits of that year and derived from the source in connection with which the loss was incurred. Prior to 2007, losses incurred by any company other than those in agricultural business and upstream petroleum industry can be carried forward for a maximum period of four years. This restriction was removed for all companies with the exemption of insurance companies in 2007	
Tax group	N/A	
Tax rate	• Company Income tax rate is 30% plus 2% Tertiary Education Tax • 1% of profit before tax payable by GSM companies and others in telecom industry • 85% for petroleum operations carried out under a JV arrangement with the Nigerian National Petroleum Corporation (NNPC) or any non-production sharing contract (PSC) over 5 years • 65.75% for non PSC operation in its first 5 years during which the company has not fully amortized all pre-production capitalized expenditure • 50% for petroleum operations under PSC with the NNPC	

III   TAXES FOR INDIVIDUALS

<table>
<tr><td rowspan="10">Income Tax</td><td></td><td>Residents</td><td>Non-residents</td></tr>
<tr><td>General description</td><td colspan="2">Personal income tax (PIT) is levied on the chargeable income of every chargeable person residing in Nigeria in a year of assessment</td></tr>
<tr><td>Taxable entities and taxable income</td><td>Income derived from business, employment, or investments accruing from, brought into, or received in Nigeria</td><td>Income derived from business, employment, or investments accruing in or derived from Nigeria</td></tr>
<tr><td>Types of taxable income</td><td colspan="2">• Employment income
• Income from business activities
• Income from investments (eg interest, dividends, rent and royalties)</td></tr>
<tr><td>Calculation of income</td><td colspan="2">Gross emolument less Consolidated Relief Allowance (CRA) of ₦200,000 or 1% of gross income whichever is higher plus 20% of gross income, child allowance of ₦2,500 for each child up to a maximum of four children, provided none is above 16 years or married and ₦2,000 for each dependent relative up to a maximum of two relatives who are widowed or infirm. However, a relief can be granted for a child over 16 years if the child is in a recognized school, under artisanship or learning a trade

Other allowable deductions are

A) National Housing Fund contribution

B) National Health Insurance Scheme Contribution

C) Life Assurance Premium

D) National pension Scheme Contribution

E) Gratuities</td></tr>
<tr><td>Tax year, tax assessment and tax payment</td><td colspan="2">• Year of assessment is the calendar year from 1 January to 31 December
• A return of income must be filed no later than the 10th day of the month following the month of deduction. For employment income a fixed monthly Pay As You Earn (PAYE) regime is in place
• Every employer is required to file a return of all emoluments paid to his employees not later than 31 January of every year in respect of all employees in his employment in the preceding year. A return in respect of the current year must also be filed within 90 days of the fiscal year</td></tr>
<tr><td>Losses</td><td colspan="2">None</td></tr>
<tr><td>Tax rates</td><td colspan="2">

Personal Income Tax	Rate (%)
First ₦300,000	7%
Next ₦300,000	11%
Next ₦500,000	15%
Next ₦500,000	19%
Next ₦1,600,000	21%
Above ₦3,200,000	24%

</td></tr>
</table>

		Capital Gains Tax (CGT)
Capital Gains Tax (CGT)	General description	Capital gains tax accrues on an actual year basis and it pertains to all gains accruing to a tax payer from the disposal of chargeable assets
	Taxable entities and chargeable assets	Payable on capital gains accruing to any person, company or individual from the disposal of chargeable assets
		Chargeable assets: Option, debts and incorporeal property generally, any currency other than Nigerian currency, any form of property created by the person disposing of it or otherwise coming to be owned without being acquired, goodwill, copyrights, buildings, chattels etc. Options, debts, stocks and shares, Nigerian government securities, life assurance policies, main residence or dwelling house of an individual etc are exempted from capital gains tax
	Calculation of gain	Computation of capital gains tax is done by deducting from the sum received or recoverable the cost of acquisition to the person realizing the chargeable gain plus expenditure incurred on its improvement and expenses incidental to the realization of the asset. Premiums paid under a policy of insurance taken against any risk or damage to, or depreciation of or loss of an asset and expenses deductible under Companies Income Tax Act or Personal Income Tax Act are non-allowable deductions
		Rollover relief can be claimed in certain circumstances and for certain classes of asset
	Losses	No relief granted
	Tax rates	10% of the net capital gains

IV   WITHHOLDING TAXES (WHT)

WHT is an advance payment of income tax deductible at source on specified transactions. It can be applied as tax credit against income tax liability.

Transactions	Companies	Individuals
Dividend, Interest & Rent	10%	10%
Royalties	10%	5%
Commissions, consultancy, Professional & Management fees	10%	5%
Technical fees	10%	5%
Building, construction & related activities	2.5%*	5%
All types of contract of supplies & agency arrangements, other than sales in the ordinary course of business	5%	5%
Directors' fees	N/A	5%

* The 2.5% WHT rate does not apply on activities relating to survey, design and deliveries performed by companies.

Note: The rate of WHT on dividend, interest and royalty is reduced to 7.5% when paid to a corporate recipient resident in a treaty country. In the case of individuals, 7.5% is applied on dividend and interest and 5% on royalty.

Administration
- The currency in which the tax is to be paid is the currency in which the contracts, consultancy and agency arrangement were awarded and in which the tax was deducted.
- The payment should be accompanied with the schedule showing relevant information about the transaction.
- Payment for individuals should be made to the State Board of Inland Revenue (SBIR) where the individual resides, while that of companies should be to the Federal Inland Revenue Service (FIRS).
- The time within which the withholding tax is to be remitted to FIRS is 21 days from the date the duty to deduct arose. However, in practice, remittance is done 21 days following the end of the month in which the duty to deduct arose.
- Failure to deduct and remit withholding taxes due to FIRS carries a penalty of 10% pa and interest at Central Bank rate in addition to the principal tax due.
- Failure to remit withholding taxes due to the SBIR is a fine of ₦5,000 or 10% of tax due, whichever is higher in addition to the principal tax due and interest at bank lending rate.

V   INDIRECT TAXES

		Residents	Non-residents
Value Added Tax (VAT)		Value Added Tax (VAT) in Nigeria is a consumption tax that was instated by the VAT Act of 1993. VAT is charged on most goods and services provided in Nigeria and also on goods imported into Nigeria	Non-resident companies are expected to register with the VAT office using the address of the person or business that they are doing business with in Nigeria. They are also required to include VAT in their services to the person or business they are doing business with in Nigeria and the VAT is to be remitted in the currency of the contract
	General description	VAT is a consumption tax chargeable on the supply of taxable goods and services except items specifically stated as exempt or zero-rated	
	Entities obliged to deduct VAT at source	• Oil and gas companies including oil services companies • Government, government agencies and departments • Resident entities in respect of transactions with non-residents	
	Taxable activities	Any supply of taxable goods and services except items specifically stated as exempt or zero-rated	
	Zero-rated items	• Non-oil export • Goods and services purchased by diplomats • Goods purchased for humanitarian donor-funded projects	
	Exempted goods and services	• Medical and pharmaceutical products • Oil exports • Plants, machinery and goods imported for use in the export processing zones or free trade zones • Plants, machinery and equipment purchased for utilization of gas in downstream petroleum operations • Baby products • Basic food items • Books and educational materials • Tractors, ploughs and agricultural implements purchased for agricultural purposes • Fertilizers locally produced agricultural and veterinary medicine, farming machinery and farming transportation equipment • Medical services • Plays and performances conducted by educational institutions as part of learning • Services rendered by community banks, peoples banks and mortgage institutions • All exported services	

		Residents	**Non-residents**
Value Added Tax (VAT) - contd	Exemption by policy	Section 34(b) of the VAT Act allows the Minister of Finance powers to grant exemptions through fiscal policy measures. Some of the exemptions granted are: 1. Locally manufactured biscuits 2. Plant, machinery and equipment (including steel structures) for the manufacture of cement and allied products 3. Vegetable oil 4. Motorcycles (CKD)/Bicycle (SKDs) and their spare parts 5. Corporate bonds and government securities (10 years from 2 January 2012) 6. Commissions on transactions in the Nigeria Stock Exchange from 25 July 2014 (5 years from 25 July 2014)	
	Refund of VAT	Subject to certain conditions, the commissioner of VAT upon receipt of an application may pay VAT refunds	
	Tax liability	The tax liability is the excess of output VAT over input VAT in any reporting period	
	Tax rates	VAT is calculated at a flat rate of 5% on all chargeable supplies of taxable goods and services	
	Administrative obligations	Returns should be filed on or before the 21st day of the month following the month of transaction. The tax is administered by the FIRS	
Real Property Taxes		This generally varies with the value and location of the property, as well as the local government authority involved	
Stamp Duty		This is a tax levied on most legal instruments including agreements, awards, bonds, leases and receipts. It is levied at a normal rate on the transfer of shares or stocks. Stamp duty of 50k is now levied on all bank transactions above ₦1,000 (from 20 January 2016)	

Norway

(Kjell A. Nordli, BHL DA, kan@bhl.no)

I   MAIN LEGAL FORMS

Legal form / Characteristics	Partnership and Limited Liability Partnership (KS)	Private corporation (AS) and Public corporation (ASA)
Partners/shareholders • Number • Restrictions	• Two or more • None	• One or more • None
Directors	Generally managed by partners but may elect to have a board of directors	Managed by the board of directors and a general manager[1]
Establishment	Partnership agreement	Memorandum of incorporation, appointment of board members and auditor, registration with the Register of Business Entities (*Foretaksregisteret*)
Registration	The Register of Business Enterprises[2]	
Minimum capital	None	NOK30,000 for AS and NOK1m for ASA
Liability	Unlimited[3]	Limited to capital
Governance	Partners, partnership meeting and Board of Directors (if elected)	General Assembly, Company Assembly, Board of Directors and General Manager

---

1   A private corporation should have at least 1 director (board member). It is not necessary to appoint a general manager. A public corporation must have at least 3 board members and a general manager. If a private or public company is required to have a corporate assembly (a requirement when the number of employees exceeds 200), the number of board members should be at least 5.
2   Private and public limited companies are required to register with the Register of Business Enterprises within 3 months of formation as a condition for establishment of the company. Partnerships are also required to register but registration is not a condition for establishment. Companies and partnerships may also be required to register for VAT and in the Register of Employers and Employees.
3   For KS unlimited liability will apply to at least one partner. Other partners' liability may be limited to their capital.

Legal form / Characteristics	Partnership and Limited Liability Partnership (KS)	Private corporation (AS) and Public corporation (ASA)
Audit requirements[4]	Required[5]	Required[6]
Taxation	Transparent	Companies resident in Norway are liable to corporation tax

---

4 Audit is required for all companies and businesses except companies and businesses with operating income less than MNOK 5.
5 Required for KS if the general partner is a corporate body, and total assets are more than MNOK 20, or more than 10 FTEs (average). Required for unlimited partnerships when all of the partners are corporate bodies. Required for all partnerships with more than 5 participants, or if annual turnover is MNOK 5 or more.
6 Private corporations can unselect audit if

   • operating income is less than MNOK 5, and
   • total assets are less than MNOK 20, and
   • the average FTEs are fewer than 10 employees.

All three of the above criteria must be met to be exempt from the audit requirement. The exception does not apply if the limited company must prepare consolidated financial statements, or is a parent company.

II CORPORATION TAX

Description \ Legal Form	Resident corporation	Permanent establishment (PE)
General description	Norwegian corporation tax	
Taxable entities	Companies incorporated in Norway and/or foreign companies with central management and control located in Norway	PE located in Norway
Taxable income	Worldwide profits	Profits derived by the PE in Norway
Calculation of taxable profits	Accounting profit is adjusted for various tax items, including depreciations and non-deductible costs, to arrive at profits chargeable to corporation tax	
Interest payments	Deductible provided that funding arrangements are at arm's length	Deductible provided that funding arrangements are made at arm's length. Deduction limitation on intragroup interest when total net interest expense exceeds MNOK 5

Interest paid by a PE to its main office abroad is normally not tax deductible |
| Related party transactions | All related party transactions must take place on arm's-length basis | |
| Tax year, return and payment | Tax period normally coincides with accounting period. Accounting period normally follows the calendar year unless the company's parent company or the PE's main office applies a different accounting period

Tax return is due by 31 May in the year following the end of each accounting period

Advance tax payments to be made in equal instalments on 15 February and 15 April in the year following the tax year. Remaining tax to be paid within 3 weeks of the annual tax settlement (normally due in November) | |
| Capital gains and dividends | Capital gains are subject to corporation tax at normal rates

Capital gains arising on business assets may be entered over a profit and loss account whereby 20% of remaining balance is entered as income each year

Capital gains arising on shares (with origin within the EEA) are generally not taxable. Capital gains arising on shares with origin outside the EEA are taxable at normal rate[7]

3% of dividends on shares with origin within the EEA are taxable at normal rate. The remaining 97% are not taxable. Dividends on shares with origin outside the EEA area are taxable at normal rate | |

---

7 Capital gains arising on shares in limited companies or partnerships resident in Norway or any other country within the EEA are tax-free. This tax exemption only applies if the taxpayer is itself a limited company. Participation exemption rules apply to capital gains on shares in companies and partnerships resident outside of the EEA. Capital gains arising on shares in companies and partnerships resident in low tax jurisdictions outside the EEA are taxable at normal rates. Capital gains arising on shares in companies and partnerships resident in low tax jurisdictions within the EEA are taxable if the target company is not genuinely established and conducting business in the relevant EEA-country.

Legal Form / Description	Resident corporation	Permanent establishment (PE)
Losses	Losses are generally deductible for tax purposes	
	Losses arising on business assets must be entered over a profit and loss account whereby 20% of remaining balance is deductible each year	
	Losses arising on shares are deductible only to the extent a gain on the same shares would be taxable[8]	
	Net losses can be carried forward without time limit and offset against future profits arising from the same entity. Net losses may also be offset against income in other tax group companies through group contributions. Group contributions may only be distributed if the distributing company has sufficient equity and liquidity to distribute dividends	
Tax group	A group comprises a parent company and its more than 90% subsidiaries	
	Foreign entities with Norwegian PE can also be included in the group	
Tax rate	25%	

8   Losses arising on shares are not tax deductible to the same extent as capital gains are not taxable. There are certain differences as regards participation exemption rules concerning shares in companies and partnerships resident outside the EEA.

III   TAXES FOR INDIVIDUALS

<table>
<tr><td colspan="2"></td><th>Residents</th><th>Non-residents</th></tr>
<tr><td rowspan="8">Income Tax</td><td>General description</td><td colspan="2">Tax levied on the chargeable income of a chargeable person for a year of assessment</td></tr>
<tr><td>Taxable entities and taxable income</td><td>Individuals who are resident in Norway are liable to tax on their worldwide income</td><td>Individuals who are not resident in Norway are liable to tax on income from a Norwegian source, subject to provisions in double taxation treaties</td></tr>
<tr><td>Types of taxable income</td><td colspan="2"><ul><li>Property income</li><li>Trading income of a trade, profession or vocation</li><li>Savings and investment income</li><li>Employment income</li><li>Income from trusts or estates</li><li>Miscellaneous income – annual profits or gains not taxed elsewhere</li></ul></td></tr>
<tr><td>Calculation of income</td><td colspan="2"><ul><li>Employment – income/benefit received</li><li>Other income – accrual basis</li></ul></td></tr>
<tr><td>Tax year, tax assessment and tax payment</td><td colspan="2">The tax year follows the calendar year

Individual tax returns for each tax payer to be filed by 30 April, or 31 May if the tax payer has business income or participates in a partnership

Advance tax payments made in 4 instalments through the year if salary withholding tax is not sufficient to cover estimated taxes. Final taxes due in 2 instalments after the announcement of the tax assessment for the year in question (August or October)</td></tr>
<tr><td>Losses</td><td colspan="2">Net losses may be carried forward indefinitely</td></tr>
<tr><td>Tax rates</td><td colspan="2">Net income subject to 25% tax

Employment income and business profits exceeding certain threshold is subject to additional high bracket tax of 9% or 12%</td></tr>
<tr><td rowspan="6">Capital Gains Tax (CGT)</td><td>General description</td><td colspan="2" rowspan="6">Capital gains and losses are treated as part of ordinary net income. Norway does not levy any particular capital gains tax</td></tr>
<tr><td>Taxable entities and chargeable assets</td></tr>
<tr><td>Calculation of gain</td></tr>
<tr><td>Tax year, tax assessment and tax payment</td></tr>
<tr><td>Losses</td></tr>
<tr><td>Tax rates</td></tr>
</table>

		Domiciled	**Non-domiciled**
Inheritance Tax (IHT)	General description	Tax charged on a chargeable transfer of value made by a lifetime gift or estate on death	
	Taxable entities and chargeable assets	Inheritance tax is eliminated effective from 1 January 2014. The amendment has significance for inheritance and gifts given after 31 December 2013. No requirement to notify the Tax Administration of inheritance and gifts in 2014 or later	
	Calculation of charge		
	Taxable events		
	Allowances	Tax positions on inheritance or gifts will be transmitted by tax continuity. Tax continuity implies that the heir or gift recipient acquires the historical input value, as well as other tax positions related to the transferred asset. This will have an impact on a later sale[9]	
	Tax rates		

9 Property, leisure property, farms and forestry that could be sold tax free by the giver or the testator at the date of the gift or death date are exempt under the rules for tax continuity. The input value of residential and leisure property should be set at the market value at the date of transmission. For typical farm or forestry, the maximum input value can be set to ¾ of the property's estimated market value.

IV WITHHOLDING TAXES

Under domestic law	Payments to residents	Payments to non-residents
Dividends	Nil	25%
Interest	Nil	Nil
Royalties	Nil	Nil
On payments to artists and sportsmen/women	Nil[10]	15%[11]

Reduced rate available under the relevant Double Taxation Treaty					
Country	Dividend	Interest	Royalties	Mother/ Subsidiary	Criteria for reduced tax rate
Albania	15%	Nil	Nil	5%	25% ownership
Argentina	15%	Nil	Nil	10%	25% ownership
Australia	15%	Nil	Nil	5% 0	10% voting shares listed companies fulfilling conditions of article no 10
Austria	15%	Nil	Nil	0%	
Azerbaijan	15%	Nil	Nil	10%	30% ownership and investment in the country of minimum USD 100,000
Bangladesh	15%	Nil	Nil	10%	10% ownership
Barbados	15%	Nil	Nil	5%	10% ownership
Belgium	15%	Nil	Nil	25%	25% ownership
Benin	20%	Nil	Nil	20%	
Bosnia and Herzegovina	15%	Nil	Nil	15%	
Brazil	25%	Nil	Nil	25%	
Bulgaria	15%	Nil	Nil	5%	10% ownership
Canada	15%	Nil	Nil	5%	10% of voting shares
Chile	15%	Nil	Nil	5%	25% of voting shares
China	15%	Nil	Nil	15%	
Croatia	15%	Nil	Nil	15%	
Cyprus	5%	Nil	Nil	0%	10% ownership
Czech Republic	15%	Nil	Nil	0%	10% ownership
Denmark	15%	Nil	Nil	0%	10% ownership
Egypt	15%	Nil	Nil	15%	
Estonia	15%	Nil	Nil	5%	25% ownership
Faroe Islands	15%	Nil	Nil	0%	10% ownership
Finland	15%	Nil	Nil	0%	10% ownership

10 Salary withholding tax may be applicable if the artist or sportsman is considered to be employed by the organiser of the arrangement.

11 Artists and sportsmen resident in an EEA member country may opt for ordinary taxation as a non-resident taxpayer.

Reduced rate available under the relevant Double Taxation Treaty					
Country	Dividend	Interest	Royalties	Mother/ Subsidiary	Criteria for reduced tax rate
France	15%	Nil	Nil	0%	25% share capital
				5%	>10%, <25% share capital
Gambia	15%	Nil	Nil	5%	25% ownership
Georgia	10%	Nil	Nil	5%	10% ownership
Germany	15%	Nil	Nil	0%	25% ownership
Greece	20%	Nil	Nil	20%	
Greenland	15%	Nil	Nil	5%	10% ownership
Hungary	10%	Nil	Nil	10%	
Iceland	15%	Nil	Nil	0%	10% ownership
India	10%	Nil	Nil	10%	
Indonesia	15%	Nil	Nil	15%	
Ireland	15%	Nil	Nil	5%	10% ownership
Israel	15%	Nil	Nil	5%	50% voting shares
Italy	15%	Nil	Nil	15%	
Ivory Coast	15%	Nil	Nil	15%	
Jamaica	15%	Nil	Nil	15%	
Japan	15%	Nil	Nil	5%	25% voting shares
Kazakhstan	15%	Nil	Nil	5%	10% ownership
Kenya	25%	Nil	Nil	15%	25% voting shares
Latvia	15%	Nil	Nil	5%	25% ownership
Lithuania	15%	Nil	Nil	5%	25% ownership
Luxembourg	15%	Nil	Nil	5%	25% ownership
Macedonia, Republic of	15%	Nil	Nil	10%	25% ownership
Malawi	15%	Nil	Nil	5%	
Malaysia	Nil	Nil	Nil	0%	
Malta	15%	Nil	Nil	0%	10% ownership, 24 months
Mexico	15%	Nil	Nil	0%	25% ownership
Montenegro	15%	Nil	Nil	15%	
Morocco	15%	Nil	Nil	15%	
Nepal	15%	Nil	Nil	5%	25% share capital
				10%	>10%, <25% share capital
Netherlands	15%	Nil	Nil	0%	10% ownership
Netherlands Antilles	15%	Nil	Nil	5%	25% ownership
New Zealand	15%	Nil	Nil	15%	
Nordic countries	15%	Nil	Nil	0%	10% ownership
Pakistan	15%	Nil	Nil	15%	
Philippines	25%	Nil	Nil	15%	10% ownership
Poland	15%	Nil	Nil	0%	10% ownership, 24 months

Reduced rate available under the relevant Double Taxation Treaty					
Country	Dividend	Interest	Royalties	Mother/ Subsidiary	Criteria for reduced tax rate
Portugal	15%	Nil	Nil	5%	10% ownership the last 12 months
Qatar	15%	Nil	Nil	5%	10% ownership
Republic of Korea	15%	Nil	Nil	15%	
Romania	10%	Nil	Nil	10%	
Russia	10%	Nil	Nil	10%	
Senegal	16%	Nil	Nil	16%	
Serbia	15%	Nil	Nil	5%	25% ownership
Sierra Leone	5%	Nil	Nil	0%	50% voting shares
Singapore	15%	Nil	Nil	5%	25% ownership
Slovakia	15%	Nil	Nil	5%	25% ownership
Slovenia	15%	Nil	Nil	0%	15% ownership
South Africa	15%	Nil	Nil	5%	25% ownership
Spain	15%	Nil	Nil	10%	25% ownership
Sri Lanka	15%	Nil	Nil	15%	
Sweden	15%	Nil	Nil	0%	10% ownership
Switzerland	15%	Nil	Nil	0%	10% ownership
Tanzania	20%	Nil	Nil	20%	
Thailand	15%	Nil	Nil	10%	10% ownership
Trinidad and Tobago	20%	Nil	Nil	10%	25% voting shares
Tunisia	20%	Nil	Nil	20%	
Turkey	15%	Nil	Nil	5%	20% ownership assuming dividends are exempted from tax in the other country
Uganda	15%	Nil	Nil	10%	25% ownership
Ukraine	15%	Nil	Nil	5%	25% ownership
United Kingdom	15%	Nil	Nil	0%	10% ownership
United States	15%	Nil	Nil	15%	
Venezuela	10%	Nil	Nil	5%	10% ownership
Vietnam	15%	Nil	Nil	5% 10%	70% ownership >25%, <70% share capital
Zambia	15%	Nil	Nil	15%	
Zimbabwe	20%	Nil	Nil	15%	25% ownership

Note: the above rates are only available provided the specific Treaty criteria are satisfied. It is possible that lower rates than those shown above may be available provided that certain criteria are satisfied. As treaties will not be identical, guidance should be sought in all cases.

V   INDIRECT TAXES

		Residents	Non-residents
Value Added Tax (VAT)	General description	Tax on the supply of goods and services	
	Entities obliged to levy VAT	Any individual, partnership, corporation or other body, which carries out taxable activities in Norway, subject to turnover limit of NOK50,000 Other situations may also arise, eg distance selling and sale of assets	
	Taxable activities	Supply of goods and services, import of goods, etc	
	Taxable activities – zero-rated (examples)	• Export of goods and services • Deliveries of goods to offshore petroleum installations	
	Exemptions (examples)	• Transactions related to the sale or lease of any property located in Norway (option to register for VAT available for letting of commercial property) • Banking and insurance services • Educational services • Certain welfare services including hospital and medical care services	
	Refund of VAT	VAT paid on supplies and services is deductible as input tax, if incurred in the course or furtherance of a taxable business There is no credit for input tax incurred which relates to a business activity exempt from VAT Where mixed supplies occur (taxable and exempt supplies), subject to de minimis provisions, input tax must be apportioned and recovered according to a partial exemption method	Refund available for business that does not have a taxable place of business in Norway, provided the business would have been subject to VAT in Norway if the business had been connected to a taxable place in Norway Strict time limits apply
	Tax liability	Normally the supplier of goods and services is responsible for charging VAT Reverse charge for certain supplies of goods and services (eg consultancy services received from businesses established outside Norway)	
	Tax rates	Standard rate 25% Food articles 15% Passenger transport, hotel rooms, movie theatres 10%	

		Residents	Non-residents
	Administrative obligations	Formal requirements concerning business records and invoices Bi-monthly self-assessment VAT return plus bi-monthly payment of any VAT liability to tax authorities (smaller businesses may apply for annual VAT return and VAT payment) VAT groups are allowed subject to certain requirements VAT identification number must be shown on all invoices issued	Registration for VAT purposes, if making supplies of goods and services in Norway Appointment of fiscal tax representative obligatory
Real Property Taxes		Municipal property tax in effect in some municipalities	
Stamp Duty		2.5% stamp duty on transfer of title to real property	

Pakistan

(Sarfraz Mahmood, Riaz Ahmad and Company, sm@racopk.com)

I MAIN LEGAL FORMS

Legal form / Characteristics	Partnership and Limited Liability Partnership (LLP)	Private corporation (Ltd) and Public corporation (Plc)
Partners/ shareholders • Number • Restrictions	• Minimum two partners and limits the number of its partners to 20, except for professional firms • Draft Notification for establishment of LLP in Pakistan is pending for approval	• One shareholder/member in a Single Member Company Private Limited (SMC-PVT) • Other private companies should have at least two members and limits the number of its members to 50 not including persons who are in the employment of the company. Prohibits any invitation to the public to subscribe for the shares, if any, or debentures of the company • Plcs which are not listed on Stock Exchange should have at least three members. No restriction on maximum number of members • Listed Plcs should have at least seven members. No restriction on maximum numbers
Directors	N/A	• Minimum one director in SMC-PVT • Minimum two directors in other private companies • Minimum three directors in Plcs which are not listed on Stock Exchange • Minimum seven directors in a Listed Plc. No restriction on maximum number of directors
Establishment	Partnership Deed	Companies are established under the Companies Ordinance 1984
Registration	Registrar of Firms	Both private and public companies are registered with Registrar of Companies, Securities and Exchange Commission of Pakistan (SECP)
Minimum capital	Not required	Different requirements for different types of companies Every shareholder must have at least one ordinary share

Legal form Characteristics	Partnership and Limited Liability Partnership (LLP)	Private corporation (Ltd) and Public corporation (Plc)
Liability	Unlimited	The liability of members in limited companies is limited up to their investment in share capital of the company
Governance	Registrar of Firms	The companies are governed by SECP in accordance with the provisions of Companies Ordinance 1984
Audit requirements	Not Mandatory	• Private companies with share capital having Pak Rupees 3 million or more are required to appoint an auditor who is a member of the Institute of Chartered Accountants of Pakistan (ICAP) • Public or a private company which is a subsidiary of a public company is required to appoint an auditor who is a member of ICAP • For public companies listed on stock exchanges, auditors should have a satisfactory quality control review rating from ICAP • All private limited companies having paid-up capital of Rupees 7.5 million or more are required to file annual audited accounts and directors' report with the SECP
Taxation	Partnership profits are assessed to income tax under Income Tax Ordinance, 2001. Share in profit of each partner is exempt	Profit of a company is subject to tax under the Income Tax Ordinance, 2001. Dividend income of shareholder is also taxed at the rate of 12.5% for the tax year 2015 and onwards. For further detail, visit our website at www. racopk.com

II CORPORATION TAX

Description \ Legal form	Resident corporation	Permanent establishment (PE)
Taxable entities	Corporations incorporated in Pakistan	PE located in Pakistan
Taxable income	Worldwide profits with consideration of double taxation treaties	Profits derived by PE in Pakistan
Calculation of taxable profits	Accounting profit is adjusted for various tax add-backs and allowances to arrive at profits chargeable to tax	
Interest payments	Interest payments can be claimed as expense in computing the taxable income In the case of a foreign controlled resident company other than banking company, foreign debt to foreign equity ratio should not exceed 3:1. Otherwise, deduction on account of interest payment will be disallowed on that part of the debt which exceeds the ratio of 3:1	
Related party transactions	Arm's length basis	
Tax year, return and payment	• Tax year is a period of 12 months normally ending on 30 June • Universal Self Assessment • Tax return is due on 31 December if income year-end falls between 1 January and 30 June, otherwise due on 30 September • The estimated tax liability for the year is to be paid in advance in four instalments as given below: *Quarter* *Due date of instalment* September on or before 25 September December on or before 25 December March on or before 25 March June on or before 15 June • Balance amount of tax is payable at the time of filing of return of income or within 30 to 45 days of receipt of tax demand notice if assessment is amended by the Commissioner Inland Revenue	
Capital gains	Gains on movable assets are treated as income. However, gains on capital assets (other than immoveable properties and shares listed on stock exchanges) held for more than one year are restricted to 75%. Gain on disposal of securities and immovable property is charged to tax at fixed rate as separate block of income	
Losses	• Net operating tax losses may be carried forward for 6 years and set off against taxable income • Depreciation losses may be carried forward without any restriction of number of years	
Tax group	Wholly owned subsidiaries and holding company can file a single return	
Tax rate	For banking companies – 35% For small and *modaraba* companies – 25% For other companies – 31%	

III   TAXES FOR INDIVIDUALS

		Residents	Non-residents
Income Tax	General description	Tax levied on the taxable income of a taxpayer for a tax year	
	Taxable entities and taxable income	Residents are taxed on their worldwide income	Non-residents are taxed on income derived in Pakistan subject to relevant double tax treaties
	Types of taxable income	• Salary • Income from property • Income from business • Capital gains • Income from other sources (interest, sale of goodwill, dividend, royalty, annuities, etc)	
	Tax year, tax assessment and tax payment	• Tax year is a period of 12 months from 1 July to 30 June • Universal Self Assessment • Tax is payable at the time of filing of return of income or within 30 to 45 days of receipt of tax demand notice if assessment is amended by the Commissioner Inland Revenue • Tax return is due on 31 August for salaried persons • Tax return is due on 30 September for other cases	
	Losses	• Business losses can be set off against any other income except income from salary and property for the same year. Thereafter, tax losses may be carried forward for the next 6 years and set off against taxable income • Depreciation losses may be carried forward for indefinite period	
	Tax rates	Business individuals and association of persons: • Income exceeding Rs. 400,000 is subject to tax at graduated rates ranging from 7% to 35% Salaried individuals: • Income exceeding Rs. 400,000 is subject to tax at graduated rates ranging from 2% to 30%	
Capital Gains Tax (CGT)	General description	Gains on disposal of capital assets, immovable property, securities	
	Taxable entities and chargeable assets	Taxable residents	
	Calculation of gain	Gain is calculated by subtracting cost of the asset from consideration received on disposal of the asset. Net gains on disposal of capital assets in the same year are chargeable to tax. If the asset is held for more than one year the gain is reduced to 75%	

		Residents	Non-residents
Capital Gains Tax (CGT) – contd	Tax year, tax assessment and tax payment	• Tax year is a period of 12 months from 1 July to 30 June • Tax is payable at the time of filing of return of income or within 30 to 45 days of receipt of tax demand notice if assessment is amended by the Commissioner Inland Revenue • Tax return is due on 30 September	
	Losses	Capital losses may be carried forward but not more than 6 years and can be set off against capital gains only	
	Tax rates	• Gains arising on disposal of immovable property are charged to tax at 10% of net gain if holding period of property is one year, at 7.5% where holding period of property is more than one year but not more than two years, and at 5% where holding period of property is more than two years but not more than three years. However, 0% tax rate is applicable if holding period is more than three years • Gains arising on disposal of shares of companies listed on stock exchanges and securities (corporate debt securities, all kinds of debt instruments issued by any corporation registered in Pakistan, Government debt securities, all kinds of debt instruments issued by Federal, Provincial Governments, local authorities or other statutory bodies, etc) are charged to tax at 15% if holding period is less than 12 months, at 12.5% if holding period is between 12 and 24 months, at 7.5% if holding period is between two and four years, and 0% if holding period is more than four years	
		Domiciled	**Non-domiciled**
Inheritance Tax (IHT)	General description	There is no IHT in Pakistan	

IV   WITHHOLDING TAXES

	Payments to residents	Payments to non-residents[1]
Dividends	7.5%,12.5%	7.5%,12.5%
Interest	10%	10%
Royalties	Nil	15%
On payments to artists and sportsmen	10%	10%

Reduced rate available under the relevant Double Taxation Treaty			
Country	Dividends	Interest	Royalties
Austria	10%, 15%	10%, 15%	10%
Azerbaijan	10%	10%	10%
Bahrain	10%	10%	10%
Bangladesh	10%, 15%	10%, 15%	15%
Belarus	10%, 15%	10%	15%
Belgium	10%, 15%	10%, 15%	15%, 20%
Bosnia-Herzegovina	10%	20%, 10%	15%
Canada	10%, 15%, 20%	15%, 10%, 25%	15%, 20%
China	10%	10%	12.5%
Denmark	15%, 10%	15%, 10%	12%
Egypt	15%, 30%	15%	15%
Finland	12%, 15%, 20%	10%, 15%	10%
France	12%, 15%, 20%	10%, 15%	10%
Germany	10%, 15%	10%, 20%	10%
Hungary	15%, 20%	15%	15%
Indonesia	10%, 15%	15%	15%
Iran	5%	10%	10%
Ireland	Exempt, 10%	Exempt, L, 10%	Nil, Exempt, 15%
Italy	10%, 15%, 25%	10%, 30%	15%, 30%
Japan	10%, 5%, 7.5%	10%	10%
Jordan	10%	10%	10%
Kazakhstan	10%, 12.5%, 15%	10%, 12.5%	15%
Kuwait	10%	10%	10%
Lebanon	10%	10%	15%, 7.5%
Malaysia	10%, 15%, 25%	10%, 15%	15%
Malta	10%, 15%	10%	10%
Mauritius	10%	10%	12.5%
Morocco	10%	10%	10%
Netherlands	10%, 20%	10%, 15%, 20%	5%, 15%
Nigeria	10%, 12.5%, 15%	10%, 15%	15%
Norway	10%, 15%	10%	12%, 15%
Oman	10%, 12.5%	10%	12.5%, 15%
Philippines	10%, 15%, 25%	10%, 15%	15%, 25%
Poland	15%	L	15%, 20%
Portugal	10%, 15%	10%	10%, 15%

---

1   Reduced rates of withholding tax may apply where there is an appropriate double tax treaty.

Reduced rate available under the relevant Double Taxation Treaty			
Country	Dividends	Interest	Royalties
Qatar	10%, 5%	10%	15%, 10%
Republic of Korea	10%	12.5%	10%
Romania	10%	10%	12.5%, 15%
Saudi Arabia	10%, 5%	10%	15%, 10%
Singapore	10%, 12.5%, 15%	10%, 12.5%	10%, 15%
South Africa	10%, 15%	10%	10%, 15%
Sri Lanka	10%, 15%	10%	15%, 20%
Sweden	10%, 15%	10%, 15%	10%, 15%
Switzerland	10%, 20%	10%	10%, 15%
Syria	10%	10%	15%, 8%, 10%
Tajikistan	10%, 5%	10%	10%, 15%
Thailand	10%, 15%, 25%	25%, 10%	15%, 10%, 20%
Tunisia	10%	10%, 13%	10%, 15%
Turkey	10%, 15%	10%	10%, 15%
Turkmenistan	10%	10%	10%, 15%
United Arab Emirates	10%, 15%	10%	12%, 15%
United Kingdom	10%, 15%, 20%	10%, 15%	12.5%, 15%
United States	Exempt	Exempt	Exempt
Uzbekistan	10%	10%	15%
Vietnam	10%, 15%	10%, 15%	15%
Yemen	10%	10%	10%, 15%

L: Local rates apply.

Note: the above rates are only available provided the specific Treaty criteria are satisfied. It is possible that lower rates than those shown above may be available provided that certain criteria are satisfied. As treaties will not be identical, guidance should be sought in all cases.

V   INDIRECT TAXES

		Residents	Non-residents
Value Added Tax (VAT)	General description	Tax on the supply of goods and services	
	Entities obliged to levy VAT	In Pakistan, VAT is commonly known as Sales Tax and is levied on importers, manufacturers, retailers and wholesalers. Federal Government has powers to levy sales tax on goods, and Provincial Governments have powers to levy sales tax on services	
	Taxable activities	Taxable activity involves supply of goods, rendering of services, business, trade, manufacture and distributors	
	Taxable activities – zero-rated (examples)	Exports of goods and supplies of certain prescribed goods	
	Exemptions (examples)	Certain prescribed goods including supply of live animals, meat of bovine animals	
	Refund of VAT	Excess of input tax over output tax on account of zero-rated local supplies or exports is refundable within 45 days of filing of refund claim	
	Tax liability	Output tax minus input tax	
	Tax rates	• Standard rate = 17% Different Provinces of Pakistan have different rates for sales tax on services • Exports = 0%	
	Administrative obligations	Chief Commissioner, Commissioner, Additional and Deputy Commissioner Inland Revenue, etc	
Real Property Taxes		Real property tax rates are based on gross annual rental value of land / building used for residential / commercial purposes	
Stamp Duty		Following instruments are chargeable with stamp duty: • Every instrument mentioned in the schedule of the Stamp Act, 1899 executed in Pakistan including bonds, affidavit, agreement, title deeds, conveyance, etc • Bill of exchange otherwise payable on demand • Promissory notes made or drawn outside Pakistan but presented for payment in Pakistan, etc • Any instrument for the sale, transfer or other disposition, either absolutely or by way of mortgage or otherwise, of any ship or vessel, or any part, interest, share or property of or in any ship or vessel registered under the Merchant Shipping Act, 1894 or under Act XIX of 1838, or the Registration of Ships Act, 1841, as amended by subsequent Acts	

Panama

(Bartolomé Mafla H, Nexia Auditores (Panama), bmafla@nexiapanama.com)

I   MAIN LEGAL FORMS

Legal form / Characteristics	Partnership and Limited Liability Partnership (LLP)	Private corporation (Ltd) and Public corporation (Plc)
Partners/shareholders • Number • Restrictions	Partnership: no limit LLP: only shareholders are allowed	No limit
Directors	Two as a minimum	Three as a minimum
Establishment	Articles of Incorporation	
Registration	Before a Public Notary and registered at the Public Registry	
Minimum capital	US$5,000	US$10,000
Liability	Limited to capital	Only limited to unpaid subscribed capital. In general shareholders are not liable for the company's debts. The only liability a shareholder may have is limited to the extent of any unpaid shares of stock if they were subscribed by the shareholder but never paid
Governance	A legal representative needs to be appointed	
Audit requirements	Audited financial statements for all businesses	
Taxation	Corporation tax	

II   CORPORATION TAX

Description \ Legal Form	Resident corporation	Permanent establishment (PE)
General description	Corporation tax	Income tax derived by PE in Panama
Taxable entities	Anyone deriving Panamanian sourced income	
Taxable income	Income from goods and services provided in Panama	
Calculation of taxable profits	Taxable profits are defined as the higher of: • Gross income minus deductions (traditional method) or Presumptive income tax • Gross income minus 95.33% (4.67%) Only applies to Businesses with revenues exceeding US$1.5m (see Tax rate below)	
Interest payments	Normally deductible	
Related party transactions	Study of transfer pricing by transactions with foreign related parties	
Tax year, return and payment	Three months after taxation year end; on request, extension is granted for one month	
Capital gains	10% of earnings, with down payment of 5% of sales price; can choose to make 5% of sales price the final liability	
Losses	May be carried forward for 5 following years and used up to 20% per year	
Tax group	No consolidation is possible	
Tax rate	25% on the higher of: • Net income or • Gross income minus 95.33% (approximately 1.1675% of gross income) whichever is greater	

III TAXES FOR INDIVIDUALS

		Residents	Non-residents
Income Tax	General description	Subject to income tax on income of US$11,000 and up	Non-residents pay income tax on about 50% of what was received, and are taxed at the individual taxation rates
	Taxable entities and taxable income	Individuals and legal entities are taxable	Individuals and legal entities are taxable
	Types of taxable income	Every kind of income derived from any source	
		A very extensive definition of income has been traditionally taken by the Tax Authorities	
	Calculation of income	Aggregate income	
	Tax year, tax assessment and tax payment	Three months after taxation year-end is the deadline to file tax returns	
		An automatic extension (2 months) is granted if requested before such date	
	Losses	May be carried forward 5 years and used up to 20% in each of these years	
	Tax rates	0–25% for individuals	0–25% for individuals
Capital Gains Tax (CGT)	Taxable entities and chargeable assets	All assets other than inventory	
	Calculation of gain	Ordinary income if more than 10 sales are made of a given asset per year	
		When an asset other than inventory is sold the buyer withholds 5% of the purchase price	
		The seller decides whether to be taxed either at 10% on the net capital gain realised or considers the 5% withholding at source as a final payment	
		Should the 10% option be taken, a refund may be claimed due to losses and/or the 10% rate on the net capital gain being lower than the 5% withholding	
	Tax year, tax assessment and tax payment	Immediately upon sale for assets other than inventory	
	Losses	Should the 10% option be taken, a refund may be claimed due to losses and/or the 10% rate on the net capital gain being lower than the 5% withholding	
	Tax rates	10% of gain or 5% of selling price	
		Domiciled	**Non-domiciled**
Inheritance Tax (IHT)	General description	No inheritance taxes	
	Taxable entities and chargeable assets		
	Calculation of charge		
	Taxable events		
	Allowances		
	Tax rates		

IV   WITHHOLDING TAXES

Under domestic law	Payments to residents	Payments to non-residents
Dividends	10%	Nil
Interest	Nil	12.50%
Royalties	Nil	12.50%
On payments to artists and sportsmen	Nil	12.50%

Reduced rate available under the relevant Double Taxation Treaty			
Country	Dividends	Interest	Royalties
Barbados	7.5%	7.5%	7.5%
Czech Republic	10%	10%	10%
France	15%	5%	5%
Ireland	5%	5%	5%
Israel	15%	15%	15%
Italy	10%	10%	10%
Korea, Republic of	15%	5%	10%
Luxembourg	15%	5%	5%
Mexico	7.5%	10%	10%
Netherlands	15%	5%	5%
Portugal	15%	10%	10%
Qatar	6%	6%	6%
Singapore	5%	5%	5%
Spain	10%	5%	5%
United Arab Emirates	5%	5%	5%
United Kingdom	15%	5%	5%

Where the domestic rate is lower than the treaty rate the domestic rate usually applies.

Note: the above rates are only available provided the specific Treaty criteria are satisfied. It is possible that lower rates than those shown above may be available provided that certain criteria are satisfied. As treaties will not be identical, guidance should be sought in all cases.

These are the maximum rates established in the treaties with these countries. In all cases it is a credit to the country of origin.

V   INDIRECT TAXES

		Residents	Non-residents
Value Added Tax (VAT)	General description	Indirect taxes are paid in accordance with value of product or service, custom tax, production, sales and consumption taxes and stamp duty	
	Entities obliged to levy VAT	Any taxpayers with gross receipts in excess of US$36,000	
	Taxable activities	Services rendered in Panama and goods (other than intangibles and real property) whose passage of title occurs in Panama	
	Taxable activities – zero-rated (examples)	No zero rate is applicable since refunds are given through coupons usable to pay VAT. This certificate is limited to: • taxpayers exclusively dedicated to the pharmaceutical industry • taxpayers whose only activity is the food industry	
	Exemptions (examples)	• Goods from nature • Food • Medicine • Intangibles and their use • Services whose final consumer is located abroad • Restaurants not selling alcohol	
	Refund of VAT	Not possible	Not possible
	Tax liability	Any consumer must pay VAT on goods purchased	
	Tax rates	• 7% (general rate) • 10% alcohol, hospitality • 15% cigarettes	
	Administrative obligations	Filing a monthly VAT return This obligation is fulfilled every 3 months by liberal professionals	
Real Property Taxes		From 0.75% to 2.10%	
Stamp Duty		US$1 for every US$1,000 invoiced in activities not covered by VAT	

Peru

(Florentino Urbizagástegui Pacheco, Urbizagastegui & Asociados S Civil R L, furbizagasteguip@nexiaperu.com.pe)

I MAIN LEGAL FORMS

Legal form / Characteristics	Partnership and Limited Liability Partnership (LLP)	Private corporation (Ltd) and Public corporation (Plc)
Partners/shareholders • Number • Restrictions	• Two or more • None	• Two or more • None
Directors	Two or more	Two or more
Establishment	Partnership deed	Articles of Incorporation
Registration	Recorded at the Public Registry	
Minimum capital	None	
Liability	The liability of the contracting parties is determined by the General Corporations Law and Articles of Incorporation, depending on the type of entity	
Governance	The governing bodies are determined by the General Corporations Law and Articles of Incorporation, depending on the type of entity	
Audit requirements	According to the standards of the Peruvian Securities Commission (SMV), publicly traded companies or entities established under the General Companies Act and those companies or entities whose annual income from the sale of goods or provision of services or whose total assets as at the end of the 2015 period are equal to or greater than 5,000 Peruvian Tax Units (UIT) must present audited annual financial statements[1] Starting from the 2016 period, companies or entities whose annual income from the sale of goods or provision of services or whose total assets as at the end of the 2016 period are equal to or greater than 3,000 UIT will be obliged to present audited annual financial statements The UIT applicable to determine this obligation will be the UIT in force on 1 January of the year after the respective financial period[2]	

1 For the 2014 period, companies whose annual income from the sale of goods or provision of services or whose total assets as at the end of the 2014 period are equal to or greater than 10,000 Peruvian Tax Units – UIT (equivalent to S/. 38,500,000.00) are obliged to present audited annual financial statements.
2 The Tax Units to determine the obligation to present audited financial statements for the 2014 period is the tax unit for the 2015 period, which is S/. 3,850 (equivalent to US$1,290).

Legal form Characteristics	Partnership and Limited Liability Partnership (LLP)	Private corporation (Ltd) and Public corporation (Plc)
Taxation	Corporate taxes on worldwide income	Corporate taxes on worldwide income
Usage	No restrictions	No restrictions

II CORPORATION TAX

Legal form / Description	Resident corporation	Permanent establishment (PE)
General description	Corporation tax	
Taxable entities	Corporations resident in Peru, branches of companies and banks	PE trading in Peru
Taxable income	Worldwide profits with considerations for double taxation treaties	Income arising in Peru
Calculation of taxable profits	Accounting profit is adjusted for various tax add-backs and allowances to arrive to profits chargeable to corporation tax (PCTCT)	
Interest payments	Interest payments to related parties are not deductible when the debt to equity ratio exceeds 3:1 limit	
Related party transactions	All related party transactions must take place on an arm's length basis	
Tax year, return and payment	Mandatory 1 January to 31 December tax year. Return and payment within the 3 months following the end of the tax year	
Capital gains	Includes those gains produced by rent, sub-leasing, assignment of goods, interest on capital placements, royalties, etc	
Losses	Losses can be carried forward for 4 years, being used up whenever profit arises	
Tax group	None	
Tax rate	In order to promote the revitalisation of the economy, the Peruvian Government has established a gradual reduction from the 30% rate for Third Category Income Tax in force as at 31 December 2014, as follows: Tax Period: Rate: 2015–2016 28% 2017–2018 27% 2019 onwards 26%	

III TAXES FOR INDIVIDUALS

<table>
<tr><td colspan="2"></td><th>Residents</th><th>Non-residents</th></tr>
<tr><td rowspan="8">Income Tax</td><td>General description</td><td colspan="2">Tax levied on the chargeable income of a chargeable person for a year of assessment</td></tr>
<tr><td>Taxable entities and taxable income</td><td>Residents are taxed on their worldwide income</td><td>Certain types of income arising in Peru</td></tr>
<tr><td>Types of taxable income</td><td colspan="2"><ul><li>Property income (usually rent)</li><li>Income from capital investment (interest, sale of goodwill, dividends, royalties, annuities)</li><li>Income from business activities</li><li>Employment from personal services or pensions</li></ul></td></tr>
<tr><td>Calculation of income</td><td colspan="2">Based on the consolidated income from capital, income as an independent professional and as an employee</td></tr>
<tr><td>Tax year, tax assessment and tax payment</td><td colspan="2">Mandatory 1 January to 31 December tax year

Payments on account are made monthly. The final accounting and payment is made within the 3 months following the end of each tax year</td></tr>
<tr><td>Losses</td><td colspan="2">Losses on real estate are offset against future income during the 4 years following occurrence</td></tr>
<tr><td>Tax rates[7]</td><td colspan="2"><ul><li>Net capital income (gross income less 20% for first[3] and second[4] category income) is taxed at 6.25%</li><li>Net income from work (for fourth[5] and fifth[6] category income), according to the following scale:</li><li>Up to 27 UIT[7] = 15%</li></ul>27–54 UIT = 21%

More than 54 UIT = 30%</td></tr>
</table>

3 First category income: income resulting from leasing or subleasing property, temporary lease or assignment of real estate and movable assets.

4 Second category income: interest from placement of capital, as well as any capital instruments or readjustments, whatever their denomination and method of payment may be. Royalties: Definite or temporary assignment of goodwill, brands, patents, royalties or similar aspects. Capital gains, any gain or income from transactions made with derived financial instruments; income from regular transfers, redemptions or surrenders of shares and interest that represents capital, investment shares, certificates, securities, bonds and commercial papers, as the case may be.

5 Fourth category income: income obtained by an independent individual who exercises any profession, art, science, trade or activities that are not expressly included in the third category. Performing the duties of a company director, trustee, agent, business manager, executor or similar activities.

6 Fifth category income: income earned by employees including public servants, elected or not, such as wages, salaries, allowances, emoluments, premiums, travel allowances, bonuses, incentives, Christmas bonuses, commissions, compensation in cash or benefits. Profit sharing, whether from annual assignment or any other benefit awarded.

7 The UIT (Tax Unit) is the basis for measuring the tax scale in Peru, and for 2014 it amounts to PEN 3,800 or $1,310.

		Residents	Non-residents
Capital Gains Tax (CGT)	General description	Normally taxed as income	
	Taxable entities and chargeable assets		
	Calculation of gain		
	Tax year, tax assessment and tax payment		
	Losses		
	Tax rates		
		Domiciled	**Non-domiciled**
Inheritance Tax (IHT)	General description	No inheritance taxes	
	Taxable entities and chargeable assets		
	Calculation of charge		
	Taxable events		
	Allowances		
	Tax rates		

IV   WITHHOLDING TAXES

Under domestic law	Payments to residents	Payments to non-residents[8]
Dividends	A gradual increase of the current rate of 4.1% applicable to the sharing of third category dividends and any other form of profit sharing by legal entities residing in the country has been established according to the following scale: Range: Rate: 2015–2016 6.8% 2017–2018 8.0% 2019 onwards 9.3% The new established rates will be applied to the distribution of dividends that are adopted or made available in cash or in kind starting 1 January 2015 However, the 4.1% rate will continue to be applied to accumulated results or other assessable dividends obtained until 31 December 2014 that form part of the distribution of dividends	
Interest	30%	30%[9] 4.99%[10]
Royalties	Nil	30%
On payments to artists and sportsmen	Nil	In the case of live shows with the participation of non-resident artists and performers, 15% In the case of sportsmen, they are included in the regime of Section III

---

8   Reduced rates of withholding tax may apply where there is an appropriate double tax treaty.

9   Article 54 of the Income Tax Law establishes that non-domiciled natural people and undivided estates are subject to tax on their income from a Peruvian source at the following rate: interest, when paid or credited by a third-category income generator that is domiciled, incorporated or established in the country is 30%.

10 Article 56 of the Income Tax Law establishes that tax for non-domiciled legal entities is determined by applying the following rates: interest from external credit – 4.99%, whenever the following requirements are met: (1) for cash loans, the entry of foreign currency into the country must be accredited; and (2) the credit must not accrue annual simple interest higher than the predominant preferential rate in the market of original plus three points.

Reduced rate available under the relevant Double Taxation Treaty			
Country	Dividends	Interest	Royalties
Andean Community[13]	Local source taxation applies	Local source taxation applies	Local source taxation applies
Brazil[11]	15%[12]	15%	15%
Canada[14]	15%[12]	15%	15%
Chile[14]	15%[12]	15%	15%
Korea[15]	15%	15%	15%
Mexico[15]	15%	15%	15%
Portugal[15]	15%	15%	15%
Switzerland[15]	15%	15%	15%

Note: the above rates are only available provided the specific Treaty criteria are satisfied. It is possible that lower rates than those shown above may be available provided certain criteria are satisfied. As treaties will not be identical, guidance should be sought in all cases.

11 In the case of dividends, a 10% rate of the net amount of dividends is applied if the effective beneficiary is a corporation that directly or indirectly controls no less than 25% of the voting shares of the company that pays said dividends, and 15% of the gross amount of the dividends in all other cases.
12 In force since 1 January 2004.
13 Applicable since 1 January 2004.
14 Applicable since 1 January 2005.
15 Applicable from January 2015.

V   INDIRECT TAXES

<table>
<tr><td></td><td></td><th>Residents</th><th>Non-residents</th></tr>
<tr><td rowspan="11" style="writing-mode: vertical-rl;">Value Added Tax</td><td>General description</td><td colspan="2">Tax on the supply of goods and services</td></tr>
<tr><td>Entities obliged to levy VAT</td><td colspan="2">• Central government
• Ministry of Economy and Finance
• National Superintendent of Tax Administration</td></tr>
<tr><td>Taxable Activities[16]</td><td colspan="2">All entities, companies, branches, etc that carry out third category income activities</td></tr>
<tr><td>Taxable activities – zero-rated (examples)</td><td colspan="2">• Sales of real estate
• Providing services within the country
• Construction contracts
• First sale of real estate made by builder
• Import of goods</td></tr>
<tr><td>Exemptions (examples)</td><td colspan="2">• Export of goods
• Export of services indicated in the law
• Transfer of goods resulting from business reorganisations</td></tr>
<tr><td>Refund of VAT</td><td colspan="2">• Advance recovery regimen
• Credits in favour of exporter
• Drawbacks</td></tr>
<tr><td>Tax liability</td><td colspan="2">Those corporations and individuals that carry out taxable activities</td></tr>
<tr><td>Tax rates</td><td colspan="2">Standard rate = 18%</td></tr>
<tr><td>Administrative obligations</td><td colspan="2">Monthly payments of a definitive nature</td></tr>
<tr><td colspan="2">Real Property Taxes</td><td colspan="2">Monthly payments of a definitive nature</td></tr>
<tr><td colspan="2">Stamp Duty</td><td colspan="2">Monthly payments of a definitive nature</td></tr>
</table>

---

16 Third category income is considered as income from trade, industry and other activities expressly contemplated by law.

Philippines

(Francisco G. Tagao, Maceda Valencia & Co., ftagao@mvco.com.ph)

I MAIN LEGAL FORMS

Legal form / Characteristics	Partnership and Limited Liability Partnership (LLP)	Private corporation (Ltd) and Public corporation (Plc)
Partners/shareholders • Number • Restrictions	Minimum of 2 persons, at least 1 must be a general partner	Incorporators should not be less than 5 but not more than 15 persons. The majority should be residents of the Philippines
Directors	Management by partners	Elected from among the stockholders of the corporation. Every director must own at least 1 share of the capital stock of the corporation
Establishment	Partnership deed	A corporation begins from the date the Securities and Exchange Commission issues a certificate of incorporation
Registration	Securities and Exchange Commission	Securities and Exchange Commission
Minimum capital	PHP3,000, unless the pertinent law or regulation provides for a higher capital	PHP5,000, unless the pertinent law or regulation provides for a higher capital
Liability	Liability of a general partner is unlimited. For a limited partner, only to the extent of his contribution	Directors who wilfully and knowingly vote for or assent to patently unlawful acts of the corporation, or who are guilty of gross negligence or bad faith in directing the affairs of the corporation, or acquire any personal or pecuniary interest in conflict with their duty as such directors, shall be liable jointly and severally for all damages resulting therefrom suffered by the corporation, its stockholders and other persons
Governance	Partners	Shareholders/directors

Characteristics \ Legal form	Partnership and Limited Liability Partnership (LLP)	Private corporation (Ltd) and Public corporation (Plc)
Audit requirements	Audited financial statements are required if quarterly sales exceed PHP150,000	Audited financial statements are required if quarterly sales exceed PHP150,000
Taxation	Partnerships are generally taxed as corporations and the share of the partners in the net profits of the partnerships is taxable as dividends. There are exceptions to being treated as a corporation, such as a professional partnership, joint venture or consortium formed for the purpose of undertaking construction projects (subject to certain limitations) or engaging in energy-related activities pursuant to a service contract with the government. In such cases the partnership is not taxable as a corporation, but the partners are subject to income tax of their share in the net profits of the partnership	Taxed on worldwide profits

II CORPORATION TAX

Legal Form / Description	Resident corporation[1]	Permanent Establishment (PE)[2]
General description	Corporate income tax	
Taxable entities	Domestic corporations organised in and existing under the laws of the Philippines	A PE located within the Philippines
Taxable income	Worldwide profits	Profits attributable to the PE in the Philippines
Calculation of taxable profits	Gross income xx Less allowable deductions yy Taxable income zz	
Interest payments	Interest incurred is allowed as deduction from gross income subject to a reduction of 33% of the interest income subject to final tax or disallowance of interest between related parties if the conditions for disallowance are met	
Related party transactions	Must adhere to the arm's length principle. There are now formal transfer pricing methodologies, procedures and requirements adopted by the government	
Tax year, return and payment	Tax year – calendar or fiscal year Annual and quarterly (for the first three quarters) corporate income tax return Quarterly prepayments, final payment based on annual return (paid on or before the 15th day of the fourth month following the close of the taxable year)	
Capital gains	Taxed as part of corporate income, except capital gains on certain transactions subject to special tax rates	
Losses	Net operating loss can be carried forward for the next 3 consecutive years. No carry back is possible	
Tax group	Taxes are imposed on individual corporate entities, and not on consolidated entities	
Tax rate	Normally 30%, except for certain kinds of income as discussed below	

1 The term resident corporation should be understood as being limited to domestic corporations organised and existing under the laws of the Philippines to differentiate it from permanent establishment of a foreign corporation.

2 The term 'permanent establishment' should be understood to include foreign corporations authorised or licensed to do business (by establishing a branch or as a resident foreign corporation) as well as foreign corporations although not licensed to do business but actually engaged in trade or business in the Philippines for which tax treaty relief has been obtained from the Philippine Internal Revenue Service that it has a permanent establishment under the pertinent tax treaty between the country of which it is a resident and the Philippines. Absent the tax treaty relief or licence to do business, such foreign corporations are treated as non-resident foreign corporations taxable on gross income without any allowable deduction. However, the Supreme Court has issued another decision that there is no need to obtain prior tax treaty relief to avail of the benefits of a tax treaty. Tax treaties must be honoured by the Philippine government and failure to secure such tax treaty relief would only subject the tax treaty resident to penalties for failure to obtain tax treaty relief. Such recent Supreme Court decision is already final as it is ruled against the motion for reconsideration filed by the Philippine government. Notwithstanding this recent Supreme Court decision, the Philippine Internal Revenue is still requiring the filing of a tax treaty relief application, not necessarily prior to the availment of the tax treaty benefits, in order to claim the tax treaty benefits. With this development, the treaty applicant might have to go to the courts to claim the tax treaty benefits in the absence of an approved tax treaty relief from the tax authorities.

III   TAXES FOR INDIVIDUALS

<table>
<tr><th></th><th></th><th>Residents</th><th>Non-residents</th></tr>
<tr><td rowspan="9">Income Tax</td><td>General description</td><td colspan="2">Tax levied on the total taxable income of a taxable person for the year of assessment</td></tr>
<tr><td>Taxable entities and taxable income</td><td>Resident citizens are taxable on their worldwide income. Resident aliens are taxable only on their Philippine source income</td><td>Non-resident citizens and non-resident aliens are taxed only on their taxable income derived from all sources within the Philippines</td></tr>
<tr><td>Types of taxable income</td><td colspan="2">Taxable income for individuals includes but is not limited to the following: 1) compensation for services (eg fees, salaries, wages, commissions); 2) income derived from the conduct of trade or business or the exercise of profession; 3) gains derived from dealings in property; 4) interests; 5) rents; 6) royalties; 7) dividends; 8) annuities; 9) prizes and winnings</td></tr>
<tr><td>Calculation of income</td><td colspan="2">Generally cash for salaried employees; accrual or modified cash basis if running a business or self-employed</td></tr>
<tr><td>Tax year, tax assessment and tax payment</td><td colspan="2">Tax year: calendar (1 January to 31 December)

Tax payment: for salaries – monthly withholding by the employer

Tax payment: for those engaged in business or self-employed individuals – quarterly prepayments (for the first three quarters), final payment based on annual return (paid on or before the 15th day of April of each year)

Tax assessment: after the return is filed, it is examined and assessed if the correct amount of tax is not paid</td></tr>
<tr><td>Losses</td><td colspan="2">Generally, losses can be offset against taxable income of the following 3 years</td></tr>
<tr><td>Tax rates</td><td colspan="2">

Income (PHP)	Tax (%)
Less than 10,000	5%
Over 10,000 but less than 30,000	500 + 10% of the excess over 10,000
Over 30,000 but less than 70,000	2,500 + 15% of the excess over 30,000
Over 70,000 but less than 140,000	8,500 + 20% of the excess over 70,000
Over 140,000 but less than 250,000	22,500 + 25% of the excess over 140,000
Over 250,000 but less than 500,000	50,000 + 30% of the excess over 250,000
Over 500,000	125,000 + 32% of the excess over 500,000

</td></tr>
</table>

		Residents	Non-residents
Capital Gains Tax (CGT)	General description	Gains derived from the disposal of assets not otherwise subject to individual income tax or corporate income tax	
	Taxable entities and chargeable assets	Residents taxable on gains on assets located in the Philippines derived in the period	
	Calculation of gain	The excess of the selling price from disposals of capital assets over their costs	
	Tax year, tax assessment and tax payment	Reported in the tax return on an annual basis by the seller. Sales of real property and shares must be reported and the tax paid within 30 days of sale	
	Losses	Losses set off against gains arising in the period	
	Tax rates	• Real properties treated as capital assets: 6% of the gross selling price or zonal value, whichever is higher • For shares of stock in a domestic corporation not listed and traded in the local stock exchange, on the net capital gains: – Not over PHP100,000 – 5% – Any amount in excess of PHP100,000 – 10% • For shares listed and traded through the local stock exchange, there is a 0.5% transaction tax based on the gross selling price, other than sales by a dealer in securities • For all types of capital assets other than those stated above, the tax rate is graduated ranging from 5% to 32% for individuals and 30% for corporations	

		Domiciled	Non-domiciled
Inheritance Tax (IHT) (Estate Tax)[3]	**General description**	Tax charged on the estate on death or on certain lifetime gifts	
	Taxable entities and chargeable assets	• Real or immovable property, wherever located • Tangible personal property, wherever located • Intangible personal property, wherever located	• Real or immovable property located in the Philippines • Tangible personal property located in the Philippines • Intangible personal property with a situs in the Philippines
	Calculation of charge	Net Estate Tax is calculated based on the fair market value of the properties at the time of the deceased's death, less allowances and deductions	
	Taxable events	Upon death of the deceased	
	Allowance	The current fair market value of the family home not to exceed PHP1,000,000	

Tax rates — If the net estate is:

Over	But not over	The tax shall be	Plus	Of the excess over
	PHP200,000	Exempt		
PHP200,000	PHP500,000	PHP0	5%	PHP200,000
PHP500,000	PHP2,000,000	PHP15,000	8%	PHP500,000
PHP2,000,000	PHP5,000,000	PHP135,000	11%	PHP2,000,000
PHP5,000,000	PHP10,000,000	PHP465,000	15%	PHP5,000,000
PHP10,000,000		PHP1,215,000	20%	PHP10,000,000

3 No inheritance tax is imposed in the Philippines but an estate tax is imposed. The tax is imposed on the deceased, whether resident or non-resident in the Philippines at the time of death, on all property wherever situated, except that, in the case of a non-resident who at the time of his/her death was not a citizen of the Philippines, only that part of the entire gross estate which is situated in the Philippines is subject to estate tax.

IV   WITHHOLDING TAES

Under domestic law	Payments to residents	Payments to non-residents
Dividends	10% Nil for resident corporations	30%
Interest	20%	30%
Royalties	25%	30%
On payments to artists and sportsmen	15%	25%

Reduced rate available under the relevant Double Taxation Treaty			
Country	**Dividends**	**Interest**	**Royalties**
Australia	15% / 25%	10% / 15%	15% / 25%
Austria	10% / 25%	10% / 15%	10% / 15%
Bahrain	10% / 15%	10%	10% / 15%
Bangladesh	10% / 15%	15%	15%
Belgium	10% / 15%	10% / 15%	15%
Brazil	15% / 25%	10% / 15%	15% / 25%
Canada	15% / 25%	10% / 15%	25%
China	10% / 15%	10%	15%
Czech Republic	10% / 15%	10%	10% / 15%
Denmark	10% / 15%	10%	15%
Finland	15% / 30%	10% / 15%	15% / 25%
France	10% / 15%	10% / 15%	15%
Germany	10% / 15%	10% / 15%	10% / 15%
Hungary	15% / 20%	15%	15%
India	15% / 20%	10% / 15%	15% / 30%
Indonesia	15% / 20%	15%	15% / 25%
Israel	10% / 15%	10%	15%
Italy	15%	10% / 15%	15% / 25%
Japan	10% / 15%	10%	10% / 15%
Kuwait	10% / 15%	10%	20%
Malaysia	15%	10% / 15%	15% / 25%
Netherlands	10% / 15%	10% / 15%	10% / 15%
New Zealand	15%	10%	15%
Nigeria	12.5% / 15%	15%	20%
Norway	15% / 25%	15%	10% / 25%
Pakistan	15% / 25%	10% / 15%	10% / 25%
Poland	10% / 25%	10% / 15%	15% / 25%
Qatar	10% / 15%	10%	15%
Republic of Korea	15% / 25%	10% / 15%	10% / 15%
Romania	10% / 15%	10% / 15%	10% / 15% / 25%
Russia	15%	15%	15%
Singapore	15% / 25%	10% / 15%	15% / 25%
Spain	10% / 15%	10% / 15%	10% / 15% / 20%
Sweden	10% / 15%	10%	15%
Switzerland	10% / 15%	10%	15%
Thailand	15%	10% / 15%	15% / 25%

Reduced rate available under the relevant Double Taxation Treaty			
Country	Dividends	Interest	Royalties
United Arab Emirates	10% / 15%	10%	10%
United Kingdom	15% / 25%	10% / 15%	15% / 25%
United States of America	20% / 25%	10% / 15%	15% / 25%
Vietnam	10% / 15%	15%	15%

Note: The above rates are only available provided the specific Treaty criteria are satisfied. It is possible that lower rates than those shown above may be available provided that certain criteria are satisfied. As treaties are not identical, guidance should be sought in all cases.

V   INDIRECT TAXES

		Residents	Non-residents
Value Added Tax (VAT)	General description	VAT is a tax on the supply of goods and services	
	Entities obliged to levy VAT	Any person who, in the course of trade or business, sells, barters or exchanges goods or property or engages in the sale or exchange of services are obliged to pay VAT where: • their gross sales or receipts for the past 12 months, other than those that are exempt from VAT, have exceeded PHP1,919,500 effective 1 January 2012 • there are reasonable grounds to believe that their gross sales or receipts for the next 12 months, other than those that are VAT exempt, will exceed PHP1,919,500 effective 1 January 2012	
	Taxable activities	Generally, all types of goods and services	
	Taxable activities – zero-rated (examples)	A zero rate applies to the export of goods and services, foreign currency denominated sale and sale to persons or entities deemed tax-exempt under special law or international agreement	
	Exemptions (examples)	The following are exempt from VAT: • Sale or importation of agricultural and marine food products in their original state • Sale or importation of fertilizers, seeds, livestock and poultry feeds • Services by agricultural contract growers and milling for others • Medical, dental, hospital and veterinary services except those rendered by professionals Educational services rendered by private educational institutions duly accredited by the Department of Education • Sales by agricultural cooperatives • Lending activities by credit or multi-purpose cooperatives • Sale of real properties not primarily held for sale to customers or held for lease in the ordinary course of business • Sale, importation or lease of passenger or cargo vessels and aircraft • Importation of life-saving equipment, safety and rescue equipment and communication and navigational safety equipment used for shipping transport operations • Importation of fuel, goods and supplies engaged in international shipping or air transport operations • Services of banks and non-bank financial intermediaries performing quasi-banking functions	
	Refund of VAT	By way of tax credit or cash refund only on input VAT attributable to zero-rated or effectively zero-rated sales or upon cancellation of VAT registration	
	Tax liability	The liability is that of the supplier but the burden of paying the VAT could be passed on to the buyer or customer	
	Tax rate	12%	
	Administrative obligations	Precise accounting and documentation required	
Real Property Taxes		Levied by the provincial, city and municipal governments depending on the use of the land	

	Residents	Non-residents
Stamp Duty	A tax on certain documents, instruments, loan agreements and papers evidencing the acceptance, assignment, sale or transfer of an obligation, right or property. Imposed at either a fixed rate or at ad valorem rates	

Poland

(Katarzyna Klimkiewicz-Deplano, Advicero Tax Sp. z o.o. kklimkiewicz@ advicero.eu, www.advicero.eu)

I   MAIN LEGAL FORMS

Legal form / Characteristics	Spólka jawna (RP – Registered Partnership) and spólka komandytowa (LP – Limited Partnership)	Sp. z o.o. (LLC – private corporation) and SA (PLC – public corporation)
Partners/ shareholders • Number • Restrictions	• A minimum of two individuals or legal persons • None	• One or more individuals or legal persons • The only restriction states that a Limited Liability Company (LLC) and PLCPLC cannot be established solely by another single-member LLC
Directors	RP: partners LP: general partner and limited partner	LLC: Board of Directors PLC: Board of Directors and supervisory board (no less than three people)
Establishment	The partnership is established upon its registration Notarial deed	Registration in the National Court Register Notarial deed
Registration	In the National Court Register	
Minimum capital	No restrictions	LLC: PLN 5,000[1] PLC: PLN 100,000[2]
Liability	RP: Unlimited liability LP: Limited to capital except for the general partner	Limited to capital

---

1   The par value of one share at least PLN 50.
2   The par value of one share at least PLN 0.01.

Legal form / Characteristics	Spólka jawna (RP – Registered Partnership) and spólka komandytowa (LP – Limited Partnership)	Sp. z o.o. (LLC – private corporation) and SA (PLC – public corporation)
Governance	RP: Every partner has the right to represent the partnership Every partner has the right and obligation to manage the partnership's affairs LP: General partner; limited partner can represent only as a plenipotentiary and has no right to manage partnership affairs unless the Articles of Association provide otherwise	Board of Directors conducts the company's affairs and is authorised to represent the company
Audit requirements	No audit requirement, unless in the preceding financial year at least two of the following criteria were met: • the total assets amount to at least €2.5m • the net revenue amounts to at least €5m • the annual average number of full-time employees amounted to at least 50 people	No audit requirement for LLC, unless in the preceding financial year two of the following criteria were met: • the total assets amount to at least €2.5m • the net revenue amounts to at least €5m • the annual average number of full-time employees amounted to at least 50 people PLC: The financial statement is required to be audited and published every year
Taxation	Transparent[3]	Corporation income tax
Usage	Suited for small-scale service provision or production Limited partnership is a form of organisation that is used by professionals who want to limit their liability for partnership debts	LLC: Suited for small- and medium-scale ventures that do not need to pool capital from a large group of investors PLC: Mainly intended for large-scale ventures

---

3 Personal income tax or corporate income tax for partners.

II CORPORATION TAX

Legal form / Description	Resident corporation	Permanent establishment (PE)
General description	Tax on income of legal persons and organisational units with legal personality. Corporate income tax does not apply to: • revenue earned on agricultural activity, with the exception of income from special branches of agricultural production • revenue earned on forestry activities within the limits of the Forestry Act • revenue earned on activities, which cannot constitute the subject of a legally effective contract	
Taxable entities	CT applies to all legal entities, including: • corporations, • corporations under organization, • 'organizational units with no corporate status' (with the exception of partnerships) which conduct business activities, • foreign entities with no corporate status, provided that are treated as corporations and subject to unlimited tax liability in their home countries • limited joint-stock partnerships	PE located in Poland
Taxable income	Worldwide income	Income derived by a PE in Poland
Calculation of taxable profits	Taxable profit is based on accounting profit adjusted under the tax law	
Interest payments	Generally, interest may be considered tax deductible when paid or capitalized Thin capitalization rules apply (two possible methodologies): • to loans granted by a related party (ie all direct and indirect shareholders having at least 25% share participation) in case of interest on indebtedness exceeding debt-to-equity (1:1) ratio; • alternatively (solution chosen by taxpayer): to all loans granted by both related and unrelated companies (in this case, special calculation of interest based on (i) the value of assets and (ii) the reference interest rate of the National Bank of Poland should be prepared)	

Legal form / Description	Resident corporation	Permanent establishment (PE)
Related party transactions	Starting mostly from 1 January 2017, new regulations regarding subject as well as entity-based scope of TP documentation, thresholds and types of documentation, shall come into force. These are: • modification of the definition of related parties – thresholds of capital share shall increase from 5% to 25% • exemption from the documentation requirement for entities with revenues or costs less than €2m in the previous year • obligation to prepare TP documentation for transactions which have a significant impact on the taxpayer's business activity • new types of transaction on which documentation obligation exists (eg cash pooling agreements, joint venture agreements) • obligation to prepare benchmarking analyses for some transactions performed by entities with revenues or costs above €10m • new types of TP documentation depending on the overall level of revenues or costs of a taxpayer • confirmation through a signed statement, to be filed by a competent tax authority, that the documentation requirements were fulfilled (the statement should be submitted no later than within the date for submission of the annual CIT return) • pursuant to the statement of Ministry of Finance – beginning from 1 July 2016, intensification of tax audits regarding transfer pricing issues	
Tax year, return and payment	Tax year – calendar year or different business year Annual return filed within 3 months after the end of the tax year Tax advance payments due monthly/quarterly.[4] Simplified tax advance payments possible upon certain conditions	
Capital gains	Capital gains are taxable at regular tax rates	
Losses	Losses may be carried forward for 5 years, up to 50% of the loss may be set off in each year. Loss carry back is not allowed	
Tax group	Resident companies with an average share capital of at least PLN 1m may form a tax group. A tax group must be formed for a period of at least 3 years	
Tax rate	Standard rate of 19% Decreased tax rate of 15% applicable to income earned by taxpayers whose revenues (gross, with VAT) did not exceed €1.2m in the previous tax year and new taxpayers in the tax year in which they commenced economic activity Penalty tax rate of 50% may be applied for profit adjustment in relation to transaction concluded with related parties (transfer pricing)	

4   Quarterly tax payments are beneficial for small entities (small entity with gross turnover for the previous financial year of less than the Polish zloty equivalent of €1.2m).

III TAXES FOR INDIVIDUALS

<table>
<tr><th></th><th></th><th>Residents</th><th>Non-residents</th></tr>
<tr><td rowspan="8">Income Tax</td><td>General description</td><td colspan="2">Tax is assessed on the income of natural persons</td></tr>
<tr><td>Taxable entities and taxable income</td><td>Individuals whose place of residence is in Poland are liable to tax on worldwide income (unlimited tax liability)</td><td>Non-residents are liable to tax on income arising in Poland, subject to provisions in double taxation agreements</td></tr>
<tr><td>Types of taxable income</td><td colspan="2"><ul><li>Employment income</li><li>Income deriving from self-employment in recognised professions</li><li>Other self-employment income, except agriculture</li><li>Income deriving from certain non-mainstream types (known as special sectors) of agriculture, such as heated greenhouses, beekeeping, fur farming, battery farming of poultry, etc</li><li>Income deriving from real estate (including assigning and granting leases and subleases)</li><li>Capital gains and income deriving from other property rights</li><li>Saving and investment income (eg bonds, shares, deposits)</li></ul></td></tr>
<tr><td>Calculation of income</td><td colspan="2"><ul><li>Income is determined by earnings minus costs. Income reduction by payment to the social security insurance</li><li>The tax may be reduced by the national health insurance premium</li></ul>Income deriving from more than one source is added together and subject to taxation. However, there are some exceptions to this rule that refer to the following:<ul><li>revenue (income), which is subject to lump-sum taxation</li><li>income which is subject to flat-rate tax</li></ul></td></tr>
<tr><td>Tax year, tax assessment and tax payment</td><td colspan="2">Tax year – calendar year

During the tax year, taxpayers or tax remitters are obliged to make advance payments for income tax (by the 20th day of the following month for the preceding month) and, after the end of the given tax year, taxpayers pay the tax due in a final amount (ie not later than by 30 April of the following year)

Tax return – by 30 April of the following year; joint tax return for spouses possible</td></tr>
<tr><td>Losses</td><td colspan="2">Losses may be carried forward for five years. Only 50% of the loss may be set off in each year and only for the same sources of income. No carry back is allowed</td></tr>
<tr><td>Tax rates</td><td colspan="2"><ul><li>Personal allowance (tax-free earnings) – depending on the actual income up to PLN 6,600 (in case of income exceeding PLN 127,000, no tax-free earnings available)</li><li>Progressive tax rate<ul><li>18% for income up to PLN 85,528 minus PLN 556.02 (free of tax)</li><li>32% for income over PLN 85,528</li></ul></li><li>Flat tax rate 19% (optional for entrepreneurs)</li><li>Savings and investment income – 19%</li></ul></td></tr>
<tr><td rowspan="2">Capital Gains Tax (CGT)</td></tr>
<tr><td>General description</td><td colspan="2">Capital gains such as interest, dividends, income from capital funds, income from sale of shares are subject to a 19% flat rate tax</td></tr>
</table>

		Domiciled	Non-domiciled
Inheritance Tax (IHT)	General description	Tax charged on a chargeable transfer of value originated by estate on death	
	Taxable entities and chargeable assets	Estate worldwide	Estate situated in Poland
	Calculation of charge	Tax is levied on the net market value of all assets received	
	Taxable events	Estates on death	
	Allowances	Depending on the relationship of the parties. There are four different kinds of relationship: • without limit of value of transfer for spouses, parents and children (also adopted children), grandparents, grandchildren, brothers and sisters and step-parents • PLN 9,637 or PLN 7,276 (other family member, depending on the relation) • PLN 4,902 for others	The transfer is not taxable if the transfer takes place in Poland but neither the transferor nor the transferee is a Polish citizen or resident of Poland
	Tax rates	3–20%	N/A

IV   WITHHOLDING TAXES

Under domestic law	Payments to residents[6]	Payments to non- residents[5,6]
Dividends	19%	19%
Interest	19%	20%
Royalties	19%	20%
On payments to artists and sportsmen	19%	20%

Reduced rate available under the relevant Double Taxation Treaty			
Country	Dividends	Interest	Royalties
Albania	10%	10%	5%
Armenia	10%	5%	10%
Australia	15%	10%	10%
Austria	15%	5%	5%
Azerbaijan	10%	10%	10%
Bangladesh	15%	10%	10%
Belarus	15%	10%	Nil
Belgium	15%	5%	5%
Bosnia & Herzegovina (Yugoslavian Treaty)	15%	10%	10%
Bulgaria	10%	10%	5%
Canada	15%	10%	10%
Chile	15%	15%	15%
China	10%	10%	10%
Croatia	15%	10%	10%
Cyprus	5%	5%	5%
Czech Republic	5%	5%	10%
Denmark	15%	5%	5%
Egypt	12%	12%	12%
Estonia	15%	10%	10%
Finland	15%	5%	5%
France	15%	Nil	10%
Georgia	10%	8%	8%
Germany	15%	5%	5%
Greece	19%	10%	10%
Hungary	10%	10%	10%
Iceland	15%	10%	10%
India	10%	10%	15%
Indonesia	15%	10%	15%
Iran	7%	10%	10%
Ireland	15%	10%	10%

5   Reduced rates foreseen for withholding tax or exemptions may apply where there is an appropriate double tax treaty.
6   Payments of dividends, interest and royalties are reduced to nil following the fulfilment of several conditions.

Reduced rate available under the relevant Double Taxation Treaty			
Country	Dividends	Interest	Royalties
Israel	10%	5%	10%
Italy	10%	10%	10%
Japan	10%	10%	10%
Jordan	10%	10%	10%
Kazakhstan	15%	10%	10%
Korea, Republic of	10%	10%	5%
Kyrgyzstan	10%	10%	10%
Kuwait	5%	5%	15%
Latvia	15%	10%	10%
Lebanon	5%	5%	5%
Lithuania	15%	10%	10%
Luxembourg	15%	5%	5%
Macedonia	15%	10%	10%
Malaysia	15%	15%	15%
Malta	10%	5%	5%
Mexico	15%	15%	10%
Moldova	15%	10%	10%
Mongolia	10%	10%	5%
Montenegro (Yugoslavian Treaty)	15%	10%	10%
Morocco	15%	10%	10%
Netherlands	15%	5%	5%
New Zealand	15%	10%	10%
Norway	15%	5%	5%
Pakistan	15%	20%	20%
Philippines	15%	10%	15%
Portugal	15%	10%	10%
Romania	15%	10%	10%
Russia	10%	10%	10%
Saudi Arabia	5%	5%	10%
Serbia (Yugoslavian treaty)	15%	10%	10%
Singapore	10%	5%	5%
Slovakia	10%	10%	5%
Slovenia	15%	10%	10%
South Africa	15%	10%	10%
Spain	15%	Nil	10%
Sri Lanka	15%	10%	10%
Sweden	15%	Nil	5%
Switzerland	15%	5%	5%
Syria	10%	10%	18%
Tajikistan	15%	10%	10%
Thailand	19%	10%	15%
Tunisia	10%	12%	12%
Turkey	15%	10%	10%

Reduced rate available under the relevant Double Taxation Treaty			
Country	Dividends	Interest	Royalties
Ukraine	15%	10%	10%
United Arab Emirates	5%	5%	5%
United Kingdom	10%	5%	5%
United States	15%	Nil	10%
Uzbekistan	15%	10%	10%
Vietnam	15%	10%	15%
Zimbabwe	15%	10%	10%

Note: the above rates are only available provided the specific Double Tax Treaty criteria are satisfied. It is possible that lower rates than those shown above may be available provided that certain criteria are satisfied. As treaties will not be identical, guidance should be sought in all cases. According to the provisions foreseen in the most of Double Tax Treaties the relevant reduction of rate / exemption from withholding taxation could be applied solely to the payments of interest/royalties being a subject to withholding tax if a transaction takes place on arm's length basis.

V   INDIRECT TAXES

		Residents	Non-residents
Value Added Tax (VAT)	General description	There are three indirect taxes in Poland: tax on goods and services (VAT), excise duty, game tax	
	Entities obliged to levy VAT	Legal entities, individuals in business and organisational units without a legal entity who: • are required to pay customs duty • make intra-Community acquisitions of goods • are the recipients of the services supplied by the taxpayers whose registered office or fixed place of business is located outside the territory of Poland • acquire goods, if the goods are supplied on the territory of Poland by a taxpayer who has no registered office, fixed place of business on the territory of Poland • are the purchasers of new vehicles The exception to this rule applies to entities whose estimated annual turnover does not exceed PLN 150,000 (in case of specific business activities the said exemption could be not applied)	
	Taxable activities	Supply of goods for consideration inside the territory of Poland defined as the transfer of economic ownership Rendering services for consideration inside the territory of Poland The following activities are also taxable: • a commitment to refrain from performing activities, or to tolerate activities or situations • the transfer of intangible rights • the provision of services in accordance with an order issued, a public government organ or an organ acting on its behalf, or an order arising by virtue of the law • the free of charge rendering of services for the taxpayer's personal needs or the personal needs of its current and former employees, partners, shareholders, etc	
	Taxable activities – zero-rated (examples)	• Export of goods and services • Intra-Community supply transactions • Some international transportation services	
	Exemptions (examples)	• Financial and Banking services • Land which has not been built on, other than building land or land designated for development • Buildings or their part (in specified cases) • Educational services • Development of technology	
	Refund of VAT	• Usually within 60 days from submission of tax return • In some cases these period could be shorted to 25 days – certain statutory requirements should be fulfilled (eg in general, all purchase invoices should be paid through a bank account of the taxpayer, the entity which applies for VAT refund should be registered as active VAT taxpayer for at least 12 month, and it should have filed all due VAT returns) • In case that a tax payer does not declare any output VAT in a given return, the VAT refund is executed within 180 days	

Value Added Tax (VAT) – contd	Tax liability	• Normally the supplier of goods and services is responsible for charging VAT • Reverse charge for certain supplies of goods and services (eg factoring services received from businesses established outside Poland)
	Tax rates	The standard tax rate is 23%. There are three reduced rates[7]
	Administrative obligations	• Monthly or quarterly self-assessment VAT return • Monthly VAT payments (for small entities, possible quarterly payments) • Obligation to formal registration before the execution of first activity being subject to VAT (in practice, possible also backward registration, but not in case of cross-border supplies of goods) • Formal requirements concerning invoices • VAT identification number must be shown on all invoices • Recapitulative statement • In case of purchase invoices not paid within 150 days from payment deadline, no possibility to deduct a relevant input VAT
Real Property Taxes		Annual tax rates are determined by resolutions of the local government and may be different in each administrative area The following constitute the tax base: • for land – its area • for buildings and their parts – their usable area • for other types of constructions (so-called structures) – their value However, the tax charges in the year 2017 cannot be higher than: • PLN 0.89 /square metre – for land • PLN 22.86 /square metre – for buildings used for business activities • PLN 0.75 / square metre – for residential buildings • 2% of its value – for other types of constructions (structures)
Stamp Duty		Entrepreneurs are obliged to pay stamp duty due on activities associated with certain transactions with the authorities. The most common are applications, certificates, permits (licences), etc and other filings associated with registration of legal documents There are many different charges, eg VAT registration – PLN 170

Nexia International does not accept liability for any loss arising from any action taken, or omission, on the basis of this publication. Professional advice should be obtained before acting or refraining from acting on the contents of this publication. Membership of Nexia International, or associated umbrella organizations, does not constitute any partnership between members, and members do not accept any responsibility for the commission of any act, or omission to act by, or the liabilities of, other members.

Nexia International is the trading name of Nexia International Limited, a company registered in the Isle of Man. Company registration number: 53513C. Registered office: 2nd floor, Sixty Circular Road, Douglas, Isle of Man, IM1 1SA

---

7   8% rate refers mainly to some goods connected with passenger transportation, groceries, services connected with housing construction, hotel services.
5% rate is applied to the sale of certain unprocessed or semi-processed products of agriculture, specialist books.
0% rate refers to export of goods and intra-Community supply of goods.

Portugal

(Pedro Alves, and Ricardo Coelho, Nexia, CPLA & Associados, SROC, Lda, pedro.alves@nexia.pt, ricardo.coelho@nexia.pt)

I MAIN LEGAL FORMS

Characteristics / Legal form	Partnership and Limited Liability Partnership (LLP)	Private corporation (Ltd) and Public corporation (Plc)
Partners/shareholders • Number • Restrictions	General partnership (*Sociedade em Nome Colectivo*): • Minimum number of partners: two Limited partnership (*Sociedade em Comandita*): • Minimum number of partners: two, or five if capital is represented by shares	Single Person Private Limited Liability (*Sociedade Unipessoal por Quotas*): • Number of quotaholders: one Private Limited Liability (*Sociedade por Quotas*): • Minimum number of quotaholders: two Corporation (*Sociedade Anónima*) (SA): • Minimum number of shareholders: five
Directors	Management attributed to the partners or to entities appointed as directors, who may or may not be partners	• Director: management attributed to one or more directors, who may or may not be quotaholders General meeting takes the relevant decisions and the directors take day-to-day decisions • Unitary System: Board of Directors, or a single director overseen by an Audit Committee or an Individual Qualified Auditor (*Conselho Fiscal* or *Fiscal Único*) • Dual system: management powers shared between a single manager or a Board with a maximum number of five managers and an Advisory Board (*Conselho Geral*), overseen by an individual qualified auditor

Legal form / Characteristics	Partnership and Limited Liability Partnership (LLP)	Private corporation (Ltd) and Public corporation (Plc)
Establishment	Minimal	Mainly small and medium-sized companies adopt this legal form. SA tends to be for larger/listed companies
Registration	Companies have to register at: • Registry of Company Names (*Registo Nacional de Pessoas Colectivas*) • Commercial Company Registrar (*Registo Comercial*) • Tax authorities declaring the start of activity	
Minimum capital	No minimum share capital	No minimum capital (*Sociedade por Quotas*) €50,000 (SA only)
Liability	General partnership: unlimited Limited partnership: unlimited for individual partners and unlimited for partners that have the legal form of Private Limited Liability or Corporation	Limited to capital
Governance	Partners	Board of Directors
Audit requirements	N/A	Audit is optional for limited liability companies unless two of the following three limits are exceeded in 2 consecutive years, companies are required to appoint a qualified auditor (*Revisor Oficial de Contas*): • total net assets: €1.5m • total net sales and other profits: €3m • number of employees: 50 Audit is compulsory for corporations. Depending on the governance model adopted, audit requirements for corporations may differ
Taxation	Transparent	Corporation tax

II CORPORATION TAX

Legal form / Description	Resident corporation	Permanent establishment (PE)
General description	Corporation tax	
Taxable entities	Corporations incorporated or effectively managed in Portugal	PE located in Portuguese territory
Taxable income	Worldwide income	Income attributable to the Portuguese territory
Calculation of taxable profits	Accounting profit is adjusted for various tax add-backs and allowances to arrive at taxable income/tax losses	
Interest payments	Interest Barrier rule (Art° 67 CIRC): The deductibility of net financial expenses is limited to the higher of: (i) €1 million, or (ii) 30% of EBITDA The limit applies to all financing costs, regardless of the existence of special relations between the debtor and creditor, and the residence of the creditor (ie financing from EU resident lenders is not excluded) A transitional provision established a phase-in system, according to which the EBITDA limit was 40% during 2016	
Related party transactions	All related party transactions must take place on arm's length basis	
Tax year, return and payment	Tax follows the calendar year but companies may ask for a different annual period Tax return are filed up to the fifth month following the tax year end Three payments on account are made during the year, based on previous year's assessment, the balance being paid when filing the tax return A special payment on account is also due (that may be paid in two instalments) based on previous year's turnover with a cap, deducted from previous year's payments on account Three additional payments on account are due by entities subject to State Surcharge, based on the previous year taxable income (over €1.5 million)	
Capital gains	Included in the computation of the taxable income Capital gains arising from the disposal of fixed and specific financial assets complying with certain requirements may be reduced to 50% provided the sale proceeds are reinvested in the acquisition of qualifying assets in the year prior to the disposal, in the year of the disposal, or in the 2 following years Capital gains derived from the sale of participations representing at least 10% of the subsidiary's share capital or voting rights, and held for a minimum period of 1 year, are exempt of CIT	
Losses	Tax losses recorded until 2016 may be carried forward for a 12-year period, and those recorded as of 2017 may be carried forward for a 5-year period. Small-medium companies (PMEs) may benefit from the 12-year period for all tax losses Only 70% of the taxable profit of each year may be offset by losses carried forward	

Legal form / Description	Resident corporation	Permanent establishment (PE)
Tax group	The tax group is applicable for Portuguese companies held by a parent company, directly or indirectly, controlling at least 70% of the share capital and more than 50% of the voting rights of the subsidiary. Other requirements apply	
Tax rate	21% standard rate. A reduced 17% rate applies to the first €15,000 of the taxable income for small-medium companies. As of 2017, this reduced rate may be 12.5% for small-medium companies located in inland regions Municipal surtax may be applicable, up to a maximum of 1.5% of the taxable profits A state surtax will apply as follows: – 3% on taxable profits exceeding €1.5 million – 5% on taxable profits exceeding €7.5 million – 7% on taxable profits exceeding €35 million	

III TAXES FOR INDIVIDUALS

		Residents	Non-residents
Income Tax	General description	Tax levied on the chargeable income of a chargeable person for a year of assessment	
	Taxable entities and taxable income	Residents are taxed on their worldwide income	Non-residents are taxable on all income deemed to arise in Portugal
	Non habitual residents	Liable on their net employment and self-employment income from 'high value added activities' at a flat rate of 20%. Foreign-source income may be exempt under certain conditions	
	Types of taxable income	• Real estate income (usually rental income) • Investment income (interest, dividends, royalties) • Capital gains and other accretions in net worth • Income from business activities • Employment income or pensions	
	Calculation of income	Taxpayer is entitled to make deductions from the sum of the different natures of income (eg employment income, business income, property income, dividends, etc) resulting in the taxable income which is subject to progressive tax rates	
	Tax year, tax assessment and tax payment	Tax year – calendar year Individual taxpayers must file annual returns between March and May of the following year, the timing depends on the combination of income sources The computation of taxable business and self-employment income is based: (a) on the rules of the so-called 'simplified regime'; (b) on the rules applicable to isolated acts of business and self-employment services; or (c) on formal accounting records Individuals with business and self-employment income may have to make advance payments in July, September and December Employment and pension income is subject to withholding tax at the time of payment, as prepayment of the ultimate tax liability On the other hand, under some conditions, self-employment, real estate, and specific capital investment income are also subjected to withholding taxes Non-residents must appoint a tax representative under certain conditions (except for residents in the EU or the EEA, in the latter case if co-operation in the field of taxation similar to that in force in the EU is in place)	
	Losses	Losses computed in the context of business and self-employment activities (based on accounting records) can be offset against income in the subsequent 12 years However, only 70% of the taxable profit of each year may be offset by losses carried forward Capital losses computed in the context of disposal of real estate can be offset against positive income of same nature in the subsequent 5 years	

		Residents	Non-residents
Income Tax – *contd*	Tax rates	Tax Income (€) ... Marginal tax rate (%) ... Deduction (€)	

	Tax rates	Residents	
		Tax Income *(€)*	*Marginal tax rate* *(%)*	*Deduction* *(€)*

Under the Residents column for Tax rates:

Tax Income (€)	Marginal tax rate (%)	Deduction (€)
0–7,091	14.5	0
7,091–20,261	28.5	992.74
20,261–40,522	37	2,714.93
40,522–80,640	45	5,956.69
80,640+	48	8,375.89

Extraordinary surtax is applicable to income subject to PIT exceeding the annual amount of (€20,261):

20,261–40,522	0.88%
40,522–80,640	2.25%
80,640+	3.21%

A 'solidarity surcharge' of 2.5% applies to taxable income in excess of €80,000 and 5% to taxable income in excess of €250,000

Tax regime for non-habitual residents

Taxation rules

Employment and self-employment income derived from 'high value-added activities of a scientific, artistic or technical nature' earned by non-habitual residents in Portugal will be taxed at a flat rate of 20%

Full tax exemption for foreign-sourced income, such as pensions, employment income, self-employment income, rental income, interest, dividends as well as other investment income, under certain specific conditions

The regime is applicable for a period of ten consecutive years

Conditions

The regime applies to individuals who become Portuguese tax residents in year and have not qualified as tax residents in any of the previous five years

		Residents	Non-residents
Capital Gains Tax (CGT)	General description	Capital gains in excess of capital losses are subject to taxation annually (eg disposal of real estate, shares, bonds)	
	Taxable entities and chargeable assets	Worldwide income qualified as capital gains under Portuguese tax legislation obtained by individuals	Income attributable to Portuguese territory obtained by individuals (eg sale of real estate located in the Portuguese territory, disposal of shares in Portuguese companies)
	Calculation of gain	Examples: • Gains on real estate used as permanent residence are not taxable if sale proceeds are reinvested within 36 months, or in the previous 24 months, in real estate with the same purpose in the EU or in a EEA country bound to provide administrative cooperation on taxation • Gains on securities acquired before 1989 are not taxed • Only 50% of gains from real estate and related rights are taxable	
	Tax year, tax assessment and tax payment	Tax year corresponds to calendar year Income included in annual tax return to determine tax liability	

		Residents	Non-residents
Capital Gains Tax (CGT)	Tax rates	• Capital gains on the disposal of shares, bonds and certain other financial instruments – taxation at a flat 28% rate • Capital gains not attributable to a PE in Portugal obtained by non-residents are taxed at a flat 28% rate, but in the case of disposal of securities, capital gains may be exempt under a specific tax benefit provision Other capital gains, obtained by individuals qualifying as tax residents, are subjected to the progressive tax rates	
		Domiciled	**Non-domiciled**
Inheritance Tax (IHT)	General description	The inheritance tax was abolished. Nonetheless, assets and rights received by individuals by inheritance or gifts are subject to a 10% Stamp Tax rate Spouses, ascendants and descendants are exempt from Stamp Tax on such gratuitous transfers	

IV WITHHOLDING TAXES

Under domestic law	Payments to residents	Payments to non-residents
Dividends[1]	Individuals 28% Companies 25%	Individuals 28% Companies 25%
Interest	28%	25%
Royalties	Individuals 16.5% Companies 25%	25%
On payments to artists and sportsmen	25%	25%
Service fees	Nil	15% (except for fees not deemed to arise within the Portuguese territory, which is always the case with finance, transportation and communication services, among others, or fees due to entities resident in countries with which Portugal has a Double Tax Treaty in force)

Reduced rate available under the relevant Double Taxation Treaty			
Country	Dividends	Interest	Royalties
Algeria	15%	15%	10%
Austria	15%	10%	10%
Belgium	15%	15%	10%
Brazil	15%	15%	15%
Bulgaria	15%	10%	10%
Canada	15%	10%	10%
Cape Verde	10%	10%	10%
Chile	15%	15%	10%
China	10%	10%	10%
Colombia	10%	10%	10%
Croatia	10%	10%	10%
Cuba	10%	10%	5%
Cyprus	10%	10%	10%
Czech Republic	15%	10%	10%

1 A participation exemption regime applies to inbound and outbound dividends.
  To qualify for the WHT exemption for outbound dividend payments, the main criteria will be:
  (i)   10% of the share capital or voting rights of the Portuguese company;
  (ii)   1 year holding period before distribution (may be satisfied after the income is paid but refund may be requested);
  (iii) available for shareholders that are resident in EU/EEA (excluding EEA which do not exchange tax information with Portugal) or any jurisdiction with which Portugal has signed a tax treaty with exchange of information mechanism; and
  (iv)   company receiving the dividends should be subject either to CIT, taxes listed in the EU Parent-Subsidiary Directive, or a tax comparable to the Portuguese CIT at a nominal rate, corresponding to at least 60% of the Portuguese rate (ie 13.8%).

Reduced rate available under the relevant Double Taxation Treaty			
Country	Dividends	Interest	Royalties
Denmark	10%	10%	10%
Estonia	10%	10%	10%
Finland	15%	15%	10%
France	15%	12%	5%
Georgia	10%	10%	5%
Germany	15%	15%	10%
Greece	15%	15%	10%
Guinea-Bissau	10%	10%	10%
Hong Kong	10%	10%	5%
Hungary	15%	10%	10%
Iceland	15%	10%	10%
India	15%	10%	10%
Indonesia	10%	10%	10%
Ireland	15%	15%	10%
Israel	15%	10%	10%
Italy	15%	15%	12%
Japan	10%	10%	5%
Korea (Republic of)	15%	15%	10%
Kuwait	10%	10%	10%
Latvia	10%	10%	10%
Lithuania	10%	10%	10%
Luxembourg	15%	15%	10%
Macao	10%	10%	10%
Malta	15%	10%	10%
Mexico	10%	10%	10%
Moldova	10%	10%	8%
Morocco	15%	12%	10%
Mozambique	10%	10%	10%
Netherlands	10%	10%	10%
Norway	15%	10%	10%
Panama	15%	10%	10%
Pakistan	15%	10%	10%
Peru	15%	15%	15%
Poland	15%	10%	10%
Qatar	10%	10%	10%
Romania	15%	10%	10%
Russia	15%	10%	10%
Saudi Arabia	10%	10%	8%
Senegal	10%	10%	10%
Singapore	10%	10%	10%
Slovakia	10%	10%	10%
Slovenia	15%	10%	5%
South Africa	15%	10%	10%
Spain	15%	15%	5%
Sweden	10%	10%	10%

Reduced rate available under the relevant Double Taxation Treaty			
Country	**Dividends**	**Interest**	**Royalties**
Switzerland	15%	10%	5%
Tunisia	15%	15%	10%
Turkey	15%	15%	10%
Ukraine	15%	10%	10%
United Arab Emirates	15%	10%	5%
United Kingdom	15%	10%	5%
United States	15%	10%	10%
Uruguay	10%	10%	10%
Venezuela	15%	10%	12%

Note: the above rates are only available provided the specific Treaty criteria are satisfied. It is possible that lower rates than those shown above may be available provided that certain criteria are satisfied. As treaties will not be identical, guidance should be sought in all cases.

Double Taxation Treaty – not yet in force			
Country	**Dividends**	**Interest**	**Royalties**
Bahrain	10%–15%	10%	5%
Barbados	5%–15%	10%	5%
East Timor	5%–10%	10%	10%
Ethiopia	5%–10%	10%	5%
Ivory Coast	10%	10%	5%
Oman	5%–10%–15%	10%	8%
San Marino	10%–15%	10%	10%
Sao Tome and Principe	10%–15%	10%	10%
Vietnam	5%–10%–15%	10%	7.5%–10%

V INDIRECT TAXES

<table>
<tr><td rowspan="10">Value Added Tax (VAT)</td><td></td><td>Residents</td><td>Non-residents</td></tr>
<tr><td>General description</td><td colspan="2">Tax on the supply of goods and services</td></tr>
<tr><td>Entities obliged to levy VAT</td><td colspan="2">• Individuals, companies, collective bodies who independently and regularly engage in the production/commerce of goods or in the supply of services
• Persons who engage in occasional transactions which qualify as commercial transactions
• Importers</td></tr>
<tr><td>Taxable activities</td><td colspan="2">Supply of goods and services and importation of goods</td></tr>
<tr><td>Taxable activities – zero-rated (examples)</td><td colspan="2">Exports</td></tr>
<tr><td>Exemptions (examples)</td><td colspan="2">Financial transactions, real estate rental, transactions subject to Property Transfer Tax</td></tr>
<tr><td>Refund of VAT</td><td colspan="2">As a general rule, when VAT credit exceeds approximately €250, after a period of credit of 12 months, or without any time limitation if it exceeds €3,000

Payment within 2 months</td></tr>
<tr><td>Tax liability</td><td colspan="2">In general, 5 days after the delivery of goods or the rendering of services or, if advance payments are made, at the moment the payment is received</td></tr>
<tr><td>Tax rates</td><td colspan="2">• Mainland
  – Standard rate = 23%
  – Intermediate rate = 13%
  – Reduced rate = 6%
• Madeira[2] = 22%/12%/5%
• Azores = 18%/10%/5%</td></tr>
<tr><td>Administrative obligations</td><td colspan="2">Tax returns due on a monthly basis if annual turnover is equal or higher than €650,000 or on a quarterly basis if turnover is lower than that amount

Annual tax return summarising the annual activities, including the identification of clients and suppliers with annual transactions exceeding €25,000</td></tr>
</table>

---

2 In force since 1 April 2012, as a consequence of the Economic and Financial Adjustment Programme signed between Madeira and the Central Government.

	Residents	Non-residents
Real Property Taxes	Stamp tax is due on the acquisition of ownership or other rights on real estate – 0.8%	
	Property Transfer Tax is levied on the transfer of real estate:	
	• urban property not exclusively for residential purposes – 6.5% • urban property exclusively for permanent residential purposes (acquisition value higher than €574,323) – 6%. Lower progressive tax rates apply to smaller amounts • rural property – 5% • property acquired by residents in tax havens – 10%	
	Municipal Property Tax is levied on an annual basis, due by the property owner:	
	• urban property (appraised under the former legislation) – 0.5%–0.8% • urban property (appraised under current legislation) – 0.3%–0.45% • rural property – 0.8% • property owned by residents in tax havens – 7.5%	
	As of 2017, an additional real property tax (AIMI) applies to urban property appraised over €600,000 (0.7% if owned by individuals and 0.4% if owned by companies; in both cases, a 1% marginal rate is levied on properties over €1 million)	
Stamp Duty	Levied on deeds, acts and other situations specified in the Code, including gifts and donations, as mentioned above under IHT	
	Specific tax rates depending on the taxable event	

Puerto Rico

(Gabriel J. Viera Pina, Nexia Puerto Rico, PSC, gabriel.viera@nexiapr.com)

I MAIN LEGAL FORMS

Legal form / Characteristics	Partnership and Limited Liability Partnership (LLP)	Limited Liability Corporation (LLC)	Private corporation (Ltd) and Public corporation (Plc)
Partners/shareholders • Number • Restrictions	Two minimum Foreign persons may be partners/members, subject to special withholding rules	One minimum	One minimum
Directors	Might be one managing partner and one limited/unlimited partner	Might be sole member or more	Might be sole director or board
Establishment	Partnership agreement	Certificate of Organization	Certificate of Organization or Articles of Incorporation
Registration	Registration with tax authorities, social security authorities and state payroll tax		
Minimum capital	No minimum capital is required		
Liability	LLP: Limited Liability General Partnership: general partner has unlimited liability	General Rule: Limited to capital	General rule: limited to capital
Governance	Not mandatory	Operating Agreement	Ltd or Plc: President or Board of Directors
Audit requirements	Required if gross sales exceed $3,000,000	Required if gross sales exceed $3,000,000	Required if gross sales exceed $3,000,000

Legal form / Characteristics	Partnership and Limited Liability Partnership (LLP)	Limited Liability Corporation (LLC)	Private corporation (Ltd) and Public corporation (Plc)
Taxation	Partnerships formed or that began operations after 2011 are considered 'pass-through' tax entities. Any partner (including non-residents) of a partnership doing business in Puerto Rico is considered to be engaged in a trade or business in Puerto Rico regarding their distributive share of income, gain, loss, deductions or credits	General rule: Taxable as corporations May elect to be treated as a partnership. An LLC that is treated as a pass-through entity outside Puerto Rico is not able to elect corporate treatment	Ltd or Plc: Taxable on worldwide income
Informative Income Tax Returns	Partnerships, LLPs and LLCs may use calendar or fiscal year. Returns are filed on the 15th day of the third month after the year end. Partner/Member's Withheld Income Tax is paid quarterly in advance		Corporations may use calendar or fiscal year. Returns are filed on the 15th day of the fourth month after the year end

II CORPORATION TAX

Legal Form / Description	Domestic corporation	Foreign Corporation (FC)
General description	Corporate Income Tax	Branch Income Tax
Taxable entities	Corporations incorporated in Puerto Rico	FC trading in Puerto Rico
Taxable income	Worldwide profits	Income effectively connected to Puerto Rico
Calculation of taxable profits	Accounting net income is adjusted for various tax add-backs and allowances to arrive at profits subject to corporation tax	
Interest payments	Deductible	
Related party transactions	All related party transactions must take place on arm's length basis	
Tax year, return and payment	Companies may use calendar or fiscal year. Returns are due by the 15th day of the fourth month after the year end. Tax is paid quarterly in advance	
Capital gains	General rule: capital gains subject to income tax of 20%	
Losses	Net operating losses can be carried forward for ten years and set off against taxable profits but limited to 80% of the normal tax net income	
Tax group	Tax consolidation is not permitted	
Tax rate	A 20% tax will be levied, collected and paid on the net income subject to normal tax. If the net income is more than $25,000 a surtax will be applicable as follows:	

Surtax Net Income is:		Your Surtax is:		
Over	But not over		Plus	Of the Excess Over
$0	$75,000	5%		
$75,000	$125,000	$3,750	15%	$75,000
$125,000	$175,000	$11,250	16%	$125,000
$175,000	$225,000	$19,250	17%	$175,000
$225,000	$275,000	$27,750	18%	$225,000
$275,000		$36,750	19%	$275,000

Alternative Minimum Tax	Excess of highest Tentative Minimum Tax (TMT) over regular income tax
	Highest TMT:
	TMT 1= 30% of Alternative minimum net income plus additional tax on gross income
	TMT 2= Progressive tax from 2.5% up to 6.5% on Intercompany purchases plus 20% on Intercompany charges from Home Office

CORPORATION TAX INCENTIVES

General Description	The 'Export Services Act 20' provides benefits for services provided from Puerto Rico to outside markets
Eligibility	Research and development, Advertising and public relations, Economic, scientific, environmental, technological, managerial, marketing, human resources, engineering, information systems, auditing and consulting services, Consulting services for any trade or business, Commercial art and graphic services, Production of engineering and architectural plans and designs, and related services, Professional services such as legal, tax and accounting services, Centralized managerial services, including, but not limited to, strategic direction, planning and budgeting, provided by regional headquarters or a headquarters company engaged in the business of providing such services, Services performed by electronic data processing centres, Development of licensee computer software, Telecommunications voice and data between persons located outside Puerto Rico, Call centres, Shared service centres, Medical, hospital and laboratories services, Investment banking and other financial services, and any other service designated by the Secretary of the Department of Economic Development and Commerce of Puerto Rico
Tax rate	A 4% (or 3% in case of strategic services) fixed rate of income tax will be levied, collected and paid on the net income subject to normal tax
Alternative Minimum Tax	No additional tax will be imposed
Dividends	0% Dividend Tax Rate for Non-Puerto Rico shareholders
	6% Dividend Tax Rate for Puerto Rico shareholders
Personal Property Tax	90% tax exemption from personal property taxes
Real Property Tax	90% tax exemption from real property taxes
Municipal Tax	60% tax exemption on municipal taxes
Exempt Period	Tax Exemption Decrees for up to 45 years

III TAXES FOR INDIVIDUALS

<table>
<tr><td rowspan="20">Income Tax</td><td></td><td colspan="2">Residents</td><td>Non-residents</td></tr>
<tr><td>General description</td><td colspan="3">Tax levied on the chargeable income of a chargeable person for a year of assessment</td></tr>
<tr><td>Taxable entities and taxable income</td><td colspan="2">Residents are taxed on their worldwide income</td><td>Non-residents are taxable for income arising in Puerto Rico</td></tr>
<tr><td>Types of taxable income</td><td colspan="3">• Rental income
• Income from capital investment (sale of goodwill, real and personal property, and stocks)
• Dividends, royalties and annuities
• Income from business activities
• Employment from personal services or pensions</td></tr>
<tr><td>Calculation of income</td><td colspan="3">Gross income as reduced by deductible items and allowances</td></tr>
<tr><td>Tax year, tax assessment and tax payment</td><td colspan="3">Tax year is the calendar year. Individual income tax returns must be filed by the 15th day of the fourth month of the following year. The total tax liability is due on or before the return's filing date</td></tr>
<tr><td>Losses</td><td colspan="3">Can be carried forward</td></tr>
<tr><td>Tax rates</td><td>If the net taxable income is</td><td>Your tax will be:</td><td rowspan="6">US Citizens will be subject to a 20% income tax

Non US Citizens will be subject to a 29% income tax</td></tr>
<tr><td></td><td>≤ $9,000</td><td>0%</td></tr>
<tr><td></td><td>Over $9,000, but ≤ $25,000</td><td>7% of the excess over $9,000</td></tr>
<tr><td></td><td>Over $25,000, but ≤ $41,500</td><td>$1,120 plus 14% of the excess over $25,000</td></tr>
<tr><td></td><td>Over $41,500, but ≤ $61,500</td><td>$3,430 plus 25% of the excess over $41,500</td></tr>
<tr><td></td><td>> $61,500</td><td>$8,430 plus 33% of the excess over $61,500</td></tr>
</table>

		Residents	Non-residents
Capital Gains Tax (CGT)	General description	Gains realised from the difference between the acquisition and disposal price of an asset	
	Taxable entities and chargeable assets	• Taxed at the lesser of regular tax or special 15% tax • If the gross income is in excess of $150,000, the resulting amount will be subject to a minimum tax called Alternate Basic Tax • Except for real estate	Only assets located in Puerto Rico
	Calculation of gain	Difference between sales price and tax basis of capital asset	
	Tax year, tax assessment and tax payment	The tax year is the calendar year and tax is paid quarterly in advance	
	Losses	Capital losses may be deducted from capital gains or carried forward 5 years. Losses of up to $1,000 may be deducted from ordinary income	
	Tax rates	• Short-term capital gains (assets held less than six months) are taxed as ordinary income subject to normal tax rates • Long-term capital gains (assets held six or more months) are taxed at 10% • If the gross income is in excess of $150,000, the resulting amount will be subject to a minimum tax. Alternate Basic Tax is: – From $150,000 to $250,000 – 10% – Over $250,000 but not over $500,000 – 15% – Over $500,000 – 24%	

		Domiciled	Non-domiciled
Inheritance Tax (IHT)	General description	Tax on the transfer of property	
	Taxable entities and chargeable assets	All worldwide assets included	PR assets
	Calculation of charge	Gross estate less allowances	
	Taxable events	Transfer by gift or by bequest at death	
	Allowances	The value of the property located in Puerto Rico	$10,000 (non-resident alien)
		$1,000,000 reduced by the value of the property located in Puerto Rico	$30,000 (US Citizens non-resident)
	Tax rates	10% of taxable amount	Tax will be the maximum amount of credit allowed by the foreign country where the taxpayer is resident

TAX INCENTIVES FOR INDIVIDUALS

Income Tax	General description	Act No 22 provides tax exemptions to eligible individuals residing in Puerto Rico. To avail from such benefits, an individual needs to become a resident of Puerto Rico and apply for a tax exemption decree	
	Eligibility	The benefits of Act No 22 are only available to bona fide residents of Puerto Rico that were not bona fide residents of Puerto Rico for the 15-year period preceding the enactment of the Act on 12 January 2012	
	Types of eligible taxable income	• Interest • Dividends • Short-term and Long-term Capital Gains	
Incentives Tax Rate	Capital Gains	0% tax on short-term and long-term capital gains for New Puerto Rico Residents	
	Dividends	0% tax on dividends income for New Puerto Rico Residents	
	Interest	0% tax on interest income for New Puerto Rico Residents	
	Federal Taxes	0% federal taxes on Puerto Rico source income	

IV WITHHOLDING TAXES

Under domestic law	Payments to residents	Payments to non-residents
Dividends	15%	15%, generally
Interest	• If it is not subject to withholding, is taxable as ordinary income • If it is subject to withholding from financial institutions the tax rate will be 10% • Interest from Individual Retirement Account is subject to rate of 17%, if the withholding is made by the financial institution	20% US Citizens 29% Non US Citizens
Royalties	10%	20% US Citizens 29% Non US Citizens
On payments to artists and sportsmen	Sportsmen 20% Artists (regular tax table rates)	Sportsmen 20% Artists: 20% US Citizens 29% Non US Citizens

There are no Double Taxation Treaties which reduce the rate of withholding tax.

V   INDIRECT TAXES

		Residents	Non-residents
Sales and Use Tax (SUT)	General description	Tax on the sale and use of goods and services	
	Entities obliged to levy VAT	Puerto Rico does not impose a Value Added Tax, rather the state and each municipality imposes a base tax rate of 11.5% sales and use tax on taxable transactions. Base tax rate is imposed upon the introduction or the purchase of goods and taxable services. B2B services, other than taxable services and designated professional services, are subject to a special tax rate of 4%	
	Taxable activities	Sale of personal property (goods), taxable services, admission fees, combined transactions, prepared food, B2B services, and designated professional services	
	Exemptions (examples)	An Exempt Certification shall be requested: • Services to the Government • Exports • Manufacturing articles • Food • Medicine • Certain legal services A person engaged in the manufacture of taxable items may request and obtain a waiver from the requirement to collect, withhold and deposit the sales tax on the sale of taxable items to a wholesale distributor A reseller of taxable items, upon compliance with certain requirements, could qualify for a reseller certificate which would allow the merchant to claim a credit for the sales and use tax paid on the purchases of taxable items for resale. The credit is not available for taxes paid on the purchase of services	
	Taxable Services	The following services rendered to a person engaged in trade or business: • Bank charges to commercial customers for managing demand or other deposit accounts to cover specific transaction costs and excess pre-established limit costs • Collection services • Security services • Cleaning services • Laundry services • Repair and maintenances services of real and tangible personal property. As described below, under certain circumstances, the service provider may not be required to collect the tax, in which case the liability for payment of the tax would fall on the purchaser of the service • Telecommunication services • Waste management services • The leasing of motor vehicles under an operating lease that constitutes a 'daily rental', other than those equivalents to a purchase	
	Tax liability	The supplier of the goods and services is responsible for charging the tax, except for a supplier who is not a resident of PR and is not engaged in business in PR. In this case, the registered merchant shall auto impose (reverse charge) the use tax on services received by a foreign entity	
	Administrative obligations	Apply for registration File monthly returns on or before the 20th day of the following month. There are two different forms available to file the base tax and the special tax rate	

	Residents	Non-residents
Real Property Taxes	Real property tax rates vary for each municipality. Rates fluctuate between 8.08% and 11.58% depending upon the location of the property. This tax is imposed by the Municipality based on 1958 appraised value and payable in two equal instalments. This tax is assessed by government and no return needs to be filed. Principal residence is exempt from real property tax up to $150,000 on the historical cost	
Stamp Duty	The rate of stamp duty depends on the type of goods sold since there is a different rate for each product. In some cases the law of Puerto Rico states a minimum rate and in other cases it can be negotiable between the parties	

Nexia International does not accept liability for any loss arising from any action taken, or omission, on the basis of this publication. Professional advice should be obtained before acting or refraining from acting on the contents of this publication. Membership of Nexia International, or associated umbrella organizations, does not constitute any partnership between members, and members do not accept any responsibility for the commission of any act, or omission to act by, or the liabilities of, other members.

Nexia International is the trading name of Nexia International Limited, a company registered in the Isle of Man. Company registration number: 53513C. Registered office: 2nd floor, Sixty Circular Road, Douglas, Isle of Man, IM1 1SA

Romania

(Luminita Ristea, CRG NEXIA, luminita.ristea@crgnexia.ro)

I MAIN LEGAL FORMS

Legal Form / Characteristics	Partnership and Limited Liability Partnership (LLP)	Private corporation (Ltd) and Public corporation (Plc)
Partners/shareholders • Number • Restrictions	A limited partnership consists of one or more general partners who manage the business of a partnership and one or more limited partners who contribute to capital	Ltd: from 1–50 partners Plc: at least two shareholders
Directors	The general partner provides the professional management of the partnership	Ltd: directors/managers are appointed in the Articles of Association or by the General Assembly Plc: directors are appointed by the General Assembly of shareholders, which establishes their empowerment and accountability, for a maximum period of 4 years
Establishment	Various documents submitted to the Local Trade Registry The procedure for setting up a company usually takes usually 5 days, from the date the whole requested documentation is submitted, but the period may be longer	
Registration	The company is a legal entity from the date of its registration with the Trade Register and therefore each legal entity has the obligation to apply for registration with the Trade Register where the entity is located (their head office). Every change of shareholders' structure, locations, object of activity, directors, auditors, etc must be filled in on the basis of entity's application registration forms	
Minimum capital	No legal provisions	Ltd: at least RON 200 Plc: at least RON 90,000
Liability	Unlimited liability for partnerships LLP – limited to partnership capital	Limited to the company's capital

Characteristics / Legal Form	Partnership and Limited Liability Partnership (LLP)	Private corporation (Ltd) and Public corporation (Plc)
Governance	General partners ensure the administration of the company	• Ltd and Plc: the management is assumed by a Board of Directors • If the company is audited according to the law, it must have at least three administrators • The administrators cannot be employed on the basis of a labour contract as an employee • Plc can be managed by a dual system: Board of Directors and a Supervision Council as well

Audit requirements	Generally not required	Required in some circumstances:
		• Plc only in case of dual system
		• listed (quoted) companies
		• companies (Plc, Ltd) meeting two of three criteria:
		  – total assets over €3.65m;
		  – net turnover over €7.3m;
		  – number of employees more than 50

Taxation	Transparent	Corporation tax
Usage	Rarely used	Commonly used

II CORPORATION TAX

Legal form / Description	Resident corporation	Permanent establishment (PE)
General description	Corporation tax	
Taxable entities	Corporations incorporated and managed in Romania	PE located in Romania
Taxable income	Worldwide taxable profits with considerations for double taxation treaties for Romanian companies	Taxable profits assigned to the PE derived in Romania with specific regulation in case of more than one PE
Calculation of taxable profits	Accounting profit is adjusted for various tax add-backs and allowances to arrive to profits chargeable to corporation tax (PCTCT)	
Interest payments	For long-term loan agreements, interest expenses are fully deductible where the debt to equity ratio is less than three; excess amount may be carried forward. For loans obtained from other entities, interest deductible limited to: a) interest rate monetary policy of the National Bank of Romania of the last month of the quarter for loans in lei; and b) the annual interest rate of 4% for foreign currency loans	
Related party transactions	All related party transactions must be taken into consideration on arm's length basis	
Tax year, return and payment	Tax year – calendar year Tax year may be different from calendar year for: • subsidiaries which belong to a foreign legal person (except credit institutions, non-banking financial institutions, insurance companies, insurance-reinsurance companies and reinsurance companies, etc) • the consolidated branches of the parent company, as well as for the branches of branches (except credit institutions, non-banking financial institutions, insurance companies, insurance-reinsurance companies and reinsurance companies, etc) if the financial year is different for the parent company Payments are due on the 25th of the month following each quarter Final date for submitting the annual tax return is 25 March of the following year Returns must be filed with the accounts on a quarterly basis Taxpayers can choose to declare and pay the annual tax on profit through quarterly prepayments The option for quarterly prepayments for tax on profit shall be maintained for at least two consecutive fiscal years	
Capital gains	Treated as income	
Losses[1]	Starting on 1 January 2009, fiscal losses may be carried forward 7 years	
	Tax losses recorded by legal entities that cease to exist as a result of a merger or division shall be recovered by the newly established taxpayer or by those acquiring the patrimony of merged/divided firm, proportionally to the assets and liabilities transferred to recipient legal entity, according to merger/division project	

---

1   There are special rules allowing the company to utilise other losses such as capital losses and loan relationship deficits.

Legal form / Description	Resident corporation	Permanent establishment (PE)
Tax group	Not available	
Tax rate	16%	
Taxation of specific activities[2]	This specific tax is computed based on a standard tax and on certain coefficients that depend on the class of the city/village where the activity is performed, usable commercial surface and seasonality. The value of these items differs depending on the type of activity performed The declaration and payment of this specific tax is performed biannually, until the 25th of the following month. The amount to be paid is half of the annual specific tax	

---

2   Starting with 1 January 2017, Companies that will pay this tax are those that have the following activities listed as their main or secondary business activities: hotels and other similar accommodation units; accommodation units for short-term rent; trailer parks, camping sites and others; other types of accommodation units; restaurants and catering businesses; bars and other types of establishments.

III TAXES FOR INDIVIDUALS

		Residents	Non-residents
Income Tax	General description	Tax levied on the chargeable income of a chargeable person for a fiscal year	
	Taxable entities and taxable income	Residents are taxed on their worldwide income	Non-residents are taxed on the income obtained from Romania
	Types of taxable income	• Property income (usually rent) and real estate transactions income • Intellectual property rights • Income from capital investments (interest, stocks, bonds, dividends, annuities, income from company's liquidation) • Income from business activities • Wage and salary • Pensions • Income from agriculture • Other incomes	
	Calculation of income (examples)	• Property income (usually rent): 60% of the net income from rental is imposed with a flat quota of 16% • Property income from real estate transactions: different quota (1%–3%) applied to the transaction value taking into consideration the ageing of property held and the transaction value (less than RON200,000 or more than RON200,000) • Intellectual property income: 60% of the net income from intellectual property income minus social contributions is imposed with a flat quota of 16% • In case of incomes derived from the creation of works of monumental art: 60% of the net income minus social contributions is imposed with a flat quota of 16% • Income from capital investment (interest, stocks, bonds, dividends, annuities, income from company's liquidation) after deducting the support expenses, is imposed with a flat quota of 16% • Income from business activities: gross income minus deductible expenses minus fiscal loss carried forward for 7 years is imposed with a flat quota of 16% • Wages and salaries: gross income minus social contributions minus personal allowance minus certain other items is imposed with a flat quota of 16%	
	Tax year, tax assessment and tax payment	Tax year – calendar year Tax return must be filled by 25 May in the following year Payments are made in advance on a quarterly or half-yearly basis according to the income	
	Losses	Losses can be offset against income of the same source in the subsequent 5 years (until 2009) and 7 years (after 2009)	
	Tax rates	16% applied on taxable income for all income, except: • Real estate transaction – the quota is 1%–3% applied on the transaction's value taking into consideration the ageing of property held and the transaction value (less than Lei 200,000 or more than Lei 200,000) • Capital gains from stocks sold are taxable at 16% • Gambling income – 1%; 16%; 25% applied on gross income instalments by applying the quota on each gross income received by each participant, from an organiser or from a payer of incomes from gambling, at the time of each payment	

		Residents	Non-residents
Capital Gains Tax (CGT)	General description	No capital taxes	
Inheritance Tax (IHT)	General description	Inheritance asset	
	Taxable entities and chargeable assets	Individuals for real estate	
	Calculation of charge	If the inheritance is debated upon and completed within 2 years of the date of death no tax is paid	
		In case of failure to complete the succession proceedings within the above mentioned timeframe, the inheritors have to pay a 1% tax calculated at the value of the net worth of the estate	
	Taxable events	Individuals inheriting real estate properties, if the property is not debated within the 2-year period	
	Allowances	If the inheritance asset is debated within 2 years, no tax is due	
	Tax rates	1%	

IV WITHHOLDING TAXES

Under domestic law	Payments to residents	Payments to non-residents
Dividends	5% or exemption	5% or exemption[1] or the rate applicable in any double tax treaty
Interest	16% individuals	16% exemption[2]
Royalties	Nil	16% exemption[3]
On payments to artists and sportsmen	16%	16%[4]

Reduced rate available under the relevant Double Taxation Treaty			
Country	Dividends	Interest	Royalties
Albania	15%	10%	15%
Algeria	15%	15%	15%
Armenia	10%	10%	10%
Australia	15%	10%	10%
Austria	5%	3%	3%
Azerbaijan	10%	8%	10%
Bangladesh	15%	10%	10%
Belarus	10%	10%	15%
Belgium	15%	10%	5%
Bulgaria	15%	15%	15%
Canada	15%	10%	10%
Czech Republic	10%	7%	10%
China	10%	10%	7%
Cyprus	10%	10%	5%
Croatia	5%	10%	10%
Denmark	15%	10%	10%
Ecuador	15%	10%	10%
Egypt	10%	15%	15%
Estonia	10%	10%	10%
Finland	5%	5%	5%

1 5% or the rate applicable in any double tax treaty.
  Exemption: EU and AELS – if the respective person holds at least 10% of shares in the Romanian legal entity for an uninterrupted period of 1 year.
  50% if the incomes are paid in a state with which Romania has not signed a legal instrument under which to exchange information.
2 16% or the rate applicable in any double tax treaty.
  Exemption: EU and AELS – if the respective person holds at least 25% of shares in the Romanian legal entity for an uninterrupted period of 2 years.
3 16% or the rate applicable in any double tax treaty.
  50% if the incomes are paid in a state with which Romania has not signed a legal instrument under which to exchange information.
  Exemption: EU and AELS – if the respective person holds at least 25% of shares in the Romanian legal entity for an uninterrupted period of 2 years.
4 16% or the rate applicable in any double tax treaty.

Reduced rate available under the relevant Double Taxation Treaty			
Country	Dividends	Interest	Royalties
France	10%	10%	10%
Georgia	8%	10%	5%
Germany	15%	3%	3%
Greece	25%	10%	5%
Hungary	15%	15%	10%
India	20%	15%	22.5%
Indonesia	15%	12.5%	15%
Jordan	15%	12.5%	15%
Iran	10%	8%	10%
Ireland	3%	3%	3%
Israel	15%	10%	10%
Italy	10%	10%	10%
Japan	10%	10%	15%
Kazakhstan	10%	10%	10%
Korea, Republic of	10%	10%	10%
Kuwait	1%	1%	20%
Lebanon	5%	5%	5%
Lithuania	10%	10%	10%
Luxembourg	15%	10%	10%
Macedonia	5%	10%	10%
Malaysia	10%	15%	12%
Malta	30%	5%	5%
Morocco	10%	10%	10%
Mexico	10%	15%	15%
Moldova	10%	10%	15%
Namibia	15%	15%	15%
Netherlands	15%	Nil	3%
Nigeria	12.5%	12.5%	12.5%
Norway	10%	10%	10%
North Korea	10%	10%	10%
Pakistan	10%	10%	12.5%
Philippines	15%	15%	25%
Poland	15%	10%	10%
Portugal	15%	10%	10%
Qatar	3%	3%	5%
Russia	15%	15%	10%
San Marino	10%	3%	3%
Serbia and Montenegro	10%	10%	10%
Singapore	5%	5%	5%
Syria	15%	10%	12%
Slovakia	10%	10%	15%
Slovenia	5%	5%	5%
South Africa	15%	15%	15%
Spain	15%	10%	10%
Sri Lanka	12.5%	10%	10%

Reduced rate available under the relevant Double Taxation Treaty			
Country	Dividends	Interest	Royalties
Sweden	10%	10%	10%
Switzerland	10%	10%	10%
Sudan	10%	5%	5%
Thailand	20%	25%	15%
Tunis	12%	10%	12%
Turkey	15%	10%	10%
Turkmenistan	10%	10%	15%
Ukraine	15%	10%	15%
United Arab Emirates	3%	3%	3%
United Kingdom	15%	10%	10%
United States	10%	10%	10%
Uzbekistan	10%	10%	10%
Vietnam	15%	10%	15%
Zambia	10%	10%	15%

Note: the above rates are only available provided the specific Treaty criteria are satisfied. It is possible that lower rates than those shown above may be available provided certain criteria are satisfied. As treaties will not be identical, guidance should be sought in all cases.

V   INDIRECT TAXES

		Residents	Non-residents
Value Added Tax (VAT)	General description	Tax on the supply of goods and services	
	Entities obliged to levy VAT	All legal entities performing an economic activity in the production, commerce and services sector, or persons practising freelance activities, are subject to VAT	
	Taxable activities	All supply of goods and services	
	Taxable activities – zero-rated (examples)	No zero-rated activities	
	Exemptions (examples)	There are three categories: • exempt operations without credit (deduction): public interest activities, such as hospitals, education, mailing; and also other activities, such as financial and banking services, gambling, insurance, rental and sale of real estate properties (with the possibility of option for taxation) • exempt operations with credit (deduction), such as export of goods, services in connection with the export, international transportation of persons, intra-Community delivery (under certain conditions) • exempt import operations, such as the import of goods whose delivery in Romania is exempted	
	Refund of VAT	Romanian VAT – registered entities in scope of VAT or using a fiscal representative or empowered person are entitled to reclaim VAT	
	Tax liability	• Taxable entities who perform taxable activities whose place is, or is considered to be, in Romania • The beneficiary of intangible services (chargeable persons) provided by another chargeable entity established abroad • Non-resident EU entities liable to pay VAT can appoint a fiscal representative • Non-resident non-EU entities must appoint a fiscal representative	
	Tax rates	Standard rate = 19%[5] Reduced rates = 9%; 5%	
	Administrative obligations	• Registration • VAT identification code	• Registration • Appoint a fiscal representative
Real Property Taxes		Notarial fees are applied	
Stamp Duty		Notarial fees are applied	

---

5 Starting on 1 January 2017, the standard rate will be 19%.

	Residents	Non-residents
M1SS[6]	To support companies providing electronic services, telecommunications, broadcasting, a new special scheme called Mini One Stop Shop (M1SS) will become operational from 1 January 2015(Council Implementing Regulation (EU) No 1042/2013)	

Nexia International does not accept liability for any loss arising from any action taken, or omission, on the basis of this publication. Professional advice should be obtained before acting or refraining from acting on the contents of this publication. Membership of Nexia International, or associated umbrella organizations, does not constitute any partnership between members, and members do not accept any responsibility for the commission of any act, or omission to act by, or the liabilities of, other members.

Nexia International is the trading name of Nexia International Limited, a company registered in the Isle of Man. Company registration number: 53513C. Registered office: 2nd floor, Sixty Circular Road, Douglas, Isle of Man, IM1 1SA

© Nexia International 2017

---

6 M1SS will allow companies to register, submit statements and pay VAT due to Member State of consumption via the web portal provided by the Member State of identification (usually the Member State in which the company has established its business activity). Simplification is the opportunity that a company no longer registers in each Member State where it is liable to pay VAT, but to benefit from the electronic services through the web portal of the Member State of identification. Also, companies will be charged VAT at the rate applicable in the Member State of consumption.

Russia

(Natalia Malofeeva, ICLC, Moscow, malofeeva@mkpcn.ru)

I MAIN LEGAL FORMS

Legal form / Characteristics	Partnerships	Private corporation and Public corporation (Plc)
Partners/shareholders • Number • Restrictions	Investment Partnership (IP): Only individual entrepreneurs and (or) legal entity may be participant of IP. In some cases, established by the federal law, non-profit organizations may also be a participant of the IP May include no more than 50 participants Full Partnership (FP): Consists of full partners. Only individual entrepreneurs and (or) legal entity may be participant of FP No restrictions as to the number of partners. One may participate as a full partner in only one partnership Partnership in commendam (PC): Consists of full partners and partners in commendam. Only individual entrepreneurs and (or) legal entity may be full partner May contain 1–20 participants in commendam Legal entities and individuals may be partners in commendam	Limited liability company (LLC) and Joint-Stock Company (JSC) Legal entities and individuals may be participants of LLC LLC may be founded by one person, who becomes its sole participant LLC cannot have as a sole participant another business company consisting of one person LLC may contain from 1 to 50 participants but no more than 50. Otherwise, LLC must be converted into JSC during a year After this period, LLC will be liquidated in court, if the number of participants will not be reduced to a specified limit (to 50, but no less than 1) JSC may be founded by one shareholder. Legal entity and individual may be shareholders of JSC. JSC has no restrictions as to the number of shareholders JSC which is placing its shares and securities, converted into shares, in public subscription are Public Joint-Stock Companies (PJSC). Other JSC are Non-Public Joint-Stock Companies (NPJSC)

Legal form / Characteristics	Partnerships	Private corporation and Public corporation (Plc)
Directors	IP: Management by few persons (control partners) or one person (control partner) FP: Management by mutual agreement of all partners PC: Management by full partners	LLC may be managed by the: – sole executive body (general director, president and others), elected on the General participants meeting. Only individual can be the sole executive body OR – collegial executive body (board, directorate and others), elected on the General participants meeting. Only individual can be a member of the collegial executive body JSC may be managed by the: – sole executive body (director, general director) OR – sole executive body (director, general director) and collective executive body (governing board, directorate). Executive bodies are accountable to the Board of Directors and to the general meeting of shareholders OR – managing company or individual entrepreneur by the decision of General shareholders meeting
Establishment	IP: Established on the basis of an investment partnership contract signed by all partners FP: Established on the basis of a foundation contract signed by all partners PC: Established on the basis of a foundation contract signed by all full partners	LLC: Established by the decision of the meeting of participants or by the decision of the sole participant JSC: Established by the decision of the general meeting or by the decision of the sole shareholder
Registration	In order to be registered, an entity should submit the following documents to tax authorities: • application according to the form • foundation documents (Charter, foundation contract, if any) • decision on establishment of an entity (minutes, contract, etc) • document certifying payment of state duty In case one of the founders is a foreign legal entity: • extract from companies' register of the country of origin	
Minimum capital	No requirements as to the *minimum* capital, although there should be some joint capital	LLC: 10,000 rubles NPJSC: 10,000 rubles PJSC: 100,000 rubles

Characteristics \ Legal form	Partnerships	Private corporation and Public corporation (Plc)
Liability	IP: Partners jointly and severally bear the liability for the general obligations not arising from the contract (with the exception of income tax liabilities). Partners are liable with all their own property for the general tax liability in accordance with the legislation on taxes and fees	LLC and JSC is liable for its obligations with all property belonging to it LLC and JSC shall not be liable for the obligations of its participants (LLC)/ shareholders (JSC)
	Each partner-investor bears the liability for the common obligations (related to the investment) in proportion to the value of belonging to him a share in the ownership of the common property of the partners and is not responsible with his own property (except if IP does not have enough property to satisfy creditors' claims)	
	FP: Partners jointly and severally bear subsidiary liability with their property for the obligations of the partnership	
	PC: Full partners jointly and severally bear subsidiary liability with their property for the obligations of the partnership. Partners in commendam only bear the risk of losses associated with the activities of the partnership up to amount of their investments	
Governance	IP: Management by few persons (control partners) or one person (control partner) FP: Management by mutual agreement of all partners PC: Management by full partners	LLC: General meeting of participants (the highest body) Board of Directors (Supervisory Board) which may be provided by the charter Executive body (sole executive body or collegial executive body) JSC: General meeting of shareholders (the highest body) Board of Directors (overall management of the company) Executive body (sole executive body or sole executive body and collective executive body or managing company or individual entrepreneur by the decision of General shareholders meeting)

Legal form / Characteristics	Partnerships	Private corporation and Public corporation (Plc)
Audit requirements	JSP: Obligatory audit is prescribed by law	
	Other entities: In some cases may be subject to obligatory audit	
Taxation	Common order of taxation for all legal forms	
Usage	Rarely used	LLC and NPJSC: used in small and medium-sized business
		PJSC: Used in large business

II CORPORATION TAX

Legal form / Description	Resident corporation	Permanent establishment of foreign entity
General description	Corporate profit tax	
Taxable entities	Legal entities established under the legislation of the Russian Federation (RF)	Foreign entities doing business through permanent representative office
Taxable income	Enterprises registered under Russian legislation are liable to tax on their worldwide profits	Foreign enterprises are subject to tax only on profits derived from business activities of a permanent representative office within the Russian Federation
Calculation of taxable profits	All types of income are included in gross income. Generally, taxable profit is computed by deducting from the total profit the total of incurred expenses and allocations to the reserve funds, listed in the Tax Code	Taxable profit of the PE derived from business activities exercised in the RF
	There are some differences between financial and fiscal accounting rules	
	Profit[1] of a foreign company (including foreign organization without forming a separate legal entity), controlled by Russian tax-residents[2]	
	Profit of controlled foreign company shall not be subject to corporate income tax to the extent permitted by the law	
Interest payments	Generally, interest payments are calculated based on effective rate	
	Interest payments on bonds of any kind for related party transactions are calculated based on effective rate following transfer pricing rules	
Related party transactions	Arm's length pricing prevails, but adherence to the specific domestic rules is required	

---

1 Profit of controlled foreign company shall mean an amount of profit before taxation according to its financial statements, prepared under its personal law, if the audit report on this financial statement was not modified or if domicile of this controlled foreign company is a foreign state (territory) which is party to an international treaty with the Russian Federation on taxation and the country (territory) provides information interchange for tax purposes. In other cases or under the decision of controlling person, profit of controlled foreign company shall mean an amount of profit determined by general rules of the Tax Code.
 The controlling person should submit to tax authorities notification about each controlled foreign company annually until 20 March in case the accounting profit or tax profit calculated under Russian tax requirements exceeds 50 million rubles of such company.
2 Legal entities and individuals should submit to tax authorities notification about their participation in foreign company in case their share exceeds 10%. This notification should be submitted during three months of acquisition or change in it.
 Individuals or legal entities shall be recognised as controlling persons of a foreign company (including unincorporated foreign structure) if the investment share in such organisation is either over 25%, or over 10% provided that investment shares of all persons recognised as Russian tax residents in such organisation is over 50%.

Legal form / Description	Resident corporation	Permanent establishment of foreign entity
Tax year, return and payment	*Calendar year – tax period* Reporting periods are: • for taxpayers that compute their monthly tax advances proceeding from profit received – one month, 2 months, 3 months and so on until the end of the calendar year. Advance payments of tax are made not later than 25 day of month following the past reporting period • for other taxpayers – first quarter, half a year and 9 months of the calendar year. Generally, advance payments are set off as a result of previous reporting period. Quarterly advance payments of tax are made in equal shares no later than the 28th day of each month during a report period	
Capital gains	The corporate tax rate for income in the form of a capital gain (profit from a sale of shares) is identical to the rate on regular income, ie 20%	
Losses	Current losses may reduce current profits for the current tax year Losses can be carried forward for 10 years following the year in which the loss was made	
Tax group	A Russian holding company can consolidate its Russian subsidiaries into a consolidated group of taxpayers for profits tax purposes if it holds (directly or indirectly) at least 90% of the shares in them	
Tax rate	Basic rate of 20% is allocated as follows: • federal budget – 2% • regional budget – 18% The regional part may be lower in accordance with the regional law, but not lower than 13.5% Dividends are taxed at the following rate: • 0% for dividends received from Russian legal entities, provided that, by the day of receipt, the recipient has possessed not less than 50% of the payer's charter capital for not less than 365 days Tax legislation sets special tax rates for some type of profits received by a resident corporation, for example: – 13% for dividends received from Russian legal entities (except those listed above) and foreign legal entities and income received as a stock dividend, provided that the share right shall be certified by a depositary receipt – 15% for profit in the form of interest received from state and municipal securities – 0%[3] for profit from a sale (redemption) of shares (stock) of a Russian company in cases specified in tax legislation	Standard corporate tax rate is 20% For some types of profit, there are other tax rates, for example: • 15% for profits in the form of dividends received from Russian entities and interest received from state and municipal securities

---

3 Not applicable in respect of income in the form of dividends.

III TAXES FOR INDIVIDUALS

<table>
<tr><th></th><th></th><th>Residents</th><th>Non-residents</th></tr>
<tr><td rowspan="5">Income Tax</td><td>General description</td><td>Income tax</td><td></td></tr>
<tr><td>Taxable entities and taxable income</td><td>• Natural persons who have been living in the RF not less than 183 days during 12 consecutive months
• Worldwide income</td><td>• Natural persons who have been living in the RF less than 183 days during 12 consecutive months
• Income from sources in the RF</td></tr>
<tr><td>Types of taxable income</td><td>• Employment income
• Profit of controlled foreign company
• Dividends and interest
• Rental income
• Insurance payments
• Royalties
• Income from sale of immovable property, shares, rights on demand, other individual's property</td><td></td></tr>
<tr><td>Calculation of income</td><td>There are several types of tax deduction:

• social deduction – expenses on charity, medical treatment, and education may be deducted from the sum of income in determined limits
• property deduction – income from property sales, sums spent on acquisition of plots of land for residential construction or on which residential houses are allocated (or shares of it), on purchasing and construction of houses (apartments, rooms) may be deducted (in determined limits)
• professional deduction – such categories of taxpayers as individual entrepreneurs, individuals receiving author's emoluments and some others may deduct expenses on profit gaining from income

Investment deduction –

1) in the amount of beneficial financial result received by a taxpayer during the tax period from sales (redemption) of shares traded on an organized security market and be owned by a taxpayer for more than 3 years (applies to shares acquired after 1 January 2014) (in determined limits)

2) in the amount of funds paid by a taxpayer during the tax period to his personal investment account (in determined limits)

3) in the amount of income received on transactions on personal investment account (provided that agreement for account management occurred after 1 January 2015 for the period not less than 3 years)</td><td>No tax deductions</td></tr>
</table>

		Residents	**Non-residents**
Income Tax – *contd*	Tax year, tax assessment and tax payment	Taxable period is the calendar year Legal entities and individual entrepreneurs paying income to natural persons are obliged to withhold tax at source Tax returns should be submitted in certain cases, for example by entrepreneurs, or individuals in case of selling property, or when tax was not derived in the source of income. Tax return (declaration) is due not later than 30 April of the following year. Tax is paid not later than 15 July of the following year	
	Losses	Not taken into account when determining tax base	
	Rates	• Basic rate of 13% for residents, including income in the form of dividends • 35% is applicable to certain incomes, eg interest yields, winnings, prizes	• 30% is basic tax rate for non-residents • 13% is applicable for profits from labour activity by highly skilled workers in accordance with the legislation of the Russian Federation • 15% is applicable for profits in the form of dividends received from Russian entities
	Capital gains	Income derived from the sale (redemption) of shareholdings in the authorised capital or stocks of Russian companies are exempt from taxation if, by the date of sale (redemption) of such stocks (shareholdings), they have been in a taxpayer's permanent possession for over five years, on the basis of the right of ownership or other real right. This exception shall apply in respect of income derived from the sale (redemption) of shares (stocks) of a Russian company if the shares (stocks) are bought after 1 January 2011 and held for more than five years	
Personal property tax		The tax is local and concerns the owners of the real estate. The following kinds of real estate are subject to individual property tax: dwelling houses, flats, country cottages, garages and other buildings and premises Tax rates are established by the Tax Code of the RF within the limit of 0.1, 0.5 and 2% from the cadastral cost depending on kind of property or 2% from the inventory cost of property. Specific rates and kinds of assessment base (cadastral or inventory cost) are determined by regional and local authorities	
Capital Gains Tax (CGT)	General description	No capital gains taxes	

		Domiciled	**Non-domiciled**
Inheritance Tax (IHT)	General description	No IHT in Russia	

IV WITHHOLDING TAXES

Under domestic law	Payments to residents	Payments to non-residents[4]
Dividends	0%[5] for legal entities 13% for legal entities and individuals	15% for legal entities and individuals
Interest	13% (basic tax rate)/35%[6] for individuals 20% (basic tax rate)/15%[7] for legal entities	30% (basic tax rate) 20% (basic tax rate)/15%[7] for legal entities
Royalties	13% for individuals 20% for legal entities	30% for individuals 20% for legal entities
On payments to artists and sportsmen	13% for individuals	30% for individuals

Reduced rate available under the relevant Double Taxation Treaty			
Country	Dividends	Interest	Royalties
Albania	10%	10%	10%
Algeria	15%	15%	15%
Argentina	15%	15%	15%
Armenia	10%	10%	Nil
Australia	15%	10%	10%
Austria	15%	Nil	Nil
Azerbaijan	10%	10%	10%
Belarus	15%	10%	10%
Belgium	10%	10%	Nil
Botswana	10%	10%	10%
Bulgaria	15%	15%	15%
Canada	15%	10%	10%
Chile	10%	15%	10%
China	10%	Nil	6%
Croatia	10%	10%	10%
Cuba	15%	10%	5%
Cyprus	10%	Nil	Nil
Czech Republic	10%	Nil	10%
Denmark	10%	Nil	Nil
Egypt	10%	15%	15%

4 Reduced rates of withholding tax may apply where there is an appropriate double taxation treaty.

5 0% is applicable only by Russian legal entities for dividends received from Russian legal entities provided that, by the day of receipt, the recipient has possessed not less than 50% of the payer's charter capital for not less than 365 days.

6 35% for individuals concerning interest on bank deposits, as regards the excess of the amount of interest accrued under the terms of a contract over the amount of interest calculated for deposits in roubles on the basis of the refinancing rate of the Central Bank of the Russian Federation increased by five percentage points, or on the basis of 9% annual receipts for deposits in foreign currency.

7 15% is applicable for profit in the form of interest received from state and municipal securities.

Reduced rate available under the relevant Double Taxation Treaty			
Country	Dividends	Interest	Royalties
Finland	12%	Nil	Nil
France	15%	Nil	Nil
Germany	15%	Nil	Nil
Greece	10%	7%	7%
Hungary	10%	Nil	Nil
Iceland	15%	Nil	Nil
India	10%	10%	10%
Indonesia	15%	15%	15%
Iran	10%	7.5%	5%
Ireland	10%	Nil	Nil
Israel	10%	10%	10%
Italy	10%	10%	Nil
Japan	15%	10%	10%
Kazakhstan	10%	10%	10%
Korea, Republic of	10%	Nil	Nil
Kuwait	5%	Nil	10%
Kyrgyzstan	10%	10%	10%
Latvia	10%	10%	5%
Lebanon	10%	5%	5%
Lithuania	10%	10%	10%
Luxembourg	15%	Nil	Nil
Macedonia	10%	10%	10%
Malaysia	15%	15%	15%
Mali	15%	15%	Nil
Malta	10%	5%	5%
Mexico	10%	10%	10%
Moldova	10%	Nil	10%
Mongolia	10%	10%	–
Montenegro	15%	10%	10%
Morocco	10%	10%	10%
Namibia	10%	10%	5%
Netherlands	15%	Nil	Nil
New Zealand	15%	10%	10%
North Korea	10%	Nil	Nil
Norway	10%	10%	Nil
Philippines	15%	15%	15%
Poland	10%	10%	10%
Portugal	15%	10%	10%
Qatar	5%	5%	Nil
Romania	15%	15%	10%
Saudi Arabia	5%	5%	10%
Serbia	15%	10%	10%
Singapore	10%	7.5%	7.5%
Slovakia	10%	Nil	10%
Slovenia	10%	10%	10%

Reduced rate available under the relevant Double Taxation Treaty			
Country	Dividends	Interest	Royalties
South Africa	15%	10%	Nil
Spain	15%	5%	5%
Sri Lanka	15%	10%	10%
Sweden	15%	Nil	Nil
Switzerland	15%	Nil	Nil
Syria	15%	10%	18%
Tajikistan	10%	10%	Nil
Thailand	15%	10%	15%
Turkey	10%	10%	10%
Turkmenistan	10%	5%	5%
Ukraine	15%	10%	10%
United Kingdom	10%	Nil	Nil
United States	10%	Nil	Nil
Uzbekistan	10%	10%	Nil
Venezuela	15%	10%	15%
Vietnam	15%	10%	15%

Note: the above rates are only available provided the specific Treaty criteria are satisfied. Some treaties provide lower rates than those shown above, which may be available provided certain criteria are satisfied. As treaties will not be identical, guidance should be sought in all cases.

V   INDIRECT TAXES

		Residents	Non-residents
Value Added Tax (VAT)	Entities obliged to levy VAT	Legal entities and individual entrepreneurs	
	Taxable activities	• Sales of goods, works, services and property rights in the RF • Import of goods	
	Taxable activities – zero-rated (examples)	• Goods placed under customs export regime • Services involved in international carriage of commodities • Works (services) carried out (rendered) by the organisations engaged in pipeline transportation of oil and oil products • Works (services) involved in processing commodities placed under the customs procedure of processing in the customs territory • Works or services directly connected with the carriage or transportation of goods placed under the customs procedure of customs transit when carrying foreign goods from the customs authority at the place of arrival at the territory of the Russian Federation to the customs authority at the place of their departure from the territory of the Russian Federation • Other activities specified in tax legislation	
	Refund of VAT	Where input VAT exceeds output VAT, a refund is due	
	Tax liability	Amount of tax due to payment is calculated as the difference between output and input VAT. Input VAT may be claimed if the following rules are observed: • goods, works, services and property rights were purchased in order to conduct operations subject to VAT • the mentioned goods have been entered into books • the taxpayer keeps the VAT invoice	Calculated and paid by tax agent based on the profit from sale
	Tax rates	• 10% tax rate is levied on goods of basic necessity to society: major foodstuffs, goods for children, medical goods produced in Russia and imported, print periodicals (except erotic and advertising) • 18% tax rate is imposed on other goods (work, services) not mentioned above	

	Residents	Non-residents
Administrative obligations	There is a special order of VAT accounting in Russia: • All taxpayers are obliged to draw up invoices, keep record books of received and issued invoices, keep purchase books and sale books • Tax period is one quarter. Payment should be made in equal shares no later than the 25th day of each of 3 months following the past tax period • Tax return is submitted not later than the 25th day of the month following the past tax period	• Accounting, declaring and payment is made by tax agent • Payment of tax is made by the tax agent together with transfer of funds • Tax return is submitted by tax agent not later than the 25th day of the month following the past tax period

Saudi Arabia

(Al Tala CPA – Nexia International, yaser.s@altala.com.sa, www.altala.com.sa)

I MAIN LEGAL FORMS

Legal form / Characteristics	Partnership and Limited Liability Partnership (LLP)	Private corporation (Ltd) and Public corporation (Plc)
Partners/shareholders • Number • Restrictions	Partnership: Unlimited number of general partners – KSA nationals only – minimum two LLP: One general Partner and unlimited number of limited partners – KSA nationals only	Ltd: At least two shareholders, no more than 50, and can be 100% non-KSA nationals, or KSA and non-KSA nationals Plc: At least five shareholders can be KSA and non-KSA nationals
Directors	Partnership: One or more managing director(s), can be one of the partners LLP: At least one general partner	Ltd: One or more managing director(s), can be one of the partners Plc: Board of directors of at least three persons (including the CEO)
Establishment	Partnership deed	Ltd/Plc: Notarize the Articles of Association with a Notary public & Chamber of Commerce & General Organization for Social Insurance & Register with the Department of Zakat & Tax 'for non-KSA nationals must have approval from investment authority'
Registration	Partnership & LLP: • Ministry of Commerce • Chamber of Commerce • General Organization for Social Insurance • Register with the Department of Zakat	Ltd/Plc: • Ministry of Commerce • SAGIA for non-KSA national • Chamber of Commerce • General Organization for Social Insurance • Register with the Department of Zakat & Tax

Legal form / Characteristics	Partnership and Limited Liability Partnership (LLP)	Private corporation (Ltd) and Public corporation (Plc)
Minimum capital	No Minimum capital required	Ltd: No Minimum capital required but according to company activity
		For non-KSA nationals, minimum capital is SAR 2m for most industries, SAR 25m for agricultural companies and SAR 5m for factories
		Plc: Minimum shear capital required is SAR 10m for public joint stock companies, but for a private joint stock company the minimum shear capital required is SAR 2m
Liability	Partnership & LLP: General partners are jointly and severally liable to the extent of all their assets for the liabilities of the entity. Limited partners are liable for the company's liabilities to the extent of their respective shares in the capital only	Ltd: Each member is liable to the extent of his respective shareholding. If they lose more than 50% of the capital, the company should go to liquidation
		If the company is not placed into liquidation, members become jointly and severally liable to the extent of all their assets for the liabilities of the company
		Plc: Each member is liable to the extent of his respective shareholding
Governance	Partnership: Deed of Partnership or Memorandum of Association LLP: General Partner Or Deed of Partnership or Memorandum of Association	Ltd: Managing Director – Board of Directors Plc: Managing Director – Board of Directors Shareholders' general meeting
Audit requirements	Not generally required	Ltd: Independent audit required by law Plc: Public joint stock company – Two auditors required Private joint stock company – Independent audit required by law
Taxation & Zaka	Income Tax does not apply for KSA nationals but Zaka applies for KSA nationals only	Ltd/Plc: Income Tax does not apply for KSA nationals but applies for non-KSA nationals according to their shares in the capital only, and Zaka applies for KSA nationals only

II CORPORATION TAX

Description \ Legal form	KSA resident corporation	Non-resident corporation
General description	No Tax Applies Only Zaka	Tax levied on taxable profit (adjusted net profit), only from foreign companies and foreign partners in a resident company
Taxable entities	None	Only from foreign companies and foreign partners in a resident company
Taxable income	None	Net profit of the foreign companies and foreign partners in a resident company from its operations
Calculation of taxable profits	None	Accounting profit is adjusted to arrive at taxable profit
Interest payments	Interest paid is accepted as an expense if it is paid to Saudi Bank	Interest paid is accepted as expenses according to tax calculation
Related party transactions	For any transactions where payment is made abroad for services, 5% has to be deducted, otherwise no tax	On any transactions where the payment is made abroad to a related party, 5% has to be deducted
Tax year, return and payment	None	Tax period is 12 months Tax return must be submitted to authorities not later than 120 days from end of the financial year Delay penalty from 5% to 25% + SAR 20,000 as non-submission penalty
Capital gains	None	None
Losses	The losses of a year can be carried forward until fully utilised	The losses of a year can be carried forward and set against 25% of the following years' profits until fully utilised
Tax group	None	Non-resident group is taxed and treated as one company
Tax rate	None	20% of taxable profit

III   TAXES FOR INDIVIDUALS

		Residents	Non-residents
Income Tax	General description	None	None
	Taxable entities and taxable income	None	None
	Types of taxable income	None	None
	Calculation of income	None	None
	Tax year, tax assessment and tax payment	None	None
	Losses	None	None
	Tax rates	None	None
Capital Gains Tax (CGT)	General description	None	None
	Taxable entities and chargeable assets	None	None
	Calculation of gain	None	None
	Tax year, tax assessment and tax payment	None	None
	Losses	None	None
	Tax rates	None	None
		KSA domiciled	Non-KSA domiciled
Inheritance Tax (IHT)	General description	None	None
	Taxable entities and chargeable assets	None	None
	Calculation of charge	None	None
	Taxable events	None	None
	Allowances	None	None
	Tax rates	None	None

IV   WITHHOLDING TAXES

Under domestic law	Payments to residents	Payments to non-residents
Dividends	Nil	5%
Interest	Nil	5%
Royalties	Nil	20% for management fees / 15% transactions to a head office or related parties abroad / 5% for rents, services, insurance etc / 15% for any other payments
On payments to artists and sportsmen	Nil	Nil

Reduced rate available under the relevant Double Taxation Treaty			
Country	Dividends	Interest	Royalties
Austria	5%	5%	10%
Bangladesh	10%	7.5%	10%
Belarus	5%	5%	10%
China, People's Republic of	5%	10%	10%
France	0%	0%	0%
Greece	5%	5%	10%
India	5%	10%	10%
Ireland	0%/5%	0%	5%/8%
Italy	5%/10%	5%	10%
Japan	5%/10%	10%	5%/10%
Luxembourg	5%	0%	5%/7%
Malaysia	5%	5%	8%
Malta	5%	0%	5%/7%
Netherlands	5%/10%	5%	7%
Pakistan	5%/10%	10%	10%
Poland	5%	5%	10%
Romania	5%	5%	10%
Russia	5%	5%	10%
Singapore	5%	5%	8%
South Africa	5%/10%	5%	10%
South Korea	5%/10%	5%	5%/10%
Spain	0%/5%	5%	8%
Syria	0%	7.5%	15%
Tunisia	5%	2.5%/5%	5%
Turkey	5%/10%	10%	10%
Ukraine	5%/15%	10%	10%
United Kingdom	5%/15%	0%	5%/8%
Uzbekistan	7%	7%	10%
Vietnam	5%/12.5%	10%	7.5%/10%

Note: the above rates are only available provided the specific Treaty criteria are satisfied. It is possible that lower rates than those shown above may be available provided certain criteria are satisfied. As treaties will not be identical, guidance should be sought in all cases.

V   INDIRECT TAXES

		Residents	Non-residents
Value Added Tax	General description	Nil	Nil
	Entities obliged to levy VAT	Nil	Nil
	Taxable activities	Nil	Nil
	Taxable activities – zero-rated (examples)	Nil	Nil
	Exemptions (examples)	Nil	Nil
	Refund of VAT	Nil	Nil
	Tax liability	Nil	Nil
	Tax rates	Nil	Nil
	Administrative obligations	Nil	Nil
Real Property Taxes		Nil	Nil
Stamp Duty		Nil	Nil

Nexia International is the trading name of Nexia International Limited, a company registered in the Isle of Man. Company registration number: 53513C. Registered office: 2nd floor, Sixty Circular Road, Douglas, Isle of Man, IM1 1SA

Senegal

(Papa Alboury NDAO, RMA Senegal, p.ndao@rmasenegal.com)

I MAIN LEGAL FORMS

Legal form / Characteristics	Limited Liability Partnership (SARL)	Public and private Corporations (SA)
Partners/ shareholders	Two choices: • SUARL (sole proprietorship) – 1 partner • SARL – 2 or more partners	Two choices: • SA Unipersonnelle – 1 shareholder **only** • SA – 2 or more shareholders
Number	• SUARL – maximum 1 • SARL – none	• SA Unipersonnelle – Maximum 1 • SA – None
Restrictions	Minors	None
Directors	Managed by Partners or any other individual chosen by the partners	The Director must be a physical individual
Establishment	Charter of Incorporation (Statut)	Charter of Incorporation (Statut)
Registration	Centralized at APIX: • Tax ID from the Fiscal Administration • Company registration number from the courts	Centralized at APIX: • Tax ID from the Fiscal Administration • Company registration number from the courts
Minimum capital	No minimum	Private: CFA 10,000,000 Public: CFA 100,000,000
Liability	Limited to capital for all partners	Limited to capital for all shareholders
Governance	Partner's meeting	Board of directors Meeting (Conseil D'administration)
Audit requirements	Two out of three must be met: • Revenues over CFA 250 million • Total Assets over CFA 125 million • More than 50 employees	Mandatory
Taxation	SUARL – Taxed at the individual rate unless they opt to be taxed at the corporate rate SARL – Taxed at the corporate rate of 30%	Corporate tax of 30% except entities which have the status of 'Société Franche d'exportation' which export more than 80% of their production. Those entities are taxed at 15%[1]

---

1 The entities eligible for the 15% tax rate are those that had the status before the fiscal reform of 2013. Any company deemed to be a 'Société Franche d'exportation' after the reform will be taxed at the normal rate of 30%.

II   CORPORATION TAX

Legal form / Description	Resident corporation and Permanent Establishment
General Description	The corporate tax is applicable to all corporations, permanent establishments and limited liability partnerships except SUARL who do not opt to be taxed at the corporate rate
Taxable entities	The Corporation
Taxable income	All revenues
Calculation of taxable profits	Accounting Profit +/- Tax timing differences +/- Tax permanent differences Senegalese Taxation Income
Interest payments	Interest paid is deductible in all cases except if the interest is paid to a financial institution or individual located in a tax haven. In such a case the interest is only deductible if the corporation can prove that it relates to a real transaction
Related party transactions	Strict adherence to arm's length principle

Tax year, return and payment	• Tax year – 2014
	• Return – 30 April 2015
	• Payment
	  – 15 February 2015 (greater of IMF (see Losses below) or 1/3 of corporate tax)
	  – 30 April 2015 (1/3)
	  – 30 June 2015 (1/3)

Capital gains	Taxed at the corporate tax rate. Investment firms for which the capital gain on stock held within the first three years of existence are exempt from capital gains tax. Also Companies are exempt from capital gains tax if the company has a plan to reinvest the proceeds of the sale within three years
Losses	Alternative Minimum Tax (IMF). In cases of losses, companies are taxed at 0.5% of revenues with a minimum of CFA 500,000 and a ceiling of CFA 5,000,000 Losses can be carried forward for three years
Tax group	N/A
Tax rate	30%

III TAXES FOR INDIVIDUALS

		Residents	Non-residents
Income Tax	Taxable entities and taxable income	All individuals disposing of income and residing in Senegal or any other individual disposing of Senegalese sourced income	
	Types of taxable income	• Income tax • Rental income • Capital Gains • Dividends • Royalties • Profit from Agricultural activities	
	Calculation of income	Global Income – Deductible expenses = Taxable income net of 'abattement' A standard deduction of 30% of the annual income with a ceiling of CFA 900,000 is allowed. A reduction of taxes is also given depending on the number of dependants which the tax payer has and a taxpayer can be given up to 5 'part' calculated in 0.5 increments for each spouse and child he/she has. The taxpayer is counted as 1 part	

	Tax year, tax assessment and tax payment	• Tax Year – 2014
		• Income tax declaration deadline – 1 May 2015
		• Payment –
		  – Salary – on a monthly basis
		  – Others – 1 May 2015	

	Losses	Losses are carried forward for up to three years but are only imputable to gains of the same nature	
	Tax rates	CFA Franc 0 to 630,000 → 0% 630,001 to 1,500,000 → 20% 1,500,001 to 4,000,000 → 30% 4,000,001 to 8,000,000 → 35% 8,000,001 to 13,500,000 → 37% More than 13,500,001 → 40%	

		Residents	Non-residents
Capital Gains Tax (CGT)	General description	Tax on the sale of assets which have appreciated or depreciated in value	
	Taxable entities and chargeable assets	The tax is applicable to all individuals	
	Calculation of gain	Sales price – acquisition price. No differentiation between long-term or short-term capital gain as it is all considered as capital gain	
	Tax year, tax assessment and tax payment	The tax on capital gains is due at the time the Corporate or individual tax returns are due Individual – 1 May at time of declaration	
	Losses	Losses are carried forward for up to three years and are only imputable to capital gains	
	Tax rates	The tax rate is progressive and is calculated in the same nature as the personal income tax, as it all should be declared in the same schedule and share the same tax rate	

		Domiciled	Domiciled
Inheritance Tax (IHT)	General description	Estate tax on assets passed down through generations. It is not a tax per se. It is a registration tax to change the proprietor on the asset	
	Taxable entities and chargeable assets	The tax is imposed on the person receiving the asset	
	Calculation of charge	The taxable portion of the estate is calculated by deducting all debts of the dead as well as all agricultural-related assets from the total assets to be passed down. A standard deduction is allowed up to CFA 200 million	
	Taxable events	All property passed down, with the exception of agricultural-related assets (farmland, for example), is subject to inheritance tax If the farmland is shared between the descendants, inheritance tax becomes payable	
	Allowances	Standard deduction of CFA 200 million, agricultural land	
	Tax rates	Registration tax varies from 1% to 7% depending on the nature of the asset passed down	

IV WITHHOLDING TAXES

Under domestic law	Payments to residents	Payments to non-residents
Dividends	10% withheld by the paying corporation	
Interest	8% – if interest from a financial institution 13% – interest on bond obligations 16% – for all other interest	
Royalties	20%	
On payments to artists and sportsmen	20%	

Reduced rate available under the relevant Double Taxation Treaty			
Country	Dividends	Interest	Royalties
Belgium	0–16%	0–16%	0–10%
Canada	0–15%	0–20%	0–15%
France	0–15%	0–15%	0–15%
Mauritius	0–15%[2]	0%[2]	0%[2]
Spain	0–15%	0–20%	0–15%
UEMOA	0–10%	0–15%	0–15%

Note: the above rates are only available provided the specific Treaty criteria are satisfied. It is possible that lower rates than those shown above may be available provided certain criteria are satisfied. As treaties will not be identical, guidance should be sought in all cases.

2 Depending if the company receiving the interest, dividends or royalties has an entity representing it in Senegal.

V   INDIRECT TAXES

		Residents
Value Added Tax	General description	Value Added tax is applicable on all sales of goods or services rendered and used in Senegal
	Entities obliged to levy VAT	All entities for which their activity is not exempt of VAT
	Taxable activities	Sale of goods and services except sale of goods of first necessity such as rice, sugar and educational institutions, etc
	Taxable activities – zero-rated (examples)	A zero rate applies to the sale of goods or services used outside of Senegal
	Exemptions (examples)	Corporations whose 80% of production / manufactured is imported
		Certain Goods and services are exempt from VAT (for example, rice, sugar, educational institutions)
	Refund of VAT	Corporations can ask for a VAT refund within two years of the purchase for which VAT was levied
	Tax liability	The company providing the service or selling the goods is liable of VAT when service is rendered or goods delivered
	Tax rates	10% for companies in the hotel industry
		18% for all other companies
	Administrative obligations	• VAT Declaration on a monthly basis due 15 days after month end
		Precise accounting and documentation required
Real Property Tax		Real property tax is calculated based on its annual rental value:
		• Buildings – 5% of the annual rental value
		• Plant – 7.5% of annual rental value
Real Property Taxes		• Stamp duty is mandatory on various administrative transactions. The amount depends on the nature of the transaction

Serbia

(Vesna Stanković - v.stankovic@lbrev.com, Zvezdan Božinović - z.bozinovic@lbrev.com)

I MAIN LEGAL FORMS

Legal form / Characteristics	Partnership (O.D.) and Limited Liability Partnership (K.D.)	Private corporation (D.O.O.) and Public corporation (A.D.)
Partners/shareholders • Number • Restrictions	• Two or more • None	• One or more • None
Directors	Management by partners	Management by director(s)
Registration	In Business Register Agency according to Registration Law	
Minimum capital	None	D.O.O. RSD 100 A.D. RSD 3,000,000 unless it is otherwise provided by law for specific activities
Liability	Unlimited for all partners of O.D. and general partner of K.D., limited for limited partner of K.D.	Limited to capital
Governance	• Partners • General meeting	• Managing director/Board of directors • Shareholders' meeting • Supervisory board (additionally for A.D.)
Audit requirements	Audit is required by Law for all medium-sized and large entities,[1] for public companies regardless of their size and all legal entities and entrepreneurs whose operating income is more than EUR 4,400,000 (which is calculated in RSD according to National Bank of Serbia exchange rate) Audit of consolidated financial statements is obligatory for parent company	

---

1 Medium-sized entities – at least two of the three conditions are satisfied: number of employees is between 50 and 250, turnover is between EUR 8.8m and EUR 35m, total assets are between EUR 4.4m and EUR 17.5m.
Large entities – at least two of the three conditions are satisfied: number of employees exceeds 250, turnover exceeds EUR 35m, total assets exceed EUR 17.5m.

Legal form / Characteristics	Partnership (O.D.) and Limited Liability Partnership (K.D.)	Private corporation (D.O.O.) and Public corporation (A.D.)
Taxation	Serbian resident partnerships are subject to corporate income tax on a worldwide basis	Serbian resident companies are subject to corporate income tax on a worldwide basis
Usage	Not popular	D.O.O. popular especially for SMEs A.D. is legal form for public companies, less popular for others

II CORPORATION TAX

Description \ Legal form	Resident corporation	Permanent establishment (PE)
General description	Tax is levied on the taxable profit generated within a tax year	Tax is levied on the taxable profit earned in Serbia generated within a tax year
Taxable entities	Companies incorporated in Serbia or companies with effective place of management located in Serbia	PE constituted in Serbia
Taxable income	Worldwide principle	Territorial principle
		Income generated in Serbia
Calculation of taxable profits	Accounting profit is adjusted for various tax add-backs, allowances and exemptions to arrive at the taxable profit	
Interest payments	Interest between related parties is subject to referential interest rate published by National Bank of Serbia. Such published interest rate is considered to be at arm's length. Penalty interest is calculated as 8% + referential interest rate	
	Thin capitalisation rules apply. Thin capitalisation ratio of 1:4 applies	
	Interest payments to certain low tax jurisdictions are not deductible for corporate income tax purposes	
Related party transactions	All related party transactions must take place on an arm's length basis from an income tax point of view	
Tax year, return and payment	Tax year generally coincides with the business year, but may also differ from business year	
	Corporate income tax return must be submitted to tax authorities within 180 days after the end of the tax year	
	During the tax year, corporate income tax is prepaid on a monthly basis	
Capital gains	Capital gains are subject to corporation tax at normal rates	
Losses	Within-year losses can be offset against future tax profits. Current year tax loss may be carried forward for five years	
Tax group	Consolidated tax group is possible only where all connected entities are resident	Not applicable
	Must be applied for at least five years	
Tax rate	For 2013 and onwards: 15%	

III TAXES FOR INDIVIDUALS

		Residents	Non-residents
Income Tax	General description	Personal income tax is levied on the qualifying income of an individual for a year of assessment	
	Taxable entities and taxable income	Resident individuals are liable to tax on their worldwide income	Non-resident individuals are liable to tax only on the income with a source in Serbia Double taxation may be eliminated by application of Double Taxation Agreements
	Types of taxable income	Income from employment Professional income Income from copyright, rights related to copyright and industrial property rights Income from capital Income from real estate Annual income Capital gains Other income	
	Calculation of income	In general, income is earned when: payment is received, payment is made, or the benefit has been provided	
	Tax year, tax assessment and tax payment	Tax year equals calendar year All payers of the income report the income paid after every payment and at the end of year Tax assessment is calculated as income of an individual adjusted for various tax add-backs, allowances and exemptions to arrive at the taxable income Tax is paid on self-taxation principle	
	Losses	Capital losses may be carried forward for five years	
	Tax rates	Income from employment: 10% Professional income: 10% Income from copyright, rights related to copyright and industrial property rights: 20% Income from capital: 15% Capital gains: 15% Income from real estate: 20% Other income: 20%, except for income that person derives from insurance: 15% Annual tax on citizen income: progressive tax rate from 10%–15%[2]	

---

2   The highest rate is due where the taxable annual income is six times higher than average income.

		Residents	Non-residents
Capital Gains Tax (CGT)	General description	Capital gains tax is levied on gains earned by disposal of capital	
	Taxable entities and chargeable assets	All residents earning capital gains worldwide are subject to capital gains tax	Non-resident individuals are liable to tax only on the income with the source in Serbia
		Real estate, securities, shares in capital, copyrights and investment coupons are considered as capital[3]	Real estate, securities, shares in capital, copyrights and investment coupons are considered as capital
	Calculation of gain	Sales price reduced for purchase price of the capital represents the tax basis for capital gains tax. The purchase price is adjusted with the consumer price index	
	Tax year, tax assessment and tax payment	Tax on capital gains is paid following the decision of the tax administrator Tax return must be submitted within 30 days from: • Agreement of transfer of immovable property • Agreement of an assignment of copyright, rights related to copyright and industrial property rights • Agreement on the transfer of shares in the capital • The end of each calendar half-year in which individual completed the transfer of securities	
	Losses	Capital gains tax: tax losses may be carried forward for five years	
	Tax rates	General tax rate is 15%	
		Domiciled	**Non-domiciled**
Inheritance Tax (IHT)	General description	Tax for recipients of inheritances and lifetime gifts	
	Taxable entities and chargeable assets	Individual or legal entities that receive assets based on inheritance or gift	Individual or legal entities that receive assets located in the territory of Serbia based on inheritance or gift
	Calculation of charge	Normally market value reduced for all debts and costs which the taxable person is obligated to pay from inherited assets	
	Taxable events	Inheritances or lifetime gifts of net assets located worldwide	Inheritances or lifetime gifts of assets located in Serbia
		Tax liability for inheritance tax crystallises when court decision becomes effective	Tax liability for inheritance tax crystallises when court decision becomes effective
		Tax liability for gift tax crystallises on the signature of contract or actual receipt of the gift	Tax liability for gift tax crystallises on the signature of contract or actual receipt of the gift

---

3 Since 2012 it is not required to calculate or pay capital gains tax on rights, shares and securities which were in a taxable entity's portfolio for at least ten years before selling.

		Domiciled	**Non-domiciled**
Inheritance Tax (IHT) – *contd*	Allowances	Where inheritance or gifts are received by children, spouses or parents (first rank of inheritance)	
		Where inheritance or gift will be used for agriculture, taxi or rent-a-car activities	
		Where inheritance or gift is donated from an entity in a higher inheritance rank who then renounces ownership	
		Where the inheritance or gift is to the Republic or the municipalities	
		Where the inheritance or gift is an asset which is received from the Republic or the municipalities	
	Tax rates	First inheritance rank: 0%	
		Second inheritance rank: 1.5%	
		Other: 2.5%	

IV   WITHHOLDING TAXES

Under domestic law	Payments to residents[4]	Payments to non-residents[5]
Dividends	Generally exempt	20%
Interest	Generally exempt	20%
Royalties	Generally exempt	20%
Copyright, rights related to copyright and industrial property rights	Generally exempt	20%

Reduced rate available under the relevant Double Taxation Treaty					
	Dividends				
Country	Capital share 25% to 100%[6]	Other cases[7]	Unique tax rate[8]	Interest	Royalties
Albania	5%	15%	–	10%	10%
Austria	5%	15%	–	10%	5% / 10%[9]
Azerbaijan	–	–	10%	10%	10%
Belgium	10%	15%	–	15%	10%
Belarus	5%	15%	–	8%	10%
Bosnia and Herzegovina	5%	10%	–	10%	10%
Bulgaria	5%	15%	–	10%	10%
Canada	5%	15%	–	10%	10%
China	–	–	5%	10%	10%
Croatia	5%	10%	–	10%	10%
Cyprus	–	–	10%	10%	10%
Czech Republic	–	–	10%	10%	5% / 10%[9]
Denmark	5%	15%	–	10%	10%
Egypt	5%	15%	–	15%	15%
Estonia	5%	10%	–	10%	5% / 10%[10]
Finland	5%	15%	–	–	10%
France	5%	15%	–	–	–
Georgia	5%	10%	–	10%	10%
Germany	–	–	15%	–	10%
Greece	5%	15%	–	10%	10%
Hungary	5%	15%	–	10%	10%

4   Refers to legal entities.
5   Withholding tax rates may be reduced by application of Double Tax Agreements which are implemented in Serbian tax regulation.
6   Tax rate which applies in cases when recipient of dividend is legal entity.
7   Tax rate which applies in cases when recipient of dividend is legal entity (with lower share in capital) or individual.
8   Tax rate which applies in cases when recipient of dividend is legal entity (regardless of share in capital) or individual.
9   Withholding tax rate which must not be higher than 5% refers to intellectual property rights, while tax rate which must not be higher than 10% refers to industrial property rights.
10 Withholding tax rate which must not be higher than 5% refers to intellectual property rights, while tax rate which must not be higher than 10% refers to industrial property rights.

	Reduced rate available under the relevant Double Taxation Treaty				
Country	Dividends			Interest	Royalties
	Capital share 25% to 100%[6]	Other cases[7]	Unique tax rate[8]		
India	5%	15%	–	10%	10%
Iran	–	–	10%	10%	10%
Ireland	5%	10%	–	10%	5% / 10%[10]
Italy	–	–	10%	10%	10%
Korea (Democratic People's Republic of)	–	–	10%	10%	10%
Kuwait	5%	10%	–	10%	10%
Latvia	5%	10%	–	10%	5% / 10%[10]
Libya	5%	10%	–	10%	10%
Lithuania	5%	10%	–	10%	10%
Macedonia, Republic of	5%	15%	–	10%	10%
Malaysia	–	–	10%	10%	10%
Malta	5%	10%	–	10%	5% / 10%[10]
Moldova	5%	15%	–	10%	10%
Montenegro	–	–	10%	10%	5% / 10%[10]
Morocco	–	–	10%	10%	10%
Netherlands	5%	15%	–	–	10%
Norway	–	–	15%	–	10%
Pakistan	–	–	10%	10%	10%
Poland	5%	15%	–	10%	10%
Qatar	5%	10%	–	10%	10%
Romania	–	–	10%	10%	10%
Russian Federation	5%	15%	–	10%	10%
Slovakia	5%	15%	–	10%	10%
Slovenia	5%	10%	–	10%	5% / 10%[10]
Sri Lanka	–	–	12,5%	10%	10%
Spain	5%	10%	–	10%	5% / 10%[10]
Sweden	5%	15%	–	–	–
Switzerland	5%	15%	–	10%	10%
Tunisia	–	–	10%	10%	10%
Turkey	5%	15%	–	10%	10%
Ukraine	5%	10%	–	10%	10%
United Arab Emirates	5%	10%	–	10%	10%
United Kingdom and Northern Ireland	5%	15%	–	10%	10%
Vietnam	10%	15%	–	10%	10%

Note: the above rates are only available provided the specific Treaty criteria are satisfied. It is possible that lower rates than those shown above may be available provided certain criteria are satisfied. As treaties will not be identical, guidance should be sought in all cases.

V INDIRECT TAXES

		Residents	Non-residents
Value Added Tax	General description	General tax on supply which is calculated and paid on delivery of goods and services, in all phases of manufacturing and trade in Serbia, and also on importation of goods	
	Entities obliged to levy VAT	Entities which conduct the supply of goods and services in Serbia, as taxable activities in order to maintain a business activity	
	Taxable Activities	Supply of goods and services, import of goods	
		Place of supply of goods and services must be in Serbia, apart from exemptions which are predicted by law (mostly regarding transport and services)	
	Taxable activities – zero-rated (examples)	Export of goods and services to entities which are not located in Serbia or do not have place of management in Serbia	
	Exemptions (examples)	Banking and insurance services	
		Services related to investment funds and pension funds	
		Activities in the public interest (hospital and medical care, welfare and security work, public education, dental services, cultural and scientific services, etc)	
		Transactions related to the sale of immovable property, which have already been used	
		Leases of flats for living	
	Refund of VAT	VAT paid on supply of goods and services, or from import, is deductible as input tax, if incurred in the course or improvement of the business and for the purpose of making taxable supplies of goods and services (including zero-rated supplies)	
		Exemptions: purchase of cars (for companies whose core activity is not transport), entertainment expenses, etc	
	Tax liability	Normally accounted for by the supplier of goods and services	
		Reverse charge for import of goods and services	
	Tax rates	Standard rate = 20%	
		Reduced rate = 10% (eg food, medicines, books, hotel accommodation, public transport, etc)	
	Administrative obligations	VAT identification number is required	
		There are formal requirements concerning business records and invoices	
		Monthly tax self-assessment is required plus an annual tax return (for smaller companies self-assessment is either quarterly or not required)	

	Residents	Non-residents
Real Property Taxes	Tax is levied on the individual or legal entities which are holders of the property right, or are users or holders of the property in Serbia (land, residential and commercial buildings, flats and garages). This tax is also levied on lessees Tax rates: For taxable entities which are obliged to keep business records: up to 0.40% (all properties) For taxable entities which are not obliged to keep business records: up to 0.30% (land) For taxable entities which are not obliged to keep business records (every property except land): – Under RSD 10,000,000: up to 0.40% – From RSD 10,000,000 to RSD 25,000,000: up to 0.60% – From RSD 25,000,000 to RSD 50,000,000: up to 1.00% – Over RSD 50,000,000: up to 2.00% Tax declaration for entities which are obliged to keep business records must be submitted before 31 March Tax is payable quarterly for all entities (within 45 days of beginning of quarter)	
Real Property Transfer Tax	Tax is payable on real property transactions in Serbia and outside of Serbia Tax is calculated on sales price, but it must not be lower than market value Taxable person is the seller of the real estate Tax rate is 2.5% Tax declaration should be submitted to the tax authorities within 30 days The tax should be paid within 15 days of receipt of tax authorities' decision	Tax is payable on real property transactions in Serbia Tax is calculated on sales price, but it must not be lower than market value Taxable person is the seller of the real estate Tax rate is 2.5% Tax declaration should be submitted to the tax authorities within 30 days The tax should be paid within 15 days of receipt of tax authorities' decision
Insurance tax	Insurance tax at rate of 5% is applicable for non-life insurance contracts, with some exemptions	

Singapore

(Henry Tan, Nexia TS, henrytan@nexiats.com.sg)

I   MAIN LEGAL FORMS

Legal form / Characteristics	Partnership and Limited Liability Partnership (LLP)	Private corporation (Pte Ltd) and Public corporation (Limited)
Partners/shareholders • Number • Restrictions	Partnership: • Between two and 20 partners • Restriction on transferability of ownership • Non-perpetual existence LLP: • Minimum two partners, no maximum limit LP: • At least two partners, with at least one general partner and one limited partner. No maximum limit	Pte Ltd: • Minimum one shareholder and not more than 50 shareholders • Restriction on rights to transfer shares Limited: Minimum one shareholder
Directors	Management by partners LLP: • At least one manager who is ordinarily resident in Singapore LP: • At least one manager who is ordinarily resident in Singapore must be appointed if all the general partners are not ordinarily resident in Singapore	Pte Ltd and Limited: At least one director and secretary who is ordinarily resident in Singapore
Establishment	Partnership Agreement Limited Liability Partnerships Act Limited Partnerships Act	Memorandum and Articles of Association Companies Act
Registration	Accounting and Corporate Regulatory Authority (ACRA)	
Minimum capital	N/A	S$1.00

Legal form Characteristics	Partnership and Limited Liability Partnership (LLP)	Private corporation (Pte Ltd) and Public corporation (Limited)
Liability	Partnership: • Unlimited • Partners are jointly and severally liable for all debts and obligations LLP: • Limited to capital • Partners personally liable for debts and losses resulting from their own careless action but not personally liable for debts and losses of LLP incurred by other partners LP: • General partner personally liable for debts and losses of the LP • Limited partner not personally liable for the debts or obligations of LP beyond amount of his agreed contribution	Pte Ltd and Limited: Limited
Governance	Partners' meetings	Directors' meetings Shareholders' meetings
Audit requirements	None	Mandatory except for dormant companies and small exempt private companies ('EPC') with annual revenue not exceeding S$5 million An EPC is a private company in which no beneficial interests are held, directly or indirectly, by any corporation and which has not more than 20 members The above rule for audit exemption is replaced by a small company concept for financial years commencing on or after 1 July 2015. A company qualifies as a small company if it is a private company in the financial year in question and it meets at least two of the following three criteria for the immediate past two consecutive financial years: a) total annual revenue does not exceed S$10million; b) value of total assets does not exceed S$10million; c) Number of employees does not exceed 50. If the company is a part of a corporate group, the company must qualify as a small company and the entire group must meet at least two of the above three criterial on a consolidated based for the immediate past two consecutive financial years

	Partnership and Limited Liability Partnership (LLP)	Private corporation (Pte Ltd) and Public corporation (Limited)
Taxation	Transparent	Pte Ltd and Limited: Profits taxed at corporate tax rates
Usage	Professional practices	Small and medium-sized enterprises (SMEs) and listed companies

II   CORPORATION TAX

Description \ Legal form	Singapore resident corporation	Permanent establishment (PE)
General description	Singapore corporate income tax	
Taxable entities	Singapore incorporated corporations and corporations managed and controlled in Singapore	PE located in Singapore
Taxable income	Revenue income accruing in or derived from Singapore or received in Singapore from outside Singapore, unless specifically exempted under the Income Tax Act Foreign-sourced dividends, foreign branch profits and foreign-sourced service income received in Singapore are exempt from tax, subject to conditions	Revenue income accruing in or derived from Singapore or received in Singapore from outside Singapore, unless specifically exempted under the Income Tax Act
Calculation of taxable profits	Accounting profit before taxes after various tax adjustments and allowances to arrive at profits chargeable to corporation tax	
Interest payments	Interest incurred on capital employed in acquiring income and not in connection with expenses specifically disallowed for tax deduction under Section 15 of the Income Tax Act is generally tax deductible Interest expense relating to non-income/exempt - income producing assets is not tax deductible	
Related party transactions	All related party transactions must be conducted on an arm's length basis There is a statutory requirement to prepare contemporaneous transfer pricing ('TP') documents unless the taxpayer's situation falls under one of the specified situations in the TP Guidelines. The Inland Revenue Authority of Singapore ('IRAS') expects taxpayers to keep their TP documentation and submit it to the IRAS within 30 days upon request. In the event of non-compliance, the taxpayer may suffer adverse consequences such as record-keeping penalties, fines on conviction and, in default of payment, to imprisonment, adjustments to profits under the Income Tax Act and rejection of year-end and self-initiated retrospective TP adjustments	
Tax year, return, objections and payment	The tax year in which income tax is calculated and charged is known as the year of assessment (YA) which runs from 1 January to 31 December The basis period for any YA refers to the period on the profits of which tax for that year falls to be assessed (ie the immediate preceding year). For corporations, the basis period would be the accounting period ended in the year preceding the YA The tax return must be filed by 30 November of the YA Objections to the Notice of Assessment must be lodged within 2 months from the day of the Notice of Assessment, failing which the assessment raised by the IRAS will be regarded as finalised and completed Income tax payment is due within one month after the service of the Notice of Assessment	
Capital gains	No capital gains tax	

Description / Legal form	Singapore resident corporation	Permanent establishment (PE)
Losses	Trading losses may be carried forward without time limit for set-off against future profits, subject to conditions	
	Trading losses of up to S$100,000 may be carried back to the YA immediately preceding the current YA, subject to conditions	
Tax group	Group relief only available for Singapore incorporated companies, subject to conditions	Overseas-incorporated entities with Singapore PE do not qualify for group relief
Tax rate	YA 2010 onwards – 17%	

III   TAXES FOR INDIVIDUALS

		Residents	Non-residents
Income Tax	General description	Tax is levied on the chargeable income of a chargeable person for a YA	
	Taxable entities and taxable income	Individuals who normally reside in Singapore except for temporary absences (ie the qualitative test) and individuals who exercise employment in Singapore (excluding the board director of a company) or were physically present in Singapore for 183 days or more in the calendar year immediately preceding the YA concerned (ie the quantitative test) Administrative concessions have been granted by the IRAS to allow individuals who do not meet the above tests to be regarded as tax residents for income tax purposes	Individuals who do not satisfy the qualitative test or quantitative test or who do not wish to avail themselves of the administrative concessions granted by the IRAS
		Revenue income accruing in or derived from Singapore, unless specifically exempted under the Income Tax Act	
	Types of taxable income	Singapore-sourced income: • Income from a trade, business, profession or vocation • Employment income • Rental income • Interest received from any sources except for deposits made with approved banks and/or finance companies in Singapore • Royalty, pension, annuity, etc Foreign-sourced income received in Singapore by resident and non-resident individuals is generally tax-exempt except for foreign-sourced income received by resident individuals through a partnership in Singapore	
	Calculation of income	Taxable income after deducting any allowable expenses and/or allowances is assessed to tax	
		Personal relief available	Personal relief not available
	Tax year, tax assessment, objections and tax payment	The tax year in which income tax is calculated and charged is known as the year of assessment (YA), which runs from 1 January to 31 December	
		The basis period for any YA refers to the period on the profits of which tax for that year falls to be assessed (ie the immediate preceding year). All income except for trade/business/profession/vocation income is subject to tax on a preceding calendar year basis. For businesses whose accounts are made up to a date other than 31 December, the basis period would be the accounting period ending in the year preceding the YA	
		The tax return must be filed by 15 April of the YA	
		Objections to the Notice of Assessment must be lodged within 30 days from the day of the Notice of Assessment, failing which the assessment raised by the IRAS will be regarded as finalised and completed	
		Income tax payment is due within one month after the service of the Notice of Assessment	

		Residents	**Non-residents**
Income Tax – *contd*	Losses	Trading losses may be carried forward without time limit for set-off against future profits, subject to conditions Trading losses of up to S$100,000 may be carried back to the YA immediately preceding the current YA, subject to conditions	
	Tax rates	Progressive tax rates ranging from 0% to 20% for YA 2016 Progressive tax rates ranging from 0% to 22% with effect from YA 2017	Employment income (excluding directors' fee) – higher of 15% or resident rates All income other than employment income – 20% With effect from YA 2017, the tax rate for all income other than employment income will be raised to 22%
Capital Gains Tax (CGT)	General description	No CGT	

		Singapore domiciled	**Non-Singapore domiciled**
Inheritance Tax (IHT)	General description	Estate duty has been removed for deaths occurring on or after 15 February 2008	

IV   WITHHOLDING TAXES

Under domestic law	Payments to residents	Payments to non-residents[1]
Dividends	Nil	No withholding tax on dividend payment
Interest	Nil	15% (see note below)
Royalties	Nil	10% (see note below)
On payments to public entertainers (eg artistes and sportsmen, etc)	Nil	15% of gross income (or 10% if the income is due and payable to the non-resident public entertainer during the period from 22 February 2010 to 31 March 2020) for services performed in Singapore

Note: These withholding tax rates apply when the income is not derived by the non-resident person through its operations carried out in Singapore. They are to be applied on the gross payment and the resultant tax payable is a final tax. For operations carried out in Singapore, the tax rates applicable on the gross payment are as follows:

- Non-resident persons (other than individuals): prevailing corporate tax rate (currently 17%)
- Non-resident individuals: 20% (from YA 2017, the rate will be increased to 22%).

Reduced rate available under the relevant Double Taxation Treaty			
Country	Dividends[2]	Interest[3]	Royalties[3,4]
Albania	Nil	5%	5%
Australia	Nil	10%	10%
Austria	Nil	5%	5%
Bahrain	Nil	5%	5%
Barbados	Nil	12%	8%
Bangladesh	Nil	10%	10%
Belgium	Nil	5%	5%
Bermuda[7]	Nil	15%	10%
Belarus	Nil	5%	5%
Brazil[6]	Nil	15%	10%
Brunei	Nil	10%	10%
Bulgaria	Nil	5%	5%
Canada	Nil	15%	10%
Chile[5]	Nil	15%	10%
China	Nil	10%	10%
Cyprus	Nil	10%	10%

1   Reduced rates of withholding tax may apply where there is an appropriate double tax treaty.
2   Singapore does not impose withholding tax on dividends payable to non-residents.
3   The non-treaty rate (a final tax) is applicable if non-residents do not carry on business in Singapore or have a PE in Singapore. The rate may be further reduced by tax incentives.
4   Different rates may apply for literary or artistic copyrights, including film royalties.
5   Treaty with Chile covers only international ship operations. The rates reflected above are based on the domestic withholding tax rates.
6   Treaties with Hong Kong and the United States cover only shipping and air transport activities. The rates reflected above are based on the domestic withholding tax rates.
7   Treaty with Bermuda covers only the exchange of information. The rates reflected above are based on the domestic withholding tax rates.

Reduced rate available under the relevant Double Taxation Treaty			
Country	Dividends[2]	Interest[3]	Royalties[3,4]
Czech Republic	Nil	Nil	10%
Denmark	Nil	10%	10%
Ecuador	Nil	10%	10%
Egypt	Nil	15%	10%
Estonia	Nil	10%	7.5%
Fiji	Nil	10%	10%
Finland	Nil	5%	5%
France	Nil	10%	Nil
Georgia	Nil	Nil	Nil
Germany	Nil	8%	8%
Guernsey	Nil	12%	8%
Hong Kong[6]	Nil	15%	10%
Hungary	Nil	5%	5%
India	Nil	15%	10%
Indonesia	Nil	10%	10%
Ireland	Nil	5%	5%
Isle of Man	Nil	12%	8%
Israel	Nil	7%	5%
Italy	Nil	12.5%	10%
Japan	Nil	10%	10%
Jersey	Nil	12%	8%
Kazakhstan	Nil	10%	10%
Korea, Republic of	Nil	10%	10%
Kuwait	Nil	7%	10%
Latvia	Nil	10%	7.5%
Libya	Nil	5%	5%
Liechtenstein	Nil	12%	8%
Lithuania	Nil	10%	7.5%
Luxembourg	Nil	10%	10%
Malaysia	Nil	10%	8%
Malta	Nil	10%	10%
Mauritius	Nil	Nil	Nil
Mexico	Nil	15%	10%
Mongolia	Nil	10%	5%
Morocco	Nil	10%	10%
Myanmar	Nil	10%	10%
Netherlands	Nil	10%	Nil
New Zealand	Nil	10%	5%
Norway	Nil	7%	7%
Oman	Nil	7%	8%
Pakistan	Nil	12.5%	10%
Panama	Nil	5%	5%
Papua New Guinea	Nil	10%	10%
Philippines	Nil	15%	10%
Poland	Nil	5%	5%

Reduced rate available under the relevant Double Taxation Treaty			
Country	Dividends[2]	Interest[3]	Royalties[3,4]
Portugal	Nil	10%	10%
Qatar	Nil	5%	10%
Romania	Nil	5%	5%
Russian Federation	Nil	7.5%	7.5%
Rwanda	Nil	10%	10%
San Marino	Nil	12%	8%
Saudi Arabia	Nil	5%	8%
Seychelles	Nil	12%	8%
Slovakia	Nil	Nil	10%
Slovenia	Nil	5%	5%
South Africa	Nil	Nil	5%
Spain	Nil	5%	5%
Sri Lanka	Nil	10%	10%
Sweden	Nil	15%	Nil
Switzerland	Nil	5%	5%
Taiwan	Nil	15%	10%
Thailand	Nil	15%	10%
Turkey	Nil	10%	10%
Ukraine	Nil	10%	7.5%
United Arab Emirates	Nil	7%	5%
United Kingdom	Nil	10%	10%
United States[6]	Nil	15%	10%
Uzbekistan	Nil	5%	8%
Vietnam	Nil	10%	10%

Note: There may be rules and exemptions available for the withholding taxes. It is possible that lower rates than those shown above may be available provided that certain criteria are satisfied. As treaties are not identical, guidance is recommended to be sought in all cases.

V INDIRECT TAXES

		Residents	Non-residents
Goods and Services Tax (GST)	General description	Tax on local supply of goods and services	
	Entities obliged to levy GST	GST-registered persons	
	Taxable activities	Generally levied on the supply of goods and services made in Singapore	
	Taxable activities – zero-rated (examples)	Providing international services and exporting goods out of Singapore	
	Exemptions (examples)	Sale and lease of residential properties and certain financial services	
	Refund of GST	Input tax incurred is generally claimable if all of the prescribed conditions for claiming input tax are satisfied. However, input tax incurred on certain prescribed expenses is not claimable	
		A GST-registered person making both taxable and exempt supplies may be entitled to claim all input tax incurred (including those used in the making of exempt supplies), subject to the de minimis rule	
	Tax liability	A GST-registered person supplying goods and services locally is responsible for accounting for GST	
	Tax rate	With effect from 1 July 2007 – 7%	
	Administrative obligations	GST returns generally filed quarterly	
Real Property Taxes		Levied annually at 10% on the annual value of non-residential properties, and at progressive tax rates from 0% to 20% on the annual value of residential properties	
Stamp Duty		Stamp duty is applicable on executed documents relating to immovable properties, stocks or shares. Additional Buyer's Stamp Duty and Seller's Stamp Duty at 4% to 16% may be applicable on acquisition/sale of certain immovable properties	

Slovakia

(Mag. Branislav Kováč, VGD SLOVAKIA s.r.o. (legal successor of RECTE AUDÍT s.r.o., after a merger as of 1 January 2016) branislav.kovac@vgd.eu)

I MAIN LEGAL FORMS

Legal form / Characteristics	Partnership and Limited Liability Partnership (LLP)	Private corporation (Ltd), Public corporation (Plc) and Simplified joint stock company (SSC)
Partners/shareholders • Number • Restrictions	Partnership – at least two partners LLP – at least one unlimited partner and at least one limited partner	Ltd – at least one, maximum 50 shareholders. A company with a single partner/shareholder must not be the single founder or partner/shareholder in another company. A natural person may be a single partner in maximum three companies Plc – at least one legal person or at least 2 natural persons SSC – at least one natural person or legal person
Directors	Partnership – all shareholders LLP – unlimited partner	Ltd – at least one executive Plc – at least one member of the Board of Directors SSC – at least one member of the Board of Directors
Establishment	Partnership agreement	Ltd – Articles of Association or deed Plc – Establishment contract or deed SSC – Establishment contract or deed
Registration	The request for registration to the Commercial Register must be filed within 30 days after establishment of the company	Ltd, Plc, SSC – request for registration to the Commercial Register shall be filed within 30 days after establishment of the company
Minimum capital	Partnership – no requirements LLP – no requirements regarding the minimum capital, but the contribution of the partner with limited liability must be at least €250	Ltd – at least €5,000, each shareholder minimum contribution €750 Plc – at least €25,000 Plc with floating stock capital – at least €125,000, eg investment funds SSC – at least €1

Legal form / Characteristics	Partnership and Limited Liability Partnership (LLP)	Private corporation (Ltd), Public corporation (Plc) and Simplified joint stock company (SSC)
Liability	Partnership – unlimited liability of partners and company LLP – unlimited partner has unlimited liability; limited partner has restricted liability	Ltd – Shareholders up to the sum of unpaid value of shareholder's contribution registered in the Commercial Register Plc – no liability of shareholders SSC – no liability of shareholders
Governance	No specific rules	Ltd – shareholders agreement/General meeting Plc – shareholders agreement, Board of Directors, Supervisory Board, General Meeting SSC – General Assembly, Board of Directors, Supervisory Board

Audit requirements	Audit is obligatory only in case of an LLP, when the accounting entity:
	
	• is a corporation which has fulfilled in the last year at least two of these criteria:
	  – its average calculated number of employees exceeded 30 in a single accounting period
	  – its total assets exceeded €1,000,000
	  – its net turnover exceeded €2,000,000
	• has securities admitted to trading on a regulated market
	• is subject to special rules
		Ltd, Plc, SSC – audit is obligatory, when the accounting entity:
		
		• is a corporation, which has fulfilled in the last year at least two of these criteria:
		  – its average calculated number of employees exceeded 30 in a single accounting period
		  – its total assets exceeded €1,000,000
		  – its net turnover exceeded €2,000,000
		• has stock admitted to trading on a regulated market
		• is subject to special rules
		• (Plc only) prepares its financial statements according to IFRS (eg bank, branch of foreign bank, asset management company, insurance company, Stock Exchange and payment institution, etc); Ltd and SSC are excluded from being such regulated entity

Characteristics \ Legal form	Partnership and Limited Liability Partnership (LLP)	Private corporation (Ltd), Public corporation (Plc) and Simplified joint stock company (SSC)
Taxation	Corporate income tax rate: 21% with effect from 1 January 2017, for tax periods starting on 1 January 2017 and later. For the tax year 2016, the 22% tax rate will still apply	Corporate income tax rate: 21% with effect from 1 January 2017, for tax periods starting on 1 January 2017 and later. For the tax year 2016, the 22% tax rate will still apply
	Regulation regarding tax licences (amount of minimum corporate income tax):	**Regulation regarding tax licences (amount of minimum corporate income tax):**
	– If, at the last day of a taxable period, the tax payer is not a VAT payer and has annual revenues not exceeding €500,000, the minimum tax amount shall be €480	– If, at the last day of a taxable period, the tax payer is not a VAT payer and has annual revenues not exceeding €500,000, the minimum tax amount shall be €480
	– If, at the last day of a taxable period, the tax payer is a VAT payer and has annual revenues not exceeding €500,000, the minimum tax amount shall be €960	– If, at the last day of a taxable period, the tax payer is a VAT payer and has annual revenues not exceeding €500,000, the minimum tax amount shall be €960
	– If for a taxable period the tax payer has annual revenues higher than €500,000, the minimum tax amount shall be €2,880	– If for a taxable period the tax payer has annual revenues higher than €500,000, the minimum tax amount shall be €2,880
	The tax licence is due within the period for filing the tax return	The tax licence is due within the period for filing the tax return
	The tax licence (amount of minimum corporate income tax) will apply for the last time for the tax period of 2017	The tax licence (amount of minimum corporate income tax) will apply for the last time for the tax period of 2017
	The taxpayer has the right to include tax licence to tax calculated in tax return for the tax period of 2017 and for previous accounting periods in the subsequent tax periods of 2018–2020	The taxpayer has the right to include tax licence to tax calculated in tax return for the tax period of 2017 and for previous accounting periods in the subsequent tax periods of 2018–2020

II CORPORATION TAX

Description \ Legal Form	Resident corporation	Permanent Establishment (PE)
General description	Corporate tax	Corporate tax
Taxable entities	Corporations incorporated in the Slovak Republic and/or overseas companies with central management and control located in the Slovak Republic	PE located in the Slovak Republic
Taxable income	Income from worldwide sources	Income arising in the Slovak Republic
Calculation of taxable profits	Taxable profit is based on accounting profit adjusted under tax law	Taxable profit is calculated on the basis of difference between income and costs
Interest payments	All interest payments are considered to be business expenses and are deductible

As of 1 January 2015, thin capitalisation rules were introduced. Tax deductible interest payments are accepted up to 25% of the profit before tax, depreciation and interest (tax EBITDA) | All interest payments are considered to be business expenses and are deductible

As of 1 January 2015, thin capitalisation rules were introduced. Tax deductible interest payments are accepted up to 25% of the profit before tax, depreciation and interest (tax EBITDA) |
| Related party transactions | All related party transactions must take place on arm's length basis. A transfer pricing documentation is required, including local (within Slovakia) transactions | All related party transactions must take place on arm's length basis. A transfer pricing documentation is required, including local (within Slovakia) transactions |

Legal Form / Description	Resident corporation	Permanent Establishment (PE)
Tax year, return and payment	Tax year is calendar year. Slovak companies may stipulate in Articles of Association that the tax year is any 12-month (full calendar months) period. Corporate income tax return must be filed with the Tax Office at the end of three calendar months after the end of tax year. The corporate income tax must be paid in the same term (without notice of assessment) Prolongation of the above mentioned term is possible: • by up to three whole calendar months, based on a written notification submitted to the relevant tax administration – the taxable party shall specify the new term, which represents the end of the calendar month, in which a corporate tax return shall be filed. Within this new term, the corporate tax shall also be paid • with a written notification to the relevant tax administration by up to six whole calendar months, provided that the taxable party has income part of which is also income originating from sources abroad – the taxable party shall specify this fact and the new term, which represents the end of the calendar month, in which a corporate tax return shall be filed and in which the corporate income tax shall be paid Advance payment must be made monthly or quarterly in advance. Calculation of advance payments depends on the amount of corporate income tax of the preceding tax period: • quarterly advance payment shall be paid if the amount of corporate income tax for preceding tax period was between €2,500 and €16,600 • monthly advance payment shall be paid if the amount of corporate income tax for preceding tax period was over €16,600	Tax year is calendar year. Corporate income tax return must be filed with the Tax Office at the end of three calendar months after the end of tax year. The corporate income tax must be paid in the same term (without notice of assessment) Prolongation of the above mentioned term is possible: • by up to three whole calendar months, based on a written notification submitted to the relevant tax administration – the taxable party shall specify the new term, which represents the end of the calendar month, in which a corporate tax return shall be filed and within this new term, the tax shall also be paid • with a written notification to relevant tax administration by up to six whole calendar months, provided that the taxable party has income part of which is also income originating from sources abroad – the taxable party shall specify this fact and the new term, which represents the end of the calendar month, in which a corporate tax return shall be filed and in which the corporate income tax shall be paid Advance payment must be made monthly or quarterly in advance. Calculation of advance payments depends on the amount of corporate income tax of the preceding tax period: • quarterly advance payment shall be paid if the amount of corporate income tax for preceding tax period was between €2,500 and €16,600 • monthly advance payment shall be paid if the amount of corporate income tax for preceding tax period was over €16,600

Legal Form / Description	Resident corporation	Permanent Establishment (PE)
Capital gains	Treated as income	Treated as income
Losses	Starting from 2014, it is possible to amortize tax losses evenly within up to 4 following taxable periods It is possible to deduct unamortized tax losses for 2010 to 2013 or the sum of such unamortized tax losses only evenly (25% of the sum of the tax loss) and only for a period of 4 years (starting in 2014)	Starting from 2014, it is possible to amortize tax losses evenly within up to 4 following taxable periods It is possible to deduct unamortized tax losses for 2010 to 2013 or the sum of such unamortized tax losses only evenly (25% of the sum of the tax loss) and only for a period of 4 years (starting in 2014)
Tax group	None	None
Tax rate	As of 1 January 2017, the corporate income tax rate is 21% **For the regulation regarding tax licences (amount of minimum corporate income tax), see Section I above (Taxation)**	As of 1 January 2017, the corporate income tax rate is 21% **For the regulation regarding tax licences (amount of minimum corporate income tax), see Section I above (Taxation)**

III TAXES FOR INDIVIDUALS

		Residents	Non-residents
Income Tax	General Description	Tax levied on the chargeable income of a chargeable person for a year of assessment	
	Taxable entities and taxable income	Residents are taxed on their worldwide income	Non-resident individuals are subject to income tax
	Types of taxable income	• Property income (usually rent) • Income from capital investment (interest, sale of goodwill, royalties, annuities) • Income from business activities • Employment income • Profit share (dividends) • Share on proceeds from liquidation	
	Calculation of income	Employment income – all payments in cash, most benefits, including benefits and income in kind. Only a limited number of benefits are not taxable From the income you have to deduct: • health care insurance: 4% • permanent health insurance: 1.4% • old age insurance: 4% • disability insurance: 3% • unemployment insurance: 1% Individuals have the right to deduct a non-taxable sum of tax base (depending on the value of income yearly up to €3,803.33 for 2017) from their income, to pay tax from a lower sum – deduction of a non-taxable sum can be used 1/12th in one month by only one employer (subject to restrictions). In case of income exceeding €19,809 in the year, the non-taxable sum shall be reduced	
	Tax year, tax assessment and tax payment	Tax year is the calendar year Tax return must be filed by 31 March of the following year and the income tax due also paid in this term Prolongation of the term is possible: • by up to three whole calendar months, based on a written notification submitted to the relevant tax administration – the taxable party shall specify the new term, which represents the end of the calendar month, in which a tax return shall be filed and within this new term, the income tax shall also be paid • with a written notification to the relevant tax administration by up to six whole calendar months, provided that the taxable party has income, part of which is also income originating from sources abroad – the taxable party shall specify this fact and the new term, which represents the end of the calendar month, in which a tax return shall be filed and in which the income tax shall be paid	
	Losses	Starting from 2014, it is possible to amortize tax losses evenly within 4 subsequent tax periods It is possible to deduct unamortized tax losses for 2010 to 2013 or the sum of such unamortized tax losses only evenly (25% of the sum of the tax loss) and only for a period of 4 subsequent years (starting in 2014) Valid only for individuals who carry on a trade licence	

		Residents	Non-residents
Income Tax – *contd*	Tax rates	Income tax rate: 19%–25%	Income tax rate: 19%–25%
		With effect from 1 January 2013 the income tax rate is: 19% up to income tax base amounting to €35,022.31 and 25% for part of tax base exceeding €35,022.31	With effect from 1 January 2013 the Income tax rate is: 19% up to income tax base amounting to €35,022.31 and 25% for part of tax base exceeding €35,022.31
		Some capital gains (mostly interests) having source in foreign states: 19%, without progression	
Capital Gains Tax (CGT)	General description	No chargeable Gains Tax. Realized capital gain is taxable, treated as other income	No chargeable Gains Tax. Realized capital gain is taxable, treated as other income
	Taxable entities and chargeable assets		
	Calculation of gain		
	Tax year, tax assessment and tax payment		
	Losses		
	Tax rates		
		Domiciled	**Non-domiciled**
Inheritance Tax (IHT)		No Inheritance Tax	

IV WITHHOLDING TAXES

Under domestic law	Payments to residents	Payments to non-residents
Dividends	Natural person:	Natural person:
	Dividends subject to 7% tax rate, from accounting periods started as of 1 January 2017 or later, and accounting periods before 31 December 2003	Dividends subject to 7% tax rate, from accounting periods started as of 1 January 2017 or later, and accounting periods before 31 December 2003
	Dividends from accounting periods between 2004 and 2016 remain without taxation	Dividends from accounting periods between 2004 and 2016 remain without taxation
	Dividends subject to 35% tax rate, if received from foreign sources from non-contracting states (non EU member state, no double tax treaty nor agreement on exchange of information)	Dividends subject to 35% tax rate, if received from foreign sources from non-contracting states (non EU member state, no double tax treaty nor agreement on exchange of information)
	Note: a contribution will be paid to health care insurance for dividends relating to the years 2012 to 2016. Rate: 14%; maximum assessment base per year is average monthly salary from the second preceding calendar year multiplied by 60. This affects only individuals subject to the statutory health insurance system in Slovakia	Note: a contribution will be paid to health care insurance for dividends relating to the years 2012 to 2016. Rate: 14%; maximum assessment base per year is average monthly salary from the second preceding calendar year multiplied by 60. This affects only individuals subject to the statutory health insurance system in Slovakia
Interest	19%	19%
		With effect from 1 March 2014, a 35% tax rate is applied to income that is paid out, remitted or credited to a tax payer of a non-contracting country (non-EU member state, no double tax treaty nor agreement on exchange of information)
Royalties	19% if author has not concluded an agreement with the publisher about not applying the withholding tax	19%
		With effect from 1 March 2014, a 35% tax rate is applied to income that is paid out, remitted or credited to a tax payer of a non-contracting country (non-EU member state, no double tax treaty nor agreement on exchange of information)
On payments to artists and sportsmen	Nil	19%
		With effect from 1 March 2014, a 35% tax rate is applied to income that is paid out, remitted or credited to a tax payer of a non-contracting country (non-EU member state, no double tax treaty nor agreement on exchange of information)

Reduced rate available under the relevant Double Taxation Treaty			
Country	Dividends	Interest	Royalties
Australia	19%	10%	10%
Austria	15%	Nil	5%
Belgium	10%	10%	5%
Bosnia and Herzegovina	5% / 15%	Nil	10%
Belarus	10%–15%	10%	10%
Brazil	15%	15%	25%
Bulgaria	10%	10%	10%
Canada	5%–15%	10%	10%
China	10%	10%	10%
Croatia	5%–10%	10%	10%
Cyprus	10%	10%	10%
Czech Republic	5%–15%	Nil	Nil
Denmark	15%	Nil	Nil
Egypt		Not yet ratified	Not yet ratified
Estonia	10%	10%	10%
Finland	5% / 15%	Nil	Nil
France	10%	Nil	Nil
Georgia	5% / 15%	5%	5%
Germany	19%	Nil	Nil
Greece	5% / 15%	10%	10%
Hungary	15% / 25%	Nil	Nil
India	10%	15%	15%
Indonesia	0% / 10%	10%	10%
Ireland	5% / 10%	Nil	Nil
Israel	5% / 10%	10%	10%
Iceland	15%	Nil	Nil
Italy	10% / 15%	Nil	Nil
Japan	5% / 10%	10%	10%
Kazakhstan	10% / 15%	10%	10%
Korea, Republic of	10%	10%	10%
Kuwait	10% / 15%	10%	10%
Libya	0%	10%	10%
Latvia	10%	10%	10%
Lithuania	10%	10%	10%
Luxembourg	5% / 15%	Nil	Nil
Malta	5%	Nil	Nil
Mexico	0%	10%	10%
Macedonia	5%	10%	10%
Moldova	5% / 15%	10%	10%
Montenegro	5% / 15%	10%	10%
Mongolia	0%	Nil	Nil
Netherlands	0% / 10%	Nil	Nil
Nigeria	12.5% / 15%	15%	15%
Norway	5% / 15%	Nil	Nil
Poland	5% / 10%	10%	10%

Reduced rate available under the relevant Double Taxation Treaty			
Country	Dividends	Interest	Royalties
Portugal	10% / 15%	10%	10%
Romania	10%	10%	10%
Russia	5% / 15%	Nil	Nil
Serbia	5% / 10%	10%	10%
Singapore	5% / 15%	Nil	Nil
Slovenia	5% / 15%	10%	10%
South Africa	5% / 15%	Nil	Nil
Spain	15%	Nil	Nil
Sri Lanka	0% / 10%	10%	10%
Sweden	5% / 15%	Nil	5%
Switzerland	5%	10%	5%
Syria	5%	10%	12%
Taiwan	10%	10%	10%
Tunisia	10% / 15%	12%	15%
Turkey	5% / 10%	10%	10%
Turkmenistan	10%	10%	10%
Ukraine	10%	10%	10%
United Kingdom	5% / 15%	Nil	10%
United States	5% / 15%	Nil	10%
Uzbekistan	10%	10%	10%
Vietnam	5% / 10%	10%	15%

Note: the above rates are only available provided the specific Treaty criteria are satisfied. It is possible that lower rates than those shown above may be available provided that certain criteria are satisfied. As treaties will not be identical, guidance should be sought in all cases.

The applicable rate for dividends shall not exceed 7%, whereby dividends from years 2004 till 2016 shall be excluded from income tax.

V   INDIRECT TAXES

		Residents	Non-residents
Value Added Tax (VAT)	General description	Tax on the supply of goods and services	
	Entities obliged to levy VAT	20% on the entities that are VAT registered	
	Taxable activities	Supplies of goods and services in Slovakia by a taxable subject, imports of goods, acquisition of goods for consideration within the territory of Slovakia from another Member State of the EU etc	
	Taxable activities – zero-rated (examples)	Postal and financial services, healthcare, social help services, education, services related to sport, culture, export of goods and services, insurance services, etc	
	Exemptions (examples)	None	
	Refund of VAT	Possible only on VAT – registered subjects, after request submission	Possible only on VAT –registered subjects, after request submission
	Tax liability	VAT-registered subjects. The registration is due when the subject's turnover exceeds €49,790 within a period of any subsequent 12 months (valid as of 1 July 2009)	
	Tax rates	• Standard rate = 20 % • Reduced rate: 10% for pharmaceuticals, books As of 1 January 2016, the reduced 10% VAT rate is applied to the following goods: Fresh or cooled beef, pork meat, meat from sheep, meat from goats, rabbits, meat from domestic fowls, fresh or cooled fishes, fish fillets and other fish meat, milk, butter and cream, and fresh bread • Zero rate = 0% (export of goods and services)	
	Administrative obligations	Registration (see Tax liability above)	Registration (see Tax liability above)

	Residents	Non-residents
Real Property Taxes	Include: • *land tax* (arable land, hop gardens, vineyard, orchards; perennial grasslands; gardens; forestland covered by forests used for commercial purposes, fish-breeding ponds and other bodies of water in commercial use; built-up areas and courtyards; building plots; other areas except for building plots) The land tax shall be calculated as the product of the value of the land (calculated by multiplying the land area (m²) and the soil rate per m²) and the annual land tax rate • *tax on buildings* (residential buildings and minor structures complementary to the main building; buildings used for agricultural production, greenhouses, water management structures, buildings for the storage of own agricultural produce, including office buildings; recreational and garden cottages and sheds used for private recreational purposes; standalone garages and parking buildings and structures intended or used for parking purposes, built as detached from residential buildings; industrial buildings, energy industry structures, buildings used in the construction industry, buildings used for the storage of own production, including office buildings; buildings used for other business and gainful activities, as well as for storage and administration related to such other business or gainful activities; other buildings) The tax on buildings shall be calculated as the product of the building's built-up area in m² and the annual rate of the tax on buildings • *tax on apartments and non-residential premises within apartment buildings* The apartment tax shall be calculated as the product of the floor area of the apartment or non-residential premises in m² and the annual rate of the apartment tax	
Stamp Duty	None	

Slovenia

(Alan Maher and Simon Seibert, Cautela Pros d.o.o. –
alan.maher@cautelapros.si, simon.seibert@cautelapros.si)

I MAIN LEGAL FORMS

Legal form / Characteristics	Partnership and Limited Liability Partnership (LLP)	Private corporation (Ltd) and Public corporation (Plc)
Partners/shareholders	Two or more	One or more
• Number	None	None
• Restrictions		
Directors	Management by partners[1]	Management by director(s)
Establishment	No formal requirements[2]	Notarial deed of incorporation[3]
Registration	Trade register and tax authorities	Trade register and tax authorities
Minimum capital	None	€7,500 (Ltd – d.o.o.)
		€25,000 (Plc – d.d.)
Liability	Unlimited[4]	Limited to capital[5]
Governance	Partners, general meeting, works council	Managing director/Board of directors, supervisory board, shareholders' meeting, works council
Audit requirements	No audit requirements	No audit requirement if, for 2 consecutive years, at least two of the three conditions below were not exceeded: • Turnover does not exceed €8.0m • Total assets do not exceed €4.0m • Number of employees does not exceed 50
Taxation	Slovenian resident partnerships are subject to corporate income tax based on world wide principle	Slovenian resident companies are subject to corporate income tax based on worldwide principle

---

1 Limited partner may not legally represent the company, however he/she may be nominated as proxy.
2 Relations among partners are regulated by partnership agreement.
3 In single shareholder Ltd (d.o.o.) companies no notarial deed is required.
4 In limited liability partnership unlimited liability must apply to at least one partner. Limited partners liability is limited up to their share in the capital of the company.
5 Managers may become liable in case of misconduct.

II   CORPORATION TAX

Description / Legal Form	Resident corporation	Permanent Establishment (PE)
General description	Tax is levied on the taxable profit generated within a tax year	Tax is levied on the taxable profit earned in Slovenia generated within a tax year
Taxable entities	Companies incorporated in Slovenia or companies with effective place of management located in Slovenia	PE constituted in Slovenia
Taxable income	Worldwide principle	Territorial principle. Income generated in Slovenia
Calculation of taxable profits	Accounting profit is adjusted for various tax add-backs, allowances and exemptions to arrive at the taxable profit Dividends from qualifying participations are exempt from taxation	
Interest payments	Interest between related parties are subject to referential interest rate published on a monthly basis by the Ministry of Finance. Such published interest rate is considered to be at arm's length Thin capitalisation rules apply. Thin capitalisation ratio of 1:4 applies Interest payments to certain low tax jurisdictions are not deductible for corporate income tax purposes	
Related party transactions	All related party transactions must take place on arm's length basis	
Tax year, return and payment	Tax year generally coincides with the business year, but may also differ from business year Corporate income tax return must be submitted to tax authorities within 3 months after the beginning of the current tax year During the tax year, the corporate income tax is prepaid on a monthly basis	
Capital gains	Capital gains are subject to corporation tax at normal rates Capital gains on qualifying participations are exempt	
Losses	Within a year losses can be offset against future tax profits. However, not more than 50% of the taxable income in any tax year. Current year tax loss may be carried forward for unlimited period of time	
Tax group	Consolidated tax returns are not possible	
Tax rate	17% for 2016 19% for 2017 and onwards[11]	

III TAXES FOR INDIVIDUALS

<table>
<tr><td rowspan="13" style="writing-mode: vertical-lr">Income Tax</td><td></td><th>Residents</th><th>Non-residents</th></tr>
<tr><td>General Description</td><td colspan="2">Personal income tax is levied on a qualifying income of an individual for a year of assessment</td></tr>
<tr><td>Taxable entities and taxable income</td><td>Resident individuals are liable to tax on their worldwide income</td><td>Non-resident individuals are liable to tax only on the income with the source in Slovenia. Double taxation may be eliminated by application of Double Taxation Agreements</td></tr>
<tr><td>Types of taxable income</td><td colspan="2">Income from employment

Professional income

Income from agricultural and forestry activity

Income from letting of property and transfer of property rights

Income from capital

Other income</td></tr>
<tr><td>Calculation of income</td><td colspan="2">In general, income is earned when payment is received, when payment is made or when the benefit has been provided</td></tr>
<tr><td>Tax year, tax assessment and tax payment</td><td colspan="2">Tax year equals calendar year

Generally, all payers of the income to individuals file withholding tax returns to tax authorities by the date of payment of the income at the latest

On an annual basis, Personal Income Tax is assessed by an informative calculation which is provided by the tax authority

Should informative tax calculation not be objected to, personal income tax liability for the year becomes final

Tax is paid within the tax year and based on the decision of the tax authority</td></tr>
<tr><td>Losses</td><td colspan="2">Professional income: tax losses may be carried forward for unlimited period of time, but may be utilized only up to 50% of the tax basis calculated in the tax year</td></tr>
<tr><td>Tax rates</td><td colspan="2">Income from employment: progressive 16% up to 50%

Professional income: progressive 16% up to 50%[11]

Income from agriculture and forestry activity: progressive 16% up to 50%

Income from letting of property and transfer of property rights: 25%

Income from capital: 25%[6]

Other income: 25%</td></tr>
</table>

---

6 Income from capital consists of capital gains, interest income and dividend income. Tax rates for capital gains tax are digressive. It will be reduced by 10 percentage points for the first 5 years of holding and further 5 percentage points for every 5 years of holding. After 20 years of holding, capital gains become exempt from taxation. Interest income of up to €1,000 is exempt from taxation.

7 Disposal of shares by a non-resident exceeding 10% participation in the capital of the company or in the voting rights is subject to taxation.

		Residents	**Non-residents**
Capital Gains Tax (CGT)	General description	Capital gains tax is levied on gains earned by disposal of capital	
	Taxable entities and chargeable assets	All residents earning capital gains worldwide are subject to capital gains tax Real estate, securities, shares in capital and investment coupons are considered as capital	In general, capital gains of non-residents on securities, shares in capital and investment coupons are exempt from taxation[7]
	Calculation of gain	Sales price reduced for purchase price of the capital represents tax basis for capital gains tax Tax basis may be reduced for lump sum costs which apply for purchase price as well as sales price[8]	
	Tax year, tax assessment and tax payment	Capital gains earned by residents are declared by the end of February for the previous tax year The tax is assessed by the tax authorities by a decision The tax is due within 30 days from the receipt of the decision of the tax authorities	In general non-residents must declare capital gains within 15 days after the disposal of capital
	Losses	Capital gains tax: tax losses may be carried forward for unlimited period of time	
	Tax rates	General tax rate: 25%[6] After 5 years of holding: 15% After 10 years of holding: 10% After 15 years of holding: 5% After 20 years of holding: 0%	

---

8 Special rules apply on determination of purchase price, depending on date of acquisition of the capital.

9 Inheritance or donation of estate with value not exceeding €5,000 (except real estate) is not subject to tax.

		Domiciled	Non-domiciled
Inheritance Tax (IHT)	General description	Tax is levied on a chargeable transfer of value made by a lifetime gift or estate on death	
	Taxable entities and chargeable assets	Individuals or legal entities that receive estate based on inheritance or donation[9]	Individuals or legal entities that receive estate located in the territory of Slovenia based on inheritance or donation[9]
	Calculation of charge	The value of the estate, reduced for eventual corresponding debt and costs represents the basis for tax[10]	
	Taxable events	Tax liability for inheritance tax incurs when court decision becomes effective Tax liability for gift tax incurs on the signature of contract or actual receipt of the gift	
	Allowances	Gifts subject to personal income tax or corporate income tax are exempt from taxation Inheritance or gifts received by children or spouses Charities	
	Tax rates	Children and spouses: 0%; Parents, brothers, sisters: 5%–14% progressive rate; Grandparents: 8%–17% progressive rate; Other persons: 12%–39% progressive rate	

10 The value of immovable property represents market value of the received inheritance or gift. The tax basis for movable property is market value reduced for €5,000.
11 Under a special scheme, companies and individual entrepreneurs earning professional income of generally less than €50,000 may opt for lump-sum expense deduction (expense is calculated as 80% of taxable revenues) whereby tax rate is 20% (17% for companies in 2016 and 19% in 2017 and onwards) and the tax calculated is final. This scheme is subject to special conditions.

IV   WITHHOLDING TAXES

	Payments to residents[12]	Payments to non-residents[13]
Dividends	Generally exempt	15%
Interest	Generally exempt	15%
Royalties	Generally exempt	15%
On payments to artists and sportsmen	Subject to personal income tax as professional income	Subject to personal income tax as professional income

Reduced rate available under the relevant Double Taxation Treaty			
Country	Dividends	Interest[14]	Royalties
	Individuals, companies		
Albania	10%	7%[15]	7%
Armenia	10%	10%	5%
Austria	15%	5%[16]	5%
Azerbaijan	8%	8%	10%[17]
Belarus	5%	5%[16]	5%
Belgium	15%	10%	5%
Bosnia and Herzegovina	10%	7%[16]	5%
Bulgaria	10%	5%	10%[18]
Canada	15%	10%	10%
China	5%	10%	10%
Croatia	5%	5%	5%
Cyprus	5%	5%[16]	5%
Czech Republic	15%	5%	10%
Denmark	15%	5%	5%
Estonia	15%	10%	10%
Finland	15%	5%	5%
France	15%	5%[19]	5%[18,19]

12 The payment of dividend to a resident is exempt from taxation if resident recipient provides the tax number to the payer of the income (which is normally the case). Same applies to payments of interest and royalties among resident companies.

13 Withholding tax rates may be reduced by application of Double Tax Agreements or EU Directives 90/435/EEC, 2003/123/EC and 2003/49/EC which are implemented in Slovenian tax regulation.

14 Many treaties provide for an exemption for certain types of interest, eg interest paid to the state, local authorities, the central bank, export credit institutions or in relation to sales on credit. Such exemptions are not considered in this column.

15 The zero rate applies, inter alia, to interest paid by a public body and to interest paid on a loan granted by an approved insurance or financial institution.

16 The lower rate applies to interest paid by public bodies.

17 A rate of 5% applies to royalties paid for the use of computer software, any patent, design or model, plan, secret formula or process, or for information concerning industrial, commercial or scientific experience.

18 The lower rate applies to copyright royalties, excluding cinematograph films, and to equipment rentals.

19 The zero rate applies if: (a) the French recipient is a company that holds directly at least 20% of the capital of the Slovenian company, or vice versa; or (b) a third French or Slovenian company holds directly at least 20% of the capital of both the payer and the recipient company.

Reduced rate available under the relevant Double Taxation Treaty			
Country	**Dividends**	**Interest**[14]	**Royalties**
Georgia	5%	5%	5%
Germany	15%	5%	5%
Greece	10%	10%	10%
Hungary	15%	5%	5%
Iceland	15%	5%	5%
India	15%	5%	10%
Iran[20]	7%	5%	5%
Ireland	15%	5%	5%
Israel	15%	5%	5%
Italy	15%	10%[16]	5%
Korea, Republic of	15%	5%	5%
Kosovo	10%	5%	5%
Kuwait	5%	5%	10%
Latvia	15%	10%	10%
Lithuania	15%	10%	10%
Luxembourg	15%	5%	5%
Macedonia (FYR)	15%	10%	10%
Malta	15%	5%	5%
Moldova	10%	5%	5%
Montenegro[21]	10%	10%	10%[22]
Netherlands	15%	5%	5%
Norway	15%	5%	5%
Poland	15%	10%	10%
Portugal	15%	10%	5%
Qatar	5%	5%	5%
Romania	5%	5%	5%
Russia	10%	10%	10%
Serbia[21]	10%	10%	10%[22]
Slovakia	15%	10%	10%
Singapore	5%	5%	5%
Spain	15%	5%	5%
Sweden[23]	15%	Nil	Nil
Switzerland	15%	5%[24]	5%[25]
Thailand	10%	15%[26]	15%[18]

20 Effective from 1 January (in case of Slovenia) and 21 March 2015 (in case of Iran).
21 The treaty concluded between Slovenia and the former Serbia and Montenegro.
22 The lower rate applies to copyright royalties, including films, etc.
23 Treaty concluded by the former Yugoslavia. Slovenia continues to honour such treaties and, in general, treaty parties continue to apply the treaties with respect to Slovenia.
24 The zero rate applies, inter alia, if interest is paid (i) in respect of a loan made, approved, guaranteed or insured by an institution which is authorized under the internal law of insurance and financing of international business transactions; (ii) by a bank to another bank; or (iii) to or by an affiliated company (under conditions).
25 The zero rate applies to royalties paid to affiliated companies (under conditions).
26 The lower rate applies to interest paid to any financial institution (including an insurance company).

Reduced rate available under the relevant Double Taxation Treaty			
Country	**Dividends**	**Interest**[14]	**Royalties**
Turkey	10%	10%	10%
Ukraine	15%	5%	10%[27]
United Arab Emirates	5%	5%	5%
United Kingdom	15%	5%[28]	5%
United States	15%	5%	5%
Uzbekistan	8%	8%	10%

Note: the above rates are only available provided the specific Treaty criteria are satisfied. It is possible that lower rates than those shown above may be available provided that certain criteria are satisfied. As treaties will not be identical, guidance should be sought in all cases.

27 The higher rate applies to copyrights for literary or artistic works, including films, etc.
28 The lower rate applies to interest paid by public bodies. It also applies where the payer and the recipient are both companies and either company owns directly at least 20% of the capital of the other company, or a third company, being a resident of a contracting state, holds directly at least 20% of the capital of both the paying company and the recipient company.

V INDIRECT TAXES

<table>
<tr><th></th><th></th><th>Residents</th><th>Non-residents</th></tr>
<tr><td rowspan="20">Value Added Tax (VAT)</td><td>General description</td><td colspan="2">Tax on the supply of goods and services based on the EU VAT Directive</td></tr>
<tr><td>Entities obliged to levy VAT</td><td colspan="2">Any individual, partnership, corporation or other body, which carries out taxable activities in Slovenia

Other situations may also arise, eg distance selling, sale of assets, acquisitions from other EU Member States</td></tr>
<tr><td>Taxable activities</td><td colspan="2">Supply of goods and services, import of goods, intra-Community acquisition of goods, etc

Place of supply of goods and services must be in Slovenia</td></tr>
<tr><td>Taxable activities – zero-rated (examples)</td><td colspan="2">Supply of goods or services to companies residing in another EU Member State

Export of goods and certain services to bodies outside the EU</td></tr>
<tr><td>Exemptions (examples)</td><td colspan="2">Transactions related to the sale of any Slovenian immovable property used for more than 2 years and the lease of any Slovenian immovable property (also option to tax)

Banking and insurance services

Certain activities in the public interest (eg hospital and medical care, welfare and security work, public education, etc)</td></tr>
<tr><td>Refund of VAT</td><td>VAT paid on supplies and services is deductible as input tax, if incurred in the course or furtherance of the business and for the purpose of making taxable supplies (including zero-rated supplies)

There is no credit for input tax incurred which relates to the provision of exempt supplies

Where mixed supplies occur (taxable and exempt supplies), input tax must be apportioned and recovered according to a partial exemption method</td><td>EC Directive refund system for non-resident businesses established within the EU, providing its business is not otherwise required to be registered in Slovenia

EC Directive refund system for non-resident businesses established outside the EU (a limited list of countries with which Slovenia has reciprocity with regard to VAT refunds), providing its business is not otherwise required to be registered in Slovenia (from 1 July 2012, VAT refund claims must be filed electronically)</td></tr>
<tr><td>Tax liability</td><td colspan="2">Normally the supplier of goods and services is liable to charge VAT

Reverse charge for imports and intra-Community acquisitions of goods and services if those transactions are deemed to take place in Slovenia

Reverse charge in case of supply of:
• Construction services
• Supply of staff for the purposes of construction services
• Supply of old real estate if taxable persons agree to charge VAT
• Supply of waste materials and related services (metals)</td></tr>
<tr><td>Tax rates</td><td colspan="2">Standard rate = 22%

Reduced rate = 9.5% (eg food, supply of water, medicine, etc)</td></tr>
</table>

		Residents	Non-residents
Value Added Tax (VAT) – contd	Administrative obligations	Formal requirements concerning business records and invoices Monthly or quarterly self-assessment VAT returns plus payment of any VAT liability to tax authorities No VAT grouping possible VAT identification number must be shown on all invoices issued EU invoicing directive must be adhered to	Registration for VAT purposes if making supplies of goods and services in Slovenia (no threshold applies for taxable persons with a seat outside of Slovenia) Appointment of fiscal tax representative possible, but obligatory only for non-resident businesses established outside the EU
Real estate transfer tax		Tax is payable on real property transactions and on establishment and transfer or letting out the building title (right of superficies) for a consideration. Taxable person is the seller of the real estate. Tax rate is 2% on value of the transaction and in some cases exemptions apply. Tax is calculated based on the sales price of the real estate. Tax declaration must be filed with the tax authorities. Tax authorities issue the assessment within 30 days upon filing. The tax is due within 30 days of receipt of the assessment	
Insurance tax		Insurance tax at the rate of 8.5% is applicable for insurance contracts, with some exemptions	
Financial Services Tax		*Subject to tax:* • Provision of monetary credits or loans as well as loan intermediary, management of monetary loans or credits, when loan or credit management is performed by the lender • Issuing of credit warranties and provision of other monetary warranties as well as their management • Transactions including financial intermediaries with respect to deposits, bank accounts, payments, debts, checks and other payment instruments • Transactions including financial intermediaries with respect to legal tenders such as currency, bank notes and coins • Services of insurance agents and intermediaries *Taxable persons*: Liable to tax are legal entities and individuals performing above-mentioned financial services in Slovenia. A financial service is subject to tax when it was provided by: • Legal entities with registered seat or branch office in Slovenia or individuals with permanent address or habitual abode in Slovenia • Other foreign legal entities or individuals that may perform financial services in Slovenia directly when financial services are provided to persons with registered seat, branch office, and permanent address or habitual abode in Slovenia Tax base is fees received for provision of financial services The rate is 8.5% Services subject to VAT, insurance premium tax and services performed by or to Central Banks, Diplomatic or EU Institutions are exempt	

South Africa

(Bashier Adam, Nexia SAB&T, bashier@nexia-sabt.co.za)

I MAIN LEGAL FORMS

Legal form / Characteristics	Partnership and Limited Liability Partnership (LLP)	Private corporation ((Pty) Ltd) and Public company (Ltd)
Partners /shareholders • Number • Restrictions	Maximum 20 Both natural and juristic persons can be members No LLP-type entity exists under South African law	Private company ((Pty) Ltd): minimum one and no maximum Public company (Ltd): minimum one and no maximum Both natural and corporate persons are permitted to be shareholders
Directors	N/A	(Pty) Ltd: minimum one and maximum subject to Memorandum of Incorporation Ltd: minimum three and maximum subject to Memorandum of Incorporation
Company Secretary	N/A	(Pty) Ltd: not required Ltd: company must appoint a company secretary
Establishment	By partnership agreement	(Pty) Ltd and Ltd: registration with Companies and Intellectual Property Commission (CIPC) and adopting a Memorandum of Incorporation
Registration	N/A	Registration with CIPC Annual return fee payable by companies to CIPC
Minimum capital	N/A	1 share
Liability	No limited liability	Both have limited liability
Governance	Partnership agreement	Per King III (Draft King IV), Companies Act 2008, as amended, and the Memorandum of Incorporation

Legal form \ Characteristics	Partnership and Limited Liability Partnership (LLP)	Private corporation ((Pty) Ltd) and Public company (Ltd)
Audit requirements	No audit required	Public companies are required to be audited
		Private companies are not required to comply with extended accountability requirements (audit), except to the extent that the Memorandum of Incorporation provides otherwise
		Private companies with a public interest score of more than 350 or part of a publicly listed group will be required to be audited
Taxation	Transparent, members are taxed individually	Corporation tax on worldwide profits
Usage	Used by professionals and small registered businesses	(Pty) Ltd: small businesses, investment holding
		Ltd: all types of businesses including publicly listed entities

II CORPORATION TAX

Description \ Legal form	Resident corporation	Permanent establishment (PE)
General description	Levied on taxable income	
Taxable entities	Entities incorporated in South Africa	Branches or agencies of foreign entities
Taxable income	Worldwide income subject to certain exemptions for activities undertaken outside South Africa	South African source income
Calculation of taxable profits	Taxable profits less allowable deductions	
Interest payments	Deductible, subject to thin capitalisation rules. Debt-to-equity should not exceed 3:1 From 1 March 2015, a final withholding tax of 15% is imposed on interest paid to a non-resident from a South African source	
Related party transactions	Transactions not carried out at arm's length may fall into the ambit of the anti-avoidance legislation	
Tax year, return and payment	Any financial year of the company ending during the calendar year in question. Tax returns need to be submitted and filed within 12 months of the year end of the company. Taxes paid based on an estimated value with two provisional instalments	
Capital gains	2013 onwards: 66.6%	
Losses	Losses may be carried forward indefinitely provided entity is trading	
Tax group	No tax consolidation of profits. Each legal entity needs to submit their own tax return	
Tax rate	• Standard rate 28% • Allowances for small business • 2012 – 33% for branches of overseas companies, 2013 – 28%	

III   TAXES FOR INDIVIDUALS

<table>
<tr><td rowspan="10">Income Tax</td><td></td><td>Residents</td><td>Non-residents</td></tr>
<tr><td>General description</td><td>Taxed on worldwide income</td><td>Taxed on income from South African sources or deemed South African sources</td></tr>
<tr><td>Taxable entities and taxable income</td><td>A natural person ordinarily resident in South Africa or anyone who stays in the country more than 91 days per tax year in the current year and in the previous 5 years and in aggregate more than 915 days during the previous 5 tax years</td><td>A natural person ceases to be a resident on the day he leaves South Africa if he remains outside South Africa for a continuous period for at least 330 days</td></tr>
<tr><td>Types of taxable income</td><td>• Employment income
• Business income
• Interest
• Rentals
• Royalties
• Pensions</td><td>• Pensions
• Rentals
• Royalties
• Employment income South African sourced</td></tr>
<tr><td>Calculation of income</td><td colspan="2">Aggregate of gross income less exempt income less deductions and allowances</td></tr>
<tr><td>Tax year, tax assessment and tax payment</td><td colspan="2">1 March to the last day of February

No return is required for persons whose sole income is derived from remuneration that does not exceed R350,000 per annum, provided that:

• There is only one employer (but, if there are two employers or income sources, eg late spouse/partner pension income, exam marking income, moonlighting income, there is still no need to file, even if the total in still under R350,000)
• The individual has no car allowance or interest or rental income
• There are no tax-related deductions (eg medical expenses, retirement annuity contributions, travel expenses, etc)
• Interest received from a source in South Africa does not exceed
  ○ R23,800 if below the age of 65 years or
  ○ R34,500 if 65 years or older
• Dividends were received and the individual is non-resident

Remuneration subject to monthly PAYE deductions, but taxpayers obliged to also become provisional taxpayers if income from other sources exceeds certain levels

Provisional taxes payable based on an estimated value with two instalments and a final top up</td></tr>
<tr><td>Losses</td><td colspan="2">May be carried forward indefinitely. Farming losses may be limited to farming income only and not offset against other taxable income</td></tr>
<tr><td>Tax rates</td><td colspan="2">Progressive block rates
Maximum marginal rate of 41%</td></tr>
</table>

		Residents	**Non-residents**
Capital Gains Tax (CGT)	General description	Receipts and accruals of a capital nature subject to CGT with effect from 1 October 2001	
	Taxable entities and chargeable assets	Capital gains made on disposal of assets owned anywhere in the world	Capital gains made on disposal of fixed property situated in South Africa, including any interest in fixed property
	Calculation of gain	Aggregate gain set off against assessed capital gain losses brought forward less rebate (annual exclusion: 2013–2016: R30,000; 2017: R40,000) Net gain is multiplied by inclusion rate and then included in income	
	Tax year, tax assessment and tax payment	Individuals – 1 March to last day of February Taxpayers obliged to become provisional taxpayers if capital gain exceeds certain levels. Taxes payable on second instalment	
	Losses	Carried forward indefinitely	
	Tax rates	Natural persons and special trusts: 2013–2016: 33.3%; 2017: 40% (previously 25%)	

		Domiciled	**Non-domiciled**
Estate Duty	General description	Estate duty and donations taxes are levied	
	Taxable entities and chargeable assets	Estate duty: all assets of deceased estates, as well as amounts regarded as property of the estate Donations tax payable by donor on any gratuitous disposal subject to exemptions	Only applicable to South African assets Exempt from donations tax
	Calculation of charge	Estate duty: total value of estate, after various deductions Donations tax – market value of asset	All non-South African assets are ignored
	Taxable events	Duty payable on a deceased estate Donations tax payable when donation is made	Duty payable on a deceased estate Exempt from donations tax
	Allowances	Estate duty: abatement of R3.5m and certain other deductions Donations tax: certain entities are exempt Different levels of allowances exist	Estate duty: abatement of R3.5m and certain other deductions Donation tax: unlimited
	Tax rates	Estate duty – 20% Donations tax – 20%	Estate duty – 20% Donations tax – 0%

IV   WITHHOLDING TAXES

Under domestic law	Payments to residents	Payments to non-residents[1]
Dividends	15%	15%
Interest	Nil	15% from 1 January 2015, unless DTA applies
Royalties	Nil	12% 15% from 1 January 2015
On payments to artists and sportsmen	Nil	15%

Reduced rate available under the relevant Double Taxation Treaty			
Country	Dividends	Interest	Royalties
Algeria	15% (other beneficial owners) 10% (Minimum holding of 25% of capital by a beneficial owner which is a company)	10%	10%
Australia	15% (other beneficial owners) 5% (Minimum holding of 10% of voting power (directly) by a beneficial owner which is a company)	10%	5%
Austria	15% (other beneficial owners) 5% (Minimum holding of 25% of capital (directly) by a beneficial owner which is a company)	Nil	Nil
Belarus	15% (other beneficial owners) 5% (Minimum holding of 25% of capital (directly/indirectly) by a beneficial owner which is a company)	10%	10%
Belgium	5% (Minimum holding of 25% (directly/indirectly) of capital by a beneficial owner which is a company) 15% (other beneficial owners)	10%	Nil
Botswana	15% (other beneficial owners) 10% (Minimum holding of 25% of capital by a beneficial owner which is a company)	10%	10%
Brazil	15% (other beneficial owners) 10% (Minimum holding of 25% of capital by a beneficial owner which is a company)	15%	15%
Bulgaria	15% (other beneficial owners) 5% (Minimum holding of 25% of capital (directly) by a beneficial owner which is a company)	5%	10%
Canada	15% (other beneficial owners) 5% (Minimum holding of 10% of capital (directly) by a beneficial owner which is a company. The beneficial owner must also control a minimum of 10% of the voting power (directly/indirectly) but this does not apply to non-resident owned investment corporations resident in Canada)	10%	10%
China	5%	10%	10%

1   Reduced rates of withholding tax may apply where there is an appropriate double tax treaty.

Reduced rate available under the relevant Double Taxation Treaty			
Country	Dividends	Interest	Royalties
Croatia	10% (other beneficial owners) 5% (Minimum holding of 25% of capital by a beneficial owner which is a company)	Nil	5%
Cyprus	10% (other beneficial owners) 5% (Minimum holding of 10% of capital by a beneficial owner which is a company)	Nil	Nil
Czech Republic	15% (other beneficial owners) 5% (Minimum holding of 10% of capital by a beneficial owner which is a company)	Nil	10%
Denmark	15% (other beneficial owners) 5% (Minimum holding of 10% of capital by a beneficial owner which is a company)	Nil	Nil
Egypt	15%	12%	15%
Ethiopia	10%	8%	20%
Finland	15% (other beneficial owners) 5% (Minimum holding of 10% of capital by a beneficial owner which is a company)	Nil	Nil
France	15% (other beneficial owners) 5% (Minimum holding of 10% of capital (directly) by a beneficial owner which is a company)	Nil	Nil
Germany	15% (other beneficial owners) 7.5% (Minimum holding of 25% of voting shares (directly) by a beneficial owner which is a company)	10%	Nil
Ghana	15% (other beneficial owners) 5% (Minimum holding of 10% of capital by a beneficial owner which is a company)	10%	10%
Greece	15% (other beneficial owners) 5% (Minimum holding of 25% of capital (directly) by a beneficial owner which is a company)	8%	7%
Hong Kong	10% (other beneficial owners) 5% (Minimum holding of 10% of capital (directly) by a beneficial owner which is a company)	10%	5%
Hungary	15% (other beneficial owners) 5% (Minimum holding of 25% of capital (directly) by a beneficial owner which is a company)	Nil	Nil
India	10%	10%	10%
Indonesia	15% (other beneficial owners) 10% (Minimum holding of 10% of capital by a beneficial owner which is a company)	10%	10%
Iran	10%	5%	10%
Ireland	10% (other beneficial owners) 5% (Minimum holding of 10% of capital by a beneficial owner which is a company)	Nil	Nil
Israel	25%	25%	15%

Reduced rate available under the relevant Double Taxation Treaty			
Country	**Dividends**	**Interest**	**Royalties**
Italy	15% (other beneficial owners)	10%	6%
	5% (Minimum holding of 25% of capital by a beneficial owner which is a company and minimum 12-month holding period prior to dividend payment)		
Japan	15% (other beneficial owners)	10%	10%
	5% (Minimum holding of 25% of voting shares by a beneficial owner which is a company and minimum six-month holding period prior to end of accounting period during which the dividend is declared)		
Kenya	10% (all beneficial owners)	Nil	Nil
Korea, Republic of	15% (other beneficial owners)	10%	10%
	5% (Minimum holding of 25% of capital by a beneficial owner which is a company)		
Kuwait	Nil	Nil	10%
Lesotho	15%	10%	10%
Luxembourg	15% (other beneficial owners)	Nil	Nil
	5% (Minimum holding of 25% of capital (directly) by a beneficial owner which is a company)		
Malawi	No provision	10%	Nil
Malaysia	10% (other beneficial owners)	10%	5%
	5% (Minimum holding of 25% of capital by a beneficial owner which is a company)		
Malta	10% (other beneficial owners)	10%	10%
	5% (Minimum holding of 10% of capital by a beneficial owner which is a company)		
Mauritius	10% (all beneficial owners)	Nil	Nil
Mexico	10% (other beneficial owners)	10%	10%
	5% (Minimum holding of 10% of capital by a beneficial owner which is a company)		
Mozambique	15% (other beneficial owners)	8%	5%
	8% (Minimum holding of 25% of capital by a beneficial owner which is a company)		
Namibia	15% (other beneficial owners)	10%	10%
	5% (Minimum holding of 25% of capital by a beneficial owner which is a company)		
Netherlands	10% (other beneficial owners)	Nil	Nil
	5% (Minimum holding of 10% of capital by a beneficial owner which is a company)		
New Zealand	15% (other beneficial owners)	10%	10%
	5% (Minimum holding of 25% of capital by a beneficial owner which is a company)		
Nigeria	10% (other beneficial owners)	7.5%	7.5%
	7.5% (Minimum holding of 10% of capital by a beneficial owner which is a company)		

Country	Reduced rate available under the relevant Double Taxation Treaty		
	Dividends	Interest	Royalties
Norway	15% (other beneficial owners)	Nil	Nil
	5% (Minimum holding of 25% of capital by a beneficial owner which is a company)		
Oman	0% Paid to the Government of the other Contracting State	Nil	8%
	5% (Minimum holding of 10% of capital by a beneficial owner which is a company)		
	10% (Other beneficial owners (excluding Government))		
Pakistan	15% (other beneficial owners)	10%	10%
	10% (Minimum holding of 10% of capital by a beneficial owner which is a company)		
Poland	15% (other beneficial owners)	10%	10%
	5% (Minimum holding of 25% of capital by a beneficial owner which is a company)		
Portugal	15% (other beneficial owners)	10%	10%
	10% (Minimum holding of 25% of capital (directly) by a beneficial owner which is a company and minimum two-year uninterrupted holding period prior to dividend payment)		
Romania	15%	15%	15%
Russia	15% (other beneficial owners)	10%	Nil
	10% (Minimum holding of 30% of capital (directly) by a beneficial owner which is a company)		
Rwanda	20% (other beneficial owners)	10%	10%
	10% (Minimum holding of 25% of capital by a beneficial owner resident in the same state and minimum direct investment of $100.00)		
Saudi Arabia	10% (other beneficial owners)	5%	10%
	5% (Minimum holding of 10% of capital (directly) by a beneficial owner which is a company)		
Seychelles	10% (other beneficial owners)	Nil	Nil
	5% (Minimum holding of 10% of capital by a beneficial owner which is a company)		
Singapore	0% (Paid to the Government of the other contracting State)	Nil	5%
	5% (Minimum holding of 10% of capital by a beneficial owner which is a company)		
	15% (Other beneficial owners)		
Slovakia	15% (other beneficial owners)	Nil	10%
	5% (Minimum holding of 25% of capital (directly) by a beneficial owner which is a company)		
Spain	15% (other beneficial owners)	5%	5%
	5% (Minimum holding of 25% of capital (directly) by a beneficial owner which is a company)		

Reduced rate available under the relevant Double Taxation Treaty			
Country	**Dividends**	**Interest**	**Royalties**
Swaziland	15% (other beneficial owners) 10% (Minimum holding of 25% of capital by a beneficial owner which is a company)	10%	Nil
Sweden	15% (other beneficial owners) 5% (Minimum holding of 10% of capital by a beneficial owner which is a company)	Nil	Nil
Switzerland	15% (other beneficial owners) 5% (Minimum holding of 20% of capital (directly) by a beneficial owner which is a company)	5%	Nil
Taiwan	15% (other beneficial owners) 5% (Minimum holding of 10% of capital (directly) by a beneficial owner which is a company)	10%	10%
Tanzania	20% (other beneficial owners) 10% (Minimum holding of 15% of capital by a beneficial owner which is a company)	10%	10%
Thailand	15% (other beneficial owners) 10% (Minimum holding of 25% of capital by a beneficial owner which is a company)	15%	15%
Tunisia	10%	12%	10%
Turkey	15% (other beneficial owners) 10% (Minimum holding of 25% of capital by a beneficial owner which is a company)	10%	10%
Uganda	15% (other beneficial owners) 10% (Minimum holding of 25% of capital by a beneficial owner which is a company)	10%	10%
Ukraine	15% (other beneficial owners) 5% (Minimum holding of 20% of capital by a beneficial owner which is a company)	10%	10%
United Kingdom	5% (Minimum holding of 10% of capital by a beneficial owner which is a company) 15% (Qualifying dividends paid by a property investment company) 10% (other beneficial owners)	Nil	Nil
United States	0% (Contracting State, and any political sub-division or local authority etc – see article 10(8) for details) 5% (Minimum holding of 10% of voting power (directly) by a beneficial owner which is a company) 15% (other beneficial owners)	Nil	Nil
Zambia	No provision	Nil	15%
Zimbabwe	No provision	10%	15%

Note: the above rates are only available provided the specific Treaty criteria are satisfied. It is possible that lower rates than those shown above may be available provided that certain criteria are satisfied. As treaties will not be identical, guidance should be sought in all cases.

V INDIRECT TAXES

		Residents	Non-residents
Value Added Tax (VAT)	Entities obliged to levy VAT	Any vendor whose taxable supplies exceed R1,000,000 per annum	
	Taxable activities	Any activity carried on in South Africa in the furtherance of an enterprise, other than exempt supplies	
	Taxable activities – zero-rated (examples)	• Exports of goods and services • Supply of an enterprise or part of as a going concern • Petrol and distillate fuel oil • Certain foodstuffs	
	Exemptions (examples)	• Supply of accommodation in any dwelling by letting • Supply of transport by road or rail to fare-paying passengers • Educational services	
	Refund of VAT	Upon assessment	At Customs upon departure
	Tax liability	Settlement by due date of return	
	Tax rates	Standard rate of 14%	
	Administrative obligations	Submission of returns	Maintain documentary evidence for a period of five years
Transfer Duty		Payable by natural persons and legal entities: • On property value to R750,000 – Nil • R750,000–R1,250,000 – 3% of value above R750,000 • R1,250,001–R1,750,000 – R15,000 plus 6% of value above R1,250,000 • R1,750,001–R2,250,000 – R45,000 plus 8% of value above R1,750,000 • R2,250,001–R10,000,000 – R85,000 plus 11% of value above R2,250,000 • R10,000,001 and above – R937,500 plus 13% of value above R10,000,000 • No Transfer duty payable if transaction is subject to VAT	
Real Property Taxes		Local rates levied by local government (municipality)	
Stamp Duty		No stamp duty on leases of immovable property	

Nexia International is the trading name of Nexia International Limited, a company registered in the Isle of Man. Company registration number: 53513C. Registered office: 2nd floor, Sixty Circular Road, Douglas, Isle of Man, IM1 1SA

Spain

(Nexia Spanish Desk (Eva Olivencia, eo@laudis.es;
Roberto Peluso, rp@laudis.es))

I MAIN LEGAL FORMS

Legal form / Characteristics	Limited Partnership entities (Sociedad Colectiva, Sociedad Comanditaria Simple, Sociedad Comanditaria por Acciones)	Limited Liability Company ('Sociedad de Responsabilidad Limitada', 'SL') and Corporation ('Sociedad Anónima', 'SA')
	There are three forms of limited partnership entities: *Sociedad Colectiva* ('SC'), which is similar to a general partnership; *Sociedad Comanditaria* ('SCm'), which is similar to a limited partnership; and *Sociedad Coman-ditaria por Acciones* ('SCmpa'), which is similar to a limited partnership in which the participation of the limited partners is represented by shares	• *Sociedad de Responsabilidad Limitada* (SL) is the most common form of legal entity suited for companies with few shareholders, family business or subsidiaries of foreign companies The share capital of an SL is divided into shares (known as *'participaciones'*) that can only be transferred through public deed • *Sociedad Anónima* (SA). The capital is represented by shares that can be easily transferred. The SA is the corporate form for big companies and compulsory for listed companies

Legal form / Characteristics	Limited Partnership entities (Sociedad Colectiva, Sociedad Comanditaria Simple, Sociedad Comanditaria por Acciones)	Limited Liability Company ('Sociedad de Responsabilidad Limitada', 'SL') and Corporation ('Sociedad Anónima', 'SA')
Partners/ shareholders • Number • Restrictions	Minimum two partners • SC: partners only individuals with two kind of partners: active partners, who work in the entity, and capital partners • SCm: two kinds of partner: (i) general partners, with the same status, rights and obligations as partners in an SC (ie jointly and unlimited liability of all debts); and (ii) limited partners, whose liability is limited to their contributions • SCmpa is similar to SCm, except for the capital contributed by the limited partners which is divided into shares	May vary from one shareholder to an unlimited number
Directors	• SC: unless otherwise stipulated, all the partners are directors • SCm and SCmpa: only can be managed by the general partners	Both SA and SL may be managed by: • a sole director • several directors acting severally • two directors acting jointly or • a Board of Directors (between 3 and 12 for SL and unlimited numbers for SA). The Board of Directors may delegate most of its functions to one or more members
Establishment	Articles of Incorporation or Partnership deed	
Registration	All entities must be registered in the Commercial Register of the province where the entity is domiciled	
Minimum capital	SCmpa: €60,000	SA: €60,000 (At least 25% must be disbursed at the time of incorporation) SL: €3,000 (The share capital must be completely disbursed at incorporation)
Liability	Partners in an SC are exposed to unlimited liability for the payment of business debts, as are the general partners in an SCm or an SCmpa. The limited partners of SCm and SCmpa are limited to their contributions	Limited to the amount of capital contributed by each shareholder and, in the case of a liquidation, liability may not be greater than the sum received on liquidation of the company
Governance	Partners	Shareholders' meeting and the directors (executive governing body)

Legal form / Characteristics	Limited Partnership entities (Sociedad Colectiva, Sociedad Comanditaria Simple, Sociedad Comanditaria por Acciones)	Limited Liability Company ('Sociedad de Responsabilidad Limitada', 'SL') and Corporation ('Sociedad Anónima', 'SA')
Audit requirements	• SC and SCm: not compulsory, unless all the partners are companies • SCmpa: the same criteria as for SL and SA apply to be audited	Financial statements must be audited by independent auditors when the company meets at least two of the following three criteria in two consecutive years: • assets > €4m • turnover > €8m • employees > 50
Taxation (stamp tax)	No taxation for the incorporation, increase of capital and issue premium, direct contribution of the shareholders to the company's equity and direct contribution of the shareholder to offset losses The decrease or reduction of the share capital is taxed at 1% of the amount paid out to the shareholders	
Usage	SC, SCm and SCmpa are rarely used	SL is the most common legal form for a small or medium-sized business, but only SA may be quoted

II   CORPORATION TAX

Legal form / Description	Resident corporation	Permanent establishment (PE)
General description	Corporation tax	Non-residents income tax
Taxable entities	Corporations incorporated and managed in Spain	PE located in Spain
Taxable income	Worldwide profits with considerations for double taxation treaties. Exemption for income (and losses) proceeding from PE under certain conditions	Profits earned in Spain
Calculation of taxable profits	Accounting profit is adjusted for various tax add-backs and allowances to arrive to profits chargeable to corporation tax (PCTCT)	
Interest payments	Net financial expenses under €1m deductible. If higher, deductible up to 30% of the Operating Profit of the year	
	Interest from Group loans for Group shares acquisition non-deductible	
	Participative loan: some restrictions have been introduced for PLs granted from 20 June 2014. When inter-company PLs are involved, interest is not deductible as it is regarded as a dividend	
Related party transactions	All related party transactions must take place on an arm's length basis	
Tax year, return and payment	• Companies may choose their own tax year (maximum 12 months) • Returns must be filed within 25 calendar days after a period of 6 months following the end of the taxable year • Tax liability must be paid at the time of filing	
Capital gains	Treated as income	
Losses[1]	Net operating tax losses may be carried forward without time limitation	
Tax group	Group relief allowed within a Spanish group	
Tax rate	• 25% Companies incorporated from 1 January 2015 onwards can apply a reduced rate (15%) during the first two years of profit	

---

1   2016: 60% of taxable base with a minimum deduction of €1 million (50% for taxpayer whose turnover of the 12 months preceding the start of the fiscal year is more than €20 million and less than €60 million; 25% for taxpayer whose turnover of the 12 months preceding the start of the fiscal year is more than €60 million); 2017 onwards: 70% of adjusted taxable base with a minimum deduction of €1 million (50% for taxpayer whose turnover of the 12 months preceding the start of the fiscal year is more than €20 million and less than €60 million; 25% for taxpayer whose turnover of the 12 months preceding the start of the fiscal year is more than €60 million).

III TAXES FOR INDIVIDUALS

		Residents	Non-residents
Income Tax	General description	Tax levied on the taxable income of a taxable person for a year of assessment	Tax levied on each taxable income separately
	Taxable entities and taxable income	Residents are taxed on their worldwide income	Non-residents are taxable on all income arising in Spain
	Types of taxable income	General taxable income: • employment from personal services or pensions • income from business activities • income from real estate Savings taxable income: • income from capital investments (interest, sale of goodwill, dividends, royalties, annuities) except from related entities • capital gains	No distinction between General and Savings income
	Tax year, tax assessment and tax payment	• Tax year is the calendar year • Entrepreneurs and professionals must file returns and make advance payments quarterly. All residents prepare an annual return • Return must be filed in May/June each year • Tax liability must be paid at the time of filing, or 60% could be paid at the time of filing and 40% in November	• A return must be filed for each income obtained, though they might be grouped quarterly under some conditions. Certain income must be declared annually
	Losses	Losses can be offset against income in the subsequent 4 years under certain conditions and limits	No possibility to offset losses
	Tax rates	• General income (it depends on the autonomous regions), Up to €12,450 – 19% €12,450–€20,200 – 24% €20,200–€35,200 – 30% €35,200–€60,000 – 37% Over €60,000 – 45% • Savings income: 19% for the first €6,000 21% from €6,000 to €50,000 23% for the rest	• General tax rate is 24% (for EU tax residents: 19%) • Interest, dividends and capital gains: 19% • There are some special regimes • Should there be a double tax treaty, its rate will prevail
Capital Gains Tax (CGT)	General description	There is no specific capital gains tax. Capital gains are included as part of either the personal income tax or the non-residents income tax	They are taxed at a flat rate of 19%

		Spanish resident	Non-Spanish resident
Inheritance and Gift Tax (IGT)	General description	The inheritance and gift tax (IGT) applies to transfers of property on death or by inter vivos gift, including amounts received from certain life insurance policies when the beneficiary is not the contracting party. IGT is imposed on the recipient of the transfer. The tax is levied only if the recipient is an individual	
	Taxable entities and chargeable assets	If the beneficiary is a corporation, such transfers will be deemed to give rise to capital gains subject to corporate income tax (CIT)	
	Calculation of charge	The taxable amount is equal to the real value of the assets received minus deductible debts, liens, and burdens corresponding to each heir, legatee, donee or beneficiary	
	Taxable events	• Wealth transfers on death • Wealth transfers by inter vivos gift	
	Allowances	The law provides for a system of general allowances, depending on circumstances. The autonomous regions may establish different systems provided these do not result in a reduction of the total tax burden for IGT purposes	
	Tax rates	The tax rates depend on: the amount received by the heir, legatee, donee or beneficiary; his/her relationship with the deceased, donor or contracting party and the net worth of the recipient prior to the acquisition. The tax rate also depends on the competent Autonomous Region concerned	

IV WITHHOLDING TAXES

Under domestic law	Payments to residents	Payments to non-residents
Dividends	19%	19%[2]
Interest	19%	19%[3]
Royalties	[5]	24%[4] (for EU tax residents: 19%)
On payments to artists and sportsmen and others	15%	24% (for EU tax residents: 19%)

Reduced rates of withholding tax may apply where there is an appropriate double tax treaty and a tax residence certificate.

Reduced rate available under the relevant Double Taxation Treaty			
Country	Dividends	Interest	Royalties
Albania	10%	6%	Nil
Algeria	15%	5%	14%
Argentina	15%	12%	15%
Armenia	10%	5%	10%
Australia	15%	10%	10%
Austria	15%	5%	5%
Barbados	Nil	Nil	Nil
Belgium	15%	10%	5%
Bolivia	15%	15%	15%
Bosnia & Herzegovina	10%	7%	7%
Brazil	10%	15%	12.5%
Bulgaria	15%	Nil	Nil
Canada	15%	10%	10%
Columbia	5%	10%	10%
Costa Rica	12%	10%	10%
Croatia	15%	Nil	8%
Chile	10%	15%	10%
China	10%	10%	10%
Cyprus	5%	Nil	Nil
Cuba	15%	10%	5%
Czech Republic	15%	Nil	5%
Denmark	15%	10%	6%
Ecuador	15%	10%	10%
Egypt	12%	10%	12%

2 0% under EU Directive if prerequisites are met (that is, paid to a company, acquisition cost is more than €20 million or 5% held for more than 1 year).
3 0% under EU Directive.
4 0% if royalties are paid to a EU resident holding where the recipient holds a shareholding of more than 25%.
5 Depends on their nature: 19% or 24%.

Reduced rate available under the relevant Double Taxation Treaty			
Country	Dividends	Interest	Royalties
El Salvador	12%	10%	10%
Estonia	15%	10%	10%
Finland	15%	10%	5%
Former USSR States	18%	Nil	5%
France	15%	10%	5%
Georgia	10%	Nil	Nil
Germany	15%	10%	5%
Greece	10%	8%	6%
Hong Kong	10%	5%	5%
Hungary	15%	Nil	Nil
Iceland	15%	5%	5%
India	15%	15%	20%
Indonesia	15%	10%	10%
Iran	10%	7%	5%
Ireland	15%	10%	10%
Israel	10%	10%	7%
Italy	15%	12%	8%
Jamaica	10%	10%	10%
Japan	15%	10%	10%
Kazakhstan	15%	10%	10%
Korea	15%	10%	10%
Kuwait	5%	Nil	5%
Latvia	15%	10%	10%
Lithuania	15%	10%	10%
Luxembourg	15%	10%	10%
Macedonia	15%	5%	5%
Malaysia	5%	10%	7%
Malta	5%	Nil	Nil
Mexico	15%	15%	10%
Moldova	10%	5%	8%
Morocco	15%	10%	10%
Netherlands	15%	10%	6%
New Zealand	15%	10%	10%
Nigeria	10%	7.5%	7.5%
Norway	15%	10%	5%
Oman	10%	5%	8%
Pakistan	10%	10%	7.5%
Panama	10%	5%	5%
Philippines	15%	15%	20%
Poland	15%	Nil	10%
Portugal	15%	15%	5%
Romania	15%	10%	10%
Russia	15%	5%	5%
Saudi Arabia	5%	5%	8%
Serbia	10%	10%	10%

Reduced rate available under the relevant Double Taxation Treaty			
Country	**Dividends**	**Interest**	**Royalties**
Singapore	5%	5%	5%
Slovenia	15%	5%	5%
South Africa	15%	5%	5%
Sweden	15%	15%	10%
Switzerland	15%	Nil	5%
Thailand	10%	15%	15%
Trinidad & Tobago	10%	8%	5%
Tunisia	15%	10%	10%
Turkey	15%	15%	10%
United Arab Emirates	15%	Nil	Nil
United Kingdom	10%	Nil	Nil
United States	15%	10%	Nil
Uruguay	5%	10%	10%
Uzbekistan	10%	5%	5%
Venezuela	10%	10%	5%
Vietnam	15%	10%	10%

Note: the above rates are only available provided the specific Treaty criteria are satisfied. It is possible that lower rates than those shown above may be available provided certain criteria are satisfied. As treaties will not be identical, guidance should be sought in all cases.

V   INDIRECT TAXES

		Residents	Non-residents
Value Added Tax (VAT)	General description	Tax on the supply of goods and services (VAT)	
	Entities obliged to levy VAT	VAT is chargeable on the supply of goods and services by entrepreneurs and professionals	
	Taxable activities	Supply of goods and services	
	Taxable activities – zero-rated (examples)	There is a specific list of zero-rated operations	
	Exemptions (examples)	• Exports and other transactions related to international goods traffic • Intra-EU supplies of goods • Certain public interest activities (it covers certain medical and sanitary supplies, the supply of services for the benefit of the community, educational services, athletic or cultural services, and the supply of certain waste products for recycling) • Financial and insurance transactions • Certain real estate transactions. The general principle regarding transfers of ownership of land is that it will be taxable only when it is possible to use it for building purposes – Second and further transfers of buildings are also exempt subject to certain conditions Other exemptions: public lotteries, postal services, or services rendered by temporary unions of entrepreneurs (UTEs), Economic Interest Groups (EIGs), or European Economic Interest Groups (EEIGs) to their members provided, among other requirements, the services rendered by the members are also exempt	
	Refund of VAT	Taxpayers with excess input VAT may carry forward the excess and deduct it on subsequent tax returns. In the tax return corresponding to the last assessment period of the year, a taxpayer may choose between claiming a refund of the excess VAT paid or carrying the excess forward to subsequent periods. The tax authorities must pay refunds within 6 months. After this period, the tax authorities must pay delay interest. In most cases, refunds are subject to substantial delays Taxpayers can ask for a monthly VAT return, which means submitting VAT liquidation every month, and the tax authorities must pay refunds within 6 months. Electronic books must be submitted with the return under such an option	
	Tax rates	• Standard rate = 21% • Reduced rate = 10% • Exports = 0% • Necessities = 4%	
Real Property Taxes		A local tax is levied by municipalities	
Transfer Tax and Stamp Duty		Transfer tax and stamp duty covers three different taxes: • property transfer tax which is designed to tax all non-business transfers of property • tax on corporate events • tax on documented legal acts which is levied as a consequence of the issuance of certain kinds of documents to execute a transaction	

Nexia International does not accept liability for any loss arising from any action taken, or omission, on the basis of this publication. Professional advice should be obtained before acting or refraining from acting on the contents of this publication. Membership of Nexia International, or associated umbrella organizations, does not constitute any partnership between members, and members do not accept any responsibility for the commission of any act, or omission to act by, or the liabilities of, other members.

Nexia International is the trading name of Nexia International Limited, a company registered in the Isle of Man. Company registration number: 53513C. Registered office: 2nd floor, Sixty Circular Road, Douglas, Isle of Man, IM1 1SA

Sri Lanka

(Sanjanya Bandara, B. R. De Silva & Co, brds@eureka.lk)

I   MAIN LEGAL FORMS

Characteristics \ Legal form	Partnership and Limited Liability Partnership (LLP)	Private corporation (Ltd) and Public corporation (Plc)
Partners/shareholders • Number • Restrictions	• Minimum: two • Maximum: 20 No concept of LLPs	• Minimum: one • Maximum: no limit
Directors	N/A	Minimum: one
Establishment	Partnership Ordinance	Companies Act No 07 of 2007
Registration	With local authority	With Registrar of Companies
Minimum capital	Not specified	
Liability	Unlimited	Limited to share capital
Governance	• Partnership Ordinance • Local authority law	Companies Act No 07 of 2007
Audit requirements	Not compulsory	Compulsory
Taxation	Transparent, partners are taxed on the share of income	Worldwide profits

II   CORPORATION TAX

Legal form / Description	Resident corporation	Permanent establishment (PE)
General description	Corporation tax	
Taxable entities	Companies incorporated in Sri Lanka or overseas companies with management and control exercised in Sri Lanka	PE in Sri Lanka
Taxable income	Worldwide profits	Income arising or derived from Sri Lanka
Calculation of taxable profits	Accounting profit adjusted for various tax add-backs and allowances	
Interest payments	Business interest can be deducted, subject to thin capitalisation rules	
Related party transactions	Must be at arm's length value	
Tax year, return and payment	• Tax year runs from 1 April to 31 March • Tax payable based on taxable income of current year of assessment • Final liability must be paid within 6 months of the end of the year of assessment • Return of income must be submitted on or before 30 November	
Capital gains	Exempt from tax	
Losses	Adjusted business losses can be set off against the total statutory income up to 35% of total statutory income. Balance can be carried forward	
Tax group	12% concessionary rate may not be available for a group of companies	
Tax rate	• Companies with taxable income of less than SLR 5 million taxed at 12% (other than manufacturing and services) • Turnover not exceeding SLR 750 million taxed at 12% (other than buying and selling business) • Other companies: 28% unless an exemption or concessionary rate is available • Dividend tax is 10% on gross dividend	

III   TAXES FOR INDIVIDUALS

		Residents	Non-residents
Income Tax	General description	Tax levied on chargeable income for the year	
	Taxable entities and taxable income	Persons present in Sri Lanka for 183 days or more during any year of assessment Residents taxed on worldwide income	Non-residents are taxed on income arising in Sri Lanka
	Types of taxable income	• Employment income • Business income • Interest income • Net annual value • Dividend income	
	Calculation of income	Certain expenditure incurred for the production of business income can be deducted	
	Tax year, tax assessment and tax payment	• Tax year runs from 1 April to 31 March • Tax return filing deadline is 30 November • Tax paid on PAYE basis with the employer liable for any shortfall in remittance • Tax payable in four quarterly instalments in August, November, February and May following the tax year	
	Losses	May be carried forward and set off against the total statutory income up to 35% of total statutory income. Balance can be carried forward	
	Tax rates	Income tax – progressive rates from 4%–24%	
Capital Gains Tax (CGT)	Taxable entities and chargeable assets	No capital gains tax	

		Domiciled	Non-domiciled
Inheritance Tax (IHT)	General description	There is no IHT in Sri Lanka	

IV   WITHHOLDING TAXES

	Payments to non-residents	Payments to non-residents[1]
Dividends	10%	10%
Interest	Individuals, Charitable Institutions – 2.5% Partnerships and body of persons – 8% Companies – 10%	20% 15% on a loan granted to any person in Sri Lanka
Royalties	10%	20%
On payments to artistes and sportsmen	Nil	12%

Reduced rate available under the relevant Double Taxation Treaty			
Country	Dividends	Interest	Royalties
Australia	15%	10%	10%
Bangladesh	15%	15%	15%
Belgium	15%	10%	10%
Canada	15%	15%	10%
China	10%	10%	10%
Denmark	15%	10%	10%
Finland	15%	10%	10%
France	15%	10%	10%
Germany	15%	10%	10%
India	15%	10%	10%
Indonesia	15%	15%	15%
Iran	10%	10%	8%
Italy	15%	15%	10%
Japan	10%	15%	7.5%
Korea, Republic of	15%	10%	10%
Malaysia	15%	10%	10%
Mauritius	15%	15%	10%
Nepal	15%	15%	15%
Netherlands	15%	15%	10%
Norway	15%	10%	10%
Pakistan	15%	10%	20%
Philippines	10%	10%	10%
Poland	15%	10%	10%
Qatar	10%	10%	10%
Romania	12.5%	10%	10%
Russia	15%	10%	10%
Singapore	15%	10%	15%
Sweden	15%	10%	10%

---

1   Reduced rates of withholding tax may apply where there is an appropriate double tax treaty.

Reduced rate available under the relevant Double Taxation Treaty			
Country	Dividends	Interest	Royalties
Switzerland	15%	10%	10%
Thailand	15%	10%	15%
United Arab Emirates	10%	10%	10%
United Kingdom	15%	10%	10%
United States	15%	10%	10%
Vietnam	10%	10%	15%

Note: the above rates are only available provided the specific Treaty criteria are satisfied. It is possible that lower rates than those shown above may be available provided that certain criteria are satisfied. As treaties will not be identical, guidance should be sought in all cases.

V   INDIRECT TAXES

		Residents	Non-residents
Value Added Tax (VAT)	General description	Goods imported into Sri Lanka and goods and services supplied within the territorial limits of Sri Lanka are liable to Value Added Tax (VAT)	
	Entities obliged to levy VAT	Individual, partnership, company and body of person	
	Registration Threshold	SLR 3 million per taxable period (one month or three months) or SLR 12 million per annum SLR 12.5 million per quarter – For wholesale or retail trade	
	Taxable activities	The supply of goods and services and import of goods	
	Taxable activities – zero-rated (examples)	Exports, repair of foreign ships or aircraft, international transportation of goods and passengers	
	Exemptions (examples)	Pharmaceutical products and locally manufactured drugs, rice, rice flour, green leaf	
	Refund of VAT	Refunds are entitled only for zero-rated suppliers subject to simplified VAT (SVAT)	
	Tax liability	Supplier charges VAT on the supply of goods and services	
	Tax rates	0%, 15%	
	Administrative obligations	Submit VAT returns on monthly/quarterly basis	
Real Property Taxes		None	
Stamp Duty		Levied on the transfer of immovable property and certain documents	
Nation Building Tax (NBT)	Entities obliged to levy NBT	Individual, partnership, company and body of person	
	Taxable activities	• imports of any article; or • carries on the business of manufacture of any article; or • carries on the business of providing a service of any description; or • carries on the business of wholesale or retail sale of any article	
	Threshold of Liable Turnover	SLR 3 million per quarter	
	Tax Rate	2% on turnover	
	Exemptions (examples)	Exports of any article, pharmaceutical products and drugs, fertilizer	
	Input tax credit	Only manufacturers are entitled to this	
	Administrative obligations	Submit NBT returns on quarterly basis	

		Residents	Non-residents
Economic Service Charge (ESC)	General description	Any person or partnership is liable to pay Economic Service Charge in every quarter of every year of assessment in respect of every part of relevant turnover	
	Entities obliged to levy ESC	Every person and every partnership	
	Relevant turnover	'Relevant turnover' in relation to any person or partnership and to any relevant quarter means the aggregate turnover for that relevant quarter of every trade, business, profession or vocation carried on or exercised by such person or partnership in Sri Lanka whether directly or through an agent or more than one agent	
	Threshold of Liable Turnover	SLR 50 million per quarter	
	Exemptions (examples)	Distributors, dealers in lottery, unit trusts or mutual funds, all airlines and shipping lines	
	Tax rates	0.25%	
	Administrative obligations	Submit ESC returns on yearly basis	

Nexia International does not accept liability for any loss arising from any action taken, or omission, on the basis of this publication. Professional advice should be obtained before acting or refraining from acting on the contents of this publication. Membership of Nexia International, or associated umbrella organizations, does not constitute any partnership between members, and members do not accept any responsibility for the commission of any act, or omission to act by, or the liabilities of, other members.

Nexia International is the trading name of Nexia International Limited, a company registered in the Isle of Man. Company registration number: 53513C. Registered office: 2nd floor, Sixty Circular Road, Douglas, Isle of Man, IM1 1SA

Sweden

(Per-Åke Bois, Nexia Revision Stockholm, perake.bois@nexia.se)

I MAIN LEGAL FORMS

Legal form / Characteristics	Partnership and Limited Partnership	Private corporation (Ltd) and Public corporation (Plc)
Partners/shareholders • Number • Restrictions	• Two or more • None	• One or more • None
Directors	Management by partners	Management by directors[1]
Establishment	Registration with Swedish Companies Registration Office	
Registration	Swedish Companies Registration Office (*Bolagsverket*) and the Swedish Tax Agency (*Skatteverket*)	
Minimum capital	None	Ltd: SEK50,000 Plc: SEK500,000
Liability	Unlimited Limited for LLPs	There is no personal liability, unless half of the share capital is depleted
Governance	None	Ltd: Board of Directors can appoint a CEO, but it is not mandatory Plc: Board of Directors must appoint a CEO
Audit requirements	Audit required: • When owned by corporation • For large business	Audit required: • Ltd: by approved /authorised public accountant. Some exceptions for small businesses • Plc: by authorised public accountant
Taxation	Partners are subject to taxation on their net income	Subject to corporation tax on net income
Usage	Smaller businesses and start-ups	Ltd: small, medium-sized and large businesses Plc: medium-sized and large businesses

---

1 Private companies must have at least one director. Public companies must have at least three directors.

II   CORPORATION TAX

Legal form / Description	Swedish resident corporation	Permanent establishment (PE)
General description	Federal tax on profit	
Taxable entities	Corporations registered with the Swedish Companies Registration Office	PE located in Sweden
Taxable income	Worldwide profits	Profits arising from the Swedish PE
Calculation of taxable profits	Accounting profit is adjusted for various tax add-backs and allowances to arrive at profits chargeable to corporation tax (PCTCT)	
Interest payments	Deductible. No thin capitalisation rules. Interest on intercompany loans is subject to limitations	
Related party transactions	All related party transactions must be accounted for on an arm's length basis	
Tax year, return and payment	Financial year must cover 12 months, commencing on the first of any month. The tax returns are due 6 to 9 months after the end of the financial year (due dates – 1 March, 1 July, 1 November and 15 December). For example, the deadline for a 31 December year-end would be 1 July as it is this date that falls within 6 to 9 months. Preliminary tax payments are due monthly from the first to the fourth month of the financial year until the month after the end of the financial year	
Capital gains	Capital gains are normally subject to taxation. Capital gains on shares covered by the Swedish participation exemption regime are tax exempt. Capital losses are not deductible	
Losses[2]	Net operating losses may be carried forward indefinitely but must be offset against the first available profit	
Tax group	Each company is a separate tax entity. However, it is possible to use group contributions when a parent company owns 90% of its subsidiaries[3]	PE: N/A
Tax rate	22%	

2   There are special rules allowing the company to utilise other losses such as capital losses and loan-related deficits.
3   For group relief purposes.

III TAXES FOR INDIVIDUALS

		Residents	Non-residents
Income Tax	General description	Tax levied on the chargeable income of a chargeable person for a year of assessment	
	Taxable entities and taxable income	Residents are taxed on their worldwide income	Income arising in Sweden
	Types of taxable income	• Income from capital investment (interest, sale of goodwill, dividends, royalties, annuities), property income • Income from business activities • Earned income or pensions	
	Calculation of income	Partly on cash basis, partly on earnings basis Certain limitations on the deduction of costs	
	Tax year, tax assessment and tax payment	Tax year is the calendar year in which the income is generated with assessments made in the following year Tax return must be filed by 2 May during the year of assessment Income not subject to withholding tax is pre-assessed and tax is paid in instalments. Preliminary tax payable is 110% of the amount in the previous year, or 105% if the final tax in the previous year was less than the preliminary tax paid Date of tax payment: preliminary payments are made on a monthly basis. If the full amount hasn't been paid by the following February interest will become payable. If the individual receives the tax calculation before 30 August then the remainder will be due before 12 November and if after, 12 December	
	Losses	Losses can be offset against income of the same source in the same year	
	Tax rates	Up to SEK452,100 = 30%[4] SEK452,100–SEK657,900 = 50% Over SEK657,900 = 55%	20%
		Additionally, certain groups of foreign individuals will be eligible for tax relief, eg executives and specialists	
		Residents	**Non-residents**
Capital Gains Tax (CGT)	General description	Tax on increase in the value of asset between acquisition and disposal	
	Taxable entities and chargeable assets	Residents who disposed of: • shares • investments • real property	Non-residents who disposed of real property in Sweden
	Calculation of gain	• 22/30ths of gain on personal related real property is taxable • 90% of gain on business-related real property is taxable • 100% of gain of shares (with some exceptions)	
	Tax year, tax assessment and tax payment	Tax year is the calendar year when the income is generated with assessments made in the following year Tax return must be filed by 2 May following the year of assessment Tax payment on 12 February, final payment in autumn	
	Losses	70% of the losses are deductible (with certain exceptions)	

---

4 The municipal rate ranges between 29% and 34% depending on the municipality of residence of an individual (30% has been used in the table above). National tax applies to income earned above SEK452,100 (20% between SEK452,100 and SEK657,900, and 25% above SEK657,900).

		Residents	Non-residents
	Tax rates	• 30%	
		Domiciled	**Non-domiciled**
Inheritance Tax (IHT)	General description	No inheritance tax	

IV WITHHOLDING TAXES

Under domestic law	Payments to residents	Payments to non-residents[5]
Dividends	30%	30%
Interest	30%	Nil
Royalties	30%–57%	57%
On payments to artists and sportsmen	30%–57%	15%

Reduced rate available under the relevant Double Taxation Treaty			
Country	Dividends	Interest	Royalties
Albania	15%	Nil	5%
Argentina	15%	Nil	15%
Australia	15%	Nil	10%
Austria	10%	Nil	10%
Bangladesh	15%	Nil	10%
Barbados	15%	Nil	5%
Belarus	10%	Nil	10%
Belgium	15%	Nil	Nil
Bolivia	15%	Nil	15%
Botswana	15%	Nil	15%
Brazil	25%	Nil	25%
Bulgaria	10%	Nil	5%
Canada	15%	Nil	10%
Chile	10%	Nil	10%
China	10%	Nil	10%
Cyprus	15%	Nil	Nil
Czech Republic	10%	Nil	5%
Denmark	15%	Nil	Nil
Egypt	20%	Nil	14%
Estonia	15%	Nil	10%
Faroe Islands	15%	Nil	Nil
Finland	15%	Nil	Nil
France	15%	Nil	Nil
Gambia	15%	Nil	12.5%
Germany	15%	Nil	Nil
Greece	Nil	Nil	5%
Hungary	15%	Nil	Nil
Iceland	15%	Nil	Nil
India	10%	Nil	10%

---

5   Reduced rates of withholding tax may apply where there is an appropriate double tax treaty.

Reduced rate available under the relevant Double Taxation Treaty			
Country	Dividends	Interest	Royalties
Indonesia	15%	Nil	15%
Ireland	15%	Nil	Nil
Israel	15%	Nil	Nil
Italy	15%	Nil	5%
Jamaica	22.5%	Nil	10%
Japan	15%	Nil	10%
Kazakhstan	15%	Nil	10%
Kenya	25%	Nil	20%
Korea, Republic of	15%	Nil	15%
Latvia	15%	Nil	10%
Lithuania	15%	Nil	10%
Luxembourg	15%	Nil	Nil
Macedonia	15%	Nil	Nil
Malaysia	15%	Nil	8%
Malta	15%	Nil	Nil
Mauritius	15%	Nil	15%
Mexico	15%	Nil	10%
Namibia	15%	Nil	15%
Netherlands	15%	Nil	Nil
New Zealand	15%	Nil	10%
Norway	15%	Nil	Nil
Pakistan	30%	Nil	10%
Philippines	15%	Nil	15%
Poland	15%	Nil	5%
Portugal	10%	Nil	10%
Romania	10%	Nil	10%
Russia	15%	Nil	Nil
Singapore	15%	Nil	Nil
Slovakia	10%	Nil	5%
South Africa	15%	Nil	Nil
Spain	15%	Nil	10%
Sri Lanka	15%	Nil	10%
Switzerland	15%	Nil	Nil
Taiwan	10%	Nil	10%
Tanzania	25%	Nil	20%
Thailand	30%	Nil	15%
Trinidad and Tobago	20%	Nil	20%
Tunisia	20%	Nil	15%
Turkey	20%	Nil	10%
Ukraine	10%	Nil	10%

Note: the above rates are only available provided the specific Treaty criteria are satisfied. It is possible that lower rates than those shown above may be available provided that certain criteria are satisfied. As treaties will not be identical, guidance should be sought in all cases.

V INDIRECT TAXES

		Residents	Non-residents
Value Added Tax (VAT)	General description	Tax on the supply of goods and services	
	Entities obliged to levy VAT	Entities selling goods and services if they engage in economic activity	
	Taxable activities	• Importing goods • Supply of taxable goods and services by an entrepreneur • Intra-Community acquisition of goods and services (EU)	
	Taxable activities – zero-rated (examples)	Exports to outside the EU	
	Exemptions (examples)	Leasing and transfer of ownership of real property	
	Refund of VAT	Deductible as input tax and a refund to the tax account after filing of the return	Goods purchased for business outside Sweden
	Tax liability	Normally suppliers of goods and services; reverse charge for certain suppliers of goods and services (eg construction companies)	
	Tax rates	• Standard rate = 25% • Food, restaurants and tourism = 12% • Newspapers, transport and entertainment = 6% • Pharmaceuticals on prescription, gold for investment purposes, a number of financial services including insurance and reinsurance = 0%	
	Administrative obligations	Application to the Swedish Tax Agency for VAT registration PAYE must usually be filed monthly	Application to the Swedish Tax Agency for VAT registration or refund
Real Property Taxes		Special fees depending on property	
Stamp Duty		Standard rate 1.5%, legal entity 4.25% (eg transfer of real property)	

Switzerland

*(Andreas Baumann, ABT Treuhandgesellschaft AG, andreas.baumann@abt.ch;
Patricia Handschin, ABT Treuhandgesellschaft AG, patricia.handschin@abt.ch)*

I MAIN LEGAL FORMS

Legal form / Characteristics	Partnership and Limited Partnership	Private corporation (Sarl/GmbH) and Public corporation (SA/AG)
Partners/shareholders • Number • Restrictions	*General partnership:* • must be formed by at least two individuals • general partnership can only be set up by individuals and not by corporations *Limited partnership:* • unlimited number of partners • at least one partner with unlimited liability • unlimited liability partners can only be individuals, whereas those with limited liability may be corporations	Must be formed by one or more individuals or legal entities, ie companies
Directors	No legal provisions	At least one managing officer or other person capable of representing the corporation with legal domicile in Switzerland must be registered in the register of commerce
Establishment	Partnership contract	Adoption of the Articles of Incorporation, and by appointment of management
Registration	Commercial Register	Commercial Register of its domicile

Legal form / Characteristics	Partnership and Limited Partnership	Private corporation (Sarl/GmbH) and Public corporation (SA/AG)
Minimum capital	None	*Sarl/GmbH*: minimum fixed and fully paid in capital of CHF 20,000 with a minimum investment of CHF 100 by each shareholder *SA/AG*: minimum fixed capital of CHF 100,000. At least 20% or CHF 50,000, whichever is higher, has to be paid up prior to the first shareholders' meeting. Bearer shares must be fully paid up
Liability	Unlimited[1]	Limited to the company's assets
Governance	No rules, usually by partners Governance rule for partners for collective investments	Strong governance rules for listed companies
Audit requirements	No audit requirement, except for the partners with collective investments	With effect from 1 January 2012, the limits have changed so that an audit is required for companies that exceed two of the following thresholds in two successive financial years: • yearly turnover exceeds CHF 40m • total assets exceed CHF 20m • more than 250 full-time employees If the requirements for an ordinary audit are not met, but the company has more than 10 full-time employees on annual average, the company must have its annual accounts reviewed by an auditor in a limited audit If a company has less than 10 full-time employees, the company can renounce to the audit Special requirements for listed companies
Taxation	Transparent[2] Foreign partnerships can be taxed as corporations[3]	Corporate income and capital tax
Usage	Small and medium-sized businesses	Corporations (especially Sarl/GmbH) are the most common type of business entity in Switzerland. But SA/AG have the better reputation than Sarl/GmbH due to the higher share capital.

---

1 The limited partner's liability is restricted to his investment.
2 Income and capital are assigned to the partners.
3 Cantonal practices differ between the foreign domicile of a partnership or foreign domicile of ownership.

II CORPORATION TAX

Description \ Legal form	Resident corporation	Permanent establishment (PE)
General description	Resident companies and PEs are subject to: • federal income tax • cantonal/municipal income tax • cantonal/municipal net worth taxes	
Taxable entities	• Companies registered in Switzerland • Central management located in Switzerland	PE in Switzerland
Taxable income	Worldwide income, excluding PEs and real estate abroad	At least income derived from Switzerland (foreign losses not allowable against Swiss gains)
Calculation of taxable profits	Commercial financial statements according to Swiss civil law serve as the basis for taxation. It may be adjusted by the tax authorities according to specific provisions in the tax laws (eg depreciation, accruals, contributions to reserves, open or hidden profit distributions and non-business benefits to third parties, etc) The corporate net worth tax is based on the value of a corporate entity's net assets, normally equal to shareholders' net equity	
Interest payments	Subject to the debt-to-equity rules, interest payments are deductible. Interest rates may not exceed arm's length rates. The Federal tax administration publishes safe haven rates every year	
Related party transactions	Switzerland does not have statutory transfer pricing rules but OECD standards are accepted. Inter-company charges should follow the arm's length principle and be justified and documented	
Tax year, return and payment	• Financial year = tax year • Tax returns must be filled in after year end. Deadline and payment varies between the cantons	
Capital gains	Capital gains realised on the disposal of movable business assets as well as capital gains realised on financial transactions are generally included in taxable income at the federal and cantonal levels. Special rules may apply for capital gains on real estate assets and on participations	
Losses	Tax losses may be carried forward 7 years. All kinds of losses incurred in the usual course of business are deductible. In the case of financial restructuring, there is no time limit for the utilization of losses	
Tax group	None	
Tax rate	• Federal corporate income tax is levied at a flat rate of 8.5% of taxable income. Because tax is deductible, the effective tax rate is approximately 7.8% (on gain before tax) Rates at cantonal level vary considerably The total effective tax rate (on gains before tax – federal, canton, municipality) ranges from 12.5% (Zug, Sarnen, Wollerau) to 24% (Geneva) depending on canton and municipality • A varying rate of 0.01% to 0.5% of the company's net equity is levied annually by the canton. No federal capital tax is levied	

III   TAXES FOR INDIVIDUALS

<table>
<tr><td></td><td></td><td>Residents</td><td>Non-residents</td></tr>
<tr><td rowspan="8">Income Tax</td><td>General description</td><td colspan="2">Federal, cantonal and/or nominal tax on the chargeable income of a chargeable person for a year of assessment</td></tr>
<tr><td>Taxable entities and taxable income</td><td>Individuals having their fiscal domicile or fiscal residence in Switzerland are liable to income tax on their worldwide income[4]

• Resident individuals are subject to personal income and net wealth taxes
• Income taxes are levied by the confederation and also by the 26 cantons and their municipalities</td><td>All non-residents are only limited tax liable based on an economic affiliation, eg member of partnership, holder of PE, owner of real estate, broker of real estate, foreign workers, etc[5]

• Non-resident taxpayers are subject only to Swiss taxes on certain source income (limited tax liability to Swiss derived income)</td></tr>
<tr><td>Types of taxable income</td><td colspan="2">• Investment income
• Employment income
• Pensions
• Income from real estate
• Business and professional income
• Participation income</td></tr>
<tr><td>Calculation of income</td><td colspan="2">Addition of earnings and deduction of expenses. Some special rules apply</td></tr>
<tr><td>Tax year, tax assessment and tax payment</td><td colspan="2">• Taxes are assessed for the calendar year
• All taxpayers must file a tax return after the end of each tax period, normally the end of March. The deadline can be extended in most cantons until the end of November
• Each canton applies its own rule regarding payments</td></tr>
<tr><td>Losses</td><td colspan="2">Losses related to a business activity may be carried forward 7 years. In cases of restructuring there is no time limit for the consideration of losses. Special rules may apply for capital losses on real estate assets

Losses on private equity may not be carried forward and cannot be credited against income, as gains – with a few exceptions – are not taxable</td></tr>
<tr><td>Tax rates</td><td colspan="2">• In general, Swiss income tax rates are progressive. Different rates apply for married and single taxpayers, as income of husband and wife is aggregated and taxed as one income
• The maximum federal income tax rate is 11.5%
• The cantonal and municipal tax rate varies considerably. The maximum cantonal and municipal income tax rate varies between 15% and 32%, depending on the respective canton
• Income from participations is taxed on a reduced tax rate (federal 60%) depending on the canton (in general 50% reduction) of the taxpayer's domicile</td></tr>
</table>

4   Fiscal domicile: a person has the intention of permanently staying in Switzerland. Fiscal residence: a person works in Switzerland for a period of at least 30 days or stays in Switzerland (without working) for a period of at least 90 days.
5   Tax treaty allocation to be observed.

		Residents	Non-residents
Flat rate withholding tax; Agreements with Austria and UK			The Swiss banks deduct an amount annually on an anonymous basis from income or assets equivalent to Austrian or UK income tax. The deduction has the effect of satisfying any tax liability in Austria or UK
Capital Gains Tax (CGT)	General description	Capital gains are tax exempt except for gains on real estate and some special rules for gains on participation	
	Taxable entities and chargeable assets	An individual is always tax liable Private assets: • capital gains realised on the disposal of immovable assets are subject to real estate gains tax. Real estate gains tax is levied on the transfer of ownership of real estate (land or land and building) with some exemptions • capital gains realised on some special taxable participation transactions are taxed together with the ordinary income Business assets: • capital gains realised on the disposal of movable business assets are generally included in taxable income at the federal and cantonal levels • capital gains realised on the disposal of immovable assets are subject to income tax. Some cantonal regimes, however, apply a real estate gains tax	
	Calculation of gain	Special rules apply to define the real estate gains tax. For capital gains on business assets the difference between the sales price and book value of an asset is taxed	
	Tax year, tax assessment and tax payment	• Tax year: see notes for income tax • For gains realised on the disposal of immovable assets, a special tax declaration may be filed • The tax is owed according to the federal and cantonal rules	
	Losses	Losses on gains realised on the disposal of movable business property may be carried forward (see notes for income tax)	
	Tax rates	• See rates on income tax of residents • Tax rates for real estate gains depend on the amount of the gain and the period of ownership and vary considerably from canton to canton	
Wealth Tax	General description	Tax on net wealth	
	Tax liability	Yes	Yes for real estate and business assets located in Switzerland
	Computation of value	Difference between assets and liabilities	
	Tax rate	• In general, Swiss wealth tax rates are progressive • No federal wealth tax applies • The cantonal and municipal tax rate varies considerably. The cantonal and municipal wealth tax rate amounts between 0.5% to 3%, depending on the respective canton	

		Domiciled	Non-domiciled
Inheritance Tax (IHT)	General description	The tax is applied on net asset transfers by inheritance and donation	
	Taxable entities and chargeable assets	• Heirs – domiciled or non-domiciled – are tax liable in the domicile (canton) in which the testator resided at the time of his death • IHT on real estate property is levied on the location of the real estate in consideration of the net worth of the whole inheritance	
	Calculation of charge	The tax is levied on the accretion of wealth by virtue of the statutory right of inheritance or by virtue of dispositions mortis causa	
	Taxable events	Transfers by inheritance or donation	
	Allowances	Most cantons do not levy this tax on net asset transfers to spouses or children or provide special deductions	
	Tax rates	• Tax rates vary, according to the value of the inheritance and the degree of relationship between the deceased and the heir (the closer the blood relationship, the lower the inheritance tax) • On cantonal level the rates vary from canton to canton, eg one canton does not even levy any IHT. Usually the cantons provide for progressive rates between 0% and 54%	

IV WITHHOLDING TAXES

Under domestic law	Payments to residents[6]	Payments to non-residents[7]
Dividends	Dividends are subject to withholding tax of 35%	
Interest	Interest from banks and similar institutes is subject to withholding tax of 35%	
	Other interest (eg inter-company) is not subject to withholding tax	
Royalties	Nil	
On payments to artists and sportsmen	Nil	Payments to artists and sportsmen are subject to a federal and cantonal withholding tax. The tax rates vary from canton to canton

Reduced rate available under the relevant Double Taxation Treaty		
Country	Dividends (normal rate)	Interest	Royalties (Switzerland does not withhold tax on royalties)
Albania	15%	5%	Nil
Algeria	15%	10%	Nil
Argentina	15%	12%	Nil
Armenia	15%	10%	Nil
Australia	15%	10%	Nil
Austria	15%	Nil	Nil
Azerbaijan	15%	10%	Nil
Bangladesh	15%	10%	Nil
Belarus	15%	8%	Nil
Belgium	15%	10%	Nil
Bulgaria	10%	5%	Nil
Canada	15%	10%	Nil
Chile	15%	15%	Nil
China	10%	10%	Nil
Colombia	15%	10%	Nil
Croatia	15%	5%	Nil
Czech Republic	15%	Nil	Nil
Denmark	15%	Nil	Nil
Ecuador	15%	10%	Nil
Egypt	15%	15%	Nil
Estonia	15%	10%	Nil
Finland	10%	Nil	Nil
France	15%	Nil	Nil
Georgia	10%	Nil	Nil

6 If residents declare dividends and interests, the withholding tax will be refunded.
7 Reduced rates of withholding tax may apply where there is an appropriate double tax treaty. Dividends to corporate shareholders domiciled in the EU could benefit from the EU Parent/ Subsidiary Directive.

Reduced rate available under the relevant Double Taxation Treaty			
Country	**Dividends (normal rate)**	**Interest**	**Royalties** (Switzerland does not withhold tax on royalties)
Germany	15%	Nil	Nil
Ghana	15%	10%	Nil
Greece	15%	7%	Nil
Hong Kong	10%	Nil	Nil
Hungary	15%	Nil	Nil
Iceland	15%	Nil	Nil
India	10%	10%	Nil
Indonesia	15%	10%	Nil
Iran	15%	10%	Nil
Ireland	15%	Nil	Nil
Israel	15%	10%	Nil
Italy	15%	12.5%	Nil
Ivory Coast	15%	15%	Nil
Jamaica	15%	10%	Nil
Japan	10%	10%	Nil
Kazakhstan	15%	10%	Nil
Korea, Republic of	15%	10%	Nil
Kuwait	15%	10%	Nil
Kyrgyzstan	15%	5%	Nil
Latvia	15%	10%	Nil
Liechtenstein	Nil	Nil	Nil
Lithuania	15%	10%	Nil
Luxembourg	15%	10%	Nil
Macedonia	15%	10%	Nil
Malaysia	15%	10%	Nil
Malta	Nil	10%	Nil
Mexico	15%	10%	Nil
Moldova	15%	10%	Nil
Mongolia	15%	10%	Nil
Montenegro	15%	10%	Nil
Morocco	15%	10%	Nil
Netherlands	15%	Nil	Nil
New Zealand	15%	10%	Nil
Norway	15%	Nil	Nil
Pakistan	20%	10%	Nil
Peru	15%	15%	Nil
Philippines	15%	10%	Nil
Poland	15%	5%	Nil
Portugal	15%	10%	Nil
Qatar	15%	Nil	Nil
Romania	15%	5%	Nil
Russian Federation	15%	Nil	Nil
Serbia	15%	10%	Nil

Reduced rate available under the relevant Double Taxation Treaty			
Country	Dividends (normal rate)	Interest	Royalties (Switzerland does not withhold tax on royalties)
Singapore	15%	5%	Nil
Slovakia	15%	5%	Nil
Slovenia	15%	5%	Nil
South Africa	15%	5%	Nil
Spain	15%	Nil	Nil
Sri Lanka	15%	10%	Nil
Sweden	15%	0%	Nil
Tadzhikistan	15%	10%	Nil
Taiwan	15%	10%	Nil
Thailand	15%	15%	Nil
Trinidad & Tobago	20%	10%	Nil
Tunisia	10%	10%	Nil
Turkey	15%	10%	Nil
Turkmenistan	15%	10%	Nil
Ukraine	15%	10%	Nil
United Arab Emirates	15%	Nil	Nil
United Kingdom	15%	Nil	Nil
United States	15%	Nil	Nil
Uruguay	15%	10%	Nil
Uzbekistan	15%	5%	Nil
Venezuela	10%	5%	Nil
Vietnam	15%	10%	Nil

Note: the above rates are only available provided the specific Treaty criteria are satisfied. It is possible that lower rates than those shown above may be available provided that certain criteria are satisfied. As treaties will not be identical, guidance should be sought in all cases.

V   INDIRECT TAXES

<table>
<tr><td rowspan="9">Value Added Tax (VAT)</td><td></td><td colspan="2" align="center">Residents</td></tr>
<tr><td></td><td align="center">Residents</td><td align="center">Non-residents</td></tr>
<tr><td>General description</td><td colspan="2">Provisions basically follow, with some exemptions, the rules of the 6th EU Directive</td></tr>
<tr><td>Entities obliged to levy VAT</td><td colspan="2">Any person who carries on a business (independently performs a professional or commercial activity) with the purpose of the sustainable earning form supplies and acts externally under his own name

Anyone with a taxable turnover of less than CHF 100,000 a year and who is not registered is exempt from tax liability. However such person has the right to register optional. If registered they must declare any taxable turnover without exception</td></tr>
<tr><td>Taxable activities</td><td colspan="2">Domestic tax
• Supplies (services, deliveries) made by taxable persons in Switzerland against consideration
Acquisition tax (reverse charge)
• Services with place of supply in Switzerland rendered by foreign enterprises
• Deliveries in Switzerland by foreign enterprises where no import tax applied
Import tax
• On the import of goods including the services and rights contained therein</td></tr>
<tr><td>Taxable activities – zero-rated (examples)</td><td colspan="2">• Export of goods
• Services to foreign recipients in general</td></tr>
<tr><td>Exemptions (examples)</td><td colspan="2">Similar to EU Directive:
• supply of postal services
• hospital and medical care
• education (school, courses, etc)
• cultural activities (theatre, museum, libraries, etc)
• insurance and reinsurance transactions
• granting and negotiation of credits
• transactions in shares and other securities
• real estate transfers
• letting and leasing of real estate</td></tr>
<tr><td>Refund of VAT</td><td>Recovery through VAT declaration provided that there is VAT charged expense for taxable services. Exceptions according to the VAT Law</td><td>Non-resident enterprises can recover Swiss VAT in two ways:
• through VAT declaration (see residents) or
• if certain conditions are met by annual VAT-refund request. The request must be filed annually using standard forms, by 30 June, following the end of the related calendar year</td></tr>
</table>

		Residents	Non-residents
Value Added Tax (VAT) – contd	Tax liability	• Taxable persons • Liquidators • Directors • Companies in respect of group taxation • Liability limitation until the amount due	
	Tax rates	• 8% standard rate • 2.5% reduced rate for certain essential goods of daily consumption • 3.8% accommodation provision	
	Administrative obligations	• File in the quarterly tax declarations • Payment of tax within the legal terms	Ordinary declaration: • fiscal representative • file in the quarterly tax declarations • payment of tax within the legal terms • declaration by yearly request (see refund of VAT): special conditions apply
Real Property Taxes		• Subject to tax is transfer of ownership of real estate (land or building) as well as economic transfer of ownership (eg sale of majority of shares of a real estate company) with some exemptions • The tax is levied by the cantons or the municipalities where the property is situated • The rate varies from canton to canton and can range from 0% to 3.3% of the consideration or estimated worth of property transferred	
Stamp Duties		• One-time capital contribution tax of 1%: – On Swiss shares (zero rate for amounts under CHF 1m) • Securities turnover tax: – On the sale or exchange of securities involving a Swiss-registered securities dealer – The rate varies from 0.15% (Swiss securities) to 0.3% (foreign securities) • Redeemable capital insurance tax with single premium for Swiss policy holders: – The rate varies from 2.5% (life insurance) to 5% (others)	

Taiwan

(Maurice, Nexia Sun Rise CPAs & Co, nexia168@gmail.com)

I MAIN LEGAL FORMS

Legal form / Characteristics	Partnership	Limited Company, Private Corporation (Ltd by shares) and Public Limited Company (Plc)
Partners/shareholders • Number • Restrictions	• Two • None	One shareholder for Ltd and two individual shareholders or one corporate shareholder for Ltd by shares and Plc
Directors	None	One to three directors for Ltd and at least three directors and one supervisor for Ltd by shares and Plc
Establishment	Partnership deed	Articles of Incorporation
Registration	City Government	Ministry of Economic Affairs or City Government
Minimum capital	None	None, however the capital must at least be able to pay the set-up expenses at the time of incorporation
Liability	Unlimited	Limited
Audit requirements	None • Annual sales revenue over NT$100m tax return audit required	• Capital over NT$30m financial audit required and • Annual sales revenue over NT$100m tax return audit required
Taxation	The enterprise shall pay half the amount of income tax payable. Net income minus half of the amount of income tax payable will be assessed directly on partners	Corporation tax on worldwide profits

II CORPORATION TAX

Legal form / Description	Resident corporation	Permanent establishment (PE)
General description	Corporation tax	
Taxable entities	Corporations with a head office in Taiwan	PE located in Taiwan
Taxable income	Worldwide profits with considerations for double taxation treaties	Income arising in Taiwan
Calculation of taxable profits	Accounting profit is adjusted for various tax add-backs and allowances to arrive to profits chargeable to corporation tax (PCTCT)	
Interest payments	Interest on loans is deductible. Capitalisation of interest is possible if the loans are for the purpose of the purchase of fixed assets and land or building construction for the period before the ownership of assets transferred Interest on loans from related parties is not deductible if the loans from related parties are over 3 times net equity	
Related party transactions	All related party transactions must take place on arm's length basis	
Tax year, return and payment	Tax year is the calendar year. Non-calendar year allowed with pre-approval from the tax authority	
Capital gains	• Capital gain from sale of company stocks and/or land is tax-free in regular corporation tax. However, capital gain from sale of company stocks is taxable for separate alternative minimum tax • Capital gain from sale of house property is taxable After 2016: • If the transferred house and land are acquired on or after 1 January 2014, and have been held for a period of no more than 2 years, and are acquired on or after 1 January 2016, the capital gain is taxable	
Losses	Net operating losses may be carried forward for 10 years if proper procedures are followed	
Tax group	Not available	Not available
Tax rate	After 2012: • Under NT$120,000 = 0% • NT$120,001 and above = 17%	

III TAXES FOR INDIVIDUALS

<table>
<tr><td rowspan="9" style="writing-mode: vertical-rl;">Income Tax</td><td></td><td>Residents</td><td>Non-residents</td></tr>
<tr><td>General description</td><td colspan="2">Tax levied on the chargeable income of a chargeable person for a year of assessment</td></tr>
<tr><td>Taxable entities and taxable income</td><td>Residents are taxed on their worldwide income if the worldwide income is over NT$1m</td><td>Income arising in Taiwan</td></tr>
<tr><td>Types of taxable income</td><td colspan="2">• Property income (usually rent)
• Income from capital investment (interest, sale of goodwill, dividends, royalties, annuities) (interest under NT$270,000 non-taxable)
• Income from business activities
• Employment from personal services or pensions</td></tr>
<tr><td>Calculation of income</td><td>Gross consolidated income less standard deductions or itemised deductions and personal exemptions

In addition to regular individual income tax, under a separate alternative minimum tax system, offshore income over NT$1m is required to file; and alternative minimum tax is imposed when the domestic and offshore income is over NT$6 million</td><td>Tax is withheld at source</td></tr>
<tr><td>Tax year, tax assessment and tax payment</td><td>Tax year is the calendar year</td><td>Tax is withheld at source</td></tr>
<tr><td>Losses</td><td>Losses from sale of house property and company stocks can be offset against income of the same source in the subsequent 3 years</td><td>Nil</td></tr>
<tr><td>Tax rates</td><td colspan="2">• For residents, the amount of income tax payable is calculated as a percentage of net taxable income less a 'progressive difference' for each tax layer. Individual income tax rates are as follows:</td></tr>
</table>

Income (NT$)	Tax rate
Up to 520,000	5%
520,001–1,170,000	12%
1,170,001–2,350,000	20%
2,350,001–4,400,000	30%
4,400,001–10,000,000	40%
Over 10,000,000	45%

• For non-residents, the tax is withheld / levied according to withholding tax rates

		Residents	Non-residents
Capital Gains Tax (CGT)	General description	Gains realised from the difference between the acquisition and disposal price of an asset	
	Taxable entities and chargeable assets	House, land, property, intangible assets, company stocks, etc Capital gains derived from securities transactions ceased to be taxed from 2016	
	Calculation of gain	Transaction price less the related cost If the transferred house and land are acquired on or after 1 January 2014, and have been held for a period of more than 2 years, or are acquired before 1 January 2014, the gain from the disposal house can be calculated by the current value of the house multiplied by a constant ratio in some situations	
	Tax year, tax assessment and tax payment	Treated as income	
	Losses	Losses from sale of house property and company stocks can be offset against income of the same source in the subsequent 3 years	Nil
	Tax rates	• For residents, capital gain is consolidated with personal income when filing individual income tax return • For non-residents, 20% After 2016: Capital gains derived from transactions of house and land shall be taxed as follows:	
		Holding period < 1 year 45% >1 year but < 2 years 35% >2 years but < 10 years 20% >10 years 15%	Holding period < 1 year 45% >1 year 35%
		Domiciled	**Non-domiciled**
Inheritance Tax (IHT)	General description	10% on worldwide assets	10% on Taiwan assets

IV WITHHOLDING TAXES

Under domestic law	Payments to residents	Payments to non-residents[1]
Dividends	Nil	20%
Interest	10%	15–20%
Royalties	10% / Nil[2]	20%
On payments to artists and sportsmen	10%	20%
Wages	Rate determined in accordance with Regulations or 5%	18% 6%(if salary amount < 1.5 baseline salary)

Reduced rate available under the relevant Double Taxation Treaty			
Country	Dividends	Interest	Royalties
Non-treaty Countries	20%	15%–20%	20%
Australia	10%–15%	10%	12.5%
Belgium	10%	10%	10%
Demark	10%	10%	10%
France	10%	10%	10%
Gambia	10%	10%	10%
Germany	10%	10%–15%	10%
Hungary	10%	10%	10%
India	12.5%	10%	10%
Indonesia	10%	10%	10%
Israel	10%	7%–10%	10%
Macedonia	10%	10%	10%
Malaysia	12.5%	10%	10%
New Zealand	15%	10%	10%
Netherlands	10%	10%	10%
Paraguay	5%	10%	10%
Senegal	10%	15%	12.5%
Singapore	40%	Nil	15%
Slovakia	10%	10%	5%–10%
South Africa	5%–15%	10%	10%
Swaziland	10%	10%	10%
Sweden	10%	10%	10%
Switzerland	10%–15%	10%	10%
Thailand	5%–10%	10%–15%	10%
United Kingdom	10%	10%	10%
Vietnam	15%	10%	15%

Note: the above rates are only available provided the specific Treaty criteria are satisfied. It is possible that lower rates than those shown above may be available provided that certain criteria are satisfied. As treaties will not be identical, guidance should be sought in all cases.

---

1 Reduced rates of withholding tax may apply where there is an appropriate double tax treaty.
2 Royalties paid by a resident company to another resident company are exempt from withholding tax.

V   INDIRECT TAXES

		Residents	Non-residents
Value Added Tax (VAT)	General description	Tax on the supply of goods and services	
	Entities obliged to levy VAT	• Business entities which sell goods or services • The receivers or holders of imported goods • Those who receive services provided by foreign enterprises	
	Taxable activities	Any transaction involving goods or services within the territory of Taiwan (ROC) including importation of goods is subject to VAT	
	Taxable activities – zero-rated (examples)	• Exports • Services related to exports or services supplied within the ROC but used in foreign countries • International transportation	
	Exemptions (examples)	• Sale of land • Medical services • Nursing services • Education services • Textbooks • Newspapers, magazines, etc • Raw agricultural, forestry, fishing, etc • Services rendered by post and telecommunication offices	
	Refund of VAT	Tax overpaid: • on goods or services subject to 0% • on purchase of fixed assets • due to merger or consolidation, business transfer, dissolution or cessation of business	
	Tax rates	• Financial businesses = 5% • Reinsurance = 1% • Exports = 0% • Nightclubs and restaurants with entertainment = 15% • Saloons and shops offering companionship services = 25% • Agricultural businesses = 0.1% • Small and other specific businesses = 1% • Other entities = 5%–10% (5% since 1985)	
Land Tax		Ranges from 1%–5.5%, with some privileged rates from 0.2%–1% for land used in residential, public or approved projects	
Stamp Duty		Monetary receipts: 0.4%	
		Contracting agreements: 0.1%	
		Contracts for the sale of real estate: 0.1%	
		Contracts for the sale of movables: NT$12 per piece	

Nexia International is the trading name of Nexia International Limited, a company registered in the Isle of Man. Company registration number: 53513C. Registered office: 2nd floor, Sixty Circular Road, Douglas, Isle of Man, IM1 1SA

Tanzania

(Sujata Jaffer, Nexia SJ Tanzania, info@nexiasjtz.com)

I MAIN LEGAL FORMS

Legal Form / Characteristics	Partnership and Limited Liability Partnership (LLP)	Private Corporation (Ltd) and Public Corporation (Plc)
Partners/shareholders • Number • Restrictions	There are no restrictions as to the number of partners No concept of LLPs	For Private Limited Company 'Ltd', the maximum number of shareholders is 50 For Public Liability Company 'Plc', the minimum number of shareholders is 7 Local shareholders are required in certain sectors such as mining, banking, telecommunications, insurance, shipping and construction
Directors	Management by partners	A minimum of 2 directors is required, either a resident or non-resident Appointment of director is at any age above 21 years and retirement at the age of 70 years unless exemption is given Directors are responsible for producing the accounts of the company
Establishment	Registration at BRELA (Business Registration and Licensing Authority) of the partnership name and its partners	Registration at the Registrar of Companies of Public Companies (PLC), Private Limited Companies and Companies Limited by Guarantee or company with un-limited liability Governing statute – Companies Act 2002

Legal Form / Characteristics	Partnership and Limited Liability Partnership (LLP)	Private Corporation (Ltd) and Public Corporation (Plc)
Registration	Partnership name Registration at BRELA – Business Names (Registration) Cap 213 To be governed by an agreement between the partners or by the rules set out in the Law of Contract (345) in the absence of a contract	Registration of the Incorporation charter, ie Memorandum and Articles of Association The following are required: - Memorandum and Articles of Association - Shareholders - Directors - Company Secretary - Registered office
Minimum capital	There is no minimum capital requirement	Authorised share capital with a minimum of TZS 20,000 Specific sectors have minimum share capital requirements, such as for banks where the minimum core capital must not be less than TZS 15 billion and an existing bank with a core capital of less than the prescribed amount is required to increase its core capital within a period of 3 years For public listed companies, paid up share capital of at least TZS 1 billion is required for entities listed on the MIM (Main Investment Market) and TZS 200 million for entities listed on the EGM (Enterprise Growth Market)
Liability	Every partner is liable for all debts and obligations incurred while he is a partner in the usual course of business by or on behalf of the partnership	Limited to share capital, or unlimited for companies with un-limited liability
Governance	Partners in general meetings	The following are mandatory: - Register of members - Shareholders'/directors' meeting and record-keeping of their minutes - Filing of resolutions - Annual filing of returns - Annual audit For public listed entities, the following are specific corporate governance practices: - The board of directors to include at least one-third non-executive directors) - Establishing audit committee of at least 3 non-executive directors - Executive directors to have fixed employment contract not exceeding 5 years with a provision for renewals

Characteristics / Legal Form	Partnership and Limited Liability Partnership (LLP)	Private Corporation (Ltd) and Public Corporation (Plc)
Audit requirement	Audit required if turnover greater than TZS 20 million	Audit is compulsory for all companies However, certain sectors such as banking require periodic rotation of external auditors every 4 years
Taxation	Transparent	A locally incorporated company will be taxed on all income and expenses incurred, including expenses incurred on behalf of the local company by the holding company, provided these expenses are incurred for business purposes and are fully supported On the other hand, a branch of a foreign company is considered as a Permanent Establishment (PE) and will be taxed on all income and expenses derived in the United Republic of Tanzania and are calculated separately from its owners
Usage	Micro-enterprises and Professional practices	Not suitable for micro-enterprises due to annual compliance and other servicing costs

II   CORPORATION TAX

Legal Form / Description	Resident Corporation	Permanent Establishment (PE)
General description	Corporation tax	Corporation tax
Taxable entities	Corporations incorporated and managed in Tanzania	PE located in Tanzania
Taxable income	Worldwide profits with a provision for double taxation relief	Profit earned in Tanzania
Calculation of taxable profits	Accounting profit is adjusted for various tax add-backs and fiscal allowances to arrive at profits chargeable to corporation tax (PCTCT) **Tax incentives and grants:** **(a) Tanzania Investment Centre (TIC)** Tax incentives are provided by the TIC for sectors such as agriculture and livestock, tourism, manufacturing, telecommunications and infrastructure. The minimum requirements to qualify for a TIC certificate are: <ul><li>Minimum fixed investment capital for new rehabilitation or expansion projects of at least US$100,000 in case of fully owned by Tanzanian citizens and US$500,000 where projects are jointly or wholly owned by foreign investors</li><li>For strategic or major investment, the investment capital requirements are US$20 million in case of fully owned by Tanzanian citizens and US$50 million where projects are jointly or wholly owned by foreign investors</li></ul> **(b) Export Processing Zone Authority (EPZA)** The EPZA also grants incentives to businesses located in EPZs that manufacture and export industrial products and to companies that provide infrastructure necessary for the development of EPZs. The criteria for investing in an EPZ include: <ul><li>At least 80% of the goods produced within the EPZ must be sold to export markets</li><li>Annual turnover from the exported goods must be at least US$100,000 for local investors and US$500,000 for foreign investors</li></ul> Incentives offered by EPZA include: <ul><li>Exemption from corporate tax, withholding tax and all other taxes and levies imposed by local government authorities in respect of products produced in EPZs for a period of 10 years</li><li>Exemption from VAT on utilities and wharfage charges</li><li>The right to obtain work permits for 5 foreign nationals on the project</li><li>Remission of customs duty, VAT and any other tax payable in respect of goods purchased for use as raw materials, equipment and machinery, including all goods and services directly related to manufacturing in the EPZs</li></ul> **(c) Special Economic Zones (SEZ)** The EPZA also grants incentives to set up businesses in SEZs such as industrial parks, export processing zones, free trade zones, free ports, tourist parks, or science and technology parks The minimum capital requirements are US$1 million for local investors and US$5 million for foreign investors	

Legal Form / Description	Resident Corporation	Permanent Establishment (PE)
	Incentives provided depend on the category of licence that is provided, which can be summarized as below:	
	1: Category A investors – incentives for the development of infrastructure:	
	• Exemption from payment of taxes and duties for machinery, equipment, heavy duty articles, buildings and construction materials and other goods of capital nature that are used for purposes of development of SEZ infrastructure	
	• Exemption from payment of corporation tax, withholding tax and property tax for an initial period of 10 years	
	• The right to obtain work permits for 5 foreign nationals on the project	
	• Remission of customs duty, VAT and any other tax payable in respect of importation of one administrative vehicle, ambulance, fire-fighting equipment, fire-fighting vehicle and up to two buses for employees' transportation to and from the SEZs	
	Exemption of VAT on the utility charges	
	2: Category B investors – incentives offered for sale of manufactured goods within the customs territory:	
	Remission of customs duty, VAT and any other tax payable in respect of raw materials goods of capital nature related to production in the SEZ	
	Exemption from payment of withholding tax on interest on foreign-sourced loan	
	Remission of customs duty, VAT and any other tax payable in respect of importation of one administrative vehicle, ambulance, fire-fighting equipment, fire-fighting vehicle and up to two buses for employees' transportation to and from the SEZs	
	The right to obtain work permits for 5 foreign nationals on the project	
Interest payments	Deductible if connected with the production of income, subject to 'thin capitalisation' restrictions	
Related party transactions	These can be subjected to transfer pricing adjustments	
Tax year, return and payment	Tax year is aligned with the normal calendar year. However, the government's financial year runs from 1 July to 30 June. Commissioner's private ruling must be sought for the company's first year of income if the accounting period end will be other than 31 December. The first year of income can be less than 12 months but not more than 18 months from the date of incorporation	
	Corporation tax is payable in advance in quarterly instalments whereby the aggregate of provisional taxes paid should amount to at least 80% of the final tax liability. The provisional return and first provisional tax are due for submission at the end of first quarter of the financial year	
	However, a tax payer can revise estimate of income for a financial year at any point in time during the year of income	
	The return of income and final payment of corporate tax is due 6 months after year-end	
Capital gains	Taxed upon realisation	

Description / Legal Form	Resident Corporation	Permanent Establishment (PE)
Losses	Losses can be carried forward indefinitely	
	There is Alternative Minimum Tax (AMT) at 0.3% of turnover for companies with unrelieved losses for three consecutive years of income (excluding entities in agricultural business and entities providing education or health services)	
Tax group	Not applicable	
Tax rate	(a) Standard rate – 30%	(a) Standard rate – 30%
	(b) Newly listed companies with at least 30% of their shareholding listed on the DSE for three consecutive years from the date of listing – 25%	(b) Newly listed companies with at least 30% of their shareholding listed on the DSE for three consecutive years from the date of listing – 25%
		(c) Deemed repatriated profit – 10%

III TAXES FOR INDIVIDUALS

		Residents	Non-residents
Income Tax	**General description**	Tax levied on the chargeable income of a chargeable person for a year of assessment. In personal allowances, system is not used	
	Taxable entities and taxable income	Individuals who have been resident for less than 2 years can be taxed as non-residents on the Tanzanian derived income only at the rate of 15%	Tax levied income arising in Tanzania
	Type of taxable income	- Property income (usually rents and royalties) - Income from capital investment (interest, sale of goodwill, dividends, and annuities) - Income from business activities - Income from employment or services rendered and pensions - Capital gains	
	Calculation of income	Income is calculated on the basis of gross total income less expenditure wholly and exclusively incurred in producing the gross income Tax depreciations, incentive deductions and other specific deductions are available, as discussed above Income from the following sources are taxed in the following manner: • Property – accrual basis • Trading – accrual basis or cash basis for individuals, according to choice • Savings – cash basis for individuals • Employment – cash basis • Capital gains – on the date of realisation	
	Tax year, tax assessment and tax payment	The tax year is to 31 December but this can be varied on application to the Tax Commissioner	
	Losses	Losses are available for carry forward indefinitely	
	Tax rates	**Pay As You Earn (PAYE)**	**Non-residents** Flat rate of 15%
		Individual **Residents** *Income (TZS)* *Tax rate (%)* < 170,000 0 170,000–360,000 9% 360,000–540,000 TZS 17,100 + 20% on the excess of TZS 360,000 540,000–720,000 TZS 53,100 + 25% on the excess of TZS 540,000 > 720,000 TZS 98,100 + 30% on the excess of TZS 720,000	
	Other taxes relating to employment (borne by the employer)	Skills Development Levy (SDL) which is charged at 4.5% of the gross salary for private sectors with 4 or more employees Workers Compensation Fund is charged at 1% of the gross salary of the employees for private sectors and 0.5% for public sectors	

		Residents	**Non-residents**
Capital Gains Tax (In TZ - Assets Realization Gains)	General description	Gains realised from the difference between the acquisition and disposal price of an asset	
	Taxable entities and taxable income	Any entity making disposal of an asset	
	Calculation of income	Difference between cost and realised amount Gain not exceeding TZS 15m is exempted on sale of a private residential house provided the owner has resided in that property for a minimum of 3 years. In addition, an interest in land held by an individual that has market value of less than TZS 10m at the time it is realised, and has been used for agricultural purposes for at least two of the three years prior to realisation, is exempted Taxation is at the individual or corporate rate	
	Tax year, tax assessment and tax payment	To be declared on the individual's income tax return	
	Losses	Losses can be carried forward to be set-off against corresponding future capital gains	
	Tax rates	Taxed at an initial instalment payment of 10% on registration of the title transfer. The balance is payable with submission of the tax return and taxed at: • marginal rates for individuals • rate of 30% for corporate entities	For non-residents, the rate is 20%

		Tanzania domiciled	**Non-Tanzania domiciled**
Inheritance Tax (IHT) (In Tanzania–Assets Realisation Gains)	General description	Voluntary and involuntary dispositions	
	Taxable entities and chargeable assets	All entities and persons effecting transfers as above	When the asset is situated in Tanzania
	Calculation of charge	Difference between cost and realised amount/market value	
	Taxable events	On sale, exchange, transfer, death, dissolution or when ownership ceases	
	Allowances	Gain not exceeding TZS 10m for sale of landed property used for residential purpose / agricultural land is exempt	
	Tax rates	At the marginal tax rate of the individual	

IV WITHHOLDING TAXES

	Payments to residents	Payments to non-residents
Dividends	10%	10%
Dividends (PLCs) at DSE	5%	5%
Rent – individual ordinary	10%	10%
Rent – business Rent – Aircraft Lease	Individual marginal rate or corporate rate of 30%	Corporate rate of 30%
Dividends to companies controlling 25% or more of the share capital	5% (exempted before 30 June 2012)	10%
Interest	10%	10%
Royalties	15%	15%
On payments to artists and sportsmen	Nil (taxed directly)	15%
Services – Mining Oil and Gas Sector	5%	15%
Director Fee	15%	15%

Reduced rate available under the relevant Double Taxation Treaty[1]			
Country	Dividends	Interest	Royalties
Canada	25%	15%	20%
Denmark	15%	12.5%	20%
East African Community (Burundi, Kenya, Rwanda, and the Republic of Uganda)[2]	5%	10%	10%
Finland	20%	15%	20%
India	15%	12.5%	20%
Italy	10%	15%	15%
Norway	20%	15%	20%
South Africa	20%	10%	10%
Sweden	25%	15%	20%
Zambia	Nil	Nil	Nil

Note: the above rates are only available provided the specific Treaty criteria are satisfied. It is possible that lower rates than those shown above may be available provided that certain criteria are satisfied. As treaties will not be identical, guidance should be sought in all cases.

1 The lower of the domestic rate and the treaty rate will apply.
2 This treaty is yet to be fully ratified.

V   INDIRECT TAXES

		Residents	Non-residents
Value Added Tax (VAT)	General description	Tax on the supply of goods and services	
	Entities obliged to levy VAT	All entities supplying goods and services for consideration	
	Taxable activities	All supplies of goods and services by any entity	
	Taxable activities – zero-rated (examples)	Export of goods and services, generally and specifically services to the following: • Ships engaged on international transportation • Aircraft • Supply of goods and services outside mainland Tanzania • Supply of goods and services directly related to land located outside Tanzania	
	Exemptions (examples)	• Intermediary services • Government entities and institutions • Educational materials and services • Agricultural inputs and implements • Livestock, basic agricultural products and foods for human consumption • Fisheries and bee-keeping implements • Dairy equipment • Medicine or pharmaceutical products (not including food supplements and vitamins) • Articles designed for people with special needs • Health care • Immovable property • Petroleum products • Supply of water, except bottled or canned or similarly presented water • Transportation of person by any means of conveyance other than taxi, rental cars or boat charters • Supply of arms and ammunitions, parts and accessories to the armed forces • Funeral services such as coffins, shrouds, transportation, mortuary and disposal of human remains • Gaming supply • Supply of tourist guiding, game driving, water safaris, animal and bird watching, park fees and ground transport services • Supply of solar panels • Supply of air charter services • Agricultural, horticultural or forestry machinery for soil preparation or cultivation except lawn mowers or sports ground rollers and parts • Harvesting or threshing machinery except machines under HS Code 433.11.00, 8433.19.00 • Unprocessed edible animal products • Unpasteurized or pasteurized cow milk except with additives and long life milk • Unpasteurized or pasteurized goat milk except with additives and long life milk • Unprocessed cereals, tobacco, cashew nuts, coffee, tea, pyrethrum, cotton, sisal, sugarcane, plants and seeds thereof • Maize, wheat or meslin flour, soya beans, ground nuts, sunflower seeds, oil seeds and plants and seeds thereof	
	Refund of VAT	Claims shall be certified by an Auditor registered by the National Board of Accountants and Auditors as well as a tax consultant registered by the Tanzania Revenue Authority	

		Residents	Non-residents
	VAT payment	Effective from July 2016, VAT returns should be submitted and liability to be paid by the 20th of the month following the month of collection	
	VAT tax rates	Standard rate = 18%	
		Export = 0%	
	Administrative obligations	Registration threshold when annual turnover reaches TZS 100 million	
Stamp Duty		This is levied on specific instruments that are executed in Tanzania such as: • Leases • Debentures • Mortgages • Powers of Attorney • Share transfer forms • Conveyances or any transfer of property This is calculated based on 1% on the carrying values	
Excise Duty		This is levied on an ad-valorem basis on specific goods and services manufactured locally or imported such as wines, beer, spirits, soft drinks, cigarettes, tobacco, petroleum products, recorded DVD, VCD, CD, audio tapes, cosmetics, firearms, plastic bags Ad-valorem rates are 0%, 5%, 10%, 15%, 17%, 20%, 25%, 30% and 50%	
Customs Duty		This is levied on importation of certain goods at an ad-valorem rate based on the value of goods imported	
City Service Levy		Levy administered by municipal council which is charged at 0.3% of turnover which is to be remitted on a quarterly basis	

Thailand

(Khanit Kitinan, Thai Advisory Office Co., Ltd, khanitk@thaiadvisory.com)

I   MAIN LEGAL FORMS

Characteristics / Legal form	Partnership and Limited Liability Partnership (LLP)	Private corporation (Ltd) and Public corporation (Plc)
Partners/shareholders • Number • Restrictions	Thailand provides for three types of partnerships: • Unregistered ordinary partnerships, in which all partners are jointly and wholly liable for all obligations of the partnership • Registered ordinary partnerships. If registered, the partnership becomes a legal entity, separate and distinct from an individual partner. The ordinary partnership is the kind of partnership in which all the partners have joint and several liability • Limited partnerships. Individual partner liability is restricted to the amount of capital contributed to the partnership. Limited partnerships must be registered	Ltd: at least three people to be subscribers to the Memorandum of Association Plc: at least 15 shareholders subscribing to at least 5% of the shares
Directors	Partners	Board of Directors
Establishment	Partnerships Deed. Registered ordinary partnerships and limited partnerships are governed by the Civil and Commercial Code	Private companies are governed by the Civil and Commercial Code, and public companies by the Public Company Act
Registration	Registration with the Commerce Department	
Minimum capital	No minimum requirements	15 Baht for private companies No minimum requirement for Plc
Liability	Unlimited except in case of partners whose liabilities are limited to the amount as they may respectively undertake to contribute to the limited partnerships	Limited to share capital
Governance	Partners	Board meetings

Legal form / Characteristics	Partnership and Limited Liability Partnership (LLP)	Private corporation (Ltd) and Public corporation (Plc)
Audit requirements	No audit requirement if the registered ordinary partnerships and limited partnershipshave: 1. registered capital not more than THB 5 million 2. total assets not more than THB 30 million and 3. total revenue not more than THB 30 million However, the Revenue Department still requires those registered ordinary partnerships or limited partnerships having tax auditor to review and approve their financial statements before filing with the Revenue Department	Financial statements must be certified by an authorised auditor and must be approved by shareholders at the annual general meeting within 4 months of the end of the fiscal year and filed with the Commerce Department within 5 months of the end of the fiscal year
Taxation	An unregistered ordinary partnership is required to pay tax on the same progressive tax rates as an individual person For registered ordinary partnership and limited partnership, corporate income tax is calculated in accordance with generally accepted accounting principles as adjusted by the specific rules of income tax law	Corporate income tax is calculated in accordance with generally accepted accounting principles as adjusted by the specific rules of income tax law

II   CORPORATION TAX

Description / Legal form	Resident corporation	Permanent establishment (PE)
General description	Corporation tax	
Taxable entities	Corporations incorporated in Thailand	PE trading in Thailand
Taxable income	Worldwide profits	Income arising in Thailand
Calculation of taxable profits	Accounting profit is adjusted for various tax add-backs and allowances to arrive at profits chargeable to corporation tax (PCTCT)	
Interest payments	Interest should be calculated at the market value on the lending date	
Related party transactions	All related party transactions must take place on arm's length basis	
Tax year, return and payment	Companies may choose their year-end Semi-annual income tax returns are filed together with tax payment within 2 months from the end of the first 6 months of the period, and annual income tax returns within 150 days of the year-end	
Capital gains	Included as part of taxable income	
Losses	Net operating losses can be carried forward for up to 5 consecutive years	
Tax group	None	

Legal form / Description	Resident corporation	Permanent establishment (PE)
Tax rate	1. Normal tax rate is 20% 2. For year 2015, the corporate income tax of acompany thathas paid-up capital of not more than THB 5 million, and has sale or service income in each accounting period not exceeding THB 30 million, shall be reduced as follows: *Net taxable profit (baht)* *Tax rate* 0–300,000 = exempted Over 300,000 = 10%* * Pursuant to the cabinet resolution dated 13 October 2015, this applies regardless of whether the company has registeredwith the Revenue Department pursuant to the law governing the exemption and tax compliance support under the Revenue Code 3. Effective on 1 January 2016, the corporate income tax of acompany thathas paid-up capital of not more than THB 5 million, and has sale or service income in each accounting period not exceeding THB 30 million, shall be exemptedorreduced as follows: *Net taxable profit (baht)* *Tax rate for year 2016* Exempted *Net taxable profit (baht)* *Tax rate for year 2017* 0–300,000 = exempted Over 300,000 = 10% *Net taxable profit (baht)* *Tax rate for year 2018 onwards* 0–300,000 exempted 300,001–3,000,000 15% Over 3,000,000 20% Provided that the following qualifications must be complied with: 1. No capital paid-up at any last accounting date more than THB 5 million and the income derived from sale and service in any accounting period not higher than THB 30 million 2. Register with the Revenue Department pursuant to the law governing the exemption and tax compliance support under the Revenue Code 3. Does not repeal such exemption pursuant to the law governing the exemption and tax compliance support under the Revenue Code 4. Those who do not register with the Revenue Department shall be subject to corporate income tax for year 2016 and 2017 as follows: *Net taxable profit (baht)* *Tax rate for year 2016* 0–300,000 exempted Over 300,000 10% *Net taxable profit (baht)* *Tax rate for year 2017 onwards* 0–300,000 exempted 300,001–3,000,000 15% Over 3,000,000 20%	

III TAXES FOR INDIVIDUALS

		Residents	Non-residents
Income Tax	General description	Tax levied on the chargeable income of a chargeable person for a year of assessment	
	Taxable entities and taxable income	Every person, resident or non-resident, who derives income from employment or business in Thailand, or assets located in Thailand is subject to personal income tax, whether such income is paid in or outside of Thailand Individuals residing for 180 days or more in Thailand in any calendar year are also subject to income tax on income from foreign sources if that income is brought into Thailand during the same taxable year that they are a resident	Income arising in Thailand
	Types of taxable income	• Property income • Income from capital investment (interest, sale of goodwill, dividends, royalties, annuities) • Income from business activities • Employment from personal services or pensions	
	Calculation of income	Taxable income arising in the year	
	Tax year, tax assessment and tax payment	Tax year is the calendar year Returns must be filed before 31 March of the following year	
	Losses	No allowance of or tax credits for losses	
	Tax rates	*Progressive rates (normal rate) for year 2016 are as follows:* Baht — % 0–150,000 — 0 150,001–300,000 — 5 300,001–500,000 — 10 500,001–750,000 — 15 750,001–1,000,000 — 20 1,000,001–2,000,000 — 25 2,000,001–4,000,000 — 30 >4,000,000 — 35 Effective on 1 January 2017, the progressive tax rates (according to the cabinet resolution) shall be as follows: Baht — % 0–150,000 — 0 150,001–300,000 — 5 300,001–500,000 — 10 500,001–750,000 — 15 750,001–1,000,000 — 20 1,000,001–2,000,000 — 25 2,000,001–5,000,000 — 30 >5,000,000 — 35	

		Residents	Non-residents
Capital Gains Tax (CGT)	General description	Gains realised from the difference between the acquisition and disposal price of an asset	
	Taxable entities and chargeable assets	Capital gains derived from non-listed securities are taxable	
	Calculation of gain	Proceeds less allowable costs	
	Tax year, tax assessment and tax payment	Calendar year	
	Losses	No allowance of or tax credits for losses	
	Tax rates	Progressive tax rates to be applied for capital gains from sale of securities outside Stock Exchange of Thailand	15% for capital gains from sale of securities outside Stock Exchange of Thailand
		For individual person, gains from sale of securities in Stock Exchange of Thailand, not including income from sale of debentures and bonds are exempted from personal income tax	For individual person, gains from sale of securities in Stock Exchange of Thailand, not including income from sale of debentures and bonds are exempted from personal income tax
		Domiciled	**Non-domiciled**
Inheritance Tax (IHT)	General description	IHT was already enforced on February 2016. The tax rate is 10% levy on bequests of more than THB 100 million Under this law, the persons who are required to pay IHT are: 1. Thai nationals 2. Foreign nationals but resident in Thailand in accordance with the law governing immigration 3. Foreign nationals but receiving the heritage which is asset situated in Thailand IHT shall apply to the following assets: 1. Real Property situated in Thailand 2. Securities issued by juristic person registered in Thailand or by juristic person incorporated under the laws of Thailand 3. Deposit in bank account in Thailand 4. Vehicles which are registered in Thailand and 5. Other assets as determined by Royal Decree	

IV WITHHOLDING TAXES

Under domestic law	Payments to residents	Payments to non-residents[1]
Dividends	10%	10%
Interest	15%	15%
Royalties	Deduct at income tax rates	15%
On payments to artists and sportsmen	5%	Deduct at income tax rates

Reduced rate available under the relevant Double Taxation Treaty			
Country	Dividends	Interest	Royalties
Armenia	10%	15%	15%
Australia	20%	25%	15%
Austria	20%	25%	15%
Bahrain	10%	15%	15%
Bangladesh	15%	15%	15%
Belarus	10%	15%	15%
Belgium	20%	25%	15%
Bulgaria	10%	15%	15%
Canada	20%	25%	15%
Chile	10%	15%	15%
China, People's Republic of	20%	15%	15%
Cyprus	10%	15%	15%
Czech Republic	10%	15%	15%
Denmark	10%	15%	15%
Estonia	10%	15%	10%
Finland	20%	25%	15%
France	20%	15%	15%
Germany	20%	25%	15%
Hong Kong	10%	15%	15%
Hungary	20%	25%	15%
India	20%	25%	15%
Indonesia	20%	25%	15%
Ireland	10%	15%	15%
Israel	15%	15%	15%
Italy	20%	15%	15%
Japan	20%	25%	15%
Korea	10%	15%	15%
Kuwait	10%	15%	20%
Laos	15%	15%	15%
Luxembourg	15%	15%	15%
Malaysia	20%	25%	15%
Mauritius	10%	15%	15%
Myanmar	10%	15%	15%
Nepal	15%	15%	15%

1 Reduced rates of withholding tax may apply where there is an appropriate double tax treaty.

Reduced rate available under the relevant Double Taxation Treaty			
Country	**Dividends**	**Interest**	**Royalties**
Netherlands	25%	25%	15%
New Zealand	15%	15%	15%
Norway	15%	15%	15%
Oman	10%	15%	15%
Pakistan	25%	25%	20%
Philippines	20%	25%	25%
Poland	20%	15%	15%
Romania	20%	25%	15%
Russia	15%	15%	15%
Seychelles	10%	15%	15%
Singapore	20%	25%	15%
Slovenia	10%	15%	15%
South Africa	15%	15%	15%
Spain	10%	15%	15%
Sri Lanka	20%	25%	15%
Sweden	20%	25%	15%
Switzerland	15%	15%	15%
Taiwan	10%	15%	15%
Tajikistan	10%	15%	15%
Turkey	15%	15%	15%
Ukraine	15%	15%	15%
United Arab Emirates	10%	15%	15%
United Kingdom	20%	25%	15%
United States	15%	15%	15%
Uzbekistan	10%	15%	15%
Vietnam	15%	15%	15%

Note: the above rates are only available provided the specific Treaty criteria are satisfied. It is possible that lower rates than those shown above may be available provided certain criteria are satisfied. In cases where the ceiling rate is higher than that prescribed in the Revenue Code, the rate prescribed in the Revenue Code applies. There are several rules and exemptions regarding the levels of withholding taxes and as treaties will not be identical, guidance should be sought in all cases.

V   INDIRECT TAXES

		Residents	Non-residents
Value Added Tax (VAT)	General description	Tax on the supply of goods and services	
	Entities obliged to levy VAT	Businesses with revenue above THB 1.8 million per annum	
	Taxable activities	VAT is collected from the sale of goods and services	
	Taxable activities – zero-rated (examples)	Export of goods and services	
	Exemptions (examples)	• Operators earning yearly income less than THB 1.8 million • Sale or import of agricultural products, livestock fertiliser and feed • Sale or import of published material and books • Educational services Exemption rate which is equivalent to zero rate but the operator is not entitled to claim purchase tax	
	Refund of VAT	The registered operator can obtain a tax refund by cash or as tax credit to the following month	
	Tax liability	Sale tax – purchase tax = tax liability or tax credit/refund	
	Tax rates	• Sale of goods and services = 7% (7% is the current rate, maximum rate is 10%) • Exports = 0%	
	Administrative obligations	A monthly tax return must be filed with the revenue department by the 15th day of the following month, regardless of whether there is a tax payment	
Real Property Taxes		None	
Stamp Duty		Rate depends on the contract and provider	

Tunisia

(Mourad Abdelmoula, AFINCO, afinco@afinco.net)

I MAIN LEGAL FORMS

Legal form / Characteristics	Partnerships	Private corporation (Ltd) and Public corporation (Plc)
Partners/shareholders • Number • Restrictions	*Société en nom collectif (SENC):* General SENC: • At least two members • Maximum 50 members Limited SENC: • At least 2 active members, and the remainder can be sleeping members • Maximum 50 members	*Private Limited Company (SARL):* At least 2 shareholders *Unipersonal Limited Company (SUARL):* 1 shareholder *Public Limited Company (SA):* At least 7 shareholders
Directors	One or more general manager(s) named by assembly or in Articles of Association	• Board of Directors named by shareholders' assembly • President and Chief Executive Officer of Board of Directors (President may be separately named)
Establishment	• Signature of Articles of Association or partners' meeting minutes • Obtaining an investment declaration (or other agreement depending on activity) • Obtaining a fiscal ID • Obtaining a trade register matriculation • Advertising in the Official Gazette • Obtaining a custom ID	
Registration	The registration is completed ahead of the trade register of the tribunal	
Minimum capital	No minimum capital	• SARL: TND1,000 • SA: TND5,000 For the SA, at least one quarter of the share capital must be paid-up at incorporation date

Legal form / Characteristics	Partnerships	Private corporation (Ltd) and Public corporation (Plc)
Liability	General SENC: • Unlimited for all members Limited SENC: • Unlimited for all active members • Limited to capital participation for sleeping members	SA and SARL: • Limited to shareholder's participation in share capital
Governance		Appointment of a supervisory council (*Conseil de surveillance*) is optional
Audit requirements	Designation of a statutory auditor is mandatory when two of the following three conditions are reached: • Balance sheet total: TND100,000 • Total sales: TND300,000 • Employees average number: 10	For SA, designation of a statutory auditor is mandatory For SARL, designation is mandatory when conditions (as mentioned in partnership section) are reached
Taxation	Transparent	Corporate income tax

II CORPORATION TAX

Description \ Legal form	Resident corporation	Permanent establishment (PE)
General description	Corporation income tax	
Taxable entities	Companies established in Tunisia	PE established in Tunisia
Taxable income	Worldwide profits	Territorial basis – all income derived in Tunisia only is taxable
Calculation of taxable profits	Taxable profits = accounting profits + add-backs – deductions	
Interest payments	Interest payments are subject to withholding tax of 20% or 25% if paid to a country considered, by law, as a tax haven (interest receivable on foreign currency investments in Tunisian banks are exempted)	
Related party transactions	Arm's length principle	
Tax year, return and payment	Tax year: from 1 January to 31 December. However, company may choose a different accounting year-end date	
	Tax return must be filed by day 25 of the third month following the end of the accounting year	
	Tax is payable in quarterly instalments based on prior year income tax	
	Balance of tax is payable on the tax return filing date	
Capital gains	Taxable at the corporate income tax rate	
Losses	Tax losses may be carried forward for 5 years and deducted from future taxable profits. Loss carryback is not permitted	
	The loss arising from tax depreciation can be carried forward indefinitely	
Tax group	Tax consolidation applicable for a parent and its 75% subsidiaries	Not available
Tax rate	• Headline rate is 25% • 35% rate for banks, insurance, oil and gas service companies, telecommunication activities • Between 50% and 75% for oil and gas companies • 10% rate for agriculture, healthcare, handicraft and educational activities • Companies that are wholly or partially engaged in export are exempted from corporate tax for 10 years if the registration of the company is done before 31 December 2013 and the first exporting operation is carried out during 2014. Otherwise the tax rate is 10%	

III   TAXES FOR INDIVIDUALS

<table>
<tr><td colspan="2"></td><th>Residents</th><th>Non-residents</th></tr>
<tr><td rowspan="9">Income Tax</td><td>General description</td><td>Residing in Tunisia more than 183 days or having a main residence in Tunisia</td><td>Residing less than 183 days in Tunisia and not having main residence in Tunisia</td></tr>
<tr><td>Taxable entities and taxable income</td><td>Residents are taxed on their worldwide income (under provision of particular specifications provided in double tax treaty)</td><td>Non-residents are taxed on all income arising in Tunisia (under provision of particular specifications provided in double tax treaty)</td></tr>
<tr><td>Types of taxable income</td><td colspan="2">• Industrial and commercial profits
• Non-commercial benefits (fees)
• Agriculture and fishing profits
• Salaries and wages
• Property (real estate) revenues
• Capital gains</td></tr>
<tr><td>Calculation of income</td><td colspan="2">The total of the categories above after taking into account add-backs and allowances</td></tr>
<tr><td>Tax year, tax assessment and tax payment</td><td colspan="2">Tax year is the calendar year

Tax return must be filed the year after the year in question, and before:

• 25 February for capital gains and property revenues
• 25 April for commerce revenues
• 25 May for non-commercial revenues or for individuals realising different kind of revenues
• 25 July for handcraft revenues
• 25 August for agricultural or fishing revenues
• 5 December for salaries

Tax on commercial profits is payable in three quarterly instalments based on prior year tax

Balance of tax is payable on the tax return filing date (after deducting tax instalments and/or withholding taxes)

For salaries and wages, tax is payable through the withholding operated by the employer</td></tr>
<tr><td>Losses</td><td colspan="2">Losses are carried forward for 5 years

Losses originated from tax depreciation are carried forward indefinitely</td></tr>
<tr><td>Tax rates</td><td>– On the basis of the individual income tax scale with progressive rates:

Income (TND)   *Tax rate (%)*
0–5,000   0
5,001–20,000   26
20,001–30,000   28
30,001–50,000   32
50,001+   35
– Income gain from shares sale is subject to a 10% rate</td><td>– Non-residents receiving salaries from companies that are wholly exporters or hydrocarbons companies, or non-residents working for less than 6 months, may choose the flat tax rate of 20%

Otherwise, salaries are subject to the progressive scale rates as applied for residents</td></tr>
</table>

		Residents	Non-residents
Capital Gains Tax (CGT)	General description	Gains arising from chargeable assets	
	Taxable entities and chargeable assets	Chargeable assets include: • immovable property • securities and shares • business assets	
	Calculation of gain	• Real estate sale: Proceeds less acquisition costs, improvement costs, incidental legal fees and an additional deduction of 10% of the acquisition cost for each year since acquisition, acquisition cost	
	Tax year, tax assessment and tax payment	Tax year is the calendar year Tax return must be filed before 25 February of the year following the calendar year	
	Losses	Loss on disposal of shares is deductible from business profit	
	Tax rates	On the basis of the individual income tax scale, except: • profit on disposal of shares: exempt up to TND10,000, 10% thereafter • profit on disposal of real estate: 10% (up to 10 years' possession) and 5% (more than 10 years' possession)	

		Domiciled	Non-domiciled
Inheritance Tax (IHT)	General description	Applied to the value of the estate at date of death, depending on degree of succession	
	Taxable entities and chargeable assets	For a resident person, inheritance tax is based on properties and goods located in Tunisia Properties and goods located abroad are included if the deceased was tax-resident in Tunisia However, properties and goods located abroad which are already subject to inheritance tax of the jurisdiction of their location are exempted in Tunisia	For a non-resident person, inheritance tax is based on properties and goods located in Tunisia
	Calculation of charge	For the tax calculation basis, debts duly proved are admitted in deduction	
	Taxable events	Death of an individual or gift to an individual	
	Allowances	None	
	Tax rates	• 2.5% to direct ascendant, descendant or spouse • 5% between brothers and sisters • 25% between uncles and aunts, between nephews and nieces, between cousins • 35% between relatives at fourth degree or non-relative persons	Same rates applied as those for residents

IV   WITHHOLDING TAXES

Under domestic law	Payments to residents	Payments to non-residents[1]
Dividends	5% on dividends paid by companies to resident individuals	5% on dividends paid by companies to non-resident individuals and non-established companies
Interest	20%	20% 5% on interest paid to non-resident banks 25% to beneficiaries established in tax havens (amongst countries listed by law)
Royalties	15%	15% 25% to beneficiaries established in tax havens (amongst countries listed by law)
Fees	15% or 5% (if paid to companies or individuals submitted to real tax regime) or 2.5% (if paid by totally exporting companies)	15% 25% to beneficiaries established in tax havens (amongst countries listed by law)
Gain on disposal of shares	Nil	25% on margin realized on disposal of shares price for non-resident companies (with a maximum of 5% of sale price) and 10% for non-resident individuals (with a maximum of 2.5% of sale price) 25% to beneficiaries established in tax havens (amongst countries listed by law)
On payments to artists and sportsmen	Sportsmen: 15% Artists: 15% or 5% (for those submitted to real tax regime)	15%
Lottery and games of chance	25%	25%

Reduced rate available under the relevant Double Taxation Treaty			
Country	Dividends	Interest	Royalties
Algeria	5%	20%	15%
Austria	5%	10%	15%
Belgium	5%	15%	15%
Canada	5%	15%	15%
China	5%	10%	10%
Czech Republic	5%	12%	15%
Denmark	5%	12%	15%
Egypt	5%	10%	15%
France	5%	12%	15%
Germany	5%	10%	15%
Greece	5%	15%	12%
Hungary	5%	12%	12%
Indonesia	5%	12%	15%
Iran	5%	10%	8%
Italy	5%	12%	12%

1   Reduced rates of withholding tax may apply where there is an appropriate double tax treaty.

Reduced rate available under the relevant Double Taxation Treaty			
Country	Dividends	Interest	Royalties
Jordan	5%	20%	15%
Kuwait	5%	10%	5%
Lebanon	5%	5%	5%
Libya	5%	20%	15%
Luxembourg	5%	10%	12%
Mali	5%	5%	10%
Mauritania	5%	20%	15%
Morocco	5%	20%	15%
Netherlands	5%	10%	11%
Norway	5%	12%	20%
Oman	5%	10%	5%
Pakistan	5%	13%	10%
Poland	5%	12%	12%
Portugal	5%	15%	10%
Qatar	5%	20%	5%
Republic of Korea	5%	12%	15%
Romania	5%	10%	12%
Saudi Arabia	5%	5%	5%
Senegal	5%	20%	Nil
South Africa	5%	12%	12%
Spain	5%	10%	10%
Sweden	5%	12%	15%
Switzerland	5%	10%	10%
Syria	5%	10%	18%
Turkey	5%	10%	10%
United Arab Emirates	5%	0%	7.5%
United Kingdom	5%	12%	15%
United States	5%	15%	15%
Yemen	5%	10%	7.5%

Note: the above rates are only available provided the specific Treaty criteria are satisfied; as treaties will not be identical, guidance should be sought in all cases. It is possible that lower rates than those shown above may be available provided certain criteria are satisfied.

V   INDIRECT TAXES

		Residents	Non-residents
Value Added Tax (VAT)	General description	VAT is levied on the supply of goods and services and import of certain goods	
	Entities obliged to levy VAT	Companies and individuals exerting commercial activity, except those complying with certain conditions (revenues less than TND100,000; retailers)	Non-resident companies operating commercial activity in Tunisia
	Taxable activities	Supply of goods and services	Services/works rendered in Tunisia by non-residents
	Taxable activities – zero-rated (examples)	• Agricultural products	Public bids executed by non-residents and financed by international donation
	Exemptions (examples)	• Export of goods and services • Oil and gas activity	
	Refund of VAT	Refund of VAT is mainly applied in cases where: • VAT credit remaining for a minimum of 6 months • VAT credit due to export operations • VAT credit due to withheld tax operated by the state or public company	
	Tax liability	VAT to be paid before day 28 of the month following the relevant month	
	Tax rates	Standard rate = 18% Other rates = 0%, 6%, 12%	
	Administrative obligations	Obligation to include on invoice: • VAT rate • VAT amount • Tax ID	
Real Property Taxes		Only at local level	
Stamp Duty		Duties varying from TND0.500 to TND150, depending on the type of document or authorisation	

Turkey

(Tugrul Ozsut, AS CPA & Auditing Co./Nexia Turkey, tozsut@nexiaturkey.com.tr)

I   MAIN LEGAL FORMS

Legal form / Characteristics	Partnership	Joint stock company (AS) and Limited liability company (Ltd Sti)
Partners/shareholders • Number • Restrictions	• Minimum 2 • No maximum	*Ltd Sti* • Between 1 and 50 *AS* • Minimum 1, no restrictions • If more than 100 shareholders, it is deemed to be a public corporation
Directors	Partner	Minimum one director
Establishment	Partnership Agreement	Notarisation of Articles of Association and submission to Trade Registry Office
Registration	Not necessary	Trade Registry Offices
Minimum capital	Not necessary	*Ltd Sti* • TRY10,000 *AS* • TRY50,000
Liability	Unlimited: each partner is jointly and severally liable	• Limited to the partner's share ratio of the capital amount
Governance	Partner or a manager who may not be a partner	• General meetings of shareholders; meeting of the Board of management • Additional rules for public corporations
Audit requirements	Not mandatory	Mandatory
Taxation	Changes according to partnership structure	Corporation Tax

II CORPORATION TAX

Legal form / Description	Resident corporation	Permanent establishment (PE)
General description	Corporation tax on profit	
Taxable entities	The worldwide profits of resident companies in Turkey are subject to tax	The profits in Turkey are subject to tax
Taxable income	Worldwide profits	Profits derived in Turkey
Calculation of taxable profits	Sales and other income minus costs of generating the income which are allowed under the commercial code	
Interest payments	Generally deductible as a business expense	
Related party transactions	Transactions between related parties which are not under arm's length principles are considered as profit distributions and subject to tax	
Tax year, return and payment	Tax year – calendar year Tax payments are due quarterly in advance in March, June, September and December Tax return has to be submitted by 25 April following the end of the tax year	
Capital gains	Taxed at the main rate of corporate tax, with certain exemptions available The provisions of the relevant Double Taxation Agreements (DTA) should be taken into consideration	
Losses	Losses can be carried forward for 5 years	Losses can be carried forward for 5 years
Tax rate	20% corporate tax	

III TAXES FOR INDIVIDUALS

		Residents	Non-residents
Income Tax	General description	Tax levied on the chargeable income of a chargeable person for a year of assessment	
	Taxable entities	Individuals resident in Turkey are subject to income tax for all of their worldwide income	Income in Turkey is subject to tax
	Types of taxable income	• Business income • Agricultural income • Self-employment income • Returns on stocks and bonds • Property income • increase in value (sale of real property, sale of shares)	
	Calculation of income	The calculation of taxable business profits is based on income earned in a calendar year less expenses as specified by law Income from self-employment is taxable on a cash basis, not accrual basis	
	Tax year, tax assessment and tax payment	Tax year – calendar year Business and self-employment income returns on quarterly basis Tax returns are due by 25 March following the tax year and tax is payable in two instalments in March and July	
	Losses	Losses related with business and self-employment profit, may be carried forward 5 years	None
	Tax rates	*Income (TRY)* *Rate (%)* Up to 13,000 15 13,001–30,000 20 30,001–70,000 27 70,001+ 35	Self-employment income: 20% Salaries and business income are subject to same rate as residents
Capital Gains Tax (CGT)	General description	Tax on gains derived from disposal of movable and immovable property assets	
	Taxable entities and chargeable assets	Gains derived from disposal of securities held for less than 2 years, immovable property held for less than 5 years and from sales of partnership interests	
	Calculation of gain	Proceeds from the disposal of the assets, less costs of the assets and other expenses paid by the seller	
	Tax year, tax assessment and tax payment	Tax year – calendar year Tax returns are due to be filed by 25 March following the end of the tax year Tax is payable in two instalments in March and July	Declared and paid within 15 days of the gain being realised to the non-resident
	Losses	No relief is available	
	Tax rates	See income tax rates above	

		Residents	Non-residents
Inheritance Tax (IHT)	General description	Tax charged on a chargeable transfer of value made by a lifetime gift or estate on death	
	Taxable entities and chargeable assets	Inheritance is levied on an individual receiving an asset from a Turkish citizen or Turkey situs assets. Overseas assets received by a Turkish citizen are also subject to tax	Non-residents receiving Turkey situs assets are subject to tax
	Calculation of charge	Tax is computed on the value of the inherited asset less any debt attached to such assets	
	Taxable events	• Land and buildings, money, movable assets, rights and receivables on death • All types of lifetime gifts (real property, money, etc)	
	Allowances	• On death spouse and each child: TRY176,600 • Lifetime gifts: TRY4,086	
	Tax rates	Tax Base (TRY) Rate on death (%) Rate on lifetime gifts (%) 210,000 1 10 Next 500,000 3 15 Next 1,110,000 5 20 Next 2,000,000 7 25 3,820,000 10 30	

IV WITHHOLDING TAXES

Under domestic law	Payments to residents	Payments to non-residents
Dividends	15%	15% (DTA conditions taken into consideration)
Interest	Deposit rate: 10%, 12%, 13%, 15%, 18%	Deposit rate: 10%, 12%, 13%, 15%, 18%
	Treasury Bill: 10%	Treasury Bill: 10%
Royalties	17%	20%
On payments to artists and sportsmen	Payments to artists: 20%	Payments to artists: 20%
	Payments to sportsmen: 5%, 10%, 15%	Payments to sportsmen: 5%, 10%, 15%

Reduced rate available under the relevant Double Taxation Treaty			
Country	Dividends	Interest	Royalties
Albania	15%	10%	10%
Algeria	12%	10%	10%
Austria	15%	15%	10%
Australia	15%	10%	10%
Azerbaijan	12%	10%	10%
Bahrain	15%	10%	10%
Bangladesh	10%	10%	10%
Belarus	15%	10%	10%
Belgium	20%	15%	10%
Bosnia-Herzegovina	15%	10%	10%
Brazil	15%	15%	10%
Bulgaria	15%	10%	10%
Canada	20%	15%	10%
China	10%	10%	10%
Croatia	10%	10%	10%
Cyprus (North), Republic of	20%	10%	10%
Czech Republic	10%	10%	10%
Denmark	20%	15%	10%
Egypt	15%	10%	10%
Estonia	10%	10%	10%
Ethiopia	10%	10%	10%
Finland	20%	15%	10%
France	20%	15%	10%
Georgia	10%	10%	10%
Germany	15%	10%	10%
Greece	15%	12%	10%
Hungary	15%	10%	10%
India	15%	15%	15%
Indonesia	15%	10%	10%
Iran	20%	10%	10%

Reduced rate available under the relevant Double Taxation Treaty			
Country	Dividends	Interest	Royalties
Ireland	15%	15%	10%
Israel	10%	10%	10%
Italy	15%	15%	10%
Japan	15%	15%	10%
Jordan	15%	10%	12%
Kazakhstan	10%	10%	10%
Korea, Republic of	20%	15%	10%
Kosovo	15%	10%	10%
Kuwait	10%	10%	10%
Kyrgyzstan	10%	10%	10%
Latvia	10%	10%	10%
Lebanon	15%	10%	10%
Lithuania	10%	10%	10%
Luxembourg	20%	15%	10%
Macedonia	10%	10%	10%
Malaysia	15%	15%	10%
Malta	15%	10%	10%
Mexico	15%	15%	10%
Moldova	15%	10%	10%
Mongolia	10%	10%	10%
Morocco	10%	10%	10%
Netherlands	20%	15%	10%
New Zealand	15%	15%	10%
Norway	30%	15%	10%
Oman	15%	10%	10%
Pakistan	15%	10%	10%
Poland	15%	10%	10%
Portugal	15%	15%	10%
Qatar	15%	10%	10%
Romania	15%	10%	10%
Russia	10%	10%	10%
Saudi Arabia	10%	10%	10%
Serbia	15%	10%	10%
Singapore	15%	10%	10%
Slovakia	10%	10%	10%
Slovenia	10%	10%	10%
South Africa	15%	10%	10%
Spain	15%	15%	10%
Sudan	10%	10%	10%
Sweden	20%	15%	10%
Switzerland	15%	10%	10%
Syria	10%	10%	15%
Tajikistan	10%	10%	10%
Thailand	15%	15%	15%

Reduced rate available under the relevant Double Taxation Treaty			
Country	Dividends	Interest	Royalties
Tunisia	15%	10%	10%
Turkmenistan	10%	10%	10%
Ukraine	15%	10%	10%
United Arab Emirates	12%	10%	10%
United Kingdom	20%	15%	10%
United States	20%	15%	10%
Uzbekistan	10%	10%	10%
Yemen	10%	10%	10%

Note: the above rates are only available provided the specific Treaty criteria are satisfied. It is possible that lower rates than those shown above may be available provided that certain criteria are satisfied. As treaties will not be identical, guidance should be sought in all cases.

V   INDIRECT TAXES

		Residents	Non-residents
Value Added Tax (VAT)	General description	Value added tax is levied on all goods and services supplied within the scope of commercial industrial, agricultural and independent professional activities and on the import of goods and services	
	Entities obliged to levy VAT	Any individual, partnership, corporation, association and foundation which carries out taxable activities	
	Taxable activities	• Supply of goods and services • Import of goods • Post, telephone, radio and TV services • Organising and participating in gambling	
	Taxable activities – zero-rated (examples)	Export of goods and supply of services to other countries	
	Exemptions (examples)	• Export of goods and services • Forwarding services from Turkey to other countries • Export of goods to free zones and services performed in free zones • Delivery of naval, air and road vehicles and goods and services to be used in manufacturing these vehicles	
	Refund of VAT	There is a VAT refund mechanism in transactions: • which are exempt from VAT (export sales) and • where there are rate differences in output and inputs (output rate is 1% or 8%, input rate is 18%)	• Non-residents in forwarding business can recover VAT issued for fuel, spare parts, maintenance and repair expenses • Companies in all sectors that participated in fairs can recover VAT under some conditions
	Tax liability	The supplier (company, partnership) of goods and services is responsible for charging VAT	
	Tax rates	• Standard rate = 18% • Goods that are subject to VAT at 1% such as: some vegetables, newspapers, magazines • Education Services = 8% • Textile and apparel products = 8% • Accommodation services provided at hotels, motels, holiday villages, etc = 8% • Health services, pharmaceuticals and medical devices = 8%	
Real Property Taxes		0.1%–0.4%, depending on use and location of the building	
Stamp Duty		Any agreement that is written and signed is subject to stamp tax based on the value stated in the agreement	
		0.189%–0.948%, depending on the type of document	
		Papers prepared abroad are subject to stamp duty if they are declared to official authorities	

Uganda

(Sujata Jaffer, Nexia SJ Tanzania, info@nexiasjtz.com)

I MAIN LEGAL FORMS

Legal form / Characteristics	Partnership and Limited Liability Partnership (LLP)	Private corporation (Ltd) and Public corporation (Plc)
Partners/ shareholders • Number • Restrictions	2 to 20 2 to a maximum of 50 if Professionals Not more than 20 persons for the Limited Liability Partnership	Private corporation: 2 to 100 Public corporation: 7 to Infinity
Directors	There must be one or more General Partners who shall be liable for all debts and obligations of the firm In addition to the General Partners, there should be one or more persons who shall contribute a stated amount of capital to the firm – They shall not be liable for the debts and obligations of the firm beyond the amount of capital so contributed – They shall not draw out or receive back any part of their contributions, and if one does so, one shall be liable for the debts and obligations of the Partnership up to the amount so drawn out – They shall not take part in the management of the Partnership A body corporate may be a limited liability partner	Every company, other than a Private company, should have at least 2 directors, if formed after 2012, or 1 director, if formed before Minimum age is 21 years and maximum is 70 years A single member company shall appoint 2 people: one as Nominee director, in case of death of the single member, and the other as alternate nominee, to work as Nominee director in case of non-availability of the Nominee director
Establishment	Can be formal or informal	Formal with drawn up Memorandum and Articles of Association

Legal form Characteristics	Partnership and Limited Liability Partnership (LLP)	Private corporation (Ltd) and Public corporation (Plc)
Registration	Registration of the Partnership Deed with the Uganda Registration Services Bureau (URSB) LLP should first reserve their name	Registration of the Memorandum and Articles of Association with the Uganda Registration Services Bureau The company name has to be reserved first
Minimum capital	The Partners agree as to the amount of capital each of them has to contribute	The Memorandum of Association must state the amount of capital which the company proposes to be registered and the division of the share capital into shares of a fixed amount No subscriber may take less than a share, and each subscriber must write opposite his/her name the number of shares he/she takes
Liability	The Partners are jointly and severally liable for the debts of the firm	The Company is liable for its debts as a separate legal entity The liability of the members is limited to the value of their unpaid shares. If one is fully paid up, the company must pay by itself
Governance	The Partners must participate in the management and well-being of the Partnership business	Companies are managed by Directors, who may be shareholders or not
Audit requirements	It is not a legal requirement that the books of accounts for a Partnership should be audited	The Company's books of accounts must be audited
Taxation	The firm files the business tax returns, but the tax liability is shared between the Partners according to the sharing ratio The Firm (Partnership) files Value Added Tax returns and pays/ claims Value Added Tax (VAT) The Firm (Partnership) files and pays Pay As You Earn (PAYE) deducted from the firm's employees The Partners are assessed and pay the Income Tax according to the sharing ratio	The Company, as a legal entity: – files Corporation tax returns in its name and pays/claims the resulting taxes in its name – files Value Added Tax Returns, and pays/claims the resulting taxes in its name – files Pay As You Earn Returns and pays the taxes in its name

Legal form / Characteristics	Partnership and Limited Liability Partnership (LLP)	Private corporation (Ltd) and Public corporation (Plc)
Usage	Mainly Professionals come together to form Partnership, for example: – Accountants – Doctors – Lawyers – Architects, etc	Individuals who wish to come together collectively to do business together, but with their personal liabilities limited by the Company's memorandum, only to the amount, if any, unpaid on one's shares; if the Company is limited by shares If the Company is limited by Guarantee, the liability of its members is limited by its memorandum to such amount as the members may have agreed to contribute to the liabilities of the Company

II   CORPORATION TAX

Legal form / Description	Uganda resident corporation	Permanent establishment (PE)
General description	***Corporate residence*** A company is resident in Uganda for a year of income if it meets one of the following criteria: • Is incorporated or formed under the laws of Uganda • Has its management and control exercised in Uganda at any time during the year of income • Undertakes the majority of its operations in Uganda during a year of income	***Permanent establishment (PE)*** A PE (branch) means a place where a person carries on business, and includes: • A place where a person is carrying on business through an agent, other than a general agent of independent status acting in the ordinary course of business as such • A place where a person has, is using, or is installing substantial equipment or substantial machinery • A place where a person is engaged in a construction, assembly, or installation project for 90 days or more, including a place where a person is conducting supervisory activities in relation to such a project The furnishing of services, including consultancy services, by an enterprise of a contracting state through employees or other personnel engaged in the other contracting state, provided that such activities continue for the same or a connected project for a period or periods aggregating more than four months within any 12-month period
Taxable entities	Companies, Trusts, NGOs	The branches of multinationals incorporated under the laws of Uganda The definition of a branch now includes, from the perspective of petroleum and mining operations: 'the furnishing of services, including consultancy services, through employees or personnel engaged by the person for such purpose, but only if activities of that nature continue for the same or a connected project for a period or periods aggregating more than 90 days in any 12-month period'

Legal form / Description	Uganda resident corporation	Permanent establishment (PE)
Taxable income	Chargeable income is gross income for the year less the total deductions allowed under the Income Tax Act, Cap 340

The provisions for taxation of petroleum operations in Uganda were amended, and special provisions for taxation of mining operations were introduced in the ITA

Further, the income of Global Fund for AIDS, Malaria, and Tuberculosis is now exempt from income tax | Tax is imposed on the income of a non-resident company derived from running a branch in Uganda |
| Calculation of taxable profits | Most of the taxes imposed are self-assessed

The ITA sets out the following conditions for deductibility of an expense. There must be an expenditure or loss, incurred by a person during the year of income, and must be incurred in the production of income included in gross income

Contingent liabilities are not tax-deductible in Uganda

A deduction is allowed, by class of asset, for the depreciation of the person's depreciable assets, other than minor assets, in accordance with the appropriate applicable rates. Industrial building allowances are also available at 5% per annum on a straight-line basis

Taxpayers are now denied a deduction for any expenditure above UGX 5 million in one transaction on goods and services where the supplier does not have a TIN (Taxpayer Identification Number)

A deduction of 2% of income tax payable is granted to any employer who can prove to the URA that at least 5% of their employees on a full-time basis are people with disabilities

The income tax payable by the taxpayer for a year of income is calculated by applying the relevant tax rates determined under the Act for the year of income, and from the resulting amount are subtracted any tax credits allowed to the taxpayer for the year of income | The chargeable income of a branch in Uganda is taxed at the corporation tax rate of 30% after deduction of allowable expenses

In arriving at chargeable income (taxable income), one has to go through the process of adjusting profits by taking into account deductions allowed and deductions not allowed

In addition to corporation tax, branches are subject to extra tax at a rate of 15% on any repatriated income for a year of income

The repatriated income is calculated using the $A + (B - C) - D$ approach, where A is the net assets at the beginning of the year, B is the net profit for the year, C is the tax charge for the year, and D is the net assets at the end of the year

Where a taxpayer is allowed more than one tax credit for a year of income, the credits shall be applied in the following order:
- the foreign tax credit allowed, then
- any Withholding tax deducted from the taxpayer by a designated Withholding tax agent, and
- any Provisional tax paid |

Legal form / Description	Uganda resident corporation	Permanent establishment (PE)
Interest payments	Deductible if incurred in production of income included in the company's gross income. Interest from non-trade-related debt is not deductible. Deferred interest is deductible when paid	The thin capitalisation restrictions now apply to branches of non-resident companies. These provisions do not apply if, at all times during the year, the amount of the debt does not exceed the arm's-length debt amount
	Interest charged before capital investment is put to use has to be capitalised. Interest incurred after capital investment is put to use is allowed as a deduction	Arm's-length debt amount is defined as the amount of debt that a financial institution that is not related to the company would be prepared to lend to the company, having regard to all the circumstances of the company
	The general rule is that interest income is taxable as part of business income at a rate of 30%	
	Interest income is also subject to WHT at the rate of 15%. The WHT paid in respect of the interest income is creditable where the income is subject to the corporation tax rate of 30%	
	Also, interest income earned with respect to government securities is subject to tax at 20% as a final tax	
	Where a company is financing some of its Uganda operations with foreign debt, there are thin capitalisation rules and the safe harbour debt-to-equity ratio is 1.5:1	
	Thin capitalization may not apply in respect of debentures that:	
	• were issued by the company outside Uganda for the purpose of raising a loan outside Uganda • were widely issued for the purpose of raising funds for use by the company in a business carried on in Uganda or the interest is paid to a bank or a financial institution of a public character and • the interest is paid outside Uganda	

Legal form / Description	Uganda resident corporation	Permanent establishment (PE)
Related party transactions	A return on Transfer Pricing is required where the related party transactions are disclosed	A return on Transfer Pricing is required where the related party transactions are disclosed
	The transfer pricing regulations apply to controlled transactions if a person who is a party to the transactions is located in and is subject to tax in Uganda and the other person who is a party to the transaction is located in or outside Uganda	
	The Uganda Revenue Authority (URA) Practice Note issued on 14 May 2012 gives details on the transfer pricing documentation to be maintained by the taxpayer. These include company details and transaction details, including agreements and the pricing methodology used in determining the arm's-length price	
	In addition, the anti-avoidance provisions contained in Sections 90 and 91 of the ITA require transactions between associates to be at an arm's length. These are the provisions that are often applied by the URA in instances where they are of the view that a non-resident person may be transferring profits from Uganda	
Tax year, return and payment	The ITA provides for two provisional returns within a 12-month period (financial year). The first provisional return is due within the first six months of the accounting year, while the second is due by the end of the 12th month of the accounting year	12 months ending 30 June
		Provisional Return, file by 30 June, and final return by 31 December
	The Self-Assessment Return (SAR) is due by the end of the sixth month after the end of the accounting year	There is an option to amend the return before the year end
	Electronic filing has been introduced for all tax returns	Payment is due on date of filing
Capital gains	Capital gains are included in and taxed together with the business income at a rate of 30%. There is no separate capital gains tax	Capital gains are included in and taxed together with the business income at a rate of 30%. There is no separate capital gains tax
	Capital gains arise on disposal of non-depreciable business assets as well as sale of shares	Capital gains arise on disposal of non-depreciable business assets as well as sale of shares

Legal form / Description	Uganda resident corporation	Permanent establishment (PE)

Losses	A deduction is allowed for any assessed tax losses carried forward from previous years of income. Such tax losses are carried forward and deducted against future taxable profit of the business in the subsequent years of income. The losses can be carried forward indefinitely
	
	There is no ring-fencing of losses except in the following circumstances:
	
	• Where, during a year of income, there has been a change of 50% or more in the underlying ownership of a company, as compared with its ownership one year previously, the company is not permitted to deduct an assessed loss in the year of income or in subsequent years, unless the company, for a period of two years after the change or until the assessed loss has been exhausted if that occurs within two years after the change:
	  • continues to carry on the same business after the change as it carried on before the change and
	  • does not engage in any new business or investment after the change where the primary purpose of the company or the beneficial owners of the company is to utilise the assessed loss so as to reduce the tax payable on the income arising from the new business or investment
		They are carried forward and allowed as a deduction in determining the chargeable income of the following year

	• In cases where losses relate to farming, the assessed farming loss can only be deducted from farming income of the taxpayer in the following year and not from any other income There is no provision for carryback of losses in Uganda	

Legal form / Description	Uganda resident corporation	Permanent establishment (PE)
Tax group	No tax consolidation available	
Tax rate	The income tax rate applicable to the chargeable income of companies is 30%, with the exception of: • Mining companies • Non-resident air transport, shipping, and some telecommunication services • Resident companies whose turnover does not exceed UGX 150 million ***Resident companies with turnover of less than UGX 150 million*** A rate of 1.5% of turnover is used to determine income tax payable by a resident company whose turnover is between UGX 50 million and UGX 150 million, subject to certain thresholds However, on application to the Commissioner, a resident company with a turnover of less than UGX 150 million may be taxed at 30% This category excludes professionals, public entertainment services, public utility services, or construction services	The corporation tax applicable to companies, other than mining companies, is 30% on the chargeable profits, and 15% on the repatriated branch profits ***Mining companies*** The income tax rate applicable to mining companies is calculated according to the following specified formula: Annual tax rate = $70 - (1{,}500/x)$, where x is the ratio of the company's chargeable income to the gross revenue for the year Note that the derived tax rate is subject to a minimum tax rate of 25% and a maximum tax rate of 45% ***Non-resident air transport, shipping, and some telecommunications services*** Non-resident ship operators, charterers, and air transport operators who derive income from carriage of passengers who embark, or cargo or mail that is embarked, in Uganda, as well as road transport operators who derive income from carriage of cargo or mail that is embarked in Uganda, are taxed at the rate of 2% A non-resident person who carries on the business of transmitting messages by cable, radio, fibre-optic, or satellite communication and derives income through transmission of such messages by apparatus established in Uganda, whether or not such messages originated from Uganda, is taxed on one's gross income at a rate of 5%. Similarly, a non-resident person who derives income from providing direct-to-home pay television services to subscribers in Uganda is taxed on one's gross income at a rate of 5%

Description ⟍ Legal form	Uganda resident corporation	Permanent establishment (PE)
		Under the Petroleum operations, the income tax applicable to contractors is 30%

Income tax for resident contractors on a participation dividend paid by a resident contractor to a non-resident company is 15%,and the income tax applicable to non-resident sub-contractors deriving income from Uganda-sourced services contracts is 15% |

III TAXES FOR INDIVIDUALS

<table>
<tr><td colspan="2"></td><th>Residents</th><th>Non-residents</th></tr>
<tr><td rowspan="12">Income Tax</td><td>General description</td><td>An individual who:
– has a permanent home in Uganda
– is present in Uganda for a period aggregating to 183 days or more in any 12 months that commences or ends during the year of income
– is present in Uganda during the year of income for periods averaging more than 122 days in each such year of income, or

is an employee /official of the Government of Uganda posted abroad during the year of income</td><td>If the individual is not a resident, who has no permanent home and does not stay in Uganda for the number of days mentioned which can make one to qualify as a resident, ie 183 days or more in any 12 months that commences or ends during the year of income, or periods averaging more than 122 days in each such year of in-come

According to Section 83(1) of the ITA, a tax is imposed on every non-resident person who derives any dividend, interest, royalty, rent, natural resource payment, or management charge from sources in Uganda. WHT at a rate of 15% therefore applies on gross dividend payments, interest, management fees, and royalty payments in respect of non-treaty countries

Also, the rate of WHT on interest derived by a non-resident person from government securities is 20%

Payment of re-insurance premiums to non-resident persons is subject to WHT at a rate of 10%. The requirement to withhold tax does not apply to the African Reinsurance Corporation and PTA Reinsurance Company</td></tr>
<tr><td>Taxable entities and taxable income</td><td>Persons who derive income from Uganda and worldwide</td><td>Persons who derive income from sources in Uganda</td></tr>
<tr><td>Types of taxable income</td><td>Business income, Employment income and Property income</td><td>Business income, Employment income and Property income, eg rents, royalties, interest, dividends, etc</td></tr>
<tr><td>Calculation of income</td><td>Income aggregated from all sources</td><td>Only income derived from sources in Uganda</td></tr>
<tr><td>Tax year, tax assessment and tax payment</td><td>1 July to 30 June
Self-Assessment & provisional returns with quarterly payment instalments</td><td>1 July to 30 June</td></tr>
<tr><td>Losses</td><td>All allowable losses are recognised for offset or roll over</td><td>Losses are not allowed to non-residents as they are taxed on the gross amounts</td></tr>
</table>

		Residents	**Non-residents**
Income Tax – *contd*	Tax rates	Progressive from 10%, 20% to 30% on amounts exceeding UGX 4,920,000, after allowing the threshold of UGX 2,820,000, and an additional 10% to income in excess of UGX 120,000,000	Progressive from 10% on amounts not exceeding UGX 4,020,000, UGX 402,000, plus 20% of the amount exceeding UGX 4,020,000, and UGX 582,000 plus 30% on amounts exceeding UGX 4,920,000, and an additional 10% to income in excess of UGX 120,000,000
			Income tax applicable to a non-resident person under Section 82, 83, 84, or 85, excluding interest on Government securities, is 15% on gross amounts
			Section 82 – Branch profits
			Section 83 – International payments of dividends, interest, royalty, rent, natural resources payments, or management charges
			Section 84 – Tax on payments to non-resident Public entertainers and Sports persons
			Section 85 – Payments to non-resident Contractors and Professionals
Capital Gains Tax (CGT)	General description	Capital gains tax arises where there has been a disposal of a taxable asset	
		The amount of any gain arising is the excess of the consideration received over the cost base of the asset	
		1. A taxpayer is considered as having disposed of an asset when the asset has been: – sold, exchanged, redeemed, or distributed by the taxpayer – transferred by the taxpayer by way of gift, or – destroyed or lost	
		2. A disposal of an asset includes a disposal of part of the asset	

		3. Where the Commissioner is satisfied that a taxpayer:
		   a) has converted an asset from a taxable use to a non- taxable use, or
		   b) has converted an asset from a non-taxable use to a taxable use	

		the taxpayer is deemed to have disposed of the asset at the time of the conversion for an amount equal to the market value of the asset at that time and to have immediately re-acquired the asset for a cost base equal to that same value	
		A non-resident person who becomes a resident person is deemed to have acquired all assets, other than taxable assets, owned by the person at the time of becoming a resident for their market value at that time	
		A resident person who becomes a non-resident person is deemed to have acquired all assets, other than taxable assets, owned by the person at the time of becoming a non-resident for their market value at that time	

		Residents	**Non-residents**
Capital Gains Tax (CGT) – *contd*	Taxable entities and chargeable assets	Capital gains tax, like income tax, is imposed on every person who has chargeable income for the year of income	
		'Person' includes an individual, a partnership, a trust, a company, a retirement fund, a government, a political subdivision of government, and a listed institution	
		'Listed institutions' are International Organisations operating in Uganda	
		Non-depreciable assets, such as land and buildings	
	Calculation of gain	It is the excess of the consideration over the cost base of the asset	
	Tax year, tax assessment and tax payment	Capital Gains are included in the gross income of the taxpayer and assessed as business income in a given year of income, ending 30 June	
	Losses	The losses are allowed as a deduction in determining the chargeable income of a given year	
	Tax rates	30% for Companies and Progressive from 10% to 30% for individuals, after allowing the threshold of UGX 2,820,000	
		Uganda domiciled	**Non-Uganda domiciled**
Inheritance Tax (IHT)	General description	N/A in Uganda	
	Taxable entities and chargeable assets		
	Calculation of charge		
	Taxable events		
	Allowances		
	Tax rates		

IV   WITHHOLDING TAXES

Under domestic law	Payments to residents	Payments to non-residents
Dividends	10% if payment is by a listed company to an individual; and 15% to others	15%
Interest	15% or 10% and 20% on government securities	15%, and 20% on government securities
Consultancy, agency fees, etc	6%	15%
Professional fees	6%	15%
Management Fees and Royalties	Income, included in gross income	15%
On payments to artists and sportsmen	Nil	15%
Re-Insurance Premiums	Nil	15%

Reduced rate available under the relevant Double Taxation Treaty			
Country	Dividends	Interest	Royalties	Technical/ Management fees
Denmark	10%	10%	10%	10%
India	10%	10%	10%	10%
Italy	10%	10%	10%	10%
Mauritius	10%	10%	10%	10%
Netherlands	10%	10%	10%	10%
Norway	10%	10%	10%	10%
Seychelles	10%	10%	10%	10%
South Africa	10%	10%	10%	10%
UK	15%	15%	15%	15%
Zambia	Exempt	Exempt	Exempt	Exempt
EAC*	5%	10%	10% (Pending Ratification)	10%

Note: the above rates are only available provided the specific Treaty criteria are satisfied. It is possible that lower rates than those shown above may be available provided certain criteria are satisfied. As treaties will not be identical, guidance should be sought in all cases.

* Burundi, Kenya, Rwanda, Tanzania.

V INDIRECT TAXES

		Residents	Non-residents
Value Added Tax	General description	VAT is governed by the VAT Act and administered by the Uganda Revenue Authority (URA). VAT is charged at the rate of 18% on the supply of most goods and services in the course of business in Uganda	VAT is governed by the VAT Act and administered by the Uganda Revenue Authority (URA). VAT is charged at the rate of 18% on the supply of most goods and services in the course of business in Uganda
	Entities obliged to levy VAT	The annual threshold for VAT registration is UGX 150 million. Persons who make supplies that are VATable and whose turnover exceeds UGX 150 million are required to register for VAT with the URA. VAT-registered persons are required to: • Charge VAT whenever they make supplies that are VATable • File monthly returns before the 15th day of the month following the reporting month	The VAT Act provides for the appointment of a VAT representative by a non-resident person who may be required by the Commissioner to register for VAT in Uganda but has no fixed place of business. If the non-resident person does not appoint the VAT representative within 30 days after being required to register for VAT, the Commissioner may appoint the representative for the non-resident person. The VAT representative of the non-resident person shall be a person who is ordinarily residing in Uganda, may be an agent for more than one non-resident person, and will have the responsibility for doing all things required of the non-resident person under the VAT Act A person who is not registered, but who is required to be registered or to pay VAT, is a taxable person from the beginning of the tax period immediately following the period in which the duty to apply for registration or to pay tax arose
	Taxable activities	Goods and services, other than exempt supplies	
	Taxable activities – zero-rated (examples)	The zero-rated supplies include: the supply of goods and services exported from Uganda; the supply of drugs and medicines; the supply of seeds, fertilisers, pesticides and hoes; the supply of leased aircraft, aircraft engines, spare engines, spare parts for aircraft, and aircraft maintenance equipment; and the supply of educational materials and the supply of printing services for educational materials	
	Exemptions (examples)	Some supplies are exempt from VAT, the main categories being government subsidies, some unprocessed foodstuffs, financial services, health and life insurance, re-insurance services, unimproved land, leases and sale of certain residential properties, betting and gaming, education, medical and health services, social welfare services, pesticides, petroleum products subject to excise duty, and power generated by solar	

		Residents	Non-residents
Value Added Tax – Contd	Refund of VAT	1. If, for any tax period, a taxable person's input credit exceeds his/her liability for tax for the period, the Commissioner General shall refund him/her the excess within one month of the due date for the return for the tax period to which the excess relates, or within one month of the date when the return was made if the return was not made by the due date 2. Notwithstanding the above: a) where the excess is less than UGX 5 million, except in case of an investment trader or a person providing mainly zero-rated supplies, the amount should be offset against future tax liability, and b) with the consent of the taxable person, where the excess is UGX 5 million or more, the amount may be offset against future liability or be applied in the reduction of any other tax not in dispute due from the taxpayer	
	Tax liability	The tax payable on a taxable transaction is calculated by applying the rate of tax to the taxable value of the transaction. The taxable value of a transaction is the total consideration paid in money or in kind by a person for that supply VAT becomes due depending on the time of supply. Under the VAT Act, a supply of goods or services takes place when any of the following takes place first: 1) A tax invoice is issued for the supply 2) The goods are delivered 3) The services are rendered 4) The goods are made available 5) The goods or services are paid for in whole or in part When any of the above takes place, the difference between the VAT incurred by the person (input tax) and the VAT charged by the person (output tax) is paid to, or claimed as an offset or cash refund from, the tax authority	
	Tax rates	18% for standard-rated supplies 0% for Zero-rated supplies Nil tax for Exempt supplies	
	Administrative obligations	All taxable persons are required to file a return for every tax period (ie month) within 15 days after the end of the month	
Real Property Taxes		Tax on rental income derived by an individual is assessed separately from the individual's other business incomes or employment income. The tax is 20% of the rental income amount after deducting: – 20% as allowable expenses – UGX 2,820,000 as a tax-free threshold In case of companies, the property income is included in the gross income and taxed at the year of income corporation tax rate The current corporation tax rate is 30%	

	Residents	Non-residents
Stamp Duty	Stamp Duty is imposed by the Stamps Act. It is a duty payable on any instrument (document) which upon being created, transferred, limited, extended, extinguished or recorded, confers upon any person a right or liability	
	The affected instruments (currently about 66) are listed in the Schedules to the Stamps Act. The applicable rates are either fixed or ad valorem	
	The most common instruments that attract stamp duty include:	
	– Affidavits – Agreements or Memorandums of Agreement – Company Articles and Article of Association (0.5%) – Caveats – Insurance policies – Powers of Attorney – Promissory Notes – Mortgage Deeds (0.5%) – Debentures (0.5%) – Transfer of immovable property (1%)	

Ukraine

(Andriy Kostyuk, Pavlenko & Partners Attorneys at Law,
ak@pavlenkopartners.com)

I   MAIN LEGAL FORMS

Characteristics \ Legal form	Private corporation (Ltd)	Joint Stock Company (JSC) (public or private (closed))
Partners/shareholders • Number • Restrictions	• Up to 100 (no minimum) • None • No company with single shareholder can establish another single-shareholder company	• No minimum or maximum • No company with single shareholder can establish another single-shareholder company
Directors	No restrictions	
Establishment	By the decision of founders	• decision of founders • closed (private) placement of shares • foundation meeting • registration
	Antimonopoly committee consent in specific cases	
Registration	State Registration	
	Formal procedures up to 2 weeks	Formal procedures take about 3 months
Minimum capital	No minimum share capital requirement	1,250 minimum salaries (approx 2,000,000 UAH; from January 2017, it will be approximately 4,000,000 UAH)
Liability	Limited to capital	
Governance	• General assembly • Executive body (Director or Board of Directors) • Controlling body – an audit committee	
Audit requirements	Audit of the annual financial report is obligatory	
	If annual turnover is less than 4,250 UAH, audit of the annual financial report can be made every three years	
Taxation	Taxable on worldwide profits	
Usage	Small businesses	Major establishments with numerous shareholders
		Public placement of shares

II   CORPORATION TAX

Description \ Legal form	Resident corporation	Permanent establishment (PE)
General description	Corporate Profits Tax is centralized. No additional corporate taxes are imposed at local levels	
Taxable entities	Corporations incorporated in Ukraine	PE in Ukraine
Taxable income	Worldwide income	Income arising in Ukraine
Calculation of taxable profits	Determined by adjusting (increase or decrease) the financial result, as defined in the financial statements in accordance with national or international accounting standards, in accordance with the provisions of the Tax Code of Ukraine

A taxpayer whose annual income (excluding indirect taxes) defined by the accounting rules in the last annual reporting (tax) period does not exceed 20 million UAH has the right to decide not to make such adjustments to the financial results | |
| Interest payments | Deductible, no thin capitalization restrictions. Restrictions for foreign controlled companies | |
| Related party transactions | Related party transactions must be made on an arm's length basis. Transfer pricing reporting applicable if the total income of the taxpayer and/or its associated persons exceeds 50 million UAH (excluding indirect taxes) during the tax year and the volume of transactions of the taxpayer and/or its associated persons with one contractor exceeds 5 million UAH (excluding indirect taxes) for the same tax (reporting) year | |
| Tax year, return and payment | Tax (reporting) period is the calendar quarter, calendar half of the year, calendar three-quarters and calendar year

Returns should be filed quarterly based on cumulative results, within 40 calendar days following the reporting quarter **OR** the annual return (for the whole financial year) shall be filed within 60 calendar days of the following year

Payments are made within 10 days of the filing deadline | |
Capital gains	Treated as income	
Losses	Losses may be carried forward indefinitely	
Tax group	None	
Tax rate	• Basic rate is 18% • 0 or 3% for insurance activities • 0, 4, 6, 12, 15 and 20% for non-residents	

III TAXES FOR INDIVIDUALS

		Residents	Non-residents
Income Tax	General description	Tax levied on the chargeable income of a chargeable person for a year of assessment	
	Taxable entities and taxable income	Residents are taxed on their worldwide income	Income arising in Ukraine
	Types of taxable income	• Property income (usually rent) • Income from capital investment (interest, sale of goodwill, dividends, royalties, annuities) • Income from business activities • Employment from personal services or pensions	
	Calculation of income	The total taxable revenue is any profit subject to taxation	
		The taxpayer has the right to an allowance based on results of the reporting taxation year	No allowances
	Tax year, tax assessment and tax payment	Tax year – calendar year Payer is liable for tax assessment, unless income is taxed at source Taxpayers who have income not taxed at source must file a return by 1 May the following year	
	Losses	Losses may not be carried forward	
	Tax rates	Passive income (interest, dividends, royalties, investment income): • 18% rate for passive income, including dividends on shares and/or investment certificates paid by joint investment institutions • 5% rate for income from dividends on shares and corporate rights accrued by residents taxable to income tax Such income is subject to temporary military tax at 1.5% rate	
Capital Gains Tax (CGT)	General description	Treated as part of income	

		Domiciled
Inheritance Tax (IHT)	General Description	Tax levied as if it were income on the amount received by the taxpayer as a result of the inheritance or gift of funds, property, property and non-property rights
	Chargeable Assets	Real property
		Antiques or pieces of art, jewelry, transport, other movable assets
		Commercial property (securities, shares intellectual property rights)
		Cash or funds on bank accounts
	Calculation of Charge	Residents – Value of inherited/gifted property
		Non-residents – Value of inherited/gifted property located within Ukraine
	Taxable Events	The inheritance/gift should be included within the annual tax return
		For the non-resident, a filing exemption may be available if taxes are paid before the certificate of inheritance has been received or the gift agreement verified by a notary
	Allowances	N/A
	Tax Rates	0% for the members of family of the first degree gentility
		5% for the non-family members
		18% for the inheritance from the non-resident or for the inheritance by the non-resident

IV WITHHOLDING TAXES

Under Domestic Law	Payments to residents	Payments to non-residents[1]
Dividends	–	15%
Interest	–	15%
Royalties	–	15%
On payments to artists and sportsmen	–	15%

Reduced rate available under the relevant Double Taxation Treaty			
Country	Dividends	Interest	Royalties
Algeria	15%	10%	10%
Armenia	15%	10%	0%
Austria	10%	5%	5%
Azerbaijan	10%	10%	10%
Belarus	15%	10%	15%
Belgium	15%	10%	5%
Brazil	15%	15%	15%
Bulgaria	15%	10%	10%
Canada	15%	10%	10%
China (PRC)	10%	10%	10%
Croatia	10%	10%	10%
Cyprus	15%	2%	10%
Czech Republic	15%	5%	10%
Denmark	15%	10%	10%
Egypt	12%	12%	12%
Estonia	15%	10%	10%
Finland	15%	10%	10%
France	15%	10%	10%
Georgia	10%	10%	10%
Germany	10%	5%	5%
Greece	10%	10%	10%
Hungary	15%	10%	5%
Iceland	15%	10%	10%
India	15%	10%	10%
Indonesia	15%	10%	10%
Iran	10%	10%	10%
Israel	15%	10%	10%
Italy	15%	10%	7%
Japan	15%	10%	10%
Jordan	15%	10%	10%
Kazakhstan	15%	10%	10%
Korea (ROK)	15%	5%	5%
Kuwait	5%	0%	10%
Kyrgyzstan	15%	10%	10%
Latvia	15%	10%	10%

1 Reduced rates of withholding tax may apply where there is an appropriate double tax treaty.

Reduced rate available under the relevant Double Taxation Treaty			
Country	**Dividends**	**Interest**	**Royalties**
Lebanon	15%	10%	10%
Libya	15%	10%	10%
Lithuania	15%	20%	10%
Macedonia	15%	10%	10%
Malaysia	15%	15%	15%
Mexico	15%	10%	10%
Moldova	15%	10%	10%
Mongolia	10%	10%	10%
Montenegro	10%	10%	10%
Morocco	10%	10%	10%
Netherlands	15%	10%	10%
Norway	15%	10%	10%
Pakistan	15%	10%	10%
Poland	15%	10%	10%
Portugal	15%	10%	10%
Romania	15%	10%	15%
Russian Federation	15%	10%	10%
Saudi Arabia	15%	10%	10%
Serbia	10%	10%	10%
Singapore	15%	10%	7.5%
Slovakia	10%	10%	10%
Slovenia	15%	5%	10%
South Africa	15%	10%	10%
Spain	15%	0%	5%
Sweden	10%	10%	10%
Switzerland	15%	10%	10%
Syria	10%	10%	15%
Tajikistan	10%	10%	10%
Thailand	15%	15%	15%
Turkey	15%	10%	10%
Turkmenistan	10%	10%	10%
United Arab Emirates	15%	3%	10%
United Kingdom	10%	0%	0%
United States	15%	0%	10%
Uzbekistan	10%	10%	10%
Vietnam	10%	10%	10%
Non-treaty countries	15%	15%	15%

Note: the above rates are only available provided the specific Treaty criteria are satisfied. Lower rates may be available in certain circumstances. As treaties will not be identical, guidance should be sought in all cases.

V INDIRECT TAXES

		Residents	Non-residents
Value Added Tax (VAT)	General description	Tax on the supply of goods and services	
	Entities obliged to levy VAT	Each entity which is registered as a VAT payer on voluntary basis	
		Registration as a VAT payer is compulsory for each entity carrying out taxable operations for more than 1,000,000 UAH per annum (without VAT) during the last 12 months	
	Taxable activities	• Supply of goods and services with place of supply within the territory of Ukraine • Transfer of objects of financial lease to the lessee • Export of goods and auxiliary services • Import of goods and services • International transportation services	
	Taxable activities – zero-rated (examples)	Export	
		Provision of goods:	
		• to refuel or provision some sea vessels, aircraft, space ships, carrier rockets or satellites of the Earth • to refuel (to refill) or provision land military transport or any other special personnel of the Armed Forces of Ukraine which participate in peace-keeping actions abroad or in other cases set forth in the legislation	
		Services of international transportation of passengers and baggage as well as cargo by railroad, car, sea, river and air	
		Services of maintenance of aircraft making international flights	
	Exemptions (examples)	Certain medicines and healthcare, domestically produced baby food, banking, insurance, sale of land, book publishing	
	Refund of VAT	Applicable, very sophisticated bureaucratically	No refund
	Tax rates	Standard rate = 20%	
		0% rate applies to provision of certain goods and services	
		7% rate applies to provision of medicines and medical products	
Real Property Taxes		Entities (individuals and legal entities) including non-residents, which own residential real estate, shall be taxable persons	
		Object of taxation is residential real estate in whole or part	
		The taxable base shall comprise the total space of the residential real estate object	
		The taxable base of a residential real estate object, as owned by an individual taxpayer, shall be reduced:	
		a) for apartments, by 60 square metres	
		b) for a dwelling house, by 120 square metres	
		c) for different types of residential properties (in the case of one owner), by 180 square metres	
		The tax rates shall be established by village, or city council in the amounts per 1 square metre of living space of a residential real estate object	
Stamp Duty		Entities are obligated to pay stamp duty concerning certain activities and transactions with the authorities (registrations, applications, licences, certificates, etc)	

Nexia International does not accept liability for any loss arising from any action taken, or omission, on the basis of this publication. Professional advice should be obtained before acting or refraining from acting on the contents of this publication. Membership of Nexia International, or associated umbrella organizations, does not constitute any partnership between members, and members do not accept any responsibility for the commission of any act, or omission to act by, or the liabilities of, other members.

Nexia International is the trading name of Nexia International Limited, a company registered in the Isle of Man. Company registration number: 53513C. Registered office: 2nd floor, Sixty Circular Road, Douglas, Isle of Man, IM1 1SA

United Arab Emirates

(Shahab Haider, Sajjad Haider & Associates, shahab@sajjadhaider.com)

I　MAIN LEGAL FORMS

Legal form / Characteristics	Sole Proprietorship/Civil Company	Partnership and Limited Liability Partnership (LLP)	Public corporation (Plc), Private corporation (Ltd) and Limited Liability Company (LLC)
Partners/shareholders			
• Number	*Sole Proprietorship* Can be 100% owned by non-residents only for entities engaged in specific professional type activities, Industrial and commercial activities are not allowed	*General Partnership* Two or more UAE nationals as partners	*Public Joint Stock Company* Minimum of 10 founding members
• Restrictions	Must appoint a 'local service agent'	*Partnership Limited by Shares* Owned by one or more general partners and one or more limited partners	Local partner, ie UAE national (Minimum 51% equity/ shareholding) except for designated economic zones
	The local service agent shall not own any share in the company's capital	General partners must be UAE nationals	*Private Joint Stock Company* Minimum of three founding members
	Civil Company	Limited partners may be non-UAE nationals	Local partner, ie UAE national (Minimum 51%)
	Can only practise professional business and is 100% owned by the professional partners of any nationality. Company for engineering must have one partner who is a UAE national, who owns no less than 51% of the business and must be an engineer		Shares cannot be offered to public unless conditions met
			Limited Liability Company
			Minimum of two and not more than 50 persons
			Shares can be transferred between partners or to third parties
Directors			3 to 15 directors manage the company Chairman must be a UAE National
Establishment		Partnership deed	
Registration	Must be registered with the UAE Federal Ministry of Economy commercial registry and with its relevant authority in the respective Emirate		

Legal form Characteristics	Sole Proprietorship/Civil Company	Partnership and Limited Liability Partnership (LLP)	Public corporation (Plc), Private corporation (Ltd) and Limited Liability Company (LLC)
Minimum capital	No minimum capital required	*General Partnership* No minimum capital required *Partnership Limited by Shares* AED500,000 The capital of partnerships limited by shares shall be divided into negotiable equal shares	*Public Joint Stock Company* AED10m A minimum of 20% and maximum of 45% of the share capital of the company can be listed *Private Joint Stock Company* Not less than AED2m *Limited Liability Company* Minimum share capital required is Dhs.150,000 Shareholders have the right to determine the share capital of the company
Liability	The proprietor/ partners shall be responsible for all financial obligations to the extent of their assets	General partners are jointly and severally liable to the extent of all their assets for the liabilities of the company Limited partners are liable for the company's liabilities to the extent of their respective shares in the capital only	Each member is liable to the extent of his respective shareholding
Governance	Partnership Agreement for a civil company	*General Partners* Articles/Deed of Partnership and/ or Memorandum of Association *Partnership limited by Shares* Must have a board of supervisors	Board of Directors and ultimately the equity shareholders in general meeting *Limited Liability Company* Not more than 5 managers and the method of operation for each manager must be specified

Legal form / Characteristics	Sole Proprietorship/Civil Company	Partnership and Limited Liability Partnership (LLP)	Public corporation (Plc), Private corporation (Ltd) and Limited Liability Company (LLC)
Audit requirements	None	*General Partners* Provisions in the Articles/ Deed of Partnership and/ or Memorandum of Association will apply *Partnership limited by Shares* Accounts must be audited annually	Mandatory to appoint auditors on an annual basis
Taxation	None	None	Only entities in the following sectors are required to pay taxes: • Oil, gas and petrochemical • Courier • Telecoms • Foreign banks

II CORPORATION TAX

Description / Legal Form	Resident corporation	Non-resident corporation
General description	Each Emirate has its own tax decrees, whereby all companies are required to pay tax on their earnings	Each Emirate has its own tax decrees, whereby all companies are required to pay tax on their earnings
Taxable entities (in practice)	Oil companies Telecommunication companies Courier companies	Foreign banks Oil companies
Taxable income	*Oil Companies* Calculated by reference to their concession agreements *Telecommunication companies* Rates are revised every year *Courier companies* 10% GST is levied on revenue which is fully passed on to consumers	*Foreign banks* Calculated by reference to their audited financial statements *Oil companies* Calculated by reference to their concession agreements
Calculation of taxable profits		
Interest payments		
Related party transactions		
Tax year, return and payment		
Capital gains		
Losses		
Tax group		
Tax rate	*Oil companies* Dubai up to 55% In other Emirates up to 50% *Telecom companies* Rates are 17.5%–30% for profit and 5%–15% on revenue *Courier companies* 10% GST is levied on revenue which is fully passed on to consumers	*Oil companies* Dubai up to 55% In other Emirates up to 50% *Foreign banks* Up to 20%

III   TAXES FOR INDIVIDUALS

		Residents	Non-residents
Income Tax	General description	Individual Income tax is not levied in the UAE	
	Taxable entities and taxable income		
	Types of taxable income		
	Calculation of income		
	Tax year, tax assessment and tax payment		
	Losses		
	Tax rates		
Capital Gains Tax (CGT)	General description	There is no capital gains tax	
	Taxable entities and chargeable assets		
	Calculation of gain		
	Tax year, tax assessment and tax payment		
	Losses		
	Tax rates		
		Domiciled	Non-domiciled
Inheritance Tax (IHT)	General description	There is no inheritance tax	
	Taxable entities and chargeable assets		
	Calculation of charge		
	Taxable events		
	Allowances		
	Tax rates		

IV WITHHOLDING TAXES

Under domestic law	Payments to residents	Payments to non-residents
Dividends	Nil	Nil
Interest	Nil	Nil
Royalties	Nil	Nil
On payments to artists and sportsmen	Nil	Nil

Reduced rate available under the relevant Double Taxation Treaty			
Country	**Dividends**	**Interest**	**Royalties**
Albania	Details not available	Details not available	Details not available
Algeria	Nil	Nil	Private sector up to 10% Government sector 0%
Armenia	Private sector 3% Government sector 0%	Nil	5%
Argentina	Details not available	Details not available	Details not available
Austria	Nil	Nil	Nil
Azerbaijan	5% if beneficial owner is government, political subdivision and central bank Otherwise 10%	7% 0% if beneficial owner is government, political subdivision and central bank 0% in case of UAE Abu Dhabi Investment Authority 0% in case of Azerbaijan (State Oil Fund)	5% in case of computer software, industrial and commercial or scientific experience 10% in other cases
Bangladesh	Details not available	Details not available	Details not available
Benin	Details not available	Details not available	Details not available
Belarus	5% if beneficial owner holds at least US$100,000 Otherwise 10%	5%	10%
Belgium	5% if shareholding ≥25% Otherwise 10%	5%	5% 0% if the beneficial owner is a financial institution
Bosnia and Herzegovina	0–5% if shareholding ≥10% Otherwise 10%	Nil	5%
Bulgaria	5%	2%	5%
Canada	5% if shareholding ≥10% 10% if paid from Canadian resident to UAE resident subject to a holding of ≥10% 15% in other cases	10% 0% if beneficial owner is a government, political subdivision and central bank	10%

Reduced rate available under the relevant Double Taxation Treaty			
Country	**Dividends**	**Interest**	**Royalties**
China	7% 0% if beneficial owner is a government, political subdivision and central bank	7% 0% if beneficial owner is a government, political subdivision and central bank	10%
Cyprus	Nil	Nil	Nil
Czech Republic	5% 0% if beneficial owner is a government, political subdivision, central bank and any entity where government holding is 25% or more	Nil	10%
Denmark	Details not available	Details not available	Details not available
Egypt	Nil	Private sector 10% Government sector 0%	Nil
Finland	Nil	Nil	Nil
Fiji	Details not available	Details not available	Details not available
France	Nil	Nil	Nil
Georgia	Nil	Nil	Nil
Germany	5% if shareholding ≥10% Otherwise 15%	Nil	Nil
Hellenic Republic	5% if beneficial owner is a company (other than partnership) which holds directly at least 10% of the capital Otherwise 15%	10%	5%
Hungary	Details not available	Details not available	Details not available
Hong Kong	Details not available	Details not available	Details not available
India	5% if shareholding ≥10% Otherwise 15%	5% on a bona fide banking loan In other cases 12.5% 0% for government, political subdivision and central bank	10% of gross amount
Indonesia	10%	5% 0% for government, political subdivision and central bank	5%
Ireland	Nil	Nil	Nil
Italy	5% if shareholding ≥25% Otherwise 15%	Nil	10%
Japan	Details not available	Details not available	Details not available
Jordan	Details not available	Details not available	Details not available

Reduced rate available under the relevant Double Taxation Treaty			
Country	**Dividends**	**Interest**	**Royalties**
Kazakhstan	5% if shareholding ≥10% Otherwise 10%	10%	10%
Kenya	Details not available	Details not available	Details not available
Korea	5% if shareholding ≥10% Otherwise 10%	10% 0% for government, political subdivision and central bank	Nil
Latvia	Details not available	Details not available	Details not available
Lebanon	Nil	Nil	5%
Lithuania	Details not available	Details not available	Details not available
Luxembourg	5% if shareholding ≥10% Otherwise 10%	Nil	Nil
Malaysia	10%	5% of the gross amount 0% for government, political subdivision and central bank	10%
Malta	Nil	Nil	Nil
Mauritania	Details not available	Details not available	Details not available
Mauritius	Nil	Nil	Nil
Mexico	Details not available	Details not available	Details not available
Mongolia	Nil	Nil	10%
Montenegro	0% for government sector	0% for government sector	Details not available
Morocco	Private sector 5% Government sector 0%	Private sector 10% Government sector 0%	Nil
Mozambique	Nil	Nil	5%
Netherlands	5% if shareholding ≥10% Otherwise 10%	Nil	Nil
New Zealand	15%	10% 0% if beneficial owner is a UAE government, political subdivision and central bank	10%
Norway	Details not available	Details not available	Details not available
Pakistan	10% if shareholding ≥20% Otherwise 15%	10% of gross amount 0% for Government, political subdivision and central bank	12%
Palestine	Details not available	Details not available	Details not available
Panama	Details not available	Details not available	Details not available
Philippines	10% if shareholding ≥10% Otherwise 15% 0% for government, political subdivision and government entities	10% of gross amount 0% for government, political subdivision and central bank	10% of gross amount 0% for government, political subdivision and central bank

Reduced rate available under the relevant Double Taxation Treaty			
Country	Dividends	Interest	Royalties
Poland	5% 0% if beneficial owner is a government, political subdivision, central bank and any entity where government holding is 25% or more	5% 0% if beneficial owner is a government, political subdivision and central bank	5%
Portugal	5% if shareholding ≥10% Otherwise 15%	10%	5%
Romania	3% 0% if beneficial owner is a government, and any entity where government holding is 25% or more	3% 0% if beneficial owner is a government, and any entity where government holding is 25% or more	3% 0% for approved industrial royalties
Serbia	Details not available	Details not available	Details not available
Seychelles	Nil	Nil	5%
Singapore	5%	7% 0% for government, political subdivision and central bank	5% Certain industrial royalties may be exempt subject to domestic laws
Slovenia	Details not available	Details not available	Details not available
South Africa	Details not available	Details not available	Details not available
Spain	5% if shareholding ≥10% Otherwise 15%	Nil	Nil
Sri Lanka	10% of gross amount 0% for government, political subdivision and central bank	10% of gross amount 0% for government, political subdivision and central bank	10% of gross amount
Sudan	Nil	Nil	Nil
Sweden	Details not available	Details not available	Details not available
Switzerland	5% if shareholding ≥10% Otherwise 15%	Details not available	Details not available
Syria	Nil	Private sector 10% Government sector 0%	18%
Tajikistan	Nil	Nil	10%
Thailand	10%	10% if received by financial institution (including insurance company) 15% in other cases 0% for government, political subdivision and central bank	15%

Reduced rate available under the relevant Double Taxation Treaty			
Country	Dividends	Interest	Royalties
Tunisia	Nil	Private sector 3% Government sector 0%	7.5%
Turkey	5% if beneficial owner is a government, political subdivision and central bank 10% if shareholding ≥25% 12% in all other cases	10% 0% if beneficial owner is a government, local government and central bank	10%
Turkmenistan	Nil	Nil	10%
Ukraine	5% if shareholding ≥10% 0% for government, political subdivision and central bank	3% 0% for government, political subdivision and central bank 0% in case of UAE's Abu Dhabi Investment Authority and Abu Dhabi Fund for Economic Development	10%
Uzbekistan	5% if shareholding ≥25% Otherwise 15%	10%	10%
Venezuela	5% if shareholding ≥10% Otherwise 10% 0% for government, political subdivision and central bank	10%	10%
Vietnam	5% if shareholding is > 50% or at least US$10m Otherwise 15%	10% 0% for government, political subdivision and central bank 0% in case of UAE's Abu Dhabi Investment council, Abu Dhabi Investment Authority, Dubai Investment Company and Development Funds 0% in case of State Bank of Vietnam and Vietnam Development Bank	10%
Yemen	Nil	Nil	10%

Note: the above rates are only available provided the specific Treaty criteria are satisfied. It is possible that lower rates than those shown above may be available if certain criteria are satisfied. As treaties will not be identical, guidance should be sought in all cases.

V   INDIRECT TAXES

		Residents	Non-residents
Value Added Tax (VAT)	General description	There are no consumption taxes in the UAE, but individual Emirates may charge levies on certain products	
		Customs duty is levied at different rates in each Emirate. For example, in Sharjah, 5% is levied on imports and exports (CIF Value) on majority of products	
		Tobacco and alcoholic beverages are subject to duty at higher rates:	
		• Tobacco/cigarettes (100% on CIF value) • Liquor/alcohol (50% on CIF value)	
		UAE to impose VAT on consumers from year 2018; the rates have not been finalized yet	
	Entities obliged to levy VAT		
	Taxable activities		
	Taxable activities – zero-rated (examples)		
	Exemptions (examples)		
	Refund of VAT		
	Tax liability		
	Tax rates		
	Administrative obligations		
Real Property Taxes		*Abu Dhabi*	
		Commercial: 5–10% of the annual rent	
		Residential: 5% of the annual rent	
		Dubai	
		Residential tenants: 5–15% of the annual rent	
		Commercial tenants: 5% of the annual rent	
		Banking sector: 15%	
		Sharjah	
		Residential tenants: 2% of the annual rent	
		In addition, 2% is generally charged on sale transfer of property	
Municipal Taxes		Municipal taxes are charged in some of the Emirates. In Dubai a 10% municipal tax is charged on hotel revenues and entertainment	
Stamp Duty		A land registration fee may be levied	

United Kingdom

(Rajesh Sharma, Smith & Williamson LLP, Rajesh.Sharma@smithandwilliamson.com)

1 MAIN LEGAL FORMS

Legal form Characteristics	Partnership and Limited Liability Partnership (LLP)	Private corporation (Ltd) and Public corporation (Plc)
Partners/shareholders • Number • Restrictions	• Two or more • None	• One or more • None
Directors	Management by partners (partnership) or designated members (LLP)	Management by directors[1]
Establishment	Registration with Companies House only for LLPs	Registration with Companies House or purchase off-shelf companies
Registration	Companies House and HM Revenue & Customs (HMRC)	
Minimum capital	None	£1 for Ltd and £50,000 for Plc
Liability	Partnerships: unlimited LLPs: limited to capital	Limited to capital
Governance	Partners, general meeting	Managing Director/Board of Directors, company secretary, shareholders' meeting
Audit requirements	No audit requirements for partnership No audit requirements for LLP provided: • meets definition of small LLP, and • turnover does not exceed £6.5m or • total assets do not exceed £3.26m[2]	No audit requirements for Ltd provided: • meets definition of small company, and • turnover does not exceed £6.5m or • total assets do not exceed £3.26m[2] Audit is required for Plc

---

1 Private companies must have at least one director. Public companies must have at least two directors and one secretary. Every company must have at least one director who is a natural person, ie is not a corporate body.

2 Audit exemption is also not available for subsidiaries or the parent company unless the whole group is small, nor is the exemption available for LLPs operating in certain regulated industries.

Legal form / Characteristics	Partnership and Limited Liability Partnership (LLP)	Private corporation (Ltd) and Public corporation (Plc)
Taxation	Transparent. Partners are taxed on their share of the trading profits[3]	Corporation tax on worldwide profits
Usage	Professional practices and financial organisations	Small and medium-sized enterprises usually use Ltd and larger companies seeking listing on AIM or main market use Plc

3   Investment LLPs may be treated as opaque.

II CORPORATION TAX

Legal form / Description	UK resident corporation	Permanent establishment (PE)
General description	UK corporation tax	
Taxable entities	Companies incorporated in the UK and/or overseas companies with central management and control located in the UK	PE located in the UK
Taxable income	Worldwide profits	Profits derived by PE in the UK
Calculation of taxable profits	Accounting profit is adjusted for various tax add-backs and allowances to arrive at profits chargeable to corporation tax	
Interest payments	Transfer pricing rules are in place, which require funding arrangements to be at arm's length for interest payment to remain tax deductible. From 1 April 2017, new rules will restrict interest relief for companies with net interest expense of > £2m to 30% of EBITDA	
Related party transactions	All related party transactions must take place on arm's length basis. Specific requirements to retain transfer pricing documentation with exemptions for small- and medium-sized enterprises	
Tax year, return and payment	Tax period normally coincides with accounting period, maximum of 12 months per return period Tax return must be submitted to HMRC within 12 months from the end of the accounting period Tax payment should be made 9 months and one day after the accounting period end while large companies pay tax in quarterly instalments	
Capital gains	Capital gains are subject to corporation tax at normal rates UK residential properties within the ATED regime are subject to CGT at 28%	Capital gains arising on assets used for UK trading are subject to corporation tax at normal rates UK residential properties within the ATED regime are subject to CGT at 28% Other disposals of UK residential property by a non-resident corporate are subject to CGT at 20% (NRCGT) on the portion of gains accruing during ownership on or after 6 April 2015 Gains accruing on UK residential properties since April 2015 are taxable in the UK

Description \ Legal form	UK resident corporation	Permanent establishment (PE)
Losses	Excess trading losses can be carried back against profits of the previous 12 months	Loss relief similar to resident corporations but limited to the profits of the PE
	Excess trading losses can be carried forward without time limit and offset against future profits arising from the same trade	
	These rules are being reformed from 1 April 2017 as follows:	
	• Carried-forward losses arising on or after 1 April 2017 can be set against taxable profits of different activities and taxable profits of group members • Companies with profits in excess of £5m will only be able to offset brought-forward losses (whether arising pre or post 1 April 2017) against 50% of taxable profits • More restrictive rules will apply to losses of banks	
Tax group	For group relief purposes a group comprises a parent and its 75% subsidiaries. This threshold is lowered for other corporation tax purposes	Overseas entities with UK PE can also be included in the group
Tax rate	Rate of tax will be reduced to 19% from 1 April 2017 and is expected to fall to 17% from 1 April 2020	

III   TAXES FOR INDIVIDUALS

		Residents	**Non-residents**
Income Tax	General description	Tax levied on the chargeable income of a chargeable person for a year of assessment	
	Taxable entities and taxable income	• Individuals, trustees and estates that are resident in the UK are liable to tax on their worldwide income • Special rules for non-domiciled residents	Non-residents are liable to tax on income arising in the UK, subject to provisions in double taxation agreements
	Types of taxable income	• Property income • Income from a trade, profession or vocation • Savings and investment income • Employment income • Income from trusts or estates • Miscellaneous income – annual income, profits and gains not taxed elsewhere	
	Calculation of income	• Property – accrual basis • Trading – current year basis • Savings – actual income received • Employment – income/benefit received	
	Tax year, tax assessment and tax payment	Tax year – fiscal year – 6 April to following 5 April Tax assessment – individual self-assessment returns for each taxpayer to be filed by 31 October (31 January if filed electronically) Instalments due on 31 January during and 31 July following the tax year, with the balance due on 31 January following the tax year	
	Losses	Number of reliefs available where a trading loss arises UK rental losses are pooled and carried forward to be offset against first-available rental profit, foreign rental losses pooled separately	
	Tax rates	• Personal allowance (tax-free earnings) £11,000 reduced by £1 for every £2 above £100,000 of income; increases to £11,500 beginning 6 April 2017 • Higher allowances and reliefs available for over-65s • Progressive tax rate • 20% (7.5% for dividends) for income up to the basic rate band of £32,000, increasing to £33,500 from 6 April 2017 • 40% (32.5% for dividends) for income over £32,000, increasing to £33,500 from 6 April 2017 • 45% (38.1% for dividends) for income over £150,000	Personal allowance can only be claimed by British subjects, EEA citizens and Commonwealth citizens Consultation ongoing on whether entitlement to personal allowances for non-residents should be restricted

		Residents	**Non-residents**
Capital Gains Tax (CGT)	General description	Tax on increase in the value of asset, between acquisition and disposal, not chargeable to income or corporation tax	
	Taxable entities and chargeable assets	Any person resident in the UK during the tax year in which the gain arises. Worldwide assets are chargeable for CGT	Currently no charge on assets except for gains arising on UK residential property from 6 April 2015 Temporary non-UK residents may still be charged to gains in the year they return to the UK
	Calculation of gain	• Disposal proceeds less allowable expenditure • Additional reliefs available depending on type of asset	
	Tax year, tax assessment and tax payment	Tax year – fiscal year – 6 April to following 5 April Tax assessment – reportable on same individual self-assessment as income tax (if UK residential property, also reportable on a non-resident CGT form within 30 days of sale) Tax payment due – 31 January following the tax year (or, if UK residential property, within 30 days of sale if not already within self-assessment system)	
	Losses	• Losses utilised against gains in year • Excess carried forward and set against future gains	
	Tax rates	Annual exemption – £11,100 Chargeable gain is treated as top slice of income taxed at 10% (or 18% for UK residential property or certain carried interest), or 20% (or 28% for UK residential property or certain carried interest) for the portion of the gain bringing the individual's taxable income and gains above the 20% basic rate band	
		UK domiciled	**Non-UK domiciled**[4,5]
Inheritance Tax (IHT)	General description	Tax charged on a chargeable transfer of value made by a lifetime gift or estate on death	
	Taxable entities and chargeable assets	Estate or lifetime gifts, which are not specifically excluded, situated worldwide	Estate or lifetime gifts, which are not specifically excluded, situated in the UK From 6 April 2017, UK residential property within the scope of UK IHT, regardless of ownership vehicle
	Calculation of charge	Loss in value of the donor's estate after gift has been made or value of estate on death	
	Taxable events	• Certain lifetime gifts • Estates on death and gifts made in 7 years prior to death of donor	• Certain lifetime gifts of assets situated in the UK • Assets situated in UK on death and gifts of assets situated in UK made in 7 years prior to death of donor

4 From 6 April 2017, a non-UK domiciled individual will become deemed UK domiciled for all taxes (income tax, CGT and IHT) once they have been UK resident for 15 out of the previous 20 tax years.

5 Once resident in the UK in at least 17 of the preceding 20 tax years ending with the year of transfer, treated as UK domiciled for IHT purposes. This will be reduced to 15 years from 6 April 2017.

		UK domiciled	**Non-UK domiciled**[4,5]
Inheritance Tax (IHT) – *contd*	Allowances	• Spouse exemption on all gifts • Annual exemption – £3,000 • Nil rate band – £325,000[6]	If recipient spouse is foreign domiciled and gift is from UK domiciled spouse, spouse exemption is restricted to £325,000 (on top of nil rate band of £325,000) Can elect to be treated as UK domiciled for IHT purposes
	Tax rates	• 20% on chargeable lifetime transfers • 40% on estates and gifts made 7 years prior to death of donor – the estate tax is reduced to 36% should 10% of the estate's net value be donated to an eligible UK charity • Taper relief available to gifts becoming chargeable on death	

6 An additional nil rate band for residences that pass to descendants will be introduced as follows:

2017/18	£100,000
2018/19	£125,000
2019/20	£150,000
2020/21	£175,000

The additional nil rate band is subject to a tapered reduction where the value of the estate at death exceeds £2m.

IV   WITHHOLDING TAXES

Under domestic law	Payments to residents	Payments to non-residents[7]
Dividends	Nil	Nil
Interest	Nil to corporate entities 20% to non-corporates	20%
Royalties	20%	20%[8,9]
On payments to artists and sportsmen	Normal income tax rates apply	20%

Reduced rate available under the relevant Double Taxation Treaty			
Country	Dividends[10]	Interest	Royalties[11]
Albania	Nil	6%	Nil
Antigua and Barbuda	Nil	20%	Nil
Argentina	Nil	12%	15%[12]
Armenia	Nil	5%	5%
Australia	Nil	10%	5%
Austria	Nil	Nil	Nil
Azerbaijan	Nil	10%	10%[12]
Bahrain	Nil	Nil	Nil
Bangladesh	Nil	10%	10%
Barbados	Nil	Nil	Nil[12]
Belarus[8]	Nil	Nil	Nil
Belgium	Nil	10%	Nil
Belize	Nil	20%	Nil
Bolivia	Nil	15%	15%
Bosnia-Herzegovina	Nil	10%	10%
Botswana	Nil	10%	10%
Brunei	Nil	20%	Nil
Bulgaria	Nil	5%	5%
Canada	Nil	10%[12]	10%[12]
Chile	Nil	15%	10%
China	Nil	10%[12]	10%[12]
Croatia	Nil	5%	5%
Cyprus	Nil	10%	Nil
Czech Republic	Nil	Nil	10%[12]
Denmark	Nil	Nil	Nil
Egypt	Nil	15%[12]	15%
Estonia	Nil	10%[12]	10%[12]
Ethiopia	Nil	5%	7.5%

---

7   Reduced rates of withholding tax may apply where there is an appropriate double tax treaty.
8   Payments of interest and royalties between EU associated companies (ie at least 25% interest in the share capital is required) can be made gross if the payer believes that payee is entitled to the exemption under the EU Directive.
9   Payments made after 17 March 2016 are subject to the anti-avoidance rules under the BEPS proposals.

Reduced rate available under the relevant Double Taxation Treaty			
Country	Dividends[10]	Interest	Royalties[11]
Falkland Islands	Nil	Nil[12]	Nil[12]
Faroe Islands	Nil	Nil	Nil
Fiji	Nil	10%	15%[12]
Finland	Nil	Nil	Nil
France	Nil	Nil	Nil
Gambia	Nil	15%	12.5%
Georgia	Nil	Nil	Nil
Germany	Nil	Nil[12]	Nil[12]
Ghana	Nil	12.5%	12.5%
Greece	Nil	Nil	Nil
Grenada	Nil	20%	Nil
Guyana	Nil	15%[12]	10%[12]
Hong Kong	Nil	Nil	3%
Hungary	Nil	Nil	Nil
Iceland	Nil	Nil	Nil
India	Nil	15%	15%[12]
Indonesia	Nil	10%	15%[12]
Ireland	Nil	Nil	Nil
Isle of Man	Nil	20%	20%
Israel	Nil	15%	Nil[12]
Italy	Nil	10%	8%
Ivory Coast	Nil	15%	10%
Jamaica	Nil	12.5%[12]	10%
Japan	Nil	10	Nil
Jordan	Nil	10%	10%
Kazakhstan	Nil	10%[12]	10%[12]
Kenya	Nil	15%	15%
Kiribati	Nil	20%	Nil
Korea, Republic of	Nil	10%[12]	10%[12]
Kosovo	Nil	Nil	Nil
Kuwait	Nil	Nil	10%
Latvia	Nil	10%[12]	10%
Lesotho	Nil	10%	10%
Liechtenstein	Nil	Nil	Nil
Libya	Nil	Nil	Nil
Lithuania	Nil	10%[12]	10%[12]

10 On or after 17 March 2016, no withholding taxes on outbound dividends under the domestic legislation.

11 Different rates may apply for copyright royalties for literary, dramatic, musical and artistic work.

12 There are several rules and exemptions regarding the levels of these withholding taxes; as treaties are not identical, guidance is recommended to be sought in all cases.

Reduced rate available under the relevant Double Taxation Treaty			
Country	Dividends[10]	Interest	Royalties[11]
Luxembourg	Nil	Nil	5%
Macedonia	Nil	10%	Nil
Malawi	Nil	Nil	Nil
Malaysia	Nil	10%[12]	8%
Malta	Nil	10%	10%
Mauritius	Nil	20%[12]	15%
Mexico	Nil	15%[12]	10%
Moldova	Nil	5%[12]	5%
Mongolia	Nil	10%	5%
Montenegro	Nil	10%	10%
Montserrat	Nil	20%	Nil
Morocco	Nil	10%	10%
Myanmar	Nil	20%	Nil
Namibia	Nil	20%	Nil
Netherlands	Nil	Nil	Nil
New Zealand	Nil	10%	10%
Nigeria	Nil	12.5%	12.5%
Norway	Nil	Nil	Nil
Oman	Nil	Nil	8%[12]
Pakistan	Nil	15%	12.5%
Panama	Nil	5%	5%
Papua New Guinea	Nil	10%	10%
Philippines	Nil	15%[12]	25%[12]
Poland	Nil	5%	5%
Portugal	Nil	10%	5%
Qatar	Nil	Nil	5%
Romania	Nil	10%	15%[12]
Russian Federation	Nil	Nil	Nil
St Christopher (St Kitts) and Nevis	Nil	20%	Nil
Saudi Arabia	Nil	Nil	8%[12]
Serbia	Nil	10%	10%
Sierra Leone	Nil	20%	Nil
Singapore	Nil	5%	8%
Slovakia	Nil	Nil	10%[12]
Slovenia	Nil	5%	5%
Solomon Islands	Nil	20%	Nil
South Africa	Nil	Nil	Nil
Spain	Nil	Nil	Nil
Sri Lanka	Nil	10%[12]	10%[12]
Sudan	Nil	15%	10%
Swaziland	Nil	20%	Nil
Sweden	Nil	Nil	Nil
Switzerland	Nil	Nil	Nil
Taiwan	Nil	10%	10%

Reduced rate available under the relevant Double Taxation Treaty			
Country	Dividends[10]	Interest	Royalties[11]
Tajikistan	Nil	10%	7%
Thailand	Nil	20%[12]	15%[12]
Trinidad and Tobago	Nil	10%	10%[12]
Tunisia	Nil	12%	15%
Turkey	Nil	15%	10%
Turkmenistan	Nil	Nil	Nil
Tuvalu	Nil	20%	Nil
Uganda	Nil	15%	15%
Ukraine	Nil	Nil	Nil
United States[13]	Nil	Nil	Nil
Uzbekistan	Nil	5%[12]	5%[12]
Venezuela	Nil	5%[12]	7%[12]
Vietnam	Nil	10%	10%
Zambia	Nil	10%	5%
Zimbabwe	Nil	10%[12]	10%

Note: the above rates are only available provided the specific Treaty criteria are satisfied. It is possible that lower rates than those shown above may be available provided certain criteria are satisfied. As treaties will not be identical, guidance should be sought in all cases.

---

13 The US and UK also have a FATCA agreement in place which requires non-US financial institutions to enter into an agreement with the IRS to report information on US citizens working overseas. If this information is not provided, a 30% withholding tax on US source payments will be levied.

V   INDIRECT TAXES

This section gives a brief overview of the following indirect taxes: VAT, Stamp duty land tax (SDLT) and stamp duty (SD). There are a number of other indirect taxes not covered below.

		Residents	Non-residents
Value Added Tax	General description	Tax on the supply of goods and services	
	Entities obliged to register for VAT	• Any individual, partnership, corporation or other body, which carries out taxable activities in the UK, subject to turnover threshold of £83,000 (from 1 April 2016) • On request, if turnover from taxable activities carried out in the UK is below £83,000 (from 1 April 2016) • On request, if supplies are made outside the UK by a UK established business. The supplies must be outside the scope of UK VAT with the right to recover related input tax (depending on the nature of the supplies being sold outside the UK, ie would these supplies attract VAT had they been supplied within the UK?) • Other situations may also arise, eg distance selling, sale of assets, acquisitions from other EC Member States and services received from outside the UK • For overseas traders operating in the UK, there is no VAT registration threshold	
	Taxable activities	• Supply of goods and services, import of goods, intra-Community acquisition of goods, etc unless specifically exempted • Place of supply of goods and services must be in the UK (following Title V of Directive 2006/112)	
	Taxable activities – zero-rated (examples)	• Export of goods and supply of services to another EU business • First sale or long lease (over 21 years) of new residential accommodation by developer • Sale of books and printing of leaflets, children's clothing, transport, etc	
	Exemptions (examples)	• Transactions related to the sale or lease of any property located in UK (option to tax for VAT available for commercial property) • Banking and insurance services • Educational supplies • Certain welfare services including hospital and medical care services	
	Refund of VAT	• VAT paid on supplies and services is deductible as input tax, if incurred in the course or furtherance of the business and for the purpose of making taxable supplies (including zero-rated supplies) • There is no credit for input tax incurred which relates to the provision of exempt supplies • Where mixed supplies occur (taxable and exempt supplies), subject to de minimis provisions, input tax must be apportioned and recovered according to a partial exemption method. Agreement with HMRC is required for non-standard partial exemption methods	• EC VAT refund scheme 2008/09 Directive refund system for non-established business established within the EC, providing its business is not otherwise required to be registered in the UK • EC 13th Directive VAT refund scheme for non-established business established outside the EC, providing its business is not otherwise required to be registered in the UK • Strict time limits apply to claims

		Residents	**Non-residents**
Value Added Tax – *contd*	Tax liability	• Normally the supplier of goods and services within the UK is responsible for charging VAT • Reverse charge for certain supplies of goods and services (eg consultancy services received from businesses established outside the UK)	
	Tax rates	• Standard rate = 20% • Reduced rate = 5% (eg certain residential conversions, and other supplies) • Zero rate = 0%	
	Administrative obligations	• Formal requirements concerning business records and invoices • Quarterly self-assessment VAT return plus quarterly payment of any VAT liability to HMRC (special arrangements and schemes available for smaller businesses and repayment businesses where monthly returns are possible) • VAT groups are allowed subject to certain requirements • Certain arrangements may need to be disclosed • VAT identification number must be shown on all invoices issued • EC Invoicing Directive must be adhered to • Filing of EC Sales List and Intrastat declarations (only for intra-EU transactions)	• Registration for VAT purposes, if making supplies of goods and services in the UK
Real Property Taxes		• Stamp Duty Land Tax – transactions related to the sale or lease of property located in the UK, with the purchaser liable • Tax is between 0% and 15% depending on value of transaction and whether the property is residential or not • Special rates of 15% will apply to residential properties that are owned through a non-natural person where the value exceeds £0.5 million, subject to reliefs and exemptions • A surcharge of 3% applies for additional properties acquired	
Stamp Duty		Transactions related to purchase and sale of securities	
		0.5% with a range of exemptions and reliefs	

United States

(Len Wolf, The Wolf Group, PC, l.wolf@thewolfgroup.com)

I MAIN LEGAL FORMS

Legal form / Characteristics	Partnership and Limited Liability Partnership (LLP)	Corporation (public or private)
Partners/shareholders • Number • Restrictions	• No limit on the number of partners • Foreign persons may be partner/members, subject to special withholding rules	• No limit on number of corporate shareholders • Foreign persons may own shares of a U.S. corporation
Directors	N/A	No limitation
Establishment	Partnership Agreement Articles of Organisation	Articles of Incorporation
Registration	Registration with local and state authorities may be required	
Minimum capital	No minimum capital requirements	No minimum capital requirements
Liability	LLP: limited liability General Partnership: general partner has unlimited liability	Limited to capital
Governance	By state law	
Audit requirements	No statutory audit requirements imposed	No statutory audit requirements imposed upon private companies (only public companies)
Taxation	Transparent	Taxable on worldwide income

II CORPORATION TAX

Description \ Legal form	Resident Corporation	Permanent Establishment (PE)
General description	Corporation tax	
Taxable entities	Corporations incorporated in United States	PEs trading in United States
Taxable income	Worldwide profits including income of foreign branches	Business profits attributable to a PE in the U.S. with considerations for double taxation treaties
Calculation of taxable profits	Accounting profit is adjusted for various tax add-backs and allowances to arrive at profits chargeable to corporation tax	
Interest payments	Deductible subject to thin capitalisation restrictions	
Related party transactions	All related party transactions should take place on arm's-length basis	
Tax year, return and payment	Companies may use calendar or fiscal year Returns are filed on the 15th day of the third month after the year-end Payment is due on or before the due date for the tax return	
Capital gains	Capital gains are taxed at the same rates as ordinary income and may only be offset by capital losses (excess capital loss may be carried back 3 years and forward 5 years to offset capital gains in other years, subject to certain restrictions)	
Losses	Net operating losses can be carried back 2 years and then forward 20 years (Election may be made to waive the entire carry back period by the return due date including extensions)	
Tax group	Tax consolidation permissible for 80% owned subsidiaries	
Tax rate	2016 rates: *Taxable Income ($)* *Tax rate* Up to 50,000 15% 50,001–75,000 25% 75,001–100,000 34% 100,001–335,000 39% 335,001–10,000,000 34% 10,000,001–15,000,000 35% 15,000,001–18,333,333 38% 18,333,334 and above 35%	

III TAXES FOR INDIVIDUALS

		Residents	Non-residents
Income Tax	General description	Tax levied on the chargeable income of a person for the year of assessment	
	Taxable entities and taxable income	Residents are taxed on their worldwide income	Non-residents are generally taxed on U.S. source income
	Types of taxable income	• Property income (usually rent) • Income from capital investment (interest, sale of goodwill, dividends, royalties, annuities) • Income from business activities • Income from personal services or pensions	
	Calculation of income	Gross income as reduced by deductible items and allowances	
	Tax year, tax assessment and tax payment	Tax year is generally a calendar year Individual income tax returns must be filed by 15th day of the fourth month of the following year (eg 15 April) The full tax amount is due on or before the return filing date; otherwise penalties and interest may accrue	
	Losses	Losses from a passive activity cannot offset other types of income Net operation losses ('NOLs') must be carried back 2 years and then any remaining NOL can be carried forward for up to 20 years, or the taxpayer can elect to waive the carry-back and only carry forward	
	Tax rates	2016 rates:	

2016 rates:

Filing Status: Single

Taxable Income ($)	Tax rate
Up to 9,275	10%
9,275–37,650	15%
37,650–91,150	25%
91,150–190,150	28%
190,150–413,350	33%
413,350–415,050	35%
415,050 and above	39.6%

Filing Status: Married Filing Separately

Taxable Income ($)	Tax rate
Up to 9,275	10%
9,275–37,650	15%
37,650–75,950	25%
75,950–115,725	28%
115,725–206,675	33%
206,675–233,475	35%
233,475 and above	39.6%

Filing Status: Married Filing Jointly or Qualifying Widow(er)

Taxable Income ($)	Tax rate
Up to 18,550	10%
18,550–75,300	15%
75,300–151,900	25%
151,900–231,450	28%
231,450–413,500	33%
413,500–466,950	35%
466,950 and above	39.6%

Filing Status: Head of Household

Taxable Income ($)	Tax rate
Up to 13,250	10%
13,250–50,400	15%
50,400–130,150	25%
130,150–210,800	28%
210,800–413,350	33%
413,350–441,000	35%
441,000 and above	39.6%

		Residents	**Non-residents**
Capital Gains Tax (CGT)	General description	Gains realized from the difference between the acquisition and disposal price of an asset	
	Taxable entities and chargeable assets	Assessed as part of personal income	
	Calculation of gain	Gross proceeds less adjusted tax basis and selling expenses = capital gain	
	Tax year, tax assessment and tax payment	Reported with Individual Income Tax Return (see Taxes for Individuals)	
	Losses	Capital losses may be deducted from capital gains or carried forward indefinitely Losses of up to $3,000 may be deducted from ordinary income	Cannot carry forward loss and cannot claim net loss in the current year
	Tax rates	Short-term capital gains (assets held one year or less) are taxed as ordinary income subject to ordinary tax rates Long-term (assets held more than one year) capital gains are generally taxed at 15% or 20%	Not subject to capital gains tax, unless a non-resident spends more than 182 days in the U.S. during the year and his/her tax home is in the U.S., in which case a 30% tax rate applies
		U.S. domiciled	**Non-U.S. domiciled**
Inheritance Tax (IHT)	General description	Tax on the transfer of property	
	Taxable entities and chargeable assets	All worldwide assets included	U.S. situs assets
	Calculation of charge	Gross fair market value of gifts, or net estate less allowances	
	Taxable events	Transfer by gift or upon death	
	Allowances	For 2016 Estate tax and lifetime gift tax exemption amount is $5,450,000 Annual gift tax exclusion amount is $14,000 Gifts to a U.S. citizen spouse are entitled to an unlimited marital deduction On gifts to a non-U.S. citizen spouse, the marital deduction is limited to transfers of up to $148,000	For 2016 Estate tax exemption amount is $60,000 No lifetime gift exemption but are entitled to use of the annual gift tax exclusion amount of $14,000
	Tax rates	For 2016, the top federal estate and gift tax rate is 40% State-level estate tax rate varies by state	

IV WITHHOLDING TAXES

Under domestic law	Payments to residents	Payments to non-residents
Dividends	Nil	30% or lower treaty rate
Interest	Nil	Nil
Royalties	Nil	30% or lower treaty rate
On payments to artists and sportsmen	Nil	30% or lower treaty rate

Reduced rate available under the relevant Double Taxation Treaty				
Country	Dividends		Interest	Royalties
	Dividends paid by U.S. corporations in general	Dividends qualifying for direct dividend rate		
Australia	15%	5%	10%	5%
Austria	15%	5%	Nil	Nil
Bangladesh	15%	10%	10%	10%
Barbados	15%	5%	5%	5%
Belgium	15%	5%	Nil	Nil
Bulgaria	10%	5%	5%	5%
Canada	15%	5%	Nil	Nil
China, People's Republic of	10%	10%	10%	10%
Commonwealth of Independent States (CIS)	30%	30%	Nil	Nil
Cyprus	15%	5%	10%	Nil
Czech Republic	15%	5%	Nil	Nil
Denmark	15%	5%	Nil	Nil
Egypt	15%	5%	15%	15%
Estonia	15%	5%	10%	10%
Finland	15%	5%	Nil	Nil
France	15%	5%	Nil	Nil
Germany	15%	5%	Nil	Nil
Greece	30%	30%	Nil	Nil
Hungary	15%	5%	Nil	Nil
Iceland	15%	5%	Nil	Nil
India	25%	15%	15%	15%
Indonesia	15%	10%	10%	10%
Ireland	15%	5%	Nil	Nil
Israel	25%	12.5%	17.5%	10%
Italy	15%	5%	10%	Nil
Jamaica	15%	10%	12.5%	10%
Japan	10%	5%	10%	Nil
Kazakhstan	15%	5%	10%	10%
Korea, South	15%	10%	12%	10%
Latvia	15%	5%	10%	10%
Lithuania	15%	5%	10%	10%
Luxembourg	15%	5%	Nil	Nil
Malta	15%	5%	10%	10%

Reduced rate available under the relevant Double Taxation Treaty				
Country	Dividends		Interest	Royalties
	Dividends paid by U.S. corporations in general	Dividends qualifying for direct dividend rate		
Mexico	10%	5%	15%	10%
Morocco	15%	10%	15%	10%
Netherlands	15%	5%	Nil	Nil
New Zealand	15%	5%	10%	5%
Norway	15%	15%	10%	Nil
Pakistan	30%	15%	30%	Nil
Philippines	25%	20%	15%	15%
Poland	15%	5%	Nil	10%
Portugal	15%	5%	10%	10%
Romania	10%	10%	10%	10%
Russia	10%	5%	Nil	Nil
Slovakia	15%	5%	Nil	10%
Slovenia	15%	5%	5%	5%
South Africa	15%	5%	Nil	Nil
Spain	15%	10%	15%	5%
Sri Lanka	15%	15%	10%	10%
Sweden	15%	5%	Nil	Nil
Switzerland	15%	5%	Nil	Nil
Thailand	15%	10%	15%	5%
Trinidad & Tobago	30%	30%	30%	Nil
Tunisia	20%	14%	15%	15%
Turkey	20%	15%	15%	10%
Ukraine	15%	5%	Nil	10%
United Kingdom	15%	5%	Nil	Nil
Venezuela	15%	5%	10%	10%

Note: the above rates are provided for general guidance only and only available provided the specific Treaty criteria are satisfied. It is possible that lower rates than those shown above may be available, provided certain criteria are satisfied. Please refer to IRS Publication 901 (Table 1) for a comprehensive list of reduced treaty rates.

As treaties will not be identical, guidance should be sought in all cases.

V INDIRECT TAXES

		Residents	Non-residents
Value Added Tax (VAT)	General description	Tax on the supply of goods and services	
	Entities obliged to levy VAT	The United States does not impose a VAT tax. Rather, each state (and many localities) typically imposes a sales tax on taxable sales (as defined in each state). Tax is imposed on the sale to the ultimate consumer	
	Tax rates	Each state defines its own tax rate: currently from 0%–10% depending on the state	
Real Property Taxes		Varies by state and county	

Uruguay

(Luis Rafael Normey, Maria Fernanda Normey, Normey Peruzzo & Asociados, rnormey@npyas-nexia.com.uy, fnormey@npyas.nexia.com.uy)

I MAIN LEGAL FORMS

Legal form / Characteristics	Partnership and Limited Liability Partnership (LLP)	Private corporation (Ltd) and public corporation (Plc)
Partners/shareholders • Number • Restrictions	• Two or more • None	• One or more • None
Directors	Management by partners	Management by directors
Establishment	Notarial Deed	Articles of Incorporation
Registration	Commercial Register. The shareholder must register with the Central Bank	
Minimum capital	Partnership: none LLP: none	None
Liability	Partnership: unlimited for all partners LLP: limited for all partners	Limited for all shareholders
Governance	Managing partners General partners' meeting	Board of Directors Shareholders' meetings
Audit requirements	Only for large enterprises and for those with loans greater than U$2m	
Taxation	Transparent	Corporation tax

II   CORPORATION TAX

Description \ Legal form	Resident corporation	Permanent establishment (PE)
General description	Tax on earnings derived from industrial, commercial and rural activities or services	
Taxable entities	Resident corporations or non-resident corporations with PE in Uruguay	
Taxable income	Income received in Uruguay	
Calculation of taxable profits	Accounting profit is adjusted for various tax add-backs and allowances to arrive at taxable profits	
Interest payments	No thin capitalisation rules	
Related party transactions	Transfer pricing rules apply to cross-border transactions	
Tax year, return and payment	Tax year = business year (calendar year-end or any other year-end) Payment and tax return = 4 months Monthly prepayments, final payment or refund after tax assessment	
Capital gains	Capital gains on disposal of shares and listed shares are exempt Other gains included with taxable income	
Losses	5-year loss carry back possible, with a ceiling of 5% of net tax revenue	
Tax group	None but dividends from subsidiaries are exempt	
Tax rate	25%	

Note: in late 2015, the government decided to eliminate the fiscal adjustment that was made to correct the effect of inflation. This adjustment allowed to deduct the loss (or taxed the profits) that the companies had for the effect of inflation.

III TAXES FOR INDIVIDUALS

		Residents	Non-residents
Income Tax	General description	Income tax levied on the chargeable income of a chargeable person for a year of assessment	
	Taxable entities and taxable income	Individuals with habitual residence in the country deriving income in Uruguay	Individuals without habitual residence in the country but deriving income in Uruguay
	Types of taxable income	• Property income • Income from capital investment (interest, sale of goodwill, dividends, royalties, annuities) • Income from personal services or pensions • Income derived from professional services or employment income • Gains on disposal of capital assets	
	Tax year, tax assessment and tax payment	Tax returns are filed on a fiscal basis and tax liabilities paid on a monthly basis The income tax on dividends must be paid after the income that generated is more than three years, even if the company decides not distribute it. This tax is retained by the companies	
	Losses	Losses can be carried back for 2 years and offset against similar source of income	

	Tax rates	• Standard rate = none
		• Employment income: progressive rates from 0–36%
		• Capital gains or rental income: 12%
		• Profits: 7%
		• Social security:
		  – employers 19%
		  – employees 24%
			• General rate = 12%
			• Profits: 7%

Capital Gains Tax (CGT)	General description	There is no capital gains tax in Uruguay. Gains are taxed as part of ordinary taxable income	
Inheritance Tax (IHT)	General description	No IHT in Uruguay	

IV   WITHHOLDING TAXES

Under domestic law	Payments to residents	Payments to non-residents
Dividends	7%	7%
Interest	3% deposits in local currency 12% deposits in other currency	3% or 5% deposits in local currency 12% deposits in other currency
Royalties	12%	12%
On payments to artists and sportsmen	12%	12%

Reduced rate available under the relevant Double Taxation Treaty			
Country	Dividends	Interest	Royalties
Korea	5%[4]	10%	10%
Ecuador	10%[2]	15%	10%
Finland	5%[2]	10%	5% over software 10% over copyright
Germany	5%[1]	10%	10%
India	5%	10%	10%
Liechtenstein	5%[2]	10%	5% over copyright 10% the rest
Malta	5%[2]	10%	5% over copyright 10% the rest
Mexico	5%[2]	10%	10%
Portugal	5%[2]	10%	10%
Romania	5%[2]	10%	10%
Spain	5%[3]	10%	10%
Switzerland	5%[3]	10%	10%

Note: The above rates are only available provided the specific Treaty criteria are satisfied. It is possible that lower rates than those shown above may be available provided that certain criteria are satisfied. As treaties will not be identical, guidance should be sought in all cases.

The agreement signed with France, Iceland, Canada, Denmark, Greenland, Norway is only to exchange tax information. There is also an agreement signed with Argentina and with Hungary, but they are only to exchange tax information and allow deduction of taxes, but not to reduce rates.

Uruguay has signed other international agreements, to avoid double taxation and to prevent fiscal evasion regarding income taxes and patrimony taxes, with Faroe Islands, Sweden and Greenland. These agreements are pending approval in parliament.

---

1 Only if beneficiary is a company which holds at least 10% of the capital of the company paying dividends.
2 Only if beneficiary is a company which holds at least 25% of the capital of the company paying dividends.
3 Only if beneficiary is a company which holds at least 75% of the capital of the company paying dividends.
4 Only if beneficiary is a company which holds at least 20% of the capital of the company paying dividends.

V   INDIRECT TAXES

<table>
<tr><th></th><th></th><th>Residents</th><th>Non-residents</th></tr>
<tr><td rowspan="9">Value Added Tax (VAT)</td><td>General description</td><td colspan="2">Tax on the supply of goods, services and imports</td></tr>
<tr><td>Entities obliged to levy VAT</td><td colspan="2">All corporations and individuals involved in economic activities</td></tr>
<tr><td>Taxable activities</td><td colspan="2">Supply of goods and services in Uruguay, and import of goods</td></tr>
<tr><td>Taxable activities – zero-rated (examples)</td><td colspan="2">Export of goods and services</td></tr>
<tr><td>Exemptions (examples)</td><td colspan="2">• Agricultural goods and machines
• Educational material
• Milk
• Oil
• Exports</td></tr>
<tr><td>Refund of VAT</td><td colspan="2">VAT on supplies may be refunded when a corporation has more income from exports than from supplies in Uruguay</td></tr>
<tr><td>Tax rates</td><td colspan="2">10%–22% depending on the nature of goods and services</td></tr>
<tr><td>Administrative obligations</td><td colspan="2">Monthly returns and payments</td></tr>
<tr><td colspan="2">Real Property Taxes</td><td colspan="2">4% (2% for each part of the operation: the seller, and the purchaser)</td></tr>
<tr><td colspan="2">Stamp Duty</td><td colspan="2">None</td></tr>
</table>

Venezuela

*(Luis Cardona, Cardona & Avila Contadores Públicos,
luis.cardona@nexia.com.ve)*

I MAIN LEGAL FORMS

Legal form / Characteristics	Partnership and Limited Liability Partnership (LLP)	Private corporation (Ltd) and Public corporation (Plc)
Partners/shareholders • Number • Restrictions	• Two or more, but it can be one owner after initial registration • None	• Two or more, but it can be one owner after the initial registration • None
Directors	Managed by partners – board of directors can be appointed	Managed by partners – board of directors can be appointed
Establishment	Register Offices	Register Offices
Registration	Register Offices SENIAT (Tax Authority) Foreign Investments Superintendency (only for foreign companies)	Register Offices SENIAT (Tax Authority) Foreign Investments Superintendency (only for foreign companies) Securities and Exchange Superintendency (only public companies)
Minimum Capital	Partnerships: none LLPs: VEB 2,000	None
Liability	Partnerships: Unlimited LLPs: Limited to capital	Limited to capital
Governance	Partners General Meeting	Managing Director/Board of Directors Shareholders' meeting
Audit requirements	No audit requirements	Requested for listed companies
Taxation	Partnerships: Partners are taxed on share of their partnership profit LLPs: ruled by income tax law	Ruled by income tax law

II   CORPORATION TAX

Legal Form / Description	Resident corporation	Permanent Establishment (PE)
General description	Income Tax Law	
Taxable entities	Companies incorporated within Venezuelan territory	PE located in Venezuela
Taxable income	Worldwide profits	Worldwide profits from activities within Venezuela
Calculation of taxable profits	Accounting profit is adjusted for non-taxable and non-deductible items. Also, an inflation adjustment is required, as part of the fiscal net profit calculation. The inflation adjustment is not available for banks	
Interest payments	Interest on loans invested in the production of income is deductible. Transfer pricing rules are in place, which require funding arrangements to be at arm's length for interest payments to remain tax deductible	
Related party transactions	All related party transactions must take place on an arm's length basis. The Transfer pricing system under the Income tax law is based on all the OECD guidelines and requirements	
Tax year, return and payment	Tax period must coincide with accounting period, with a maximum of 12 months per return period	
	Tax declaration and payment must be made within 3 months after the end of the accounting period	
Capital gains	Income Tax Law creates a proportional tax on dividends through taxing the payer's net income in excess of their declared net taxable income	
	Foreign companies operating through a PE will be required to pay tax of 34% on the difference between book income and net taxable income for the year, being the amount deemed remitted overseas as a dividend	
	This dividend will not be presumed where the branch proved, to the satisfaction of the Tax Administration, that the amount was reinvested. This reinvestment will need to stay in the country for at least 5 years	
Inflation Adjustment	Inflation adjustment will not apply to special taxpayers (appointed as such by tax authorities), or to banks and financial companies	
Losses	Inflation adjustment losses can be offset against profits for only 1 year	
Tax group	Groups are not considered to be a single taxpayer. Each member of the group is liable to taxation for its own profits	

Description / Legal Form	Resident corporation	Permanent Establishment (PE)
Tax rate	Corporation and limited liability companies in Venezuela are subject to progressive taxation, under Tariff No 2, based on the company's net income converted into Fiscal Units where the value of the Fiscal Unit will be adjusted by the Taxation Administration within the first 15 days of each year. The current value of the Fiscal Unit is 1 FU = VEBs. 177.00 (US\$17.70 at official rate of VEBs. 10.00:US\$1). The value of the Fiscal Unit is adjusted at the beginning of each year following the consent of the Permanent Finance Committees of the National Assembly. That annual adjustment reflects the variation in the National Consumer Price Index (NCPI), published by the Central Bank of Venezuela in accordance with the provisions of the Venezuelan Organic Tax Code	
	Tariff No 2	
	For the portion up to 2,000 FU: 15% less 0 FU	
	For the portion between 2,000 and 3,000 FU: 22% less 140 FU	
	For the portion exceeding 3,000 FU: 34% less 500 FU	
	In the case of architects, engineers, accountants, attorneys and other professional advisers organised into partnerships rather than companies, the partnerships are not subject to taxation, but the partners are taxed individually on their earnings (see Tariff No 1)	
	Special tax rates	
	Individuals and other taxpayers falling into the same category, as well as other categories of taxpayers not engaged in the exploitation of natural resources, who earn income in the form of royalties and similar payments from the exploitation of mines, are subject to a 60% tax rate. Taxpayers other than individuals and others falling into the same category, engaged in exploitation of hydrocarbons and related activities, are subject to a 67.7% tax rate (Tariff No 3) on their earnings, including those from outside Venezuela. Nevertheless, companies whether national or foreign, which are incorporated under association contracts pursuant to the Organic Law Reserving the Hydrocarbon Industry and Trade to the State or the national-interest contracts for which provision is made in the National Constitution are subject to the ordinary income tax rules established in the Income Tax Law for corporations and taxpayers treated in the same way as corporations as mentioned before	
	Proportional rate of 40% for banking and financial activities, as well as insurance and related activities	

III   TAXES FOR INDIVIDUALS

<table>
<tr><th></th><th></th><th>Residents</th><th>Non-residents</th></tr>
<tr><td rowspan="8">Income Tax</td><td>General description</td><td colspan="2">Tax levied on the chargeable income of a chargeable person for a calendar year</td></tr>
<tr><td>Taxable entities and taxable income</td><td>All individuals who reside in Venezuela, or have been more than 183 continuous days in the country, are liable to tax when their net enrichment equivalent is one thousand (1,000.00) Fiscal Units or more during the fiscal year</td><td>Also, non-residents are liable to tax on a global basis on income arising in and from activities undertaken in Venezuela, but subject to provisions in double taxation agreements</td></tr>
<tr><td>Types of taxable income</td><td colspan="2">• Employment income
• Investment income
• Business income
• Capital gains</td></tr>
<tr><td>Calculation of income</td><td>Gross income less permitted expenses. The amount is then converted into Fiscal Units (FU), which will compensate for the effects of inflation</td><td>Gross income less permitted expenses. The amount is then converted into Fiscal Units (FU), which will compensate for the effects of inflation</td></tr>
<tr><td>Tax year, tax assessment and tax payment</td><td colspan="2">Fiscal year for individual is calendar year (1 January–31 December)

Tax must be declared and paid no later than 31 March of the subsequent year</td></tr>
<tr><td>Losses</td><td colspan="2">Excess trading losses can be offset against profits for 3 subsequent periods</td></tr>
<tr><td>Tax rates</td><td>For the portion up to 1,000 FU: 6% less 0 FU

For the portion between 1,000 and 1,500 FU: 9% less 30 FU

For the portion between 1,500 and 2,000 FU: 12% less 75 FU

For the portion between 2,000 and 2,500 FU: 16% less 155 FU

For the portion between 2,500 and 3,000 FU: 20% less 255 FU

For the portion between 3,000 and 4,000 FU: 24% less 375 FU

For the portion between 4,000 and 6,000 FU: 29% less 575 FU

For the portion exceeding 6,000 FU: 34% less 875 FU</td><td>Income received by non-residents is subject to a flat 34% of tax</td></tr>
</table>

		Residents	Non-residents
Capital Gains Tax (CGT)	General description	Dividends and capital gains are included within taxable income and are subject to all above-mentioned conditions for individuals	
	Taxable entities and chargeable assets		
	Calculation of gain		
	Tax year, tax assessment and tax payment		
	Losses		
	Tax rates		

		Resident	Non-resident
Inheritance Tax (IHT)	General description	All beneficiaries of inheritances and legacies comprising movable property or estates, or gifts of immoveable property or shares/stock located in Venezuela will be subject to *Impuesto sobre Sucesiones y Donaciones*	
	Taxable entities and chargeable assets	• Stocks, bonds and securities issued in Venezuela and issued abroad by companies incorporated or domiciled in Venezuela • Stocks, bonds and other securities issued outside Venezuela by foreign companies which are owned by persons resident in Venezuela • The rights or actions that fall on property located in Venezuela • Personal rights or legal obligations whose source is in Venezuela	
	Calculation of charge	Net assets left by the deceased are determined by subtracting from total assets all liabilities, as permitted within the rules and limitations of this law In determining the net estate, exempt assets are not included. The amount of tax payable is calculated based on the net assets left by the deceased after subtracting the value of legacies and charges for the benefit of others and applying any exemptions available. The share of the legatees' taxable income is calculated as the value of the property or goods that are comprised in the legacy, less any available exemptions	
	Taxable events		
	Allowances		
	Tax rates	The rates range from 1% to 55% depending upon the taxable value and the relationship between the two persons	

IV   WITHHOLDING TAXES

Under domestic law	Payments to residents	Payments to non-residents
Dividends	34%	34%
Interest	3% less Bs. 442.50	34%
Royalties	Nil	34%
On payments to artists and sportsmen	3% less Bs. 442.50	34%

Reduced rate available under the relevant Double Taxation Treaty			
Country	Dividends	Interest	Royalties
Belgium	15%	10%	5%
Czech Republic	10%	10%	12%
France	15%	5%	5%
Germany	15%	5%	5%
Italy	10%	10%	10%
Mexico	5%	15%	10%
Netherlands	10%	5%	10%
Norway	10%	15%	12%
Portugal	10%	10%	12%
Sweden	10%	10%	10%
Switzerland	10%	5%	5%
Trinidad	10%	15%	10%
United Kingdom	10%	5%	7%
United States	15%	10%	10%

Note: the above rates are only available provided the specific Treaty criteria are satisfied. It is possible that lower rates than those shown above may be available provided certain criteria are satisfied. As treaties will not be identical, guidance should be sought in all cases.

V   INDIRECT TAXES

		Residents	Non-residents
Value Added Tax (VAT)	General description	VAT became effective on 1 June 1999 (reformed on 5 May 1999) and is applicable to economic agents	
	Entities obliged to levy VAT	The following categories of taxpayers are subject to VAT: • Individuals or companies usually selling tangible goods • Importers of tangible goods and services • Individuals or companies usually performing services of an independent nature • Public agencies or enterprises owned by the nation, the states, municipalities or independent public institutions which usually conduct taxable activities, as well as occasional taxpayers, the latter being importers of goods or services not falling into any of the preceding categories	
	Taxable activities	The obligation to pay VAT arises from the following activities: • Sales and removal or disposal of tangible personal goods located in Venezuela or nationalised • Permanent importation of tangible goods • Importation of services to be used in Venezuela • Rendering of services in Venezuela on an independent basis	
	Taxable activities – zero-rated (examples)	All activities described above will be zero-rated when those activities take place in Nueva Esparta State	
	Exemptions (examples)	• Non-permanent imports of goods which enter the country under the temporary admission and drawback regimes; sales of such personal goods as fiscal instruments, stocks, bonds • mortgage bonds, etc and, in general, transactions and services performed by banks, insurance companies and other financial institutions • Imports made by passengers and ship or aircraft crew-members when made as accompanied baggage are exempt from the tax provided the goods in question are also exempt from import duties. Imports made by organisations which operate tax-free under international agreements are also exempt. In addition, transfers of raw animal or vegetable food products, rice, flour, chicken eggs among others are exempt from VAT, as is land, ocean, river or lake and air national passenger transportation	
	Refund of VAT	Exporters and industrial projects with a pre-operating stage longer than 6 months may request reimbursement of the tax credits paid for their activities. In the specific case of industrial projects, the VAT to which they are subject shall be indexed when the entities begin operations. However, the taxpayer may waive such indexing and has the option to request a tax credit certificate	

		Residents	Non-residents
Value Added Tax (VAT) – contd	Tax liability	The activities mentioned above are taxable as follows: • In relation to sales of tangible goods, when the invoice or equivalent document is issued to record the transaction, when paid, or when the goods are delivered, whichever comes first • In relation to the permanent importation of goods and services, when they are imported into the country • In relation to rendering of services, when the invoice is issued, the service is completed, or total or partial payment is made	
	Tax rates	12% general 12% general plus an additional 10% 8%	
	Administrative obligations	Merchants shall specify what they are charging for with the merchandise or service they sell, and what the respective VAT chargeable to the sale price is. Each taxpayer receives a tax credit for the taxes paid in connection with its purchases, which is subtracted from the tax generated by the value of its billings (tax debit) Taxpayers must keep additional books, records, and files for this purpose, and must file a return setting out their transactions under accounting rules within the first 15 days of the calendar month following that of the transactions. A special account must be opened to record the tax debits and credits	
Municipal Taxes		The municipal business tax is based on gross income and rates vary between municipalities and types of economic activity, and normally have a progressive scale. In many cases, the municipal tax rate is a small percentage of gross sales. For example, the rates in force in the Capital District vary form 0.3% to 9.4% of gross income, depending on the activity. Since these taxes are set at the district (rather than the state or national) level, the different city councils have a great deal of leeway in determining the tax rates and in granting exoneration to attract companies to their jurisdictions The new Constitution of the Republic of Venezuela, which became effective on 30 December 1999, has established that the industrial, business and services economic activity could be subject to tax in the municipalities	
Stamp Duty		From 2 May 2012, Capital Stamp Tax is charged by the Mercantile Registries of the District Capital at the rate of 2% on subscribed or increased share capital There are a number of stamp duties chargeable on official documents	

Vietnam

(Le Quang Phi, NEXIA STT phi.le@nexia.vn)

I   MAIN LEGAL FORMS

Main Legal Forms / Category	Partnership	Limited Liability Company		Private Enterprise	Joint Stock Company
		Single member	**Multiple-member**		
Partners/Share-holders Number Restrictions	• At least two partners are required • Partner must be an individual and • Partner cannot be the owner of any private enterprise or partner of other partnership	• One member being an organization or an individual and • Cannot be listed	• Members being organizations or individuals • The number of members must not exceed 50 and • Cannot be listed	• Owner must be an individual and • Are not permitted to issue any type of securities	• At least three shareholders who may be organizations or individuals and • Can be listed
Director(s)/Legal Representative	Managed by partners	• Appointed or hired by Chairperson or Members' Council and • Chairperson of Members' Council can be concurrently the Director/General Director • Allowed to have more than one legal representative and only one of them is required to reside in Vietnam	• Appointed or hired by Chairperson or Members' Council and • Chairperson of Members' Council can be concurrently the Director/General Director • Allowed to have more than one legal representative and only one of them is required to reside in Vietnam	• Being the individual owner	• Appointed by Board of Management and • Cannot concurrently be the Director of other Vietnamese companies
Establishment	• Formed by individuals and • Partnership deed	• Formed by individuals and/or organizations and • The Charter	• Formed by individuals and/or organizations and • The Charter	• Formed by the individual owner	• Formed by individuals and/or organizations • The Charter • Allowed to have more than one legal representative and only one of them is required to reside in Vietnam

Registration: Licensing authority
 	
Registration Result
	• Department of Planning and Investment
	• Management boards of industrial zones, export processing zones, or hi-tech zone and economic zones
	• Two-step licensing process required for a foreign Investor:
	  ○ application for obtaining an Investment Registration Certificate ("IRC")
	  ○ registration for establishment of an enterprise by obtaining an enterprise registration certificate ('ERC')
	• ERC granted to local enterprises				

Capital or form of equity investment	• Minimum and maximum charter capitals are not required and • Minimum legal capital required for the enterprise registration of the sectors of: banking, non-bank credit institutions, real estate, debt collection services, security services, services for the Vietnamese guest workers, film production, air transportation businesses, airports business, and multilevel marketing, etc				
	May issue all types of shares	Not permitted to issue any type of securities	Cannot issue shares	Must not issue any type of securities	
Liability	Limited to the value of the capital that shareholder has contributed to the company	Fully liable before the laws in the capacity as its owner	Only liable for the debts of the company to the extent of the capital contribution they have poured into the company	Liable for all obligations of the partnership without limit	
Management Structure	General Meeting of Shareholders – a Board of Management, Directors (or General Directors) – and a Board of Controllers	The Owner-Director	Members' Council – a Chairman – and a Director/General Director	*Where the member/owner is an institution:* (i) a Chairman, a Director/General Director and Controller(s) or (ii) a Members' Council, a Director/General Director and Controller(s). *Where the member/owner is an individual:* a Chairman and a Director/General Director	Partners' Council – Director
Governance/ Authority	General Meeting of Shareholders	The Owner	Members' Council	Members' Council or Chairman	Partners' Council or Chairman
Audit requirements	• Enterprises with foreign investment • Credit institutions established and operating under the Law on Credit Institutions • Financial institutions, insurance enterprises, insurance brokerage firms • Public companies, issuers and securities trading organizations • Stated owned enterprises, except for state owned enterprises operating in the field of state secrets as prescribed by laws • Enterprises, organisations implementing the national important projects, group –A projects as stipulated in Article 7 and 8 of Decree No. 12/2009/ND-CP using the State funds, except for the projects in the field of state secrets as prescribed by laws • Enterprises and organisations with state contributed capital and projects funded by the Government and other State capital prescribed by laws • Auditing firms, branches of foreign auditing firms in Vietnam				

Main Legal Forms / Category	Partnership	Limited Liability Company		Private Enterprise	Joint Stock Company
		Single member	Multiple-member		
Other Legal Forms	Branches and Representative Offices of foreign merchants	Business Cooperation Contracts (BCCs)	Build-Operate-Transfer (BOT), Build-Transfer (BT) and Build-Transfer-Operate (BTO) Contracts	Build-Operate-Transfer (BOT), Build-Transfer (BT) and Build-Transfer-Operate (BTO) Contracts	State owned enterprises
	• all foreign businesses, which have been in operation for a year and more, will be allowed to open representative offices or branches in Vietnam • licences for representative offices and branches will be valid for five years but may be extended or re-issued upon expiry • branches shall be entitled to do business in accordance with the branch licences	• a contractual relationship signed between multiple parties, generally a foreign investor and a local company • This form of business has traditionally been used in industries where LLCs and JSCs are restricted • does not form a legal entity but permits the partners to engage in business activities on the basis of mutual allocation of responsibilities and the sharing of profits and losses	• foreign investors may sign BOT, BT and BTO contracts with state bodies to implement infrastructure construction projects in Vietnam • typically used for transportation, electricity production, water supply, drainage and waste treatment projects • The difference between BOT, BT and BOT contracts is the point in time that the project is transferred to the government		• an enterprise wholly owned by the State • must conduct periodical and extraordinary public disclosure on its web portal and its owner representative agency's web portal • information subject to periodical public disclosure includes: the charter, specific parameters of annual business plans, and audited annual and semi-annual financial statements

II   CORPORATION TAX (CORPORATE INCOME TAX)

	Resident corporation	Permanent Establishment (PE)
General description	Enterprises incorporated under the Vietnamese laws	Any PE is defined as 'a fixed place of business through which a foreign enterprise carries out a part or the whole of its business or production activities in Vietnam'
		Vietnam has a broadly worded PE definition, namely: A branch, an operating office, a factory, a workshop, means of transportation, a mine, an oil and gas field, an establishment providing services including consultancy services through its employees or other organization, individuals, etc
Taxable incomes	Income arising from Vietnam and foreign sources	Income arising in Vietnam (irrespective of whether it relates to the PE) and the taxable income generated out of Vietnam related to operations of the PEs
	Income from producing and trading goods or services	
	Other incomes from capital transfer, transfer of real estates, transfer of capital contribution rights, transfer of properties, investment projects, ownership and right to use assets, disposal of assets, revaluation of assets for capital contribution, recoveries of bad debts which have been written off, penalties/compensation of economic contract breach, production and business activities carried on outside Vietnam, gifts and donations, provisions which are not used up and reverted to expenses, etc	
Calculation of taxable profit	Total revenues X *Minus* Deductible expenses Y *Plus* Other incomes Z Taxable income T	
Non-cash payments	Non-cash payment vouchers are required for invoice of goods and services having value inclusive of VAT of VND20 million or more	
Interest payments	Interest paid to the entities/individuals not being credit institutions or economic organizations and exceeding 150% of the prime rate of the State Bank of Vietnam is excluded from deductible expenses (Y)	
Related party transactions	Compliance with the arm's length principles under Transfer Pricing regulations	
Tax year, Tax return and payment	A tax year is usually determined as the calendar year. Tax year for the assessment of CIT may be the enterprise's financial year, which is other than the calendar year, but must be ended in each quarter	
	CIT is declared and paid quarterly as the provisional assessment. Finalization and payment of CIT is made for each tax year as the final assessment by the enterprise	
Capital gains	CIT rate: 22% (20% from 1 January 2016)	

	Resident corporation	**Permanent Establishment (PE)**
Losses	Tax losses are not accounting losses	
	Tax losses can be carried forward for a period of 5 consecutive years following the year the loss incurred	
	Tax losses incurred on transfers of real estate, transfers of investment project, and transfers of the right to take part in investment project are allowed to consolidate with the taxable income of business operation in the tax period	
Tax group	N/A	
Tax rate	Standard CIT rate: 22% (20% from 1 January 2016)	
	The standard CIT rate will be reduced to 20% from 2016.	
	• A reduced CIT rate of 20% is applicable to enterprises having sales revenue of the preceding tax year not exceeding VND20 billion (approx US$1 million)	
	• CIT rate of 10% is applicable to income from socialized fields and social housing projects	
	• Oil and gas companies and companies involved in exploitation of precious minerals: 32%–50%	

III   TAXES FOR INDIVIDUALS

<table>
<tr><td rowspan="7">Income Tax (PIT)</td><td></td><th>Residents</th><th>Non-residents</th></tr>
<tr><td>Taxable entities</td><td>• All Vietnamese citizens and foreigners present in Vietnam for 183 days or more in a taxable year or in 12 consecutive months or
• Having a regular residence according to Vietnam's regulations on residence or a house rental contract with a term of 183 days or more within the tax assessment year</td><td>• Those who do not meet either of the conditions for residency</td></tr>
<tr><td>General description</td><td>Taxed on income arising inside and outside Vietnam (worldwide income)</td><td>Taxed on income arising from Vietnam regardless of where the income is paid or received. Worldwide income may be pro-rated if the income earned in Vietnam cannot be separated</td></tr>
<tr><td>Taxable income and types of taxable income</td><td colspan="2">• Business income
• Employment income
• Capital investment income
• Capital transfer income
• Real estate transfer income
• Winnings with prizes (taxable only where the value is more than VND10million/winning)
• Royalties (taxable only where the value is more than VND10 million/receipt)
• Franchising income (taxable only where the value is more than VND10million/contract)
• Inheritances (taxable only where the value is more than VND10 million/receipt)
• Gifts (taxable only where the value is more than VND10 million/receipt)

* VND10 million is approx US$460 – with the current exchange rate of Vietnam State Bank</td></tr>
<tr><td>Calculation of income</td><td>• Taxable income to be determined in variety of formulae based on the type of income
• Income for each activity shall be separately calculated for tax purposes, except for business income and employment income which shall be totalled up for tax calculation at year-end finalization</td><td>Taxable income = total income arising from Vietnam</td></tr>
<tr><td>Tax year</td><td>• Income from business and employment income: calendar year/ 12 consecutive months from date of first arrival, tax year is calendar year from the second year
• Others: as they arise</td><td>As it arises</td></tr>
</table>

		Residents	Non-residents
Income Tax (PIT) – contd	Tax assessment	Self-assessment regime. Tax inspection/tax audit is carried out either at the enterprise's request or by the tax offices, at least once every 5 years. There are penalties for non-compliance with declaration and payment of PIT	
	Tax reports, declarations and Tax payment	• Income from business and employment income: within 20 days of the succeeding month under monthly declaration basis and within 30 days of the succeeding quarter under quarterly declaration basis • Other types of income (which is paid one time/each time): within 10 days of tax obligation arising • Tax finalization at the calendar year-end: within 90 days of the succeeding year	• Income from business and employment income: within 30 days of the succeeding quarter under quarterly declaration basis • Other types of income: within 10 days of tax obligation arising but quarterly for employment income and • No tax finalization required
	Tax rates	• **Progressive rates (resident Vietnamese and foreigners)** *Monthly income (million VND)* — *Rate (%)* Up to 5 — 5 5–10 — 10 10–18 — 15 18–32 — 20 32–52 — 25 52–80 — 30 80+ — 35 • **Flat rates** *Assessable Income* — *Rate (%)* Capital investment income — 5 Royalties/franchising income — 5 Lottery winning/prizes — 10 Inheritance/gifts — 10 Real estates transfer income — 25 or 2 Capital transfer income — 20 or 0.1	*Type of Income* — *Tax rate (%)* From commercial activities — 1 From services — 5 From manufacturing, construction, transportation, and other business — 2 From employment — 20 From capital investment — 5 From capital assignment — 0.1 From real estates transfer — 2 Royalties and franchise — 5 From lottery winnings, prizes from commercial promotions, games with prizes — 10 From inheritance and gifts — 10 There is the opportunity for the application for tax treaty exemption for an expatriate who is resident of a country that has signed a tax treaty with Vietnam and the expatriate satisfies the relevant tax treaty conditions

		Residents	Non-residents
Capital Gains Tax (CGT)	General description	Covered under Personal Income Tax and Corporate Income Tax Generally, capital gains made by an enterprise will form part of the taxable income of the enterprise and will be taxed at CIT rate of 22%	
	Taxable entities and chargeable assets		
	Calculation of gain		
	Tax year, tax assessment and tax payment		
	Losses		
	Tax rates		
		Domiciled	**Non-domiciled**
Inheritance Tax (IHT)	General description	Inheritances in excess of VND10 million are subject to tax at the rate of 10%, including: – Inherited securities – Inherited capital in economic organizations and businesses and – Inherited real estate The ownership and use rights of other inherited assets must be registered with state agencies	
	Taxable entities and chargeable assets		
	Calculation of charge		
	Taxable events		
	Allowances		

IV   WITHHOLDING TAXES (FOREIGN CONTRACTOR TAX ('FCT'))

Types of incomes	Impose tax rates under domestic law
Dividends	Tax free
Interest on loan	• 5% CIT and VAT exempt
Royalties	• 10% on royalties being the income of any form paid for the use right or for the transfer of intellectual property rights or for technology transfer, software licence (including payments for the right to use and for transfers of rights of an author and rights of the owner of a work; for transfers of industrial property rights; for technology transfer; and software licence) • Exempted or reduced royalties withholding tax where a relevant tax treaty or Inter-Governmental Agreement/Donor Agreement applies

No.	Matrix of tax rates under the tax treaties signed with Vietnam (Updated on 15 July 2014)			
	Country	Dividends	Interest	Royalties
1.	Algeria	Not yet in force		
2.	Australia	10%	10%	10%
3.	Austria	5%, 10%, 15%	10%	10%
4.	Azerbaijan	Not yet in force		
5.	Bangladesh	15%	15%	15%
6.	Belarus	15%	10%	15%
7.	Belgium	5%, 10%, 15%	10%	5%, 10%, 15%
8.	Brunei Darussalam	10%	10%	10%
9.	Bulgaria	15%	10%	15%
10.	Canada	5%, 10%, 15%	10%	10%
11.	China	10%	10%	10%
12.	Cuba	5%, 10%, 15%	10%	10%
13.	Czech Republic	10%	10%	10%
14.	Denmark	5%, 10%, 15%	10%	5%, 15%
15.	Egypt	Not yet in force		
16.	Finland	5%, 10%, 15%	10%	10%
17.	France	7%, 10%, 15%	10%	10%
18.	Germany	5%, 10%, 15%	10%	10%
19.	Hong Kong	10%	10%	7%, 10%
20.	Hungary	10%	10%	10%
21.	Iceland	10%, 15%	10%	10%
22.	India	10%	10%	10%
23.	Indonesia	15%	15%	15%
24.	Ireland	Nil	10%	15%
25.	Israel	10%	10%	5%, 15%
26.	Italy	5%, 10%, 15%	10%	10%
27.	Japan	10%	10%	10%
28.	Kazakhstan	Not yet in force		
29.	Korea	10%	10%	5%, 15%

No.	Matrix of tax rates under the tax treaties signed with Vietnam (Updated on 15 July 2014)			
	Country	Dividends	Interest	Royalties
30.	Kuwait	10%, 15%	15%	20%
31.	Laos	10%	10%	10%
32.	Luxembourg	5%, 10%, 15%	10%	10%
33.	Macedonia	Not yet in force		
34.	Malaysia	10%	10%	10%
35.	Mongolia	10%	10%	10%
36.	Morocco	10%	10%	10%
37.	Mozambique	Not yet in force		
38.	Myanmar	10%	10%	10%
39.	Netherlands	5%, 10%, 15%	10%	5%, 10%, 15%
40.	New Zealand	5%, 15%	10%	10%
41.	North Korea	10%	10%	10%
42.	Norway	5%, 10%, 15%	10%	10%
43.	Oman	5%, 10%, 15%	10%	10%
44.	Pakistan	15%	15%	15%
45.	Palestine	10%	10%	10%
46.	Philippines	10%, 15%	15%	15%
47.	Poland	10%, 15%	10%	10%, 15%
48.	Qatar	5%, 12.5%	10%	5%, 10%
49.	Romania	15%	10%	15%
50.	Russia	10%, 15%	10%	15%
51.	San Marino	Not yet in force		
52.	Saudi Arabia	5%, 12.5%	10%	7.5%, 10%
53.	Serbia	Not yet in force		
54.	Seychelles	10%	10%	10%
55.	Singapore	5%, 7%, 12.5%	10%	5%, 10%
56.	Slovakia	5%, 10%	10%	5%, 10%, 15%
57.	Spain	7%, 10%, 15%	10%	10%
58.	Sri Lanka	10%	10%	15%
59.	Sweden	5%, 10%, 15%	10%	5%, 15%
60.	Switzerland	7%, 10%, 15%	10%	10%
61.	Taiwan	15%	10%	15%
62.	Thailand	15%	10%, 15%	15%
63.	Tunisia	10%	10%	10%
64.	Turkey	Not yet in force		
65.	United Arab Emirates	5%, 15%	10%	10%
66.	Ukraine	10%	10%	10%
67.	United Kingdom	7%, 10%, 15%	10%	10%
68.	Uzbekistan	15%	10%	10%

Note: the above rates are only available provided the specific tax treaty conditions are satisfied. It is possible that lower rates than those shown above may be available provided that certain criteria are satisfied. As treaties will not be identical, guidance should be sought in all cases.

V   INDIRECT TAXES

		Residents	Non-residents
Value Added Tax (VAT)	General description	VAT applies to goods and services used for production, trading and consumption in Vietnam (including goods and services purchased from abroad)	
	Entities obliged to pay VAT	All organizations and individuals producing, trading or importing goods and rendering services	
	Taxable activities	Most of goods or services used for production, trading and consumption in Vietnam	
	Taxable activities – zero-rated (examples)	• Exported sales of goods and services • International transportation service enjoys VAT rate of 0%	
	Exemptions (examples)	• Certain agricultural products, including those imported • Essential products/services for community living needs (Life insurance, re-insurance, Medical and veterinary services) • Encouraged products/services (Training, education, Publication, importation and distribution of newspapers, magazines etc) • Financial/Credit Activities (Security trading; Capital transfer etc, including credit activity of tax payers which are not credit institutes) • Transfer of land use right; transfer of right to capital contribution (including right to contribute capital) • Domestic software products/services • Sales of debts • Exported products being unprocessed exploited natural resources, and minerals	
	Refund of VAT	• Only applicable for application of VAT by the credit method • VAT shall be refunded by way of tax credit in the chain of company activity or in cash or via bank transfer where certain VAT refund conditions are satisfied • Tax assessment for VAT refund shall be conducted before or after the VAT refund • Foreigners purchasing goods in Vietnam are allowed a refund of VAT when leaving Vietnam	
	VAT filing method	• VAT by the credit method • VAT by the direct method (direct taxation on value added) Note: business establishments must apply same method for 2 consecutive years	
	Tax declaration	• Monthly basis: on or before 20th day of the succeeding month or • Quarterly basis: on or before 30th day of the succeeding month after the declaration quarter • No annual filing is required	
	Tax rates	• 0%, 5%, and 10% are varied depending on type of goods or services • 10% is the standard rate for most goods and services	
	Administrative obligations	• Vietnamese Accounting System to be applied • Good conduct of tax compliance • Registration of the tax code within 10 days from the issuance date of Investment Certificate • Notification of the use of bank accounts and tax invoices	
Property Taxes		N/A	
Stamp Duty		N/A	

Special Consumption Tax (SCT)	Levied on organizations or individuals producing or importing, and subsequently trading, certain goods and services subjected to SCT, such as cigarettes, wine, alcohol, beer, aircraft, casino, etc
Environmental Protection Tax (EPT)	Levied on products, goods exerting adverse effect on the environment such as: gasoline, oil, grease; coal; HFCF solution; nylon bag; restricted substances
	EPT shall be calculated at a fixed amount on each unit of taxable products, goods (absolute tax rates)

Nexia International does not accept liability for any loss arising from any action taken, or omission, on the basis of this publication. Professional advice should be obtained before acting or refraining from acting on the contents of this publication. Membership of Nexia International, or associated umbrella organizations, does not constitute any partnership between members, and members do not accept any responsibility for the commission of any act, or omission to act by, or the liabilities of, other members.

Nexia International is the trading name of Nexia International Limited, a company registered in the Isle of Man. Company registration number: 53513C. Registered office: 2nd floor, Sixty Circular Road, Douglas, Isle of Man, IM1 1SA